# ECONOMIC FREEDOM OF THE WORLD:
# 1975-1995

AUG 6 1996

# ECONOMIC FREEDOM OF THE WORLD: 1975-1995

*by*
*James Gwartney*
*Robert Lawson*
*Walter Block*

DOUGLAS COLLEGE LIBRARY

Copyright © 1996 by The Fraser Institute. All rights reserved. No part of this book may be reproduced in any manner whatsoever without written permission except in the case of brief quotations embodied in critical articles and reviews.

The authors of this book have worked independently and opinions expressed by them, therefore, are their own, and do not necessarily reflect the opinions of the members or the trustees of The Fraser Institute.

Printed in Canada.

**Canadian Cataloguing in Publication Data**

Gwartney, James D.
  Economic Freedom of the World, 1975-1995

  Includes bibliographical references.
  ISBN 0-88975-157-9

  1. Free enterprise.  2. Economic history—1971-1990.  3. Economic history—1900-  4. Economic development—Measurement.  I. Lawson, Robert A. (Robert Allen), 1967-  II. Block, Walter, 1941-  III. Fraser Institute (Vancouver, B.C.)  IV. Title
HB95.G92 1995          330.9′045          C95-911182-4

# TABLE OF CONTENTS

# FOREWORD

Freedom is a big word, and economic freedom not much smaller. To talk about economic freedom is easy; to measure it, to make fine distinctions, assign numbers to its attributes, and combine them into one overall magnitude—that is a very different and much more difficult task, as we found out when we started on this quest some thirteen years ago (see Michael Walker's introduction).

James Gwartney, Robert Lawson, and Walter Block deserve great credit for having brought this quest to so satisfactory a temporary conclusion—I say temporary because this study of economic freedom for more than 100 countries provides a cornucopia for students of the relation between economic freedom, political freedom, and civil freedom, and for further explorations of the relation between economic freedom and the level and rate of economic growth. The resulting studies will surely make revised editions necessary, both to bring the indexes of economic freedom up to date and to incorporate the additional understanding that will be generated.

For many of us, freedom—economic, political, civil—is an end in itself not a means to other ends—it is what makes life worthwhile. We would prefer to live in a free country even if it did not provide us and our fellow citizens with a higher standard of life than an alternative regime. But I am firmly persuaded that a free society could never survive under such circumstances. A free society is a delicate balance, constantly under attack, even by many who profess to be its partisans. I believe that free societies have arisen and persisted only because economic freedom is so much more productive economically than other methods of controlling economic activity.

It did not require the construction of an index of economic freedom for it to be widely believed that there is a close relation between economic freedom and the level and rate of economic growth. Theoretical considerations gave reason to expect such a relation, and little more than casual observation sufficed to show that what theory suggested, experience documented. We have not in a sense learned any **big** thing from this book that we did not know before. What we have done is to acquire a set of data that can be used to explore just how the relation works, and what are the essential connections, and that will enable skeptics to test their views objectively.

To achieve these advantages, it was essential that the measure of economic freedom not beg any questions by depending on outcomes; it was essential that it depend only on objective characteristics of an economy. This may seem obvious but I assure you that it is not. After all, the rate of economic growth or the level of living may be an excellent proxy for economic freedom, just as an auto's maximum speed may be an excellent proxy for the power of its motor. But any such connections must be demonstrated not assumed or taken for granted. There is nothing in the way the indexes are calculated that would prevent them from having no correlation whatsoever with such completely independent numbers as per capita GDP and the rate of growth of GDP. Yet the actual correlation between the indexes and the level and rate of economic growth documented in some of the extraordinarily informative graphs in the book (e.g., Exhibit S-2) is most impressive. No qualitative verbal description can match the power of that graph.

Milton Friedman
The Hoover Institution
Stanford University

# List of Exhibits

# About the Authors

**James Gwartney** is a Professor of Economics and Policy Sciences at Florida State University. His Ph.D. in Economics is from the University of Washington (1969). He is the co-author (with Richard Stroup) of *Economics: Private and Public Choice*, a widely-used university level text and *What Everyone Should Know About Economics and Prosperity*, a popular book that has already been translated to ten foreign languages. He is also the author of several other books and articles published in the leading professional journals of economics.

**Robert Lawson** is an Associate Professor of Economics at Shawnee State University. He received his Ph.D. from Florida State University in 1992. In addition to the study of economic systems, freedom and growth, his major area of research is public choice.

**Walter Block** is an Associate Professor of Economics at the College of the Holy Cross. His Ph.D. in economics is from Columbia University (1972). Senior Economist at The Fraser Institute from 1978 to 1991, he is the author (or co-author) of six books and the editor (or co-editor) of twelve others. He is currently the co-editor of two journals, *The Review of Austrian Economics* and *The Journal of Libertarian Studies*. He has also served as the guest editor of *The Journal of Labor Economics* and *Cultural Dynamics*.

# Acknowledgments

This project is the fruition of a team effort. It is an outgrowth of a series of six conferences jointly sponsored by the Fraser Institute of Vancouver, British Columbia and the Liberty Fund of Indianapolis, Indiana. We owe an enormous debt to both the sponsors and conference participants. The free wheeling discussions stimulated our thinking and provided us with several ideas, many of which are incorporated into our measure of economic freedom.

While we benefitted from discussions and papers presented by numerous participants, we must mention the specific contributions of three. First, Mike Walker provided the entrepreneurial insight for the topic, the energy to organize the conference series, and the persuasiveness to attract several of today's finest intellects to address the topic. Without his contribution, we would probably have not even thought about the measurement of economic freedom, much less undertaken the task. His Introduction to the book presents the historical background that proceeded our work on this topic.

Second, the contribution of Alvin Rabushka was also crucial. His enthusiasm for the project supported it during the early days. His paper, "Preliminary Definition of Economic Freedom" presented at the second conference, outlined the key attributes of economic freedom and provided us with invaluable guidance concerning how they should be measured. More recently as our work developed, he has given us additional direction and encouragement.

Third, we would like to thank Milton Friedman. No words can fully express our debt to him. He attended each of the Fraser/Liberty Fund conferences and his ferocious love for intellectual inquiry was an inspiration to all participants. His pointed and often revealing criticisms challenged us to work harder and think deeper. His directions have helped us avert at least a few of the treacherous swamps that inevitably accompany a project of this type.

We would also like to express our appreciation to the Policy Sciences Center of Florida State University for providing the research and word processing support that made the project feasible. Barbara Morgan and Frank Keuchel assisted with data gathering, calculations, and the checking of the figures in the manuscript. Kristin McCahon, Director of Publications at the Fraser Institute, did an excellent job of coordinating the design and publication of the book. Finally, no one will be happier to see this project completed than Valerie N. Colvin, Senior Art/Production Specialist. She maintained her patience during numerous occasions when data were updated, a variable or a country added, or an exhibit redesigned. It was a challenging task and she handled it well.

James Gwartney
Robert Lawson
Walter Block

# Executive Summary

1.  The central elements of economic freedom are personal choice, protection of private property, and freedom of exchange. The goal of this study is to construct an index that is (a) a good indicator of economic freedom across countries and (b) based on objective components that can be updated regularly and used to track future changes in economic freedom.

2.  An index containing 17 components was designed to provide an empirical measure for economic freedom. The components were grouped into four major areas: I. Money and Inflation, II. Government Operations and Regulations, III. Takings and Discriminatory Taxation, and IV. Restrictions on International Exchange. Exhibit 1-1 provides a description of the specific components of the index. Data were assembled and procedures adopted to rate countries on a zero to ten scale for each of the components. Chapter 1 indicates the data sources used and explains how the each of the component ratings were derived. See Appendix II for the tables containing the underlying data and the ratings for each of the 17 components.

3.  Since there is not a single "best way" to weight the components into an aggregate summary rating, three alternative summary indexes were derived. See Exhibit 1-2 for the component weights used to derive each of the three indexes.

4.  Exhibit 2-1 presents the 1993-1995 ratings for each of the 17 components in our index, as well as area ratings, and the three alternative summary indexes (and the average of the three). With the exception of the high-income industrial countries, the three alternative summary ratings yield similar results. In the case of the industrial countries, the summary index that allocates only a very small weight to the size of government consumption expenditures and transfers and subsidies *as a share of the economy* yielded ratings that were approximately one unit higher than the two other summary ratings.

5.  In terms of economic freedom, Hong Kong is the highest rated country in the world. Since Hong Kong's average for the three alternative ratings in 1993-1995 was significantly higher than any other country, it was given a letter grade of A+. New Zealand, Singapore, and United States earned a grade of A. The following ten countries were assigned a grade of B: Switzerland, United Kingdom, Canada, Australia, Ireland, Japan, Netherlands, Germany, Belgium, and Malaysia. Exhibit S-1A (Graphic Summary) indicates the average of the three indexes for each country and their ranking. Exhibit S-1B provides the same information for the Is1 index.

6.    At the other end of the spectrum, the following 27 countries earned a grade of F-: Brazil, Haiti, Nicaragua, Venezuela, Hungary, Iran, Romania, Syria, Nepal, Algeria, Benin, Burundi, Central African Republic, Congo, Cote d'Ivoire, Madagascar, Morocco, Niger, Nigeria, Rwanda, Sierra Leone, Tanzania, Togo, Uganda, Zaire, Zambia, and Zimbabwe. The policies and institutional arrangements of these countries were inconsistent with economic freedom in almost every area.

7.    In addition to the mid-1990s ratings, indexes were also derived for 1975, 1980, 1985, and 1990. Exhibit 2-2 presents the summary rating Is1 for the Top 15, Bottom 15, and selected middle-rated countries for these years as well as for 1995. Some of the top-rated countries were able to maintain their high rating throughout the 1975-1995 period, but there was also a great deal of both upward and downward mobility. Several top-ranked countries in 1975 and 1985 fell well down the rankings in later years (for example, Honduras and Venezuela). Correspondingly, several economies with low ratings in 1975, 1980, or 1985 substantially improved their scores in recent years (for example, New Zealand, Thailand, South Korea, and Costa Rica).

8.    The five countries that improved their economic freedom rating the most during the 1975-1990 period were: Chile, Jamaica, Iceland, Malaysia, and Pakistan. See Exhibit 3-1 for more a complete list of countries that improved substantially during the 1975-1990 period. The five countries for which the economic freedom rating declined the most during the 1975-1990 period were: Nicaragua, Somalia, Iran, Honduras, and Venezuela. See Exhibit 3-2 for a more complete list of these countries.

9.    The summary indexes indicate that there was little change in the average economic freedom rating for the more than 100 countries of our study during the 1975-1985 period. However, since 1985 there is evidence of an increase in economic freedom. The average summary ratings of both industrial and less developed countries rose during the last decade. The primary factors contributing to this improvement were: greater price level stability, greater freedom to maintain foreign currency bank deposits, improved credit market policies, lower top marginal tax rates, reductions in taxes (tariffs) on international trade, liberalization of exchange rate controls, and relaxation of restrictions on the movements of capital. See Exhibits 3-6 and 3-7 for details. Also see Exhibit S-7 in the Graphic Summary.

10.   Economic theory indicates that economic freedom will enhance the gains from trade and entrepreneurship. Therefore, if economic freedom is measured properly, a positive impact on economic growth is the expected result. The data are consistent with this view. As Exhibit 4-1A shows, the 14 countries that earned a summary rating grade of either A or B in 1993-1995, achieved an average annual

growth rate in per capita real GDP of 2.4% during 1980-1994 and 2.6% during 1985-1994. In contrast, the average annual growth of per capita real GDP for the 27 countries with a summary rating of F- in 1993-1995 was *minus* 1.3 percent during 1980-1994 and *minus* 1.6 percent for the 1985-1994 period. Twenty-one of the 27 experienced *declines* in real per capita GDP during 1980-1994. See Exhibits 4-1B for additional details. Also see Exhibit S-2 in the Graphic Summary for evidence that differences in economic freedom (and the accompanying grade level) exert a positive impact on both income levels and growth rates.

11.   Since increases in economic freedom and maintenance of a high level of freedom will positively influence growth, countries that achieve and sustain high levels of economic freedom over a lengthy time period will tend to be high-income countries. The six countries (Hong Kong, Switzerland, Singapore, United States, Canada, and Germany) with *persistently* high ratings throughout the 1975-1995 period were all in the Top Ten in terms of 1994 per capita GDP. **No country with a persistently high economic freedom rating during the two decades failed to achieve a high level of income.** In contrast, no country with a persistently low rating was able to achieve even middle income status. See Exhibit 4-2 and Exhibit S-3 in the Graphic Summary for additional details.

12.   The countries with the largest *increases* in economic freedom during the period, achieved impressive growth rates. As Exhibit 4-3 shows, the 15 countries (actually there are 17 because of a tie) with the most improvement in the index of economic freedom during the 1975-1990 period experienced an average growth rate in per capita GDP of 2.7 percent during 1980-1990 (and 3.1% during 1985-1994). **All 17 of the countries in the most improved category experienced positive growth rates.** In contrast, the average real per capita GDP *declined* at an annual rate of 0.6% in the 15 countries (there were also 16 in this group due to a tie) for which the index of economic freedom fell the most during the same period. Eleven of the 16 countries with the largest declines in economic freedom experienced declines in real per capita GDP during 1980-1994. See Exhibit 4-4 and Graphic Exhibit S-5 for additional details.

13.   Countries that achieved a one unit increase in the Is1 economic freedom rating between 1975 and 1985 and maintained that increase during the next decade grew at a average rate of 3.5% during 1985-1994. Mauritius, Pakistan, Japan, Chile, Jamaica, Singapore, Portugal, United Kingdom and Turkey comprised this category. In contrast, the growth rates of the countries where economic freedom declined during 1975-1985 were persistently negative. The pattern was similar for the countries that achieved and sustained increases in economic freedom between 1980 and 1990 compared to those experiencing declines in freedom. See Exhibits 4-5 and 4-6 for additional details. Also see Exhibits S-4C and S-4D in the Graphics Summary section.

14.    Chapter 5 presents detailed data for both economic freedom ratings and recent indicators of economic performance for many of the countries included in our study.

# Graphic Summary

## of

# Major Findings

# Exhibit S-1A: The Average of the Three 1993-95 Summary Index Ratings of Economic Freedom

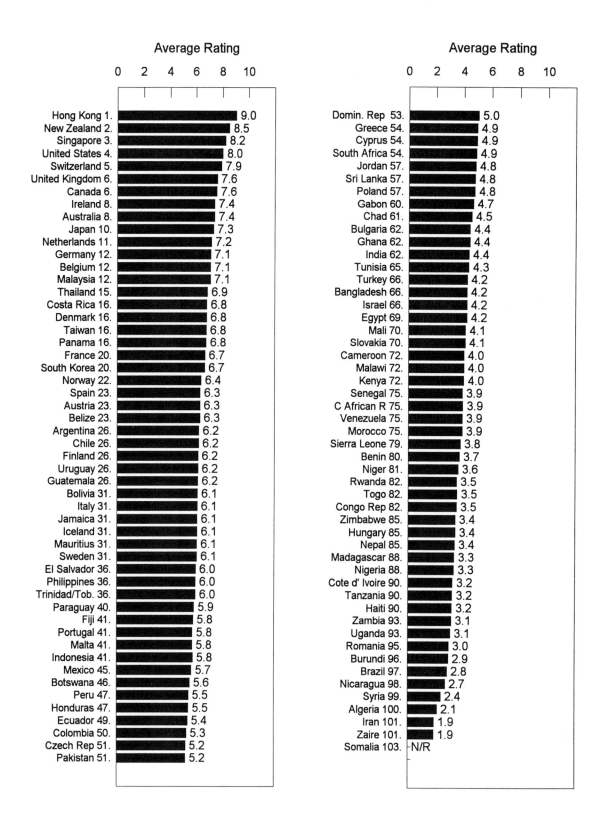

Average Rating

| Country | Rating |
|---|---|
| Hong Kong 1. | 9.0 |
| New Zealand 2. | 8.5 |
| Singapore 3. | 8.2 |
| United States 4. | 8.0 |
| Switzerland 5. | 7.9 |
| United Kingdom 6. | 7.6 |
| Canada 6. | 7.6 |
| Ireland 8. | 7.4 |
| Australia 8. | 7.4 |
| Japan 10. | 7.3 |
| Netherlands 11. | 7.2 |
| Germany 12. | 7.1 |
| Belgium 12. | 7.1 |
| Malaysia 12. | 7.1 |
| Thailand 15. | 6.9 |
| Costa Rica 16. | 6.8 |
| Denmark 16. | 6.8 |
| Taiwan 16. | 6.8 |
| Panama 16. | 6.8 |
| France 20. | 6.7 |
| South Korea 20. | 6.7 |
| Norway 22. | 6.4 |
| Spain 23. | 6.3 |
| Austria 23. | 6.3 |
| Belize 23. | 6.3 |
| Argentina 26. | 6.2 |
| Chile 26. | 6.2 |
| Finland 26. | 6.2 |
| Uruguay 26. | 6.2 |
| Guatemala 26. | 6.2 |
| Bolivia 31. | 6.1 |
| Italy 31. | 6.1 |
| Jamaica 31. | 6.1 |
| Iceland 31. | 6.1 |
| Mauritius 31. | 6.1 |
| Sweden 31. | 6.1 |
| El Salvador 36. | 6.0 |
| Philippines 36. | 6.0 |
| Trinidad/Tob. 36. | 6.0 |
| Paraguay 40. | 5.9 |
| Fiji 41. | 5.8 |
| Portugal 41. | 5.8 |
| Malta 41. | 5.8 |
| Indonesia 41. | 5.8 |
| Mexico 45. | 5.7 |
| Botswana 46. | 5.6 |
| Peru 47. | 5.5 |
| Honduras 47. | 5.5 |
| Ecuador 49. | 5.4 |
| Colombia 50. | 5.3 |
| Czech Rep 51. | 5.2 |
| Pakistan 51. | 5.2 |

Average Rating

| Country | Rating |
|---|---|
| Domin. Rep 53. | 5.0 |
| Greece 54. | 4.9 |
| Cyprus 54. | 4.9 |
| South Africa 54. | 4.9 |
| Jordan 57. | 4.8 |
| Sri Lanka 57. | 4.8 |
| Poland 57. | 4.8 |
| Gabon 60. | 4.7 |
| Chad 61. | 4.5 |
| Bulgaria 62. | 4.4 |
| Ghana 62. | 4.4 |
| India 62. | 4.4 |
| Tunisia 65. | 4.3 |
| Turkey 66. | 4.2 |
| Bangladesh 66. | 4.2 |
| Israel 66. | 4.2 |
| Egypt 69. | 4.2 |
| Mali 70. | 4.1 |
| Slovakia 70. | 4.1 |
| Cameroon 72. | 4.0 |
| Malawi 72. | 4.0 |
| Kenya 72. | 4.0 |
| Senegal 75. | 3.9 |
| C African R 75. | 3.9 |
| Venezuela 75. | 3.9 |
| Morocco 75. | 3.9 |
| Sierra Leone 79. | 3.8 |
| Benin 80. | 3.7 |
| Niger 81. | 3.6 |
| Rwanda 82. | 3.5 |
| Togo 82. | 3.5 |
| Congo Rep 82. | 3.5 |
| Zimbabwe 85. | 3.4 |
| Hungary 85. | 3.4 |
| Nepal 85. | 3.4 |
| Madagascar 88. | 3.3 |
| Nigeria 88. | 3.3 |
| Cote d' Ivoire 90. | 3.2 |
| Tanzania 90. | 3.2 |
| Haiti 90. | 3.2 |
| Zambia 93. | 3.1 |
| Uganda 93. | 3.1 |
| Romania 95. | 3.0 |
| Burundi 96. | 2.9 |
| Brazil 97. | 2.8 |
| Nicaragua 98. | 2.7 |
| Syria 99. | 2.4 |
| Algeria 100. | 2.1 |
| Iran 101. | 1.9 |
| Zaire 101. | 1.9 |
| Somalia 103. | N/R |

Note: Chapter 1 explains how the three summary indexes (Ie, Is1, and Is2) are derived. The rating above is the average of these three. See Exhibit 2-1 for each of the three ratings.

## Exhibit S-1B: The 1993-95 Summary Index (Is1) of Economic Freedom

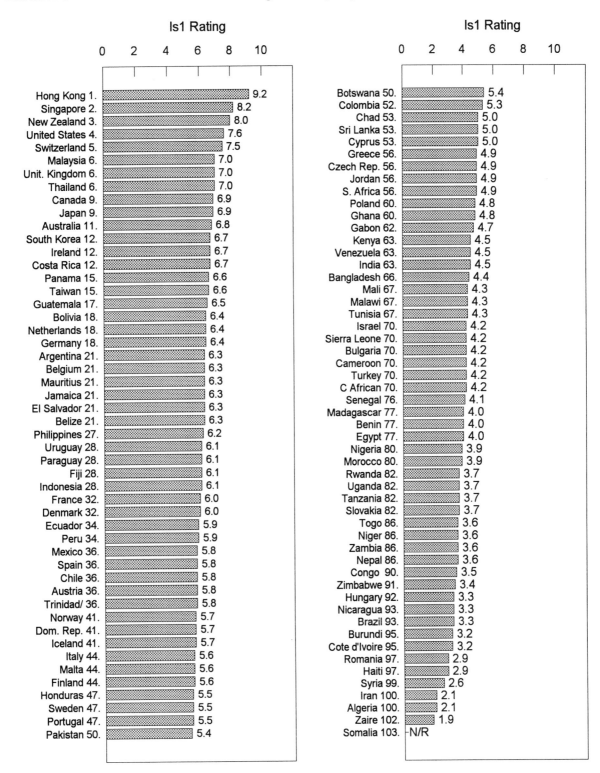

Note: Chapter 1 explains how this rating was derived. See Exhibit 2-1 for information on the components that underlay the rating. In the judgment of the authors, the Is1 index is the most reliable indicator of differences in economic freedom across a wide range of countries.

**Exhibit S-2: The 1995 Economic Freedom, Grade Level Per Capita GDP, and Growth**

A. Average Per Capita GDP by
   1995 Economic Freedom Grade

*The graph at the right indicates the average per capita GDP of countries grouped according to their 1995 economic freedom grade. On average, countries with more economic freedom have a higher per capita GDP. (The GDP figures are derived by the purchasing power parity method, Summers and Heston, Penn World Tables data). They are measured in 1985 U.S. dollars.*

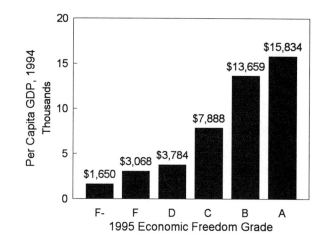

B. The Average Growth Rate of Per
   Capita GDP Between 1980 and 1994
   by 1995 Economic Freedom Grade

*Here we illustrate the annual growth rate of per capita GDP by economic freedom grade. Not only do countries with more economic freedom have a higher per capita GDP (see above), they also generally grow more rapidly.*

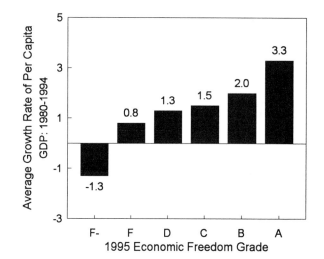

## Exhibit S-3: The Income Levels and Growth Rates of Persistently High and Persistently Low Rated Countries

*As the graphs below indicate, countries with persistently high economic freedom ratings during the last two decades have a very high per capita GDP while those with persistently low ratings have extremely low incomes. The growth rates of the persistently high-rated group are also positive, while those for the low-rated group are low and often negative.*

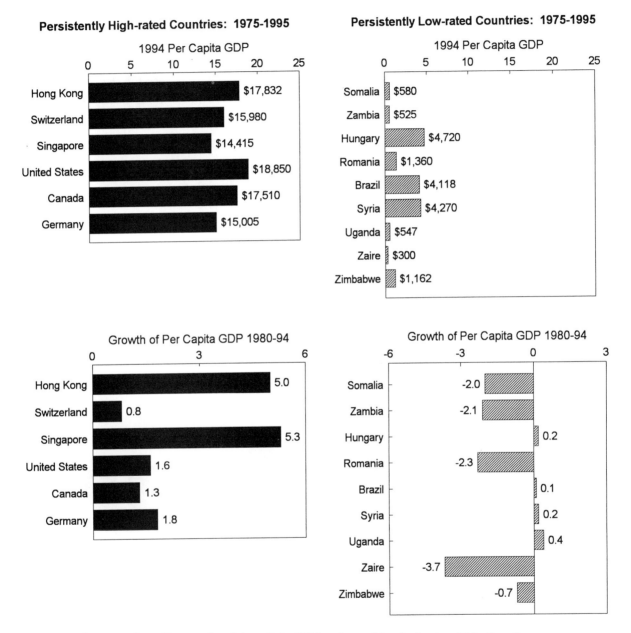

**Persistently High-rated Countries: 1975-1995**

1994 Per Capita GDP

| Country | GDP |
|---|---|
| Hong Kong | $17,832 |
| Switzerland | $15,980 |
| Singapore | $14,415 |
| United States | $18,850 |
| Canada | $17,510 |
| Germany | $15,005 |

**Persistently Low-rated Countries: 1975-1995**

1994 Per Capita GDP

| Country | GDP |
|---|---|
| Somalia | $580 |
| Zambia | $525 |
| Hungary | $4,720 |
| Romania | $1,360 |
| Brazil | $4,118 |
| Syria | $4,270 |
| Uganda | $547 |
| Zaire | $300 |
| Zimbabwe | $1,162 |

Growth of Per Capita GDP 1980-94

| Country | Growth |
|---|---|
| Hong Kong | 5.0 |
| Switzerland | 0.8 |
| Singapore | 5.3 |
| United States | 1.6 |
| Canada | 1.3 |
| Germany | 1.8 |

Growth of Per Capita GDP 1980-94

| Country | Growth |
|---|---|
| Somalia | -2.0 |
| Zambia | -2.1 |
| Hungary | 0.2 |
| Romania | -2.3 |
| Brazil | 0.1 |
| Syria | 0.2 |
| Uganda | 0.4 |
| Zaire | -3.7 |
| Zimbabwe | -0.7 |

Note: The countries with a grade of A or B in 1995 and a ranking in the top 15 in the other years comprise the persistently high-rated group. Countries with a summary economic freedom rating (Is1) of less than 4.0 for every year throughout the 1975-1995 period comprise the persistently low-rated group. See Exhibits 2-3 and 4-2 for additional details. The GDP per capita figures (measured in 1985 U.S. dollars) are updates of the Summers and Heston data. They were derived by the purchasing power parity method.

**Exhibit S-4A: The Economic Freedom Ratings (Is1) During 1975-1995 and Growth Rate for High-Rated Non-Industrial Economies**

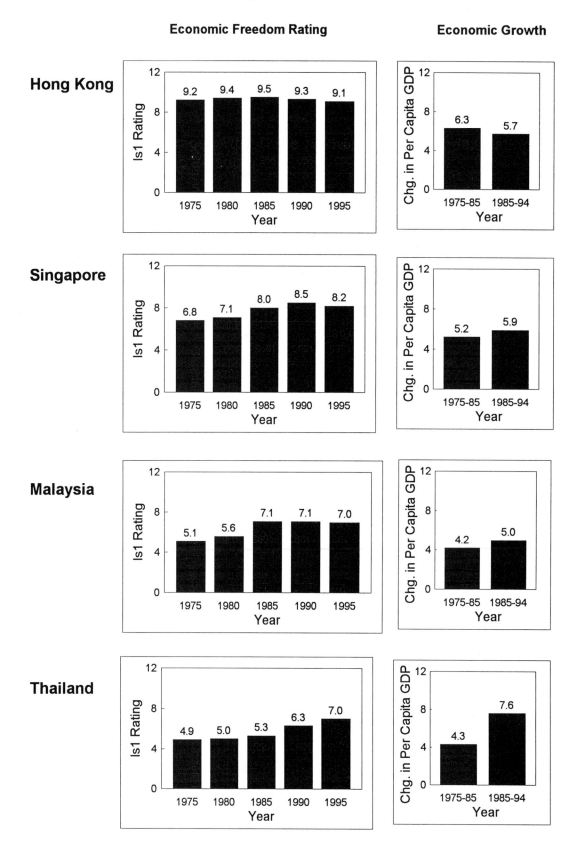

**Exhibit S-4B:  The Economic Freedom Ratings (Is1) During 1975-1995 and Growth Rate for Low-Rated Non-Industrial Economies**

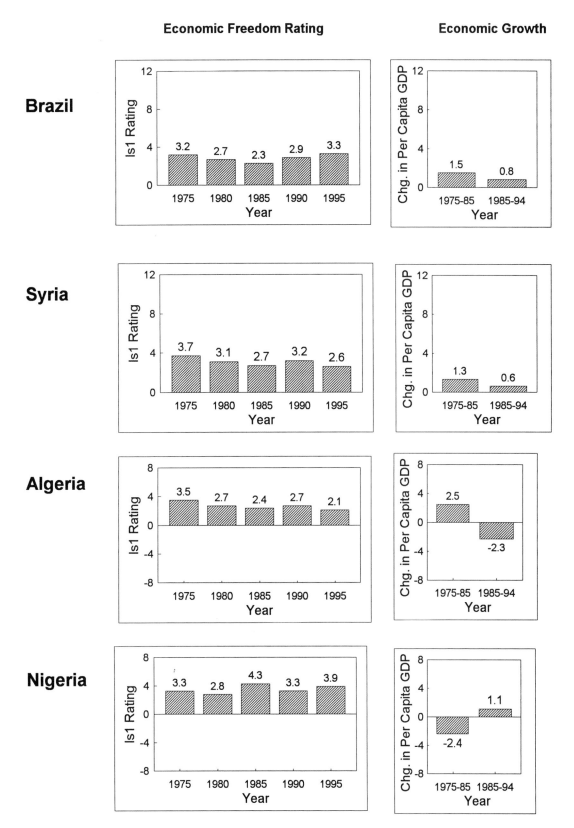

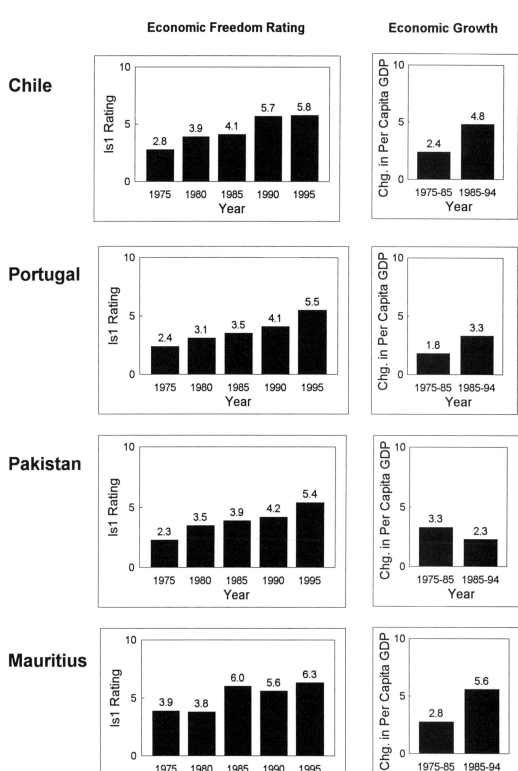

**Exhibit S-4D: The Economic Freedom Ratings (Is1) and Growth Rates of Less-Developed Economies That Became Less Free During 1975-1995**

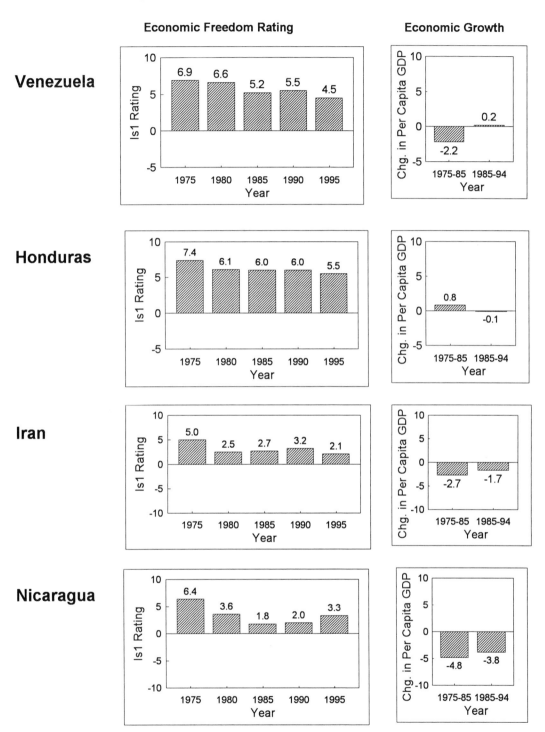

**Exhibit S-5: Growth Rates During 1980-1994 of the Ten Countries with the Largest Increases and Largest Declines in Economic Freedom During 1975-1990**

### Ten Countries with Largest Increase in Economic Freedom Ratings: 1975-1990
(Change in Is1 rating in parentheses.)

*All of these countries achieved positive growth rates. Their average increase in per capita GDP was 2.7%. (See Exhibit 4.3 for additional details.)*

### Ten Countries with Largest Decline in Freedom Ratings: 1975-1990
(Change in Is1 rating in parentheses.)

*Nine of the 11 countries with the largest declines in economic freedom during 1975-1990 also experienced declines in per capita GDP. On average, their per capita GDP declined approximately 1% annually during 1980-1994. (See Exhibit 4-4 for additional details.)*

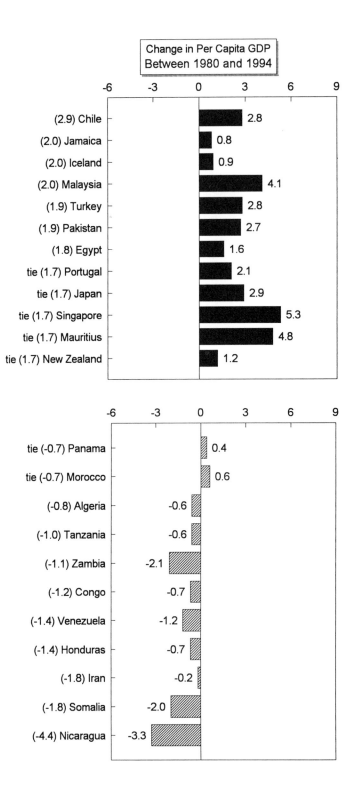

Change in Per Capita GDP Between 1980 and 1994

Ten Countries with Largest Increase:
- (2.9) Chile — 2.8
- (2.0) Jamaica — 0.8
- (2.0) Iceland — 0.9
- (2.0) Malaysia — 4.1
- (1.9) Turkey — 2.8
- (1.9) Pakistan — 2.7
- (1.8) Egypt — 1.6
- tie (1.7) Portugal — 2.1
- tie (1.7) Japan — 2.9
- tie (1.7) Singapore — 5.3
- tie (1.7) Mauritius — 4.8
- tie (1.7) New Zealand — 1.2

Ten Countries with Largest Decline:
- tie (-0.7) Panama — 0.4
- tie (-0.7) Morocco — 0.6
- (-0.8) Algeria — -0.6
- (-1.0) Tanzania — -0.6
- (-1.1) Zambia — -2.1
- (-1.2) Congo — -0.7
- (-1.4) Venezuela — -1.2
- (-1.4) Honduras — -0.7
- (-1.8) Iran — -0.2
- (-1.8) Somalia — -2.0
- (-4.4) Nicaragua — -3.3

**Exhibit S-6:** **The Growth of Per Capita GDP During 1980-1990 for the Countries That Had a One Unit Increase in the Is1 Economic Freedom Rating Between 1975 and 1985 (and Maintained that Increase into the 1990s) Compared to the Growth of Countries with a One Unit Decline During 1980-1990**

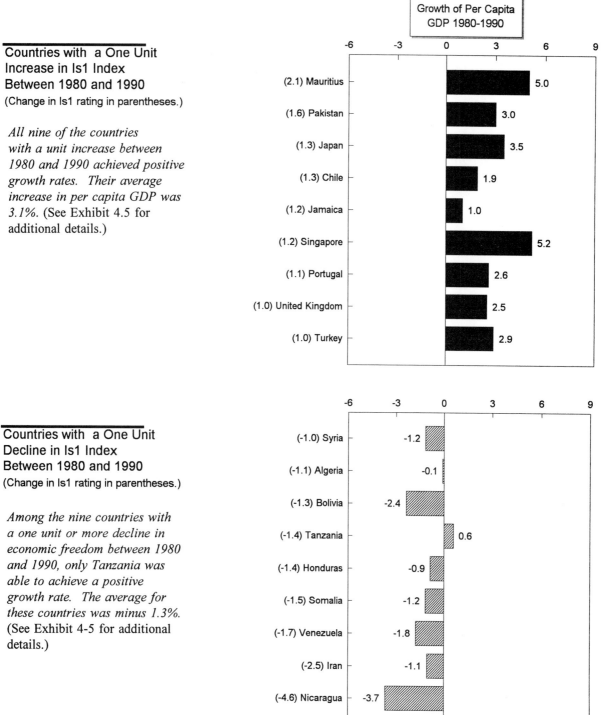

Countries with a One Unit
Increase in Is1 Index
Between 1980 and 1990
(Change in Is1 rating in parentheses.)

*All nine of the countries
with a unit increase between
1980 and 1990 achieved positive
growth rates. Their average
increase in per capita GDP was
3.1%. (See Exhibit 4.5 for
additional details.)*

Growth of Per Capita
GDP 1980-1990

(2.1) Mauritius — 5.0
(1.6) Pakistan — 3.0
(1.3) Japan — 3.5
(1.3) Chile — 1.9
(1.2) Jamaica — 1.0
(1.2) Singapore — 5.2
(1.1) Portugal — 2.6
(1.0) United Kingdom — 2.5
(1.0) Turkey — 2.9

Countries with a One Unit
Decline in Is1 Index
Between 1980 and 1990
(Change in Is1 rating in parentheses.)

*Among the nine countries with
a one unit or more decline in
economic freedom between 1980
and 1990, only Tanzania was
able to achieve a positive
growth rate. The average for
these countries was minus 1.3%.
(See Exhibit 4-5 for additional
details.)*

(-1.0) Syria — -1.2
(-1.1) Algeria — -0.1
(-1.3) Bolivia — -2.4
(-1.4) Tanzania — 0.6
(-1.4) Honduras — -0.9
(-1.5) Somalia — -1.2
(-1.7) Venezuela — -1.8
(-2.5) Iran — -1.1
(-4.6) Nicaragua — -3.7

Note: See Exhibits 3-3 and 4-5 for details.

# Exhibit S-7: Changes in the Average Country Rating for the Summary Indexes and the Components: 1975-1995

## A: Average Summary Rating of Countries, 1975-1995

*The average country rating increased by only a small amount (0.3 or less) between 1975 and 1985, but it rose by a larger amount (approximately 1.0) between 1985 and 1995. (Note that each of our three indexes followed this same pattern.) This suggests that there has been a modest move toward economic freedom during the last decade.*

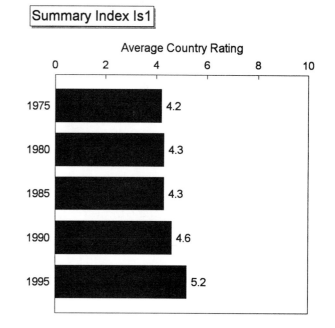

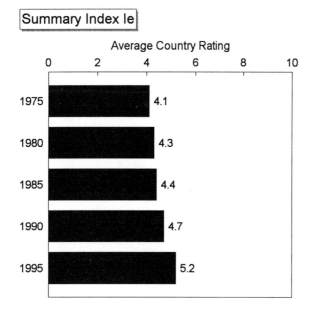

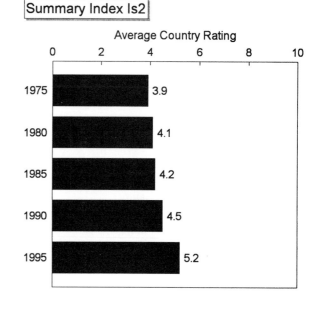

## B. Average Component Rating of Countries:

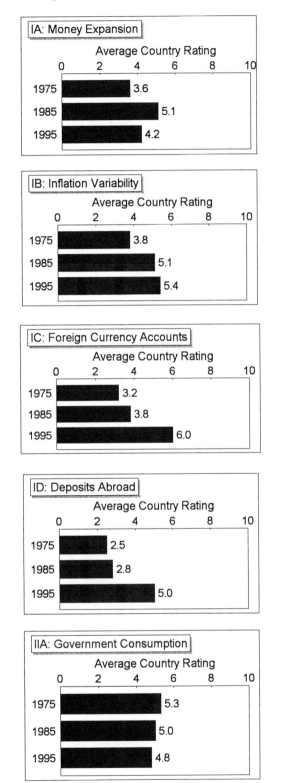

**IA: Money Expansion**
Average Country Rating

| Year | Rating |
|------|--------|
| 1975 | 3.6 |
| 1985 | 5.1 |
| 1995 | 4.2 |

**IB: Inflation Variability**
Average Country Rating

| Year | Rating |
|------|--------|
| 1975 | 3.8 |
| 1985 | 5.1 |
| 1995 | 5.4 |

**IC: Foreign Currency Accounts**
Average Country Rating

| Year | Rating |
|------|--------|
| 1975 | 3.2 |
| 1985 | 3.8 |
| 1995 | 6.0 |

**ID: Deposits Abroad**
Average Country Rating

| Year | Rating |
|------|--------|
| 1975 | 2.5 |
| 1985 | 2.8 |
| 1995 | 5.0 |

**IIA: Government Consumption**
Average Country Rating

| Year | Rating |
|------|--------|
| 1975 | 5.3 |
| 1985 | 5.0 |
| 1995 | 4.8 |

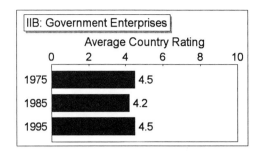

**IIB: Government Enterprises**
Average Country Rating

| Year | Rating |
|------|--------|
| 1975 | 4.5 |
| 1985 | 4.2 |
| 1995 | 4.5 |

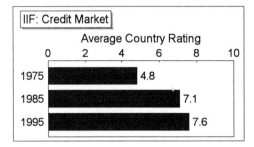

**IIF: Credit Market**
Average Country Rating

| Year | Rating |
|------|--------|
| 1975 | 4.8 |
| 1985 | 7.1 |
| 1995 | 7.6 |

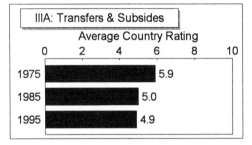

**IIIA: Transfers & Subsides**
Average Country Rating

| Year | Rating |
|------|--------|
| 1975 | 5.9 |
| 1985 | 5.0 |
| 1995 | 4.9 |

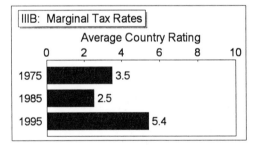

**IIIB: Marginal Tax Rates**
Average Country Rating

| Year | Rating |
|------|--------|
| 1975 | 3.5 |
| 1985 | 2.5 |
| 1995 | 5.4 |

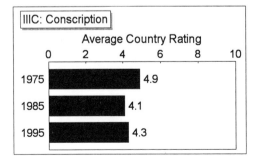

**IIIC: Conscription**
Average Country Rating

| Year | Rating |
|------|--------|
| 1975 | 4.9 |
| 1985 | 4.1 |
| 1995 | 4.3 |

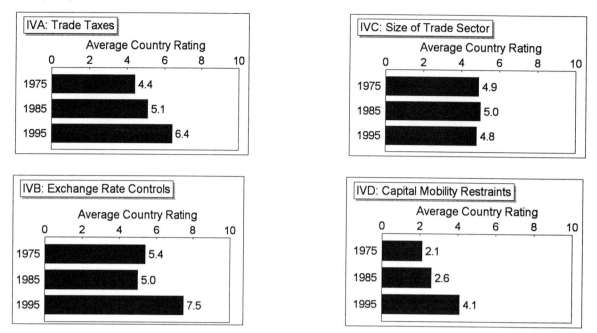

*The component ratings indicate that the major areas of improvement during the last 20 years were greater price stability (IB), increased freedom to maintain foreign currencies both domestically and abroad (IC and ID), more orderly credit markets, lower marginal tax rates (since 1985), lower taxes on international trade (IVA), relaxation of foreign exchange controls (since 1985), and fewer restrictions on capital mobility. Larger government consumption and transfer sectors (IIA and IIIA) were areas of declining economic freedom.*

Note:  See Exhibit 3-6 for additional details.

# INTRODUCTION:

## The Historical Development of The Economic Freedom Index

by Michael A. Walker

The current volume is the culmination of a process which began at the 1984 meetings of the Mont Pelerin Society in Cambridge, England. In the course of a comment on a paper by Paul Johnson, I made reference to the famous passage in *Capitalism and Freedom* written by Milton Friedman and Rose Friedman, in which the authors note that, "Historical evidence speaks with a single voice on the relation between political freedom and a free market. I know of no example in time or place of a society that has been marked by a large measure of political freedom, and that has not also used something comparable to a free market to organize the bulk of economic activity."

There then ensued a discussion about the relationship between economic and political freedom led by the late Max Thurn, a long time member of the Society. It became clear during the course of this discussion that while Milton and Rose Friedman's comment had been extant for three decades there had been no serious attempt to explore the relationship between economic and political freedoms in a scholarly way. At the meeting I approached Milton and Rose Friedman to invite them to co-host a symposium to investigate these relationships. They agreed and subsequently Dr. Neil McLeod, President of the Liberty Fund, Inc. of Indianapolis agreed to provide the funding to bring a group of distinguished economists from all over the world to the Napa Valley, California in 1986.

The proceedings of this first symposium were published in a book which I edited entitled, *Freedom, Democracy and Economic Welfare*, published by the Fraser Institute in 1988. Meanwhile, Alvin Rabushka, Milton Friedman's colleague at the Hoover Institution who had been concerned about these issues for nearly a decade because of his direct involvement in the study and

1

documentation of the economic development of Hong Kong, held a series of Liberty Fund conferences. One, on "Taxation and Liberty" was held in Santa Fe, New Mexico in 1985 and another on "Taxation, Democracy, and Threats to Liberty" in Savannah, Georgia in 1987. Alvin Rabushka was also a participant in the 1986 Napa Valley Conference and he was to play a central role in developing the symposium series.

Milton Friedman had suggested to me that I should invite to the first meeting in the Napa Valley a representative from Freedom House because they had expanded their 1982 Annual Report on political and civil liberties around the world to include, on an experimental basis, ratings for economic freedom. Raymond Gastil, then the President of Freedom House and Lindsay Wright, a young economist working for the organization, came and presented a paper on their findings on economic freedom at the first conference.

As Gastil and Wright shared their views on economic liberty, it was obvious that they differed significantly from those of most conference participants. The Gastil-Wright approach reflected the Freedom House perspective that democratic political procedures and civil liberties were the most important aspects of freedom. According to this philosophy, highly progressive taxation and large income transfers are entirely consistent with individual liberty, if policies in these areas are approved by democratic majorities of legislative bodies.[1] Several of the participants in this first conference, including myself, Walter Block, and Alvin Rabushka, believed that the Freedom House approach trivialized and distorted economic freedom, making it dependent on the political process. We came away even more convinced that development of a sound measure of economic freedom was a vitally important project.

My colleague Walter Block and Alvin Rabushka had a subsequent meeting in which they decided to suggest that a series of follow up symposia be held in order to explore the weaknesses of the Freedom House approach and to develop an index of economic freedom that was consistent with the history and proper meaning of economic liberty. The long term objective would be to develop a measure of economic freedom that would be published on a regular basis just like the Freedom House's annual survey of political and civil liberties.

It was then left for me to persuade Milton and Rose Friedman to co-host a series of symposia to properly elucidate the subject and to persuade the Liberty Fund to provide the financing. The new President of Liberty Fund, Inc., Mr. W. W. Hill was quite excited by the project, could see its implications, and happily agreed to fund a further five meetings in which international experts would build up an intellectual base from which the index might be formed.

The second conference of the series was held in Vancouver in July of 1988 and centred on a paper presented by Alvin Rabushka on how economic freedom should be defined.[2] Building on the work of John Locke, Adam Smith, Milton Friedman, Murray Rothbard, and his own extensive empirical and theoretical analysis, Rabushka examined the attributes of economic freedom and the nature of policies consistent with that freedom. He argued that private property and rule of law provided the foundation—the institutional basis—for economic freedom. Rabushka applied the concept of economic freedom to five basic areas—taxation, public spending, economic regulation of business and labour, money, and foreign trade—and outlined some ideas about how it might be measured in each of these areas. This work proved to be quite important in focusing subsequent discussion at the other symposia.

Also at the second meeting came the first attempt to provide empirical measures with a paper by Zane Spindler and Laurie Still. In their paper they added to the taxonomy suggested by Alvin Rabushka and provided a first-cut try at evaluating the Freedom House Index and adding to it a measure of freedom based on involuntary military service and freedom of foreign trade and investment. One of the consequences of the discussion of this paper was the suggestion that all of the participants produce a list of factors that they felt should go in to an index of economic freedom and there resulted a list of indicators which might be used for this purpose.

The third meeting was held in 1989 at Banff, Alberta and represented the first real attempt to construct both theoretical and empirical measures which were derived from the principles sketched out by Rabushka at the second session. Sectoral papers explored the construction of indices for labour markets, international trade and money markets. The discussions were mostly interesting for the direction they would provide for the papers presented at the fourth meeting held at Sea Ranch, California in 1990.

The fourth symposium saw the investigation proceed to a much higher level of understanding both empirically and theoretically. A theoretical paper by Ronald Jones and Alan C. Stockman built upon two papers by Stephen Easton to specifically consider freedom as part of the standard economic model. Their analysis put to rest a confusion which often attends such discussions and that is the difference between wealth and freedom. They showed that there could simultaneously be a reduction in freedom and an increase in wealth.

Also at the fourth symposium there was the beginning of the index which is presented in this book. James Gwartney worked with Walter Block and Robert Lawson to produce the first comprehensive index which ranked 79 countries in the sectors which Rabushka had outlined and which were further discussed at the third symposium. The fourth symposium also involved, in a paper by Zane Spindler and Joanna Miyake, the consideration of the list of indices of freedom which had been devised during the second symposium.

One of the most interesting aspects of the fourth symposium was a survey of economic freedom conducted by Milton and Rose Friedman. Each of the symposium participants was asked to rank 11 countries which would be familiar to all participants. Milton and Rose then analyzed the ranking during the evening and presented it the following day. This simple survey and analysis of it proved to be quite helpful in discovering the dispersion of estimates of the freedom of countries that were neither very free nor very unfree but somewhere in between. The classic problem of distinguishing amongst things that are similar was also seen to plague the task of measuring freedom.

One of the conclusions that emerged from the Sea Ranch meeting was that there are two ways in which to construct an index of freedom. The "low tech," judgmental way in which a number of individuals are asked to provide their subjective ranking of a group of countries and the "high tech" way in which a large number of criteria, based on a series of measurable quantities, are applied to produce the rating.

By way of testing further the low tech approach, it was decided to have a future meeting consider a group of countries and to have individuals who were familiar with the countries rank them on a freedom scale. The fifth symposium held in 1991 at Monterey California focused on a series of papers which had been constructed in this way. Essentially, groups of respondents in Asia, Latin America, Africa, Europe and North America were asked to rank countries in their region as well as countries outside their region which were common to all of the lists. In this way it was hoped that an integrated picture might emerge of the economic freedom rankings of all countries considered.

While this exercise produced some interesting insights, in general it was found that respondents did not possess enough information about the countries they were asked to rank and it was quite difficult to find people in a given region who were knowledgeable about more than one or two countries. While there were many interesting insights generated from the various regions, it did not prove possible to derive a coherent index from the components.

In a separate survey conducted by Stephen Easton and myself, members of the Mont Pelerin Society were also asked to rank countries in their region and this survey did prove to be coherent. However, it was in general felt that more success might be achieved by reverting to the "high tech" method and the use of many index series for each country which Gwartney, Block and Lawson had begun in the fourth session. This objectification of the measurement process would overcome the problems of subjectivity and the difficulty of finding knowledgeable people to do the rating.

However, a serious problem remained. Namely, to find the weights that should be attached to the various data series in the Gwartney, Block and Lawson index. In partial response to the recognition of this problem, Easton and I undertook another survey of the Mont Pelerin Society membership in which we asked the respondents to rank each country's performance in a number of general areas such as international trade, monetary freedom, etc. The sixth symposium focused entirely on the revised Gwartney, Block and Lawson paper and the second paper which Easton and I had constructed.

The sixth symposium was held in Sonoma California in 1993 and the focus of discussion was a greatly revised Gwartney,

Block and Lawson paper and the paper Easton and I had written to report the results of our second survey. Many suggestions for improvement were advanced and a number of approaches to the problem of weighting the components of the index were discussed. The Index of Freedom which is presented in this volume reflects the valuable contributions of the participants toward resolving the difficulties which were identified.

All told, 61 people have contributed to the Rating Economic Freedom program of the Fraser Institute. We feel that it would be appropriate to acknowledge their contribution to the process and they are therefore named at the end of this introduction. However, it goes without saying that they are not responsible for the resulting index nor do they necessarily endorse it or its implications.

Recently, the Heritage Foundation of Washington, D.C., has published an index of Economic Freedom. There is some question, therefore, as to why we should produce another, seemingly competing index. The answer is simple.

First of all, as The Heritage Foundation was careful to note in their publication, the research which has been produced by the Rating Economic Freedom Project of the Fraser Institute is of a fundamental kind and attempts to deal with the key methodological issues involved in the creation of such an index. The Heritage Foundation index reflects some of this research but is not as complete or as comprehensive as the index published here. It is hoped that the Heritage Foundation will incorporate the advances in the state of research which are reflected in this index.

Secondly, this index provides a historical measurement of economic freedom. It is possible therefore to use this index to undertake analysis of the relationship between economic freedom and other variables through time. This is a very important consideration.

Finally, we believe that this index represents the "state of the art" in the measurement of economic freedom and that it establishes both a new bench mark for economic freedom and a new starting point for research that will improve our understanding of this vital aspect of the human condition.

Endnote:

1. For the presentation of this view, see Lindsey M. Wright, "A Comparative Survey of Economic Freedoms" in *Freedom in the World: Political Rights and Civil Liberties*, 1982, ed. Raymond D. Gastil (Westport and London: Greenwood Press, 1982), pp. 51-90 and Raymond D. Gastil and Lindsey M. Wright, "The State of the World: Political and Economic Freedom," in *Freedom, Democracy and Economic Welfare*, ed. Michael Walker (Vancouver: The Fraser Institute, 1988), pp. 85-119. For a detailed criticism of this view, see Alvin Rabushka "Freedom House Survey of Economic Freedoms," in *Economic Freedom: Toward a Theory of Measurement*, ed. Walter Block (Vancouver: The Fraser Institute, 1991), pp.57-71.

2. For those interested in the papers and a summary of the discussion from the entire Fraser Institute/Liberty Fund series, see Michael A. Walker, ed., *Freedom, Democracy, and Economic Welfare*, (Vancouver: Fraser Institute, 1988); Walter Block, ed., *Economic Freedom: Toward and Theory of Measurement*, (Vancouver: Fraser Institute, 1991); and Stephen T. Easton and Michael A. Walker, eds., *Rating Global Economic Freedom*, (Vancouver: Fraser Institute, 1992).

## Participants in Fraser Institute/Liberty Fund Series:

James Ahiakpor
Professor of Economics
California State University
at Hayward

Armen Alchian
Professor of Economics
University of Calif.—Los
Angeles

Peter Bauer
Professor Emeritus of
Economics
London School of
Economics

Gary S. Becker
Professor of Economics
University of Chicago

Juan F. Bendfeldt
Executive Secretary
Centro de Estudios
Economico-Sociales
Guatemala

Walter Block
Professor of Economics
College of the Holy Cross

Jack Carr
Institute for Policy Analysis
University of Toronto

John F. Chant
Professor of Economics
Simon Fraser University

Edward Crane
President, Cato Institute

William C. Dennis
Liberty Fund, Inc.

Arthur T. Denzau
Professor of Economics
Washington University

Governor Ramon P. Diaz
Central Bank of Uruguay

Thomas J. DiLorenzo
Professor of Economics
Loyola College—Baltimore

Stephen Easton
Professor of Economics
Simon Fraser University

David Friedman
University of Chicago Law
School

Milton Friedman
The Hoover Institution
Stanford University

Rose Friedman
The Hoover Institution
Stanford University

Raymond Gastil
Freedom House

John C. Goodman
President, National Center
for Policy Analysis

John G. Greenwood
Chairman/Chief Economist
G.T. Capital Management

Herbert Grubel
Professor of Economics
Simon Fraser University

James D. Gwartney
Professor of Economics
Florida State University

William Hammett
Manhattan Institute

Arnold Harberger
Professor of Economics
University of Chicago

W.W. Hill
Liberty Fund., Inc.

Edward L. Hudgins
Heritage Foundation

Ronald W. Jones
Professor of Economics
University of Rochester

Professor Brian Kantor
Professor of Economics
University of Capetown

Henry Kierzkowski
Professor of Economics
Grad. Inst. of International
Studies
Geneva, Switzerland

Henri LePage
President, Institut de
L' Entreprise
Paris, France

Robert Lawson
Professor of Economics
Shawnee State University

Assar Lindbeck
Professor of Economics
Inst. for International
Economic Studies
University of Stockholm

Tibor Machan
Professor of Philosophy
Auburn University

Henry Manne
Dean, School of Law
George Mason University

Antonio Martino
Professor of Economics
University of Rome

Hugo Maul
Professor of Economics
Centro de Estudios
Economico-Sociales
Guatemala

Richard B. McKenzie
Professor of Economics
Graduate School of
Management
University of California,
Irvine

Charles Murray
American Enterprise
Institute

Douglass C. North
Professor of Economics
Washington University

Simon Ogus
G.T. Management (Asia)
Limited
Hong Kong

Filip Palda
Professor of Economics
Ecole nationale
d'administration publique
Montreal, Quebec

Ellen Paul
Professor of Philosophy
Bowling Green State
University

Michael Parkin
Professor of Economics
University of Western
Ontario

Gramoz Pashko
Deputy Prime Minister
Government of Albania

Svetozar Pejovich
Professor of Economics
Texas A & M University

Sally Pipes
President, Pacific Research
Institute

Robert Poole
Editor, *Reason*

Alvin Rabushka
The Hoover Institution
Stanford University

Gerald Radnitsky
Professor of Philosophy
University of Trier

Richard W. Rahn
President, Novecon Corp.

Alan Reynolds
Hudson Institute

Gerald W. Scully
Professor of Economics
School of Management
University of Texas at
Dallas

Bernard Siegan
Professor of Law
Univ. of San Diego School
of Law

Zane Spindler
Professor of Economics
Simon Fraser University

Ingemar Stahl
Professor of Economics
University of Lund
Lund, Sweden

Alan C. Stockman
Professor of Economics
University of Rochester

Richard L. Stroup
Professor of Economics
Montana State University

Melanie Tammen
Cato Institute

Gordon Tullock
Professor of Economics
University of Arizona

Michael Walker
Executive Director
Fraser Institute

Sir Alan Walters
The World Bank

Lindsay Wright
Freedom House

# CHAPTER 1

## Construction of the Economic Freedom Index

*Measurement is the making of distinction; precise measurement is making sharp distinctions.*
-Enrico Fermi[1]

Most people prefer to choose for themselves. This indicates that freedom, including economic freedom, has intrinsic value. Adam Smith noted that human beings have a natural inclination to "truck and barter." Restrictions on the freedom to choose and engage in voluntary exchange deny human beings something they value—something that is an integral part of their humanity. In addition, economic theory indicates that economic freedom affects incentives, productive effort, and the effectiveness of resource use. Since the time of Smith, economists have argued that the freedom to choose, supply resources, compete in business, and trade with others is a central ingredient—perhaps the fundamental element—of economic progress.

If economic freedom is this important, why have we invested so little time attempting to measure it? The obvious answer is that economic freedom is multi-dimensional and therefore its measurement is a difficult—some would say impossible—task. These same arguments were presented prior to the development of the national income accounts used to measure gross domestic product. Of course, there is a parallel here. Since most thought measurement of output with any degree of accuracy was an impossible task, it was 150 years after Smith's *Wealth of Nations* before a comprehensive measure was developed.

If we are unable to measure economic freedom, we are in a poor position to judge its significance as a source of progress. Clearly, the degree of economic freedom present is influenced by numerous factors. No single statistic will be able to fully capture all of them and their interrelations. However, we believe that it is possible to devise measures and develop indicators that will capture the most important elements of economic freedom and provide a reasonably good measure of differences in economic freedom across countries and time periods.[2] As the quotation of Professor Fermi indicates, measurement involves making distinctions. When something is difficult to measure precisely, the distinctions may not be as refined as we would like. This is the case with economic freedom. The measures developed in this study might best be viewed as approximations rather than precise measures. Therefore, *small differences* between countries and across time periods should not be taken very seriously.

This chapter addresses three topics. We begin with a discussion of the concept of economic freedom. The second section describes the various components of our indexes and indicates how the economic freedom ratings for each of the components are derived. The final section considers the problems that arise when the components are aggregated into a summary index and explains how the three summary indexes of economic freedom are derived.

## THE CONCEPT OF ECONOMIC FREEDOM

The central elements of economic freedom are personal choice, protection of private property, and freedom of exchange. Individuals have economic freedom when (a) property they acquire without the use of force, fraud, or theft is protected from physical invasions by others and (b) they are free to use, exchange, or give their property to another as long as their actions do not violate the identical rights of others.[3] Thus, an index of economic freedom should measure the extent to which rightly acquired property is protected and individuals are free to engage in voluntary transactions. In an economically free society, the fundamental function of government is the protection of private property and the enforcement of contracts. When a government fails to protect private property, takes property itself without full compensation, or establishes restrictions that limit voluntary exchange, it violates the economic freedom of its citizens.[4]

*An index of economic freedom should measure the extent to which rightly acquired property is protected and individuals are free to engage in voluntary transactions.*

This concept of economic freedom reflects the prior work of others. Alvin Rabushka, a pioneer researcher and leading scholar in this area, highlighted the relationship between private property and economic freedom in the following manner:

*Private property is the common denominator that underpins every liberal philosophical treatment of individual economic freedom. John Locke regarded the existence of private property as the proper condition of man in a state of nature; the primary function of civil society, to which man granted the rights he enjoyed in the state of nature, was to protect and preserve private property. Most important, the state has no right to take any part of a man's property without his consent.*[5]

Lindsey Wright of the Freedom House has also stressed the central role of private property. In the 1982 Freedom House annual report, she stated:

*The freedom to have property and control its use is fundamental to the ability of individuals and groups to make economic choices independent of arbitrary intervention by others.*[6]

Freedom of exchange and the autonomy of the individual are also integral elements of economic freedom. As Alvin Rabushka put it:

*The free and voluntary exchange of property titles goes hand in hand with the rights of private property. Unless each individual controls the use of his property, including his right to transfer it to another party in exchange for some consideration, the notion of private ownership and use has little meaning. Thus, freedom of contract is inherent in private property.... A free society affords every individual freedom of contract in contrast with, say, an aristocratic society in which only the nobility can enter into contracts to exchange titles.*[7]

It is useful to view economic freedom within the framework of protective rights and intrusive rights.[8] Protective rights provide individuals with a shield against others who would invade and/or take what does not belong to them. Since they are nonaggression rights, all citizens can simultaneously possess them. In order to maintain protective rights, preventing people from initiating aggression against others is all that is required. In contrast, intrusive rights (or "positive rights" as they are sometimes called), such as a "right" to food, clothing, medical services, housing, or a minimal income level impose "forced labor" requirements on others. If A has a right to housing, for example, this logically implies that he has a right to force B to provide the housing. But A has no right to the labor of B or any other individual. Thus, A cannot possibly have a right to housing and other things that can only be

*Intrusive rights such as a "right" to food, clothing, medical services, housing, or a minimal income level impose "forced labor" requirements on others. Alleged "rights" of this type are simply disguised demands for the forced transfers of income and wealth.*

supplied if they are provided by other people. Intrusive rights therefore conflict with economic freedom because such "rights" imply that some have a right to the labor and possessions of others. In reality, alleged "rights" of this type are simply disguised demands for the forced transfers of income and wealth.

It is important to distinguish economic freedom from political and civil liberties. Political freedom has to do with the procedures that are used to elect government officials and decide political issues. Political liberty is present when all adult citizens are free to participate in the political process (vote, lobby, and choose among candidates), elections are fair and competitive, and alternative parties are allowed to participate freely. Civil liberty encompasses the freedom of the press and the rights of individuals to assemble, hold alternative religious views, receive a fair trial, and express their views without fear of physical retaliation. A country may have a substantial amount of both political and civil liberty—it may be highly democratic and the major civil liberties may be protected—and still adopt policies that conflict with economic freedom. Countries like Israel, Sweden, and India illustrate this point. Political and civil liberties are present in such countries, but nonetheless, their policies—for example, the levels of taxation, government spending, and regulations—are often in conflict with economic freedom.

## THE COMPONENTS OF OUR INDEX OF ECONOMIC FREEDOM

*Our goal is to construct an index that is (a) a good indicator of economic freedom across countries and (b) based on objective components that can be updated regularly.*

Our goal is to construct an index that is (a) a good indicator of economic freedom across a large number of countries and (b) based on objective components that can be updated regularly. To the extent possible, we want to avoid having to make "judgment calls" when rating the policies, legal structures, and institutions of a country.

As Exhibit 1-1 indicates, our index has 17 components that are allocated to four major areas: (1) money and inflation, (2) government operations and regulations, (3) takings and discriminatory taxation, and (4) international exchange.[9] Since we want the ratings to be easily comparable across countries and time

14

periods, a zero to ten rating scale was used for each component in the index. A ten represents the highest possible rating and a zero the lowest.

Because the structure of the underlying data used to derive the ratings was not always the same, three alternative methods were used to derive them. A continuous variable provided the underlying data for seven of the components. When this was the case, the data for 1985—our base year—were arrayed from the highest to the lowest values and divided into eleven groups containing an equal number of countries. Nations in those 11 groups were then assigned ratings ranging from ten to zero. For example, if there were 99 countries (for which the required data were available), then the nine countries that rated best in this category in 1985 would receive a rating of ten, the next nine would receive a rating of nine, and so on.[10] The cutoff points between groups in the 1985 data were then used to rate each country in the other years (1975, 1980, 1990 and 1995). To determine the interval cutoff points between, say, a ten and a nine rating, we calculated the midpoint in the 1985 data between the country with the lowest ten rating and the country with the highest nine rating.

The advantage of using only the base year 1985 to derive the conversion table is that this approach allows the ratings of countries to either improve or worsen in the other years. Thus, while the rating system judges countries relative to one another during the 1985 base year, the rating of a country can move up or down in the other years. If most countries improve (or regress) relative to the base year, this system allows their ratings to reflect this improvement.

A binary variable provided the underlying data for three of the components. This would be the case, for example, when a restriction was either present or absent (or when an act was either legal or illegal). If the condition consistent with economic freedom was present, the country was assigned a rating of ten. Alternatively, if the condition was absent, the country was assigned a zero.

Finally, in some cases a classification-rating system was developed and underlying data used to classify and rate each country. This method was employed when the underlying data were multi-dimensional. For example, both the top marginal tax

15

**Exhibit 1-1: Components of the Index of Economic Freedom**

I.  **MONEY AND INFLATION** (Protection of money as a store of value and medium of exchange)
    A.  Average Annual Growth Rate of the Money Supply During the Last Five Years Minus the Potential Growth Rate of Real GDP
    B.  Standard Deviation of the Annual Inflation Rate During the Last Five Years
    C.  Freedom of Citizens to Own a Foreign Currency Bank Account Domestically
    D.  Freedom of Citizens to Maintain a Bank Account Abroad

II. **GOVERNMENT OPERATIONS AND REGULATIONS** (Freedom to decide what is produced and consumed)
    A.  Government General Consumption Expenditures as a Percent of GDP
    B.  The Role and Presence of Government-Operated Enterprises
    C.  Price Controls—the Extent that Businesses are Free to Set Their Own Prices (This variable is included in only the 1990 and 1995 Indexes.)
    D.  Freedom of Private Businesses and Cooperatives to Compete in Markets (This variable is included only in the 1995 Index.)
    E.  Equality of Citizens Under The Law and Access of Citizens to a Nondiscriminatory Judiciary (This variable is included only in the 1995 Index.)
    F.  Freedom from Government Regulations and Policies that Cause Negative Real Interest Rates

III. **TAKINGS AND DISCRIMINATORY TAXATION** (Freedom to keep what you earn)
    A.  Transfers and Subsidies as a Percent of GDP
    B.  Top Marginal Tax Rate (and income threshold at which it applies)
    C.  The Use of Conscripts to Obtain Military Personnel

IV. **RESTRAINTS ON INTERNATIONAL EXCHANGE** (Freedom of exchange with foreigners)
    A.  Taxes on International Trade as a Percent of Exports Plus Imports
    B.  Difference Between the Official Exchange Rate and the Black Market Rate
    C.  Actual Size of Trade Sector Compared to the Expected Size
    D.  Restrictions on the Freedom of Citizens to Engage in Capital Transactions with Foreigners

rate and the income level at which the rate took affect were used to rate tax structures. The various countries were placed into rating categories reflecting both of these variables. When this method was used, the zero to ten rating range was still retained.

16

The underlying data and the country ratings for each of the 17 components are presented in the tables of Appendix II. (Note: the labeling of the tables for each of the components presented in Appendix II matches the labels of Exhibit 1-1.) We now turn to a discussion of the components in each of the four major areas of our index and the explanation of precisely how the country ratings for each of the 17 components were derived. We will begin with the money and inflation area.

## I. Money and Inflation

Since money plays such a central role in the exchange process, monetary institutions and arrangements exert an important impact on the security of property and freedom of exchange. Money makes it possible for people to engage in complex exchanges involving the receipt of income or payment of a purchase price across lengthy time periods. It also provides a means of storing purchasing power into the future.

The relationship between monetary arrangements and policies and economic freedom is a matter of some controversy. Some would argue that any government action whatsoever in this area necessarily conflicts with economic freedom.[11] Proponents of this view argue that if coinage of money and the business of banking were left completely to the private sector, firms would tie the value of money they issue to precious metals (like gold and silver) and follow strategies designed to maintain purchasing power stability in order to protect their reputation (brand name) and the future demand for their product. According to this perspective, the competitive process would lead to monetary stability because people would be reluctant to use money issued by institutions that lacked credibility. In turn, the credibility of banking institutions would be dependent upon their ability to develop and maintain a monetary unit with stable, predictable purchasing power.

Others argue that provision of a stable monetary framework is a legitimate function of government and if the government provides a stable monetary unit with predictable value, its actions are consistent with economic freedom.[12] The proponents of this view often argue for constitutional provisions that would commit the monetary authorities to stable money and limit their ability to expand the supply of money.

*Money makes it possible for people to engage in complex exchanges involving the receipt of income or payment of a purchase price across lengthy time periods.*

17

There is some common ground between these two camps. First, both would agree that economic freedom is diminished when monetary disturbances and unexpected price changes alter the value of money and the terms of time-dimension agreements involving money. Such actions involve, in effect, the taking of property. In many such cases, wealth is taken from one private party and given to another. In other cases, it is taken from individuals and transferred to the government.

*The general ingredients of economic freedom in the monetary area are: (1) slow monetary expansion that maintains and protects the value of money, (2) price level (or inflation rate) stability, and (3) the absence of restrictions limiting the use of alternative currencies.*

Second, there is also widespread agreement that government actions which deter the use of alternative currencies infringe on the freedom of contract and therefore economic freedom. The right of trading partners to conduct their business affairs in any currency—domestic or foreign; private or issued by a government—is an important right. Thus, laws conflict with economic freedom when they require trading partners to use a certain currency or prohibit the ownership and use of alternatives. In turn, the freedom to maintain and use alternative currencies limits the power of the national monetary authorities. When trading partners can easily shift to other means of exchange, they are better able to protect themselves against a central monetary authority that follows inflationary and unpredictable policies.

Today, almost every government in the world issues money and operates a central bank that conducts monetary policy. Therefore, if we want to establish gradations of economic freedom in this area, we must evaluate these policies. Our discussion highlights three general ingredients of economic freedom in the monetary area: (1) slow monetary expansion that maintains and protects the value of money, (2) price level (or inflation rate) stability, and (3) the absence of restrictions limiting the use of alternative currencies. We proceed to an explanation of how the four monetary components of our index were derived.

**I-A: The Average Annual Growth Rate of the Money Supply during the last five years Minus the Annual Growth Rate of Potential GDP.**

Authorities that issue money have an implicit responsibility to maintain the purchasing power of the outstanding units. When the supply of a currency is increased rapidly relative to the availability of goods and services, wealth is taken from the people holding money (and assets yielding a fixed nominal return). In essence, rapid growth in the money supply "waters down" the value of the outstanding monetary units and thereby erodes its value. This is wrongful seizure of property. Therefore, countries with high rates of monetary growth relative to real GDP are given low ratings.

*Data Sources and Methodology.* The compound average annual growth rate of the money supply (M1) during the 5-year period just prior to each rating year *minus* the average growth of real GDP during the last ten years was calculated. A country's real GDP growth rate during the last ten years was perceived to be a good estimator for the growth of potential GDP. The money supply and GDP data were from the World Bank, *World Tables, 1994* and the International Monetary Fund, *Monthly International Financial Statistics.* The latter source was generally used to update the data series for the more recent years. The statistics for this measure of monetary growth are presented by country for each of the five periods in Table I-A of Appendix II.

When a country's monetary authorities expand the money supply slowly (rapidly) relative to potential GDP, this variable will be small (large) and the country will receive a high (low) rating.[13] The data for the 1985 base year period were arranged in ascending order and divided into eleven groups of equal size. Since the 1985 money supply data were available for 101 countries, the nine countries with the lowest rate of monetary expansion were given a rating of ten. The nine countries with the next lowest rate of monetary expansion were given a rating of nine, and so on. The midpoints between intervals were then used to derive the range for each of the zero-to-ten ratings for the 1985 base year. The transformation table containing these values is included in the source note accompanying Table I-A (Appendix II). These base-year rating intervals were then used to assign ratings for the other four periods. These ratings are presented along with the actual money growth data for each of the five periods in Table I-A (Appendix II).

## I-B: The Standard Deviation of Annual Inflation Rate during the last five years.

The efficacy of money is directly related to the stability of its value. When the inflation rate is constantly changing in an unpredictable manner—when it is 10% in one year, 40% the next, and 20% the year after that, it is extremely difficult to plan for the future and undertake exchanges that involve a time dimension (e.g., payment for the purchase of an automobile or house over a period

*The efficacy of money is directly related to the stability of its value.*

of years). Since unpredictable changes in the rate of inflation undermine the efficacy of money, countries with the most stable—and therefore most easily predictable—rates of inflation are given the highest ratings. Correspondingly, countries with the highest variability in their inflation rates are given the lowest ratings.[14]

*Data Sources and Methodology.* Data for the GDP Deflator from the World Bank, *World Tables, 1994* supplemented with recent data from the International Monetary Fund, *Monthly International Financial Statistics* were used to calculate the inflation rate of each country by year. Then the standard deviation of the inflation rate was calculated for each 5-year period prior to the rating year. Following the procedures adopted for continuous variables, the base-year 1985 data were divided into eleven intervals of equal size and these intervals were then used to determine the country ratings for each period. Data for both the standard deviation of the inflation rate and the corresponding rating by country for each of the five periods of our study are presented in Table II-B of Appendix II. The conversion table derived from the base year data is also presented in the note at the end of this table.

## I-C: Freedom of Residents to Own Foreign Money Domestically.

Money offered by other monetary authorities is a substitute for money issued by the government of a given country. When residents are allowed to maintain bank accounts in foreign currencies, it is easier for them to avoid the uncertainties accompanying an unstable domestic monetary regime. Thus, citizens have more economic freedom if they are allowed to maintain domestic bank accounts in other currencies.

*Data Sources and Methodology.* The *World Currency Yearbook*, which was published bi-annually throughout the 1975-1990 period contains a "front matter" table which lists each country and indicates whether it is legal for the citizens of the country to own foreign currency bank accounts domestically. This information was used to rate each country for 1975, 1980, 1985, and 1990. An Annual Report, *Exchange Arrangements and Exchange Restrictions*, published by the International Monetary

Fund, also provides information on the legality of foreign currency bank accounts for each country. The 1994 Report provided the source for this component during the most recent period (1993-1995).

Since this is a binary variable—generalized holdings of foreign currency accounts are either legal or illegal—a country is given a rating of 10 if citizen ownership of a foreign currency bank account is legal. If such an account is illegal, the country is given a rating of zero.

## I-D: Freedom of Residents to Maintain Bank Accounts Abroad.

Ownership of a bank account abroad provides another alternative method of storing purchasing power for future use. From a security standpoint, this option may be preferable to the domestic ownership of a foreign currency bank account because an account abroad is less vulnerable to confiscation by one's own government. When the monetary arrangements of a country have a history of instability, many citizens may prefer to deposit their funds with a bank elsewhere. Freedom to own a bank account abroad provides them with this option and thereby reduces their government's power to utilize monetary expansion as a method of extracting wealth from them. Thus, countries that permit their citizens to maintain bank accounts abroad are given a higher rating.

*Data Sources and Methodology.* As was the case for the previous component, the *International Currency Yearbook* and the *Exchange Arrangements and Exchange Restrictions—Annual Report* are the source of this variable. When it is legal for the citizens of a country to own a bank account abroad, the country is given a rating of 10. When ownership of these accounts is illegal, the country is given a rating of zero.

## II. Government Operations and Regulations

Market exchange is based on a voluntary agreement among trading partners. Unless all parties agree, the transaction will not take place. No private business firm, regardless of its size, can force potential consumers to purchase its products. Government is fundamentally different. Unlike business firms, governments can take (tax) some of your wealth and transfer it to others or use it to operate government agencies or enterprises. Governments can also set prices, limit entry into markets and occupations, mandate provision of services by private parties (usually businesses), and impose numerous other regulations on individuals.

There are two broad functions of government that are consistent with economic freedom: (1) protection of individuals and their property against invasions by intruders, both domestic and foreign and (2) provision of a few select goods—what economists call public goods—which have characteristics that make them difficult for private business firms to produce and market. Nobel laureate James Buchanan refers to these functions as the protective and productive functions of government.

Government's protective function seeks to prevent individuals from physically harming the person or property of another and to maintain an infrastructure of rules within which people can interact peacefully. The crucial ingredients of this infrastructure include the enforcement of contracts and the avoidance of restrictions, regulations, and differential or excessive taxes that would restrain exchange.

The productive function of government involves the provision of public goods—goods that have two distinguishing characteristics: (1) supplying them to one individual simultaneously makes them available to others, and (2) it is difficult, if not impossible, to restrict their consumption to paying customers only. National defense, flood control projects, and mosquito abatement programs are examples of public goods.[15]

When governments move beyond these protective and productive functions into the provision of private goods, they restrict consumer choice and economic freedom. Most modern states are heavily involved in directing production toward more of some goods and less of others, operation of enterprises, the protection of government firms from the discipline of competition, the imposition of price controls, and numerous other expenditures and regulatory activities that have nothing to do with either the protection of property rights or the provision of public goods.

Given the breadth and magnitude of government operations and regulations, precise measurement of these activities is an impossible task. However, our index includes six components that provide insight into the relationship between government activity and

*There are two broad functions of government that are consistent with economic freedom: (1) protection of individuals against invasions by intruders, both domestic and foreign, and (2) provision of a few select goods—what economists call public goods.*

economic freedom in several important areas. While these components are far from inclusive, they provide an indication of the degree to which governmental operations conflict with economic freedom.

## II-A: Government General Consumption Expenditures as a Share of GDP.

When government consumption expenditures increase as a share of GDP, political decision-making is substituted for market choices and coordination. Ceteris paribus, more public sector spending means less spending by individuals and families.

As government expenditures increase, more and more of these expenditures tend to be channelled toward activities outside of the protective and productive functions of government. Big-spending governments generally tend to be more heavily involved in projects designed to benefit local constituents, organized special interests, and other favored groups—including government bureaucrats and officials. Therefore, as coercive political decision-making allocates more resources and non-coercive market decision-making allocates fewer, economic freedom shrinks.

*Data Sources and Methodology.* The World Bank, *World Tables*, provided the primary source of the data for this variable. In a few cases, data were obtained from the International Monetary Fund, *Monthly International Financial Statistics,* since current data were sometimes more readily available from this source.[16] Since government consumption as a share of GDP is a continuous variable, the general procedures that we previously outlined were utilized to derive the rating transformation in 1985. In turn, the 1985 intervals were used to rate the countries in the other years. The transformation table containing these intervals is presented in the note at the end of Table II-A of Appendix II. The country ratings for this variable are also presented in this table.

## II-B: Government-Operated Enterprises as a Share of the Economy.

Government-operated enterprises also involve the substitution of political coercion for market decision-making. Government enterprises are fundamentally different from private businesses. Their start-up capital is coercively obtained from taxpayers, whereas the initial funds of private firms are voluntarily obtained from investors willing to risk their own wealth. Subsequent investment decisions of public sector firms are made by political officials playing with funds that belong to taxpayers, rather than entrepreneurs capable of attracting financial capital voluntarily from investors. Subsidies, favorable tax treatment, and regulations are often used to protect state-operated firms from private competitors. If the government project fails to generate enough revenue to cover its costs, there is no bankruptcy mechanism to bring it to a halt. Thus, public sector enterprises tend to stifle market forces and substitute political choices for market decision-making.

Data on government expenditures will substantially understate the intervention of government when state-operated enterprises are widespread. To the extent the current operating expenditures of government enterprises are covered by sales revenue, they generally do not appear in the national budget. Only the subsidy (or revenue surplus) enters into the budgetary accounts. Inclusion of this variable helps to correct a major deficiency of general government consumption expenditures as a measure of the size and intrusiveness of the state.

*Data Sources and Methodology.* Ideally, it would be nice to have a continuous variable like the proportion of output (or employment) of government-operated enterprises as a share of the economy. To our knowledge, data of this sort are unavailable from a single source for a large number of countries. However, there has been a great deal of research on government-operated enterprises in recent years and empirical data are increasingly becoming available. The Organization for Economic Cooperation and Development (OECD) has done a number of studies of its members on this topic. The World Bank recently conducted a similar study of African countries.[17] Our research on the topic also turned up several country studies of government-operated enterprises and privatization during the last two decades. In addition, the International Monetary Fund, *Government Finance Statistics Yearbook*, provides a listing of the enterprises operated by the central governments of various countries.[18]

We analyzed these various sources and used them to classify countries into six different categories that were assigned ratings ranging from zero to ten. Countries with very few government-operated enterprises that were estimated to produce less than 1 percent of the country's output were assigned a rating of ten. As the estimated size and breadth of the government enterprise sector

*Data on government expenditures will substantially understate the intervention of government when state-operated enterprises are widespread.*

increased, countries were assigned lower ratings. A rating of 8 was assigned when there were few government-operated enterprises except for power-generating or similar industries where economies of scale might reduce the effectiveness of competition. A rating of 6 was assigned when the government enterprises also spread into transportation, communications, and the development of energy sources, but private enterprises dominated other sectors of the economy. A rating of 4 was given when most of the large enterprises of the economy were operated by the government and these enterprises generally comprised between 10 and 20 percent of the total non-agricultural employment and output. The assigned rating declined to 2 when government enterprises were estimated to comprise between 20 and 30 percent of the total non-agricultural employment and output and to zero when the estimated share of the public sector businesses exceeded 30 percent of the economy. The source note at the end of Table II-B of Appendix II provides additional details on these rating categories as well as the country ratings for each of our rating years.

### II-C: Price Controls—The Extent that Businesses Are Free to Set Their Own Prices.

The freedom of individuals to use their own property and engage in voluntary exchange can be substantially reduced by regulations that limit the scope of business activity and the use of privately-owned property. Price controls interfere with the freedom of buyers and sellers to undertake exchanges even though the terms of trade are mutually agreeable. Price controls also, in effect, take property from a private owner. For example, if price controls on rental housing cut the rate of return of a property in half, in essence, they take half of the property's value from the owner. Since price controls both constrain exchange and take property from owners, they are inconsistent with economic freedom.

*Price controls interfere with the freedom of buyers and sellers to undertake exchanges even though the terms of trade are mutually agreeable.*

*Data Sources and Methodology.* Two major data sources were utilized to rate countries in this area. First, the *World Competitiveness Report* published by The World Economic Forum contains survey data indicating the "extent to which companies can set their prices freely". This source provided data for 32 countries in 1989 and 41 countries in 1994. Since this was the most comprehensive empirical indicator on the breadth of price controls we could find, we used it to rate the countries covered by the

World Economic Forum surveys. The list of countries rated from this source is supplied in the note accompanying Table II-C of Appendix II.[19]

In addition, Price Waterhouse's *Doing Business in...* publication series provides a verbal description of the imposition of price controls in various product categories for countries covered by the series. When available, this information was used to rate the countries not covered by the data from the *World Competitiveness Report*. In some instances, supplementary information from country sources was also used. These descriptive data were used to place countries into various categories indicating the coverage of price controls as a share of the economy. The more widespread the use of price controls throughout the economy, the lower the rating.

The country ratings for this variable and additional details concerning their derivation are provided in Table II-C of Appendix II. Since the source data for this variable were only available in 1990 and 1994, it was not included in the 1975, 1980, and 1985 indexes.

## II-D: Freedom to Enter and Compete in Markets.

The freedom to enter and compete in product and labor markets is highly important. Governments often require licenses and/or impose other restraints that limit the entry of firms into various business activities and of individuals into various occupations.

*Data Source and Methodology.* The data source of this rating was the Freedom House, *Freedom in the World: The Annual Survey of Political Rights and Civil Liberties, 1994-95*. In recent years the Freedom House annual survey used to rate the political and civil liberties of countries has included a sub-category on the economic freedom of businesses and cooperatives to compete in the marketplace (Item 9 on the Freedom House checklist of 13 civil liberty categories). Each country was given a rating of 0 to 4 with a rating of 4 indicating the countries for which businesses and cooperatives were most free to compete.[20] We transformed the 0 to 4 rating of Freedom House to our 0 to 10 scale (0 = 0, 1 = 2.5, 2 = 5, 3 = 7.5 and 4 = 10). The ratings for each country are presented in Table II-D of Appendix II.

26

## II-E: Equality of Citizens Under The Law and Access of Citizens to a Nondiscriminatory Judiciary.

A legal structure that clearly defines property rights, enforces contracts, and provides a mutually agreeable mechanism for the settlement of contractual and property right disputes provides the foundation for a market economy. To the extent countries provide such a legal system, they are given higher ratings.

*Data Sources and Methodology.* The rating data for this component are also found in the annual survey of political and civil liberties conducted by the Freedom House. (See Freedom House, *Survey of Political Rights and Civil Liberties, 1994-95.*) Item 5 of the 13 item civil liberties checklist is: "Are citizens equal under the law, do they have access to an independent, non-discriminatory judiciary, and are they respected by the security forces?" Countries were given ratings ranging from 0 to 4. The higher the rating, the greater the degree of equality under the law. As in the case of the previous component, we transformed the 0 to 4 ratings of the Freedom House to our 0 to 10 scale. Since this variable was unavailable prior to 1994, it was only included in our 1995 index.

## II-F: Freedom from Government Regulations and Policies that Cause Negative Real Interest Rates.

This component seeks to measure the impact of credit market regulations, interest rate controls, and government operation of the banking system on the freedom of citizens to borrow and lend. Many government regulations restrict entry into various banking activities and increase the cost of transactions between borrowers and lenders. As a result, the differential between the borrowing and the lending (or deposit) rate is unnecessarily large and exchange between borrowers and lenders is retarded.

Probably the most damaging way that government regulations and controls restrict exchanges in the credit market is through the combination of an inflationary monetary policy and interest rate controls. When the inflation rate exceeds the fixed interest rate, *negative real* interest rates occur. With negative real interest rates, the purchasing power of the principal and interest of savers actually declines when wealth is held in the form of domestic savings

*Probably the most damaging way that government regulations and controls restrict exchanges in the credit market is through the combination of an inflationary monetary policy and interest rate controls.*

27

deposits or bonds. Thus, there is little incentive to save and thereby supply funds to the domestic capital market. "Capital flight" will result as domestic residents seek positive returns abroad and foreigners shun the country. Such policies will both diminish economic freedom and undermine the operation of the capital market.

*Data Sources and Methodology.* Our objective is to develop a rating for this component that will reflect both regulations that drive a wedge between the borrowing and lending interest rates and policies that lead to destructive negative real interest rates. First, we obtained the inflation rate, deposit interest rate, and lending interest rate data for each country from the International Monetary Fund, *International Financial Statistics Yearbook* (or the monthly version of this publication). These data were used to estimate real interest rates. The differential between the nominal deposit and lending interest rates was used as the estimate of the respective real rates.

The data on the real deposit and lending rates (and the differential between the two) during the three years prior to a rating year were then used to classify credit markets. Countries were given rating of ten when their real interest rates were consistently low and positive and the differential between the borrowing and lending rates relatively small. A slightly lower rating (an 8) was given if the differential between the two rates was larger (8% or more), while the deposit and lending real rates remained persistently positive. Countries with persistently *negative real* deposit and lending interest rates were assigned still lower ratings. The larger the negative rate, the lower the rating. If either the deposit or lending real interest rate was persistently negative by a single-digit amount, a country was given a score of 6. If both were persistently negative by a single-digit amount, 4 was assigned. If either the deposit or lending real interest rate was persistently negative by a double-digit amount, the country was given a rating of 2. A zero was assigned if both the borrowing and lending real interest rates were persistently negative by double-digit amounts or if hyperinflation had virtually eliminated the operation of the credit market. Table II-F of Appendix II provides the country rating for this component. (See the note at the end of that table for additional details on the derivation of the ratings.)

28

## III. Takings and Discriminatory Taxation

When a government plays favorites—when it takes from one group in order to make transfers to others or when it imposes the costs of public services disproportionately on various groups—the government becomes an agent of plunder. Such actions conflict with economic freedom. This is equally true whether the policies are undertaken by a dictatorial political leader or a legislative majority.

Much of what modern states do involves taking from some in order to make transfers to others (often with the intent of "buying" their votes). This is true for both the budgetary and regulatory policies of government. We have identified three areas where discriminatory actions in the political sphere are particularly important and where measurement is possible. These three areas are (a) subsidies and income transfers, (b) marginal tax rates, and (c) conscription.

### III-A: Transfers and Subsidies as a Percent of GDP.

Transfers and subsidies violate the freedom of individuals to keep the value of their productivity. When governments tax income from one person in order to transfer it to another, they are denying individuals the fruits of their labors. This is true whether funds are transferred from the rich to the poor (or as is often the case, from the poor to the rich), from one racial group to another, or from the politically disorganized to the politically powerful. The taking of property (including labor services) without fully compensating the rightful owner is a *per se* violation of economic freedom.[21] The ratio of transfers and subsidies to GDP indicates the degree to which various countries use the budget to engage in taking and transfer activities. Thus, countries with large transfer sectors are given low ratings.

*Data Sources and Methodology.* Data on transfers and subsidies are supplied by the International Monetary Fund, *Government Finance Statistics Yearbook*, (various years). The GDP data are from the World Bank, *World Tables, 1994*. In addition, supplementary data on transfers and subsides from Inter-American Development Bank, *Economic and Social Progress in Latin America, 1994 Report* were also utilized. Special care was

*Much of what modern states do involves taking from some in order to make transfers to others (often with the intent of "buying" their votes).*

taken to ensure that the subsidies and transfers for all levels of government were counted, and that intergovernmental transfers were omitted in order to avoid double-counting.

Following the general procedures used for other continuous variables, the 1985 data on transfers and subsidies as a percent of GDP were arranged from highest to lowest and used to form a zero to ten conversion table. Countries with a small (large) transfer sector were rated high (low). The raw data, the ratings, and the conversion table showing the relationship between the size of the transfer sector and the rating for each year are presented in Table III-A (Appendix II).

### III-B: Top Marginal Tax Rate (and Income Threshold at Which It Applies).

*In essence, high marginal tax rates seize wealth from taxpayers without providing them an equivalent increase in service.*

High marginal tax rates discriminate against productive citizens and deny them the fruits of their labor. In essence, such rates seize wealth from taxpayers without providing them an equivalent increase in service. To the extent that they raise revenue, high marginal tax rates force some people to pay for services provided to others.

Generally, high marginal rates are a very inefficient form of raising government revenue, since people will often reduce their work effort and make other adjustments when a large proportion of their additional earnings is taxed away. Thus, high marginal tax rates impose an additional cost (and loss of freedom) over and above the revenues transferred to the government. Perhaps the following example will help illustrate this point. Suppose that the government threw everyone who earned more than $100,000 per year in jail for six months. In essence, this is a very high marginal tax rate. A tax scheme like this would substantially reduce economic freedom over and above the revenue it generated for the government. In fact, it probably would not raise much revenue. Nonetheless, the impact on economic freedom would be substantial. So it is with high marginal tax rates—they impose a discriminatory cost on people over and above the cost of the revenue they generate.

*Data Sources and Methodology.* Data on the top marginal taxes and the income threshold at which they apply were assembled from

30

Price Waterhouse, *Individual Taxes: A Worldwide Summary,* (various issues). The exchange rate at beginning of the year was used to convert the income threshold data to U.S. dollars, and the U.S. Consumer Price Index was used to convert the threshold to real 1982-84 dollars. A conversion table was designed and used to assign each country a zero to ten rating *based on the country's top marginal tax rate and the income threshold at which the rate took effect.* Countries with low marginal tax rates and a high income threshold for the initial application of the top rate were given high scores (toward the ten end of the scale). Correspondingly, countries with high marginal tax rates and low income thresholds were assigned a low rating (toward the zero end of the scale).[22] The data on the top marginal tax rates and their effective income thresholds, as well as the associated ratings for each country are presented in Table III-B of Appendix II. The conversion table used to derive the ratings from the tax rate and income threshold data is presented in the source note at the end of this table.

### III-C: The Use of Conscripts to Obtain Military Personnel.

Conscription prevents individuals from selling their labor services to those who offer them the most attractive compensation package. In essence, military conscription denies draftees the property right to their labor services. While national defense is an acceptable activity for a "protective and productive" state, the cost of that protection should be imposed on all citizens. Singling out a specific group (for example, young men or young women) to pay for something that benefits all is a clear "taking" and a discriminatory form of taxation. The military draft falls into this category and, as such, is a violation of economic freedom.[23]

*Data Sources and Methodology.* International Institute for Strategic Studies, *The Military Balance,* (various issues) indicate countries which use conscription to obtain military personal. This publication provided the source material for this component. There are only two possible values for this component— conscription is either present or absent. Nations that rely on wage payments rather than conscription to obtain military personnel are given a rating of 10. Those that utilize conscription earn a zero. Appendix II, Table III-C indicates whether countries utilize conscription and provides the ratings for each country.

## IV. Restraints On International Exchange

Since the time of Adam Smith, economists of almost all persuasions have recognized the efficiency gains derived from free trade. Free trade makes it possible for the citizens of different countries to gain from division of labor, economies of scale, and specialization in areas where they have a comparative advantage. As a result, trading partners can produce a larger joint output and each can derive mutual gain.[24]

This standard economic argument, however, is not our major focus. We are interested in international trade because freedom of exchange is also a central tenet of economic freedom. It makes no difference if the potential trading partners live in different countries. Restrictions on exchange—both domestic and international—are per se violations of economic freedom.[25]

*It makes no difference if the potential trading partners live in different countries. Restrictions on exchange—both domestic and international—are a per se violation of economic freedom.*

Prodded by interest groups, governments use a variety of devices to restrain international trade. Tariffs, export duties, quotas, exchange rate controls, "buy-local" policies, marketing boards, restrictions on foreign ownership (or on the repatriation of the capital, interest, or dividends to owners), monopoly grants to domestic citizens, and discriminatory licensing or taxation that limits access to credit, foreign exchange, or other markets—all of these devices retard the ability of domestic citizens to engage in exchange activities with foreigners. Thus, they are a violation of economic freedom. Our task is to measure the extent to which various countries have imposed such restrictions. Toward this end, we will focus on four general types of restrictions: tariffs and other taxes on international trade, exchange rate controls, regulations that reduce the volume of trade, and regulations limiting capital market transactions.

### IV-A: Taxes on International Trade as a Percent of Exports Plus Imports.

Taxes on international trade limit the freedom of domestic residents to trade with foreigners. Tariffs and taxes on exports drive a wedge between what the seller receives and what the buyer pays. Thus, they reduce the volume of international trade, lower consumer and producer surplus, and, most relevant to our concerns, retard economic freedom.

*Data Sources and Methodology.* Data on revenue derived from "taxes on international trade transactions" were obtained from the International Monetary Fund, *Government Finance Statistics Yearbook,* (various issues). These data along with the information on exports and imports (World Bank, *World Tables, 1994)* were used to derive an average tax rate on international trade. As this tax wedge increases, the freedom of domestics to trade with foreigners is retarded and therefore the country is given a lower rating.[26] As long as a nation's taxes on international trade are in the normal range—that is, in the range where higher tax rates lead to an increase in tax revenues—there will be a direct relationship between revenues from taxes imposed on international trade and the restrictive effects of the taxes on trade (and thus, economic freedom). However, if taxes on some goods are raised so high that they are in the prohibitive range—the range where higher taxes mean less revenues—then the revenues from trade taxes will understate the restrictive effects of the taxes and their adverse impact on economic freedom.

*Taxes on international trade reduce the volume of trade, lower consumer and producer surplus, and, most relevant to our concerns, retard economic freedom.*

Table IV-A of Appendix II presents tax revenues on international trade as a percent of exports plus imports for the years of our study. Following our usual procedures for continuous variables, the 1985 statistics were arrayed from lowest to highest and used to derive the conversion intervals for the base year (1985). These intervals were then used to rate each country in the other years. Of course, countries with the lowest average tax rates on international trade were given the highest ratings. See Table IV of Appendix II for the trade tax data and accompanying country ratings.

**IV-B: Difference Between the Official Exchange Rate and the Black Market Rate.**

If people in a country are going to trade with outsiders, they must be able to convert their domestic currency to foreign exchange (other currencies). Exchange rate controls often make it difficult for them to do so. Currency convertibility is no problem if a nation permits its domestic currency to be freely and legally converted to other currencies in the foreign exchange market. Many governments, however, fix the price of their currency and prohibit currency exchanges at other prices.

Fixed exchange rates need not interfere with the free convertibility of a currency if a country is willing to subject its monetary policy to maintenance of the fixed rates. Put another way, a country can either (1) follow an independent monetary policy and allow its exchange rate to fluctuate or (2) tie its monetary policy to the maintenance of the fixed exchange rate. It cannot, however, maintain convertibility if it is going to both fix the exchange rate value of its currency and follow an independent monetary policy. It must either give up its monetary independence or allow its exchange rate to fluctuate if its currency is going to be fully convertible with other currencies.

Some countries, particularly small ones, have chosen to forgo monetary independence and tie the exchange rate value of their domestic currency to a widely accepted currency like the U.S. dollar, the German mark, or the French franc.[27] Fixing the exchange rate value of one's currency works fine as long as the country is willing to forgo control over its monetary policy.

*The black market exchange rate provides an indicator of the degree to which exchange rate controls limit trade with foreigners.*

Problems arise, however, when a country attempts to both fix the exchange rate value of its currency *and* conduct an independent monetary policy, particularly if the latter is inflationary. When this happens, the fixed exchange rate value of the domestic currency will exceed the market level. Since the prices of foreign currencies are fixed below equilibrium, a shortage of foreign exchange will result and black markets will develop. The more a currency is out of line with the forces of supply and demand, the larger the black market premium and greater the adverse impact of the exchange rate controls on the volume of international trade. Thus, the black market exchange rate provides an indicator of the degree to which exchange rate controls limit trade with foreigners.

*Data Sources and Methodology.* International Currency Analysis, Inc. *World Currency Yearbook* (various issues), provided the information on the size of the black market exchange rate premium through 1990. More recently, the monthly newsletter of this organization was the source for the black market rate between various currencies and the U.S. dollar. In turn, this rate can be used to calculate the black market premium.

The larger the black market premium, the more restrictive the impact on international trade. Thus, countries with the highest black market premiums are given the lowest ratings. Since this is a continuous variable, the 1985 data were arrayed from the lowest to the highest and the intervals that allocated an equal number of countries to each of the 11 rating categories were derived. In turn, this transformation table was used to rate the countries for the other years. The information on the black market exchange rate premium, the associated ratings for each country and transformation table are all presented in Table IV-B of Appendix II.

## IV-C: Actual Size of Trade Sector Compared to the Expected Size.

In addition to tariffs and exchange rate controls, many nations restrain trade through the use of quotas, monopoly grants, "buy local" schemes, and various other types of discriminatory regulations. Trade restrictions of this type are every bit as much a violation of economic freedom as tariffs, export duties, and exchange rate controls. Ignoring such restrictions would be a serious omission.

*Data Sources and Methodology.* Since these restrictions are numerous, complex, and heterogeneous, their direct measurement is an insurmountable task. Thus, we devised an indirect method designed to approximate their severity. Regression analysis was used to estimate the expected size of the trade sector for each country, given its geographic size, population, and location relative to potential trading partners.

We hypothesized that the expected size of a country's trade sector is a function of the following five variables: (1) geographic size, (2) population, (3) a dummy variable indicating that the country is land-locked and therefore restricted in its use of oceans for transport purposes, (4) a dummy variable indicating that the country has potential trading partners within 150 miles of its borders but less than 50 percent of its population resides within this distance from the potential trading partners, and (5) a dummy variable indicating that more than 50 percent of the country's population was located within 150 miles of a potential trading partner. The base for the last two variables is therefore countries that do *not* have a potential trading partner within 150 miles.

Since geographically large countries tend to have many producers and consumers located long distances from potential foreign trading partners, physical size tends to reduce the expected size of the trade sector. Similarly, a large population will facilitate the ability of domestic producers to sell (and domestic consumers buy) in the domestic market *while fully realizing the potential economies associated with large scale production.* Thus, a negative

*In addition to tariffs and exchange rate controls, many nations restrain trade through the use of quotas, monopoly grants, "buy local" schemes, and various other types of discriminatory regulations.*

sign is expected for the geographic size and population variables. A negative sign is also expected for land-locked countries. Finally, a positive sign is expected for the last two variables since having closer trading partners will tend to enhance the size of the trade sector. Regression analysis confirms each of these relationships.[28]

This model was then used to derive an "expected size of the trade sector" for each country which was then compared with the actual size of the country's trade sector. If the actual size of a country's trade sector as a share of GDP was significantly smaller than expected (given its geographic size, population, and locational characteristics), this is consistent with the view that its trade sector was reduced as the result of quotas and other regulatory restraints. Such countries were given low ratings. In contrast, if the actual size of a nation's trade sector as a share of GDP was large relative to the expected size, this indicates that regulatory restrictions were minimal. Therefore, countries in this category were given high ratings. The data for the various components of the regression equation and the actual size of the trade sector were from the World Bank, *World Tables* and *World Development Report.*

Table IV-C of Appendix II provides the data on the actual size of the trade sector, the expected size, and the percentage difference between the two. This latter figure was used to derive the rating transformation table in the usual manner for continuous variables. This transformation table along with the associated country ratings are also presented in Table IV-C of Appendix II.

### IV-D: Restrictions on the Freedom of Citizens to Engage in Capital Transactions with Foreigners.

*Limitations on domestic investments by foreigners and the freedom of citizens to invest abroad restrict economic freedom and often lead to side effects such as political favoritism, bribes, and other forms of corruption.*

Many countries require foreigners to get permission from the government in order to make an investment or remit its earnings. Sometimes these regulations reflect the presence of an inflexible exchange rate regime. In other instance, they are designed to protect domestic industries and/or centrally plan the investment of the economy. Often there are side effects such as political favoritism, bribes and other forms of corruption. Clearly, such regulations of capital movements are inconsistent with economic freedom.

Many governments also limit the freedom of their citizens to make either real property or financial investments abroad, or both. In some cases there is an outright prohibition and in other instances, permission to undertake an investment must be obtained from government authorities. These restrictions also conflict with economic freedom.

*Data Sources and Methodology.* International Monetary Fund, *Exchange Arrangements and Exchange Restrictions* (various issues) provides excellent descriptive data on the presence of restrictions, if any, that apply to both foreigners who want to make investments within the country and citizens wishing to make investments abroad. This descriptive information was used to classify and rate each country. A country was given a rating of ten when foreigners were free to undertake domestic investments and nationals were free to undertake investments abroad. As more and more restrictions were placed on the freedom of nationals to invest abroad and foreigners to invest domestically, a country was given a lower and lower rating. The source note at the end of Table IV-D of Appendix II provides the details on the various categories of restrictions and the ratings accompanying them. This table also provides the ratings for each country for the various years of our study.

## ATTACHING WEIGHTS TO THE COMPONENTS

We have identified 17 elements where institutional arrangements and/or public policies exert a substantial influence on economic freedom. How can we aggregate these 17 elements into a summary index? If we could accurately measure the costs of the actions that prohibit or retard voluntary exchanges and/or mandate involuntary "transactions", we could use these figures to attach weights to the various components. Of course, data limitations generally prevent us from making such calculations.

There are several alternative methods that might be used to aggregate components of economic freedom into a summary index. Unfortunately, there are problems associated with each of them. Therefore, we will develop and present results for three alternative summary indexes, each of which attaches different weights to the components. We now proceed to a discussion of how these indexes were developed and the deficiencies that accompany each.

*Equal Impact Index Ie.* The simplest alternative would be to take the position that since we do know the weight that should be

*There are several alternative methods that might be used to aggregate components of economic freedom into a summary index. Unfortunately, all of them have problems. Therefore, we will develop and present the results for three alternative summary indexes.*

attached to the various components, each should exert an equal impact on the index. Only one adjustment is required to achieve this objective—each variable must be assigned a weight equal to the inverse of its standard deviation. This is precisely what the summary index that we will refer to as Ie does. (The "e" refers to equal impact.) Each component in the Ie index is assigned a weight equal to the inverse of its standard deviation. Thus, less weight is given to a component when it has a great deal of variability across countries. Under this procedure, each of the components will exert an equal impact on the index. Exhibit 1-2 indicates both the standard deviation of the ratings across countries and the weights attached to each component when the Ie index is constructed.[29]

**Exhibit 1-2: The Weights Attached to Each Component in the Alternative Indexes**

| Component | Standard Deviation[a] | Component Weights | | |
|---|---|---|---|---|
| | | Ie[b] | Is1[b] | Is2 |
| IA: Money Expansion | 3.2 | 5.8 | 4.7 | 6.9 |
| IB: Inflation Variability | 3.2 | 5.8 | 5.3 | 6.2 |
| IC: Foreign Currency Accounts | 4.8 | 3.8 | 3.0 | 4.3 |
| ID: Deposits Abroad | 4.5 | 4.1 | 2.7 | 8.3 |
| IIA: Government Consumption | 3.2 | 5.8 | 6.2 | 0.7 |
| IIB: Government Enterprises | 2.4 | 7.7 | 6.5 | 10.4 |
| IIC: Price Controls | 2.3 | 8.0 | 7.1 | 9.7 |
| IID: Entry into Business | 2.2 | 8.3 | 6.7 | 7.6 |
| IIE: Equality Under the Law | 3.5 | 5.2 | 4.7 | 5.5 |
| IIF: Credit Market | 3.3 | 5.6 | 3.4 | 4.9 |
| IIIA: Transfers & Subsides | 3.2 | 5.8 | 10.9 | 0.5 |
| IIIB: Marginal Tax Rates | 2.5 | 7.4 | 12.7 | 4.5 |
| IIIC: Conscription | 4.9 | 3.8 | 3.6 | 5.0 |
| IVA: Trade Taxes | 3.2 | 5.8 | 6.7 | 4.8 |
| IVB: Exchange Rate Controls | 3.4 | 5.4 | 6.2 | 6.9 |
| IVC: Size of Trade Sector | 3.2 | 5.8 | 3.7 | 5.8 |
| IVD: Capital Mobility Restraints | 3.1 | 5.9 | 5.9 | 8.0 |
| TOTALS | | 100.0 | 100.0 | 100.0 |

[a] The standard deviation of the component ratings for all countries in 1985 (the base year) or the earliest year the data for the component were available.

[b] The Ie weights will result in each component exerting an equal impact on the index. In order for this to be the case, the weights for each component must be inversely related to the variation in the component ratings across countries. Thus, the Ie weights are equal to $1/\sigma \div \Sigma\, 1/\sigma$. The Is1 survey weights were also adjusted for differences in the variation in the component ratings across countries.

*Survey Index Is1*.  An alternative approach would be to ask knowledgeable people to provide their estimates for the importance of each component (the relative size of the loss in economic freedom imposed by the restrictions encompassed in the component) and to use this survey data as a basis for attaching weights.  Our summary index Is1 follows this procedure (the Is1 refers to the Index derived from the Survey 1 method).  We constructed a survey instrument which described the 17 components in our index and  asked the participants of the past three conferences on Measurement of Economic Freedom jointly sponsored by the Liberty Fund and Fraser Institute to provide us with their views concerning the weights that should be attached to each of the components.  Since all of these people attended at least one of the conferences, we were reasonably sure of their familiarity with the concept of economic freedom and the factors that influence it.

Eighteen of the 40 individuals who received the questionnaire responded.  Exhibit 1-2 (the second column under Is1) presents the average weight for each of the seventeen components derived from this survey.[30]  The respondents were instructed to assign weights summing to 100 and to insert a zero weight for any component that they did not believe contributed to economic freedom.  Nonetheless, at least 17 of the 18 respondents assigned a positive weight for each of the components.

As a comparison of the weights accompanying the Ie and Is1 indexes reveals, the survey respondents attached an above average weight to transfers and subsidies (III-A) and high marginal tax rates (III-B).  At the other end of the scale, the respondents attached the least weight to the deposits abroad (I-D), the credit market (II-F), and the size of the trade sector (IV-C).  Except for these five cases, the weights attached by the respondents to the other 12 variables were similar (prior to the adjustment for the differences in the standard deviations.)  This indicates that the respondents believed these twelve factors were of  similar importance as an indicator of economic freedom.

While this procedure is both understandable and simple, it still has a few deficiencies.  First, survey methods are generally not favorites of economists.  The views of the respondents—even knowledgeable respondents—may not accurately reflect the "true" importance of the various factors as indicators of economic freedom.  There is also a second problem—the weights (or importance of the components) will in some cases vary across countries. For example, one would expect that freedom of exchange with foreigners will be more important for residents of small countries than for large ones. This suggests that the appropriate weights should vary across countries. Therefore to a degree, the weights might be thought of as an average that would be most appropriate for a typical country.[31]

*Survey Index Is2.* A third approach to the problem of weights would be to ask a large number of people who are familiar with *specific countries* to rate those countries' overall economic freedom on a common scale (for example, zero to 100) and then attempt to regress various objective indicators of economic freedom (e.g. the ratings of our 17 components) on these country ratings in order to derive the "implicit" weights underlying the subjective aggregate ratings for each of the countries. If the subjective ratings for the various countries were "correct" then the regression coefficients would provide estimates for the weights of the components. While this option is attractive, there is a major practical problem—the number of countries is not large enough to provide for reliable simultaneous estimates of a model with 17 components. Thus, we were unable to develop a summary index based on this method.

However, we did pursue a modified form of this approach. Stephen Easton and Michael Walker conducted a survey from which they were able to derive a subjective aggregate rating for 33 countries, 31 of which are included in our analysis.[32] We calculated the simple correlation coefficient for each of the variables in our index and the subjective country ratings of the Easton-Walker survey. Each component was then weighted according to the relative size of its correlation coefficient. If the ratings of a component across the 31 countries were highly correlated with the Easton-Walker country ratings, then the component was given a large weight. In contrast, components that were poorly correlated with the Easton-Walker index were given proportionally smaller weights. The weights for the components derived by this method are presented in Exhibit 1-2, column 4. We refer to the summary index derived by this procedure as Is2—the Survey 2 approach.

When the component weights are derived by this method, the government enterprise (II-B) and price controls (II-C) components receive the largest weights, 10.4 percent and 9.7 percent respectively. In contrast, the government consumption (II-A) and transfers and subsidies (III-A) components receive very little weight, less than 1 percent.

*Some Final Thoughts on Weights.* Given that there is no ideal solution to the problem of weights for the components, we generally present each of the three summary indexes. If we had to choose among these three, our preference would be for Is1 because it reflects the views of a sample of people who have thought seriously about both economic freedom and the importance of various ingredients of that freedom. We recognize that others may have different views with regard to the importance of the components in our index. If one thinks that alternative component weights would be preferable for any country (or in aggregate), the index can be recalculated from the ratings for each component.

In conclusion, we would like to make two additional points with regard to the component weights and evaluation of the summary indexes. First, when a country has either low or high ratings for all, or almost all, of the components, the weights attached to the various components will not exert much impact on the summary index. Under these circumstances, almost any sensible set of weights will lead to a high rating when the ratings for most of the components are high (and a low rating when the ratings for most of the components are low.) As we will see, a substantial number of the countries fall into one or the other of these categories. Second, the ability of the summary indexes to explain differences in economic growth across countries also provides evidence as to their merit. Economic theory indicates that the gains from specialization, exchange, and productive efficiency associated with economic freedom will tend to generate higher income levels and growth rates. Therefore, if our measures of economic freedom are related to the level and growth of income, this will enhance our confidence in their accuracy. We will address this subject in Chapter 4.

*When a country has either low or high ratings for all, or almost all, of the components, the weights attached to the various components will not exert much impact on the summary index.*

## LOOKING AHEAD

In this chapter we defined the various components of our indexes and explained how these components are weighted in the three alternative indexes of economic freedom that we derive. The following chapter will present the country ratings for the components and the summary indexes for the 1993-95 period.

## Endnotes

1. As quoted by Milton Friedman in Walter Block (ed.), *Economic Freedom: Toward a Theory of Measurement* (Vancouver: Fraser Institute, 1991), p. 11.

2. Other researchers have also sought to quantify economic freedom across countries. See Zane Spindler and Laurie Still, "Economic Freedom Ratings," in Walter Block (ed.), *Economic Freedom: Toward a Theory of Measurement* (Vancouver: The Fraser Institute, 1991); Gerald W. Scully and Daniel J. Slottje, "Ranking Economic Liberty Across Countries," *Public Choice* (69: 121-152, 1991); and Bryan T. Johnson and Thomas P. Sheehy, *The Index of Economic Freedom*, (Washington, D. C. : Heritage Foundation, 1995).

3. Of course, the most basic property right of individuals is the property right to their person. The protection of individuals from "invasions" by others is the central element of criminal law. Since cross-country data on the safety of individuals from physical attacks on their person differ substantially and their reliability is generally questioned, our study does not attempt to deal with this factor.

4. See Ronald W. Jones and Alan C. Stockman. "On the Concept of Economic Freedom" in Stephen T. Easton and Michael A. Walker (ed.), *Rating Global Economic Freedom*, (Vancouver: The Fraser Institute, 1992) for an excellent discussion of the concept of economic freedom and an analysis of how it might be measured.

5. Alvin Rabushka, "Preliminary Definition of Economic Freedom," in *Economic Freedom: Toward a Theory of Measurement*, ed. Walter Block, (Vancouver: The Fraser Institute, 1991), pp. 87-108. This article provides an excellent foundation for the development of an empirical measure of economic freedom.

6. Lindsey M. Wright, "A Comparative Survey of Economic Freedom," in *Freedom in the World: Political Rights and Civil Liberties 1982*, ed. Raymond D. Gastil, (Westport and London: Greenwood Press, 1982), p. 55.

7. Rabushka (1991), p. 89.

8. Philosophers generally refer to protective rights as negative rights and intrusive rights as positive rights. See Roger Pilon, "Property Rights, Takings, and a Free Society," in *Public Choice and Constitutional Economics*, James Gwartney and Richard Wagner (ed.), (Greenwich, CT: JAI Press, 1988) and Walter Block, *The U.S. Bishops and Their Critics: An Economic and Ethical Perspective*, (Vancouver: The Fraser Institute, 1986) for an analysis of this topic and its importance for a free society.

9. However, the data for three components—price controls, freedom of entry into business, and equality under the law—are unavailable for the years 1975, 1980, and 1985. The latter two variables are also unavailable for 1990. Thus, our index has 14 components for the years 1975, 1980, and 1985; 15 in 1990; and 17 in 1993-95.

10. Often the total number of countries for which the data were available was not evenly divisible by eleven. When this was the case, the odd number of ratings was spread as evenly as possible among high and low ratings categories.

11. For details on this view, see Murray Rothbard, *The Mystery of Banking*, (New York: Richard and Snyder, 1983) and *What Has Government Done to Our Money*, 3rd ed. (San Rafael, CA: Libertarian Publishers, 1985).

12. See Milton Friedman, *Capitalism and Freedom*, (Chicago: University of Chicago Press, 1962), Chapter III and *Money Mischief: Episodes in Monetary History* (New York: Harcourt Brace Jovanovich, 1992).

13. While they were extremely rare during the period of our study, monetary contractions can also change the terms of trade and undermine economic exchange. Therefore, our transformation table is symmetrical. The larger a negative change in the money supply minus potential GDP, the lower the rating of a country. Further, a sizeable monetary contraction might well cause a sharp reduction in real GDP. Under these circumstances, money growth minus the change in *current-year* real GDP would lead to a higher rating than is justified. This is why we used the change in real GDP during the *last ten years* rather than the change in GDP during the current year to adjust the money growth figures for cross-country differences in the growth of potential real output. We would like to thank Milton Friedman for calling this problem to our attention and suggesting the use of the ten-year average growth rate to minimize distortions arising from this source.

14. Our thinking in this area was influenced by the rational expectations theory of Robert Lucas, Thomas Sargent, Robert Barro and others. For a review of this literature, see *The Rational Expectations Revolution: Readings From The Front Line*, edited by Preston J. Miller (Cambridge, MA: MIT Press, 1994).

15. While the public goods justification for government action represents the mainstream position, there are dissenters. See Hans-Hermann Hoppe, "Fallacies of Public Goods Theory and the Production of Security," in *The Economics and Ethics of Private Property: Studies in Political Economy and Philosophy*, (Boston: Kluwer, 1993); Tyler Cowen, ed., *The Theory of Market Failure: A Critical Examination*, (Fairfax, VA: George Mason University Press, 1988); Walter Block, "Public Finance and Taxation," *Canadian Public Administration*, Fall 1993 and Walter Block, "Taxation in the Public Finance," *Journal of Public Finance and Public Choice*, Fall 1989.

16. Both government consumption and GDP were measured in the domestic currency units of the respective countries. Government consumption expenditures include all spending on goods and services purchased by the government—things like national defense, road maintenance, wages and salaries, office space, and government-owned vehicles. Since it is obtained from the national income accounts, it includes all levels of government spending. Note, this variable does not include direct transfers and subsidies, since these do not enter into the national income accounts.

17. See particularly John R. Nellis, "Public Enterprises in Sub-Saharan Africa," *World Bank Discussion Paper*, no. 1 (Washington, DC: November, 1986); Rexford A. Ahene and Bernard S. Katz, eds., *Privatization and Investment in Sub-Saharan Africa*, (New York: Praeger, 1992); and *OECD Economic Surveys*, (Italy: Organization for Economic Cooperation and Development, January, 1994).

18. International Monetary Fund, *Government Finance Statistics Yearbook* (Washington, D.C.: IMF), annual.

19. See The World Economic Forum, *World Competitiveness Report*, (Geneva: World Economic Forum, 1994). Also see various issues of this publication for earlier years.

20. The actual ratings for the specific checklist items were unavailable in the Annual Survey publication. However, Joseph Ryan, a senior scholar at the Freedom House, graciously supplied them to us.

21. See Terry L. Anderson and P.J. Hill, *The Birth of the Transfer Society* (Palo Alto: Hoover Institution Press, 1980) and Richard A. Epstein, *Takings: Private Property and the Power of Eminent Domain* (Cambridge: Harvard University Press, 1985) for additional analysis of income transfers, the taking of private property, and economic freedom

22. When there was a range of top marginal tax rates within a country, as was sometimes the case under federal systems of government, the midpoint of the top rates for the country was used to derive the rating for this variable.

23. Some may argue that military conscription can sometimes promote economic freedom *in the long run* by helping to protect a country against an external threat imposed by an authoritarian aggressor. This may well be true, but we do not know how to measure the intensity of the potential future threat. Thus, we were unable to adjust for it.

24. See Henry George, *Protectionism or Free Trade* 1886, reprinted edition, (New York: Robert Schalkenbach Foundation, 1980) for an excellent analysis of the economies of trade restrictions.

25. See Stephen T. Easton, "Rating Economic Freedom: International Trade and Financial Arrangements," in Stephen T. Easton and Michael A. Walker (eds.), *Rating Global Economic Freedom*, (Vancouver: The Fraser Institute, 1992) for additional analysis on this topic.

26. There is one significant deficiency with this approach as a measure of the loss of freedom due to the imposition of trade taxes—extremely high taxes on goods may limit trade so much that the duties will raise little revenue. A totally prohibitive marginal tax rate on a good would generate no revenue at all.

27. For example, Hong Kong has followed this strategy: its currency is tied to the U.S. dollar. Instead of a central bank that conducts monetary policy, Hong Kong has a currency board that issues HK dollars in exchange for U.S. dollars at a fixed rate of 7.7 Hong Kong dollars = $1 U.S. dollar. The HK dollars issued by the currency board are fully convertible and 100 percent backed with U.S. dollars and U.S. bonds dominated in dollars. If people want more Hong Kong dollars, they can obtain them by providing the currency board with U.S. dollars (at the fixed rate), which the board then invests in U.S. government bonds. Other countries have also followed this approach. Singapore has tied its currency to a bundle of foreign currencies. Several African countries, including Benin, Cameroon, Central African Republic, Chad, Congo Peoples Republic, Cote d'Ivoire, Gabon, Niger, Senegal and Togo, tie their currency to the French franc.

28. With log of exports plus imports divided by GDP as the dependent variable, the following regression was used to estimate the expected size of the trade sector:

| Independent variables | Coefficient | t-ratio |
|---|---|---|
| Area in sq. kilometers (log) | −.109 | 8.83 |
| Population (log) | −.154 | 8.80 |
| Land-locked country (dummy) | −.177 | 3.37 |
| Between 1% and 50% of population within 150 miles of trading partner | .165 | 2.05 |
| Between 50% and 100% of population within 150 miles of trading partner | .194 | 2.82 |
| 1980 (dummy) | .119 | 2.09 |
| 1985 (dummy) | .036 | 0.62 |
| 1990 (dummy) | .109 | 1.90 |
| 1993 (dummy) | .130 | 2.24 |
| Intercept | 2.260 | 8.76 |
| $R^2$ | .50 | |
| Number of observations | 496 | |

This regression indicates that 50% of the variation in the size of the trade sector across countries reflects country differences in geographic size, population, and locational variables. We derived the expected size of the trade sector by plugging the country characteristics for the variables into the regression equations. This provides us with an expected size of the trade sector for each country (for each of the years of our study), given its geographic size, population, and locational characteristics.

29. An adjustment of this type is particularly important when the index includes both continuous and binary variables. Since our rating procedure for continuous variables assigns an equal number of countries to each of 11 intervals during the base year, the standard deviation of these components will be equal and they will all be assigned the same weight in the Ie index (see Exhibit 1-2.) Since the standard deviations of the three binary variables (I-C. I-D, and III-C) were greater, the weights attached to these components were smaller. Failure to make this adjustment would result in the dominance of the index by the variables with the most variability.

30. The survey weights were also adjusted for differences in the standard deviations of the various components. See previous endnote.

31. The use of uniform techniques to derive estimates that we know will have a bias under certain circumstances is not particularly unusual. For example, we recognize that our methods of deriving GDP will understate the output of less

developed countries since non-market and therefore uncounted productive activities will be greater for such countries than for modern industrial economies. In a similar manner, our index Is1 will overestimate the economic freedom of small countries with numerous restraints on international trade and underestimate the economic freedom of large countries with numerous restraints on international trade.

32. Stephen T. Easton and Michael A. Walker, "A Survey Approach to Indexes of Economic Freedom," a paper presented to the Sixth Liberty Fund-Fraser Institute Symposium on Rating Economic Freedom held November 18-21, 1993 in Sonoma, California.

# CHAPTER 2

## Rating the Economic Freedom of Countries in 1993-1995, 1990, 1985, 1980, and 1975

Having explained how the index of economic freedom is constructed, we are now ready to present the data for the 103 countries (102 prior to the separation of Czechoslovakia into the Czech Republic and Slovak Republic in 1993) for which we were able to obtain reasonably complete data. This chapter focuses on three topics. First, we will present the component ratings, area ratings, and summary indexes for the 1993-1995 period for each country. These data will allow us to identify the strengths and weaknesses of each country and make comparisons across countries. Second, we will also present the summary ratings for the Top 15, Bottom 15, and selected other countries for 1975, 1980, 1985, 1990 and 1995. These data will permit us to observe the changes in the composition of country rankings during the last two decades. Finally, we will identify two groups—the first comprised of countries with persistently high levels and the second with persistently low levels—of economic freedom throughout the entire period of our study.

## COUNTRY RATINGS IN 1993-1995

Exhibit 2-1 presents the 1993-1995 ratings for each of the 17 components in our index, as well as area ratings, and the three alternative summary indexes. The area ratings and the summary indexes merely reflect the aggregation of the  component ratings which range from zero to ten. The higher the rating, the greater the estimated degree of economic freedom.

**Exhibit 2.1: Component, Area, and Summary Index Ratings: 1993-95**

Part 1: Component Ratings: 1993-95

| | I: Money and Inflation | | | | II: Government Operations | | | | | | III: Takings | | | IV: International Sector | | | |
|---|---|---|---|---|---|---|---|---|---|---|---|---|---|---|---|---|---|
| INDUSTRIAL COUNTRIES | A | B | C | D | A | B | C | D | E | F | A | B | C | A | B | C | D |
| United States | 7 | 10 | 10 | 10 | 3 | 8 | 8 | 10.0 | 7.5 | 10 | 3 | 7 | 10 | 9 | 10 | 3 | 10 |
| Canada | 9 | 10 | 10 | 10 | 1 | 6 | 8 | 7.5 | 7.5 | 10 | 2 | 4 | 10 | 9 | 10 | 9 | 8 |
| Australia | 5 | 10 | 10 | 10 | 2 | 6 | 7 | 10.0 | 7.5 | 10 | 3 | 4 | 10 | 8 | 10 | 6 | 8 |
| Japan | 9 | 10 | 10 | 10 | 8 | 8 | 5 | 7.5 | 7.5 | 10 | 4 | 2 | 10 | 9 | 10 | 1 | 8 |
| New Zealand | 8 | 10 | 10 | 10 | 5 | 8 | 10 | 10.0 | 10.0 | 10 | 2 | 7 | 10 | 9 | 10 | 5 | 10 |
| Austria | 8 | 10 | 10 | 10 | 2 | 2 | 6 | 7.5 | 7.5 | 6 | 0 | 5 | 0 | 9 | 10 | 7 | 8 |
| Belgium | 8 | 10 | 10 | 10 | 5 | 6 | 5 | 7.5 | 10.0 | 10 | 0 | 2 | 0 | 10 | 10 | 10 | 10 |
| Denmark | 9 | 10 | 10 | 10 | 0 | 4 | 8 | 10.0 | 10.0 | 10 | 0 | 2 | 0 | 10 | 10 | 2 | 10 |
| Finland | 1 | 9 | 10 | 10 | 1 | 6 | 8 | 7.5 | 10.0 | 10 | 1 | 2 | 0 | 9 | 10 | 2 | 8 |
| France | 10 | 10 | 10 | 10 | 1 | 6 | 7 | 7.5 | 7.5 | 8 | 0 | 3 | 0 | 10 | 10 | 5 | 8 |
| Germany | 5 | 10 | 10 | 10 | 3 | 6 | 9 | 7.5 | 7.5 | 10 | 0 | 4 | 0 | 10 | 10 | 8 | 10 |
| Iceland | 4 | 5 | 10 | 10 | 1 | 4 | - | 10.0 | 10.0 | 6 | 3 | - | 10 | 6 | 8 | 1 | 5 |
| Ireland | 9 | 9 | 10 | 10 | 4 | 4 | 8 | 7.5 | 7.5 | 10 | 2 | 3 | 10 | 8 | 10 | 8 | 10 |
| Italy | 8 | 9 | 10 | 10 | 2 | 2 | 5 | 7.5 | 7.5 | 10 | 0 | 4 | 0 | 10 | 10 | 3 | 8 |
| Netherlands | 9 | 9 | 10 | 10 | 5 | 6 | 7 | 7.5 | 10.0 | 10 | 0 | 2 | 0 | 10 | 10 | 8 | 10 |
| Norway | 7 | 9 | 10 | 10 | 1 | 2 | 7 | 7.5 | 10.0 | 10 | 0 | 4 | 0 | - | 10 | 6 | 10 |
| Spain | 8 | 10 | 10 | 10 | 3 | 4 | 6 | 7.5 | 5.0 | 10 | 2 | 3 | 0 | 9 | 10 | 3 | 8 |
| Sweden | 10 | 6 | 10 | 0 | 0 | 4 | 8 | 10.0 | 10.0 | 10 | 0 | 1 | 0 | 9 | 10 | 4 | 10 |
| Switzerland | 10 | 9 | 10 | 10 | 5 | 8 | 6 | 10.0 | 10.0 | 10 | 2 | 9 | 0 | 8 | 10 | 5 | 10 |
| United Kingdom | 7 | 9 | 10 | 10 | 1 | 6 | 9 | 10.0 | 5.0 | 10 | 2 | 5 | 10 | 10 | 10 | 5 | 10 |
| **CENTRAL/- SOUTH AMERICA** | | | | | | | | | | | | | | | | | |
| Argentina | 0 | 0 | 10 | 10 | 10 | 6 | 8 | 10.0 | 2.5 | 8 | 3 | 9 | 0 | - | 10 | 0 | 10 |
| Belize | 10 | 9 | 0 | 0 | 1 | 8 | 6 | 10.0 | 7.5 | 10 | 10 | 4 | 10 | 1 | 6 | 3 | 8 |
| Bolivia | 1 | 5 | 10 | 10 | 5 | 4 | 8 | 7.5 | 2.5 | 8 | 8 | 10 | 0 | 7 | 8 | 3 | 5 |
| Brazil | 0 | 0 | 0 | 0 | 3 | 2 | 4 | 7.5 | 0.0 | 0 | 3 | 8 | 0 | 7 | 6 | 1 | 0 |
| Chile | 2 | 5 | 10 | 10 | 9 | 8 | 8 | 10.0 | 5.0 | 10 | 3 | 3 | 0 | 6 | 6 | 6 | 5 |
| Colombia | 1 | 6 | 10 | 10 | 7 | 4 | 6 | 7.5 | 0.0 | 8 | 5 | 5 | 0 | - | 8 | 3 | 5 |
| Costa Rica | 2 | 3 | 10 | 10 | 3 | 8 | 6 | 10.0 | 7.5 | 8 | 6 | 9 | 10 | 6 | 8 | 4 | 5 |
| Dominican Rep | 2 | 1 | 0 | 0 | 8 | 6 | 6 | 7.5 | 2.5 | - | 9 | 8 | 10 | - | 7 | 3 | 2 |
| Ecuador | 0 | 2 | 10 | 10 | 10 | 6 | 0 | 7.5 | 2.5 | 6 | 8 | 9 | 0 | - | 8 | 4 | 5 |
| El Salvador | 2 | 4 | 10 | 10 | 9 | 8 | 6 | 5.0 | 2.5 | 10 | 9 | 8 | 0 | 6 | 4 | 0 | 8 |
| Guatemala | 1 | 2 | 10 | 10 | 10 | 8 | 6 | 7.5 | 0.0 | 8 | 9 | 9 | 0 | 7 | 6 | 1 | 8 |
| Haiti | 2 | 1 | 10 | 10 | - | 4 | 0 | 2.5 | 0.0 | - | - | - | 10 | - | 0 | - | 2 |
| Honduras | 2 | 3 | 10 | 10 | 8 | 8 | 4 | 7.5 | 2.5 | 6 | 7 | 5 | 0 | - | 6 | 3 | 5 |
| Jamaica | 0 | 2 | 10 | 10 | 6 | 4 | 4 | 7.5 | 2.5 | 4 | 7 | 9 | 10 | - | 8 | 8 | 8 |
| Mexico | 1 | 2 | 10 | 10 | 9 | 6 | 7 | 7.5 | 0.0 | 8 | 5 | 7 | 0 | - | 10 | 3 | 5 |
| Nicaragua | 0 | 0 | 0 | 0 | 4 | 0 | 2 | 5.0 | 0.0 | 0 | 5 | 8 | 10 | 2 | 6 | 3 | 0 |
| Panama | 2 | 10 | 10 | 10 | 1 | 6 | 4 | 7.5 | 2.5 | 10 | 4 | 9 | 10 | 6 | 10 | 3 | 10 |
| Paraguay | 1 | 3 | 10 | 10 | 9 | 8 | 4 | 7.5 | 2.5 | 8 | 8 | 8 | 0 | 7 | 4 | 5 | 5 |

Exhibit 2-1 (con't)

| Part 2: Area Ratings (Is1) | | | | Part 3: Summary Indexes | | | | | |
| Money and Inflation | Govern- ment Operations | Takings | Inter- national Sector | (Ie) | (Is1) | (Is2) | Avg. | Grade a | INDUSTRIAL COUNTRIES |
|---|---|---|---|---|---|---|---|---|---|
| 9.1 | 7.6 | 5.8 | 8.6 | 7.9 | 7.6 | 8.6 | 8.0 | A | United States |
| 9.7 | 6.4 | 4.0 | 9.0 | 7.5 | 6.9 | 8.4 | 7.6 | B | Canada |
| 8.5 | 6.9 | 4.4 | 8.2 | 7.3 | 6.8 | 8.0 | 7.4 | B | Australia |
| 9.7 | 7.4 | 3.9 | 7.7 | 7.3 | 6.9 | 7.8 | 7.3 | B | Japan |
| 9.4 | 8.7 | 5.4 | 8.9 | 8.4 | 8.0 | 9.1 | 8.5 | A | New Zealand |
| 9.4 | 5.0 | 2.3 | 8.7 | 6.2 | 5.8 | 6.9 | 6.3 | C | Austria |
| 9.4 | 6.8 | 0.9 | 10.0 | 7.1 | 6.3 | 7.8 | 7.1 | B | Belgium |
| 9.7 | 6.7 | 0.9 | 8.7 | 6.7 | 6.0 | 7.7 | 6.8 | C | Denmark |
| 7.0 | 6.7 | 1.3 | 7.9 | 6.1 | 5.6 | 6.9 | 6.2 | C | Finland |
| 10.0 | 6.0 | 1.4 | 8.7 | 6.6 | 6.0 | 7.5 | 6.7 | C | France |
| 8.5 | 7.0 | 1.9 | 9.7 | 7.1 | 6.4 | 7.8 | 7.1 | B | Germany |
| 6.5 | 6.1 | 4.7 | 5.5 | 6.0 | 5.7 | 6.6 | 6.1 | C | Iceland |
| 9.4 | 6.6 | 3.5 | 9.1 | 7.4 | 6.7 | 8.1 | 7.4 | B | Ireland |
| 9.1 | 5.2 | 1.9 | 8.3 | 6.1 | 5.6 | 6.7 | 6.1 | C | Italy |
| 9.4 | 7.3 | 0.9 | 9.7 | 7.2 | 6.4 | 7.9 | 7.2 | B | Netherlands |
| 8.8 | 5.8 | 1.9 | 9.1 | 6.3 | 5.7 | 7.2 | 6.4 | C | Norway |
| 9.4 | 5.6 | 2.2 | 8.0 | 6.3 | 5.8 | 6.9 | 6.3 | C | Spain |
| 6.9 | 6.7 | 0.5 | 8.7 | 6.1 | 5.5 | 6.7 | 6.1 | C | Sweden |
| 9.7 | 7.9 | 5.0 | 8.6 | 7.9 | 7.5 | 8.3 | 7.9 | B | Switzerland |
| 8.8 | 6.8 | 4.5 | 9.2 | 7.5 | 7.0 | 8.3 | 7.6 | B | United Kingdom |
| | | | | | | | | | CENTRAL/- SOUTH AMERICA |
| 3.6 | 7.6 | 5.4 | 7.7 | 6.2 | 6.3 | 6.2 | 6.2 | C | Argentina |
| 6.0 | 6.9 | 7.2 | 4.5 | 6.3 | 6.3 | 6.3 | 6.3 | C | Belize |
| 5.6 | 5.9 | 7.9 | 6.1 | 6.1 | 6.4 | 5.9 | 6.1 | C | Bolivia |
| 0.0 | 3.2 | 4.9 | 3.9 | 2.8 | 3.3 | 2.4 | 2.8 | F- | Brazil |
| 5.9 | 8.4 | 2.6 | 5.7 | 6.3 | 5.8 | 6.5 | 6.2 | C | Chile |
| 6.0 | 5.5 | 4.3 | 5.7 | 5.3 | 5.3 | 5.4 | 5.3 | D | Colombia |
| 5.2 | 7.0 | 7.9 | 6.0 | 6.7 | 6.7 | 7.0 | 6.8 | C | Costa Rica |
| 0.9 | 6.2 | 8.7 | 4.2 | 5.1 | 5.7 | 4.3 | 5.0 | D | Dominican Rep |
| 4.3 | 5.3 | 7.4 | 5.9 | 5.4 | 5.9 | 5.0 | 5.4 | D | Ecuador |
| 5.6 | 6.6 | 7.3 | 5.0 | 6.0 | 6.3 | 5.7 | 6.0 | C | El Salvador |
| 4.6 | 6.8 | 7.8 | 6.0 | 6.2 | 6.5 | 5.8 | 6.2 | C | Guatemala |
| 4.6 | 1.7 | 10.0 | 1.0 | 3.1 * | 2.9 * | 3.5 * | 3.2 | F- | Haiti |
| 5.2 | 6.1 | 5.1 | 4.9 | 5.5 | 5.5 | 5.4 | 5.5 | D | Honduras |
| 4.3 | 4.8 | 8.3 | 8.0 | 6.0 | 6.3 | 6.0 | 6.1 | C | Jamaica |
| 4.6 | 6.4 | 5.3 | 6.5 | 5.7 | 5.8 | 5.7 | 5.7 | D | Mexico |
| 0.0 | 2.1 | 7.1 | 2.7 | 2.7 | 3.3 | 2.2 | 2.7 | F- | Nicaragua |
| 7.6 | 4.9 | 7.1 | 7.7 | 6.6 | 6.6 | 7.1 | 6.8 | C | Panama |
| 4.9 | 6.5 | 6.9 | 5.3 | 5.9 | 6.1 | 5.6 | 5.9 | D | Paraguay |

Exhibit 2-1: (Continued)

## Part 1: Component Ratings: 1993-95

| CENTRAL/- S. AMERICA (con't) | I: Money and Inflation | | | | II: Government Operations | | | | | | III: Takings | | | IV: International Sector | | | |
|---|---|---|---|---|---|---|---|---|---|---|---|---|---|---|---|---|---|
| | A | B | C | D | A | B | C | D | E | F | A | B | C | A | B | C | D |
| Peru | 0 | 0 | 10 | 10 | 10 | 6 | 6 | 7.5 | 0.0 | 2 | 8 | 8 | 0 | 6 | 8 | 1 | 8 |
| Trinidad/Tobago | 3 | 4 | 10 | 10 | 3 | 2 | 4 | 10.0 | 7.5 | 8 | 4 | 5 | 10 | - | 10 | 1 | 8 |
| Uruguay | 0 | 1 | 10 | 10 | 6 | 6 | 6 | 7.5 | 5.0 | 6 | 2 | 10 | 10 | 6 | 8 | 1 | 10 |
| Venezuela | 1 | 1 | 0 | 0 | 10 | 2 | 2 | 5.0 | 0.0 | 4 | 6 | 8 | 0 | 6 | 8 | 6 | 5 |
| **EUROPE/- MIDDLE EAST** | | | | | | | | | | | | | | | | | |
| Bulgaria | 0 | 0 | 10 | 10 | 3 | 0 | 4 | 7.5 | 7.5 | - | 2 | - | 0 | 8 | 6 | 6 | 5 |
| Cyprus | 9 | 10 | 0 | 0 | 5 | 6 | 2 | 10.0 | 7.5 | 8 | 4 | 5 | 0 | 6 | 5 | 3 | 0 |
| Czechoslovakia | - | - | - | - | - | - | - | - | - | - | - | - | - | - | - | - | - |
|   Czech Rep | 2 | 1 | 10 | 10 | 1 | 4 | 5 | 5.0 | 7.5 | 6 | - | 4 | 0 | - | 10 | 10 | 5 |
|   Slovakia | 3 | 1 | 10 | 10 | 0 | 4 | 4 | 5.0 | 5.0 | 4 | - | 3 | 0 | - | 5 | 10 | 0 |
| Egypt | 5 | 4 | 10 | 10 | 5 | 2 | 2 | 2.5 | 0.0 | 8 | 4 | 3 | 0 | 4 | 8 | 10 | 0 |
| Greece | 2 | 6 | 10 | 0 | 1 | 2 | 6 | 7.5 | 5.0 | 8 | 2 | 5 | 0 | 10 | 10 | 3 | 5 |
| Hungary | 1 | 2 | 0 | 0 | 6 | 2 | 7 | 5.0 | 7.5 | 6 | 0 | 4 | 0 | - | 5 | 7 | 0 |
| Iran | 2 | 5 | 0 | 0 | 3 | 2 | - | 2.5 | 0.0 | - | - | 4 | 0 | 2 | 1 | 3 | 0 |
| Israel | 2 | 6 | 10 | 0 | 0 | 2 | 4 | 7.5 | 5.0 | 8 | 2 | 4 | 0 | 9 | 8 | 2 | 2 |
| Jordan | 8 | 8 | 0 | 0 | 0 | 6 | 2 | 5.0 | 2.5 | 6 | 8 | - | 10 | 1 | 8 | 10 | 2 |
| Malta | 10 | 10 | 10 | 0 | 1 | 4 | 2 | 7.5 | 10.0 | 10 | 2 | 7 | 10 | 6 | 6 | 4 | 2 |
| Poland | 0 | 0 | 10 | 10 | 8 | 2 | 5 | 7.5 | 7.5 | 4 | - | 4 | 0 | - | 10 | 4 | 2 |
| Portugal | 3 | 5 | 10 | 10 | 2 | 2 | 6 | 7.5 | 7.5 | 10 | 3 | 5 | 0 | 9 | 10 | 4 | 5 |
| Romania | 0 | 0 | 10 | 0 | 5 | 0 | 4 | 5.0 | 5.0 | - | 1 | 1 | 0 | 8 | 3 | 3 | 5 |
| Syria | 2 | 4 | 10 | 0 | 5 | 2 | 0 | 2.5 | 0.0 | - | - | - | 0 | 7 | 0 | 5 | 0 |
| Turkey | 0 | 1 | 10 | 10 | 2 | 4 | 3 | 7.5 | 0.0 | 6 | 5 | 4 | 0 | 8 | 8 | 5 | 0 |
| **ASIA** | | | | | | | | | | | | | | | | | |
| Bangladesh | 4 | 8 | 0 | 0 | 6 | 6 | 0 | 7.5 | 5.0 | 10 | - | - | 10 | - | 3 | 1 | 0 |
| Fiji | 9 | 7 | 0 | 0 | 2 | 6 | 6 | 7.5 | 5.0 | 6 | 10 | 7 | 10 | 5 | 8 | 5 | 2 |
| Hong Kong | 5 | 5 | 10 | 10 | 10 | 10 | 9 | 10 | 7.5 | - | 10 | 9 | 10 | 9 | 10 | 10 | 10 |
| India | 3 | 9 | 0 | 0 | 7 | 2 | 3 | 5.0 | 2.5 | 10 | 5 | 4 | 10 | 0 | 10 | 4 | 2 |
| Indonesia | 3 | 10 | 10 | 10 | 9 | 2 | 3 | 2.5 | 0.0 | 10 | 10 | 7 | 0 | 8 | 7 | 10 | 2 |
| Malaysia | 2 | 10 | 10 | 10 | 7 | 6 | 4 | 7.5 | 2.5 | 10 | 7 | 7 | 10 | 7 | 10 | 10 | 5 |
| Nepal | 2 | 5 | 0 | 0 | 8 | 4 | - | 5.0 | 0.0 | - | - | - | 10 | - | 3 | 4 | 0 |
| Pakistan | 5 | 7 | 10 | 0 | 7 | 4 | 4 | 5.0 | 0.0 | 8 | - | 5 | 10 | - | 10 | 6 | 2 |
| Philippines | 3 | 6 | 10 | 10 | 9 | 4 | 3 | 5.0 | 0.0 | 10 | 10 | 7 | 10 | 2 | 8 | 10 | 2 |
| Singapore | 8 | 10 | 10 | 10 | 9 | 8 | 8 | 7.5 | 0.0 | 10 | 8 | 9 | 0 | 10 | 10 | 10 | 10 |
| South Korea | 5 | 8 | 10 | 10 | 8 | 6 | 4 | 7.5 | 7.5 | 8 | 8 | 5 | 0 | 8 | 10 | 5 | 5 |
| Sri Lanka | 4 | 5 | 0 | 0 | 8 | 4 | 6 | 5.0 | 0.0 | 10 | 5 | - | 10 | 4 | 10 | 6 | 0 |
| Taiwan | 10 | 10 | 10 | 10 | 4 | 4 | 7 | 7.5 | 2.5 | 10 | 5 | 7 | 0 | 8 | 10 | 5 | 5 |
| Thailand | 7 | 9 | 10 | 10 | 8 | 6 | 5 | 5.0 | 0.0 | 10 | 10 | 7 | 0 | 6 | 10 | 10 | 5 |

Exhibit 2-1 (continued)

| Part 2: Area Ratings (Is1) | | | | Part 3: Summary Indexes | | | | | |
| --- | --- | --- | --- | --- | --- | --- | --- | --- | --- |
| Money and Inflation | Govern-ment Operations | Takings | Inter-national Sector | (Ie) | (Is1) | (Is2) | Avg. | Grade a | CENTRAL/-S. AMERICA (con't) |
| 3.6 | 5.8 | 6.9 | 6.3 | 5.4 | 5.9 | 5.1 | 5.5 | D | Peru |
| 5.9 | 5.5 | 5.3 | 7.1 | 5.9 | 5.8 | 6.3 | 6.0 | C | Trinidad/Tobago |
| 4.0 | 6.2 | 6.8 | 6.8 | 6.0 | 6.1 | 6.4 | 6.2 | C | Uruguay |
| 0.6 | 3.9 | 6.1 | 6.3 | 4.0 | 4.5 | 3.2 | 3.9 | F- | Venezuela |
| | | | | | | | | | EUROPE/-MIDDLE EAST |
| 3.6 | 4.2 | 1.5 | 6.3 | 4.4 | 4.2 | 4.7 | 4.4 | F | Bulgaria |
| 6.1 | 6.2 | 3.9 | 3.7 | 5.1 | 5.0 | 4.7 | 4.9 | F | Cyprus |
| N/R | N/R | N/R | N/R | N/R | N/R | N/R | | | Czechoslovakia |
| 4.6 | 4.5 | 3.1 | 8.1 | 5.2 | 4.9 | 5.6 | 5.2 | D | Czech Rep |
| 4.9 | 3.6 | 2.3 | 4.3 | 4.1 | 3.7 | 4.5 | 4.1 | F | Slovakia |
| 6.5 | 3.0 | 3.0 | 5.0 | 4.3 | 4.0 | 4.4 | 4.2 | F | Egypt |
| 4.5 | 4.7 | 3.1 | 7.5 | 4.9 | 4.9 | 5.0 | 4.9 | F | Greece |
| 1.0 | 5.5 | 1.9 | 3.6 | 3.6 | 3.3 | 3.3 | 3.4 | F- | Hungary |
| 2.3 | 2.0 | 3.1 | 1.4 | 2.0 | 2.1 | 1.6 | 1.9 | F- | Iran |
| 4.5 | 4.1 | 2.7 | 5.7 | 4.2 | 4.2 | 4.2 | 4.2 | F | Israel |
| 5.1 | 3.4 | 8.5 | 4.7 | 4.8 | 4.9 | 4.8 | 4.8 | F | Jordan |
| 8.3 | 5.1 | 5.4 | 4.6 | 5.8 | 5.6 | 5.9 | 5.8 | D | Malta |
| 3.6 | 5.7 | 3.1 | 5.6 | 4.8 | 4.8 | 4.7 | 4.8 | F | Poland |
| 6.2 | 5.4 | 3.5 | 7.4 | 5.7 | 5.5 | 6.1 | 5.8 | D | Portugal |
| 1.9 | 3.7 | 0.9 | 5.0 | 3.1 | 2.9 | 2.9 | 3.0 | F- | Romania |
| 3.9 | 1.9 | 0.0 | 2.9 | 2.6 | 2.6 | 2.1 | 2.4 | F- | Syria |
| 4.0 | 3.8 | 3.9 | 5.4 | 4.2 | 4.2 | 4.3 | 4.3 | F | Turkey |
| | | | | | | | | | ASIA |
| 3.9 | 5.3 | 10.0 | 1.4 | 4.4 | 4.4 | 3.9 | 4.2 | F | Bangladesh |
| 5.1 | 5.4 | 8.6 | 5.0 | 5.8 | 6.1 | 5.5 | 5.8 | D | Fiji |
| 6.8 | 9.4 | 9.5 | 9.7 | 9.0 | 9.1 | 9.0 | 9.0 | A+ | Hong Kong |
| 3.9 | 4.5 | 5.2 | 3.9 | 4.5 | 4.5 | 4.1 | 4.4 | F | India |
| 7.9 | 4.1 | 7.3 | 6.5 | 5.9 | 6.1 | 5.3 | 5.8 | D | Indonesia |
| 7.6 | 6.0 | 7.4 | 7.8 | 7.1 | 7.0 | 7.1 | 7.1 | B | Malaysia |
| 2.3 | 4.5 | 10.0 | 2.1 | 3.5 | 3.6 | 3.0 | 3.4 | F- | Nepal |
| 5.8 | 4.6 | 6.1 | 6.1 | 5.3 | 5.4 | 5.0 | 5.2 | D | Pakistan |
| 6.6 | 4.9 | 8.6 | 5.0 | 6.1 | 6.2 | 5.7 | 6.0 | C | Philippines |
| 9.4 | 7.2 | 7.4 | 10.0 | 8.2 | 8.2 | 8.2 | 8.2 | A | Singapore |
| 7.8 | 6.6 | 5.5 | 7.3 | 6.7 | 6.7 | 6.6 | 6.7 | C | South Korea |
| 2.9 | 5.4 | 6.2 | 4.9 | 4.9 | 5.0 | 4.5 | 4.8 | F | Sri Lanka |
| 10.0 | 5.7 | 5.3 | 7.3 | 6.8 | 6.6 | 7.0 | 6.8 | C | Taiwan |
| 8.8 | 5.5 | 7.3 | 7.5 | 6.9 | 7.0 | 6.7 | 6.9 | C | Thailand |

Exhibit 2-1: (Continued)

## Part 1: Component Ratings: 1993-95

| | I: Money and Inflation | | | | II: Government Operations | | | | | | III: Takings | | | IV: International Sector | | | |
|---|---|---|---|---|---|---|---|---|---|---|---|---|---|---|---|---|---|
| | A | B | C | D | A | B | C | D | E | F | A | B | C | A | B | C | D |
| **AFRICA** | | | | | | | | | | | | | | | | | |
| Algeria | 2 | 2 | 0 | 0 | 2 | 4 | - | 2.5 | 0.0 | - | - | - | 0 | - | 1 | 8 | 2 |
| Benin | 3 | 10 | 0 | 0 | 7 | 4 | 2 | 5.0 | 5.0 | - | - | - | 0 | - | 8 | 2 | 0 |
| Botswana | 10 | 7 | 0 | 0 | 0 | 6 | 6 | 7.5 | 5.0 | 6 | 5 | 5 | 10 | 1 | 8 | 10 | 5 |
| Burundi | 4 | 5 | 0 | 0 | 8 | 4 | - | 2.5 | 0.0 | - | - | - | 10 | - | 2 | 1 | 0 |
| Cameroon | 9 | 5 | 0 | 0 | 6 | 4 | 2 | 5.0 | 0.0 | 8 | 8 | 1 | 10 | 3 | 8 | 2 | 0 |
| C African Rep | 3 | 7 | 0 | 0 | 8 | 6 | - | 5.0 | 2.5 | 8 | - | - | 0 | - | 8 | 1 | 0 |
| Chad | 7 | 6 | 0 | 0 | 3 | 4 | - | 5.0 | 0.0 | 8 | 10 | - | 0 | 8 | 8 | 6 | 0 |
| Congo Peoples R | 7 | 7 | 0 | 0 | 1 | 0 | 0 | 5.0 | 2.5 | 6 | - | 3 | 10 | - | 8 | 6 | 0 |
| Cote d' Ivoire | 5 | 2 | 0 | 0 | 1 | 4 | 4 | 5.0 | 0.0 | 8 | - | 3 | 0 | - | 8 | 5 | 0 |
| Gabon | 10 | 6 | 0 | 0 | 1 | 6 | 4 | 7.5 | 0.0 | 8 | 10 | 0 | 10 | 4 | 8 | 4 | 0 |
| Ghana | 1 | 2 | 10 | 0 | 7 | 2 | 6 | 5.0 | 2.5 | 8 | 7 | 7 | 10 | 2 | 7 | 2 | 0 |
| Kenya | 1 | 3 | 0 | 0 | 6 | 4 | 4 | 5.0 | 0.0 | - | 9 | 5 | 10 | 6 | 6 | 5 | 0 |
| Madagascar | 1 | 2 | 0 | 0 | 10 | 6 | - | 5.0 | 2.5 | - | 9 | - | 0 | 2 | 3 | 4 | 0 |
| Malawi | 1 | 5 | 0 | 0 | 3 | 4 | 2 | 7.5 | 5.0 | 4 | - | 7 | 10 | - | 4 | 4 | 2 |
| Mali | 7 | 5 | 0 | 0 | 7 | 4 | - | 5.0 | 0.0 | 8 | - | - | 0 | - | 8 | 5 | 2 |
| Mauritius | 6 | 9 | 0 | 0 | 7 | 6 | - | 10.0 | 7.5 | 10 | 6 | 8 | 10 | 3 | 6 | 5 | 2 |
| Morocco | 5 | 10 | 0 | 0 | 3 | 2 | 6 | 5.0 | 0.0 | - | - | 3 | 0 | - | 6 | 5 | 5 |
| Niger | 10 | 1 | 0 | 0 | 3 | 6 | - | 5.0 | 0.0 | 8 | - | - | 0 | - | 8 | 2 | 0 |
| Nigeria | 1 | 1 | 0 | 0 | 10 | 2 | 4 | 5.0 | 0.0 | 0 | - | 7 | 10 | - | 0 | 10 | 0 |
| Rwanda | 7 | 4 | 10 | 0 | 0 | 6 | - | 2.5 | 0.0 | 6 | 9 | - | 10 | 0 | 1 | 0 | 0 |
| Senegal | 8 | 2 | 0 | 0 | 7 | 6 | 4 | 5.0 | 2.5 | 8 | - | 4 | 0 | - | 8 | 2 | 0 |
| Sierra Leone | 1 | 1 | 10 | 0 | 7 | 6 | 2 | 5.0 | 0.0 | 2 | 8 | - | 10 | 2 | 8 | 1 | 0 |
| Somalia | - | 0 | 0 | 0 | - | 4 | - | 2.5 | 0.0 | - | - | - | 0 | - | - | - | 0 |
| South Africa | 3 | 9 | 0 | 0 | 1 | 4 | 4 | 5.0 | 5.0 | 10 | 6 | 4 | 10 | - | 10 | 5 | 2 |
| Tanzania | 1 | 2 | 0 | 0 | 7 | 0 | 4 | 2.5 | 2.5 | - | - | 8 | 0 | - | 6 | 10 | 0 |
| Togo | 5 | 9 | 0 | 0 | 3 | 4 | 2 | 5.0 | 0.0 | 8 | - | - | 0 | - | 8 | 3 | 0 |
| Tunisia | 10 | 10 | 0 | 0 | 3 | 4 | 6 | 5.0 | 0.0 | - | 4 | - | 0 | 1 | 6 | 6 | 5 |
| Uganda | 0 | 1 | 0 | 0 | 8 | 2 | - | 5.0 | 0.0 | - | - | 8 | 10 | - | 4 | 1 | 0 |
| Zaire | 0 | 0 | 0 | 0 | 1 | 2 | - | 2.5 | 0.0 | - | - | 1 | 10 | - | 5 | - | 2 |
| Zambia | 0 | 0 | 0 | 0 | 5 | 0 | 2 | 5.0 | 0.0 | 0 | - | 7 | 10 | - | 8 | 8 | 2 |
| Zimbabwe | 1 | 3 | 0 | 0 | 2 | 4 | 2 | 5.0 | 2.5 | 8 | - | 3 | 0 | - | 8 | 9 | 2 |

N/R = No rating because data were available for less than eleven of the seventeen components in the index for this year.

* These summary ratings should be interpreted with caution because they are based on data for only eleven of the seventeen components in the index for this year.

Exhibit 2-1 (continued)

## Part 2: Area Ratings (Is1)  Part 3: Summary Indexes

| Money and Inflation | Govern- ment Operations | Takings | Inter- national Sector | (Ie) | (Is1) | (Is2) | Avg. | Grade [a] | AFRICA |
|---|---|---|---|---|---|---|---|---|---|
| 1.3 | 2.3 | 0.0 | 3.0 | 2.2 | 2.1 | 2.1 | 2.1 | F- | Algeria |
| 4.3 | 4.5 | 0.0 | 3.6 | 3.8 | 4.0 | 3.3 | 3.7 | F- | Benin |
| 5.4 | 5.1 | 5.7 | 5.5 | 5.6 | 5.4 | 5.8 | 5.6 | D | Botswana |
| 2.9 | 3.8 | 10.0 | 1.0 | 3.0 | 3.2 | 2.6 | 2.9 | F- | Burundi |
| 4.4 | 4.0 | 5.0 | 3.4 | 4.1 | 4.2 | 3.7 | 4.0 | F | Cameroon |
| 3.3 | 5.9 | 0.0 | 3.4 | 4.1 | 4.2 | 3.5 | 3.9 | F- | C African Rep |
| 4.1 | 3.8 | 7.5 | 5.6 | 4.6 | 5.0 | 4.0 | 4.5 | F | Chad |
| 4.5 | 2.1 | 4.5 | 4.5 | 3.5 | 3.5 | 3.4 | 3.5 | F- | Congo Rep |
| 2.2 | 3.5 | 2.3 | 4.3 | 3.3 | 3.2 | 3.2 | 3.2 | F- | Cote d' Ivoire |
| 5.0 | 4.4 | 5.3 | 4.1 | 4.7 | 4.7 | 4.6 | 4.7 | F | Gabon |
| 2.9 | 5.0 | 7.4 | 2.9 | 4.5 | 4.8 | 3.9 | 4.4 | F | Ghana |
| 1.3 | 4.0 | 7.3 | 4.3 | 4.1 | 4.5 | 3.4 | 4.0 | F | Kenya |
| 1.0 | 6.1 | 6.8 | 2.1 | 3.5 | 4.0 | 2.5 | 3.3 | F- | Madagascar |
| 2.0 | 4.2 | 7.7 | 3.3 | 4.0 | 4.3 | 3.7 | 4.0 | F | Malawi |
| 3.8 | 4.7 | 0.0 | 5.1 | 4.3 | 4.3 | 3.8 | 4.1 | F | Mali |
| 4.8 | 8.0 | 7.5 | 3.9 | 6.2 | 6.3 | 5.8 | 6.1 | C | Mauritius |
| 4.9 | 3.5 | 2.3 | 5.4 | 3.9 | 3.9 | 3.8 | 3.9 | F- | Morocco |
| 3.3 | 4.3 | 0.0 | 3.6 | 3.7 | 3.6 | 3.5 | 3.6 | F- | Niger |
| 0.6 | 4.0 | 7.7 | 2.3 | 3.5 | 3.7 | 2.7 | 3.3 | F- | Nigeria |
| 5.4 | 2.8 | 9.2 | 0.3 | 3.5 | 3.7 | 3.4 | 3.5 | F- | Rwanda |
| 3.1 | 5.3 | 3.1 | 3.6 | 4.1 | 4.1 | 3.7 | 4.0 | F | Senegal |
| 2.5 | 4.0 | 8.5 | 3.0 | 3.8 | 4.2 | 3.3 | 3.8 | F- | Sierra Leone |
| 0.0 | 2.4 | 0.0 | 0.0 | N/R | N/R | N/R |  |  | Somalia |
| 3.9 | 4.4 | 5.6 | 5.8 | 4.9 | 4.9 | 4.8 | 4.9 | F | South Africa |
| 1.0 | 3.2 | 6.2 | 4.7 | 3.3 | 3.7 | 2.6 | 3.2 | F- | Tanzania |
| 4.5 | 3.5 | 0.0 | 3.8 | 3.6 | 3.6 | 3.4 | 3.5 | F- | Togo |
| 6.4 | 3.9 | 3.0 | 4.2 | 4.4 | 4.3 | 4.3 | 4.3 | F | Tunisia |
| 0.3 | 4.0 | 8.4 | 1.8 | 3.1 | 3.7 | 2.4 | 3.1 | F- | Uganda |
| 0.0 | 1.5 | 3.0 | 3.5 | 1.8 | 1.9 | 2.0 | 1.9 | F- | Zaire |
| 0.0 | 2.3 | 7.7 | 5.8 | 3.1 | 3.6 | 2.7 | 3.1 | F- | Zambia |
| 1.3 | 3.6 | 2.3 | 6.0 | 3.5 | 3.4 | 3.3 | 3.4 | F- | Zimbabwe |

[a] The average of the three ratings was used to assign the letter grade. The following conversion table was used to allocate the letter grades. Countries with an average for the three summary ratings of 8.0 or more were assigned an A (9.0 or more was assigned A+); 7.0 to 7.99 a B; 6.0 to 6.99 a C; 5.0 to 5.99 a D; 4.0 to 4.99 a F; and less than 4.0 a F-.

Note: See Exhibit 1-1 for the description of each component in the index.

## Some Reflections on the Component Ratings

*The country com-
ponent ratings
ranging from zero
to ten for each of
the 17 components
are presented in
Part 1 of
Exhibit 2-1.*

Since both the summary and area ratings are merely an aggregation of the component ratings, it is important for the reader to understand the meaning of the latter.[1] Let us look at the various component ratings for a few countries and consider their significance. France (and Sweden and Switzerland among several others) received a rating of ten for component I-A, monetary expansion adjusted for the estimated growth rate of potential output. Since the monetary expansion variable was continuous, the ten rating indicates that the rate of monetary expansion in France during the five years immediately prior to 1995 would have placed it in the top 1/11th of the countries during the base year (1985) in terms of the *least* monetary expansion adjusted for the potential growth of real output. Canada, Japan and Denmark (among others) received a rating of 9, indicating that the expansion in the money supply of these countries would have placed them in the second 1/11th of countries during the base year.

At the other end of the spectrum, Brazil received a rating of zero, indicating that the growth rate of its money supply during the five years immediately prior to 1995 would have placed it in the bottom 1/11th of countries—those with the highest growth rates of the money supply—during the base year. (Note: the *annual* growth rate of the money supply in Brazil was 1,233% during the five years immediately prior to the 1995 rating.) France, Sweden, Switzerland, Canada, Japan, Denmark and other countries with high ratings received them because they did not use monetary expansion to dilute the value of their monetary unit and thereby seize property from persons holding money during the 1990-94 period. On the other hand, Brazil, Argentina, Ecuador, Peru, Uruguay, and other countries with low ratings received them precisely because of their highly expansionary monetary policies.

The second component (I-B) in the index is the instability in the price level as measured by the standard deviation in the rate of inflation during the last five years. As previously discussed, fluctuations in the inflation rate increase uncertainty and retard time-dimension exchanges. When the rate of change in the price level is relatively constant, it will be more easily predictable; therefore it will exert less adverse impact on exchange. Thus, the countries with the lowest standard deviation (least variability) in the inflation rate are given the highest ratings. The ratings of ten of the United States, Canada, Australia and Japan, for example, indicate that the small variability in the inflation rate in each of these countries during 1990-1994 would have placed them in the top 1/11th of the countries with the least variability in the inflation rate during the base year period. The nine ratings for Finland, Ireland, and Italy indicate that while the 1990-1994 variability in the rate of inflation in these countries was low, it was slightly greater than for the countries receiving a rating of ten. At the other end of the spectrum, the zero ratings of Argentina, Brazil, and Nicaragua indicate that the fluctuations in the inflation rates of these countries during 1990-1994 would have placed them in the bottom 1/11th of all countries during the base year period.

The next two components, freedom to maintain a foreign currency bank account domestically (I-C) and freedom to maintain a bank account abroad (I-D) have only two possible outcomes—it is either legal or illegal to maintain these accounts. The ten ratings for the United States, Canada, Australia, and numerous other countries indicate that it was legal in the mid-1990s for the citizens of these countries to maintain accounts of this type. The zero ratings for Belize, Brazil, and Dominican Republic, for example, indicate that the citizens of these countries were not permitted to legally maintain these accounts in the mid-1990s.

Using the weights derived from our survey of experts (see Exhibit 1-2), the four components in the area of money and inflation (Area I) are aggregated into an Is1 area rating.[2] These results are presented in Part 2 of Exhibit 2-1. Of course, countries with high ratings for the four components in the money and inflation area will also receive a high rating in this area. For example, the money and inflation *area rating* of France was ten because it received a rating of ten for each of the four components in this area. The money and inflation area rating of Canada was slightly lower (9.7) since it received a 9 for the money expansion component (I-A) and a ten for the other three monetary components. The area ratings are merely a reflection of the component ratings that comprise them.

The country ratings for the other components in the index have a similar meaning. In each case, a higher component rating indicates that the country's institutional arrangements and/or policy choices are more consistent with economic freedom in the specific category measured by the component. A component rating of 10 indicates that for this dimension of economic freedom the nation is among the freest in the world. On the other hand, a component

*A higher component rating indicates that the country's institutional arrangements and/or policy choices are more consistent with economic freedom in the specific category measured by the component.*

rating of zero indicates that the country is among the least free in the category measured by the component.

## The Summary Ratings of Countries: 1993-1995

As we explained in Chapter 1, the 17 components were aggregated into three alternative summary indexes. Each of the three summary indexes reflects a different set of weights for the various components of the index.[3] Exhibit 1-2 indicates the various weights applied to each component under the three alternative methods of deriving a summary index.

*In order to make comparisons across countries easier, we derived an average for the three summary indexes and used it to assign letter grades.*

The summary indexes of economic freedom derived by each of the three alternative methods are presented in Part 3 of Exhibit 2-1. Except for the industrial countries, the three summary indexes generally yielded similar ratings. As Exhibit 1-2 shows, Is2 allocates only a very small weight to the components for government consumption as a share of GDP (II-A) and transfers and subsidies as a share of GDP (III-A). Since the high-income, industrial countries generally rate poorly in these two areas, the summary index rating of these countries is higher when less weight is allocated to these two components. On the other hand, Is1 allocates a relatively large weight to the transfers and subsidies (III-A) and marginal tax rate (III-B) components, two areas where many of the high-income industrial countries do poorly. This structure of weights tends to reduce the Is1 summary rating of industrial countries relative to their Is2 rating. Thus, the Is2 summary index is often approximately one unit higher than the Is1 index for these countries. For example, in the case of Sweden, the Is2 summary rating is 6.7 compared to a Is1 rating of 5.5. Similar differences between the Is1 and Is2 summary ratings are also present for other industrial countries.[4]

In order to make comparisons across countries easier, we derived an average for the three summary indexes and used it to assign letter grades. Countries with an average of 8.0 or more for the three alternative summary indexes were assigned a letter grade of "A". (An average of 9.0 or more was assigned an A+). Countries with an average for the three summary ratings between 7.0 and 7.95 were assigned a "B". Below that point, one letter grade was subtracted for each decline of 1.0 in the average of the three summary ratings. Thus, countries with a rating of less than five, were given a letter grade of "F". An F- grade, indicating little economic freedom in any of the four major areas, was assigned when the average of the three summary ratings for a country was less than 4.0.

We now turn to the consideration of these grades (and summary ratings) across countries. By a substantial margin, Hong Kong was the highest rated country in the mid-1990s. With the exception of the upper middle ratings for the monetary expansion and price stability components, Hong Kong rates high in every area. Its ratings for the three summary indexes were almost identical, either 9.0 or 9.1. The average Hong Kong summary rating was a half point higher than those for any other country. Thus, Hong Kong was given a grade of A+.

*By a substantial margin, Hong Kong was the highest rated country in the mid-1990s.*

Three other countries—the United States, New Zealand, and Singapore achieved an average for the three alternative indexes of more than 8.0. These countries were given a grade of "A". With the exception of a couple of components, these countries were consistently rated high in all categories. For example, the ratings of the United States were 7 or better for all components except government consumption (II-A), the size of transfer sector (III-A), and the size of trade sector (IV-C). These same three components were also weaknesses of New Zealand. The presence of conscription pulled down the summary ratings of Singapore. Singapore also received a very low rating for the equality under the law component (II-E).

The following ten countries were given a grade of "B" since their average for the three summary ratings was between 7.0 and 7.9: Canada, Australia, Japan, Belgium, Germany, Ireland, Netherlands, Switzerland, United Kingdom, and Malaysia. Typically the component ratings of these countries were high in the money and inflation and international categories. On the other hand, with the exception of Malaysia, the summary scores of these countries were generally pulled down by low component ratings for the size of the government consumption and transfer sectors. The presence of conscription also reduced the ratings of Belgium, Germany, Netherlands, and Switzerland. A low rating for equal treatment under the law reduced the grade level for Malaysia. Among the C rated countries; Denmark, Costa Rica, Panama, Taiwan, and Thailand had the highest average summary ratings (either 6.8 or 6.9).

At the other end of the spectrum, the following countries earned a grade of F-: Brazil, Haiti, Nicaragua, Venezuela, Hungary, Iran, Romania, Syria, Nepal, Algeria, Benin, Burundi, Central African Republic, Congo, Cote d'Ivoire, Madagascar, Morocco, Niger, Nigeria, Rwanda, Sierra Leone, Tanzania, Togo, Uganda, Zaire, Zambia, and Zimbabwe. Clearly, the policies and institutional arrangements of these countries were inconsistent with economic freedom in almost every area.

Taking a closer look at the summary ratings within regions, all of the industrial countries earned a grade of "C" or better. The record in Central and South America was not as good. No country in the region was able to earn a grade of either A or B. Eleven countries—Argentina, Belize, Bolivia, Chile, Costa Rica, El Salvador, Guatemala, Jamaica, Panama, Trinidad/ Tobago and Uruguay achieved a "C" rating in 1993-1995. As we will see later, several of these countries in the "C" category had substantially lower ratings during the earlier years of our study. At the other end of the scale, Brazil, Dominican Republic, Haiti, and Nicaragua, received either F or F- ratings. As Exhibit 2-1 (Part 1) illustrates, the ratings of Central and South American countries were often extremely low for the monetary expansion (I-A) and price stability (I-B) components.

The overall summary ratings of the non-industrial countries of Europe and the Middle East were also quite low. The D ratings of Czech Republic, Malta, and Portugal were the highest among the nations in this group. Bulgaria, Cyprus, Slovakia, Egypt, Hungary, Iran, Israel, Jordan, Poland, Romania, Syria, and Turkey all received either F or F- ratings in 1995.

In Asia, the summary index ratings were highly diverse. As we previously mentioned, Hong Kong and Singapore earned A+ or A ratings, and Malaysia a B. Taiwan and Thailand earned high "C" grades. The Philippines and South Korea also received C ratings. At the other end of the spectrum, Bangladesh, India, and Sri Lanka posted F ratings, while Nepal registered an F-.

The economic freedom ratings of the African countries were extremely low. Except for the C of Mauritius and the D of Botswana, the other 29 African nations included in our study earned grades of either F or F-. The ratings of Algeria, Burundi,

*Except for the C of Mauritius and the D of Botswana, the other 29 African nations included in our study earned grades of either F or F-.*

Congo, Cote d'Ivoire, Madagascar, Niger, Nigeria, Tanzania, Togo, Uganda, Zaire, Zambia, and Zimbabwe were among the lowest in the world.

Exhibits S-1A and S-1B in the Graphic Summary at the front of the book present the average for the three ratings and the Is1 ratings respectively—arrayed from the highest to the lowest for the 102 nations we were able to rate in 1993-1995. These exhibits make it easy to identify the relative position of various countries. As these data illustrate, the rankings of the two indexes are quite similar. Hong Kong, New Zealand, Singapore, United States, and Switzerland are the five highest ranked countries for both the average of the three indexes and the Is1 ratings. The only difference is the switching of the second and third place positions between New Zealand and Singapore. Moving down the ranking, Australia and Ireland tie for eighth in the average, but drop slightly to 11th and 12th in the Is1 ranking. On the other hand, Malaysia and Thailand tie for sixth in the Is1 ranking, compared to their 12th and 15th place ranking in the average index calculation.

The major difference between the average of the three indexes and the Is1 index is the relative rankings of industrial and non-industrial nations. As we previously discussed, the Is2 index gives very little weight to the size of the government consumption and transfer sectors (components II-A and III-A), two areas where the industrial nations generally do poorly. Therefore, inclusion of the Is2 ratings into the average increases both the ratings and rankings of the industrial relative to the less developed countries. Thus, the industrial countries generally do better when their ranking is derived by the average of the three indexes rather than the Is1 rating. For example, Germany ranks 12th in the average index, but 18th in the Is1; France is 20th in the average, but 31st in the Is1; and Italy and Sweden tie for 31st in the average; but they rank 44th and 47th respectively in the Is1 rankings. On the other hand, several non-industrial nations do better in the Is1 rankings. For example, Mexico and Indonesia rank 44th and 45th respectively when rated by the average of the three indexes, but they tie for 35th in the Is1 rankings; Peru ranks 47th in the average ratings, but 33rd in the Is1; South Korea ranks 20th when rated by the average method, but 12th in the Is1 ratings; and Philippines is 36th in the average ratings, but 27th in the Is1 rankings.

Despite these differences, the rankings of numerous countries were quite similar. For example, rankings for the average of the three indexes and the Is1 index respectively for the following countries were: Portugal, 41 and 47; South Africa, 54 and 56; India, 62 and 63; Israel and Turkey, 66 and 70 (tie); Nigeria, 88 and 81; and Brazil, 97 and 93. Syria, Iran, Algeria, and Zaire ranked 99 through 102 for both of the alternative methods. Thus, while the country rankings shift around under the two methods, the movements are not huge. Even in extreme cases, the differences are not more than 12 to 15 positions, and almost all changes of this size are in the middle of the distribution. A review of Exhibits S-1A and S-1B will provide information on the rankings of other countries.[5]

## The Pattern of the 1993-1995 Area Ratings

*The ratings of the high-income industrial countries were quite high in the money and inflation area.*

Exhibit 2-1, Part 2, indicates the Is1 area ratings for the various countries. Let us take a closer look at their pattern in 1993-1995. The ratings of the high-income industrial countries were quite high in the money and inflation area. With the exception of Finland, Iceland and Sweden, all of the industrial countries earned a rating of 8.5 or more in the money area. These high ratings are a reflection of low rates of monetary growth, low and stable rates of inflation, and the freedom of citizens to maintain foreign currency bank accounts both domestically and abroad. Among the less developed countries, Singapore, Taiwan, and Thailand had the highest ratings (8.8 or more) in the money area. The ratings of Panama, Indonesia, Malaysia, and South Korea were just slightly lower (between 7.6 and 7.9).

The component ratings for monetary expansion and inflation instability of the South and Central American countries were generally low. Of course, this is a reflection of the erratic monetary policy that has characterized this region for several decades. Several of the Middle Eastern and transitional economies of Eastern Europe were also characterized by monetary and price level instability in the first half of the 1990s (see ratings for components I-A and I-B for evidence on these points). The African countries also had very low ratings in the monetary area. In several countries (for example, Ghana, Nigeria, Sierra Leone, Tanzania, Uganda, Zaire, Zambia, and Zimbabwe), monetary instability was a contributing factor. However, restrictions limiting the use of foreign currencies were the primary reason for the low

60

ratings of most other African countries. The freedom to maintain a foreign currency bank account either domestically or abroad was almost totally absent in Africa.

The component ratings of the industrial countries in the area of government operations were mixed. Since their government consumption expenditures were generally large, with the exception of Japan, the ratings of the industrial countries were quite low for this component. The European countries (for example, Austria, Italy, Denmark, Norway, Sweden, and Spain) also received low ratings for the government enterprise component. In contrast, the ratings of the industrial countries were generally quite high for the ease of entry into business, equal treatment under the law, and credit market components. Overall, the government operations area ratings of New Zealand, Switzerland and United States were the highest (7.6 or more) among the industrial countries while the ratings of Austria, Italy, Norway, and Spain were the lowest (between 5.0 and 5.8).

In South and Central America, Argentina, Chile, and Costa Rica had the highest ratings (7.0 or more) in the government operations area, while Brazil, Haiti, and Nicaragua had the lowest. Among the other less developed countries, Hong Kong, Singapore, and Mauritius had the highest government operations area ratings. On the other hand, Egypt, Iran, Syria, Algeria, Congo, Zaire, and Zambia were among those who did the most poorly in this area.

Large transfer sectors and high marginal tax rates pulled down almost all industrial countries in the area of takings and discriminatory taxation. In addition, since most European countries utilize conscription as a means of obtaining military personnel, they also earned a low rating for this component. This combination—a large transfer sector, high marginal tax rates, and conscription—resulted in some very low ratings in the takings area. Those for Belgium, Denmark, Finland, France, Germany, Italy, Netherlands, and Sweden were among the lowest in the world. Among the non-industrial countries, the ratings of Hong Kong, Philippines, Fiji, Dominican Republic, Jamaica, and Jordan were quite high. Chile, Bulgaria, Egypt, Hungary, Israel, and Romania were among the countries with low ratings in this area.

*Large transfer sectors and high marginal tax rates pulled down the ratings of almost all industrial countries.*

In the international exchange area, with the exception of Iceland, the ratings of most industrial countries were quite high (8.0 or more). Compared to other industrial countries, the rating of

Japan was also on the low side. The ratings of several Asian countries—most notably Hong Kong, Singapore, Malaysia, and Thailand—were strong in this area. Among the South and Central American countries, Argentina, Jamaica, and Panama had the highest ratings and Brazil and Nicaragua the lowest in the international area. The Czech Republic, Greece, and Portugal also achieved high marks in this area, while those of Iran, Syria, Bangladesh, India and Nepal were relatively low. Among the African nations, Zimbabwe, Botswana, Chad, South Africa, Zambia and Zimbabwe registered the highest ratings.

## COUNTRY RANKINGS: 1975-1995

*Not only was Hong Kong the top ranked country in 1995, it was also the top-rated country during the four earlier rating years. Singapore, United States, Switzerland, Canada, and Germany were also in the Top 15 during each of the prior years.*

Exhibit 2-2 presents the economic freedom summary index Is1 for the 15 highest rated, 15 lowest rated, and selected other countries for 1975, 1980, 1985, and 1990, as well as the 1995 rankings. As discussed in Chapter 1, data for the components on entry into business (II-D) and equal treatment under the law (II-E) were only available for 1995. Similarly, the data required for the price controls component (II-C) were available only for 1990 and 1995. Thus, the summary index for 1990 has only 15 components and the indexes for 1975, 1980, and 1985 have only 14. In spite of these limitations, the summary indexes for 1975-1990 provide insight concerning the direction of changes in economic freedom during this period.

There are several interesting points about the lists of the 15 highest rated countries in the various years. First, several countries were in the Top 15 list during each of the rating years. Not only was Hong Kong the top ranked country in 1995, it also achieved this status during the four prior rating years. Singapore, United States, Canada, and Switzerland were also in the Top 15 list during each of the years. The summary ratings of these countries generally improved during the two decades. For example, the Is1 rating of Singapore rose from 6.8 in 1975 to 8.0 in 1985 and 8.5 in 1990, before receding to 8.2 in 1995. The Is1 score of the United States rose steadily throughout the period, increasing from 6.0 in 1975, 6.5 in 1985 and 7.7 in 1995.

Second, in addition to those remaining in the Top 15, there was another group of top-ranked countries that improved their relative position substantially during the last two decades.

Malaysia, Japan, United Kingdom, Costa Rica, and Thailand comprise this category. None of these countries ranked in the Top 15 in 1975. Japan moved up steadily between 1975 and 1990, climbing to a sixth place ranking in 1990, before falling back to ninth in 1995. The Is1 summary score of Japan increased from 5.2 in 1975 to 6.9 in both 1990 and 1995. The relative position of the United Kingdom increased steadily after 1980. The Is1 rating of the United Kingdom jumped from 4.5 in 1980 to 6.0 in 1985 and 7.0 in 1995. The Is1 index indicates that the economy of the United Kingdom is now the sixth most free in the world. The summary index of Malaysia jumped from 5.1 in 1975 (and 5.6 in 1980) to 7.1 in both 1985 and 1990. Costa Rica's improvement has been even more recent. Prior to 1990, Costa Rica was consistently ranked in the upper part of the middle-rated group. Actually its Is1 summary rating declined from 5.2 in 1975 to 4.8 in 1980 and 4.6 in 1985. Since 1985 the rating of Costa Rica has improved dramatically jumping to 6.6 in 1990 and 6.7 in 1995. The 1995 Is1 rating of Costa Rica places it in an twelfth place tied with South Korea and Ireland among the 103 nations in our study.

Finally, there is another group of countries that ranked in the Top 15 in 1975 that have clearly regressed. In 1975, the 7.4 rating of Honduras was exceeded only by Hong Kong. But by 1980, Honduras had slipped to tenth place and by 1990, it had fallen from the Top 15 list. By 1995 the Is1 rating of Honduras had slid to 5.5, nearly two units less than its 1975 mark. Venezuela followed a similar course. Its 6.9 summary rating was the fifth highest in 1975. By 1985 Venezuela was no longer in the Top 15 and its summary score continued to drop, plunging to 5.5 in 1990 and 4.5 in 1995.[6]

Perhaps Nicaragua provides the most dramatic illustration of a plunge in the level of economic freedom during the last two decades. In 1975 Nicaragua's Is1 summary index was the eighth highest in the world. Its rating, however, fell from 6.4 in 1975 to 3.6 in 1980. By 1985, Nicaragua's rating had declined to 1.8, third lowest among the more than 100 countries in our study. During the 1990s, Nicaragua's Is1 summary rating has rebounded modestly, reaching 3.3 in 1995.

A few countries have remained persistently on the list of 15 countries with the lowest freedom index ratings. Brazil has placed in the Bottom 15 during every year of our study. Iran and Syria have been in this group for each of the last four rating years.

*Malaysia, Japan, United Kingdom, Costa Rica, and Thailand improved their relative position and recently moved into the Top 15.*

**Exhibit 2-2: The Economic Freedom Rating (Is1) of the 15 Highest, 15 Lowest, and Selected Middle-rated Countries for 1975, 1980, 1985, 1990, and 1995**

| Fifteen Countries with the Highest Freedom Index (Is1) Ratings | | | | | | | | | |
| --- | --- | --- | --- | --- | --- | --- | --- | --- | --- |
| **1975** | | **1980** | | **1985** | | **1990** | | **1995** | |
| **COUNTRY** | | | | | | | | | |
| Hong Kong | 9.2 | Hong Kong | 9.4 | Hong Kong | 9.5 | Hong Kong | 9.3 | Hong Kong | 9.1 |
| Honduras | 7.4 | Switzerland | 7.1 | Singapore | 8.0 | Singapore | 8.5 | Singapore | 8.2 |
| Switzerland | 7.1 | Singapore | 7.1 | Switzerland | 7.3 | USA | 7.4 | New Zealand | 8.0 |
| Panama | 7.0 | Canada | 6.8 | Malaysia | 7.1 | Switzerland | 7.3 | USA | 7.7 |
| Venezuela | 6.9 | Guatemala | 6.8 | Panama | 6.6 | Malaysia | 7.1 | Switzerland | 7.5 |
| Singapore | 6.8 | Venezuela | 6.6 | USA | 6.5 | Japan | 6.9 | UK | 7.0 |
| Guatemala | 6.5 | Uruguay | 6.3 | Paraguay | 6.5 | Canada | 6.9 | Malaysia | 7.0 |
| Nicaragua | 6.4 | Panama | 6.3 | Japan | 6.5 | UK | 6.6 | Thailand | 7.0 |
| Canada | 6.1 | USA | 6.2 | Uruguay | 6.5 | Costa Rica | 6.6 | Japan | 6.9 |
| USA | 6.0 | Honduras | 6.1 | Indonesia | 6.1 | Indonesia | 6.6 | Canada | 6.9 |
| Germany | 5.9 | Paraguay | 6.1 | UK | 6.0 | Guatemala | 6.6 | Australia | 6.8 |
| Uruguay | 5.8 | Germany | 6.0 | Germany | 6.0 | Thailand | 6.5 | South Korea | 6.7 |
| Netherlands | 5.7 | Japan | 5.9 | Mauritius | 6.0 | Germany | 6.3 | Costa Rica | 6.7 |
| Paraguay | 5.6 | Belize | 5.9 | Honduras | 6.0 | Uruguay | 6.3 | Ireland | 6.7 |
| Belgium | 5.5 | Belgium | 5.7 | Australia | 5.9 | Paraguay | 6.3 | Panama | 6.6 |
|  |  | Canada | 5.9 | Bolivia | 6.3 | Taiwan | 6.6 |
|  |  |  |  | Panama | 6.3 |  |  |  |  |

| Selected Middle-Rated Countries | | | | | | | | | |
| --- | --- | --- | --- | --- | --- | --- | --- | --- | --- |
| **1975** | | **1980** | | **1985** | | **1990** | | **1995** | |
| **COUNTRY** | | | | | | | | | |
| Indonesia | 5.2 | Malaysia | 5.6 | Belgium | 5.8 | Australia | 6.0 | Netherlands | 6.4 |
| Costa Rica | 5.2 | Australia | 5.5 | Netherlands | 5.6 | New Zealand | 6.0 | Germany | 6.4 |
| Japan | 5.2 | Netherlands | 5.4 | Taiwan | 5.5 | Honduras | 6.0 | Belgium | 6.3 |
| Malaysia | 5.1 | Taiwan | 5.3 | Venezuela | 5.2 | Taiwan | 5.9 | Argentina | 6.3 |
| UK | 5.0 | Thailand | 5.0 | South Korea | 5.1 | Belgium | 5.9 | Mauritius | 6.3 |
| Mexico | 5.0 | Indonesia | 5.0 | Philippines | 4.9 | Netherlands | 5.8 | Philippines | 6.2 |
| Australia | 5.0 | New Zealand | 4.8 | Costa Rica | 4.6 | Chile | 5.7 | Indonesia | 6.1 |
| Iran | 5.0 | Costa Rica | 4.8 | South Africa | 4.5 | Philippines | 5.6 | France | 6.0 |
| Thailand | 4.9 | Philippines | 4.8 | Botswana | 4.4 | Mauritius | 5.6 | Peru | 5.9 |
| Taiwan | 4.9 | South Africa | 4.6 | Nigeria | 4.3 | France | 5.5 | Mexico | 5.8 |
| Philippines | 4.6 | UK | 4.5 | Sweden | 4.2 | Venezuela | 5.5 | Chile | 5.8 |
| New Zealand | 4.3 | France | 4.2 | Chile | 4.1 | Italy | 5.4 | Spain | 5.8 |
| France | 4.3 | Chile | 3.9 | New Zealand | 4.1 | Mexico | 5.3 | Iceland | 5.7 |
| South Korea | 4.3 | Spain | 3.9 | Mexico | 4.1 | South Korea | 5.2 | Italy | 5.6 |

Exhibit 2-2: (Con't)

## Selected Middle-Rated Countries (Con't)

| COUNTRY | 1975 | | 1980 | | 1985 | | 1990 | | 1995 |
|---|---|---|---|---|---|---|---|---|---|
| Italy | 4.1 | Mauritius | 3.8 | Spain | 4.1 | Spain | 4.7 | Sweden | 5.5 |
| South Africa | 3.9 | Greece | 3.8 | Pakistan | 3.9 | Iceland | 4.7 | Portugal | 5.5 |
| Mauritius | 3.9 | India | 3.8 | Turkey | 3.8 | South Africa | 4.6 | Honduras | 5.5 |
| Greece | 3.9 | Italy | 3.6 | Italy | 3.6 | Turkey | 4.6 | South Africa | 4.9 |
| Syria | 3.7 | Argentina | 3.6 | Sri Lanka | 3.6 | Sweden | 4.5 | Czech Rep. | 4.9 |
| Peru | 3.7 | Nicaragua | 3.6 | Portugal | 3.5 | Pakistan | 4.2 | Greece | 4.9 |
| Sri Lanka | 3.6 | Sri Lanka | 3.5 | India | 3.4 | Egypt | 4.2 | Poland | 4.8 |
| Sweden | 3.5 | Botswana | 3.5 | Peru | 3.4 | Portugal | 4.1 | India | 4.5 |
| Botswana | 3.5 | Pakistan | 3.5 | France | 3.4 | Peru | 4.0 | Venezuela | 4.5 |
| Nepal | 3.4 | Sweden | 3.4 | Egypt | 3.3 | Argentina | 3.8 | Israel | 4.2 |
| India | 3.3 | Peru | 3.4 | Iceland | 3.3 | India | 3.7 | Turkey | 4.2 |
| | | Iceland | 3.4 | Greece | 3.2 | Ghana | 3.6 | Egypt | 4.0 |
| | | | | | | Greece | 3.4 | Nigeria | 3.9 |

## Fifteen Countries with the Lowest Freedom Index (Is1) Ratings

| COUNTRY | 1975 | | 1980 | | 1985 | | 1990 | | 1995 |
|---|---|---|---|---|---|---|---|---|---|
| Jamaica | 3.2 | Portugal | 3.1 | Tunisia | 2.8 | Morocco | 3.2 | Nepal | 3.6 |
| Brazil | 3.2 | Madagascar | 3.1 | Ghana | 2.8 | Syria | 3.2 | Niger | 3.6 |
| Trinidad/Tob. | 3.2 | Syria | 3.1 | Syria | 2.7 | Iran | 3.2 | Zambia | 3.6 |
| Argentina | 3.1 | Tunisia | 3.1 | Zambia | 2.7 | Congo | 3.1 | Congo | 3.5 |
| Hungary | 3.0 | C. African R. | 3.0 | Iran | 2.7 | Israel | 3.0 | Zimbabwe | 3.4 |
| Zambia | 2.9 | Togo | 2.9 | Zimbabwe | 2.6 | Hungary | 3.0 | Hungary | 3.3 |
| Turkey | 2.8 | Burundi | 2.9 | Israel | 2.5 | Brazil | 2.9 | Brazil | 3.3 |
| Chile | 2.8 | Bangladesh | 2.8 | Argentina | 2.5 | Algeria | 2.7 | Nicaragua | 3.3 |
| Iceland | 2.7 | Egypt | 2.8 | Czechoslov. | 2.4 | Uganda | 2.5 | Burundi | 3.2 |
| Somalia | 2.6 | Jamaica | 2.8 | Algeria | 2.4 | Czechoslov. | 2.4 | Cote d'Ivoire | 3.2 |
| Ghana | 2.5 | Algeria | 2.7 | Brazil | 2.3 | Tanzania | 2.3 | Haiti | 2.9 |
| Egypt | 2.4 | Brazil | 2.7 | Poland | 2.2 | Zimbabwe | 2.3 | Romania | 2.9 |
| Portugal | 2.4 | Somalia | 2.5 | Tanzania | 1.9 | Romania | 2.2 | Syria | 2.6 |
| Pakistan | 2.3 | Iran | 2.5 | Nicaragua | 1.8 | Nicaragua | 2.0 | Iran | 2.1 |
| Israel | 2.1 | Israel | 2.3 | Uganda | 1.7 | Zambia | 1.8 | Algeria | 2.1 |
| Uganda | 1.2 | Turkey | 2.3 | Somalia | 1.1 | Bulgaria | 1.6 | Zaire | 1.9 |
| | | Ghana | 2.3 | | | Somalia | 0.8 | | |
| | | Uganda | 2.2 | | | | | | |

Source: See Appendix I for the component ratings and the summary indexes for the complete list of countries.

Uganda and (perhaps surprising to some) Israel were on the Bottom 15 list throughout the 1975-1990 period. Israel is an example of a country that even through its rating is still quite low, has shown some improvement. The 1975 summary index rating (Is1) of Israel was 2.1, the second lowest in the world. Even though it remained in the Bottom 15, its rating had risen to 3.0 by 1990 and it climbed to 4.2 in 1995. Egypt's experience was similar to that of Israel. In 1975, Egypt's 2.4 rating placed it near the bottom. But the Is1 summary index of Egypt rose to 2.8 in 1980 and 4.2 in 1990 (Egypt's 1995 rating was 4.0).

*Perhaps the most dramatic improvements among the countries in the Bottom 15 two decades ago have been registered by Chile, Iceland, and quite recently Argentina.*

Perhaps the most dramatic improvements among countries in the Bottom 15 two decades ago have been registered by Chile, Iceland, and quite recently Argentina. In 1975 the summary index (Is1) of Chile was 2.8, eighth lowest among the countries that we were able to rate during that year. But Chile has made steady improvement since that time. The Is1 summary index of Chile rose to 3.9 in 1980, 5.7 in 1990, and 5.8 in 1995. This is a three unit increase over a 20 year period. Iceland has achieved an increase of similar magnitude. The index rating of Iceland jumped from 2.7 in 1975 to 4.7 in 1990 and 5.7 in 1995. The advancement of Argentina did not really begin until the late 1980s. As recently as 1985, the Is1 summary rating of Argentina was 2.5. Since that time, the Argentine Is1 rating has jumped to 3.8 in 1990 and 6.3 in 1995, an increase of 3.8 units in a decade. In the years immediately ahead, it will be interesting to monitor the impact of this dramatic improvement on the performance of the Argentine economy.

## THE PERSISTENTLY HIGH AND PERSISTENTLY LOW RATED COUNTRIES: 1975-1995

Exhibit 2-3 identifies the countries that registered persistently high and persistently low ratings throughout the 1975-1995 period. Countries that received a letter grade of either A or B for the most recent rating year *and* ranked among the Top 15 during each of the earlier rating years comprise the persistently high-rated group. Only six countries—Hong Kong, Switzerland, Singapore, United States, Canada, and Germany—were able to achieve this status. At the other end of the spectrum, Exhibit 2-3 also provides the list of countries with persistently low rankings.

None of the nine countries included in the lower part of this exhibit were able to register a summary index rating (Is1) as high as 4.0 during any of the rating years. Their low ratings indicate that economic freedom has been stifled in almost every area. And this has been the case for at least two decades.

If free economies grow more rapidly and our index is a reasonably good measure of economic freedom, nations that are persistently free over a lengthy period of time should achieve high levels of income. Correspondingly, we would expect the income levels of the persistently unfree group to be low, as the result of the cumulative effects of slow growth and stagnation over a prolonged period of time. We will investigate this issue in Chapter 4.

*If free economies grow more rapidly, nations that are persistently free over a lengthy time period will achieve high levels of income.*

**Exhibit 2-3: Countries with Either Persistently High or Persistently Low Ratings Throughout the 1975–1995 Period**

| | Index of Economic Freedom (Is1) | | | | |
|---|---|---|---|---|---|
| | 1975 | 1980 | 1985 | 1990 | 1995 |
| **Persistently High Ratings[a]** | | | | | |
| Hong Kong | 9.2 | 9.4 | 9.5 | 9.3 | 9.1 |
| Switzerland | 7.1 | 7.1 | 7.3 | 7.3 | 7.5 |
| Singapore | 6.8 | 7.1 | 8.0 | 8.5 | 8.2 |
| United States | 6.0 | 6.2 | 6.5 | 7.4 | 7.7 |
| Canada | 6.1 | 6.8 | 5.9 | 6.9 | 6.9 |
| Germany | 5.9 | 6.0 | 6.0 | 6.3 | 6.4 |
| **Persistently Low Ratings[b]** | | | | | |
| Somalia | 2.6 | 2.5 | 1.1 | 0.8 | N/R |
| Zambia | 2.9 | 3.1 | 2.7 | 1.8 | 3.6 |
| Hungary | 3.0 | 3.2 | 3.3 | 3.0 | 3.3 |
| Romania | N/R | 3.2 | 3.2 | 2.2 | 2.9 |
| Brazil | 3.2 | 2.7 | 2.3 | 2.9 | 3.3 |
| Syria | 3.7 | 3.1 | 2.7 | 3.2 | 2.6 |
| Uganda | 1.2 | 2.2 | 1.7 | 2.5 | 3.7 |
| Zaire | 3.6 | 3.5 | 3.3 | 3.4 | 1.9 |
| Zimbabwe | N/R | 3.7 | 2.6 | 2.3 | 3.4 |

N/R = No rating because of insufficient data for several of the components during this year.
[a] This group of countries made a grade of A or B in 1993-95 *and* they were in the top 15 during 1975, 1980, 1985, and 1990.
[b] The Is1 summary rating for these countries was always less than 4.0.

## LOOKING AHEAD

We now have an overview of the ratings by country for each of the years covered by our study. In the following chapter, we will analyze the changes in economic freedom during the last two decades in more detail and attempt to determine whether the economic freedom of the world is increasing or decreasing.

### Endnotes

1. The underlying data used to derive the country ratings for each of the 17 components in our index are contained in the 17 tables of Appendix II. The Roman numeral and letter labels for these tables match the area and letter labels for the components of our index. The note at the end of each table in Appendix II provides a detailed explanation of how the ratings for the component were derived. Readers interested in the details of the relationship between the underlying data and the component ratings will want to review these tables carefully.

2. Of course, area ratings could also be derived by using the weights associated with the Ie and Is2 aggregated indexes. (See Exhibit 1-2 for the component weights associated with the alternative methods of aggregating the component ratings into area and summary ratings.) In most cases, the three alternative methods yield similar results. Thus, in the interest of preserving space, only the Is1 area ratings are presented here.

3. If the data for a component could not be obtained for a country, the weight for that component was distributed proportionally among the other components when deriving a summary index for the country.

4. Our survey respondents indicated that a high level of government consumption, a large transfer and subsidy sector, and high marginal tax rates are important infringements upon economic freedom. We agree. Thus, we believe that Is1 is a more accurate indicator of economic freedom than Is2.

5. Some may be interested in the differences between our index and that of Bryan T Johnson and Thomas P. Sheehy, *The Index of Economic Freedom*, (Washington, D.C.: Heritage Foundation, 1995). There are several differences between the two. First our index is more comprehensive—it has 17 components compared to 10 for the Johnson-Sheehy Index. Second, we developed ratings for five different years over two decades. This makes is possible to track the economic freedom of various countries over time. The Johnson-Sheehy Index covers only one year. Third, Johnson and Sheehy do not attempt to deal with the problem of how to weight the different components. They simply averaged their ten components when deriving their summary rating. Finally, our index is based on objective variables and the relationship between underlying data and a country's component ratings is clearly specified. We sought to minimize the role of judgment calls. This was not always the case with the Johnson-Sheehy index.

With regard to the results, there are both similarities and differences. Hong Kong and Singapore rank one and two in the Johnson-Sheehy Index just as they do in our Is1 index. United States, Japan, Canada, United Kingdom, and Germany rank high in both indexes. But there are also some striking differences. Johnson and Sheehy rate Uganda as the 43rd freest country among the 101 in their study. For our three indexes, Uganda ranks 92nd (Ie), 83rd (Is1), and 98th (Is2). The average of our three indexes places it in the Bottom Ten among the 102 countries in our study. Given that the monetary policy of Uganda is among the most unstable in the world, citizens are prohibited from owning foreign currencies, exchange rate controls are highly restrictive, and foreigners cannot undertake investments without the permission of the government, it is difficult for us the perceive how Uganda could possible earn a middle ranking in terms of economic freedom.

There are other differences that we find troublesome. Johnson and Sheehy rank the Czech Republic 12th, while it ranks 51st in our index. The Czech Republic has handled the transition better than any Eastern European country, but with its high level of government consumption, continued state ownership of many enterprises and assets (including approximately one-third of the housing stock), and use of conscription, we do not believe it is the 12th freest country in the world. In the Johnson and Sheehy index, Hungary and Tunisia are ranked 31 and 36, while Poland is 62nd. Both our index and knowledge of these countries suggests that the economy of Poland is more free than either Hungary or Tunisia. Despite the reservations, we admire Johnson and Sheehy for tackling this difficult problem.

6. During the last decade, several countries in South and Central America have liberalized their economies; Honduras and Venezuela are two interesting exceptions. The primary factors underlying the fall in the summary rating of Venezuela are monetary and financial—tighter restrictions on the convertibility of the domestic currency, new restrictions on the maintenance of foreign currency accounts and the mobility of capital, and greater use of price controls. In the case of Honduras, increased monetary instability, exchange rate controls, and widespread use of price controls have contributed to the rating declines.

# CHAPTER 3

## Changes in Economic Freedom During 1975-1995

Policies and institutional arrangements influence economic freedom. How has the economic freedom of various countries changed during the last two decades? Have there been changes in the economic freedom of the world in recent years? If so, what are the primary sources of these changes? How has the degree of economic freedom changed according to development status and region? This chapter will address these and related issues.

## CHANGES IN THE ECONOMIC FREEDOM OF COUNTRIES

In some ways, the *changes* in economic freedom are even more interesting than the *level*. If our index is a good measure of economic freedom, an increase in a country's summary rating indicates that it is moving toward liberalization—that the economic freedom of the citizenry is expanding. In contrast, a reduction in the summary rating would suggest a decline.

### Changes in Summary Ratings: 1975-1990

Which countries have experienced the largest changes in economic freedom in recent years? Exhibit 3-1 indicates the 15 (actually there are 17 because of a tie) nations for which the summary index (Is1) increased the most between 1975 and 1990.[1] Chile, Jamaica, Iceland, and Malaysia head the list. The Is1 summary index of these four countries increased by 2.0 or more during the 1975-1990 period. The increases of Pakistan, Turkey, Egypt, Portugal, Japan, Singapore, Mauritius, and New Zealand were only slightly less than those of the Top Four countries.

**Exhibit 3-1: The Ratings of the 15 Countries With the Largest Increase in the Index of Economic Freedom (Is1) During the 1975-1990 Period**

| Country | Index of Economic Freedom (Is1) | | | | Change Between 1975 and 1990 |
|---|---|---|---|---|---|
| | 1975 | 1980 | 1985 | 1990 | |
| Chile | 2.8 | 3.9 | 4.1 | 5.7 | +2.9 |
| Jamaica | 3.2 | 2.8 | 4.4 | 5.2 | +2.0 |
| Iceland | 2.7 | 3.4 | 3.3 | 4.7 | +2.0 |
| Malaysia | 5.1 | 5.6 | 7.1 | 7.1 | +2.0 |
| Pakistan | 2.3 | 3.5 | 3.9 | 4.2 | +1.9 |
| Turkey | 2.8 | 2.3 | 3.8 | 4.6 | +1.8 |
| Egypt | 2.4 | 2.8 | 3.3 | 4.2 | +1.8 |
| Portugal | 2.4 | 3.1 | 3.5 | 4.1 | +1.7 |
| Japan | 5.2 | 5.9 | 6.5 | 6.9 | +1.7 |
| Singapore | 6.8 | 7.1 | 8.0 | 8.5 | +1.7 |
| Mauritius | 3.9 | 3.8 | 6.0 | 5.6 | +1.7 |
| New Zealand | 4.3 | 4.8 | 4.1 | 6.0 | +1.7 |
| United Kingdom | 5.0 | 4.5 | 6.0 | 6.6 | +1.6 |
| (tie) Thailand | 4.9 | 5.0 | 5.3 | 6.3 | +1.4 |
| (tie) Indonesia | 5.2 | 5.0 | 6.1 | 6.6 | +1.4 |
| (tie) United States | 6.0 | 6.2 | 6.5 | 7.4 | +1.4 |
| (tie) Costa Rica | 5.2 | 4.8 | 4.6 | 6.6 | +1.4 |

Source: The change in the index Is1 during the 1975-1990 period was derived from the summary ratings of Appendix I: Tables A1-1 and A1-4.

United Kingdom, Thailand, Indonesia, United States, and Costa Rica round out this list of countries that, according to our summary index, moved most rapidly toward liberalization during the 1975-1990 period.

The group with the largest expansion in economic freedom is highly diverse. It includes countries from Europe, Asia, South and Central America, Oceania, and Africa. There are those with high-income industrial backgrounds like Japan, United Kingdom, New Zealand, and United States as well as those with low per capita incomes like Turkey, Egypt, Thailand, Jamaica, and Indonesia. In 1975, the economic freedom rating for some was among the lowest in the world. Chile, Iceland, Pakistan, Turkey, Egypt, and Portugal fall into this category. On the other hand, some—Singapore and United States for example—were already highly rated in 1975. Clearly, these data suggest that improvement in economic freedom can be achieved by countries with highly diverse characteristics.

Exhibit 3-2 indicates the 15 nations (there are 16 in this group as the result of a tie) for which the summary index of economic freedom (Is1) *declined* the most between 1975 and 1990. Nicaragua, Somalia, Iran, Honduras, Venezuela, and Congo head this list. This group is somewhat less diverse. Seven of the 16 countries are African; six (Nicaragua, Honduras, Venezuela, Panama, El Salvador and Brazil) are Latin American; and two (Iran and Syria) are Middle Eastern. There are no Asian countries and only one (Greece) from Europe in this group. Neither are there any high-income industrial countries on the list.

## Countries with Sustained Increases in Economic Freedom: 1975-1995

Economic theory indicates that credibility and sustained progress are important if an increase in economic freedom is going to exert its full positive impact on the performance of an economy. Neither domestic nor foreign investors are likely to risk much of their savings if they fear that, for example, a relaxation of credit market controls or a shift to a less inflationary monetary policy is likely to be reversed in the near future. Thus, countries that move steadily and consistently toward economic liberalization are likely to achieve a higher level of economic performance than those that shift back and forth between liberal and restrictive policies.

*Credibility and sustained progress are important if an increase in economic freedom is going to exert its full positive impact.*

In the next two exhibits, countries that have both *achieved* and *sustained* substantial increases in economic freedom during the period of our study will be identified. The nine nations listed in Exhibit 3-3 achieved at least a one unit increase in their Is1 summary index between 1975 and 1985 and they maintained that increase during the next decade—their rating in 1995 was at least as high as in 1985. Others may have achieved as large increases,

**Exhibit 3-2: The Ratings of the 15 Countries With the Largest Decline in the Index of Economic Freedom (Is1) During the 1975-1990 Period**

| Country | Index of Economic Freedom (Is1) | | | | Change Between 1975 and 1990 |
|---|---|---|---|---|---|
| | 1975 | 1980 | 1985 | 1990 | |
| Nicaragua | 6.4 | 3.6 | 1.8 | 2.0 | -4.4 |
| Somalia | 2.6 | 2.5 | 1.1 | 0.8 | -1.8 |
| Iran | 5.0 | 2.5 | 2.7 | 3.2 | -1.8 |
| Honduras | 7.4 | 6.1 | 6.0 | 6.0 | -1.4 |
| Venezuela | 6.9 | 6.6 | 5.2 | 5.5 | -1.4 |
| Congo | 4.5 | 4.0 | 4.0 | 3.3 | -1.2 |
| Zambia | 2.9 | 3.1 | 2.7 | 1.8 | -1.1 |
| Tanzania | 3.3 | 4.0 | 1.9 | 2.3 | -1.0 |
| Algeria | 3.5 | 2.7 | 2.4 | 2.7 | -0.8 |
| Morocco | 3.9 | 3.7 | 4.1 | 3.2 | -0.7 |
| Panama | 7.0 | 6.3 | 6.6 | 6.3 | -0.7 |
| Syria | 3.7 | 3.1 | 2.7 | 3.2 | -0.5 |
| Greece | 3.9 | 3.8 | 3.2 | 3.4 | -0.5 |
| El Salvador | 4.7 | 3.7 | 4.1 | 4.3 | -0.4 |
| (tie) Brazil | 3.2 | 2.7 | 2.3 | 2.9 | -0.3 |
| (tie) Sierra Leone | 4.2 | 3.5 | 3.9 | 3.9 | -0.3 |

Source: The change in the index Is1 during the 1975-1990 period was derived from the summary ratings of Appendix I: Tables A1-1 and A1-4.

but they were unable to maintain them. In essence, Exhibit 3-3 lists the nations that took a substantial step toward economic liberalization during 1975-1985 *and* maintained the more liberal policies into the 1990s. No other countries were able to both achieve and sustain such large increases during this period.

The largest increase was achieved by Mauritius.[2] Several factors contributed to the jump in this country's summary rating between 1975 and 1985. In the early 1970s, the economy of Mauritius was characterized by monetary expansion and a highly

**Exhibit 3-3: Countries With at Least a One Unit Increase in the Is1 Summary Rating Between 1975 and 1985 and Maintenance of This Increase Between 1985 and 1995**

| Country | Index of Economic Freedom (Is1) | | | | | Change in Is1 | |
|---|---|---|---|---|---|---|---|
| | 1975 | 1980 | 1985 | 1990 | 1995 | 1975-85 | 1985-95 |
| Mauritius | 3.9 | 3.8 | 6.0 | 5.6 | 6.3 | +2.1 | +0.3 |
| Pakistan | 2.3 | 3.5 | 3.9 | 4.2 | 5.4 | +1.6 | +1.5 |
| Japan | 5.2 | 5.9 | 6.5 | 6.9 | 6.9 | +1.3 | +0.4 |
| Chile | 2.8 | 3.9 | 4.1 | 5.7 | 5.8 | +1.3 | +1.7 |
| Jamaica | 3.2 | 2.8 | 4.4 | 5.2 | 6.3 | +1.2 | +1.9 |
| Singapore | 6.8 | 7.1 | 8.0 | 8.5 | 8.2 | +1.2 | +0.2 |
| Portugal | 2.4 | 3.1 | 3.5 | 4.1 | 5.5 | +1.1 | +2.0 |
| United Kingdom | 5.0 | 4.5 | 6.0 | 6.6 | 7.0 | +1.0 | +1.0 |
| Turkey | 2.8 | 2.3 | 3.8 | 4.6 | 4.2 | +1.0 | +0.4 |

Source: Derived from Exhibit 2-1 and Appendix I.

variable inflation rate. During 1970-1975, the growth rate of the M1 money supply (adjusted for growth of real output) averaged 30 percent and the standard deviation of the annual rate of inflation was 20 percent. Reflecting this rapid monetary expansion and price level instability, Mauritius' 1975 rating for these two components (IA and IB) was one (on our ten point scale). By the mid-1980s, Mauritius had moved toward a substantially more stable monetary policy. Its 1985 ratings for monetary expansion and inflation stability were 10 and 9 respectively, quite an improvement over the 1975 ratings. Relaxation of exchange rate controls and development of a stable competitive credit market also contributed to the improvement during the 1975-1985 period.

Pakistan, Japan, and Chile also made substantial gains between 1975 and 1985. Pakistan can credit its improvement to greater monetary stability and elimination of conscription. Japan's increase reflected less expansionary monetary policy, greater price stability, and removal of various restrictions on capital movements.

The Is1 summary index of Chile rose from 2.8 in 1975 to 4.1 in 1985 and 5.8 in 1995, an increase of 3.0 units in two decades. Several factors contributed to the improvement. In the mid-1970s, Chile's monetary policy was a disaster. Triple-digit increases in the money supply were causing triple-digit rates of inflation (and wild fluctuations in the inflation rate.) More recently, the rates of monetary expansion and price level increases have been in the 10% to 20% range, considerably less than ideal, but nonetheless a substantial improvement compared to the early 1970s. In the early 1980s, Chile legalized the use of foreign currency bank accounts both domestically and abroad. Reductions in government expenditures as a share of GDP, privatization, lower marginal tax rates,[3] and a relaxation of restrictions on the movement of capital also contributed to the improvement in the summary rating of Chile during the 1975-1995 period.

*Portugal's top marginal tax rate was sliced from 82% in 1975 (and 84% in 1980) to 69% in 1985 and 40% in 1990.*

Portugal's situation while not as dramatic was quite similar to that of Chile. Its Is1 summary rating rose from 2.4 in 1975 to 3.5 in 1985 and 5.5 in 1995, an increase of 3.1 units during the 20-year period. During the 1975-1985 period, relaxation of exchange rate controls and lower tariffs propelled Portugal's initial improvement. In 1975, Portugal imposed tight exchange rate controls and, as a result, the accompanying black market exchange rate premium was quite high (48%). These controls were liberalized throughout the period and the Portuguese escudo is now fully convertible. Portugal's average tax rate on international trade fell from 4.6% in 1975 to 1.2% in 1985 (and 0.5% in the early 1990s.) Lower marginal tax rates and deregulations of financial and capital markets have contributed to continued improvement during the last decade. The top marginal tax rate was sliced from 82% in 1975 (and 84% in 1980) to 69% in 1985 and 40% in 1990. Legislation in the late 1980s relaxed restraints on the flow of capital both into and out of the country. Finally, in the early 1990s, Portugal legalized the maintenance of foreign currency bank accounts. As Exhibits 3-1 and 3-3 show, Portugal and Chile are leaders among those that have made persistent moves toward a freer economy during the last two decades.

Exhibit 3-4 lists the ten countries that made the largest gains in economic freedom between 1980 and 1990 and sustained them into the mid-1990s. In essence, the nations of Exhibit 3-4 began their moves toward economic freedom a little later than those in Exhibit 3-3. There is some overlap between the two—Chile and Mauritius are on both lists. Jamaica, United Kingdom, Costa Rica,

**Exhibit 3-4: The Ten Countries With the Largest Increase in the Is1 Summary Rating Between 1980 and 1990 and the Maintenance of This Increase Between 1990 and 1995**

| Country | Index of Economic Freedom (Is1) | | | | Change in Index Is1 | |
|---|---|---|---|---|---|---|
| | 1980 | 1985 | 1990 | 1995 | 1980-90 | 1990-95 |
| Jamaica | 2.8 | 4.4 | 5.2 | 6.3 | +2.4 | +1.1 |
| United Kingdom | 4.5 | 6.0 | 6.6 | 7.0 | +2.1 | +0.4 |
| Costa Rica | 4.8 | 4.6 | 6.6 | 6.7 | +1.8 | +0.1 |
| Bolivia | 4.5 | 4.2 | 6.3 | 6.4 | +1.8 | +0.1 |
| Chile | 3.9 | 4.1 | 5.7 | 5.8 | +1.8 | +0.1 |
| Italy | 3.6 | 3.6 | 5.4 | 5.6 | +1.8 | +0.3 |
| Mauritius | 3.8 | 6.0 | 5.6 | 6.3 | +1.8 | +0.7 |
| Mexico | 3.8 | 4.1 | 5.3 | 5.8 | +1.5 | +0.5 |
| Norway | 3.4 | 3.9 | 4.8 | 5.7 | +1.4 | +0.9 |
| Thailand | 5.0 | 5.3 | 6.3 | 7.0 | +1.3 | +0.7 |

Bolivia, and Chile head the group of countries that registered the most improvement during the 1980s and maintained it into 1993-1995. The Is1 summary rating of Jamaica rose from 2.8 in 1980 to 5.2 in 1990 and 6.3 in 1995. Legalization of foreign currency bank accounts, persistent reductions in the top marginal tax rate (the top rate was cut from 80% in 1980 to 33% in 1990 and 25% in 1994), relaxation of exchange rate controls, and more liberal international trade policies were the primary factors underlying the gains of Jamaica. In the case of the United Kingdom, privatization, removal of restrictions on foreign bank currency accounts, and tax cuts (the top marginal tax rate was reduced from 83% in 1979 to 40% in 1989) provided the impetus for the gains. Reductions in top marginal tax rates and a more liberalized trade regime were the primary forces contributing to the recent improvement of both Costa Rica and Bolivia.

## Country Rating Increases: 1985-1995

*Since 1985, no country has moved more rapidly toward a free economy than New Zealand and Argentina.*

The economic freedom index increased substantially for quite a large number of countries between 1985 and 1995. Exhibit 3-5 (left side) presents the 1985, 1990, and 1995 ratings for the 15 countries with the largest increases in the economic freedom index (Is1) during the last decade. Since 1985, no country has moved more rapidly toward a free economy than New Zealand and Argentina. The summary ratings of these two countries have increased by almost four points. Let us take a closer look at the specific areas of change in these two countries.

Monetary reform, reductions in marginal tax rates, and de-regulation of the exchange and capital markets provided the major sources for the gains of New Zealand. In the late 1980s, New Zealand legalized the holdings of foreign currency bank accounts both domestically and abroad. The ratings for these two components jumped from zero to ten. In addition, legislation was passed instructing the central bank to maintain a low and stable rate of inflation—and the law provided for accountability. If the rate of inflation is not maintained within a specified narrow band, the governor of the central bank is subject to dismissal. Unsurprisingly, price level stability increased. The inflation rate, which had been fluctuating between 6% and 20% during the 1980s, declined sharply and remained between 1% and 3% during the first half of the 1990s. Thus, New Zealand's rating for the price stability component (I-B) jumped from 4 in 1990 to 10 in 1995. In the late 1980s, New Zealand's top marginal tax rate was pared from 66 to 33 percent. Exchange rate controls were eliminated and the restrictions on capital mobility were scrapped. Clearly, the improvement in the summary rating of New Zealand reflected widespread economic reform.

Argentina has reduced government consumption as a share of the economy, privatized several enterprises that were previously operated by the government, and virtually eliminated price controls during the last decade. The top marginal tax rate was reduced from 62% in 1985 to 35% in 1990 and 30% in 1994. Thus, the Argentine rating for this component jumped from a 2 in 1985 to a 9 in 1995. In the mid-1980s, Argentina imposed both exchange rate controls and tight restrictions on capital movements. By the mid-1990s, the Argentine peso was fully convertible and the

| Exhibit 3-5: The Fifteen Most Improved Countries During 1985-1995 and 1990-1995 | | | | | | | | |
|---|---|---|---|---|---|---|---|---|
| Most Improved During 1985-1995 | Economic Freedom Index (Is1) | | | | Most Improved During 1990-1995 | Economic Freedom Index (Is1) | | |
| | 1985 | 1990 | 1995 | Chg. | | 1990 | 1995 | Chg. |
| New Zealand | 4.1 | 6.0 | 8.0 | +3.9 | Bulgaria | 1.6 | 4.2 | +2.6 |
| Argentina | 2.5 | 3.8 | 6.3 | +3.8 | Argentina | 3.8 | 6.3 | +2.5 |
| Trinidad/ Tobago | 3.1 | 4.3 | 5.8 | +2.7 | Dominican Rep. | 3.6 | 5.7 | +2.1 |
| France | 3.4 | 5.5 | 6.0 | +2.6 | New Zealand | 6.0 | 8.0 | +2.0 |
| Poland | 2.2 | 3.3 | 4.8 | +2.6 | El Salvador | 4.3 | 6.3 | +2.0 |
| Ireland | 4.2 | 5.0 | 6.7 | +2.5 | Peru | 4.0 | 5.9 | +1.9 |
| Peru | 3.4 | 4.0 | 5.9 | +2.5 | Zambia | 1.8 | 3.6 | +1.8 |
| Iceland | 3.3 | 4.7 | 5.7 | +2.4 | Malta | 3.8 | 5.6 | +1.8 |
| Denmark | 3.7 | 4.6 | 6.0 | +2.3 | Iceland | 5.0 | 6.7 | +1.7 |
| Bolivia | 4.2 | 6.3 | 6.4 | +2.2 | Poland | 3.3 | 4.8 | +1.5 |
| El Salvador | 4.1 | 4.3 | 6.3 | +2.2 | South Korea | 5.2 | 6.7 | +1.5 |
| Costa Rica | 4.6 | 6.6 | 6.7 | +2.1 | Trinidad/ Tobago | 4.3 | 5.8 | +1.5 |
| Italy | 3.6 | 5.4 | 5.6 | +2.0 | Greece | 3.4 | 4.9 | +1.5 |
| Portugal | 3.5 | 4.1 | 5.5 | +2.0 | Portugal | 4.1 | 5.5 | +1.4 |
| Ghana | 2.8 | 3.6 | 4.8 | +2.0 | Denmark | 4.6 | 6.0 | +1.4 |
| | | | | | Tanzania | 2.3 | 3.7 | +1.4 |

Source: Derived from Exhibit 2-1 and Appendix 1: Tables A1-1 and A1-2.

restrictions on capital movements had been eliminated. All of these factors contributed to the substantial improvement in the summary rating of Argentina during the 1985-1995 period.

The summary ratings of Trinidad/Tobago have increased substantially during the last decade and most of the improvement has occurred since 1990. Monetary, exchange rate, and credit market reforms provide the under-pinnings for improved rating. Legislation was adopted legalizing the maintenance of foreign currency bank accounts both domestically and abroad in the early

1990s. The Exchange Rate Control Act of 1993 provided for a floating exchange rate and removed the restrictions on the convertibility of the Trinidad/Tobago dollar. This legislation eliminated the black market exchange rate premium, which had been running in the 40% to 60% range for more than a decade. The requirement that foreigners obtain the approval of the government prior to undertaking an investment project was scrapped. Most other restrictions on the movement of capital into and out of the country were eliminated. Trinidad/Tobago continues to be plagued by large government expenditures—particularly when compared to other low-income, less developed countries—and a large government-enterprise sector. It will be interesting to see whether the recent monetary reforms and deregulation of the foreign exchange and capital markets are sustained and, if they are, how the economy develops in the decade ahead.

As Exhibit 3-5 illustrates, several other countries have also made substantial gains during the last decade. The summary ratings (Is1) of France, Poland, Ireland, Peru, Iceland, Denmark, Bolivia, and El Salvador increased by 2.2 units or more during the 1985-1995 period. The summary ratings of Costa Rica, Italy, Portugal, and Ghana also climbed substantially during this period.

A few countries with exceedingly low ratings and modest increases prior to 1990 also registered sizeable jumps in the early 1990s. Bulgaria, Dominican Republic, Zambia, and Tanzania fall into this category.[4] At this point it is too early to tell whether these reforms will be long lasting or merely temporary. In the years immediately ahead, investors and other observers will want to keep a close eye both on these recent gainers, and those countries that began moving toward more liberal policies during the latter half of the 1980s.

## CHANGES IN THE ECONOMIC FREEDOM OF THE WORLD

Has the degree of economic freedom changed during the last 20 years? Exhibit 3-6 provides insight concerning this question. Data on the three summary indexes for the countries in our study are available for each of the rating years. There was little change in these summary indexes between 1975 and 1985. The average Is1 summary index hardly changed at all while the average for the

Ie and Is2 indexes rose by only 0.3 of a unit between 1975 and 1985. However, the picture was quite different during the 1985-1995 decade. The Is1 index rose from 4.3 in 1985 to 4.6 in 1990 and 5.2 in 1995. The other two summary indexes rose by similar amounts. Thus, each of the indexes was approximately a full point higher in 1995 than in 1985. This indicates that while there was little change in the economic freedom of the world between 1975 and 1985, a significant amount of liberalization has occurred since 1985.

The changes in the average ratings for the components of our index shed light on the nature of the increases in economic freedom. First, during the last decade there has been a substantial move toward liberalization in the money and inflation area. The rating for the variability in the inflation rate component has exceeded 5.0 during each of the last four rating periods, up from 3.8 in 1975. There has also been an increase in the freedom of citizens to maintain foreign currency bank accounts both domestically and abroad—particularly during the last ten years. The average component rating for domestic ownership of foreign currency accounts (component I-C) rose from 3.8 in 1985 to 6.0 in 1995. Simultaneously, the average rating for the freedom to maintain a bank account abroad (component I-D) rose from 2.8 in 1985 to 5.0 in 1995.[5]

In addition to the monetary area, there was a substantial increase in the average rating for the credit market component (II-F). The average rating for this component rose from 4.8 in 1975 to 7.1 in 1985 and 7.6 in 1995. This indicates that countries were much less likely to impose interest rate controls and follow inflationary policies in the mid-1990s than during the mid-1970s. Thus, credit markets today are both more integrated and more competitive than they were two decades ago.

The path of the marginal tax rate component is particularly interesting because the direction of change in the average rating reversed during the 1980s. Between 1975 and 1985, there was a tendency for countries to increase their top marginal tax rates and/or impose the top rate at a lower income level. Thus, the average rating for this component (III-B) fell from 3.5 in 1975 to 2.5 in 1985. However, this trend changed during the latter half of the 1980s. The average rating for this component rose to 4.1 in 1990 and 5.4 in 1995. In 1985, there were 48 countries that imposed a top marginal tax rate of 60% or more on personal

*In 1985, 48 countries imposed top marginal tax rates of 60% or more. By 1994, only 10 imposed such high rates.*

**Exhibit 3-6: Changes in the Average Value of the Components of the Index of Economic Freedom and the Average Summary Rating of Countries: 1975–1995**

| Components | Average Rating of Component (The number of countries rated is in parentheses.) | | | | |
|---|---|---|---|---|---|
| | 1975 | 1980 | 1985 | 1990 | 1995 |
| IA: Money Expansion | 3.6 (93) | 3.8 (97) | 5.1 (101) | 4.5 (102) | 4.2 (102) |
| IB: Inflation Variability | 3.8 (97) | 5.3 (99) | 5.1 (102) | 5.4 (102) | 5.4 (103) |
| IC: Foreign Currency Accounts | 3.2 (97) | 3.7 (100) | 3.8 (101) | 4.6 (102) | 6.0 (103) |
| ID: Deposits Abroad | 2.5 (99) | 2.9 (99) | 2.8 (101) | 3.8 (102) | 5.0 (103) |
| IIA: Government Consumption | 5.3 (96) | 5.1 (101) | 5.0 (102) | 5.1 (100) | 4.8 (101) |
| IIB: Government Enterprises | 4.5 (102) | 4.4 (102) | 4.2 (102) | 4.3 (102) | 4.5 (103) |
| IIC: Price Controls | — | — | — | 3.7 (79) | 4.9 (87) |
| IID: Entry into Business | — | — | — | — | 6.5 (103) |
| IIE: Equality Under the Law | — | — | — | — | 3.7 (103) |
| IIF: Credit Market | 4.8 (27) | 5.7 (73) | 7.1 (80) | 7.0 (89) | 7.6 (85) |
| IIIA: Transfers & Subsides | 5.9 (65) | 5.4 (77) | 5.0 (81) | 5.2 (82) | 4.9 (75) |
| IIIB: Marginal Tax Rates | 3.5 (62) | 2.4 (69) | 2.5 (78) | 4.1 (80) | 5.4 (81) |
| IIIC: Conscription | 4.9 (91) | 4.7 (101) | 4.1 (102) | 4.1 (102) | 4.3 (103) |
| IVA: Trade Taxes | 4.4 (93) | 4.5 (96) | 5.1 (90) | 5.9 (90) | 6.4 (66) |
| IVB: Exchange Rate Controls | 5.4 (102) | 5.2 (102) | 5.0 (102) | 6.1 (102) | 7.5 (102) |
| IVC: Size of Trade Sector | 4.9 (97) | 4.8 (101) | 5.0 (101) | 4.7 (102) | 4.8 (100) |
| IVD: Capital Mobility Restraints | 2.1 (99) | 2.4 (102) | 2.6 (102) | 3.0 (102) | 4.1 (103) |
| **Summary Ratings:** | | | | | |
| Index Ie | 4.1 (94) | 4.3 (99) | 4.4 (102) | 4.7 (102) | 5.2 (101) |
| Index Is1 | 4.2 (94) | 4.3 (99) | 4.3 (102) | 4.6 (102) | 5.2 (101) |
| Index Is2 | 3.9 (94) | 4.1 (99) | 4.2 (102) | 4.5 (102) | 5.2 (101) |

Source: Derived from Exhibit 2-1 and Appendix 1: Tables A1-1 and A1-2.

income. By 1994, only ten (Japan, Belgium, Denmark, Finland, Netherlands, Sweden, Romania, Cameroon, Gabon, and Zaire) imposed such high rates. The top marginal rate was 70% or more for 13 countries in 1985. None levied such a high rate on personal income in 1994.

Numerous nations have chopped their high marginal tax rates during the last decade. For example, during the 1985-1994 period, Norway cut its top rate from 64% to 42%; the top rate in Argentina was reduced from 62% to 30%; in Costa Rica from 50% to 25%; in Dominican Republic from 73% to 25%; and the top rates of both Peru and Malta fell from 65% in 1985 to 30% in 1994. The top marginal rates of several African countries have also declined sharply. Ghana recently cut its top marginal rate from 55% to 30%. Tanzania sliced its top rate from 95% in 1985 to 50% in 1990 and 30% in 1994. In Zambia, the top rate plunged from 75% in 1990 to 30% in 1994. These factors explain the increased average rating for the marginal tax rate component during the last decade. See Appendix II, Table III-B for additional information on changes in marginal tax rates.

Lower taxes on international trade, relaxation of exchange rate controls, and more liberal policies toward capital movements have also contributed to the improvement in the average summary ratings, particularly during the last decade. There was a downward trend in the average tax rate on international trade throughout the period of our study. Thus, the rating for this component (IV-A) rose from 4.4 in 1975 to 5.1 in 1985 and to 6.4 in 1995. While there was little relaxation of exchange rate controls between 1975 and 1985—the average rating for this component actually declined from 5.4 to 5.0 during this period—there has been substantial liberalization during the last decade. In 1985, there were 38 countries that imposed restrictive exchange controls such that the accompanying black market exchange rate premium was 25% or more. By 1995, there were only eleven (Haiti, Iran, Romania, Syria, Bangladesh, Nepal, Algeria, Burundi, Madagascar, Nigeria, and Rwanda) in this category (see Appendix II, Table IV-B). Reflecting these changes, the rating for the exchange rate controls component (IV-B) rose from 5.0 in 1985 to 7.5 in 1995. There was also some relaxation of the control on capital movements. The rating for this component (IV-D) rose from 2.1 in 1975 to 4.1 in 1995. Most of that increase took place during the most recent decade.

Improvement in the average component ratings was not universal. There was little change in the average rating for

*In 1985, 38 countries imposed restrictive exchange controls such that the accompanying black market exchange rate premium was 25% or more. In 1995, only eleven imposed such controls.*

government enterprises as a share of the economy. While there has been a lot of talk about privatization and a few countries have privatized a significant number of their state enterprises, the overall change has been modest. The ratings for government consumption as a share of GDP (II-B), size of the transfer-subsidy sector (III-A), and conscription (III-C) actually declined during the period, particularly during the 1975-1985 period. The average rating for transfers and subsidies as a share of the economy fell from 5.9 in 1975 to 5.0 in 1985, and there has been little change since then. The rating for the conscription component followed a similar path, declining from 4.9 in 1975 to 4.1 in 1985. Again, there was little subsequent change.

*Since 1985 the evidence indicates that the overall level of economic freedom of the world has increased.*

We are now in a position to summarize our findings with regard to the overall change in the economic freedom of the world during the last two decades. First, there was little change in economic freedom between 1975 and 1985. A few of the components in our index increased during this period but there were offsetting declines in others. Second, since 1985 the evidence indicates that the overall level of economic freedom of the world has increased. Several factors have contributed to this improvement. There has been less variability in the inflation rate. Many countries have removed prior legal restrictions against the ownership and use of foreign currency bank accounts both domestically and abroad. Credit market restrictions and other policies that lead to negative real interest rates were considerably less common in the 1990s than in the 1970s. Reductions in high marginal tax rates have enhanced the freedom of highly productive and hard-working citizens to keep what they earn. Taxes on international trade have been reduced, exchange rate controls relaxed considerably, and restrictions on the movement of capital have been liberalized in many countries around the world. As a result of these changes, international exchange is now freer than it was a decade ago.

## CHANGES IN ECONOMIC FREEDOM BY DEVELOPMENT STATUS AND REGION

Is there a difference between industrial and less-developed nations with regard to the changes in economic freedom during the last two decades? Exhibit 3-7 sheds light on this issue. As this exhibit illustrates, the average summary rating of the 20 countries classified as "industrial" increased from 4.7 to 5.0 during the 1975-1985 period.[6] During this same time period, the average rating for less developed countries was unchanged. Thus, there was very little change in the level of economic freedom in either the industrial or non-industrial countries between 1975 and 1985.

However, the situation was quite different during the following decade. The average summary rating of the 20 industrial countries rose from 5.0 in 1985 to 5.7 in 1990 and 6.4 in 1995. Thus, the average summary rating of industrial countries rose by 1.4 units between 1985 and 1995. The average rating for LDCs rose from 4.1 in 1985 to 4.4 in 1990 and 4.8 in 1995, only half as much as the increase for the industrial countries. As a result of these changes, the economic freedom gap between the industrial and less developed countries has widened during the last 20 years. In 1975, the average rating of the industrial countries was only 0.6 units higher than the average rating for the LDCs. By 1995, this gap had widened to 1.6 units.[7]

*The economic freedom gap between the industrial and less developed countries has widened during the last 20 years.*

Exhibit 3-7 also presents the average Is1 summary ratings by region. This exhibit illustrates a number of interesting points. First, the average summary rating of the 15 Asian countries in our study increased steadily—about 0.3 units every five years—through-out the period. Thus, their average rating was 6.2 in 1995, up from 4.8 in 1975. Improvements in other regions were both smaller and less consistent across time periods. Second, after languishing between 4.2 and 4.5 throughout most of the 1975-1990 period, the economic freedom rating (Is1) of the European countries in our study jumped from 4.5 in 1990 to 5.4 in 1995. The recent changes in Eastern Europe contributed substantially to this increase. Third, the average summary rating of South American countries was virtually unchanged during the 1975-1985 period, but it jumped from 4.6 to 5.9 between 1985 and 1995. The average ratings for the Central American/Caribbean region declined between 1975 and 1985, but rose during the decade following 1985. Finally, the ratings for Africa and Middle East are quite revealing. In contrast with Asia, Europe, and South America, there has been little change in their average summary ratings. In Africa, the average summary rating has been between 3.6 and 4.0 throughout the 20-year period. In the Middle East, the average rating has ranged from 3.2 to 3.6 during the same period. In 1975, the average ratings in these two regions were about 1.0 less than the average for the Asian countries. By 1995, this gap had widened to approximately 2.5 units. With the exception of two or

**Exhibit 3-7: Average Summary Rating (Is1) by Level of Development and Region: 1975-1995**

| Area | Average Summary Rating (Is1) (Number of countries rated in parentheses.) | | | | |
|---|---|---|---|---|---|
| | 1975 | 1980 | 1985 | 1990 | 1995 |
| **By Level of Development:** | | | | | |
| Industrial[a] | 4.7 (20) | 4.9 (20) | 5.0 (20) | 5.7 (20) | 6.4 (20) |
| Less Developed | 4.1 (73) | 3.9 (82) | 4.1 (82) | 4.4 (82) | 4.8 (82) |
| **By Region:** | | | | | |
| Africa | 3.6 (28) | 3.6 (31) | 3.7 (31) | 3.8 (31) | 4.0 (30) |
| Asia | 4.8 (15) | 5.0 (15) | 5.4 (15) | 5.8 (15) | 6.2 (15) |
| Europe | 4.2 (20) | 3.6 (25) | 4.1 (25) | 4.5 (25) | 5.4 (26) |
| Middle East[b] | 3.5 (5) | 3.2 (5) | 3.3 (5) | 3.6 (5) | 3.6 (5) |
| South America | 4.7 (9) | 4.7 (9) | 4.6 (9) | 5.3 (9) | 5.9 (9) |
| Central America/ Caribbean | 5.0 (12) | 4.6 (13) | 4.4 (13) | 4.9 (13) | 5.5 (13) |
| North America/ Oceania[c] | 5.4 (4) | 5.8 (4) | 5.6 (4) | 6.6 (4) | 7.4 (4) |

[a] Our classification of industrial matches that of the World Bank during the mid-1980s—the mid-point of our study. Of course, growth enlarges this group with the passage of time. See primary tables for a complete listing of the industrial countries.

[b] The following countries are included in this group: Egypt, Iran, Israel, Jordan, and Syria.

[c] The following countries are included in this group: United States, Canada, Australia, and New Zealand.

three countries that have made modest moves toward liberalization, there is little reason for optimism with regard to the future of economic freedom in these two regions.

# LOOKING AHEAD

Thus far we have presented data on both the level of economic freedom and its change. We are now ready to investigate the impact of economic freedom on the growth rate of an economy. This will be the focus of the following chapter.

## Endnotes

1. Since this chapter focuses on changes in economic freedom, we will generally present only the Is1 summary rating. There are two reasons for this. First, as previously indicated, we believe that the Is1 summary rating is a better measure of economic freedom than the other two indexes. However, there is a second and more important reason why we now focus on only one rating. As a measuring rod for *changes* in economic freedom across time periods, the three indexes follow a similar pattern. If one of the indexes for a country increases (or declines) substantially, the others almost invariably change by a similar magnitude. Given this fact, it would generally be redundant to present the tables of this chapter for each of the three indexes.

2. The 17 tables of Appendix II present the underlying data and country ratings for each of the 17 components of our index. These data can be used to pinpoint the sources of changes in the summary ratings. The "Country Profile" data of Chapter 5 also make it easy to visualize the factors contributing to changes in a country's summary rating.

3. Chile has reduced its top marginal tax rate during every five year period since 1975. In 1975 the top marginal tax rate on the personal income of individuals was 80 percent. By 1980 the rate had been reduced to 60%, and additional rate reductions to 57% in 1985, 50% in 1990 and 48% in 1994 followed.

4. As previously noted, the summary ratings of African countries are universally low. Other than the small countries of Botswana and Mauritius, probably Kenya and Ghana provide the most hope for change in this region. Both have recently taken a few constructive measures. Since 1990, Ghana has removed price controls on several commodities, reduced the top marginal personal income tax rate from 55% to 35%, and removed many of its restrictions on the convertibility of currency. Thus, the black market exchange premium for the Ghanaian Cedi has been virtually eliminated (a triple-digit premium was present throughout much of the 1980s.) However, Ghana continues to be plagued by several other factors, including monetary instability, a large government-enterprise sector, insecure property rights, and capital market restrictions.

Kenya's Is1 summary rating (4.5 in 1995) is one of the highest in Africa and its monetary and legal arrangements are more stable than most other countries in the region. However, except for a reduction in the marginal tax rate from 65% in 1985 to 40% in 1994, few constructive steps toward liberalization have been taken.

5. The number of countries allowing citizens to maintain foreign currency bank accounts domestically rose from 31 in 1975 to 38 in 1985 and 62 in 1995. The number authorizing bank accounts abroad rose from 25 in 1975 to 28 in 1985 and 51 in 1995. Thus, the number of countries where these freedoms are present has approximately doubled during the last two decades. See Tables I-C and I-D of Appendix II for additional details.

6. Of course, changes in income influence the classification of countries over time. We used the classification status of the World Bank in the mid-1980s, the mid-point of our study. At that time, 20 of the countries in our study were classified as "industrial" by the World Bank.

7. As we have already noted, the economic freedom index of several less developed countries has increased substantially during the last two decades. Inspection of Exhibits 3-1, 3-3, and 3-4 indicates that LDCs are well represented among those that have achieved substantial increases in economic freedom. Unfortunately, as Exhibit 3-2 shows, they completely dominate the list of countries that have moved in the opposite direction—those that have adopted both policies and institutional arrangements that conflict with economic freedom.

# CHAPTER 4

## Economic Freedom, Income, and Growth

*In the 1990s we have reached a point where most of the developing world has come to realize that to get economic growth we need economic freedom, and policies that attract instead of repel investment.*
-Editorial, *Wall Street Journal* (Aug. 24, 1995).


Chapter 2 presented summary ratings designed to measure differences among countries in the amount of economic freedom at various points in time. In the last chapter, we analyzed how economic freedom has changed during the last two decades. The present focus is on the linkage, if any, between economic freedom and economic growth. Do countries with more economic freedom grow more rapidly and achieve higher income levels? How do changes in economic freedom affect the growth of income?

Higher incomes and improved living standards are dependent on increases in the production of goods and services *that people value*. Without growth in the production of goods and services valued by consumers, the income of a nation will stagnate. Increases in production per capita are the basis of increases in income per capita.

There are essentially four sources of increases in productivity and income: (1) improvements in the skills of workers, (2) investment and capital formation, (3) advancements in technology, and (4) better economic organization. These four factors are interrelated and, in varying degrees, are all influenced by economic freedom. If people are not permitted to keep what they produce and earn, they will have little incentive to either upgrade their skills or invest in structures and machines designed to enhance future productivity. Additionally, if individuals are not allowed to try new ways of doing things, innovation and improvements in technology will be stifled. Most importantly, economic freedom is reflective of institutional arrangements. If an economy's institutions are consistent with economic freedom, it will be easier for people to cooperate with each other, specialize in areas where they have a comparative advantage, and realize gains from trade and entrepreneurship.[1] Correspondingly, institutional arrangements that restrain trade, increase transaction costs, weaken property rights, and create uncertainty will reduce the realization of gains from trade and also the incentive of individuals to engage in productive activities.[2]

Thus, economic theory indicates that economic freedom (and increases in that freedom) will enhance growth because it will lead to increases in the incentive to earn, higher productivity, and gains from trade and entrepreneurship. Therefore, if it is measured properly, one would expect that economic freedom will be positively related to economic growth.

## MEASUREMENT PROBLEMS AND THE RELATIONSHIP BETWEEN ECONOMIC FREEDOM AND INCOME

When considering the impact of economic freedom on the level and growth of income, it is important to keep several points in mind. First, while there are good reasons to expect that an *increase* in economic freedom will enhance, for example, the *growth rate* of real per capita GDP, the linkage is likely to be a loose one. When a nation adopts policies and institutions more consistent with economic freedom, it will take time to convince decision-makers that the changes are permanent, rather than temporary. This will be particularly true if opposition to the more liberal policies remains strong or if the nation has a history of policy shifts and instability. The effectiveness of the new policy is very much dependent on the credibility of the change. Credibility can only be earned with the passage of time and the amount of time required to earn it will be influenced by historical factors and current political conditions. Thus, the time period between the institution of a policy that influences economic freedom and its actual impact on economic growth is likely to be highly variable, and in some cases, quite lengthy. Clearly, this time lag will weaken the relationship between changes in economic freedom and changes in the growth rate of income.

Second, there are also good reasons to expect that the *level* of economic freedom will enhance growth, but this linkage too is likely to be a weak one. Growth is partly an ongoing discovery process. In a very real sense, wealth creation involves figuring out where and how resources can be transformed into goods and services that are more highly valued than the resources. Compared to the situation where restrictions are widespread, entrepreneurs in a free economy will have greater incentive to figure out better ways of doing things and greater freedom to act on their innovative ideas. Their actions will promote economic growth. However, a measure of economic freedom at a point time—our 1995 summary index for example—does not reveal how long that measured level of economic freedom has been present. Neither does the rating for a specific year reveal if the degree of economic freedom has been increasing or decreasing. Both of these factors will weaken the relationship between economic freedom and growth.[3]

Neither does a measure of economic freedom at a point in time reveal if there are signs of adverse change on the horizon. Influential political leaders may be promoting policies inconsistent with economic freedom. The political climate may be such that the likelihood of future policies restrictive of economic freedom is high. These factors will influence the security of property rights, attractiveness of investment, and level of current economic activity. Until actually instituted, however, they will not affect our measure of economic freedom. Factors of this type will also weaken the relationship between the *level* of economic freedom and the *growth* of production and income.

Finally, there are good reasons to expect that the linkage between the *level* of economic freedom *over a lengthy time period* and per capita GDP will be quite strong. As a country moves from a low to high level of economic freedom, it will experience rapid growth (once credibility is gained). This will be particularly true for low-income countries that will often be able to gain by emulating and adopting proven technologies and successful business ideas from high-income, more developed nations. Since growth is partly a discovery process, countries with more economic freedom—even those that have already achieved high levels of income—will tend to have higher growth rates than those with a persistently low level of freedom. As a result, countries with high *levels of economic freedom* over a lengthy time period will almost surely have much higher *levels of per capita GDP* than their counterparts with persistently low levels of economic freedom.

*A measure of economic freedom at a point in time does not reveal how long the level of freedom has been present, if it has been increasing or decreasing, or whether the likelihood of future restrictive policies is high or low. These omissions will weaken the relationship between freedom and growth.*

# THE LEVEL OF ECONOMIC FREEDOM, INCOME, AND GROWTH

A comprehensive analysis of precisely how economic freedom impacts the growth and level of income is beyond the focus of this research project.[4] However, we will present an overview of the data on this topic.

Let us begin by looking at the relationship between the *level* of economic freedom and *level* of income. In the Graphic Summary, we presented an exhibit which illustrated the average per capita GDP of countries according to their 1993-1995 economic freedom grade. (See Exhibit S-2A at the front of the book.) As the 1995 economic freedom grade declined, so too did the average income level. The average 1994 per capita GDP for the A rated economies was $15,834; the average for those with a grade of B was $13,659; at the C grade, it was $7,888; at the D level, it was $3,784; F grades had an average income of $3,068 and for F-, it was $1,650. Clearly, these data indicate that there is a strong linkage between *level of economic freedom* and *level of income*.

Income comparisons between the most and least free economies shed additional light on the consistency of this relationship. Exhibit 4-1A presents the 1994 per capita GDP (measured in 1985 U.S. dollars) for the 14 countries that earned an A or B economic freedom grade in 1993-1995. The average of our three summary indexes indicates that in the mid-1990s these 14 economies were the freest in the world. The 1994 per capita GDP of these countries was quite high. Only one, Malaysia, had a per capita income figure of less than $10,000 in 1994. The average per capita GDP for the 14 A or B rated countries was $14,280. Except for Malaysia, all of the 14 countries in the most free group ranked among the 21 countries with the highest incomes in the world.[5]

Exhibit 4-1B presents the income data for the 27 countries with an economic freedom grade of F- in 1993-1995. While the economically free list was dominated by high-income economies, those with extremely low incomes dominated the "least free" list. Only one (Venezuela) of the 27 in the least free group was able to achieve an income level of even $5,000.[6] Twenty-two of these 27 countries had a per capita GDP of less than $3,000. More than

**Exhibit 4-1A: The Per Capita GDP and the Growth of Per Capita GDP for the Countries with an Index Rating Grade of A or B in 1993-1995**

| Grade of A or B | Is1 1993-95 | Per Capita GDP 1994 (in 1985 U.S. dollars) | Growth of Per Capita GDP | |
|---|---|---|---|---|
| | | | 1980-94 | 1985-94 |
| Hong Kong | 9.0 | $17,832 | 5.0 | 5.7 |
| Singapore | 8.2 | 14,415 | 5.3 | 5.9 |
| New Zealand | 8.0 | 12,240 | 1.2 | 0.8 |
| United States | 7.7 | 18,850 | 1.6 | 1.6 |
| Switzerland | 7.5 | 15,980 | 0.8 | 0.7 |
| Malaysia | 7.0 | $6,510 | 4.1 | 5.0 |
| United Kingdom | 7.0 | 13,430 | 1.9 | 1.8 |
| Canada | 6.9 | 17,510 | 1.3 | 1.0 |
| Japan | 6.9 | 15,105 | 2.9 | 2.8 |
| Australia | 6.8 | 15,169 | 1.6 | 1.6 |
| Ireland | 6.7 | $10,640 | 3.2 | 4.3 |
| Netherlands | 6.4 | 13,505 | 1.3 | 1.7 |
| Germany[a] | 6.4 | 15,005 | 1.8 | 2.1 |
| Belgium | 6.3 | 13,735 | 1.5 | 1.9 |
| **Average** | | **14,280** | **2.4** | **2.6** |

[a] West Germany only.

Source: See Exhibit 2.1 for the summary rating and grade data. The per capita GDP data are from Robert Summers and Alan Heston, *Penn World Tables* (Cambridge: National Bureau of Economic Research). These figures were derived by the purchasing power parity method. The growth of per capita GDP figures were derived from the World Bank, *World Tables*. These figures were used to update the Summers and Heston data to 1994.

half (14 of the 27) had income levels below $1,000. The average per capita GDP for the least free group was $1,650, about one-ninth of the average for the most free group.

Despite the measurement problems that we previously discussed, a comparison of Exhibits 4-1A and 4-1B also indicates that there is a link between the *level* of economic freedom as measured by our index and the *growth* of real GDP. The average annual growth rate of per capita real GDP for the 14 countries with a grade of either A or B was 2.4% during the 1980-1994 period and 2.6% during 1985-1994. The growth rate of per capita GDP for every one of the 14 was positive. In contrast, the average growth rate of per capita GDP for the F- rated countries was *minus* 1.3% during the 1980-1994 period (and *minus* 1.6 during 1985-

**Exhibit 4-1B: The Per Capita GDP and the Growth of Per Capita GDP for the Countries with an Index Grade of F- in 1993—1995**

| Grade of F- | Is1 1993-95 | Per Capita GDP 1994 (in 1985 U.S. dollars) | Growth of Per Capita GDP 1980-94 | Growth of Per Capita GDP 1985-94 |
|---|---|---|---|---|
| Brazil | 3.3 | $4,118 | +0.1 | +0.8 |
| Haiti | 2.9 | 665 | -4.5 | -5.4 |
| Nicaragua | 3.3 | 1,165 | -3.3 | -3.8 |
| Venezuela | 4.5 | 6,395 | -1.2 | +0.2 |
| Hungary | 3.3 | 4,720 | -0.2 | -1.0 |
| Iran[a] | 2.1 | $3,650 | -0.2 | -1.7 |
| Romania | 2.9 | 1,366 | -2.3 | -4.9 |
| Syria[a] | 2.6 | 4,270 | +0.2 | +0.6 |
| Nepal | 3.6 | 1,005 | +2.3 | +2.4 |
| Algeria[a] | 2.1 | 2,700 | -0.6 | -2.3 |
| Benin[a] | 4.0 | $930 | -0.1 | -1.0 |
| Burundi[a] | 3.2 | 569 | +1.0 | +0.3 |
| Cent. African | 3.9 | 514 | -1.9 | -2.9 |
| Congo[a] | 3.5 | 2,200 | -0.7 | -3.1 |
| Cote d'Ivoire[a] | 3.2 | 1,065 | -3.9 | -4.3 |
| Madagascar | 4.0 | $605 | -2.8 | -1.9 |
| Morocco[a] | 3.9 | 2,150 | +0.5 | +0.5 |
| Niger[a] | 3.6 | 470 | -3.9 | -2.2 |
| Nigeria | 3.9 | 960 | -1.3 | +1.1 |
| Rwanda | 3.7 | 762 | -1.0 | -1.7 |
| Sierra Leone[a] | 4.2 | $734 | -1.2 | -1.1 |
| Tanzania[a] | 3.7 | 470 | -0.6 | +0.5 |
| Togo[a] | 3.6 | 530 | -4.2 | -4.9 |
| Uganda[a] | 3.7 | 547 | +0.5 | +0.6 |
| Zaire[a] | 1.9 | 300 | -3.7 | -5.3 |
| Zambia[a] | 3.6 | $525 | -2.1 | -1.6 |
| Zimbabwe[a] | 3.4 | 1,162 | -0.7 | -1.6 |
| **Average** | | **$1,650** | **-1.3** | **-1.6** |

[a] The per capita GDP and growth data for these countries are only through 1993.

Source: See Exhibit 2-1 for the summary rating and grade data. The data for per capita GDP are from Summers and Heston, *Penn World Tables*, (Cambridge: National Bureau of Economic Research). The growth of per capita GDP data were derived from the World Bank, *World Tables*. These figures were used to update the Summers and Heston data to the most recent year for which GDP was available.

**Exhibit 4-2: The Growth of Per Capita GDP for Countries with Persistently High and Persistently Low Economic Freedom Ratings During 1975-1995**

| Countries | Real GDP Per Capita (in 1985 U.S. dollars) | | Countries | Real GDP Per Capita (in 1985 U.S. dollars) | |
|---|---|---|---|---|---|
| | 1994 | Growth Rate 1980-94 | | 1994 | Growth Rate 1980-94 |
| **Persistently High Ratings**[a] | | | **Persistently Low Ratings**[b] | | |
| Hong Kong | $17,832 | 5.0 | Somalia[d] | $580 | -2.0 |
| Switzerland | 15,980 | 0.8 | Zambia[c] | 525 | -2.1 |
| Singapore | 14,415 | 5.3 | Hungary | 4,720 | +0.2 |
| United States | 18,850 | 1.6 | Romania | 1,360 | -2.3 |
| Canada | 17,510 | 1.3 | Brazil | 4,118 | +0.1 |
| Germany | 15,005 | 1.8 | Syria[c] | 4,270 | +0.2 |
| | | | Uganda[c] | 547 | +0.4 |
| | | | Zaire[c] | 300 | -3.7 |
| | | | Zimbabwe[c] | 1,162 | -0.7 |
| **Average** | **$16,599** | **2.6** | **Average** | **$1,954** | **-1.1** |

[a] This is the list of countries that (a) made an A or B in 1995 and (b) ranked in the top 15 during 1975, 1980, 1985, and 1990. See Exhibit 2-3 for the yearly ratings of these countries.

[b] This is the list of countries that had an economic freedom rating (Is1) of F- in 1995 and a rating of less than 4.0 for each of our rating years. See Exhibit 2-3 for the yearly ratings of these countries.

[c] The GDP data for these countries are only through 1993.

[d] The GDP data for this country are only through 1992.

Source: The per capita GDP are updates of the purchasing power parity estimates of Robert Summer and Alan Heston, *Penn World Tables* (Cambridge: National Bureau of Economic Research, 1994).

1994.) During 1980-1994, 21 of the countries with an F- rating experienced declines in real GDP per capita; only 6 were able to register a positive growth rate. Other than the 2.3% growth rate of Nepal (which was approximately equal to the average growth rate of the A/B rated countries), none of other low-rated countries was able to achieve an average growth rate in excess of 1.0% during 1980-1994. The pattern for the 1985-1994 period was similar.

Since the data of Exhibits 4-1A and 4-1B focus on country ratings at a point in time, they may be influenced by *changes* in summary ratings as well as *differences* in the levels.[7] Exhibit 4-2 attempts to eliminate the impact of the former factor. Here we present data for per capita GDP and its growth rate for countries with *persistently high* and *persistently low* ratings throughout the entire 1975-1995 period. Since the ratings for these countries did not change very much during the period, this comparison should provide us with a better indication of how persistent differences in the *level* of economic freedom influence both level of income and economic growth.

The persistently high rated-category was comprised of the countries with an economic freedom grade of either A or B in 1995 *and* a ranking in the Top 15 during each of the prior rating years of our study. Correspondingly, countries were included in persistently low category if their 1995 rating was F- *and* their summary index (Is1) was less than 4.0 during each of the prior rating years. (See Exhibit 2-3 for the yearly ratings for both of these groups). Thus, the six nations in the persistently high-rated group have been among the freest in the world for at least two decades, and probably much longer. Similarly, the nine economies in the persistently low-rated group have been among the least free over the same period of time.

*The six persistently free economies during the last decade all ranked in the Top Ten in terms of per capita income. Their average per capita GDP was ten times that of the persistently unfree group.*

First, let us consider the income level data. The 1994 per capita incomes of the persistently free group averaged $16,599; they ranged from the $14,415 of Singapore to the $18,850 of the United States. These are exceedingly high per capita incomes. The figures for United States, Hong Kong, and Canada were the three highest among the 103 countries in our study. Switzerland ranked fifth, Germany eighth, and Singapore tenth. Thus, the six persistently free economies during the last decade all ranked in the Top Ten in terms of per capita income. In contrast, the highest income among the persistently unfree group, Hungary's $4,720, was only a little more than one-fourth of the average for the free economies. Four of the nine persistently low-rated countries had a per capita GDP of less than $600. The average per capita GDP ($1,954) of the persistently unfree group was less than one-eighth the average for the persistently free group. Just as we had expected, economies that are free over a lengthy time period achieve high levels of income, while those that are unfree for extended periods have low incomes.

Turning to the growth figures, the six persistently free economies all had positive growth rates and their annual growth rate of per capita real GDP averaged 2.6% during 1980-1994. In contrast, five of the nine persistently low-rated countries had negative rates of growth and none were able to achieve growth of even a half percent annually during 1980-1994. On average, the per capita GDP of the low-rated group *declined* at an annual rate of 1.1 percent during the 1980-1994 period.

These figures provide strong evidence that the level of economic freedom exerts a positive impact on both per capita income and economic growth. When an economy is free over a long period of time, individuals achieve high and growing levels of income. Similarly, when economic freedom is stifled for lengthy periods, incomes stagnate and fall relative to those of free economies.

## CHANGES IN ECONOMIC FREEDOM AND GROWTH OF GDP

Theory indicates that a sustained increase in economic freedom will enhance growth, while a decline will retard it. Thus, one would expect countries with an expanding amount of economic freedom to have higher growth rates than those with a contracting amount of freedom. However, the immediate impact of a change in economic freedom is likely to be small—particularly in the case of an expansion in freedom. As we previously discussed, there will generally be a lag between the time when institutional arrangements and policies become more consistent with economic freedom and when they begin to exert their primary impact on economic growth. Therefore, when considering the effects of changes in economic freedom during a period, we will generally analyze their impact on growth beginning five years after the *initial* rating year.

Exhibit 4-3 presents data for the 15 countries (actually there are 17 because of a tie) that showed the most improvement in the summary index (Is1) of economic freedom between 1975 and 1990. (See Exhibit 3-1 for their yearly ratings.) Chile, Jamaica, Iceland, Malaysia, and Pakistan head the most-improved list during the 1975–1990 period. In terms of development, the most improved countries were a diverse group. As the 1980 income figures indicate, only five (Iceland, Japan, New Zealand, United Kingdom,

**Exhibit 4-3: The Economic Growth of the Fifteen Countries for Which the Index of Economic Freedom (Is1) Increased the Most During 1975-1990**

| Country | Change in Is1 1975-1990 | Per Capita GDP 1980[a] | Growth of Per Capita GDP | | |
|---|---|---|---|---|---|
| | | | 1980-90 | 1980-94 | 1985-94 |
| Chile | +2.9 | $3,892 | 1.5 | 2.8 | 4.8 |
| Jamaica[b] | +2.0 | 2,362 | 1.0 | 0.8 | 2.1 |
| Iceland | +2.0 | 11,566 | 1.0 | 0.9 | 0.6 |
| Malaysia | +2.0 | 3,799 | 3.3 | 4.1 | 5.0 |
| Pakistan | +1.9 | 1,879 | 3.0 | 2.7 | 2.3 |
| Turkey | +1.8 | $2,874 | 2.9 | 2.8 | 3.2 |
| Egypt | +1.8 | 1,645 | 2.4 | 1.6 | 0.1 |
| Portugal | +1.7 | 4,982 | 2.6 | 2.1 | 3.3 |
| Japan | +1.7 | 10,072 | 3.5 | 2.9 | 2.8 |
| Singapore | +1.7 | 7,053 | 5.2 | 5.3 | 5.9 |
| Mauritius | +1.7 | 3,988 | 5.0 | 4.8 | 5.4 |
| New Zealand | +1.7 | $10,362 | 1.0 | 1.2 | 0.8 |
| United Kingdom | +1.6 | 10,167 | 2.9 | 1.9 | 1.8 |
| (tie) Thailand | +1.4 | 2,178 | 5.9 | 6.1 | 7.6 |
| (tie) Indonesia | +1.4 | 1,281 | 3.7 | 4.0 | 3.4 |
| (tie) United States | +1.4 | 15,295 | 1.7 | 1.6 | 1.6 |
| (tie) Costa Rica | +1.4 | 3,717 | -0.4 | 0.4 | 2.1 |
| **Average Growth Rate of Per Capita GDP** | | | **2.7** | **2.7** | **3.1** |

[a] Measured in 1985 U.S. dollars.

[b] The growth of GDP data for these countries only run through 1993.

Source: The change in the Index Is1 was derived from the summary ratings of Appendix I: Tables A1-1 and A1-4. See Exhibit 3-1 for the ratings of these countries during the 1975-1990 period. The 1980 per capita GDP data are from Robert Summers and Alan Heston, *Penn World Tables* (Cambridge: National Bureau of Economic Research) and the growth of per capita GDP were derived from the World Bank, *World Tables* (various years).

and United States) of the 17 were classified as high-income industrial economies at the beginning of the period. Ten of the 17 had a per capita GDP of less than $4,000 in 1980.

Exhibit 4–4 presents similar data for the 15 countries (again there are 16 because of a tie) that regressed the most during the same period. Nicaragua, Somalia, Iran, Honduras, and Venezuela head the list of those with the largest declines in economic freedom

**Exhibit 4-4: The Economic Growth of the Fifteen Countries for Which the Index of Economic Freedom (Is1) Declined the Most During 1975-1990**

| Country | Change in Is1 1975-1990 | Per Capita GDP 1980[a] | Growth of GDP | | |
|---|---|---|---|---|---|
| | | | 1980-90 | 1980-94 | 1985-94 |
| Nicaragua | -4.4 | $1,853 | -1.2 | -3.3 | -3.8 |
| Somalia | -1.8 | 744 | -0.7 | -2.0 | — |
| Iran[b] | -1.8 | 3,434 | -1.1 | -0.2 | -1.7 |
| Honduras | -1.4 | 1,519 | -1.1 | -0.7 | -0.1 |
| Venezuela | -1.4 | 6,395 | -1.7 | -1.2 | +0.2 |
| Congo[b] | -1.2 | $1,931 | +0.2 | -0.7 | -3.1 |
| Zambia[b] | -1.1 | 971 | -2.9 | -2.1 | -1.6 |
| Tanzania[b] | -1.0 | 480 | -0.3 | -0.6 | +0.5 |
| Algeria[b] | -0.8 | 2,758 | +0.1 | -0.6 | -2.3 |
| Morocco | -0.7 | 1,941 | +1.1 | +0.6 | +0.5 |
| Panama | -0.7 | $3,392 | -1.4 | +0.4 | +0.3 |
| Syria[b] | -0.5 | 4,467 | -1.2 | +0.2 | +0.6 |
| Greece | -0.5 | 5,901 | +1.0 | +0.8 | +0.9 |
| El Salvador | -0.4 | 2,014 | -0.5 | -0.4 | +1.4 |
| (tie) Sierra Leone[b] | -0.3 | 1,139 | -0.9 | -1.2 | -1.1 |
| (tie) Brazil | -0.3 | 4,305 | -0.6 | +0.9 | +0.8 |
| **Average Growth Rate of Per Capita GDP** | | | **-0.7** | **-0.6** | **-0.6** |

[a] Measured in 1985 U.S. dollars. These data are from Summers and Heston, *Penn World Tables*, (Cambridge: National Bureau of Economic Research).

[b] The growth of GDP data for these countries are only through 1993.

Source: The change in the Index Is1 was derived from the summary ratings of Appendix I: Tables A1-1 and A1-4. See Exhibit 3-2 for the ratings of these countries during the 1975-1990 period.

between 1975 and 1990. While there were no high-income industrial countries in this group, four (Venezuela, Syria, Greece, and Brazil) of the 16 had income levels above $4,000 in 1980.

As Exhibit 4-3 indicates, the nations with the largest increases in economic freedom (Is1) during the 1975-1990 period registered an average growth in per capita GDP of 2.7% during 1980-1990. Their growth rate during the most recent ten years (1985-1994) was even higher, 3.1 percent. All 17 of these countries achieved a positive growth rate during 1980-1994 and 1985-1994. The growth of the non-industrial countries that moved toward liberalization was particularly impressive. The per capita real GDP of eight (Chile, Malaysia, Portugal, Turkey, Singapore, Mauritius, Thailand, and Indonesia) of the 12 *non-industrial* nations with the largest increases in economic freedom grew 3 percent or more during the last decade. The average growth of per capita GDP for the 12 non-industrial nations—the eight listed above plus Jamaica, Pakistan, Egypt, and Costa Rica—was 3.8 percent. At this growth rate, incomes would double every 18 years.

The economic record of the countries that restricted economic freedom during 1975-1990 stands in stark contrast to that of those liberalizing their economies. As Exhibit 4-4 indicates, average real per capita GDP *declined* at an annual rate of 0.7 percent during 1980-1990 (and by 0.6% during 1985-1994) in the 16 countries for which the index of economic freedom fell the most. The economic decline was widespread. Twelve of the 16 countries experienced reductions in real per capita GDP during the 1980-1990 period. None were able to achieve a growth rate of more than 1.1 percent, a rate less than one-half the average growth rate for those that moved toward economic freedom.

*The seven less developed countries (Mauritius, Chile, Portugal, Jamaica, Singapore, Pakistan, and Turkey) which achieved the largest increases in economic freedom between 1975 and 1985 and main-tained the increases into the 1990s grew at an annual rate of 3.9% during 1985-1994.*

As we previously discussed, maintenance of an increase in economic freedom is vitally important. Countries that shift back and forth between liberal and restrictive policies will lose credibility, which will weaken the positive effects of their more liberal policies. Therefore, if we want to isolate the real impact of economic freedom, we need to consider the performance of economies that both *increase and maintain* a higher freedom rating. Exhibit 4-5 (upper part) identifies the countries—there were only nine—in our sample that achieved at least a one unit increase in economic freedom (as measured by the Is1 index) during 1975-1985 *and* maintained the increase into the 1990s. Thus, these economies were clearly more free *throughout* 1985-1995 than they were in 1975.

How did the expansion of economic freedom influence the growth rates of these countries? As Exhibit 4-5 illustrates, the per capita GDP of these nine expanded at an annual rate of 3.1% during the 1980s and at a 3.5% rate during 1985-1994, up from 2.2% during 1975-1985. During the last decade, the slowest growth rate among the nine was the 1.8% rate of the United Kingdom. Seven of the nine were classified as less developed by the World Bank at the beginning of the period. These seven—Mauritius, Chile, Portugal, Jamaica, Singapore, Pakistan, and Turkey—grew at an average annual rate of 3.9% during 1985-1994.

**Exhibit 4-5: The Growth of Per Capita GDP for Countries with at Least a One Unit Change in the Is1 Summary Index of Economic Freedom Between 1975 and 1985**

| | Change in Is1 Rating | | Growth of Per Capita GDP | | |
|---|---|---|---|---|---|
| | 1975-85 | 1985-95 | 1975-85 | 1980-90 | 1985-94 |
| **Countries with at least a 1 Unit Increase Between 1975 and 1985 and Maintenance of the Increase During 1985-95[a]** | | | | | |
| Mauritius | +2.1 | +0.3 | +2.8 | +5.0 | +5.4 |
| Pakistan | +1.6 | +1.5 | +3.3 | +3.0 | +2.3 |
| Japan | +1.3 | +0.4 | +3.4 | +3.5 | +2.8 |
| Chile | +1.3 | +1.7 | +2.4 | +1.9 | +4.8 |
| Jamaica | +1.2 | +1.9 | -3.0 | +1.0 | +2.1 |
| Singapore | +1.2 | +0.2 | +5.2 | +5.2 | +5.9 |
| Portugal | +1.1 | +2.0 | +1.8 | +2.6 | +3.3 |
| United Kingdom | +1.0 | +1.0 | +1.5 | +2.5 | +1.8 |
| Turkey | +1.0 | +0.4 | +2.3 | +2.9 | +3.2 |
| **Average Growth Rate of Per Capita GDP** | | | **2.2** | **3.1** | **3.5** |
| **Countries with a 1 Unit Decline Between 1975 and 1985** | | | | | |
| Nicaragua | -4.6 | +1.5 | -4.8 | -3.7 | -3.8 |
| Iran | -2.5 | -0.6 | -2.7 | -1.1 | -1.7 |
| Venezuela | -1.7 | -0.7 | -2.2 | -1.8 | +0.2 |
| Somalia | -1.5 | N/R | +0.2 | -1.2 | -2.3 |
| Honduras | -1.4 | -0.5 | +0.8 | -0.9 | -0.1 |
| Tanzania | -1.4 | +1.8 | -1.7 | +0.6 | +0.5 |
| Bolivia | -1.3 | +2.2 | -2.1 | -2.4 | +0.1 |
| Algeria | -1.1 | -0.3 | +2.5 | -0.1 | -2.3 |
| Syria | -1.0 | +0.1 | -1.3 | -1.2 | +0.6 |
| **Average Growth Rate of Per Capita GDP** | | | **-1.3** | **-1.3** | **-1.0** |

[a]  All of these countries achieved at least a 1 unit increase in the Is1 summary rating between 1975 and 1985 and they were able to maintain this higher rating during the following decade.  None of the other countries in our study were able to achieve and maintain such a large increase.  See Exhibit 3-3 for the rating of these countries during each of the periods.

N/R = No rating in 1995; thus, the change between 1985 and 1995 cannot be calculated.

DOUGLAS COLLEGE LIBRARY

**Exhibit 4-6: The Growth of Per Capita GDP for the Ten Countries With the Largest Change in the Is1 Summary Rating Between 1980 and 1990**

| | Change in Is1 Rating | | Growth of Per Capita GDP | | |
|---|---|---|---|---|---|
| | 1980-90 | 1990-95 | 1980-90 | 1985-94 | 1989-94 |
| **Countries with the Largest Increase Between 1980 and 1990 and Maintenance of the Increase in 1995** | | | | | |
| Jamaica[b] | +2.4 | +1.1 | +1.0 | +2.1 | +1.9 |
| United Kingdom | +2.1 | +0.4 | +2.5 | +1.8 | +0.3 |
| Costa Rica | +1.8 | +0.1 | -0.4 | +2.1 | +2.3 |
| Bolivia[b] | +1.8 | +0.1 | -2.4 | +0.1 | +1.1 |
| Chile | +1.8 | +0.1 | +1.9 | +4.8 | +4.2 |
| Italy | +1.8 | +0.2 | +2.0 | +2.0 | +1.1 |
| Mauritius | +1.8 | +0.7 | +5.0 | +5.4 | +4.3 |
| Mexico | +1.5 | +0.5 | -0.3 | +0.1 | +1.0 |
| Norway | +1.4 | +0.9 | +1.8 | +1.3 | +2.1 |
| Thailand | +1.3 | +0.7 | +5.9 | +7.6 | +7.1 |
| **Average Growth Rate of Per Capita GDP** | | | **1.7** | **2.7** | **2.5** |
| **Countries with the Largest Decline between 1980 and 1990** | | | | | |
| Dominican Rep | -1.9 | +2.1 | -0.4 | +0.7 | +0.1 |
| Somalia[b] | -1.7 | N/R | -1.2 | -2.3 | -3.0 |
| Tanzania[b] | -1.7 | +1.4 | +0.6 | +0.5 | -0.8 |
| Nicaragua | -1.6 | +1.2 | -3.8 | -3.8 | -0.4 |
| Zimbabwe[b] | -1.3 | +1.1 | +0.2 | -1.6 | -2.0 |
| Zambia | -1.3 | +1.8 | -2.2 | -1.6 | -2.4 |
| Venezuela | -1.1 | -1.0 | -1.8 | +0.2 | +1.2 |
| Romania | -1.0 | +0.7 | -0.8 | -4.9 | -6.2 |
| Jordan | -0.9 | +0.5 | -1.9 | -3.0 | -1.5 |
| Congo[b] | -0.9 | +0.4 | +1.7 | -3.1 | -3.0 |
| **Average Growth Rate of Per Capita GDP** | | | **-1.0** | **-1.9** | **-1.8** |

[a] See Exhibit 3-4 for the Is1 ratings of these countries during 1980-1995.

[b] The 1994 GDP data were unavailable when this study was completed. Thus, the growth data only run through 1993.

Exhibit 4-5 (lower part) identifies the economies—there were also nine—where the Is1 economic freedom rating declined by one unit or more during 1975-1985. On average, the real GDP of these countries fell at an annual rate of 1% or more. During 1980-1990, eight of nine regressors experienced reductions in per capita real GDP. None was able to achieve a growth rate of more than 0.6% during either 1980-1990 or 1985-1994. Clearly, the growth rates of the countries with a one unit or more reduction in economic freedom were persistently and substantially less than those with a one unit increase.

Exhibit 4-6 is similar to Exhibit 4-5, except the focus is on the changes in economic freedom between 1980 and 1990. The upper part of the exhibit contains data for the ten countries that achieved the largest increases in economic freedom (Is1 index) during the 1980s and maintained them in 1995. It is a diverse group including three high-income industrial nations (United Kingdom, Italy, and Norway) and seven less developed economies. Among the latter group, Jamaica, Bolivia, Chile, Mauritius, and Mexico all had 1980 freedom ratings of 4.5 or less. The rating increases of Costa Rica, Bolivia, Italy, Mexico, and Thailand were concentrated in the latter half of the 1980s. In fact, the Is1 ratings of Costa Rica and Bolivia actually declined between 1980 and 1985, prior to their sizeable increase between 1985 and 1990 (see Exhibit 3-4 for the ratings throughout this period.)

During 1980-1990 Costa Rica, Bolivia, and Mexico experienced declines in per capita GDP. Interestingly, the freedom ratings of two (Costa Rica and Bolivia) of these three were declining until the latter half of the 1980s. By 1985-1994 all ten of these countries were on a positive growth path. During the last five years, the growth rates of Costa Rica, Bolivia, and Mexico were 2.3%, 1.1%, and 1.0% respectively. Each was a substantial improvement on the growth rate prior to their jump in economic freedom during the latter half of the 1980s. On average, the real GDP of the countries that improved the most during the 1980s increased by 2.7% during 1985-1994 and 2.5% during 1989-1994.

Exhibit 4-6 (lower part) presents data for the ten countries where economic freedom regressed the most during the 1980s. Seven of these ten experienced declines in per capita GDP during 1980-1990 and 1985-1994. Their average per capita growth rate was *minus* 1.9% during the latter period, 4.6% less than the rate achieved by the ten with the largest gains in economic freedom.

The gap between the two groups remained large during the most recent five year period. None of the countries with large declines in economic freedom was able to achieve a persistent positive growth rate during the 1980-1994 period.

## ECONOMIC FREEDOM AND ECONOMIC GROWTH: SOME REFLECTIONS

When considered together, the exhibits indicate a very strong relationship between economic freedom and economic growth. There is only a six country overlap between the 14 A or B rated countries of Exhibit 4-1A and the 17 most-improved countries of Exhibit 4-3. Malaysia, Japan, Singapore, New Zealand, United Kingdom, and United States are on both lists. Thus, there are 25 countries that were in either the top-rated group in 1993-1995 and/or the most-improved group during 1975-1990. The per capita GDP of every one of these 25 increased during 1980-1994 and 1985-1994. Their average growth rate of per capita GDP was 2.9% during 1985-1994.

There was considerable overlap between the 27 low-rated countries of Exhibit 4-1B and the 16 countries with the largest reductions in the summary rating included in Exhibit 4-4. Only five of the countries with the largest rating declines failed to appear among the lowest rated—those with a F- grade—in 1993-1995. Thus, there were 32 countries with either a F- rating in 1993-1995 and/or a substantial decline in rating between 1975 and 1990. Of these thirty-two, 24 had a negative growth rate for per capita GDP during the 1980-1994 period. Only Nepal which grew at an annual rate of 2.3 percent during 1980-1994 was able to achieve a growth rate greater than 1.0 percent during the period.

*Without exception, countries with either a high level or a substantial increase in economic freedom achieved positive growth rates in per capita GDP.*

Clearly, these data indicate that during the last two decades there has been a strong relationship between economic freedom and economic growth. Without exception, countries with either a *high level* or a *substantial increase* in economic freedom achieved positive growth. Correspondingly, the overwhelming majority of countries with *low* and/or *contracting* levels of economic freedom experienced declines in per capita GDP.[8]

These findings are buttressed by the linkage between a persistently high freedom rating over a lengthy time period and level of income. Without exception, countries with a persistently high level of economic freedom during the last two decades also achieved high per capita income levels. On the other hand, no country with a persistently low level of economic freedom during the last two decades was able to achieve even middle income status (see Exhibit 4-2).

Finally, countries that achieved substantial increases in economic freedom *and* then sustained those increases invariably moved to a positive growth path. This was true for the increases of 1975-1985 (Exhibit 4-5) and also for those of 1980-1990 (Exhibit 4-6). Correspondingly, when economic freedom declined, economies stagnated, and incomes fell.

Comparisons between similar countries in the same region can also provide insight on the impact of economic freedom. Exhibit 4-7 presents data of this type. Perhaps more than any other two countries, Chile and Venezuela have moved in very different directions throughout the last two decades. In 1975, the Venezuelan economy was relatively free (its Is1 rating was 6.9), while Chile was saddled with all types of economic restrictions. But the situation has changed dramatically since that time. The economic freedom rating of Chile has risen steadily from 2.8 in 1975 to 4.1 in 1985 and 5.8 in 1995. In contrast, the summary rating of Venezuela declined from 6.9 in 1975 to 5.2 in 1985 and to 4.5 in 1995. (See the Country Profile data of Chapter 5 for additional details on the factors underlying the changes in the freedom ratings of these two countries.) What has happened to the growth rates of the two countries? Chile's growth of per capita GDP accelerated throughout the period, soaring to an annual rate of 4.8% during 1985-1994. In contrast, the Venezuelan economy stagnated. Per capita GDP declined 2.2% annually between 1975 and 1985 and has changed very little since that time.

*While Chile moved toward economic liberalism, Venezuela moved in the opposite direction. During the last decade Chile's growth of GDP per capita was 4.8% compared to 0.2% for Venezuela.*

The comparison between Costa Rica and Honduras, two small Central American countries, is also revealing. Between 1975 and 1985, the freedom rating for both declined and their economies stagnated—Honduras experienced a slight increase in income while Costa Rica registered a small decline. Since 1985, Costa Rica has liberalized its economy substantially. Monetary policy has been more stable and the top tax rate was reduced from 50% to 25%. Exchange rate controls have been virtually eliminated and other barriers to trade have been reduced. Thus, the Is1 summary rating of Costa Rica jumped from 4.6 in 1985 to 6.7 in 1995.

**Exhibit 4-7: Selected Comparisons Between Countries with Increases and Decreases in Economic Freedom During Various Periods**

| | Economic Freedom Rating (Is1) | | | | | Change in Per Capita GDP | |
|---|---|---|---|---|---|---|---|
| | 1975 | 1980 | 1985 | 1990 | 1995 | 1975-85 | 1985-94 |
| **Chile** | 2.8 | 3.9 | 4.1 | 5.7 | 5.8 | +2.4 | +4.8 |
| Venezuela | 6.9 | 6.6 | 5.2 | 5.5 | 4.5 | -2.2 | +0.2 |
| **Costa Rica** | 5.2 | 4.8 | 4.6 | 6.6 | 6.7 | -0.2 | +2.1 |
| Honduras | 7.4 | 6.1 | 6.0 | 6.0 | 5.5 | +0.8 | -0.1 |
| **Ghana** | 2.5 | 2.3 | 2.8 | 3.6 | 4.8 | -1.9 | +1.4 |
| Cote d'Ivoire | 3.9 | 4.1 | 4.4 | 3.7 | 3.2 | -1.6 | -4.3 |
| **Portugal** | 2.4 | 3.1 | 3.5 | 4.1 | 5.5 | +1.8 | +3.3 |
| Greece | 3.9 | 3.8 | 3.2 | 3.4 | 4.9 | +1.8 | +0.9 |
| **Argentina** | 3.1 | 3.6 | 2.5 | 3.8 | 6.3 | -3.1 | +2.2 |
| Brazil | 3.2 | 2.7 | 2.3 | 2.9 | 3.3 | +1.5 | +0.8 |
| **Jamaica** | 3.2 | 2.8 | 4.4 | 5.2 | 6.3 | -3.0 | +2.1 |
| Panama | 7.0 | 6.3 | 6.6 | 6.3 | 6.6 | +2.3 | +0.3 |

Meanwhile, Honduras continued to move in the opposite direction. Monetary growth became more expansionary. Predicably, price level instability increased. Interest rate controls were imposed. The summary rating (Is1) of Honduras fell from 6.0 in 1985 to 5.5 in 1995. The economic performance of the two has also moved in opposite directions. Costa Rica is now on a solid growth path achieving an increase in per capita GDP of 2.1% during 1985-1994 (and 3.9% during 1992-1994). In contrast, the per capita GDP of Honduras declined during the last decade.

Ghana and Cote d'Ivoire have also moved in opposite directions during the last decade. Between 1975 and 1985, both countries had low and relatively constant freedom ratings. Both were also experiencing negative growth rates. Since 1985, Ghana has made some modest moves toward a liberal economy. Its top tax rate was cut from 60% to 35% during the decade; its very restrictive exchange rate controls were liberalized; and the size of its trade sector has grown sharply. As a result, Ghana's Is1 rating increased by two points during the last decade, while that of Cote d'Ivoire fell by more than a point. Their economies have followed suit. Ghana's real GDP per capita increased by 1.4% during 1985-1994, while Cote d'Ivoire's fell by 4.3%.

The records of the other countries included in Exhibit 4-7 are similar. The economic freedom rating of Portugal has shown steady improvement throughout the last 20 years, while prior to the 1990s the rating of Greece declined. During the last decade, the growth record of Portugal has clearly been the more impressive of the two. Economic freedom was stifled in both Argentina and Brazil until the late 1980s, when Argentina began taking decisive steps toward a freer economy. Again, economic growth responded. The recent growth record of Argentina has been stronger than that of Brazil. Like Portugal, Jamaica has moved steadily toward a freer economy since 1980, while Panama has regressed from its rating of 1975. The real GDP of Jamaica had shown strong growth since 1985 while Panama continues to struggle.

## CONCLUDING REMARKS

More precise measurement of the relationship between economic freedom and economic growth—particularly better knowledge about the length and nature of time lags between changes in economic freedom and observation of their impact on economic growth—will require additional research. Improvements in the measurement of economic freedom and its variation across countries and time periods will facilitate this research. We believe that this study is a fruitful beginning—a foundation for additional work in this area.

However, we also believe that the exhibits presented in this chapter indicate that both the level of economic freedom and changes in that level exert a consistent and potent impact on economic growth. Countries with more economic freedom tend to grow more rapidly than their counterparts adopting policies that restrict economic freedom. Furthermore, the potency of the relationship enhances our confidence that these indexes are a reasonable measure of economic freedom.

*The evidence is overwhelming— countries with more economic freedom tend to grow more rapidly than their counterparts adopting policies that restrict economic freedom.*

Finally, we believe that our findings contain an important message for both high-income industrial and low-income less developed countries. If the citizens of high-income countries want to maintain and increase their income levels, they had best not erect economic roadblocks that restrict the freedom of individuals to act and reap the benefits of their actions. Nations that choose this course can expect their growth rate and eventually their level of per capita income to fall below that of freer economies.

Correspondingly, if low-income nations are going to grow and achieve high income status, they must liberalize their economies. Low-income countries that achieved and maintained substantial increases in economic freedom during the last two decades also achieved impressive growth rates. There were no exceptions—every nation that significantly improved its rating also achieved solid economic growth. On the other hand, economies that moved away from economic freedom were characterized by sluggish growth and economic decline. The message is clear—economic freedom is the foundation for the achievement of economic growth and prosperity.

## Endnotes

1. Among modern economists, no one has stressed the importance of entrepreneurship as a source of wealth creation and economic growth more forcefully than Israel Kirzner. For a detailed analysis of this topic, see Israel M. Kirzner, *Competition and Entrepreneurship*, (Chicago: University of Chicago Press, 1973).

2. Throughout his illustrious career, 1994 Nobel laureate Douglass C. North has persuasively stressed the importance of institutional change as a source of growth and prosperity. In North's view, important institutional changes— particularly the development of the patent system and later the corporation— provided the initial ingredients for the economic growth of the West. In his recent writings, North has focused on the interrelations among economic institutions, changes in transaction costs, and economic growth. See Douglass C. North, *Institutions, Institutional Change, and Economic Performance*, (Cambridge: Cambridge University Press, 1990). Our thought process has been greatly influenced by Professor North. In a very real sense, our index of economic freedom might be viewed as an effort to evaluate the economic institutions of countries with regard to their consistency with factors that are conducive to lower transactions costs, gains from trade, and the incentive to produce.

3. Perhaps a hypothetical illustration will help clarify these points. Consider three countries A, B, and C, each with a rating of 7 on our 10 point scale. A is a high income country that achieved a rating of 7 several decades ago and has maintained it though the years; B is a high-income country that maintained a rating of 9 until a few years ago when it adopted several policies that conflicted with economic freedom; C is a low-income country that had a rating of 3 fifteen year ago. However, since that time it has moved steadily toward economic freedom. Would you expect these equally rated countries to have the same growth rate? Given its high income status and recent loss of economic freedom, we would expect B to have the lowest growth rate. Similarly, we would expect C to have the highest rate of growth, given its recent gains in economic freedom and original low-income status.

4. See The World Bank, *World Development Report*, 1983, chapter 6 and Gerald W. Scully, "The Institutional Framework and Economic Development," *Journal of Political Economy* 96 (June 1988), pp. 652-662 for prior work on this topic.

5. Except for Malaysia, all of the countries in the most free category are now classified as high-income industrial nations. However, this was not always the case. As recently as 1980, the World Bank classified three others—Hong Kong, Singapore, and Ireland—among the "developing countries" of the world. Interestingly, these four—Malaysia and the three newcomers to the high-income industrial group—have the highest growth rates in the group. Their annual increases in per capita GDP ranged between 3.2% and 5.3% throughout the 1980-1994 period. None of the long-time, high-income industrial nations achieved a growth rate greater than 2.9% during this period. This suggests that the growth rates of the industrial countries with high incomes for a long period of time have converged toward a lower long-term growth rate. Predictably, this growth rate will be lower than the growth of the newly emerging free (and formerly low-income) economies.

6. Interestingly, Venezuela is a newcomer among the least free economies. As recently as 1980, our Is1 rating ranked the Venezuelan economy as the sixth most free in the world. In 1975 it ranked fifth. Its 1980 per capita income—when it was a relatively free economy—was $7,401 (measured in 1985 dollars), well above its 1994 level. Therefore, to a large degree, Venezuela's current high-income status is merely a reflection of its past history as a relatively free economy.

7. One would expect that countries with recent *rating reductions* will be over-represented among the countries with low ratings at a point in time while countries with recent *rating increases* will be over-represented among the countries with high current ratings. Thus, some of the difference in the growth rates between the high and low rated countries may be the result of *changes in the ratings* rather than merely *differences in the rating levels*. The set of countries included in Exhibit 4-2 will tend to minimize the impact of the change in the ratings.

8. In an effort to quantify more precisely the impact of the *level* and *changes in the level* of economic freedom on economic growth, we regressed the summary index (Is1) in 1975 (the beginning of the period), changes in the index during the 1975-1990 period, and the investment/GDP ratio on the growth of per capita real GDP during 1975-1994. We included investment as a share of GDP in the regression since other researchers have shown that it is an important explanatory factor of differences in growth rates among countries. Its inclusion also provides us with a benchmark with which to judge the importance of economic freedom as a source of growth. The results were:

Growth Rate (1975-94)= -4.72 + 0.33 LEF + 1.04 CEF + 0.19 I/GDP
$\qquad\qquad\qquad\qquad$ (2.19) $\qquad$ (5.52) $\qquad$ (5.53)

$R^2 = .47$

In this equation, LEF is the 1975 level of economic freedom (Is1 rating), CEF is the change in economic freedom (Is1 rating) between 1975 and 1990, and I/GDP is the average investment/GDP ratio during the 1975-1990 period. The estimates were derived from the observations for the 90 countries for which all of the variables were available. The t-ratios for the coefficients are in parentheses. While the results should be interpreted with caution, they do suggest that economic freedom as measured by our index exerts a strong impact on economic growth. The size of the coefficient for the *level* of economic freedom indicates that a one unit increase in the initial rating increased the growth rate of per capita GDP by 0.33%. Similarly, The coefficient for the *change* in economic freedom indicates that a one unit increase in the Is1 summary index during 1975-1990 was associated with approximately a 1% increase in the growth of per capita real GDP. A unit change in the investment/GDP ratio is estimated to increase growth by 0.19%. These results indicate that a one unit increase (on a 0-10 scale) in the level of economic freedom at the beginning of the period exerts about the same impact on the growth of per capita real GDP as a two unit increase in the investment/GDP ratio (e.g., an increase from 20% to 22%). Correspondingly, a unit change in economic freedom during the period exerts about the same effect as a five unit increase (e.g., from 20% to 25%) in the investment/GDP ratio. This is particularly impressive when one considers that economic freedom will generally exert a positive impact on both the level and efficiency of investment. The $R^2$ indicates that (a) differences among countries in economic freedom (both the level and changes in the level) and (b) differences among countries in investment as a share of GDP explain almost half of the variation in growth rates across countries.

# CHAPTER 5

# Country Profiles

This chapter presents detailed data covering both economic freedom and recent performance for many of the countries in our study. Part 1 contains the three summary indexes, the Is1 area ratings (in bold), and the ratings for each of the components (and the actual data used to derive the component ratings when the underlying variable is continuous). Since this information is presented for each rating year, it makes it easy to observe the specific factors that cause a country's rating to change over time. The data sources for this information were described in Chapter 1.

Part 2 of the profile for each country presents recent (1987-1994) annual data on economic performance, including the growth of real GDP, rate of inflation, changes in the money supply, investment/GDP ratio, budget deficit as a share of GDP, and the rate of unemployment (when reliable figures were available). Except for the latter indicator, this information was from International Monetary Fund, *International Financial Statistics Yearbook* and *Monthly International Financial Statistics*. The data for the rate of unemployment were from either the Organisation for Economic Cooperation and Development (OECD), *Economic Outlook* or International Labour Organisation, *Bulletin of Labour Statistics*. Data on population (and its growth rate) and the growth of per capita real GDP for the 1980-1990 and 1985-1994 periods are also given. Finally, the 1994 (or most recent) per capita GDP measured in 1985 U.S. dollars are also presented for each country. These data are updates of the estimates of Robert Summers and Alan Heston, *Penn World Tables* (Cambridge: National Bureau of Economic Research, 1994), which were derived by the purchasing power parity method. We believe that they are the most accurate currently available set of income comparisons across countries. The Summers and Heston data generally ran through 1992. We used the 1993 and 1994 growth of per capita real GDP *measured in domestic currency* to update the 1992 country figures of Summers and Heston to 1994 (or the most recent year for which the GDP data were available). This is the same set of data and procedures that we followed when making income comparisons across countries presented in other sections of this study.

# ARGENTINA

## Part 1: The Economic Freedom Ratings for the Components and Various Area and Summary Indexes: 1975, 1980, 1985, 1990 and 1993-95.

(The numbers in parentheses indicate the actual values for the components.)

### Summary Ratings

|      | Ie  | Is1 | Is2 |
|------|-----|-----|-----|
| 1975 | 3.1 | 3.1 | 3.1 |
| 1980 | 3.3 | 3.6 | 3.4 |
| 1985 | 2.5 | 2.5 | 2.6 |
| 1990 | 3.4 | 3.8 | 3.2 |
| 1993-95 | 6.2 | 6.3 | 6.2 |

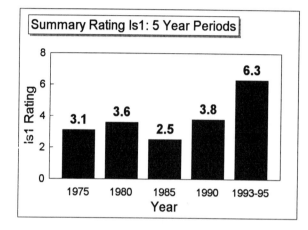

| Components of Economic Freedom | 1975 | | 1980 | | 1985 | | 1990 | | 1993-95 | |
|---|---|---|---|---|---|---|---|---|---|---|
| **I. Money and Inflation** | **3.6** | | **3.6** | | **3.6** | | **3.6** | | **3.6** | |
| (a) Annual Money Growth (last 5 yrs.) | 0 | (78.2) | 0 | (150.0) | 0 | (295.3) | 0 | (515.4) | 0 | (371.6) |
| (b) Inflation Variablity (last 5 yrs.) | 0 | (61.8) | 0 | (119.8) | 0 | (207.6) | 0 | (1185.0) | 0 | (793.4) |
| (c) Ownership of Foreign Currency | 10 | | 10 | | 10 | | 10 | | 10 | |
| (d) Maint. of Bank Account Abroad | 10 | | 10 | | 10 | | 10 | | 10 | |
| | | | | | | | | | | |
| **II. Government Operation** | **6.5** | | **3.9** | | **4.3** | | **3.8** | | **7.6** | |
| (a) Govern. Consumption (% of GDP) | 7 | (12.6) | 6 | (13.4) | 7 | (12.0) | 10 | (5.6) | 10 | (5.1) |
| (b) Government Enterprises | 6 | | 4 | | 4 | | 4 | | 6 | |
| (c) Price Controls | - | | - | | - | | 0 | | 8 | |
| (d) Entry Into Business | - | | - | | - | | - | | 10 | |
| (e) Legal System | - | | - | | - | | - | | 2.5 | |
| (f) Avoidance of Neg. Interest Rates | - | | 0 | | 0 | | 0 | | 8 | |
| | | | | | | | | | | |
| **III. Takings** | **3.5** | | **4.4** | | **2.1** | | **4.9** | | **5.4** | |
| (a) Transfers and Subsidies (% of GDP) | 4 | (7.9) | 4 | (9.7) | 3 | (11.7) | 4 | (8.5) | 3 | (12.8) |
| (b) Marginal Tax Rates (Top Rate) | 4 | (51) | 6 | (45) | 2 | (62) | 7 | (35) | 9 | (30) |
| (c) Conscription | 0 | | 0 | | 0 | | 0 | | 0 | |
| | | | | | | | | | | |
| **IV. International Sector** | **0.3** | | **2.5** | | **0.7** | | **2.8** | | **7.7** | |
| (a) Taxes on International Trade (Avg.) | 0 | (12.9) | 1 | (9.5) | 0 | (12.7) | 0 | (12.8) | - | |
| (b) Black Market Exchange Rates (Prem.) | 1 | (124) | 8 | (1) | 2 | (40) | 10 | (0) | 10 | (0) |
| (c) Size of Trade Sector (% of GDP) | 0 | (11.8) | 0 | (11.6) | 1 | (18.0) | 0 | (15.3) | 0 | (14.8) |
| (d) Capital Transactions with Foreigners | 0 | | 0 | | 0 | | 0 | | 10 | |

## Part 2: Recent Economic Indicators:

| Population 1994: | 33.9 | **Real Per Capita GDP :** | 1994 = | $6,025 |
|---|---|---|---|---|
| (in millions) | | (in 1985 U.S. dollars) | | |
| Annual Rate of Change (1980-94): | 1.3% | Avg. Growth Rate: | 1980-90 = | -2.3% |
| | | | 1985-94 = | 2.2% |

| Economic Indicators: | 1987 | 1988 | 1989 | 1990 | 1991 | 1992 | 1993 | 1994 |
|---|---|---|---|---|---|---|---|---|
| Change in Real GDP:Aggregate | 2.6 | -1.9 | -6.2 | 0.1 | 8.9 | 8.7 | 6.0 | 7.1 |
| : Per Capita | 1.3 | -3.2 | -7.5 | -1.2 | 7.6 | 7.4 | 4.7 | 5.8 |
| Inflation Rate (CPI) | 131.3 | 343.0 | 3079.8 | 2314.0 | 171.7 | 24.9 | 10.6 | 4.2 |
| Change in Money Supply: (M1) | 98.6 | 231.9 | 2765.5 | 1504.9 | 277.5 | 79.1 | 35.4 | 22.0 |
| : (M2) | 133.4 | 345.5 | 2347.3 | 1065.8 | 251.2 | 78.6 | 51.1 | - |
| Investment/GDP Ratio | 19.6 | 18.6 | 15.5 | 14.5 | 15.0 | 17.0 | 18.6 | 19.9 |
| Central Government Budget Deficit (-) or Surplus (+) As a Percent of GDP | -2.9 | -1.9 | -0.4 | - | - | +0.1 | -0.7 | -0.7 |
| Unemployment Rate | 5.3 | 6.0 | 7.4 | 7.4 | 5.8 | 6.7 | 10.1 | - |

Other than perhaps New Zealand, Argentina has moved more rapidly toward a free economy during the last decade than any other country. In both 1975 and 1985, the economic freedom rating of Argentina placed it in the Bottom Ten among the more than 100 countries in our study. Trade restrictions, monetary expansion, hyperinflation, high taxes, and government regulations characterized the Argentine economy for years. This began to change in the late 1980s. Exchange rate controls were eliminated and the Argentine peso was anchored to the U.S. dollar (1 peso=$1). Monetary policy was conducted so as to maintain this relationship. Several government enterprises were privatized; credit market restrictions were relaxed; marginal tax rates were reduced (the top rate was cut from 62% in 1985 to 35% in 1990 and 30% in 1994). Most restrictions on capital transactions with foreigners were also eliminated.

The Argentine economy was transformed and it is now on a healthy growth path. During the last two years, the annual growth of per capita GDP has averaged 5.3%, compared to *minus* 2.3% during 1980-1990. The inflation rate has decelerated sharply from over 2000% in 1990 to 25% in 1992 and 4% in 1994. While the transformation to date is impressive, the Argentine transition to a free economy is not yet finished. Argentina desperately needs a prolonged period of relative price stability. The fall out from the Mexican monetary crisis of late 1994 complicated the achievement of this objective, but thus far Argentina has managed to stay on course. In addition, movement toward a more flexible labor market is critical. Recently, the combination of dynamic change and wage inflexibility has led to rising unemployment. If Argentina can move ahead in these two areas, its economic future will be bright.

# AUSTRALIA

## Part 1: The Economic Freedom Ratings for the Components and Various Area and Summary Indexes:   1975, 1980, 1985, 1990 and 1993-95.

(The numbers in parentheses indicate the actual values for the components.

### Summary Ratings

| | Ie | Is1 | Is2 |
|------|-----|-----|-----|
| 1975 | 5.4 | 5.0 | 6.1 |
| 1980 | 6.0 | 5.5 | 6.8 |
| 1985 | 6.6 | 5.9 | 7.5 |
| 1990 | 6.5 | 6.0 | 7.3 |
| 1993-95 | 7.3 | 6.8 | 8.0 |

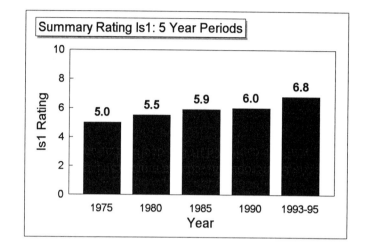

Summary Rating Is1: 5 Year Periods

| Components of Economic Freedom | 1975 | | 1980 | | 1985 | | 1990 | | 1993-95 | |
|---|---|---|---|---|---|---|---|---|---|---|
| **I.  Money and Inflation** | **7.4** | | **8.2** | | **8.7** | | **7.6** | | **8.5** | |
| (a)  Annual Money Growth (last 5 yrs.) | 7 | (7.0) | 5 | (8.7) | 8 | (3.3) | 3 | (11.9) | 5 | (9.6) |
| (b)  Inflation Variablity (last 5 yrs.) | 5 | (4.2) | 9 | (1.6) | 8 | (2.2) | 9 | (1.9) | 10 | (0.8) |
| (c)  Ownership of Foreign Currency | 10 | | 10 | | 10 | | 10 | | 10 | |
| (d)  Maint. of Bank Account Abroad | 10 | | 10 | | 10 | | 10 | | 10 | |
| | | | | | | | | | | |
| **II.  Government Operation** | **4.4** | | **5.3** | | **5.3** | | **5.5** | | **6.9** | |
| (a)  Govern. Consumption (% of GDP) | 3 | (17.2) | 2 | (18.0) | 2 | (18.9) | 2 | (17.8) | 2 | (19.0) |
| (b)  Government Enterprises | 6 | | 6 | | 6 | | 6 | | 6 | |
| (c)  Price Controls | - | | - | | - | | 6 | | 7 | |
| (d)  Entry Into Business | - | | - | | - | | - | | 10 | |
| (e)  Legal System | - | | - | | - | | - | | 7.5 | |
| (f) Avoidance of Neg. Interest Rates | 4 | | 10 | | 10 | | 10 | | 10 | |
| | | | | | | | | | | |
| **III.  Takings** | **3.9** | | **3.9** | | **3.5** | | **3.9** | | **4.4** | |
| (a)  Transfers and Subsidies (% of GDP) | 4 | (8.5) | 4 | (10.1) | 3 | (10.9) | 3 | (10.7) | 3 | (13.4) |
| (b)  Marginal Tax Rates (Top Rate) | 2 | (64) | 2 | (62) | 2 | (60) | 3 | (49) | 4 | (47) |
| (c) Conscription | 10 | | 10 | | 10 | | 10 | | 10 | |
| | | | | | | | | | | |
| **IV.  International Sector** | **5.2** | | **5.6** | | **7.1** | | **7.8** | | **8.2** | |
| (a)  Taxes on International Trade (Avg.) | 6 | (4.4) | 7 | (3.6) | 7 | (3.2) | 7 | (3.1) | 8 | (2.3) |
| (b)  Black Market Exchange Rates (Prem.) | 8 | (1) | 8 | (1) | 10 | (0) | 10 | (0) | 10 | (0) |
| (c)  Size of Trade Sector (% of GDP) | 4 | (28.8) | 5 | (33.9) | 6 | (35.2) | 5 | (34.3) | 6 | (37.4) |
| (d)  Capital Transactions with Foreigners | 2 | | 2 | | 5 | | 8 | | 8 | |

## Part 2: Recent Economic Indicators

| Population 1994: | 18.0 | **Real Per Capita GDP** : | 1994 = | $15,169 |
|---|---|---|---|---|
| (in millions) | | (in 1985 U.S. dollars) | | |
| Annual Rate of Change (1980-94): | 1.4% | A vg. Growth Rate: 1980-90 = | | 1.6% |
| | | 1985-94 = | | 1.6% |

| Economic Indicators: | 1987 | 1988 | 1989 | 1990 | 1991 | 1992 | 1993 | 1994 |
|---|---|---|---|---|---|---|---|---|
| Change in Real GDP: Aggregate | 4.9 | 4.4 | 4.4 | 1.2 | -1.1 | 2.6 | 4.1 | 5.0 |
| : Per Capita | 3.3 | 2.6 | 2.6 | -0.3 | -2.7 | 1.4 | 2.8 | 3.6 |
| Inflation Rate (CPI) | 8.5 | 7.2 | 7.6 | 7.3 | 3.2 | 1.0 | 1.8 | 1.9 |
| Change in Money Supply: (M1) | 17.1 | 24 | 19.8 | 3.5 | 8.5 | 18.1 | 17.8 | 15.4 |
| : (M2) | 12.7 | 14.3 | -26.3 | 15.8 | 5.6 | 4.7 | 6.9 | 8.1 |
| Investment/GDP Ratio | 24.1 | 25.2 | 26.7 | 22.6 | 19.6 | 19.2 | 19.6 | 20.8 |
| Central Government Budget | | | | | | | | |
| Deficit (-) or Surplus (+) | | | | | | | | |
| As a Percent of GDP | 0.0 | +1.3 | +1.4 | +0.7 | -2.6 | -3.9 | -5.0 | -4.3 |
| Unemployment Rate | 8.0 | 7.2 | 6.1 | 6.9 | 9.5 | 10.7 | 10.7 | 9.6 |

The average of our three indexes places the Australian economy in a tie with Ireland as the 8th freest in the world. Moreover, its economic freedom rating has registered modest but steady increases during the last two decades. No doubt, this relatively high ranking and consistent increases are, in large part, responsible for the high level of real GDP ($15,169 in 1994) attained by this country.

The strengths of this economy are in the financial and international areas: relatively free trade, open capital markets, relatively stable rate of inflation, and a competitive and open credit market. It also earns high marks for a relatively competitive business environment and the security of property rights, including equal treatment under the law. The major weaknesses are the high level of government consumption—19% of the GDP in 1993—and a large and growing transfer sector. Most recently, a little more than 13% of GDP was transferred from one citizen to another, up from 8.5% of GDP in 1975. Policies of this type generally culminate with large budget deficits and a high rate of unemployment. These signs are increasingly apparent in Australia. In the 1990s, the budget deficits of the central government averaged approximately 4% of GDP and the unemployment rate hovered around 10% of the labor force. Like several other high-income industrial nations, Australia must reduce the size of government and its transfer and regulatory policies that are the primary cause of its unemployment problem if it wants to achieve strong growth and continued prosperity in the future.

115

# AUSTRIA

**Part 1: The Economic Freedom Ratings for the Components and Various Area and Summary Indexes: 1975, 1980, 1985, 1990 and 1993-95.**

(The numbers in parentheses indicate the actual values for the components.)

| | Ie | Is1 | Is2 |
|---|---|---|---|
| **Summary Rating** | | | |
| 1975 | 4.8 | 4.6 | 4.9 |
| 1980 | 5.2 | 4.6 | 5.4 |
| 1985 | 5.3 | 4.6 | 5.5 |
| 1990 | 6.0 | 5.4 | 6.7 |
| 1993-95 | 6.2 | 5.8 | 6.9 |

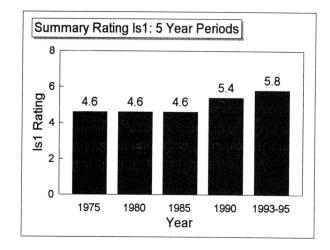

| Components of Economic Freedom | 1975 | | 1980 | | 1985 | | 1990 | | 1993-95 | |
|---|---|---|---|---|---|---|---|---|---|---|
| **I.  Money and Inflation** | **7.1** | | **8.3** | | **8.0** | | **9.4** | | **9.4** | |
| (a)  Annual Money Growth (last 5 yrs.) | 6 | (8.0) | 10 | (1.0) | 9 | (2.3) | 8 | (4.2) | 8 | (4.9) |
| (b)  Inflation Variablity (last 5 yrs.) | 10 | (1.1) | 10 | (0.6) | 10 | (1.3) | 10 | (0.9) | 10 | (0.4) |
| (c)  Ownership of Foreign Currency | 10 | | 10 | | 10 | | 10 | | 10 | |
| (d)  Maint. of Bank Account Abroad | 0 | | 0 | | 0 | | 10 | | 10 | |
| | | | | | | | | | | |
| **II. Government Operation** | **3.2** | | **3.3** | | **3.7** | | **4.1** | | **5.0** | |
| (a)  Govern. Consumption (% of GDP) | 3 | (17.2) | 2 | (18.0) | 2 | (18.9) | 2 | (17.8) | 2 | (19.0) |
| (b)  Government Enterprises | 2 | | 2 | | 2 | | 2 | | 2 | |
| (c)  Price Controls | - | | - | | - | | 5 | | 6 | |
| (d)  Entry Into Business | - | | - | | - | | - | | 7.5 | |
| (e)  Legal System | - | | - | | - | | - | | 7.5 | |
| (f)  Avoidance of Neg. Interest Rates | 6 | | 8 | | 10 | | 10 | | 6 | |
| | | | | | | | | | | |
| **III. Takings** | **2.3** | | **1.3** | | **0.9** | | **1.9** | | **2.3** | |
| (a)  Transfers and Subsidies (% of GDP) | 1 | (19.4) | 1 | (22.1) | 0 | (23.1) | 0 | (22.4) | 0 | (23.4) |
| (b)  Marginal Tax Rates (Top Rate) | 4 | (54) | 2 | (62) | 2 | (62) | 4 | (50) | 5 | (50) |
| (c)  Conscription | 0 | | 0 | | 0 | | 0 | | 0 | |
| | | | | | | | | | | |
| **IV. International Sector** | **6.6** | | **7.1** | | **7.4** | | **8.1** | | **8.7** | |
| (a)  Taxes on International Trade (Avg.) | 8 | (1.7) | 9 | (0.7) | 9 | (0.6) | 9 | (0.7) | 9 | (0.7) |
| (b)  Black Market Exchange Rates (Prem.) | 10 | (0) | 10 | (0) | 10 | (0) | 10 | 0 | 10 | (0) |
| (c)  Size of Trade Sector (% of GDP) | 6 | (63.1) | 7 | (75.6) | 9 | (81.2) | 8 | (79.1) | 7 | (77.8) |
| (d)  Capital Transactions with Foreigners | 2 | | 2 | | 2 | | 5 | | 8 | |

## Part 2: Recent Economic Indicators

| | | | | |
|---|---|---|---|---|
| **Population 1994:** | 7.9 | **Real Per Capita GDP** [a] **:** | 1994= | $13,250 |
| (in millions) | | (in 1985 U.S. dollars) | | |
| Annual Rate of Change (1980-94): | 0.2% | Avg. Growth Rate: | 1980-90= | 1.9% |
| | | | 1985-94= | 1.8% |

| Economic Indicators: | 1987 | 1988 | 1989 | 1990 | 1991 | 1992 | 1993 | 1994 |
|---|---|---|---|---|---|---|---|---|
| Change in Real GDP: Aggregate | 1.7 | 4.1 | 3.8 | 4.2 | 2.9 | 1.8 | -0.1 | 3.0 |
| : Per Capita | 1.5 | 3.8 | 3.4 | 3.0 | 1.6 | 1.1 | -1.4 | 2.8 |
| Inflation Rate (CPI) | 1.4 | 1.9 | 2.6 | 3.3 | 3.3 | 4.0 | 3.6 | 3.0 |
| Change in Money Supply: (M1) | 10.0 | 10.2 | 6.1 | 1.7 | 6.0 | 5.2 | 8.6 | 11.9 |
| : (M2) | 8.8 | 6.7 | 6.9 | 7.2 | 8.4 | 7.6 | 6.8 | 5.3 |
| Investment/GDP Ratio | 24.0 | 24.8 | 25.4 | 25.2 | 26.3 | 25.1 | 24.2 | 24.1 |
| Central Government Budget Deficit (-) or Surplus (+) As a Percent of GDP | -5.5 | -5.0 | -3.8 | -4.5 | -4.8 | -3.9 | -2.8 | -4.0 |
| Unemployment Rate | 5.6 | 5.3 | 5.0 | 5.4 | 5.8 | 5.9 | 6.8 | 6.5 |

a Derived by purchasing power parity method.

The average of our three summary indexes ranked Austria as the 23rd most free economy in 1993-1995. The Is1 index placed it 36th.

Austria's rating has improved during the last decade, primarily as the result of a reduction in the top marginal tax rate from 62% to 50% and relaxation of restrictions on capital mobility. The most recent improvement may partially reflect the change in the structure of the index, rather that a genuine move toward a freer economy. The "entry into business" and "legal structure" components are included only in the most recent index. Since the Austrian ratings for these two components are relatively high, their inclusion pushes the summary indexes upward.

The major deficiencies of this economy are its huge government consumption and transfer sectors. Government now takes over 40% of the earnings of Austrians—19% for government consumption and another 23% for transfers and subsidies. In order to finance this high level of government spending, Austria has resorted to large budget deficits. During the last decade, these deficits have averaged approximately 4% of GDP. As a result, the national debt has been increasing as a share of the economy. In turn, this soon pushes interest costs up, which makes it still more difficult to control government spending. Credit markets will not accept a continuously rising debt to GDP ratio. Therefore, like several other European nations, Austria will be forced to reduce the size of its deficit in the near future.

# BELGIUM

## Part 1: The Economic Freedom Ratings for the Components and Various Area and Summary Indexes: 1975, 1980, 1985, 1990 and 1993-95.

(The numbers in parentheses indicate the actual values for the components.)

### Summary Ratings

|         | Ie  | Is1 | Is2 |
|---------|-----|-----|-----|
| 1975    | 6.2 | 5.5 | 7.3 |
| 1980    | 6.8 | 5.7 | 8.0 |
| 1985    | 6.9 | 5.8 | 8.1 |
| 1990    | 6.7 | 5.9 | 7.5 |
| 1993-95 | 7.1 | 6.3 | 7.8 |

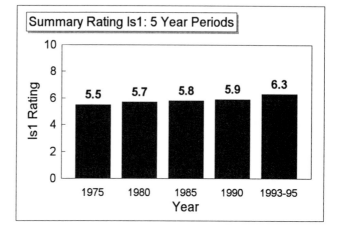

Summary Rating Is1: 5 Year Periods

| Components of Economic Freedom | 1975 | | 1980 | | 1985 | | 1990 | | 1993-95 | |
|---|---|---|---|---|---|---|---|---|---|---|
| **I. Money and Inflation** | **7.8** | | **9.7** | | **10.0** | | **9.7** | | **9.4** | |
| (a) Annual Money Growth (last 5 yrs.) | 6 | (7.9) | 10 | (1.5) | 10 | (1.7) | 9 | (2.9) | 8 | (3.3) |
| (b) Inflation Variablity (last 5 yrs.) | 7 | (3.0) | 9 | (1.6) | 10 | (0.8) | 10 | (1.0) | 10 | (0.4) |
| (c) Ownership of Foreign Currency | 10 | | 10 | | 10 | | 10 | | 10 | |
| (d) Maint. of Bank Account Abroad | 10 | | 10 | | 10 | | 10 | | 10 | |
| | | | | | | | | | | |
| **II. Government Operation** | **4.8** | | **5.3** | | **5.7** | | **5.1** | | **6.8** | |
| (a) Govern. Consumption (% of GDP) | 3 | (16.5) | 2 | (17.8) | 3 | (17.1) | 5 | (14.5) | 5 | (15.0) |
| (b) Government Enterprises | 6 | | 6 | | 6 | | 6 | | 6 | |
| (c) Price Controls | - | | - | | - | | 2 | | 5 | |
| (d) Entry Into Business | - | | - | | - | | - | | 7.5 | |
| (e) Legal System | - | | - | | - | | - | | 10 | |
| (f) Avoidance of Neg. Interest Rates | 6 | | 10 | | 10 | | 10 | | 10 | |
| | | | | | | | | | | |
| **III. Takings** | **0.9** | | **0.0** | | **0.0** | | **0.9** | | **0.9** | |
| (a) Transfers and Subsidies (% of GDP) | 0 | (28.5) | 0 | (26.0) | 0 | (27.6) | 0 | (25.0) | 0 | (26.6) |
| (b) Marginal Tax Rates (Top Rate) | 2 | (64) | 0 | (76) | 0 | (76) | 2 | (55-65) | 2 | (55-65) |
| (c) Conscription | 0 | | 0 | | 0 | | 0 | | 0 | |
| | | | | | | | | | | |
| **IV. International Sector** | **9.8** | | **10.0** | | **10.0** | | **10.0** | | **10.0** | |
| (a) Taxes on International Trade (Avg.) | 10 | (0.0) | 10 | (0.0) | 10 | (0.0) | 10 | (0.0) | 10 | (0.0) |
| (b) Black Market Exchange Rates (Prem.) | 10 | (0) | 10 | (0) | 10 | (0) | 10 | (0) | 10 | (0) |
| (c) Size of Trade Sector (% of GDP) | 9 | (107.0) | 10 | (128.3) | 10 | (151.2) | 10 | (145.0) | 10 | (135.6) |
| (d) Capital Transactions with Foreigners | 10 | | 10 | | 10 | | 10 | | 10 | |

## Part 2: Recent Economic Indicators

| | | | | |
|---|---|---|---|---|
| **Population 1994:** | 10.1 | **Real Per Capita GDP** : | 1994= | $13,735 |
| (in millions) | | (in U.S. dollars) | | |
| Annual Rate of Change (1980-94): | 0.2% | Avg. Growth Rate: | 1980-90= | 1.8% |
| | | | 1985-94= | 1.9% |

| Economic Indicators: | 1987 | 1988 | 1989 | 1990 | 1991 | 1992 | 1993 | 1994 |
|---|---|---|---|---|---|---|---|---|
| Change in Real GDP: Aggregate | 2.0 | 5.0 | 3.6 | 3.2 | 2.2 | 1.9 | -1.7 | 3.7 |
| : Per Capita | 1.9 | 4.4 | 3.3 | 2.9 | 1.9 | 1.5 | -1.4 | 3.5 |
| Inflation Rate (CPI) | 1.6 | 1.2 | 3.1 | 3.5 | 3.2 | 2.4 | 2.8 | 2.4 |
| Change in Money Supply: (M1) | 7.0 | 4.0 | 3.1 | 3.1 | 10.4 | 1.5 | 7.3 | 10.4 |
| : (M2) | 10.4 | 7.3 | 7.1 | 7.3 | 5.5 | 10.8 | 13.0 | 1.2 |
| Investment/GDP Ratio | 16.2 | 18.1 | 19.8 | 20.6 | 19.5 | 19.3 | 19.4 | 19.3 |
| Central Government Budget Deficit (-) or Surplus (+) As a Percent of GDP | -7.8 | -6.5 | -6.6 | -5.7 | -6.8 | -7.1 | -6.6 | -5.8 |
| Unemployment Rate | 11.9 | 11.1 | 10.2 | 9.6 | 10.2 | 11.2 | 13.1 | 13.8 |

Based on the average of our three indexes, the Belgium economy was the 12th freest (tied with Germany and Malaysia) in the world in the mid-1990s. (Note: its Is1 summary rating placed it in a tie for 21st place.) Its summary ratings indicate that it has made small but steady strides toward economic freedom during the last two decades.

From the viewpoint of economic freedom, monetary stability and the international sector are Belgium's strengths. In recent years, monetary expansion has been modest, prices relatively stable, and citizens are free to maintain foreign currency bank accounts. The sore spot for Belgium is its takings policy. Transfers and subsidies comprise approximately 25% of GDP. In addition, marginal tax rates, while curtailed from a high of 76% in the 1980s, continue to take approximately 60% of the marginal earnings of productive citizens. Belgium's top rates are among the highest in the world.

The growth of the welfare state has been financed with large budget deficits in recent years. Since 1987 the budget deficit of the central government has persistently exceeded 6% of GDP. This is an unsustainable level and it has drastically pushed up the government interest cost. Given that taxes are already pushing their revenue maximum level, bond markets will force the government to curtail its spending. Belgium is a high income country—its real per capita GDP in 1994 was a healthy $13,735. It is perfectly capable of cutting spending and modifying some of its welfare state practices in order to meet its financial obligations to bondholders. However, this will mean a change of direction and, if political considerations precluded this option, this country could be headed for a financial crisis.

# BOLIVIA

**Part 1: The Economic Freedom Ratings for the Components and Various Area and Summary Indexes: 1975, 1980, 1985, 1990 and 1993-95.**

(The numbers in parentheses indicate the actual values for the components.)

|      | **Summary Ratings** | | |
|------|------|------|------|
|      | **Ie** | **Is1** | **Is2** |
| 1975 | 5.3 | 5.5 | 4.9 |
| 1980 | 4.4 | 4.5 | 4.3 |
| 1985 | 3.2 | 4.2 | 2.2 |
| 1990 | 5.8 | 6.3 | 5.5 |
| 1993-95 | 6.1 | 6.4 | 5.9 |

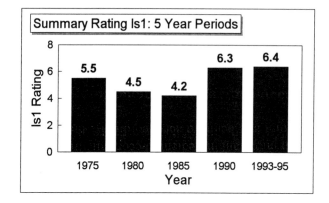

Summary Rating Is1: 5 Year Periods

| Components of Economic Freedom | 1975 | | 1980 | | 1985 | | 1990 | | 1993-95 | |
|---|---|---|---|---|---|---|---|---|---|---|
| **I. Money and Inflation** | **4.6** | | **4.6** | | **0.0** | | **3.9** | | **5.6** | |
| (a) Annual Money Growth (last 5 yrs.) | 2 | (19.3) | 1 | (21.3) | 0 | (569.5) | 1 | (38.1) | 1 | (33.0) |
| (b) Inflation Variablity (last 5 yrs.) | 1 | (21.0) | 2 | (11.0) | 0 | (4349.2) | 0 | (91.2) | 5 | (4.3) |
| (c) Ownership of Foreign Currency | 10 | | 10 | | 0 | | 10 | | 10 | |
| (d) Maint. of Bank Account Abroad | 10 | | 10 | | 0 | | 10 | | 10 | |
| | | | | | | | | | | |
| **II. Government Operation** | **7.0** | | **6.0** | | **3.9** | | **5.7** | | **5.9** | |
| (a) Govern. Consumption (% of GDP) | 8 | (10.5) | 6 | (14.1) | 6 | (13.3) | 6 | (14.0) | 5 | (15.2) |
| (b) Government Enterprises | 6 | | 6 | | 4 | | 4 | | 4 | |
| (c) Price Controls | - | | - | | - | | 6 | | 8 | |
| (d) Entry Into Business | - | | - | | - | | - | | 7.5 | |
| (e) Legal System | - | | - | | - | | - | | 2.5 | |
| (f) Avoidance of Neg. Interest Rates | - | | 6 | | 0 | | 8 | | 8 | |
| | | | | | | | | | | |
| **III. Takings** | **7.5** | | **5.0** | | **7.3** | | **7.9** | | **7.9** | |
| (a) Transfers and Subsidies (% of GDP) | 10 | (1.3) | 9 | (1.6) | 9 | (1.8) | 8 | (2.8) | 8 | (2.6) |
| (b) Marginal Tax Rates (Top Rate) | - | | 3 | (48) | 8 | (30) | 10 | (10) | 10 | (13) |
| (c) Conscription | 0 | | 0 | | 0 | | 0 | | 0 | |
| | | | | | | | | | | |
| **IV. International Sector** | **4.2** | | **2.9** | | **3.4** | | **6.5** | | **6.1** | |
| (a) Taxes on International Trade (Avg.) | 2 | (8.9) | 3 | (7.8) | 4 | (7.0) | 8 | (2.3) | 7 | (2.8) |
| (b) Black Market Exchange Rates (Prem.) | 6 | (5) | 4 | (22) | 5 | (9) | 10 | (0) | 8 | (1) |
| (c) Size of Trade Sector (% of GDP) | 8 | (58.2) | 2 | (37.7) | 2 | (30.2) | 5 | (46.8) | 3 | (40.4) |
| (d) Capital Transactions with Foreigners | 2 | | 2 | | 2 | | 2 | | 5 | |

## Part 2: Recent Economic Indicators

| Population 1994: | 7.9 | **Real Per Capita GDP** : | 1993 = | $1,730 |
|---|---|---|---|---|
| (in millions) | | (in 1985 U.S. dollars) | | |
| Annual Rate of Change (1980-94): | 2.5 | Avg. Growth Rate: | 1980-90= | -2.4% |
| | | | 1985-93= | 0.1% |

| Economic Indicators: | 1987 | 1988 | 1989 | 1990 | 1991 | 1992 | 1993 | 1994 |
|---|---|---|---|---|---|---|---|---|
| Change in Real GDP: Aggregate | 2.6 | 3.0 | 2.8 | 4.1 | 4.6 | 3.4 | 3.0 | |
| : Per Capita | 0.1 | 0.5 | 0.3 | 1.6 | 2.1 | 0.9 | 0.5 | |
| Inflation Rate (CPI) | 14.6 | 16.0 | 15.2 | 17.1 | 21.4 | 12.1 | 8.5 | - |
| Change in Money Supply: (M1) | 61.7 | 27.4 | 18.6 | 39.4 | 45.1 | 32.9 | 30.0 | 28.7 |
| : (M2) | 108.8 | 24.6 | 19.5 | 53.1 | 50.5 | 38.4 | 33.7 | 22.6 |
| Investment/GDP Ratio | 14.9 | 11.3 | 9.8 | 9.2 | 13.2 | - | - | |
| Central Government Budget | | | | | | | | |
| Deficit (-) or Surplus (+) | | | | | | | | |
| As a Percent of GDP | +0.7 | -0.6 | -1.2 | -1.5 | -0.1 | -1.8 | - | - |
| Unemployment Rate | 20.5 | 18.0 | 20.0 | 19.0 | | | | |

Historically, the potential of this poor South American country has been stifled by monetary instability and hyperinflation. In 1985 Bolivia's inflation rate soared to over 13,000% (this means that prices increased by a factor of 130 in one year). Inflation rates of this magnitude undermine economic progress, pretty much regardless of the policies in other areas.

Attempting to rebound from this catastrophic situation, Bolivia has taken a number of constructive steps in recent years. The freedom to maintain foreign currency bank accounts which was denied during the inflation of the mid-1980s has now been restored. The top marginal tax rate was reduced from 48% in 1980 to 10% in 1990 and 13% in 1994. Tariff rates were cut by approximately a third during the 1980s. Relaxation of exchange rate controls has just about eliminated the black market in this area. There has also been some relaxation of the restrictions on the movement of capital. As the result of the changes, Bolivia now ranks in the upper third among the nations in our study.

However, unless monetary policy is brought under control, a Bolivian "economic miracle" is unlikely. The growth of the M1 money supply continues to exceed 30%, a figure far too expansionary for the achievement of a low and stable rate of inflation. Stable money matters. It is an important ingredient of economic freedom. The sooner Bolivian policy makers understand this point and begin to act accordingly, the brighter the future of this troubled economy.

# BOTSWANA

**Part 1: The Economic Freedom Ratings for the Components and Various Area and Summary Indexes: 1975, 1980, 1985, 1990 and 1993-95.**

(The numbers in parentheses the actual values for the components.)

### Summary Ratings

|  | Ie | Is1 | Is2 |
|---|---|---|---|
| 1975 | 3.9 | 3.5 | 4.0 |
| 1980 | 3.8 | 3.5 | 4.1 |
| 1985 | 4.7 | 4.4 | 5.1 |
| 1990 | 4.4 | 4.3 | 4.4 |
| 1993-95 | 5.6 | 5.4 | 5.8 |

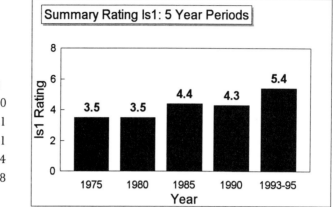

Summary Rating Is1: 5 Year Periods

| Components of Economic Freedom | 1975 | | 1980 | | 1985 | | 1990 | | 1993-95 | |
|---|---|---|---|---|---|---|---|---|---|---|
| **I. Money and Inflation** | **1.4** | | **1.6** | | **3.1** | | **1.3** | | **5.4** | |
| (a) Annual Money Growth (last 5 yrs.) | - | | 3 | (11.9) | 8 | (4.2) | 2 | (15.4) | 10 | (0.5) |
| (b) Inflation Variablity (last 5 yrs.) | 3 | (7.7) | 2 | (8.8) | 2 | (8.8) | 2 | (8.7) | 7 | (2.5) |
| (c) Ownership of Foreign Currency | 0 | | 0 | | 0 | | 0 | | 0 | |
| (d) Maint. of Bank Account Abroad | 0 | | 0 | | 0 | | 0 | | 0 | |
| | | | | | | | | | | |
| **II. Government Operation** | **5.1** | | **4.5** | | **4.9** | | **4.6** | | **5.1** | |
| (a) Govern. Consumption (% of GDP) | 2 | (18.8) | 1 | (19.3) | 0 | (24.2) | 2 | (19.1) | 0 | (24.6) |
| (b) Government Enterprises | 8 | | 8 | | 8 | | 6 | | 6 | |
| (c) Price Controls | - | | - | | - | | 6 | | 6 | |
| (d) Entry Into Business | - | | - | | - | | - | | 7.5 | |
| (e) Legal System | - | | - | | - | | - | | 5 | |
| (f) Avoidance of Neg. Interest Rates | - | | 4 | | 8 | | 4 | | 6 | |
| | | | | | | | | | | |
| **III. Takings** | **3.7** | | **3.7** | | **4.3** | | **4.7** | | **5.7** | |
| (a) Transfers and Subsidies (% of GDP) | 6 | (5.5) | 6 | (4.9) | 5 | (7.3) | 5 | (6.6) | 5 | (6.9) |
| (b) Marginal Tax Rates (Top Rate) | 0 | (75) | 0 | (75) | 2 | (60) | 3 | (50) | 5 | (40) |
| (c) Conscription | 10 | | 10 | | 10 | | 10 | | 10 | |
| | | | | | | | | | | |
| **IV. International Sector** | **3.4** | | **4.1** | | **5.0** | | **5.5** | | **5.5** | |
| (a) Taxes on International Trade (Avg.) | 1 | (10.4) | 0 | (12.8) | 3 | (7.1) | 4 | (6.6) | 1 | (9.6) |
| (b) Black Market Exchange Rates (Prem.) | 2 | (44) | 4 | (10) | 4 | (22) | 5 | (7) | 8 | (1) |
| (c) Size of Trade Sector (% of GDP) | 10 | (109.1) | 10 | (116.4) | 10 | (115.0) | 10 | (118.1) | 10 | (106.0) |
| (d) Capital Transactions with Foreigners | - | | 5 | | 5 | | 5 | | 5 | |

## Part 2: Recent Economic Indicators:

| | | | | | |
|---|---|---|---|---|---|
| **Population 1994:** | 1.5 | | **Real Per Capita GDP :** | 92 = | $3,350 |
| (in millions) | | | (in 1985 U.S. dollars) | | |
| Annual Rate of Change (1980-94): | 3.4% | | Avg. Growth Rate: | 1980-90 = | 6.4% |
| | | | | 1985-92 = | 4.6% |

| Economic Indicators: | 1987 | 1988 | 1989 | 1990 | 1991 | 1992 | 1993 | 1994 |
|---|---|---|---|---|---|---|---|---|
| Change in Real GDP:Aggregate | 8.9 | 15.3 | 13.1 | 5.7 | 8.8 | -2.9 | - | |
| : Per Capita | 5.5 | 11.9 | 9.7 | 2.3 | 5.4 | -6.3 | | |
| Inflation Rate (CPI) | 9.8 | 8.4 | 11.6 | 11.4 | 11.8 | 16.2 | 14.3 | 10.5 |
| Change in Money Supply: (M1) | 28.6 | 26.9 | 32.1 | 20.0 | 8.0 | 8.7 | 4.4 | |
| : (M2) | 38.4 | 35.5 | 38.3 | 12.0 | 20.0 | 17.8 | - | |
| Investment/GDP Ratio | 24.5 | 7.3 | 41.8 | - | - | - | - | |
| Central Government Budget Deficit (+) or Surplus (+) As a Percent of GDP | +14.2 | +15.6 | +9.6 | +11.7 | +10.0 | - | - | |
| Unemployment Rate | | | | | | | | |

This relatively small country is the freest among those on the African continent. With regard to economic freedom, a summary of the highlights would include:

- The average of the three ratings places it 46th among the countries in our study.

- Its economic freedom rating has increased substantially since 1980.

- Its strengths are a highly stable monetary policy (note the high ratings for both money expansion and price stability), absence of conscription, large trade sector, and exchange rate controls that have been relaxed considerably in recent years.

- Its major deficiencies are excessive regulation (note restrictions on foreign currency accounts, interest rates, and capital mobility), very large government consumption (particularly for a low-income nation), and high tariffs.

- Botswana's per capita GDP has grown rapidly; it increased at an annual rate of 6.4% in the 1980s and by a still healthy 4.6% since 1985.

123

# BRAZIL

## Part 1: The Economic Freedom Ratings for the Components and Various Area and Summary Indexes: 1975, 1980, 1985, 1990 and 1993-95.

(The numbers in parentheses indicate the actual values for the components.)

### Summary Ratings

|  | Ie | Is1 | Is2 |
|---|---|---|---|
| 1975 | 2.8 | 3.2 | 2.0 |
| 1980 | 2.5 | 2.7 | 1.7 |
| 1985 | 2.0 | 2.3 | 1.2 |
| 1990 | 2.1 | 2.9 | 1.4 |
| 1993-95 | 2.8 | 3.3 | 2.4 |

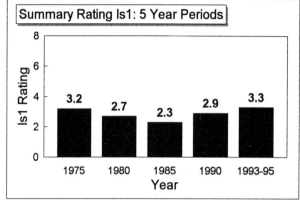

Summary Rating Is1: 5 Year Periods

| Components of Economic Freedom | 1975 | | 1980 | | 1985 | | 1990 | | 1993-95 | |
|---|---|---|---|---|---|---|---|---|---|---|
| **I. Money and Inflation** | **1.3** | | **0.6** | | **0.0** | | **0.0** | | **0.0** | |
| (a) Annual Money Growth (last 5 yrs.) | 1 | (28.9) | 1 | (41.6) | 0 | (137.8) | 0 | (648.6) | 0 | (1232.5) |
| (b) Inflation Variablity (last 5 yrs.) | 3 | (6.9) | 1 | (16.6) | 0 | (53.1) | 0 | (909.8) | 0 | (956.5) |
| (c) Ownership of Foreign Currency | 0 | | 0 | | 0 | | 0 | | 0 | |
| (d) Maint. of Bank Account Abroad | 0 | | 0 | | 0 | | 0 | | 0 | |
| | | | | | | | | | | |
| **II. Government Operation** | **6.0** | | **6.4** | | **3.9** | | **1.9** | | **3.2** | |
| (a) Govern. Consumption (% of GDP) | 8 | (10.6) | 9 | (9.2) | 8 | (9.9) | 5 | (15.5) | 3 | (16.5) |
| (b) Government Enterprises | 4 | | 4 | | 2 | | 2 | | 2 | |
| (c) Price Controls | - | | - | | - | | 0 | | 4 | |
| (d) Entry Into Business | - | | - | | - | | - | | 7.5 | |
| (e) Legal System | - | | - | | - | | - | | 0 | |
| (f) Avoidance of Neg. Interest Rates | - | | - | | 0 | | 0 | | 0 | |
| | | | | | | | | | | |
| **III. Takings** | **3.9** | | **3.1** | | **2.1** | | **5.4** | | **4.9** | |
| (a) Transfers and Subsidies (% of GDP) | - | | 3 | (12.4) | 4 | (10.0) | 3 | (10.7) | 3 | (11.8) |
| (b) Marginal Tax Rates (Top Rate) | 5 | (50) | 4 | (55) | 1 | (60) | 9 | (25) | 8 | (35) |
| (c) Conscription | 0 | | 0 | | 0 | | 0 | | 0 | |
| | | | | | | | | | | |
| **IV. International Sector** | **2.4** | | **1.7** | | **3.0** | | **2.9** | | **3.9** | |
| (a) Taxes on International Trade (Avg.) | 5 | (5.7) | 1 | (10.0) | 7 | (3.2) | 6 | (3.7) | 7 | (3.2) |
| (b) Black Market Exchange Rates (Prem.) | 2 | (49) | 4 | (18) | 2 | (49) | 4 | (10) | 6 | (5) |
| (c) Size of Trade Sector (% of GDP) | 2 | (19.0) | 2 | (20.4) | 2 | (19.3) | 0 | (12.6) | 1 | (16.5) |
| (d) Capital Transactions with Foreigners | 0 | | 0 | | 0 | | 0 | | 0 | |

## Part 2: Recent Economic Indicators:

| Population 1994: | 159.8 | | | | **Real Per Capita GDP** : | | 1994= | $4,118 |

Population 1994: 159.8 (in millions)
Annual Rate of Change (1980-94): 2.0%

Real Per Capita GDP : 1994= $4,118
(in 1985 U.S. dollars)
Avg. Growth Rate: 1980-90= -0.6%
1985-94= 0.8%

| Recent Economic Indicators: | 1987 | 1988 | 1989 | 1990 | 1991 | 1992 | 1993 | 1994 |
|---|---|---|---|---|---|---|---|---|
| Change in Real GDP: Aggregate | 3.6 | -0.1 | 3.3 | -4.4 | 0.2 | -0.8 | 4.1 | 5.7 |
| : Per Capita | 1.6 | -2.1 | 1.3 | -6.3 | -0.7 | -2.8 | 2.2 | 3.8 |
| Inflation Rate (CPI) | 229.7 | 682.3 | 1287.0 | 2937.8 | 440.9 | 1008.7 | 2148.4 | 2668.5 |
| Change in Money Supply (M1) | 149.2 | | - | - | 380.6 | 744.9 | 1584.4 | 2823.6 |
| : (M2) | 163.4 | - | - | - | - | - | - | |
| Investment/GDP Ratio | 22.2 | 22.7 | 24.8 | 21.6 | 19.0 | 19.1 | 21.0 | |
| Central Government Budget Deficit (-) or Surplus (+) As a Percent of GDP | -12.0 | -15.2 | -16.1 | -5.7 | -0.4 | -3.6 | - | - |
| Unemployment Rate | | 3.8 | 3.3 | 4.3 | 4.8 | 4.5 | 5.3 | |

The largest country in South America ranked 97th (based on the average of our three indexes; its Is1 summary rating placed it 93rd) among the 103 countries in our study. It was in the Bottom Ten for each of the five rating years covered by our study.

Brazil's policies conflict with economic freedom in almost every area. Its monetary policy is a disaster, characterized by excessive monetary growth and the consequent hyperinflation. During 1992-1994, both the money supply and the price level expanded at rates of approximately 2000%. Furthermore, it is illegal to maintain foreign currency bank accounts. Thus, Brazil's monetary policy and institutional arrangements undermine the workings of a market economy.

Nor is there much evidence of economic freedom in the area of government operations. Government consumption has increased substantially as a share of GDP during the last decade, the legal system often fails to support private property rights, and government enterprises are widespread. On a brighter note, the top marginal tax rate was reduced from 60% in 1985 to 35% in 1993-95. In addition, there were reductions in taxes on international trade (from 5.7% to 3.2% over two decades), and some relaxation of exchange rate controls.

As might be expected from its pattern of economic freedom, Brazil's growth record is dismal. Its real GDP per capita in 1994 was approximately the same as in 1980. Unless this nation makes a dramatic change, its economy will continue to stagnate.

# CAMEROON

**Part 1: The Economic Freedom Ratings for the Components and Various Area and Summary Indexes: 1975, 1980, 1985, 1990 and 1993-95.**

(The numbers in parentheses indicate the actual values for the components.)

|  | **Summary Ratings** | | |
|---|---|---|---|
|  | **Ie** | **Is1** | **Is2** |
| 1975 | 4.2 | 4.7 | 3.3 |
| 1980 | 4.7 | 5.3 | 3.7 |
| 1985 | 5.4 | 5.6 | 4.6 |
| 1990 | 4.4 | 4.5 | 3.9 |
| 1993-95 | 4.1 | 4.2 | 3.7 |

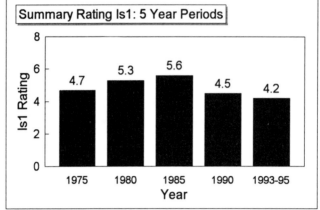

| Components of Economic Freedom | 1975 | | 1980 | | 1985 | | 1990 | | 1993-95 | |
|---|---|---|---|---|---|---|---|---|---|---|
| **I. Money and Inflation** | **2.5** | | **3.6** | | **5.1** | | **4.4** | | **4.4** | |
| (a) Annual Money Growth (last 5 yrs.) | 4 | (10.3) | 2 | (15.1) | 7 | (6.3) | 9 | (-3.2) | 9 | (-2.9) |
| (b) Inflation Variablity (last 5 yrs.) | 4 | (5.3) | 9 | (1.9) | 9 | (1.5) | 5 | (4.2) | 5 | (4.1) |
| (c) Ownership of Foreign Currency | 0 | | 0 | | 0 | | 0 | | 0 | |
| (d) Maint. of Bank Account Abroad | 0 | | 0 | | 0 | | 0 | | 0 | |
| **II. Government Operation** | **6.0** | | **6.3** | | **6.3** | | **4.8** | | **4.0** | |
| (a) Govern. Consumption (% of GDP) | 8 | (10.9) | 9 | (8.7) | 9 | (9.0) | 7 | (12.9) | 6 | (13.6) |
| (b) Government Enterprises | 4 | | 4 | | 4 | | 4 | | 4 | |
| (c) Price Controls | - | | - | | - | | 2 | | 2 | |
| (d) Entry Into Business | - | | - | | - | | - | | 5 | |
| (e) Legal System | - | | - | | - | | - | | 0 | |
| (f) Avoidance of Neg. Interest Rates | - | | 6 | | 6 | | 8 | | 8 | |
| **III. Takings** | **9.2** | | **10.0** | | **6.3** | | **5.0** | | **5.0** | |
| (a) Transfers and Subsidies (% of GDP) | 9 | (1.4) | 10 | (0.8) | 10 | (0.6) | 8 | (2.7) | 8 | (2.7) |
| (b) Marginal Tax Rates (Top Rate) | - | | - | | 2 | (60) | 1 | (60) | 1 | (60) |
| (c) Conscription | 10 | | 10 | | 10 | | 10 | | 10 | |
| **IV. International Sector** | **2.6** | | **2.7** | | **4.5** | | **3.8** | | **3.4** | |
| (a) Taxes on International Trade (Avg.) | 0 | (13.4) | 1 | (11.0) | 5 | (6.1) | 6 | (5.4) | 3 | (7.7) |
| (b) Black Market Exchange Rates (Prem.) | 7 | (2) | 7 | (2) | 8 | (1) | 6 | (4) | 8 | (1) |
| (c) Size of Trade Sector (% of GDP) | 4 | (48.2) | 3 | (51.3) | 5 | (57.6) | 2 | (41.5) | 2 | (40.6) |
| (d) Capital Transactions with Foreigners | 0 | | 0 | | 0 | | 0 | | 0 | |

## Part 2: Recent Economic Indicators:

| | | | | |
|---|---|---|---|---|
| **Population 1994:** | 12.9 | **Real Per Capita GDP :** | 1993 = | $975 |
| (in millions) | | (in 1985 U.S. dollars) | | |
| Annual Rate of Change (1980-94): | 2.8% | Avg. Growth Rate: | 1980-90 = | -0.4% |
| | | | 1985-93 = | -6.3% |

| Economic Indicators: | 1987 | 1988 | 1989 | 1990 | 1991 | 1992 | 1993 | 1994 |
|---|---|---|---|---|---|---|---|---|
| Change in Real GDP:Aggregate | -5.0 | -7.2 | -6.0 | 2.1 | -9.5 | -7.3 | -2.7 | - |
| : Per Capita | -7.8 | -10.0 | -8.8 | -0.7 | -12.3 | -10.1 | -5.5 | - |
| Inflation Rate (CPI) | 12.8 | -5.5 | 5.5 | 1.7 | 1.9 | 1.4 | - | - |
| Change in Money Supply: (M1) | -4.7 | -7.2 | 2.5 | 3.0 | -1.9 | -3.7 | -35.1 | 16.9 |
| : (M2) | -8.2 | -10.7 | 5.1 | 3.2 | 1.2 | -2.8 | -26.2 | |
| Investment/GDP Ratio | 29.0 | 27.3 | 27.3 | 28.8 | 26.8 | - | - | |
| Central Government Budget | | | | | | | | |
| Deficit (+) or Surplus (+) | | | | | | | | |
| As a Percent of GDP | - | - | -3.2 | -5.8 | -5.2 | -2.1 | - | - |
| Unemployment Rate | | | | | | | | |

After increasing from 4.7 to 5.6 between 1975 and 1985, the economic freedom rating (Is1) of Cameroon plunged to 4.2 during the last decade. Cameroon's 1993-1995 rating places it in a tie for 72nd place. The highlights include:

- Relatively stable monetary arrangements (Cameroon is part of the CFA group with currencies tied to the French franc), but prohibition of foreign currency accounts undermines confidence.

- The major strengths are absence of conscription and a largely convertible currency—black market premium in the foreign exchange market is generally small.

- The major weaknesses are widespread government enterprises, a weak and often discriminatory legal system, high marginal tax rates (the top rate has been 60% throughout the last decade), and restrictive trade practices (high tariffs, small trade sector, and extensive restrictions on the mobility of capital). With regard to the latter, direct investments abroad must be approved by the Ministry of Finance.

- As Cameroon moved to a more restrictive economy, its growth rate plunged. Since 1985, the real per capita GDP has declined at an annual rate of 6.3%.

# CANADA

## Part 1: The Economic Freedom Ratings for the Components and Various Area and Summary Indexes: 1975, 1980, 1985, 1990 and 1993-95.

(The numbers in parentheses indicate the actual values for the components.)

| | Ie | Summary Rating Is1 | Is2 |
|---|---|---|---|
| 1975 | 6.5 | 6.1 | 7.5 |
| 1980 | 7.5 | 6.8 | 8.5 |
| 1985 | 6.7 | 5.9 | 7.7 |
| 1990 | 7.5 | 6.9 | 8.5 |
| 1993-95 | 7.5 | 6.9 | 8.4 |

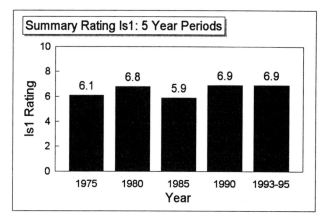

Summary Rating Is1: 5 Year Periods

| Components of Economic Freedom | 1975 | | 1980 | | 1985 | | 1990 | | 1993-95 | |
|---|---|---|---|---|---|---|---|---|---|---|
| **I. Money and Inflation** | **7.4** | | **9.7** | | **6.9** | | **9.4** | | **9.7** | |
| (a) Annual Money Growth (last 5 yrs.) | 7 | (6.0) | 10 | (1.6) | 4 | (11.3) | 8 | (4.0) | 9 | (2.5) |
| (b) Inflation Variablity (last 5 yrs.) | 5 | (4.0) | 9 | (1.9) | 6 | (3.2) | 10 | (1.1) | 10 | (1.1) |
| (c) Ownership of Foreign Currency | 10 | | 10 | | 10 | | 10 | | 10 | |
| (d) Maint. of Bank Account Abroad | 10 | | 10 | | 10 | | 10 | | 10 | |
| | | | | | | | | | | |
| **II. Government Operation** | **4.1** | | **5.3** | | **4.9** | | **5.9** | | **6.4** | |
| (a) Govern. Consumption (% of GDP) | 1 | (19.5) | 2 | (19.2) | 1 | (20.1) | 1 | (20.3) | 1 | (20.1) |
| (b) Government Enterprises | 6 | | 6 | | 6 | | 6 | | 6 | |
| (c) Price Controls | - | | - | | - | | 8 | | 8 | |
| (d) Entry Into Business | - | | - | | - | | - | | 7.5 | |
| (e) Legal System | - | | - | | - | | - | | 7.5 | |
| (f) Avoidance of Neg. Interest Rates | 6 | | 10 | | 10 | | 10 | | 10 | |
| | | | | | | | | | | |
| **III. Takings** | **4.8** | | **4.4** | | **3.5** | | **4.5** | | **4.0** | |
| (a) Transfers and Subsidies (% of GDP) | 4 | (9.1) | 3 | (14.5) | 2 | (16.3) | 2 | (15.6) | 2 | (17.7) |
| (b) Marginal Tax Rates (Top Rate) | 4 | (43-61) | 4 | (47-62) | 3 | (49-60) | 5 | (42-47) | 4 | (44-54) |
| (c) Conscription | 10 | | 10 | | 10 | | 10 | | 10 | |
| | | | | | | | | | | |
| **IV. International Sector** | **8.1** | | **8.7** | | **8.9** | | **9.0** | | **9.0** | |
| (a) Taxes on International Trade (Avg.) | 6 | (3.7) | 8 | (2.4) | 8 | (1.7) | 9 | (1.2) | 9 | (1.2) |
| (b) Black Market Exchange Rates (Prem.) | 10 | (0) | 10 | (0) | 10 | (0) | 10 | (0) | 10 | (0) |
| (c) Size of Trade Sector (% of GDP) | 9 | (47.2) | 9 | (55.1) | 10 | (54.5) | 9 | (51.2) | 9 | (54.0) |
| (d) Capital Transactions with Foreigners | 8 | | 8 | | 8 | | 8 | | 8 | |

## Part 2: Recent Economic Indicators:

| Population 1994: | 27.9 | **Real Per Capita GDP** : | 1994 = | $17,510 |
|---|---|---|---|---|
| (in millions) | | (in 1985 U.S. dollars) | | |
| Annual Rate of Change (1980-94): | 1.1% | Avg. Growth Rate: | 1980-90 = | 1.8% |
| | | | 1985-94 = | 0.9% |

| Economic Indicators: | 1987 | 1988 | 1989 | 1990 | 1991 | 1992 | 1993 | 1994 |
|---|---|---|---|---|---|---|---|---|
| Change in Real GDP: Aggregate | 4.3 | 4.9 | 2.4 | -0.2 | -2.2 | 0.6 | 3.5 | 5.6 |
| : Per Capita | 2.8 | 3.6 | 0.6 | -1.8 | -3.0 | -0.5 | 2.4 | 4.5 |
| Inflation Rate (CPI) | 4.4 | 4 | 5 | 4.8 | 5.6 | 1.5 | 1.8 | 0.6 |
| Change in Money Supply: (M1) | 14.2 | 3.6 | 4.3 | 1.7 | 5.8 | 5.4 | 6.3 | 6.1 |
| : (M2) | 9.5 | 9.8 | 11.4 | 9.8 | 7.2 | 6.9 | 11.7 | 5.2 |
| Investment/GDP Ratio | 21.7 | 22.5 | 23 | 20.7 | 19.1 | 18.1 | 18.0 | 18.3 |
| Central Government Budget Deficit (-) or Surplus (+) As a Percent of GDP | -2.5 | -2.2 | -2.5 | -4.1 | -6.6 | -7.1 | -7.1 | 2.8 |
| Unemployment Rate | 8.8 | 7.7 | 7.5 | 8.1 | 10.2 | 11.2 | 11.1 | 10.3 |

Based on the average of our three indexes, in 1993-1995 Canada placed 6th (tied with the United Kingdom) among the countries in our study. The Is1 summary rating ranked it 9th (tied with Japan). Except for a slight rating decline in 1985, which was primarily the result of monetary and price instability, Canada's rating has been steady and persistently high throughout the last two decades. In fact, Canada ranked among the ten most free economies in 1975, 1980, 1990, and 1993-1995. (See Exhibit 2-2.) Our analysis suggests that persistent economic freedom will lead to high income status. Canada's 1994 per capita GDP was the third highest in the world, behind only United States and Hong Kong, two other persistently free economies.

Our index does highlight three areas of obvious weakness: (1) a large government consumption sector—20 percent of GDP is allocated by the political process rather than markets, (2) a large and growing transfer sector, and (3) relatively high marginal tax rates, particularly in British Columbia, Nova Scotia, Ontario, and Quebec. In order to finance its huge expenditures, in the late 1980s and early 1990s the federal government ran a series of large deficits as a share of GDP (see above). In turn, the deficits pushed up the interest cost on the debt. In order to deal with this problem, Canadian governments must reduce their expenditures and rely more on the market sector. Several provinces are currently moving in this direction.

While our index does not incorporate this factor, there is evidence that the Canadian labor market is relatively inflexible. In recent years, Canada's unemployment rate has persistently exceeded that of the United States. This suggests that deregulation and a reevaluation of the system of benefit transfers to unemployed workers is in order.

# CHILE

## Part 1: The Economic Freedom Ratings for the Components and Various Area and Summary Indexes:  1975, 1980, 1985, 1990 and 1993-95.

(The numbers in parentheses indicate the actual values for the components.)

### Summary Ratings

| | Ie | Is1 | Is2 |
|------|-----|-----|-----|
| 1975 | 2.8 | 2.8 | 2.5 |
| 1980 | 4.1 | 3.9 | 3.8 |
| 1985 | 4.8 | 4.1 | 5.3 |
| 1990 | 6.1 | 5.7 | 6.3 |
| 1993-95 | 6.3 | 5.8 | 6.5 |

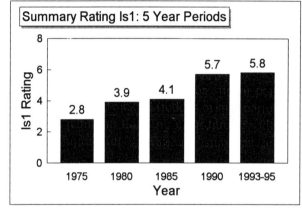

| Components of Economic Freedom | 1975 | | 1980 | | 1985 | | 1990 | | 1993-95 | |
|---|---|---|---|---|---|---|---|---|---|---|
| **I.  Money and Inflation** | **0.0** | | **1.9** | | **6.1** | | **6.0** | | **5.9** | |
| (a)  Annual Money Growth (last 5 yrs.) | 0 | 210.7) | 0 | (93.5) | 6 | (7.3) | 1 | (24.7) | 2 | (18.3) |
| (b)  Inflation Variablity (last 5 yrs.) | 0 | (234.0) | 0 | (80.6) | 2 | (9.6) | 6 | (3.2) | 5 | (4.1) |
| (c)  Ownership of Foreign Currency | 0 | | 10 | | 10 | | 10 | | 10 | |
| (d)  Maint. of Bank Account Abroad | 0 | | 0 | | 10 | | 10 | | 10 | |
| | | | | | | | | | | |
| **II.  Government Operation** | **5.0** | | **7.6** | | **7.2** | | **8.3** | | **8.4** | |
| (a)  Govern. Consumption (% of GDP) | 4 | (15.7) | 7 | (12.5) | 6 | (13.4) | 9 | (9.6) | 9 | (9.3) |
| (b)  Government Enterprises | 6 | | 8 | | 8 | | 8 | | 8 | |
| (c)  Price Controls | - | | - | | - | | 8 | | 8 | |
| (d)  Entry Into Business | - | | - | | - | | - | | 10 | |
| (e)  Legal System | - | | - | | - | | - | | 5 | |
| (f)  Avoidance of Neg. Interest Rates | - | | 8 | | 8 | | 8 | | 10 | |
| | | | | | | | | | | |
| **III.  Takings** | **1.6** | | **2.1** | | **1.3** | | **3.0** | | **2.6** | |
| (a)  Transfers and Subsidies (% of GDP) | 4 | (10.5) | 3 | (12.9) | 2 | (15.3) | 4 | (10.5) | 3 | (10.8) |
| (b)  Marginal Tax Rates (Top Rate) | 0 | (80) | 2 | (60) | 1 | (57) | 3 | (50) | 3 | (48) |
| (c)  Conscription | 0 | | 0 | | 0 | | 0 | | 0 | |
| | | | | | | | | | | |
| **IV.  International Sector** | **4.8** | | **4.9** | | **3.9** | | **6.2** | | **5.7** | |
| (a)  Taxes on International Trade (Avg.) | 6 | (5.6) | 7 | (2.8) | 5 | (5.7) | 6 | (3.7) | 6 | (3.7) |
| (b)  Black Market Exchange Rates (Prem.) | 6 | (5) | 6 | (6) | 4 | (22) | 10 | (0) | 6 | (4) |
| (c)  Size of Trade Sector (% of GDP) | 5 | (52.9) | 4 | (49.8) | 5 | (53.8) | 7 | (65.4) | 6 | (60.0) |
| (d)  Capital Transactions with Foreigners | 2 | | 2 | | 2 | | 2 | | 5 | |

130

## Part 2: Recent Economic Indicators:

| Population 1994: | 14.0 | **Real Per Capita GDP** : | 1994= | $5,250 |
|---|---|---|---|---|

(in millions)   (in 1985 U.S. dollars)

| Annual Rate of Change (1980-94): | 1.7 | Avg. Growth Rate: | 1980-90= | 1.9% |
|---|---|---|---|---|
| | | | 1985-94= | 4.8% |

| Economic Indicators: | 1987 | 1988 | 1989 | 1990 | 1991 | 1992 | 1993 | 1994 |
|---|---|---|---|---|---|---|---|---|
| Change in Real GDP: Aggregate | 6.6 | 7.3 | 10.2 | 3.0 | 6.1 | 11.0 | 6.3 | 4.2 |
| : Per Capita | 4.9 | 5.5 | 8.5 | 1.4 | 4.5 | 9.4 | 4.6 | 2.6 |
| Inflation Rate (CPI) | 19.9 | 14.7 | 17.0 | 26.0 | 21.8 | 15.4 | 12.1 | 12.0 |
| Change in Money Supply (M1) | 19.7 | 39.5 | 27.0 | 11.8 | 43.2 | 19.5 | 26.5 | 19.9 |
| : (M2) | 30.2 | 29.2 | 26.4 | 27.7 | 24.7 | 27.5 | 37.1 | 20.8 |
| Investment/GDP Ratio | 22.2 | 22.8 | 25.5 | 24.7 | 22.2 | 24.1 | 26.2 | 24.3 |
| Central Government Budget | | | | | | | | |
| Deficit (-) or Surplus (+) | | | | | | | | |
| As a Percent of GDP | 0.4 | -0.2 | 1.8 | 0.8 | 1.6 | 2.3 | 2.0 | - |
| Unemployment Rate | | | | | | | | |

The record of the Chilean economy during the last two decades illustrates the importance of economic freedom. In 1975, only 7 countries had a lower economic freedom rating (Is1) than Chile. The economy was characterized by monetary instability, hyperinflation, large government expenditures, high taxes, and various restrictions on international transactions. Things began to change for the better during the latter half of the 1970s. Between 1975 and 1990, Chile's Is1 rating jumped from 2.8 to 5.7, the largest increase among the countries in our study during this period of time.

Several factors played a role in this improvement. Even though monetary policy is still too expansionary the annual rate of monetary growth was curtailed from 216.6% during the five years prior to 1975 to approximately 20% during the last decade. Legalization of foreign currency bank accounts, privatization, a reduction in government consumption expenditures (as a share of GDP, they fell from 15.7% in 1975 to 9.3% during the latest period), a substantial reduction in the top marginal tax rate (it was reduced from a horrendous 80% in 1975 to the current 48% rate) and some relaxation of restrictions on international exchange all contributed to the improvement in Chile's economic freedom rating.

Chile's rate of economic growth changed in lock step with its improvement in economic freedom. While Chile's GDP per capita was virtually unchanged during the 1970s, it increased at an annual rate of 1.9% during the 1980s and since 1985 the rate has accelerated to 4.8%. More needs to be done. Chile needs to make its currency completely convertible and its marginal taxes are still too high. However, if Chile continues on its current path, its economic future will be bright.

# COSTA RICA

## Part 1: The Economic Freedom Ratings for the Components and Various Area and Summary Indexes: 1975, 1980, 1985, 1990 and 1993-95.

(The numbers in parentheses indicate the actual values for the components.)

|  | **Summary Ratings** | | |
|---|---|---|---|
|  | **Ie** | **Is1** | **Is2** |
| 1975 | 5.3 | 5.2 | 5.6 |
| 1980 | 4.9 | 4.8 | 5.4 |
| 1985 | 4.8 | 4.6 | 5.3 |
| 1990 | 6.5 | 6.6 | 7.1 |
| 1993-95 | 6.7 | 6.7 | 7.0 |

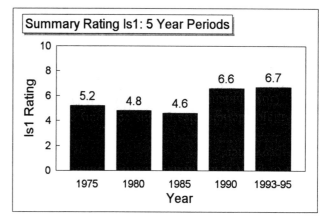

| **Components of Economic Freedom** | 1975 | | 1980 | | 1985 | | 1990 | | 1993-95 | |
|---|---|---|---|---|---|---|---|---|---|---|
| **I.  Money and Inflation** | **4.9** | | **5.9** | | **4.3** | | **6.6** | | **5.2** | |
| (a)  Annual Money Growth (last 5 yrs.) | 2 | (16.0) | 2 | (15.7) | 1 | (32.1) | 3 | (13.0) | 2 | (15.9) |
| (b)  Inflation Variablity (last 5 yrs.) | 2 | (8.9) | 5 | (4.5) | 1 | (24.2) | 6 | (3.3) | 3 | (6.1) |
| (c)  Ownership of Foreign Currency | 10 | | 10 | | 10 | | 10 | | 10 | |
| (d)  Maint. of Bank Account Abroad | 10 | | 10 | | 10 | | 10 | | 10 | |
| | | | | | | | | | | |
| **II. Government Operation** | **6.5** | | **5.1** | | **6.0** | | **3.9** | | **7.0** | |
| (a)  Govern. Consumption (% of GDP) | 5 | (15.2) | 2 | (18.2) | 4 | (15.8) | 2 | (18.2) | 3 | (17.3) |
| (b)  Government Enterprises | 8 | | 8 | | 8 | | 8 | | 8 | |
| (c)  Price Controls | - | | - | | - | | - | | 6 | |
| (d)  Entry Into Business | - | | - | | - | | - | | 10 | |
| (e)  Legal System | - | | - | | - | | - | | 7.5 | |
| (f)  Avoidance of Neg. Interest Rates | - | | - | | 6 | | 8 | | 8 | |
| | | | | | | | | | | |
| **III. Takings** | **6.1** | | **5.7** | | **4.7** | | **7.9** | | **7.9** | |
| (a)  Transfers and Subsidies (% of GDP) | - | | 5 | (6.0) | 5 | (7.2) | 6 | (5.0) | 6 | (4.7) |
| (b)  Marginal Tax Rates (Top Rate) | 5 | (50) | 5 | (50) | 3 | (50) | 9 | (25) | 9 | (25) |
| (c)  Conscription | 10 | | 10 | | 10 | | 10 | | 10 | |
| | | | | | | | | | | |
| **IV. International Sector** | **3.9** | | **2.9** | | **3.7** | | **5.8** | | **6.0** | |
| (a)  Taxes on International Trade (Avg.) | 5 | (5.9) | 6 | (5.3) | 4 | (6.9) | 4 | (7.0) | 6 | (5.0) |
| (b)  Black Market Exchange Rates (Prem.) | 5 | (8) | 1 | (69) | 3 | (24) | 10 | (0) | 8 | (1) |
| (c)  Size of Trade Sector (% of GDP) | 3 | (68.6) | 2 | (63.3) | 2 | (63.2) | 3 | (75.4) | 4 | (82.0) |
| (d)  Capital Transactions with Foreigners | 2 | | 2 | | 5 | | 5 | | 5 | |

## Part 2: Recent Economic Indicators:

| | | | | |
|---|---|---|---|---|
| Population 1994:<br>(in millions) | 3.3 | **Real Per Capita GDP** :<br>(in 1985 U.S. dollars) | 1994= | $3,785 |
| Annual Rate of Change (1980-94): | 2.4 | Avg. Growth Rate: | 1980-90 | -0.4% |
| | | | 1985-94 | 2.1% |

| Economic Indicators: | 1987 | 1988 | 1989 | 1990 | 1991 | 1992 | 1993 | 1994 |
|---|---|---|---|---|---|---|---|---|
| Change in Real GDP: Aggregate | 4.8 | 3.4 | 5.7 | 3.6 | 2.3 | 7.7 | 6.3 | 4.5 |
| : Per Capita | 2.3 | 1.9 | 3.2 | 1.2 | 0.0 | 5.7 | 3.9 | 2.1 |
| Inflation Rate (CPI) | 16.8 | 20.8 | 16.5 | 19.0 | 28.7 | 21.8 | 9.8 | 13.5 |
| Change in Money Supply: (M1) | 12.7 | 6.9 | 24.4 | 12.9 | 4.1 | 33.4 | 7.0 | 10.2 |
| : (M2) | 17.6 | 23.5 | 29.7 | 28.0 | 28.0 | 28.7 | 17.1 | 16.8 |
| Investment/GDP Ratio | 27.1 | 24.5 | 26.5 | 27.2 | 25.0 | 28.9 | 30.4 | 20.9 |
| Central Government Budget<br>Deficit (-) or Surplus (+)<br>As a Percent of GDP | -2.9 | -- | -2.1 | -3.1 | -1.3 | +0.9 | -0.2 | -4.7 |
| Unemployment Rate | | | | | | | | |

Costa Rica is another country that illustrates the importance of economic freedom as a source of progress. As recent as the mid-1980s, Costa Rica was simply another struggling Central American economy. Its per capita GDP actually declined during the 1975-1985 period. Between 1985 and 1990, its Is1 economic freedom rating rose from 4.6 to 6.6, one of the largest increases during this period and the increase was maintained in the mid-1990s. In our most recent rating year, Costa Rica's Is1 rating indicated that its economy was the 12th most free (tied with Ireland and South Korea) in the world in the mid 1990s. (Note: the average of our three ratings places it 16th.)

Two major factors contributed to the jump in Costa Rica's rating. First, the top marginal tax rate was sliced from 50% in 1985 to 25% in 1989. The lower rate remains in effect. Second, various trade restraints in the international sector have been reduced. The average tariff rate was cut from 6.9% in 1985 to 5.0% in 1993. Exchange rate controls were relaxed and the black market exchange rate premium declined. As a share of GDP, the size of the trade sector increased from 63% in 1985 to 82% in 1994. Excessive monetary growth is a continuing deficiency. The annual rate of monetary growth during the last decade was still around 15%, a rate that is far too expansionary for the achievement of stable prices.

The increase in economic freedom has fueled economic growth. During the 1985-1994 period, the per capita GDP of Costa Rica increased at an average annual rate of 2.1%, up from minus 0.3% during 1975-1985. Costa Rica has now experienced 11 straight years of growth in real GDP and during 1992-1994 the per capita growth of real GDP averaged almost 4% annually. Continued movement toward economic freedom will keep this country on a solid growth path.

# CZECH REPUBLIC (Data prior to 1993 are for former Czechoslovakia)

## Part 1: The Economic Freedom Ratings for the Components and Various Area and Summary Indexes: 1975, 1980, 1985, 1990 and 1993-95.

(The numbers in parentheses indicate the actual values for the components.)

| | **Summary Rating** | | |
|---|---|---|---|
| | **Ie** | **Is1** | **Is2** |
| 1975 | - | - | - |
| 1980 | - | - | - |
| 1985 | 2.7 * | 2.4 * | 2.4 * |
| 1990 | 2.5 | 2.4 | 2.4 |
| 1993-95 | 5.2 | 4.9 | 5.6 |

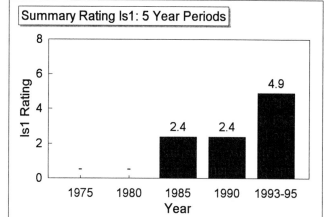

Summary Rating Is1: 5 Year Periods

*Should be interpreted with caution because it is based on only 10 of the 14 components.

| Components of Economic Freedom | 1975 | | 1980 | | 1985 | | 1990 | | 1993-95 | |
|---|---|---|---|---|---|---|---|---|---|---|
| **I. Money and Inflation** | | | | | **5.4** | | **4.7** | | **4.6** | |
| (a) Annual Money Growth (last 5 yrs.) | - | | - | | 9 | (3.0) | 10 | (0.4) | 2 | (13.9) |
| (b) Inflation Variablity (last 5 yrs.) | - | | - | | 8 | (2.2) | 5 | (4.0) | 1 | (17.4) |
| (c) Ownership of Foreign Currency | 0 | | 0 | | 0 | | 0 | | 10 | |
| (d) Maint. of Bank Account Abroad | 0 | | 0 | | 0 | | 0 | | 10 | |
| | | | | | | | | | | |
| **II. Government Operation** | | | | | **0.5** | | **0.3** | | **4.5** | |
| (a) Govern. Consumption (% of GDP) | - | | 2 | (19.5) | 1 | (20.9) | 1 | (22.5) | 1 | (22.3) |
| (b) Government Enterprises | 0 | | 0 | | 0 | | 0 | | 4 | |
| (c) Price Controls | - | | - | | - | | 0 | | 5 | |
| (d) Entry Into Business | - | | - | | - | | - | | 5 | |
| (e) Legal System | - | | - | | - | | - | | 7.5 | |
| (f) Avoidance of Neg. Interest Rates | - | | - | | - | | - | | 6 | |
| | | | | | | | | | | |
| **III. Takings** | | | | | **0.0** | | **1.9** | | **3.1** | |
| (a) Transfers and Subsidies (% of GDP) | - | | - | | - | | 0 | (37.2) | - | |
| (b) Marginal Tax Rates (Top Rate) | - | | - | | - | | 4 | (55) | 4 | (44) |
| (c) Conscription | 0 | | 0 | | 0 | | 0 | | 0 | |
| | | | | | | | | | | |
| **IV. International Sector** | | | | | **1.6** | | **3.3** | | **8.1** | |
| (a) Taxes on International Trade (Avg.) | - | | - | | - | | 6 | (4.0) | - | |
| (b) Black Market Exchange Rates (Prem.) | 0 | (359) | 0 | (387) | 0 | (423) | 2 | (61) | 10 | (0) |
| (c) Size of Trade Sector (% of GDP) | - | | - | | 7 | (69.7) | 6 | (68.8) | 10 | (110.5) |
| (d) Capital Transactions with Foreigners | 0 | | 0 | | 0 | | 0 | | 5 | |

## Part 2: Recent Economic Indicators: [a]

| | | | |
|---|---|---|---|
| **Population 1994:** | 10.3 | **Real Per Capita GDP :** | 1994 = $4,800 [b] |
| (in millions) | | (in 1985 U.S. dollars) | |
| Annual Rate of Change (1980-94): | 0.1% | Avg. Growth Rate: | 1985-94 = -1.4% |

| Economic Indicators: | 1987 | 1988 | 1989 | 1990 | 1991 | 1992 | 1993 | 1994 |
|---|---|---|---|---|---|---|---|---|
| Change in Real GDP:Aggregate | 2.1 | 2.3 | 0.7 | -1.5 | -14.0 | -6.9 | 0.0 | 2.5 |
| : Per Capita | 2.0 | 2.2 | 0.6 | -1.6 | -14.1 | -7.0 | -0.1 | 2.4 |
| Inflation Rate (CPI) | 0.1 | 0.1 | 1.4 | 10.0 | 57.7 | 10.8 | 20.8 | 9.1 |
| Change in Money Supply: (M1) | 3.6 | 6.1 | 4.7 | 0.2 | 4.2 | 25.7 | 24.0 | 20.3 |
| : (M2) | 6.0 | 6.7 | 6.3 | 3.8 | 10.7 | 27.6 | 22.5 | |
| Investment/GDP Ratio | 14.9 | 13.5 | 12.9 | 15.7 | 13.3 | - | 26.5 | |
| Central Government Budget Deficit (+) or Surplus (+) As a Percent of GDP | | | -2.4 | +0.1 | -2.0 | -3.3 | +0.0 | +1.0 |
| Unemployment Rate | - | - | - | 1.2 | 4.0 | 3.0 | 3.7 | 3.3 |

a  All data prior to 1993 are for the former Czechoslovakia. The 1993 and 1994 data are for the
the Czech Republic only. The Czech Republic comprised approximately two-thirds of
the former Czechoslovakia.
b  Estimate of the authors.

In the few short years since the yoke of Communism was lifted from the Czech Republic, it has made significant strides in the direction of economic freedom. Its 4.9 rating is no great shakes compared to the freest countries of the world—it is tied with Pakistan for 51st place—but the Czech Republic is now the economically most free of all the former Communist bloc nations.

While government ownership is still common in this former socialist country, mass privatization has moved large sectors of the economy into private hands during the last five years. In contrast with most other Eastern European nations, the Czech voucher plan successfully privatized many large state enterprises. The Czech koruna is approaching full convertibility. As trade barriers have fallen the size of the trade sector has grown dramatically in recent years. Exports plus imports now sum to 110% of GDP; substantially more than would be expected for a country of this size and location.

Of course, problems remain. The current growth of the money supply will fuel inflation unless it is curtailed. Government consumption expenditures—22.3% of the GDP in 1994—are still quite high. Both employment and income taxes are high and compliance is low and difficult to enforce in an economy where most transactions are conducted with cash rather than checks. Nonetheless, the foundation has been laid and if the Czech Republic continues to move toward economic freedom, its future will be bright.

135

# DENMARK

**Part 1: The Economic Freedom Ratings for the Components and Various Area and Summary Indexes: 1975, 1980, 1985, 1990 and 1993-95.**

(The numbers in parentheses indicate the actual values for the components.)

### Summary Ratings

| | Ie | Is1 | Is2 |
|---|---|---|---|
| 1975 | 4.1 | 3.8 | 4.3 |
| 1980 | 4.3 | 3.8 | 4.6 |
| 1985 | 4.1 | 3.7 | 4.4 |
| 1990 | 5.4 | 4.6 | 6.4 |
| 1993-95 | 6.7 | 6.0 | 7.7 |

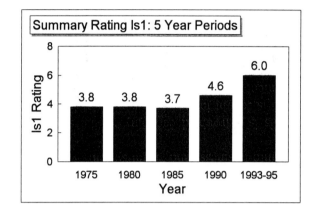

Summary Rating Is1: 5 Year Periods

| Components of Economic Freedom | 1975 | | 1980 | | 1985 | | 1990 | | 1993-95 | |
|---|---|---|---|---|---|---|---|---|---|---|
| **I.  Money and Inflation** | **4.5** | | **5.5** | | **3.6** | | **8.8** | | **9.7** | |
| (a)  Annual Money Growth (last 5 yrs.) | 5 | (9.6) | 7 | (7.0) | 3 | (12.5) | 6 | (7.3) | 9 | (2.4) |
| (b)  Inflation Variablity (last 5 yrs.) | 9 | (2.1) | 10 | (0.8) | 8 | (2.4) | 10 | (0.8) | 10 | (0.4) |
| (c)  Ownership of Foreign Currency | 0 | | 0 | | 0 | | 10 | | 10 | |
| (d)  Maint. of Bank Account Abroad | 0 | | 0 | | 0 | | 10 | | 10 | |
| | | | | | | | | | | |
| **II.  Government Operation** | **3.3** | | **3.7** | | **3.7** | | **4.4** | | **6.7** | |
| (a)  Govern. Consumption (% of GDP) | 0 | (24.6) | 0 | (26.7) | 0 | (25.3) | 0 | (25.3) | 0 | (25.3) |
| (b)  Government Enterprises | 4 | | 4 | | 4 | | 4 | | 4 | |
| (c)  Price Controls | - | | - | | - | | 6 | | 8 | |
| (d)  Entry Into Business | - | | - | | - | | - | | 10 | |
| (e)  Legal System | - | | - | | - | | - | | 10 | |
| (f)  Avoidance of Neg. Interest Rates | 8 | | 10 | | 10 | | 10 | | 10 | |
| | | | | | | | | | | |
| **III.  Takings** | **1.3** | | **0.4** | | **0.4** | | **0.0** | | **0.9** | |
| (a)  Transfers and Subsidies (% of GDP) | 2 | (17.8) | 1 | (20.8) | 1 | (20.4) | 0 | (22.6) | 0 | (24.6) |
| (b)  Marginal Tax Rates (Top Rate) | 1 | (63) | 0 | (66) | 0 | (73) | 0 | (68) | 2 | (65) |
| (c)  Conscription | 0 | | 0 | | 0 | | 0 | | 0 | |
| | | | | | | | | | | |
| **IV.  International Sector** | **6.7** | | **6.7** | | **7.7** | | **7.5** | | **8.7** | |
| (a)  Taxes on International Trade (Avg.) | 9 | (0.9) | 10 | (0.1) | 10 | (0.0) | 10 | (0.0) | 10 | (0.0) |
| (b)  Black Market Exchange Rates (Prem.) | 8 | (1) | 7 | (2) | 10 | (0) | 10 | (0) | 10 | (0) |
| (c)  Size of Trade Sector (% of GDP) | 3 | (61.1) | 3 | (66.5) | 4 | (73.0) | 3 | (65.5) | 2 | (66.4) |
| (d)  Capital Transactions with Foreigners | 5 | | 5 | | 5 | | 5 | | 10 | |

## Part 2: Recent Economic Indicators:

| Population 1994: | 5.2 | **Real Per Capita GDP** : | 1994= | $14,800 |
|---|---|---|---|---|
| (in millions) | | (in 1985 U.S. dollars) | | |
| Annual Rate of Change (1980-94): | 0.3% | Avg. Growth Rate: | 1980-90= | 2.0% |
| | | | 1985-94= | 1.5% |

| Recent Economic Indicators: | 1987 | 1988 | 1989 | 1990 | 1991 | 1992 | 1993 | 1994 |
|---|---|---|---|---|---|---|---|---|
| Change in Real GDP: Aggregate | 0.3 | 1.2 | 0.6 | 1.4 | 1.0 | 1.2 | 1.2 | 4.4 |
| : Per Capita | 0.0 | 0.9 | 0.3 | 1.1 | 0.7 | 0.9 | 0.9 | 4.1 |
| Inflation Rate (CPI) | 4 | 4.6 | 4.8 | 2.6 | 2.4 | 2.1 | 1.3 | 2.0 |
| Change in Money Supply: (M1) | 7.7 | 45.6 | 0.4 | 8.1 | 5.6 | -0.8 | 10.5 | -1.3 |
| : (M2) | 4.5 | -1.5 | 2.2 | 6.6 | 3.6 | -0.8 | 19.7 | -9.9 |
| Investment/GDP Ratio | 19 | 17.9 | 18.4 | 17.3 | 16.1 | 15.1 | 13.7 | 15.1 |
| Central Government Budget | | | | | | | | |
| Deficit or Surplus (% of GDP) | 2.4 | 0.6 | -0.5 | -1.5 | -2.1 | -2.4 | -4.5 | -4.3 |
| Unemployment Rate | 7.8 | 8.6 | 9.3 | 9.6 | 10.5 | 11.2 | 12.2 | 11.5 |

The average of our three summary indexes ranked Denmark as the 16th most free economy in 1993-1995; the Is1 index placed it 32nd. Thus, Denmark ranks in the upper third among the more than 100 nations in our study.

Denmark's rating has improved during the last decade, primarily as the result of a freer and more stable monetary regime. During the last five years, monetary expansion has been low (less than 5%) and the inflation rate has been steady at an annual rate of approximately 2%. The former restrictions on the maintenance of foreign currency bank accounts have been abolished. Removal of prior restrictions limiting the mobility of capital have also contributed to Denmark's recent improvement.

The major deficiencies of this economy are its huge government consumption and transfer sectors. Government now takes over 50% of the earnings of Danes—25% for government consumption and another 25% for transfers and subsidies. Denmark is now caught is the vicious cycle of large government expenditures, budget deficits, and rising interest costs that fuel still more government expenditures. Higher taxes will not solve this problem. The current top marginal tax rate of 65% is already the highest in the world except for the 66% rate imposed in the tiny African nation of Gabon. Predictably, the high taxes and large government expenditures have reduced private investment (down to only 15% of GDP) and led to high unemployment (11.5% in 1994 and 10.5% in mid-1995).

# EGYPT

**Part 1: The Economic Freedom Ratings for the Components and Various Area and Summary Indexes: 1975, 1980, 1985, 1990 and 1993-95.**

(The numbers in parentheses indicate the actual values for the components.)

### Summary Ratings

|         | Ie  | Is1 | Is2 |
|---------|-----|-----|-----|
| 1975    | 2.7 | 2.4 | 3.0 |
| 1980    | 3.5 | 2.8 | 3.9 |
| 1985    | 3.9 | 3.3 | 4.2 |
| 1990    | 4.7 | 4.2 | 4.7 |
| 1993-95 | 4.3 | 4.0 | 4.4 |

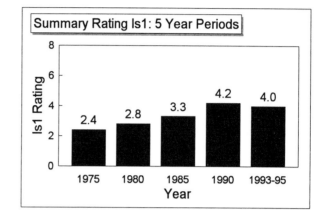

Summary Rating Is1: 5 Year Periods

| Components of Economic Freedom | 1975 | | 1980 | | 1985 | | 1990 | | 1993-95 | |
|---|---|---|---|---|---|---|---|---|---|---|
| **I. Money and Inflation** | **2.6** | | **5.6** | | **7.5** | | **8.5** | | **6.5** | |
| (a) Annual Money Growth (last 5 yrs.) | 2 | (13.8) | 1 | (21.5) | 6 | (7.8) | 6 | (7.3) | 5 | (8.4) |
| (b) Inflation Variablity (last 5 yrs.) | 6 | (3.5) | 5 | (4.4) | 6 | (3.4) | 9 | (1.6) | 4 | (5.4) |
| (c) Ownership of Foreign Currency | 0 | | 10 | | 10 | | 10 | | 10 | |
| (d) Maint. of Bank Account Abroad | 0 | | 10 | | 10 | | 10 | | 10 | |
| | | | | | | | | | | |
| **II. Government Operation** | **2.0** | | **3.2** | | **3.2** | | **3.9** | | **3.0** | |
| (a) Govern. Consumption (% of GDP) | 0 | (24.9) | 4 | (15.7) | 3 | (17.2) | 7 | (11.7) | 5 | (15.0) |
| (b) Government Enterprises | 4 | | 2 | | 2 | | 2 | | 2 | |
| (c) Price Controls | - | | - | | - | | 2 | | 2 | |
| (d) Entry Into Business | - | | - | | - | | - | | 2.5 | |
| (e) Legal System | - | | - | | - | | - | | 0 | |
| (f) Avoidance of Neg. Interest Rates | - | | 4 | | 6 | | 6 | | 8 | |
| | | | | | | | | | | |
| **III. Takings** | **0.0** | | **0.8** | | **2.1** | | **2.5** | | **3.0** | |
| (a) Transfers and Subsidies (% of GDP) | 0 | (25.0) | 2 | (17.2) | 3 | (13.9) | 4 | (8.9) | 4 | (10.6) |
| (b) Marginal Tax Rates (Top Rate) | - | | 0 | (80) | 2 | (65) | 2 | (65) | 3 | (50) |
| (c) Conscription | 0 | | 0 | | 0 | | 0 | | 0 | |
| | | | | | | | | | | |
| **IV. International Sector** | **3.8** | | **3.0** | | **1.9** | | **3.7** | | **5.0** | |
| (a) Taxes on International Trade (Avg.) | 0 | (16.7) | 0 | (13.1) | 1 | (12.1) | 5 | (5.9) | 4 | (6.4) |
| (b) Black Market Exchange Rates (Prem.) | 8 | (1) | 5 | (9) | 1 | (146) | 2 | (56) | 8 | (1) |
| (c) Size of Trade Sector (% of GDP) | 10 | (61.5) | 10 | (73.4) | 8 | (52.0) | 10 | (65.0) | 10 | (65.1) |
| (d) Capital Transactions with Foreigners | 0 | | 0 | | 0 | | 0 | | 0 | |

## Part 2: Recent Economic Indicators:

| | | | | |
|---|---|---|---|---|
| **Population 1994:** | 57.0 | **Real Per Capita GDP :** | 1994= | $1,915 |
| (in millions) | | (in 1985 U.S. dollars) | | |
| Annual Rate of Change (1980-94) | 2.4% | Avg. Growth Rate: | 1980-90= | 0.1% |
| | | | 1985-94= | 2.4% |

| Economic Indicators: | 1987 | 1988 | 1989 | 1990 | 1991 | 1992 | 1993 | 1994 |
|---|---|---|---|---|---|---|---|---|
| Change in Real GDP: Aggregate | 6.4 | 5.4 | 5.0 | 5.7 | 1.1 | 4.4 | 3.0 | 3.9 |
| : Per Capita | 4.0 | 3.0 | 2.6 | 3.3 | -1.3 | 2.0 | 0.8 | 1.7 |
| Inflation Rate (CPI) | 19.7 | 17.7 | 21.3 | 16.8 | 19.7 | 13.6 | 12.1 | 8.2 |
| Change in Money Supply (M1) | 8.7 | 15.5 | 10.7 | 14.6 | 12.9 | 6.3 | 9.4 | 10.7 |
| : (M2) | 12.8 | 25.6 | 17.8 | 22.8 | 28.0 | 15.2 | 15.9 | 11.2 |
| Investment/GDP Ratio | 26.1 | 33.2 | 31.3 | 29.4 | 24.0 | 19.8 | 16.2 | 16.6 |
| Central Government Budget Deficit (-) or Surplus (+) As a Percent of GDP | -5.1 | -7.7 | -5.4 | -5.7 | -1.0 | -3.5 | - | - |
| Unemployment Rate | | | 6.9 | 8.6 | | | | |

Source: United Nations, Statistical Yearbook, 1992 (New York 1994).

Only three countries (Uganda, Israel, and Portugal) had lower economic freedom ratings than Egypt in 1975. Between 1975 and 1990, Egypt's Is1 economic freedom rating rose slowly from 2.4 to 4.2, prior to receding to 4.0 in our most recent rating year. Based on the average of our three indexes, Egypt placed 69th in the mid-1990s. Its Is1 summary rating places it 77th. Thus, Egypt ranks in the lower-middle group among our 103 countries.

What accounts for Egypt's low rating? Monetary instability, numerous government enterprises, price controls, a 50% top marginal tax rate (this is down from 80% in 1980), a legal system that often fails to support private property rights, conscription, and capital market restrictions all contributed to this country's low rating. The trade sector is a lone bright spot. The average tariff rate was cut in half during the last decade. The black market foreign exchange premium evaporated after soaring to near 150% in the mid-1980s. The size of the trade sector is significantly larger than one would expect, given the country size and locational characteristics.

After struggling during the early 1980s, the economy grew at a 2.4% clip during the last decade. Egypt has a number of things going for it. A decisive move toward a freer economy and sound policies in other areas would almost certainly put it on a strong growth path.

# FINLAND

## Part 1: The Economic Freedom Ratings for the Components and Various Area and Summary Indexes: 1975, 1980, 1985, 1990 and 1993-95.

(The numbers in parentheses indicate the actual values for the components.)

**Summary Ratings**

|         | Ie  | Is1 | Is2 |
|---------|-----|-----|-----|
| 1975    | 4.0 | 3.9 | 4.0 |
| 1980    | 5.0 | 4.6 | 5.2 |
| 1985    | 4.9 | 4.4 | 5.1 |
| 1990    | 5.5 | 4.8 | 6.3 |
| 1993-95 | 6.1 | 5.6 | 6.9 |

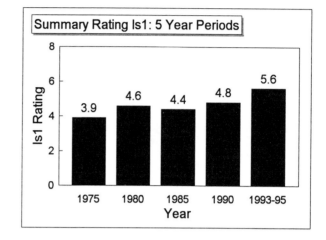

| Components of Economic Freedom | 1975 | | 1980 | | 1985 | | 1990 | | 1993-95 | |
|---|---|---|---|---|---|---|---|---|---|---|
| **I. Money and Inflation** | **3.9** | | **7.0** | | **6.1** | | **9.1** | | **7.0** | |
| (a) Annual Money Growth (last 5 yrs.) | 2 | (18.9) | 7 | (5.5) | 4 | (10.3) | 7 | (6.8) | 1 | (29.1) |
| (b) Inflation Variablity (last 5 yrs.) | 4 | (5.5) | 9 | (1.9) | 9 | (1.9) | 10 | (0.9) | 9 | (1.9) |
| (c) Ownership of Foreign Currency | 10 | | 10 | | 10 | | 10 | | 10 | |
| (d) Maint.of Bank Account Abroad | 0 | | 0 | | 0 | | 10 | | 10 | |
| | | | | | | | | | | |
| **II. Government Operation** | **4.5** | | **4.9** | | **4.9** | | **5.2** | | **6.7** | |
| (a) Govern. Consumption (% of GDP) | 3 | (17.0) | 2 | (18.0) | 1 | (20.2) | 1 | (21.1) | 1 | (22.4) |
| (b) Government Enterprises | 6 | | 6 | | 6 | | 6 | | 6 | |
| (c) Price Controls | - | | - | | - | | 6 | | 8 | |
| (d) Entry Into Business | - | | - | | - | | - | | 7.5 | |
| (e) Legal System | - | | - | | - | | - | | 10 | |
| (f) Avoidance of Neg. Interest Rates | - | | 8 | | 10 | | 10 | | 10 | |
| | | | | | | | | | | |
| **III. Takings** | **2.1** | | **1.7** | | **1.3** | | **0.8** | | **1.3** | |
| (a) Transfers and Subsidies (% of GDP) | 3 | (14.1) | 3 | (14.3) | 2 | (15.8) | 2 | (16.0) | 1 | (21.1) |
| (b) Marginal Tax Rates (Top Rate) | 2 | (61-68) | 1 | (65-71) | 1 | (64-70) | 0 | (63-69) | 2 | (55-61) |
| (c) Conscription | 0 | | 0 | | 0 | | 0 | | 0 | |
| | | | | | | | | | | |
| **IV. International Sector** | **5.8** | | **6.2** | | **6.6** | | **6.3** | | **7.9** | |
| (a) Taxes on International Trade (Avg.) | 8 | (1.6) | 9 | (0.8) | 9 | (0.4) | 9 | (0.6) | 9 | (0.6) |
| (b) Black Market Exchange Rates (Prem.) | 8 | (1) | 8 | (1) | 10 | (0) | 10 | (0) | 10 | (0) |
| (c) Size of Trade Sector (% of GDP) | 4 | (54.0) | 5 | (67.2) | 4 | (58.1) | 2 | (47.6) | 2 | (52.5) |
| (d) Capital Transactions with Foreigners | 2 | | 2 | | 2 | | 2 | | 8 | |

## Part 2: Recent Economic Indicators:

| Population 1994: | 5.1 | **Real Per Capita GDP :** | 1994= | $12,000 |
| (in millions) | | (in 1985 U.S. dollars) | | |
| Annual Rate of Change (1980-94): | 0.5% | Avg. Growth Rate: 1980-90= | | 2.7% |
| | | 1985-94= | | 0.3% |

| Economic Indicators: | 1987 | 1988 | 1989 | 1990 | 1991 | 1992 | 1993 | 1994 |
|---|---|---|---|---|---|---|---|---|
| Change in Real GDP: Aggregate | 4.1 | 4.9 | 5.7 | 0.0 | -7.1 | -3.8 | -2.6 | 3.5 |
| : Per Capita | 3.6 | 4.6 | 5.3 | -0.4 | -7.9 | -3.9 | -3.0 | 3.0 |
| Inflation Rate (CPI) | 4.1 | 5.1 | 6.6 | 6.1 | 4.1 | 2.6 | 2.1 | 1.1 |
| Change in Money Supply: (M1) | 9.0 | 15.9 | 15.3 | 14.8 | 173.9 | 3.3 | 6.7 | 10.8 |
| : (M2) | 10.7 | 14.1 | 18.4 | 8.5 | -4.9 | 1.6 | 0.1 | 2.1 |
| Investment/GDP Ratio | 24.0 | 26.6 | 29.7 | 28.1 | 20.5 | 16.7 | 13.2 | 15.4 |
| Central Government Budget Deficit (-) or Surplus (+) As a Percent of GDP | -1.7 | +0.4 | +1.8 | +0.2 | -7.0 | -14.8 | -12.4 | -12.8 |
| Unemployment Rate | 5.0 | 4.5 | 3.4 | 3.4 | 7.5 | 13.0 | 17.7 | 18.6 [a] |

a First 10 months of the year.

In 1993-1995, the average of our three indexes ranked the Finnish economy as the 26th most free in the world. Its Is1 summary rating placed it 44th. Other than modest improvement in the monetary area and some relaxation of the restrictions on capital mobility, there is little evidence of movement toward a freer economy. (Note: most of the increase in the government operations rating between 1990 and 1993-1995 reflects the inclusion of the "entry into business" and "legal system" variables into our index for the first time.)

This is a troubled economy. Like several other "big government" European nations, Finland is caught in the vicious cycle of large government expenditures, budget deficits (the government deficit exceeded 10% of GDP during 1992-1994) that soon push up interest costs, and rising expenditures on interest that fuel still more government spending. Higher taxes will not solve this problem. Finland's current top marginal tax rate of approximately 60% is already one of the highest in the world. Weak private investment and high unemployment are typically side effects of large government expenditures, rising interest costs, and high taxes. Changing trade patterns associated with the collapse of the former Soviet Union created an additional transition problem that drove the Finnish unemployment rate to record levels (nearly 20%) in 1994. The budgetary situation is going to force Finland to make some difficult decisions in the near future. If it is going to prosper, its needs to reduce the size of government and allow markets to coordinate more of its economic activity.

# FRANCE

**Part 1: The Economic Freedom Ratings for the Components and Various Area and Summary Indexes: 1975, 1980, 1985, 1990 and 1993-95.**

(The numbers in parentheses indicate the actual values for the components.)

|          | **Summary Ratings** | | |
|----------|------|------|------|
|          | **Ie** | **Is1** | **Is2** |
| 1975     | 4.4  | 4.3  | 4.4  |
| 1980     | 4.6  | 4.2  | 4.7  |
| 1985     | 3.9  | 3.4  | 4.1  |
| 1990     | 6.2  | 5.5  | 7    |
| 1993-95  | 6.6  | 6.0  | 7.5  |

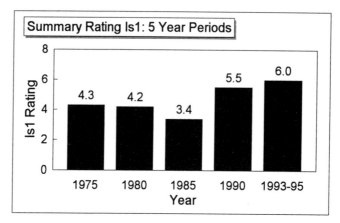

Summary Rating Is1: 5 Year Periods

| Components of Economic Freedom | 1975 | | 1980 | | 1985 | | 1990 | | 1993-95 | |
|---|---|---|---|---|---|---|---|---|---|---|
| **I. Money and Inflation** | **3.9** | | **4.6** | | **4.5** | | **9.7** | | **10.0** | |
| (a) Annual Money Growth (last 5 yrs.) | 5 | (8.4) | 4 | (10.2) | 6 | (8.1) | 9 | (3.0) | 10 | (-1.2) |
| (b) Inflation Variablity (last 5 yrs.) | 7 | (2.6) | 10 | (0.8) | 8 | (2.3) | 10 | (0.9) | 10 | (0.5) |
| (c) Ownership of Foreign Currency | 0 | | 0 | | 0 | | 10 | | 10 | |
| (d) Maint. of Bank Account Abroad | 0 | | 0 | | 0 | | 10 | | 10 | |
| | | | | | | | | | | |
| **II. Government Operation** | **4.5** | | **4.1** | | **3.7** | | **5.2** | | **6.0** | |
| (a) Govern. Consumption (% of GDP) | 3 | (16.6) | 2 | (18.1) | 1 | (19.4) | 2 | (17.9) | 1 | (19.8) |
| (b) Government Enterprises | 4 | | 4 | | 4 | | 6 | | 6 | |
| (c) Price Controls | - | | - | | - | | 6 | | 7 | |
| (d) Entry Into Business | - | | - | | - | | - | | 7.5 | |
| (e) Legal System | - | | - | | - | | - | | 7.5 | |
| (f) Avoidance of Negative Interest Rates | 8 | | 8 | | 8 | | 8 | | 8 | |
| | | | | | | | | | | |
| **III. Takings** | **2.3** | | **1.4** | | **0.5** | | **1.4** | | **1.4** | |
| (a) Transfers and Subsidies (% of GDP) | 0 | (24.0) | 0 | (26.1) | 0 | (26.8) | 0 | (25.2) | 0 | (26.9) |
| (b) Marginal Tax Rates (Top Rate) | 5 | (48) | 3 | (60) | 1 | (65) | 3 | (53) | 3 | (57) |
| (c) Conscription | 0 | | 0 | | 0 | | 0 | | 0 | |
| | | | | | | | | | | |
| **IV. International Sector** | **6.9** | | **6.0** | | **6.1** | | **7.9** | | **8.7** | |
| (a) Taxes on International Trade (Avg.) | 10 | (0.1) | 10 | (0.1) | 10 | (0.0) | 10 | (0.0) | 10 | (0.0) |
| (b) Black Market Exchange Rates (Prem.) | 10 | (0) | 6 | (3) | 6 | (4) | 10 | (0) | 10 | (0) |
| (c) Size of Trade Sector (% of GDP) | 4 | (54.0) | 5 | (67.2) | 6 | (47.1) | 5 | (46.1) | 5 | (45.0) |
| (d) Capital Transactions with Foreigners | 2 | | 2 | | 2 | | 5 | | 8 | |

## Part 2: Recent Economic Indicators:

| | | | | |
|---|---|---|---|---|
| **Population 1994:** | 58.0 | **Real Per Capita GDP** : | 1994= | $13,910 |
| (in millions) | | (in 1985 U.S. dollars) | | |
| Annual Rate of Change (1980-84): | 0.7% | Avg. Growth Rate: | 1980-90= | 1.9% |
| | | | 1985-94= | 1.6% |

| Economic Indicators: | 1987 | 1988 | 1989 | 1990 | 1991 | 1992 | 1993 | 1994 |
|---|---|---|---|---|---|---|---|---|
| Change in Real GDP: Aggregate | 2.3 | 4.5 | 4.3 | 2.5 | 0.8 | 1.2 | -0.9 | 1.8 |
| : Per Capita | 1.6 | 3.8 | 3.6 | 1.8 | 0.2 | 0.6 | -1.4 | 1.3 |
| Inflation Rate (CPI) | 3.3 | 2.7 | 3.5 | 3.4 | 3.2 | 2.4 | 2.1 | 1.7 |
| Change in Money Supply: (M1) | 4.6 | 1.9 | 5.4 | 3.9 | -4.7 | 0.0 | 1.4 | 1.6 |
| : (M2) | 6.6 | 5.6 | 2.5 | 3.4 | 0.6 | 0.5 | 1.6 | 4.1 |
| Investment/GDP Ratio | 20.2 | 21.4 | 22.3 | 22.5 | 21.4 | 19.7 | 17.5 | 18.7 |
| Central Government Budget Deficit (-) or Surplus (+) As a Percent of GDP | -1.2 | -2.3 | -1.9 | -2.1 | -2.2 | -3.9 | -5.8 | -5.9 |
| Unemployment Rate | 10.5 | 10.0 | 9.4 | 8.9 | 9.4 | 10.4 | 11.6 | 12.1 |

Based on the average of our three indexes, the French economy tied with South Korea for 20th place on the most free list. Its Is1 summary rating places it 32nd.

France's economic freedom rating improved during the last decade mostly as the result of a reduction in monetary growth, greater price stability, and legalization of foreign currency bank accounts. Like most of the European welfare state economies, France achieved high ratings in the monetary and international sectors, but low ratings for government operations and takings, particularly the latter. The ratings for all three of the components in the takings areas were exceedingly low. Transfers and subsidies have consistently taken more than one-quarter of GDP from the person who earned it and transferred it to another. The 57% top marginal tax bracket is one of the highest in the world. Combine these two factors with conscription, and you have a very low rating in the takings area.

A large transfer sector generally leads to two unpleasant side effects—large budget deficits and high unemployment rates. The French economy is plagued with both. The budget deficits of the 1990s have averaged approximately 4% of GDP, a level that is unsustainable for a country with a real growth rate of less than two percent. The deficit along with the double digit unemployment rates, will almost certainly lead to pressure for change in the years immediately ahead.

# GERMANY

## Part 1: The Economic Freedom Ratings for the Components and Various Area and Summary Indexes: 1975, 1980, 1985, 1990 and 1993-95.

(The numbers in parentheses indicate the actual values for the components.)

**Summary Ratings**

|        | Ie  | Is1 | Is2 |
|--------|-----|-----|-----|
| 1975   | 6.4 | 5.9 | 7.3 |
| 1980   | 6.6 | 6.0 | 7.6 |
| 1985   | 6.9 | 6.0 | 8.0 |
| 1990   | 7.0 | 6.3 | 7.8 |
| 1993-95| 7.1 | 6.4 | 7.8 |

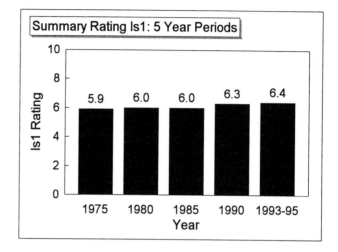

Summary Rating Is1: 5 Year Periods

| Components of Economic Freedom | 1975 | | 1980 | | 1985 | | 1990 | | 1993-95 | |
|---|---|---|---|---|---|---|---|---|---|---|
| **I. Money and Inflation** | **8.8** | | **9.4** | | **9.7** | | **8.5** | | **8.5** | |
| (a) Annual Money Growth (last 5 yrs.) | 6 | (7.5) | 8 | (4.5) | 9 | (3.1) | 5 | (9.6) | 5 | (8.7) |
| (b) Inflation Variablity (last 5 yrs.) | 10 | (0.9) | 10 | (0.5) | 10 | (1.0) | 10 | (0.7) | 10 | (0.6) |
| (c) Ownership of Foreign Currency | 10 | | 10 | | 10 | | 10 | | 10 | |
| (d) Maint. of Bank Account Abroad | 10 | | 10 | | 10 | | 10 | | 10 | |
| | | | | | | | | | | |
| **II. Government Operation** | **4.5** | | **4.9** | | **4.9** | | **6.4** | | **7.0** | |
| (a) Govern. Consumption (% of GDP) | 1 | (20.5) | 1 | (20.3) | 1 | (20.1) | 2 | (18.3) | 3 | (17.5) |
| (b) Government Enterprises | 6 | | 6 | | 6 | | 6 | | 6 | |
| (c) Price Controls | - | | - | | - | | 9 | | 9 | |
| (d) Entry Into Business | - | | - | | - | | - | | 7.5 | |
| (e) Legal System | - | | - | | - | | - | | 7.5 | |
| (f) Avoidance of Neg. Interest Rates | 8 | | 10 | | 10 | | 10 | | 10 | |
| | | | | | | | | | | |
| **III. Takings** | **2.7** | | **2.2** | | **1.3** | | **2.2** | | **1.9** | |
| (a) Transfers and Subsidies (% of GDP) | 2 | (17.4) | 2 | (17.6) | 1 | (19.0) | 2 | (17.9) | 0 | (22.4) |
| (b) Marginal Tax Rates (Top Rate) | 4 | (56) | 3 | (56) | 2 | (56) | 3 | (56) | 4 | (53) |
| (c) Conscription | 0 | | 0 | | 0 | | 0 | | 0 | |
| | | | | | | | | | | |
| **IV. International Sector** | **8.8** | | **8.8** | | **9.8** | | **9.7** | | **9.7** | |
| (a) Taxes on International Trade (Avg.) | 10 | (0.0) | 10 | (0.0) | 10 | (0.0) | 10 | (0.0) | 10 | (0.0) |
| (b) Black Market Exchange Rates (Prem.) | 10 | (0) | 10 | (0) | 10 | (0) | 10 | (0) | 10 | (0) |
| (c) Size of Trade Sector (% of GDP) | 6 | (46.5) | 6 | (53.3) | 9 | (61.5) | 8 | (58.0) | 8 | (59.9) |
| (d) Capital Transactions with Foreigners | 8 | | 8 | | 10 | | 10 | | 10 | |

## Part 2: Recent Economic Indicators:

**Population 1994:** 80.9  **Real Per Capita GDP :** 1994= $15,005 [a]

(in millions)  (in 1985 U.S. dollars)

Annual Rate of Change (1980-94): 0.2%  Avg. Growth Rate: 1980-90= 2.1%

1985-94= 2.1%

| Economic Indicators: | 1987 | 1988 | 1989 | 1990 | 1991 | 1992 | 1993 | 1994 |
|---|---|---|---|---|---|---|---|---|
| Change in Real GDP: Aggregate | 2.3 | 4.5 | 4.3 | 2.5 | 0.8 | 1.2 | -0.9 | 3.3 |
| : Per Capita | 2.1 | 4.3 | 4.1 | 2.3 | 0.6 | 1.0 | -1.1 | 3.1 |
| Inflation Rate (CPI) | 3.3 | 2.7 | 3.5 | 3.4 | 3.2 | 2.4 | 2.1 | 2.3 |
| Change in Money Supply: (M1) | 4.6 | 1.9 | 5.4 | 5.7 | -1.1 | -0.9 | - | 3.7 |
| : (M2) | 7.0 | 5.8 | 4.5 | 12.9 | 10.4 | 8.6 | 8.5 | 1.4 |
| Investment/GDP Ratio | 20.2 | 21.4 | 22.3 | 22.5 | 21.4 | 19.7 | 17.5 | 24.5 |
| Central Government Budget Deficit (-) or Surplus (+) As a Percent of GDP | -1.2 | -2.3 | -1.9 | -2.1 | -1.3 | -3.8 | -2.6 | - |
| Unemployment Rate | 6.3 | 6.3 | 5.7 | 5.0 | 4.2 | 4.6 | 5.8 | 6.5 |

a Data are for West Germany.

Based on the average of our three indexes, the German economy was the 12th freest (tied with Belgium and Malaysia) in the world in the mid-1990s. Both the summary rating and ranking of this country have been steady throughout the last two decades. No doubt, this relatively high economic freedom rating over a lengthy time period has contributed to the high income level of this country. Its $15,005 GDP per capita in 1994 was the 8th highest in the world.

Monetary and price stability (note the 10 ratings throughout for this component), freedom to maintain bank accounts in other currencies, a stable and competitive credit market, and a relatively free trade sector constitute the strengths of this economy. There are three major weaknesses—a high level of government consumption, a large transfer sector, and high tax rates. Throughout most of the last two decades, government consumption has taken approximately 20% of the GDP. Another 20% is taxed away from its earner and transferred to someone else. Thus, approximately 40% of the German GDP is channelled through the government; earners get to keep less than 60% of what they earn. The top marginal personal income tax rate is currently 53%, down only modestly from 56% in 1990. Since several other high-income industrial countries have reduced their top rates substantially during the last decade, the German rate is now one of the highest in the world.

Given its price stability, strong and competitive trade sector, and high investment rate, this economy will probably continue to perform reasonably well in the future. However, other economies that have adopted more liberal policies will almost surely achieve higher growth rates. Therefore, if Germany continues on its present course, its income *relative to other countries* is likely to decline in the future.

# GHANA

**Part 1: The Economic Freedom Ratings for the Components and Various Area and Summary Indexes: 1975, 1980, 1985, 1990 and 1993-95.**

(The numbers in parentheses indicate the actual values for the components.)

|  | **Summary Ratings** | | |
|---|---|---|---|
|  | **Ie** | **Is1** | **Is2** |
| 1975 | 2.1 | 2.5 | 1.3 |
| 1980 | 1.8 | 2.3 | 1.0 |
| 1985 | 2.1 | 2.8 | 1.0 |
| 1990 | 3.3 | 3.6 | 2.6 |
| 1993-95 | 4.5 | 4.8 | 3.9 |

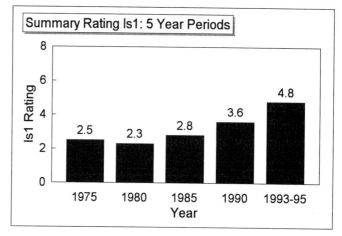

| Components of Economic Freedom | 1975 | | 1980 | | 1985 | | 1990 | | 1993-95 | |
|---|---|---|---|---|---|---|---|---|---|---|
| **I. Money and Inflation** | **1.0** | | **0.6** | | **0.3** | | **3.9** | | **2.9** | |
| (a) Annual Money Growth (last 5 yrs.) | 1 | (25.6) | 1 | (42.8) | 1 | (43.9) | 1 | (37.9) | 1 | (25.0) |
| (b) Inflation Variablity (last 5 yrs.) | 2 | (8.7) | 1 | (16.9) | 0 | (38.2) | 5 | (4.8) | 2 | (8.6) |
| (c) Ownership of Foreign Currency | 0 | | 0 | | 0 | | 10 | | 10 | |
| (d) Maint. of Bank Account Abroad | 0 | | 0 | | 0 | | 0 | | 0 | |
| | | | | | | | | | | |
| **II. Government Operation** | **3.4** | | **2.7** | | **3.5** | | **3.0** | | **5.0** | |
| (a) Govern. Consumption (% of GDP) | 7 | (13.0) | 7 | (11.2) | 9 | (9.4) | 8 | (10.9) | 7 | (11.7) |
| (b) Government Enterprises | 0 | | 0 | | 0 | | 2 | | 2 | |
| (c) Price Controls | - | | - | | - | | 0 | | 6 | |
| (d) Entry Into Business | - | | - | | - | | - | | 5 | |
| (e) Legal System | - | | - | | - | | - | | 2.5 | |
| (f) Avoidance of Neg. Interest Rates | - | | 0 | | 0 | | 2 | | 8 | |
| | | | | | | | | | | |
| **III. Takings** | **4.5** | | **5.0** | | **5.8** | | **5.5** | | **7.4** | |
| (a) Transfers and Subsidies (% of GDP) | 8 | (3.1) | 8 | (2.4) | 10 | (1.3) | 8 | (2.6) | 7 | (3.3) |
| (b) Marginal Tax Rates (Top Rate) | 0 | (70) | 1 | (60) | 1 | (60) | 2 | (55) | 7 | (35) |
| (c) Conscription | 10 | | 10 | | 10 | | 10 | | 10 | |
| | | | | | | | | | | |
| **IV. International Sector** | **0.4** | | **0.0** | | **0.3** | | **1.8** | | **2.9** | |
| (a) Taxes on International Trade (Avg.) | 0 | (20.6) | 0 | (17.3) | 0 | (21.7) | 1 | (11.6) | 2 | (8.6) |
| (b) Black Market Exchange Rates (Prem.) | 1 | (67) | 0 | (304) | 1 | (142) | 5 | (7) | 7 | (2) |
| (c) Size of Trade Sector (% of GDP) | 1 | (37.8) | 0 | (17.6) | 0 | (21.2) | 1 | (39.4) | 2 | (42.8) |
| (d) Capital Transactions with Foreigners | 0 | | 0 | | 0 | | 0 | | 0 | |

146

## Part 2: Recent Economic Indicators:

| | | | | |
|---|---|---|---|---|
| **Population 1994:** | 16.8 | **Real Per Capita GDP** : | 1993= | $975 |
| (in millions) | | (in 1985 U.S. dollars) | | |
| Annual Rate of Change (1980-94): | 3.2% | Avg. Growth Rate: | 1980-90 = | -1.1% |
| | | | 1985-93 = | 1.4% |

| Economic Indicators: | 1987 | 1988 | 1989 | 1990 | 1991 | 1992 | 1993 | 1994 |
|---|---|---|---|---|---|---|---|---|
| Change in Real GDP: Aggregate | 4.8 | 5.6 | 5.1 | 3.3 | 5.3 | 3.9 | 5.0 | |
| : Per Capita | 1.6 | 2.4 | 2.7 | 0.1 | 2.1 | 0.7 | 1.8 | |
| Inflation Rate (CPI) | 39.8 | 31.4 | 25.2 | 37.3 | 18.0 | 10.1 | 25.0 | 24.9 |
| Change in Money Supply (M1) | 52.6 | 44.0 | 50.8 | 29.7 | 4.3 | 22.8 | 48.0 | 36.6 |
| : (M2) | 56.9 | 44.2 | 57.2 | 27.5 | 12.1 | 34.8 | 39.9 | 33.7 |
| Investment/GDP Ratio | 10.4 | 10.9 | 13.5 | 12.3 | 12.7 | 12.9 | 14.8 | |
| Central Government Budget Deficit (-) or Surplus (+) As a Percent of GDP | +0.5 | +0.4 | +0.7 | +0.2 | +1.5 | -4.8 | -2.5 | - |
| Unemployment Rate | | | | | | | | |

In 1990-95 the average of our three indexes placed Ghana 62nd (tied with Bulgaria and India) among the 103 countries in our study. Despite its low rating, Ghana's economy is one of the freest in Africa. Only Mauritius and Botswana are rated significantly higher. During the 1975-1985 period, this economy was beset with monetary instability, negative interest rates, high marginal tax rates, rigid exchange rate controls (the 1985 black market premium was 142%, down from 304% in 1980), and restrictive trade practices. Thus, its ratings during this period were among the lowest in the world.

During the last decade, there has been observable improvement, most notably some relaxation of both interest rate and exchange rate controls and a sharp reduction in the top marginal tax rate from 60% to 35%. Much more needs to be done. During the last five years, monetary expansion has averaged 25% annually. The predictable side effect—a high and variable rate of the inflation—continues to undermine the confidence and planning of decision-makers. Trade restrictions continue to retard international exchange and the mobility of capital. Foreign investors must obtain approval from the Ghana Investment Center prior to undertaking a project otherwise they will not be permitted to remit returns from their investment. Policies of this type must be scrapped if this poor country is going to develop in the future.

# GREECE

## Part 1: The Economic Freedom Ratings for the Components and Various Area and Summary Indexes: 1975, 1980, 1985, 1990 and 1993-95.

(The numbers in parentheses indicate the actual values for the components.)

### Summary Ratings

|  | Ie | Is1 | Is2 |
|------|------|------|------|
| 1975 | 3.7 | 3.9 | 3.2 |
| 1980 | 3.8 | 3.8 | 3.5 |
| 1985 | 3.5 | 3.2 | 3.4 |
| 1990 | 3.5 | 3.4 | 3.5 |
| 1993-95 | 4.9 | 4.9 | 5.0 |

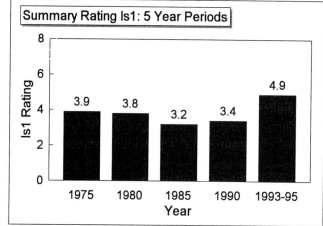

Summary Rating Is1: 5 Year Periods

| Components of Economic Freedom | 1975 | | 1980 | | 1985 | | 1990 | | 1993-95 | |
|---|---|---|---|---|---|---|---|---|---|---|
| **I. Money and Inflation** | **3.8** | | **5.2** | | **5.2** | | **4.9** | | **4.5** | |
| (a) Annual Money Growth (last 5 yrs.) | 3 | (12.9) | 2 | (14.1) | 2 | (16.5) | 2 | (18.6) | 2 | (16.5) |
| (b) Inflation Variablity (last 5 yrs.) | 3 | (7.3) | 8 | (2.4) | 8 | (2.3) | 7 | (2.9) | 6 | (3.4) |
| (c) Ownership of Foreign Currency | 10 | | 10 | | 10 | | 10 | | 10 | |
| (d) Maint. of Bank Account Abroad | 0 | | 0 | | 0 | | 0 | | 0 | |
| | | | | | | | | | | |
| **II. Government Operation** | **3.6** | | **3.6** | | **2.5** | | **2.0** | | **4.7** | |
| (a) Govern. Consumption (% of GDP) | 5 | (15.2) | 4 | (16.4) | 1 | (20.4) | 1 | (21.1) | 1 | (19.7) |
| (b) Government Enterprises | 2 | | 2 | | 2 | | 2 | | 2 | |
| (c) Price Controls | - | | - | | - | | 0 | | 6 | |
| (d) Entry Into Business | - | | - | | - | | - | | 7.5 | |
| (e) Legal System | - | | - | | - | | - | | 5 | |
| (f) Avoidance of Neg. Interest Rates | 4 | | 6 | | 6 | | 8 | | 8 | |
| | | | | | | | | | | |
| **III. Takings** | **3.5** | | **2.6** | | **1.3** | | **1.9** | | **3.1** | |
| (a) Transfers and Subsidies (% of GDP) | 4 | (8.5) | 3 | (12.5) | 2 | (18.0) | 0 | (27.1) | 2 | (15.6) |
| (b) Marginal Tax Rates (Top Rate) | 4 | (52) | 3 | (60) | 1 | (63) | 4 | (50) | 5 | (40) |
| (c) Conscription | 0 | | 0 | | 0 | | 0 | | 0 | |
| | | | | | | | | | | |
| **IV. International Sector** | **4.6** | | **4.3** | | **4.7** | | **5.6** | | **7.5** | |
| (a) Taxes on International Trade (Avg.) | 7 | (3.5) | 7 | (3.2) | 9 | (0.3) | 10 | (0.1) | 10 | (0.1) |
| (b) Black Market Exchange Rates (Prem.) | 6 | (3) | 5 | (7) | 3 | (25) | 6 | (3) | 10 | (0) |
| (c) Size of Trade Sector (% of GDP) | 2 | (43.7) | 2 | (47.1) | 4 | (53.9) | 3 | (54.2) | 3 | (56.1) |
| (d) Capital Transactions with Foreigners | 2 | | 2 | | 2 | | 2 | | 5 | |

## Part 2: Recent Economic Indicators:

| | | | | |
|---|---|---|---|---|
| **Population 1994:** | 10.5 | **Real Per Capita GDP** : | 1994= | $6,783 |
| (in millions) | | (in 1985 U.S. dollars) | | |
| Annual Rate of Change (1980-94): | 0.5% | Avg. Growth Rate: | 1980-90= | 0.9% |
| | | | 1985-94= | 0.9% |

| Economic Indicators: | 1987 | 1988 | 1989 | 1990 | 1991 | 1992 | 1993 | 1994 |
|---|---|---|---|---|---|---|---|---|
| Change in Real GDP: Aggregate | -0.5 | 4.5 | 3.5 | -1.1 | 3.3 | 0.9 | -0.5 | 1.1 |
| : Per Capita | -0.7 | 4.2 | 3.2 | -1.6 | 2.1 | -0.1 | -1.0 | 0.6 |
| Inflation Rate (CPI) | 16.4 | 13.5 | 13.7 | 20.4 | 19.5 | 15.9 | 14.4 | 10.9 |
| Change in Money Supply: (M1) | 18.7 | 14.5 | 21.5 | 23.3 | 15.6 | 15.5 | 13.1 | 28.1 |
| : (M2) | 21.5 | 23.6 | 22.1 | 18.5 | 7.4 | 12.4 | 4.1 | 24.8 |
| Investment/GDP Ratio | 17.6 | 19.3 | 20.9 | 19.9 | 20.4 | 19.8 | 19.3 | 19.5 |
| Central Government Budget Deficit (-) or Surplus (+) As a Percent of GDP | -13.7 | -15.2 | -26.4 | -28.9 | -18.9 | -12.0 | -15.7 | - |
| Unemployment Rate | 6.4 | 6.0 | 6.5 | 6.4 | 7.3 | 8.7 | 9.8 | 10.1 |

Greece may well be the cradle of democracy, but it still has a long way to go in the area of economic freedom. Throughout 1975-1990, Greece's summary ratings were just slightly better than those of the Bottom Ten. (See Exhibit 2-2 for evidence on this point.) Its rating jumped substantially in the 1990s. Based on the average of our three indexes, the Greek economy now ranks 54th (tied with Cyprus and South Africa) among the 103 countries of our study.

The major factors underlying this recent improvement were:

- elimination of price controls in several areas;
- reduction of the top marginal tax rate to 40%, down from 63% in 1985 and 50% in 1990;
- movement to a fully convertible currency in the foreign exchange market; and
- relaxation of various restrictions limiting the mobility of capital.

Much more needs to be done. Monetary policy continues to be far too expansionary. (Note that the monetary aggregates have continued to grow at approximately 20% annually in recent years.) Huge budget deficits (these deficits have averaged 20% of GDP during the five years) fuel the pressure for monetary expansion, drain funds from the capital market, and undermine confidence in the governmental authorities. Greece needs to follow the path of Portugal, another relatively poor member of the European Union. During the last two decades, Portugal has taken a number of steps toward economic freedom and it has paid off with a handsome rate of economic growth. It is time for Greece to travel this same road.

# GUATEMALA

## Part 1: The Economic Freedom Ratings for the Components and Various Area and Summary Indexes: 1975, 1980, 1985, 1990 and 1993-95.

(The numbers in parentheses indicate the actual values for the components.)

### Summary Ratings

|      | Ie  | Is1 | Is2 |
|------|-----|-----|-----|
| 1975 | 5.9 | 6.5 | 5.3 |
| 1980 | 6.4 | 6.8 | 6.0 |
| 1985 | 5.6 | 5.7 | 5.1 |
| 1990 | 6.3 | 6.6 | 6.0 |
| 1993-95 | 6.2 | 6.5 | 5.8 |

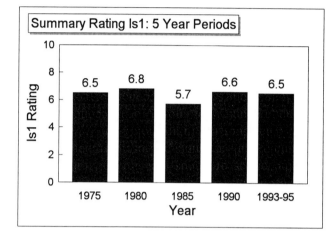

| Components of Economic Freedom | 1975 | | 1980 | | 1985 | | 1990 | | 1993-95 | |
|---|---|---|---|---|---|---|---|---|---|---|
| **I. Money and Inflation** | **4.2** | | **6.9** | | **6.2** | | **4.6** | | **4.6** | |
| (a) Annual Money Growth (last 5 yrs.) | 5 | (9.7) | 4 | (10.7) | 4 | (10.1) | 2 | (18.3) | 1 | (21.1) |
| (b) Inflation Variablity (last 5 yrs.) | 3 | (7.8) | 6 | (3.6) | 4 | (5.3) | 1 | (15.2) | 2 | (13.2) |
| (c) Ownership of Foreign Currency | 0 | | 10 | | 10 | | 10 | | 10 | |
| (d) Maint. of Bank Account Abroad | 10 | | 10 | | 10 | | 10 | | 10 | |
| | | | | | | | | | | |
| **II. Government Operation** | **9.0** | | **8.4** | | **8.8** | | **7.9** | | **6.8** | |
| (a) Govern. Consumption (% of GDP) | 10 | (6.9) | 9 | (8.0) | 10 | (7.1) | 10 | (6.8) | 10 | (6.4) |
| (b) Government Enterprises | 8 | | 8 | | 8 | | 8 | | 8 | |
| (c) Price Controls | - | | - | | - | | 6 | | 6 | |
| (d) Entry Into Business | - | | - | | - | | - | | 7.5 | |
| (e) Legal System | - | | - | | - | | - | | 0 | |
| (f) Avoidance of Neg. Interest Rates | - | | 8 | | 8 | | 8 | | 8 | |
| | | | | | | | | | | |
| **III. Takings** | **8.2** | | **7.7** | | **6.3** | | **6.9** | | **7.8** | |
| (a) Transfers and Subsidies (% of GDP) | 10 | (0.8) | 10 | (1.2) | 10 | (1.3) | 9 | (1.8) | 9 | (1.9) |
| (b) Marginal Tax Rates (Top Rate) | 9 | (34) | 8 | (40) | 5 | (48) | 7 | (34) | 9 | (25) |
| (c) Conscription | 0 | | 0 | | 0 | | 0 | | 0 | |
| | | | | | | | | | | |
| **IV. International Sector** | **4.5** | | **4.4** | | **2.5** | | **6.3** | | **6.0** | |
| (a) Taxes on International Trade (Avg.) | 6 | (5.6) | 6 | (4.8) | 3 | (7.5) | 7 | (3.6) | 7 | (3.6) |
| (b) Black Market Exchange Rates (Prem.) | 4 | (10) | 4 | (10) | 1 | (89) | 10 | (0) | 6 | (4) |
| (c) Size of Trade Sector (% of GDP) | 2 | (45.3) | 1 | (47.1) | 0 | (25.0) | 1 | (43.4) | 1 | (45.0) |
| (d) Capital Transactions with Foreigners | 5 | | 5 | | 5 | | 5 | | 8 | |

## Part 2: Recent Economic Indicators:

| **Population 1994:** | 10.2 | | **Real Per Capita GDP** : | | 1994= | $2,300 |
| (in millions) | | | (in 1985 U.S. dollars) | | | |
| Annual Rate of Change (1980-94): | 2.9 | | Avg. Growth Rate: | | 1980-90= | -2.0% |
| | | | | | 1985-93= | 0.6% |

| Economic Indicators: | 1987 | 1988 | 1989 | 1990 | 1991 | 1992 | 1993 | 1994 |
|---|---|---|---|---|---|---|---|---|
| Change in Real GDP: Aggregate | 3.5 | 3.9 | 3.9 | 3.1 | 3.6 | 4.8 | 4.0 | 4.0 |
| : Per Capita | 0.6 | 1.0 | 1.0 | 0.2 | 0.7 | 1.9 | 1.1 | 1.0 |
| Inflation Rate (CPI) | 12.3 | 10.8 | 11.4 | 41.2 | 33.2 | 10.0 | 11.8 | 10.5 |
| Change in Money Supply (M1) | 13.7 | 10.2 | 14.4 | 32.7 | 19.1 | 16.6 | 18.1 | 34.1 |
| : (M2) | 14.0 | 15.6 | 15.9 | 21.3 | 35.1 | 47.4 | 12.1 | 10.6 |
| Investment/GDP Ratio | 13.9 | 13.7 | 13.5 | 13.6 | 14.3 | 18.2 | 18.7 | 16.4 |
| Central Government Budget | | | | | | | | |
| Deficit (-)or Surplus (+) | | | | | | | | |
| As a Percent of GDP | -1.3 | -1.7 | -2.9 | -2.1 | 0.0 | 0.0 | -1.7 | -1.4 |
| Unemployment Rate | | | | | | | | |

Based on the average for our three indexes, Guatemala ranks 26th (tied with several other countries) among the countries in our study. Except for a decline during the mid-1980s that was primarily the result of higher trade taxes, more restrictive exchange rate controls, and a decline in the size of the trade sector, Guatemala's summary rating has been steady throughout the last two decades.

The major weaknesses of this economy are monetary instability, insecure property rights, and an absence of the rule of law. During the last decade, budget deficits financed with the creation of money have become a habit. The money supply has been increasing at an annual rate of approximately 20 percent. Predictably this policy leads to a high and variable rate of inflation which undermines investment and other exchanges involving a time dimension. (Note: Effective in 1995, a new constitutional provision prohibits the central bank from extending credit to the government. This is a positive step toward more stable monetary arrangements.) The legal system often grants political officials discretionary authority. This undermines the rule of law and inevitably leads to political corruption and loss of confidence in the system.

Some modest steps toward economic freedom have been taken. Between 1985 and 1994, the top marginal tax rate was reduced from 48% to 25%. Unfortunately the rate was increased to 30% in 1995. Taxes on international trade have declined slightly during the last decade. However, without monetary stability and a more even-handed legal system, it will be difficult for this poor country to find the path to consistent economic growth.

# HONDURAS

## Part 1: The Economic Freedom Ratings for the Components and Various Area and Summary Indexes: 1975, 1980, 1985, 1990 and 1993-95.

(The numbers in parentheses indicate the actual values for the components.)

### Summary Ratings

|         | Ie  | Is1 | Is2 |
|---------|-----|-----|-----|
| 1975    | 7.1 | 7.4 | 6.8 |
| 1980    | 6.1 | 6.1 | 6.1 |
| 1985    | 6.2 | 6.0 | 6.0 |
| 1990    | 5.9 | 6.0 | 5.7 |
| 1993-95 | 5.5 | 5.5 | 5.4 |

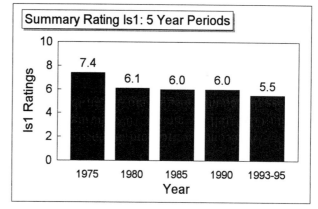

Summary Rating Is1: 5 Year Periods

| Components of Economic Freedom | 1975 | | 1980 | | 1985 | | 1990 | | 1993-95 | |
|---|---|---|---|---|---|---|---|---|---|---|
| **I. Money and Inflation** | **7.1** | | **6.9** | | **9.7** | | **5.2** | | **5.2** | |
| (a) Annual Money Growth (last 5 yrs.) | 7 | (6.4) | 3 | (12.9) | 9 | (2.6) | 2 | (15.7) | 2 | (17.8) |
| (b) Inflation Variablity (last 5 yrs.) | 4 | (5.4) | 7 | (3.0) | 10 | (1.3) | 3 | (6.7) | 3 | (6.7) |
| (c) Ownership of Foreign Currency | 10 | | 10 | | 10 | | 10 | | 10 | |
| (d) Maint. of Bank Account Abroad | 10 | | 10 | | 10 | | 10 | | 10 | |
| | | | | | | | | | | |
| **II. Government Operation** | **7.5** | | **7.5** | | **7.7** | | **7.6** | | **6.1** | |
| (a) Govern. Consumption (% of GDP) | 7 | (12.4) | 7 | (12.7) | 6 | (13.1) | 7 | (12.9) | 8 | (10.6) |
| (b) Government Enterprises | 8 | | 8 | | 8 | | 8 | | 8 | |
| (c) Price Controls | - | | - | | - | | - | | 4 | |
| (d) Entry Into Business | - | | - | | - | | - | | 7.5 | |
| (e) Legal System | - | | - | | - | | - | | 2.5 | |
| (f) Avoidance of Neg. Interest Rates | - | | - | | 10 | | 8 | | 6 | |
| | | | | | | | | | | |
| **III. Takings** | **9.5** | | **8.4** | | **5.9** | | **5.9** | | **5.1** | |
| (a) Transfers and Subsidies (% of GDP) | 10 | (0.5) | - | | 9 | (2.3) | 9 | (2.2) | 7 | (4.0) |
| (b) Marginal Tax Rates (Top Rate) | 9 | (27) | 8 | (40) | 5 | (46) | 5 | (46) | 5 | (46) |
| (c) Conscription | - | | 10 | | 0 | | 0 | | 0 | |
| | | | | | | | | | | |
| **IV. International Sector** | **5.4** | | **3.1** | | **0.9** | | **5.1** | | **4.9** | |
| (a) Taxes on International Trade (Avg.) | 6 | (5.3) | 4 | (6.7) | - | | - | | - | |
| (b) Black Market Exchange Rates (Prem.) | 10 | (0) | 4 | (20) | 1 | (65) | 10 | (0) | 6 | (3) |
| (c) Size of Trade Sector (% of GDP) | 5 | (70.4) | 5 | (80.3) | 2 | (54.1) | 5 | (75.2) | 3 | (65.3) |
| (d) Capital Transactions with Foreigners | 0 | | 0 | | 0 | | 0 | | 5 | |

152

## Part 2: Recent Economic Indicators:

**Population 1994:**        5.7      **Real Per Capita GD :**     1994=   $1,335

   (in millions)                     (in 1985 U.S. dollars)

Annual Rate of Change (1980-94):   3.1%        Avg. Growth Rate:    1980-90=   -0.9%

                                                     1985-94=   -0.1%

| Economic Indicators: | 1987 | 1988 | 1989 | 1990 | 1991 | 1992 | 1993 | 1994 |
|---|---|---|---|---|---|---|---|---|
| Change in Real GDP: Aggregate | 6.0 | 4.6 | 4.3 | 0.1 | 3.3 | 5.6 | 3.7 | -1.3 |
| : Per Capita | 2.9 | 1.5 | 1.2 | -3.0 | 0.2 | 2.5 | 0.6 | -4.5 |
| Inflation Rate (CPI) | 2.5 | 4.5 | 9.9 | 23.3 | 34.0 | 8.8 | 10.7 | 21.7 |
| Change in Money Supply: (M1) | 14.4 | 13.4 | 14.4 | 28.3 | 20.2 | 11.9 | 19.2 | 36.6 |
| : (M2) | 15.9 | 20.0 | 11.9 | 19.8 | 21.7 | 18.4 | 18.9 | 28.6 |
| Investment/GDP Ratio | 17.4 | 21.0 | 19.1 | 23.0 | 24.7 | 26.0 | 26.7 | 25.9 |
| Central Government Budget Deficit (-) or Surplus (+) As a Percent of GDP | - | -3.0 | -3.3 | -3.4 | +0.7 | +0.9 | -0.2 | -0.1 |
| Unemployment Rate | | | | | | | | |

In 1975, Honduras was one of the most economically free countries in the world. Our Is1 summary index ranked it 2nd—behind only Hong Kong—in 1975. In our other two summary indexes, its ranking was lower, but nonetheless impressive. Since that time, the rating of Honduras has slid downward. In the mid-1990s, our indexes place it 47th among the 103 nations in our study.

What accounts for the decline? An increase in monetary instability was clearly a contributing factor. In the five years prior to 1975, the M1 money supply increased at a modest annual rate of 6.4%; during the most recent period, the annual rate of increase was 17.8%. Not surprisingly, the more rapid monetary growth led to increased variability in the rate of inflation. Honduran authorities also increased the top marginal tax rates from 27% in 1975 to 46% in the 1980s. The higher rate remains in effect. Thus, the amount of marginal earnings that the most productive citizens are allowed to keep for themselves is now substantially less than was the case in 1975. Conscription was instituted beginning in the 1980s. Exchange rate controls were imposed off and on throughout the last 15 years. In the mid-1980s the controls were so rigid that the black market premium rose to 65%. All of these factors contributed to the decline in economic freedom.

As economic freedom dropped, so too, did the performance of the economy. Per capita GDP fell by almost 10% during the 1980s and there is little sign of a rebound. Unless this country begins moving in the opposite direction, its economic future is bleak.

# HONG KONG

**Part 1: The Economic Freedom Ratings for the Components and Various Area and Summary Indexes: 1975, 1980, 1985, 1990 and 1993-95.**

(The numbers in parentheses indicate the actual values for the components.)

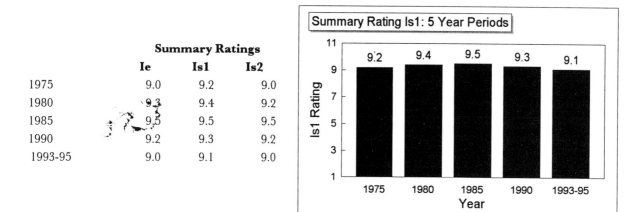

|  | **Summary Ratings** | | |
|---|---|---|---|
|  | **Ie** | **Is1** | **Is2** |
| 1975 | 9.0 | 9.2 | 9.0 |
| 1980 | 9.3 | 9.4 | 9.2 |
| 1985 | 9.5 | 9.5 | 9.5 |
| 1990 | 9.2 | 9.3 | 9.2 |
| 1993-95 | 9.0 | 9.1 | 9.0 |

| Components of Economic Freedom | 1975 | | 1980 | | 1985 | | 1990 | | 1993-95 | |
|---|---|---|---|---|---|---|---|---|---|---|
| **I. Money and Inflation** | **6.8** | | **7.7** | | **8.7** | | **7.2** | | **6.8** | |
| (a) Annual Money Growth (last 5 yrs.) | 5 | (9.3) | 9 | (2.9) | 9 | (2.9) | 4 | (10.3) | 5 | (9.9) |
| (b) Inflation Variablity (last 5 yrs.) | 5 | (3.9) | 4 | (5.2) | 7 | (2.5) | 7 | (2.9) | 5 | (4.5) |
| (c) Ownership of Foreign Currency | 10 | | 10 | | 10 | | 10 | | 10 | |
| (d) Maint. of Bank Account Abroad | 10 | | 10 | | 10 | | 10 | | 10 | |
| | | | | | | | | | | |
| **II. Government Operation** | **10.0** | | **10.0** | | **10.0** | | **10.0** | | **9.4** | |
| (a) Govern. Consumption (% of GDP) | 10 | (7.5) | 10 | (6.5) | 10 | (7.6) | 10 | (6.2) | 10 | (6.9) |
| (b) Government Enterprises | 10 | | 10 | | 10 | | 10 | | 10 | |
| (c) Price Controls | - | | - | | - | | 10 | | 9 | |
| (d) Entry Into Business | - | | - | | - | | - | | 10 | |
| (e) Legal System | - | | - | | - | | - | | 7.5 | |
| (f) Avoidance of Neg. Interest Rates | - | | - | | - | | - | | - | |
| | | | | | | | | | | |
| **III. Takings** | **10.0** | | **10.0** | | **9.5** | | **9.5** | | **9.5** | |
| (a) Transfers and Subsidies (% of GDP) | 10 | (1.1) | 10 | (0.6) | 10 | (0.9) | 10 | (0.9) | 10 | (1.2) |
| (b) Marginal Tax Rates (Top Rate) | 10 | (15) | 10 | (15) | 9 | (25) | 9 | (25) | 9 | (25) |
| (c) Conscription | 10 | | 10 | | 10 | | 10 | | 10 | |
| | | | | | | | | | | |
| **IV. International Sector** | **9.5** | | **9.5** | | **9.7** | | **9.7** | | **9.7** | |
| (a) Taxes on International Trade (Avg.) | 9 | (0.7) | 9 | (0.5) | 9 | (0.6) | 9 | (0.4) | 9 | (0.3) |
| (b) Black Market Exchange Rates (Prem.) | 10 | (0) | 10 | (0) | 10 | (0) | 10 | (0) | 10 | (0) |
| (c) Size of Trade Sector (% of GDP) | 9 | (162.5) | 9 | (180.7) | 10 | (209.5) | 10 | (262.9) | 10 | (285.8) |
| (d) Capital Transactions with Foreigners | 10 | | 10 | | 10 | | 10 | | 10 | |

## Part 2: Recent Economic Indicators:

| | | | | | |
|---|---|---|---|---|---|
| **Population 1994:** | 6.0 | **Real Per Capita GDP :** | 1994 = | $17,832 |
| (in millions) | | (in 1985 U.S. dollars) | | |
| Annual Rate of Change (1980-94): | 1.2% | Avg. Growth Rate: | 1980-90 = | 5.4% |
| | | | 1985-94 = | 5.7% |

| Economic Indicators: | 1987 | 1988 | 1989 | 1990 | 1991 | 1992 | 1993 | 1994 |
|---|---|---|---|---|---|---|---|---|
| Change in Real GDP:Aggregate | 14.5 | 8.3 | 2.8 | 3.0 | 3.9 | 5.4 | 5.4 | 5.1 |
| : Per Capita | 13.3 | 7.1 | 1.6 | 1.8 | 2.7 | 4.2 | 4.2 | 3.9 |
| Inflation Rate (CPI) | 5.3 | 7.4 | 9.7 | 9.7 | 11.0 | 9.6 | 8.7 | 8.6 |
| Change in Money Supply: (M1) | 46.0 | 8.5 | 6.8 | 13.3 | 19.5 | 21.1 | 20.6 | 6.1 |
| : (M2) | 30.7 | 14.2 | 19.9 | 22.3 | 13.3 | 10.8 | 16.0 | 12.8 |
| Investment/GDP Ratio | 26.4 | 28.6 | 26.7 | 27.4 | 27.2 | 28.5 | 27.7 | 31.8 |
| Central Government Budget Deficit (-) or Surplus (+) As a Percent of GDP | +3.3 | +4.2 | +2.1 | +0.7 | +3.4 | +2.8 | +2.1 | +0.8 |
| Unemployment Rate | 1.7 | 1.4 | 1.1 | 1.3 | 1.8 | 2.0 | 2.0 | 1.9 |

Hong Kong is the freest nation in the world and this has been the case for the last several decades. It provides a vivid reminder of what an economically free people can accomplish in a relatively short period of time. In 1960, Hong Kong's per capita GDP was $2,247, less than the comparable figures for Israel, Mexico, and Argentina, for example. Its 1960 income figure was approximately one-third that of Venezuela, Sweden, and Canada; and one-fourth that of Switzerland and United States. Three decades of sustained growth have changed all of this. In 1994, Hong Kong's per capita GDP ($17,832) was the second highest in the world, following only the United States. (Note: the per capita GDP figures are all in constant purchasing power 1985 U.S. dollars, see Summers and Heston.)

In contrast with most other high-income nations, government consumption in Hong Kong remains small (6.9% of GDP during the most recent year), transfers and subsidies are low (approximately 1% of GDP), and the top marginal tax rate is 25% with a ceiling on the average tax rate set at 15% of gross income. Clearly, the citizens of Hong Kong are permitted to keep most of what they earn. Hong Kong's economic freedom ratings is exceedingly high in every area except monetary and price stability, and even its middle rating in this area may be misleading because Hong Kong's recent inflation is the result of a structural transformation that has pushed up the prices of goods that are not traded internationally. In addition, residents are free to maintain bank accounts and use currencies other than the Hong Kong dollar if they wish to do so. What does the future hold? In 1997, the political control over Hong Kong will revert to China, a country not known for its economic freedom. Hopefully, the Chinese will look closely at Hong Kong's enviable economic record before they decide to transform the world freest economy.

# INDIA

## Part 1: The Economic Freedom Ratings for the Components and Various Area and Summary Indexes:  1975, 1980, 1985, 1990 and 1993-95.
(The numbers in parentheses indicate the actual values for the components.)

|  | **Summary Ratings** | | |
|---|---|---|---|
|  | **Ie** | **Is1** | **Is2** |
| 1975 | 3.0 | 3.3 | 2.3 |
| 1980 | 3.8 | 3.8 | 3.2 |
| 1985 | 3.5 | 3.4 | 3.1 |
| 1990 | 3.7 | 3.7 | 3.3 |
| 1993-95 | 4.5 | 4.5 | 4.1 |

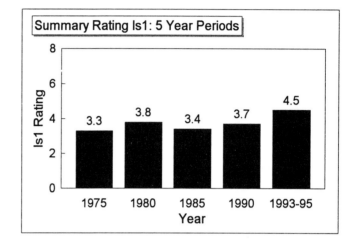

| **Components of Economic Freedom** | 1975 | | 1980 | | 1985 | | 1990 | | 1993-95 | |
|---|---|---|---|---|---|---|---|---|---|---|
| **I.  Money and Inflation** | **2.5** | | **3.5** | | **4.6** | | **4.5** | | **3.9** | |
| (a)  Annual Money Growth (last 5 yrs.) | 5 | (8.7) | 6 | (7.8) | 4 | (10.8) | 5 | (9.4) | 3 | (12.7) |
| (b)  Inflation Variablity (last 5 yrs.) | 3 | (7.2) | 5 | (4.8) | 10 | (1.1) | 9 | (1.4) | 9 | (2.1) |
| (c) Ownership of Foreign Currency | 0 | | 0 | | 0 | | 0 | | 0 | |
| (d) Maint. of Bank Account Abroad | 0 | | 0 | | 0 | | 0 | | 0 | |
|  | | | | | | | | | | |
| **II.  Government Operation** | **4.4** | | **5.1** | | **4.3** | | **3.9** | | **4.5** | |
| (a)  Govern. Consumption (% of GDP) | 9 | (9.4) | 9 | (9.6) | 7 | (11.1) | 7 | (11.6) | 7 | (11.8) |
| (b) Government Enterprises | 0 | | 0 | | 0 | | 0 | | 2 | |
| (c) Price Controls | - | | - | | - | | 3 | | 3 | |
| (d) Entry Into Business | - | | - | | - | | - | | 5 | |
| (e) Legal System | - | | - | | - | | - | | 2.5 | |
| (f) Avoidance of Neg. Interest Rates | - | | 8 | | 8 | | 8 | | 10 | |
|  | | | | | | | | | | |
| **III.  Takings** | **4.1** | | **4.2** | | **3.3** | | **4.3** | | **5.2** | |
| (a) Transfers and Subsidies (% of GDP) | 7 | (3.8) | 6 | (5.4) | 5 | (6.5) | 5 | (6.5) | 5 | (6.7) |
| (b) Marginal Tax Rates (Top Rate) | 0 | (77) | 1 | (60) | 0 | (62) | 2 | (53) | 4 | (45) |
| (c) Conscription | 10 | | 10 | | 10 | | 10 | | 10 | |
|  | | | | | | | | | | |
| **IV.  International Sector** | **2.1** | | **2.5** | | **2.0** | | **2.1** | | **3.9** | |
| (a) Taxes on International Trade (Avg.) | 0 | (14.8) | 0 | (15.5) | 0 | (24.2) | 0 | (20.7) | 0 | (17.0) |
| (b) Black Market Exchange Rates (Prem.) | 5 | (9) | 6 | (5) | 4 | (14) | 4 | (10) | 10 | (0) |
| (c) Size of Trade Sector (% of GDP) | 1 | (12.8) | 2 | (16.6) | 2 | (15.0) | 3 | (18.7) | 4 | (21.2) |
| (d) Capital Transactions with Foreigners | 2 | | 2 | | 2 | | 2 | | 2 | |

## Part 2: Recent Economic Indicators:

| | | | | | |
|---|---|---|---|---|---|
| **Population 1994:** | 918 | **Real Per Capita GDP** | | 1994 = | $1,335 |
| (in millions) | | (in 1985 U.S. dollars) | | | |
| Annual Rate of Change (1980-94): | 2.1% | Avg. Growth Rate: | 1980-90 = | 3.5% | |
| | | | 1985-94 = | 2.9% | |

| Economic Indicators: | 1987 | 1988 | 1989 | 1990 | 1991 | 1992 | 1993 | 1994 |
|---|---|---|---|---|---|---|---|---|
| Change in Real GDP:Aggregate | 4.8 | 9.9 | 6.6 | 4.9 | 1.0 | 4.6 | 3.5 | 5.3 |
| : Per Capita | 2.7 | 7.8 | 4.5 | 2.8 | -1.1 | 2.5 | 1.4 | 3.3 |
| Inflation Rate (CPI) | 8.8 | 9.4 | 6.2 | 9.0 | 13.9 | 11.8 | 6.4 | 9.9 |
| Change in Money Supply: (M1) | 14.7 | 15.1 | 18.1 | 18.9 | 17.5 | 20.2 | 9.0 | 26.1 |
| : (M2) | 17.4 | 17.0 | 17.8 | 17.9 | 16.2 | 19.8 | 13.1 | 16.5 |
| Investment/GDP Ratio | 23.7 | 25.6 | 25.6 | 26.7 | 24.0 | 25.0 | 21.3 | - |
| Central Government Budget Deficit (-) or Surplus (+) As a Percent of GDP | -8.4 | -8.1 | -7.9 | -8.2 | -5.8 | -5.2 | -7.4 | -6.7 |
| Unemployment Rate | | | | | | | | |

In the mid-1990s the average of our three indexes places India in a tie (with Bulgaria and Ghana) for 62nd place. This ranking is an improvement over prior years. Throughout the 1975-1990 period, India generally ranked just above the ten least free countries in our study (see Exhibit 2-2). Among the Asian countries in our study, India along with Nepal and Bangladesh were the least free.

Economic freedom is restricted in many areas. Double-digit monetary expansion—no doubt fueled by large budget deficits—undermines the productivity of the rupee and legal restraints limit the ability of citizens to turn to more stable currencies. Even though government consumption as a share of GDP is not particularly large (the most recent rating for this component was 7), the Indian economy is dominated by government. State-operated enterprises exist in almost every major sector of the economy. Price controls abound. Restrictions limit entry into various business activities. Investment by foreigners generally requires approval from the government. The legal system arms political decision-makers with a great deal of discretionary authority. The Indian tariff rates are among the highest in the world. (Note: the average tax rate on international trade was 17% in 1993.) All these factors serve to undermine economic freedom and the operations of markets.

In recent years, a few modest steps toward a freer economy have been taken. The top marginal tax rate has been cut from 77% in 1975 and 62% in 1985 to the current 45% rate. Exchange rate controls have been eased during the last decade. The credit market is now more fully integrated with the global market. However, much more needs to be done if this populace country is going to reach its full potential.

# INDONESIA

## Part 1: The Economic Freedom Ratings for the Components and Various Area and Summary Indexes: 1975, 1980, 1985, 1990 and 1993-95.

(The numbers in parentheses indicate the actual values for the components.)

### Summary Ratings

|         | Ie  | Is1 | Is2 |
|---------|-----|-----|-----|
| 1975    | 5.0 | 5.2 | 4.6 |
| 1980    | 4.9 | 5.0 | 4.6 |
| 1985    | 6.0 | 6.1 | 5.6 |
| 1990    | 6.5 | 6.6 | 6.0 |
| 1993-95 | 5.9 | 6.1 | 5.3 |

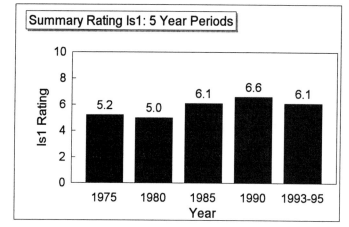

| Components of Economic Freedom | 1975 | | 1980 | | 1985 | | 1990 | | 1993-95 | |
|---|---|---|---|---|---|---|---|---|---|---|
| **I. Money and Inflation** | **4.3** | | **4.6** | | **7.5** | | **5.9** | | **7.9** | |
| (a) Annual Money Growth (last 5 yrs.) | 1 | (32.6) | 1 | (24.8) | 5 | (8.8) | 3 | (13.1) | 3 | (13.2) |
| (b) Inflation Variablity (last 5 yrs.) | 1 | (16.3) | 2 | (10.2) | 7 | (3.0) | 4 | (5.1) | 10 | (0.9) |
| (c) Ownership of Foreign Currency | 10 | | 10 | | 10 | | 10 | | 10 | |
| (d) Maint. of Bank Account Abroad | 10 | | 10 | | 10 | | 10 | | 10 | |
| | | | | | | | | | | |
| **II. Government Operation** | **5.5** | | **4.3** | | **4.4** | | **6.3** | | **4.1** | |
| (a) Govern. Consumption (% of GDP) | 9 | (9.0) | 8 | (10.5) | 7 | (11.2) | 9 | (9.0) | 9 | (8.2) |
| (b) Government Enterprises | 4 | | 2 | | 2 | | 2 | | 2 | |
| (c) Price Controls | - | | - | | - | | 6 | | 3 | |
| (d) Entry Into Business | - | | - | | - | | - | | 2.5 | |
| (e) Legal System | - | | - | | - | | - | | 0 | |
| (f) Avoidance of Neg. Interest Rates | 2 | | 2 | | - | | 10 | | 10 | |
| | | | | | | | | | | |
| **III. Takings** | **5.5** | | **4.6** | | **6.5** | | **6.9** | | **7.3** | |
| (a) Transfers and Subsidies (% of GDP) | 9 | (1.5) | 8 | (3.3) | 8 | (2.5) | 9 | (2.0) | 10 | (0.7) |
| (b) Marginal Tax Rates (Top Rate) | 4 | (48) | 3 | (50) | 7 | (35) | 7 | (35) | 7 | (35) |
| (c) Conscription | 0 | | 0 | | 0 | | 0 | | 0 | |
| | | | | | | | | | | |
| **IV. International Sector** | **5.2** | | **6.2** | | **5.8** | | **7.3** | | **6.5** | |
| (a) Taxes on International Trade (Avg. ) | 6 | (4.0) | 7 | (2.9) | 8 | (1.6) | 8 | (2.5) | 8 | (1.9) |
| (b) Black Market Exchange Rates (Prem.) | 5 | (7) | 7 | (2) | 5 | (7) | 10 | (0) | 7 | (2) |
| (c) Size of Trade Sector (% of GDP) | 9 | (44.2) | 10 | (53.3) | 9 | (42.6) | 10 | (52.6) | 10 | (55.8) |
| (d) Capital Transactions with Foreigners | 2 | | 2 | | 2 | | 2 | | 2 | |

## Part 2:  Recent Economic Indicators:

| | | | | |
|---|---|---|---|---|
| **Population 1994:** | 190 | **Real Per Capita GDP :** | 1994 = | $2,310 |
| (in millions) | | (in 1985 U.S. dollars) | | |
| Annual Rate of Change (1980-94): | 1.8% | Avg. Growth Rate: | 1980-90 = | 3.7% |
| | | | 1985-94 = | 4.6% |

| Economic Indicators: | 1987 | 1988 | 1989 | 1990 | 1991 | 1992 | 1993 | 1994 |
|---|---|---|---|---|---|---|---|---|
| Change in Real GDP:Aggregate | 4.9 | 5.8 | 7.5 | 7.2 | 6.9 | 6.3 | 6.5 | 6.8 |
| : Per Capita | 3.1 | 4.0 | 5.7 | 5.4 | 5.1 | 4.5 | 4.7 | 5.0 |
| Inflation Rate (CPI) | 9.2 | 8.0 | 6.4 | 12.5 | 9.4 | 7.5 | 9.7 | 8.5 |
| Change in Money Supply: (M1) | 11.4 | 10.0 | 24.0 | 35.8 | 12.9 | 9.6 | - | - |
| : (M2) | 20.1 | 25.5 | 29.3 | 46.8 | 24.2 | 20.6 | - | - |
| Investment/GDP Ratio | 31.4 | 31.5 | 35.2 | 36.1 | 35.0 | 34.6 | 37.3 | 34.0 |
| Central Government Budget Deficit (-) or Surplus (+) As a Percent of GDP | -0.8 | -3.0 | -1.9 | +0.4 | +0.4 | -0.4 | -0.8 | - |
| Unemployment Rate | | | | | | | | |

The average of our three indexes places Indonesia 41st among the countries in our study.  In the Asian region, it falls in the middle.  This economy is clearly less free than those of Hong Kong, Singapore, Malaysia, Thailand, South Korea, and Taiwan, but more free than India, Bangladesh, and Nepal.  There are two major areas that Indonesia must improved if it is going to achieve its full potential.  These two deficiencies are:

**Legal Structure—the Absence of Rule of Law**.  The legal structure provides public officials with too much arbitrary authority.  When the discretion of government officials replaces the rule of law, the security of property rights is undermined and corruption (for example, bribes, selective enforcement of regulations, and favoritism) becomes a way of life.  A legal structure of this type undermines market allocation.

**Excessive Regulation**.  This is a regulated economy.  Price controls, limitations on entry into business and professional practice, exchange rate controls (however, the black market premium is relatively small), and restrictions on the movement of capital are widespread.  Government enterprises—often protected from potential market competitors—operate in many sectors of the economy.

Despite these shortcomings, Indonesia's growth record during the last two decades has been outstanding.  With movement toward a freer economy, it could follow the path of Japan and become a major economic power.

# IRAN

**Part 1: The Economic Freedom Ratings for the Components and Various Area and Summary Indexes: 1975, 1980, 1985, 1990 and 1993-95.**

(The numbers in parentheses indicate the actual values for the components.)

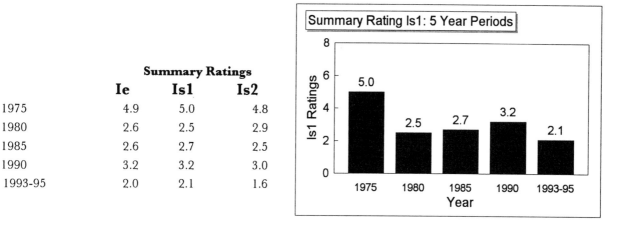

**Summary Ratings**

| | Ie | Is1 | Is2 |
|---|---|---|---|
| 1975 | 4.9 | 5.0 | 4.8 |
| 1980 | 2.6 | 2.5 | 2.9 |
| 1985 | 2.6 | 2.7 | 2.5 |
| 1990 | 3.2 | 3.2 | 3.0 |
| 1993-95 | 2.0 | 2.1 | 1.6 |

| Components of Economic Freedom | 1975 | | 1980 | | 1985 | | 1990 | | 1993-95 | |
|---|---|---|---|---|---|---|---|---|---|---|
| **I. Money and Inflation** | **2.5** | | **4.9** | | **4.9** | | **6.3** | | **2.3** | |
| (a) Annual Money Growth (last 5 yrs.) | 2 | (18.1) | 1 | (35.1) | 1 | (23.4) | 2 | (14.8) | 2 | (18.9) |
| (b) Inflation Variablity (last 5 yrs.) | - | | 3 | (6.1) | 3 | (6.8) | 6 | (3.6) | 5 | (4.3) |
| (c) Ownership of Foreign Currency | 10 | | 10 | | 10 | | 10 | | 0 | |
| (d) Maint. of Bank Account Abroad | 0 | | 10 | | 10 | | 10 | | 0 | |
| | | | | | | | | | | |
| **II. Government Operation** | **2.0** | | **1.5** | | **3.5** | | **3.6** | | **2.0** | |
| (a) Govern. Consumption (% of GDP) | 0 | (24.2) | 1 | (20.8) | 5 | (15.5) | 7 | (11.1) | 3 | (17.3) |
| (b) Government Enterprises | 4 | | 2 | | 2 | | 2 | | 2 | |
| (c) Price Controls | - | | - | | - | | 2 | | - | |
| (d) Entry Into Business | - | | - | | - | | - | | 2.5 | |
| (e) Legal System | - | | - | | - | | - | | 0 | |
| (f) Avoidance of Neg. Interest Rates | - | | - | | - | | - | | - | |
| | | | | | | | | | | |
| **III. Takings** | **5.3** | | **3.8** | | **3.2** | | **2.8** | | **3.1** | |
| (a) Transfers and Subsidies (% of GDP) | 4 | (8.9) | 5 | (7.0) | 8 | (3.0) | 7 | (4.4) | - | |
| (b) Marginal Tax Rates (Top Rate) | 8 | (40) | - | | 0 | (90) | 0 | (75) | 4 | (54) |
| (c) Conscription | 0 | | 0 | | 0 | | 0 | | 0 | |
| | | | | | | | | | | |
| **IV. International Sector** | **7.0** | | **0.6** | | **0.0** | | **1.6** | | **1.4** | |
| (a) Taxes on International Trade (Avg.) | 7 | (4.0) | 0 | (17.0) | 0 | (14.2) | 3 | (7.3) | 2 | (8.7) |
| (b) Black Market Exchange Rates (Prem.) | 7 | (2) | 1 | (164) | 0 | (533) | 0 | (2197) | 1 | (156) |
| (c) Size of Trade Sector (% of GDP) | 10 | (75.0) | 2 | (29.7) | 0 | (16.0) | 4 | (35.2) | 3 | (31.1) |
| (d) Capital Transactions with Foreigners | 5 | | 0 | | 0 | | 0 | | 0 | |

160

## Part 2: Recent Economic Indicators:

| | | | | | | |
|---|---|---|---|---|---|---|
| **Population 1994:** | 60.1 | **Real Per Capita GDP :** | 1993= | $3,650 |
| (in millions) | | (in 1985 U.S. dollars) | | |
| Annual Rate of Change (1980-94): | 2.8% | Avg. Growth Rate: | 1980-90= | -1.1% |
| | | | 1985-93= | -1.7% |

| Economic Indicators: | 1987 | 1988 | 1989 | 1990 | 1991 | 1992 | 1993 | 1994 |
|---|---|---|---|---|---|---|---|---|
| Change in Real GDP: Aggregate | 1.2 | -8.7 | 3.3 | 11.7 | 11.4 | 5.7 | 1.8 | |
| : Per Capita | -1.6 | -11.5 | 0.5 | 8.9 | 8.6 | 2.9 | -1.0 | |
| Inflation Rate (CPI) | 28.6 | 28.7 | 22.3 | 7.6 | 17.1 | 25.7 | 21.2 | 31.5 |
| Change in Money Supply: (M1) | 17.5 | 15.2 | 13.2 | 15.9 | 25.4 | 18.3 | 23.3 | 41.6 |
| : (M2) | 19.5 | 20.1 | 22.5 | 18.1 | 23.4 | 25.1 | 27.4 | 33.3 |
| Investment/GDP Ratio | 25.2 | 19.1 | 23.8 | 28.6 | 33.2 | 32.6 | 29.0 | |
| Central Government Budget | | | | | | | | |
| Deficit (-) or Surplus (+) | | | | | | | | |
| As a Percent of GDP | -7.1 | -9.2 | -3.9 | -1.8 | -2.3 | -1.4 | -0.3 | |
| Unemployment Rate | | | | | | | | |

In 1975, the Iranian economic freedom rating of 5.0 placed it in the Top Thirty among the countries in our study. That changed dramatically following the Iranian revolution and the overthrow of the Shah. Since 1980, Iran has ranked among the ten least free countries in each of our rating years. Its 1993-1995 average summary rating placed it in a tie with Zaire as the least free country in the world.

Inspection of the components makes it clear why Iran received such a low rating. Monetary policy is highly expansionary—the M1 money supply grew at an annual rate of 18.9% during the last five years. Citizens are not allowed to have foreign currency bank accounts, so the function of money as a store of value is undermined. Government consumption takes a large share (17.3%) of GDP. Government enterprises are widespread throughout the economy. Equal protection under the law is weak; political figures have a substantial amount of discretionary authority. Taxes take 54% of the marginal earnings of productive citizens—and this is down from 90% in 1985 and 75% in 1990. Conscription takes the labor of the young. The taxes on international trade are among the highest in the world. Exchange rate controls have led to a 150% black market premium. As a share of GDP, the size of the trade sector is now *less than half* its size in 1975. Foreigners are not allowed to undertake domestic investments and neither are citizens allowed to make investments abroad without the permission of the government.

The 1993 per capita real GDP of Iran was 40% *less than* the 1975 figure. Countries that stifle economic freedom pay a price.

# ISRAEL

## Part 1: The Economic Freedom Ratings for the Components and Various Area and Summary Indexes: 1975, 1980, 1985, 1990 and 1993-95.

(The numbers in parentheses indicate the actual values for the components.)

### Summary Ratings

| | Ie | Is1 | Is2 |
|------|------|------|------|
| 1975 | 2.2 | 2.1 | 2.3 |
| 1980 | 2.4 | 2.3 | 2.6 |
| 1985 | 2.4 | 2.5 | 2.5 |
| 1990 | 2.9 | 3.0 | 2.8 |
| 1993-95 | 4.2 | 4.2 | 4.2 |

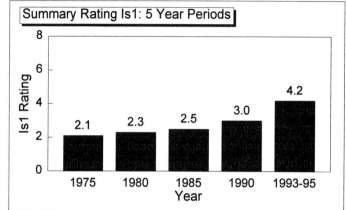

| Components of Economic Freedom | 1975 | | 1980 | | 1985 | | 1990 | | 1993-95 | |
|---|---|---|---|---|---|---|---|---|---|---|
| **I. Money and Inflation** | **3.2** | | **2.2** | | **1.9** | | **2.9** | | **4.5** | |
| (a) Annual Money Growth (last 5 yrs.) | 2 | (18.2) | 1 | (40.0) | 0 | (169.3) | 1 | (42.6) | 2 | (17.0) |
| (b) Inflation Variablity (last 5 yrs.) | 2 | (9.4) | 0 | (33.2) | 0 | (101.7) | 2 | (13.0) | 6 | (3.6) |
| (c) Ownership of Foreign Currency | 10 | | 10 | | 10 | | 10 | | 10 | |
| (d) Maint. of Bank Account Abroad | 0 | | 0 | | 0 | | 0 | | 0 | |
| | | | | | | | | | | |
| **II. Government Operation** | **1.0** | | **0.8** | | **0.8** | | **1.4** | | **4.1** | |
| (a) Govern. Consumption (% of GDP) | 0 | (40.2) | 0 | (38.5) | 0 | (34.4) | 0 | (28.8) | 0 | (27.1) |
| (b) Government Enterprises | 2 | | 2 | | 2 | | 2 | | 2 | |
| (c) Price Controls | - | | - | | - | | 0 | | 4 | |
| (d) Entry Into Business | - | | - | | - | | - | | 7.5 | |
| (e) Legal System | - | | - | | - | | - | | 5.0 | |
| (f) Avoidance of Neg. Interest Rates | - | | 0 | | 0 | | 6 | | 8 | |
| | | | | | | | | | | |
| **III. Takings** | **0.0** | | **0.9** | | **1.8** | | **2.7** | | **2.7** | |
| (a) Transfers and Subsidies (% of GDP) | - | | 1 | (20.8) | 1 | (19.7) | 2 | (16.7) | 2 | (15.2) |
| (b) Marginal Tax Rates (Top Rate) | - | | 1 | (66) | 3 | (60) | 4 | (51) | 4 | (50) |
| (c) Conscription | 0 | | 0 | | 0 | | 0 | | 0 | |
| | | | | | | | | | | |
| **IV. International Sector** | **2.3** | | **5.2** | | **4.8** | | **5.2** | | **5.7** | |
| (a) Taxes of International Trade (Avg.) | 2 | (8.0) | 6 | (5.1) | 7 | (2.9) | 9 | (0.9) | 9 | (1.1) |
| (b) Black Market Exchange Rates (Prem.) | 2 | (60) | 8 | (1) | 5 | (7) | 6 | (4) | 8 | (1) |
| (c) Size of Trade Sector (% of GDP) | 4 | (77.4) | 4 | (90.4) | 5 | (85.8) | 2 | (69.0) | 2 | (64.4) |
| (d) Capital Transactions with Foreigners | 2 | | 2 | | 2 | | 2 | | 2 | |

## Part 2:  Recent Economic Indicators:

| | | | | |
|---|---|---|---|---|
| **Population 1994:** | 5.3 | **Real Per Capita GDP :** | 1994 = | $9,970 |
| (in millions) | | (in 1985 U.S. dollars) | | |
| Annual Rate of Change (1980-94): | 2.3% | Avg. Growth Rate: | 1980-90 = | 1.8% |
| | | | 1985-94 = | 2.2% |

| Economic Indicators: | 1987 | 1988 | 1989 | 1990 | 1991 | 1992 | 1993 | 1994 |
|---|---|---|---|---|---|---|---|---|
| Change in Real GDP:Aggregate | 6.1 | 3.1 | 1.3 | 5.8 | 6.2 | 6.6 | 3.0 | 6.5 |
| : Per Capita | 3.8 | 0.8 | -1.0 | 3.5 | 3.9 | 4.3 | 0.7 | 4.2 |
| Inflation Rate (CPI) | 19.8 | 16.3 | 20.2 | 17.2 | 19.0 | 11.9 | 10.9 | 12.3 |
| Change in Money Supply: (M1) | 58.2 | 31.0 | 27.6 | 27.9 | 26.5 | 22.8 | 25.8 | 19.7 |
| : (M2) | 27.4 | 20.0 | 23.7 | 19.4 | 19.2 | 15.7 | 27.2 | 24.7 |
| Investment/GDP Ratio | 19.1 | 17.3 | 15.9 | 18.7 | 24.3 | 24.3 | 24.0 | - |
| Central Government Budget Deficit (-) or Surplus (+) As a Percent of GDP | -3.3 | -8.0 | -3.9 | -4.3 | -8.0 | -3.9 | -1.8 | - |
| Unemployment Rate | 6.1 | 6.4 | 8.9 | 9.6 | 10.6 | 11.2 | 10.0 | 7.6 [a] |

a  First 6 months of the year.

Israel may be the "bastion of democracy in the Middle East," but when it comes to economic freedom, it is not a "moral light to the nations." On the contrary, its economic freedom rating is poor, although there are some modest signs of improvement. In 1975, Israel's Isl summary rating of 2.1 was the second lowest among the countries in our study. Only Uganda had a lower rating. In 1980, 1985, and 1990, Israel's rating increased, but it continued to rank in the Bottom Ten among the more than 100 countries of our study (see Exhibit 2-2). Based on the average of our three indexes, Israel ranked 66th (tied with Turkey and Bangladesh) in 1993-1995.

Monetary expansion, price instability, a huge government consumption sector, widespread public sector enterprises, and a large transfer sector constitute the major weaknesses of this economy. The Israeli top marginal tax rate, although declining from 66% in 1980, is still at the 50% level. Countries that take one half of the marginal earnings of their most productive citizens are unlikely to reach their full potential. Put simply, the Israeli government has suffocated the market sector.

This country needs monetary stability (note the 20% recent growth in money), deregulation of its financial and capital markets, and privatization of state enterprises. The entrepreneurial spirit and market success of the Jewish people are renown around the world. If released, these forces will also lead to prosperity and growth in the Jewish homeland.

# ITALY

## Part 1: The Economic Freedom Ratings for the Components and Various Area and Summary Indexes: 1975, 1980, 1985, 1990 and 1993-95.

(The numbers in parentheses indicate the actual values for the components.)

### Summary Ratings

|        | Ie  | Is1 | Is2 |
|--------|-----|-----|-----|
| 1975   | 4.0 | 4.1 | 3.6 |
| 1980   | 3.8 | 3.6 | 3.8 |
| 1985   | 4.0 | 3.6 | 4.1 |
| 1990   | 5.9 | 5.4 | 6.4 |
| 1993-95| 6.1 | 5.6 | 6.7 |

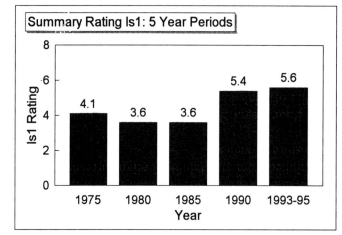

| Components of Economic Freedom | 1975 | | 1980 | | 1985 | | 1990 | | 1993-95 | |
|---|---|---|---|---|---|---|---|---|---|---|
| **I.  Money and Inflation** | **2.2** | | **3.3** | | **3.5** | | **9.1** | | **9.1** | |
| (a) Annual Money Growth (last 5 yrs.) | 3 | (12.6) | 2 | (17.2) | 5 | (9.8) | 7 | (7.0) | 8 | (3.7) |
| (b) Inflation Variablity (last 5 yrs.) | 4 | (5.2) | 8 | (2.2) | 6 | (3.8) | 10 | (0.8) | 9 | (1.7) |
| (c) Ownership of Foreign Currency | 0 | | 0 | | 0 | | 10 | | 10 | |
| (d) Maint. of Bank Account Abroad | 0 | | 0 | | 0 | | 10 | | 10 | |
| | | | | | | | | | | |
| **II.  Government Operation** | **4.4** | | **3.6** | | **3.6** | | **4.4** | | **5.2** | |
| (a) Govern. Consumption (% of GDP) | 6 | (14.1) | 5 | (14.7) | 4 | (16.4) | 3 | (17.4) | 2 | (17.6) |
| (b) Government Enterprises | 2 | | 2 | | 2 | | 2 | | 2 | |
| (c) Price Controls | - | | - | | - | | 5 | | 5 | |
| (d) Entry Into Business | - | | - | | - | | - | | 7.5 | |
| (e) Legal System | - | | - | | - | | - | | 7.5 | |
| (f) Avoidance of Neg. Interest Rates | 6 | | 4 | | 6 | | 10 | | 10 | |
| | | | | | | | | | | |
| **III.  Takings** | **3.1** | | **0.4** | | **0.0** | | **2.3** | | **1.9** | |
| (a) Transfers and Subsidies (% of GDP) | 2 | (17.5) | 1 | (20.9) | 0 | (28.5) | 0 | (27.1) | 0 | (28.6) |
| (b) Marginal Tax Rates (Top Rate) | 5 | (48) | 0 | (72) | 0 | (81) | 5 | (50) | 4 | (51) |
| (c) Conscription | 0 | | 0 | | 0 | | 0 | | 0 | |
| | | | | | | | | | | |
| **IV.  International Sector** | **6.5** | | **7.9** | | **8.0** | | **7.7** | | **8.3** | |
| (a) Taxes on International Trade (Avg.) | 10 | (0.3) | 10 | (0.0) | 10 | (0.0) | 10 | (0.0) | 10 | (0.0) |
| (b) Black Market Exchange Rates (Prem.) | 5 | (9) | 10 | (0) | 10 | (0) | 10 | (0) | 10 | (0) |
| (c) Size of Trade Sector (% of GDP) | 5 | (41.1) | 5 | (46.5) | 6 | (46.0) | 4 | (41.4) | 3 | (39.8) |
| (d) Capital Transactions with Foreigners | 5 | | 5 | | 5 | | 5 | | 8 | |

## Part 2: Recent Economic Indicators:

| | | | | |
|---|---|---|---|---|
| **Population 1994:** | 58.0 | **Real Per Capita GDP** : | 1994= | $12,920 |
| (in millions) | | (in 1985 U.S. dollars) | | |
| Annual Rate of Change (1980-94): | 0.2% | Avg. Growth Rate: | 1980-90= | 2.0% |
| | | | 1985-94= | 2.0% |

| Economic Indicators: | 1987 | 1988 | 1989 | 1990 | 1991 | 1992 | 1993 | 1994 |
|---|---|---|---|---|---|---|---|---|
| Change in Real GDP: Aggregate | 3.1 | 4.1 | 2.9 | 2.1 | 1.2 | 0.7 | -0.7 | 2.7 |
| : Per Capita | 3.1 | 4.0 | 2.9 | 2.1 | 1.2 | 0.6 | -1.0 | 2.5 |
| Inflation Rate (CPI) | 4.7 | 5.1 | 6.3 | 6.4 | 6.3 | 5.2 | 4.5 | 4.2 |
| Change in Money Supply: (M1) | 10.5 | 7.8 | 7.5 | 8.1 | 10.0 | 7.1 | 7.4 | 3.5 |
| : (M2) | 9.8 | 7.0 | 8.5 | 9.0 | 8.7 | 8.2 | 7.3 | 2.7 |
| Investment/GDP Ratio | 21.0 | 21.5 | 21.3 | 21.0 | 20.5 | 19.4 | 19.2 | 18.7 |
| Central Government Budget Deficit (-) or Surplus (+) As a Percent of GDP | -14.9 | -10.6 | -10.5 | -10.3 | -9.9 | -10.9 | -9.6 | - |
| Unemployment Rate | 10.9 | 11.0 | 11.9 | 10.3 | 9.9 | 10.5 | 10.2 | 11.6 |

After declining during 1975-1985, Italy's economic freedom rating has increased substantially during the last decade. Based on the average of our three indexes, Italy ranked 31st (tied with several other countries) in the mid-1990s. Its Is1 summary rating placed it in a tie for 44th place (with Malta and Finland.)

The primary factors underlying the recent improvement of Italy are a more stable monetary policy, removal of restrictions on the ownership of foreign currency bank accounts, and a reduction in the top marginal tax rate. Historically, Italy's monetary expansion and inflation rates have been the highest of the large industrial nations of Europe. As the steady improvement in the money expansion and inflation variability components of our index indicate, Italy has made substantial progress in this area. It also legalized the maintenance of foreign currency bank accounts, both domestically and abroad, in the late 1980s. These changes have led to a sharp increase in Italy's rating in the monetary area during the last decade. The reduction in the top marginal tax rate from a confiscatory 81% to the current 51% also helped push the summary rating upward.

Like several other European nations, the Italian economy is plagued with large government consumption and transfer sectors which are fueling a huge budget deficit that has averaged approximately 10% of GDP during the last decade. Deficits of this size cannot be maintained for very long without rapid growth in the money supply. Unless Italy gets its budget under control, the monetary instability of the past will soon be returning.

# JAPAN

## Part 1: The Economic Freedom Ratings for the Components and Various Area and Summary Indexes: 1975, 1980, 1985, 1990 and 1993-95.

(The numbers in parentheses indicate the actual values for the components.)

**Summary Ratings**

|         | Ie  | Is1 | Is2 |
|---------|-----|-----|-----|
| 1975    | 5.3 | 5.2 | 5.3 |
| 1980    | 6.4 | 5.9 | 6.4 |
| 1985    | 6.9 | 6.5 | 7.0 |
| 1990    | 7.4 | 6.9 | 7.9 |
| 1993-95 | 7.3 | 6.9 | 7.8 |

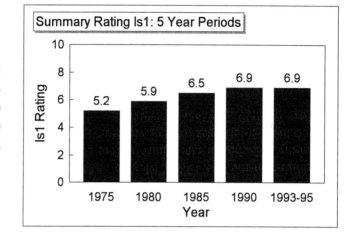

Summary Rating Is1: 5 Year Periods

| Components of Economic Freedom | 1975 | | 1980 | | 1985 | | 1990 | | 1993-95 | |
|---|---|---|---|---|---|---|---|---|---|---|
| **I. Money and Inflation** | **4.5** | | **7.6** | | **8.3** | | **9.7** | | **9.7** | |
| (a) Annual Money Growth (last 5 yrs.) | 4 | (10.8) | 9 | (2.4) | 10 | (0.9) | 9 | (2.0) | 9 | (2.4) |
| (b) Inflation Variablity (last 5 yrs.) | 4 | (5.6) | 9 | (1.7) | 10 | (0.8) | 10 | (0.9) | 10 | (0.6) |
| (c) Ownership of Foreign Currency | 10 | | 10 | | 10 | | 10 | | 10 | |
| (d) Maint. of Bank Account Abroad | 0 | | 0 | | 0 | | 10 | | 10 | |
| | | | | | | | | | | |
| **II. Government Operation** | **7.2** | | **8.4** | | **8.8** | | **7.9** | | **7.4** | |
| (a) Govern. Consumption (% of GDP) | 8 | (10.0) | 8 | (9.8) | 9 | (9.6) | 9 | (9.1) | 8 | (9.8) |
| (b) Government Enterprises | 8 | | 8 | | 8 | | 8 | | 8 | |
| (c) Price Controls | - | | - | | - | | 6 | | 5 | |
| (d) Entry Into Business | - | | - | | - | | - | | 7.5 | |
| (e) Legal System | - | | - | | - | | - | | 7.5 | |
| (f) Avoidance of Neg. Interest Rates | 4 | | 10 | | 10 | | 10 | | 10 | |
| | | | | | | | | | | |
| **III. Takings** | **3.4** | | **2.9** | | **3.4** | | **3.9** | | **3.9** | |
| (a) Transfers and Subsidies (% of GDP) | 4 | (9.6) | 4 | (10) | 4 | (10.4) | 4 | (9.9) | 4 | (10.0) |
| (b) Marginal Tax Rates (Top Rate) | 1 | (68) | 0 | (75) | 1 | (70) | 2 | (65) | 2 | (65) |
| (c) Conscription | 10 | | 10 | | 10 | | 10 | | 10 | |
| | | | | | | | | | | |
| **IV. International Sector** | **6.5** | | **6.5** | | **7.2** | | **7.7** | | **7.7** | |
| (a) Taxes on International Trade (Avg.) | 9 | (1.3) | 9 | (0.9) | 9 | (0.8) | 9 | (0.9) | 9 | (0.9) |
| (b) Black Market Exchange Rates (Prem.) | 10 | (0) | 10 | (0) | 10 | (0) | 10 | (0) | 10 | (0) |
| (c) Size of Trade Sector (% of GDP) | 3 | (25.6) | 3 | (28.3) | 3 | (25.5) | 1 | (21.0) | 1 | (18.0) |
| (d) Capital Transactions with Foreigners | 2 | | 2 | | 5 | | 8 | | 8 | |

# JAPAN

## Part 2: Recent Economic Indicators:

**Population 1994:** 125.7     **Real Per Capita GDP :**    1994= $15,105

  (in millions)           (in 1985 U.S. dollars)

Annual Rate of Change (1980-94):    0.5%      Avg. Growth Rate:   1980-90=   3.5%

                                                      1985-94=   2.8%

| Economic Indicators: | 1987 | 1988 | 1989 | 1990 | 1991 | 1992 | 1993 | 1994 |
|---|---|---|---|---|---|---|---|---|
| Change in Real GDP: Aggregate | 4.1 | 6.2 | 4.7 | 4.8 | 4.3 | 1.1 | 0.1 | 0.9 |
| : Per Capita | 3.6 | 5.8 | 4.3 | 4.5 | 3.9 | 0.8 | -0.2 | 0.4 |
| Inflation Rate (CPI) | 0.1 | 0.7 | 2.3 | 3.1 | 3.3 | 1.7 | 1.3 | 0.6 |
| Change in Money Supply: (M1) | 9.0 | 7.7 | 4.6 | 3.2 | 5.9 | 6.5 | 4.2 | 5.7 |
| : (M2) | 10.2 | 11.2 | 10.0 | 12.1 | 4.1 | 1.2 | 1.4 | 3.1 |
| Investment/GDP Ratio | 28.7 | 30.6 | 31.8 | 32.8 | 32.5 | 31.2 | 30.4 | 28.8 |
| Central Government Budget Deficit (-) or Surplus (+) As a Percent of GDP | -3.5 | -2.6 | -2.9 | -1.6 | - | - | - | - |
| Unemployment Rate | 2.8 | 2.5 | 2.3 | 2.1 | 2.1 | 2.2 | 2.5 | 2.9 |

This economic powerhouse has shown slow and steady improvement in the area of economic freedom over the last two decades. Its economic freedom summary rating (Is1) increased from 5.2 in 1975 to 6.9 in 1993-1995. Japan's Is1 rating places it ninth while the average of the three indexes ranks it 10th among the more than 100 countries in our study.

Japan's greatest strength is in the money and inflation area. Its most recent rating in this area was 9.7, up from 4.5 in 1975. For the last ten to fifteen years, Japan has been a model of monetary stability. For a high-income industrial country, Japan's government consumption expenditures are relatively small. Its rating in this area is the highest among the industrial nations. Its major weaknesses are high marginal tax rates (its top marginal rate of 65% is now out of line with the rest of the world which has been reducing rates) and non-tariff trade restraints (note how the size of the trade sector is much smaller than would be expected for a country of this size and location).

Japan's modest growth rates in the 2-4% range are probably indicative of a high-income mature economy. Of course, these growth rates would be the envy of quite a few high-income European nations. While Japan is no free market utopia, its generally positive economic record highlights the importance of monetary stability, security of ownership rights, primary reliance on market allocation, and the integration of financial markets with the world economy.

167

# KENYA

**Part 1: The Economic Freedom Ratings for the Components and Various Area and Summary Indexes: 1975, 1980, 1985, 1990 and 1993-95.**

(The numbers in parentheses indicate the actual values for the components.)

**Summary Ratings**

| | Ie | Is1 | Is2 |
|------|-----|-----|-----|
| 1975 | 3.8 | 3.4 | 3.9 |
| 1980 | 4.0 | 4.0 | 3.8 |
| 1985 | 4.7 | 4.3 | 4.6 |
| 1990 | 4.4 | 4.5 | 4.0 |
| 1993-95 | 4.1 | 4.5 | 3.4 |

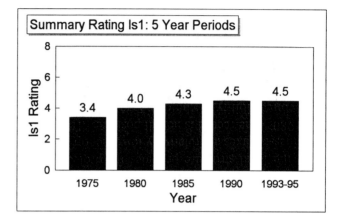

| Components of Economic Freedom | 1975 | | 1980 | | 1985 | | 1990 | | 1993-95 | |
|---|---|---|---|---|---|---|---|---|---|---|
| **I. Money and Inflation** | **3.4** | | **2.8** | | **5.8** | | **3.9** | | **1.3** | |
| (a) Annual Money Growth (last 5 yrs.) | 9 | (3.2) | 6 | (7.2) | 8 | (4.5) | 3 | (12.2) | 1 | (23.1) |
| (b) Inflation Variablity (last 5 yrs.) | 2 | (9.3) | 3 | (6.1) | 10 | (1.2) | 9 | (1.4) | 3 | (7.5) |
| (c) Ownership of Foreign Currency | 0 | | 0 | | 0 | | 0 | | 0 | |
| (d) Maint. of Bank Account Abroad | 0 | | 0 | | 0 | | 0 | | 0 | |
| **II. Government Operation** | **3.2** | | **3.7** | | **4.9** | | **3.7** | | **4.0** | |
| (a) Govern. Consumption (% of GDP) | 2 | (18.3) | 1 | (19.8) | 3 | (17.5) | 2 | (18.7) | 6 | (13.1) |
| (b) Government Enterprises | 4 | | 4 | | 4 | | 4 | | 4 | |
| (c) Price Controls | - | | - | | - | | 2 | | 4 | |
| (d) Entry Into Business | - | | - | | - | | - | | 5 | |
| (e) Legal System | - | | - | | - | | - | | 0 | |
| (f) Avoidance of Neg. Interest Rates | 4 | | 8 | | 10 | | 10 | | - | |
| **III. Takings** | **2.2** | | **5.0** | | **3.7** | | **5.9** | | **7.3** | |
| (a) Transfers and Subsidies (% of GDP) | - | | 8 | (2.3) | 6 | (4.7) | 8 | (2.8) | 9 | (1.7) |
| (b) Marginal Tax Rates (Top Rate) | 0 | (70) | 1 | (65) | 0 | (65) | 3 | (50) | 5 | (40) |
| (c) Conscription | 10 | | 10 | | 10 | | 10 | | 10 | |
| **IV. International Sector** | **4.5** | | **3.7** | | **3.6** | | **3.8** | | **4.3** | |
| (a) Taxes on International Trade (Avg.) | 6 | (5.5) | 5 | (6.1) | 3 | (7.4) | 4 | (6.3) | 6 | (3.7) |
| (b) Black Market Exchange Rates (Prem.) | 5 | (8) | 4 | (10) | 7 | (2) | 6 | (6) | 6 | (6) |
| (c) Size of Trade Sector (% of GDP) | 8 | (64.3) | 7 | (67.0) | 5 | (51.6) | 6 | (57.5) | 5 | (54.0) |
| (d) Capital Transactions with Foreigners | 0 | | 0 | | 0 | | 0 | | 0 | |

## Part 2: Recent Economic Indicators:

| | | | | | | | | |
|---|---|---|---|---|---|---|---|---|
| **Population 1994:** | 27.5 | | **Real Per Capita GDP** : | | 1993= | | $894 | |
| (in millions) | | | (in 1985 U.S. dollars) | | | | | |
| Annual Rate of Change (1980-94): | 3.6% | | Avg. Growth Rate: | | 1980-90= | | 0.6% | |
| | | | | | 1984-93= | | 0.7% | |

| Economic Indicators: | 1987 | 1988 | 1989 | 1990 | 1991 | 1992 | 1993 | 1994 |
|---|---|---|---|---|---|---|---|---|
| Change in Real GDP: Aggregate | 5.9 | 6.2 | 4.7 | 4.2 | 1.4 | 0.4 | -0.2 | 5.2 |
| : Per Capita | 2.3 | 2.6 | 1.1 | 0.6 | -2.4 | -3.2 | -3.8 | 1.6 |
| Inflation Rate (CPI) | 7.6 | 11.2 | 12.9 | 15.6 | 19.8 | 29.5 | 45.8 | 29.0 |
| Change in Money Supply: (M1) | 13.6 | 2.2 | 11.5 | 18.7 | 16.6 | 29.7 | 37.4 | 25.0 |
| : (M2) | 18.3 | 5.9 | 15.3 | 14.0 | 18.7 | 29.3 | 30.5 | |
| Investment/GDP Ratio | 19.8 | 20.1 | 19.3 | 20.8 | 19.3 | 17.1 | 15.3 | 20.6 |
| Central Government Budget Deficit (-) or Surplus (+) (As a Percent of GDP) | -6.7 | -4.4 | -6.9 | -4.0 | -2.8 | -0.4 | -4.0 | -3.4 |
| Unemployment Rate | | | | | | | | |

Based on the average of our three indexes, Kenya's economic freedom rating placed it 72nd in 1993-1995. The summary rating changed very little during the last two decades. While Kenya's ratings are poor in almost all categories, its major deficiencies are:

**Unstable Monetary Policy**. In recent years, the annual rate of monetary growth has soared above 20% and it appears to be moving higher (it exceeded 30% during 1992-1994). Of course, this fuels the inflation rate, which is now in the 30% range. Since citizens are prohibited from maintaining foreign currency bank accounts, they have no way to hold money as a store of value.

**Poor Legal Structure**. The legal structure often operates in a discriminatory manner. Public officials have a great deal of discretionary authority that is often beyond the reach of the legal structure. As the result, corruption is widespread and the security of property rights and enforcement of contracts is weak.

**Excessive Regulation**. This is a regulated economy. Price controls, exchange rate controls (the black market premium is relatively small), an under-developed credit market, and restrictions on the movement of capital (in order to assure the remittance of earnings, foreign investors must obtain a "certificate of approved enterprise") undermine the development of a market economy.

Perhaps Kenya's poor growth record (per capita GDP has increased at an average rate of 0.6% during the last 15 years) will provide stimulus for some positive changes in the near future.

# MALAYSIA

**Part 1: The Economic Freedom Ratings for the Components and Various Area and Summary Indexes: 1975, 1980, 1985, 1990 and 1993-95.**

(The numbers in parentheses indicate the actual values for the components.)

### Summary Ratings

| | Ie | Is1 | Is2 |
|------|-----|-----|-----|
| 1975 | 5.3 | 5.1 | 5.9 |
| 1980 | 6.0 | 5.6 | 6.7 |
| 1985 | 7.2 | 7.1 | 7.0 |
| 1990 | 7.3 | 7.1 | 7.4 |
| 1993-95 | 7.1 | 7.0 | 7.1 |

**Summary Rating Is1: 5 Year Periods**

| Year | 1975 | 1980 | 1985 | 1990 | 1993-95 |
|------|------|------|------|------|---------|
| Is1 Rating | 5.1 | 5.6 | 7.1 | 7.1 | 7.0 |

| Components of Economic Freedom | 1975 | | 1980 | | 1985 | | 1990 | | 1993-95 | |
|---|---|---|---|---|---|---|---|---|---|---|
| **I. Money and Inflation** | **3.9** | | **7.2** | | **7.3** | | **7.1** | | **7.6** | |
| (a) Annual Money Growth (last 5 yrs.) | 5 | (8.9) | 5 | (9.7) | 10 | (0.9) | 7 | (6.5) | 2 | (14.0) |
| (b) Inflation Variablity (last 5 yrs.) | 2 | (8.3) | 6 | (3.1) | 7 | (2.6) | 4 | (5.2) | 10 | (1.1) |
| (c) Ownership of Foreign Currency | 0 | | 10 | | 10 | | 10 | | 10 | |
| (d) Maint. of Bank Account Abroad | 10 | | 10 | | 0 | | 10 | | 10 | |
| | | | | | | | | | | |
| **II. Government Operation** | **3.0** | | **4.0** | | **6.5** | | **6.3** | | **6.0** | |
| (a) Govern. Consumption (% of GDP) | 2 | (17.7) | 3 | (16.5) | 5 | (15.3) | 6 | (14.0) | 7 | (13.0) |
| (b) Government Enterprises | 4 | | 4 | | 6 | | 6 | | 6 | |
| (c) Price Controls | - | | - | | - | | 5 | | 4 | |
| (d) Entry Into Business | - | | .. | | - | | - | | 7.5 | |
| (e) Legal System | - | | - | | - | | - | | 2.5 | |
| (f) Avoidance of Neg. Interest Rates | - | | 6 | | 10 | | 10 | | 10 | |
| | | | | | | | | | | |
| **III. Takings** | **5.2** | | **4.7** | | **7.3** | | **7.3** | | **7.4** | |
| (a) Transfers and Subsidies (% of GDP) | 5 | (6.4) | 6 | (4.8) | 8 | (3.6) | 8 | (2.4) | 7 | (4.2) |
| (b) Marginal Tax Rates (Top Rate) | 4 | (50) | 2 | (60) | 6 | (45) | 6 | (45) | 7 | (34) |
| (c) Conscription | 10 | | 10 | | 10 | | 10 | | 10 | |
| | | | | | | | | | | |
| **IV. International Sector** | **6.9** | | **6.6** | | **7.2** | | **7.8** | | **7.8** | |
| (a) Taxes on International Trade (Avg.) | 4 | (7.0) | 3 | (7.7) | 5 | (5.7) | 7 | (3.2) | 7 | (2.8) |
| (b) Black Market Exchange Rates (Prem.) | 10 | (0) | 10 | (0) | 10 | (0) | 10 | (0) | 10 | (0) |
| (c) Size of Trade Sector (% of GDP) | 10 | (86.8) | 10 | (112.6) | 10 | (104.6) | 10 | (151.2) | 10 | (154.2) |
| (d) Capital Transactions with Foreigners | 5 | | 5 | | 5 | | 5 | | 5 | |

170

## Part 2: Recent Economic Indicators:

| | | | | |
|---|---|---|---|---|
| **Population 1994:** (in millions) | 19.5 | **Real Per Capita GDP :** (in 1985 U.S. dollars) | 1994 = | $6,510 |
| Annual Rate of Change (1980-94): 2.5% | | Avg. Growth Rate: | 1980-90 = | 3.30% |
| | | | 1985-94 = | 4.98% |

| Economic Indicators: | 1987 | 1988 | 1989 | 1990 | 1991 | 1992 | 1993 | 1994 |
|---|---|---|---|---|---|---|---|---|
| Change in Real GDP:Aggregate | 5.4 | 8.9 | 9.2 | 9.7 | 8.7 | 8.5 | 8.0 | 9.9 |
| : Per Capita | 2.9 | 6.4 | 6.7 | 7.2 | 6.2 | 6.0 | 5.5 | 7.4 |
| Inflation Rate (CPI) | 3.0 | 2.6 | 2.8 | 2.6 | 4.4 | 4.8 | 3.5 | 3.7 |
| Change in Money Supply: (M1) | 12.8 | 14.4 | 17.3 | 15.6 | 9.9 | - | 22.6 | 31.6 |
| : (M2) | 3.9 | 8.8 | 15.1 | 10.7 | 15.5 | - | 21.4 | 22.4 |
| Investment/GDP Ratio | 23.2 | 26.0 | 29.0 | 32.1 | 36.3 | 35.9 | 35.0 | 38.5 |
| Central Government Budget Deficit (-) or Surplus (+) As a Percent of GDP | -6.6 | -0.3 | -0.5 | -1.3 | -0.2 | +0.7 | +1.6 | +2.3 |
| Unemployment Rate | | | | | | | | |

Between 1975 and 1985, the economic freedom of this southeast Asian nation increased substantially and the higher rating was maintained during the last decade. In the mid-1990s, the Malaysian economy ranks as one of the freest in the world. Our Is1 summary rating ranks it 6th and the average of our three ratings places it 12th. Other than Hong Kong and Singapore, no non-industrial economy has a higher rating than Malaysia.

Several factors contributed to the improvement. There was an increase in the stability of the price level (and inflation rate). Foreign currency bank accounts were legalized. During the last two decades, there has been a decline in both government consumption expenditures and transfers as a share of the economy. Not many countries can match that record. Marginal tax rates have been reduced. The top rate is now 34%, down from 60% in 1980. Tariffs have been reduced and the trade sector has grown rapidly. There are a few areas of concern, however. In the last few years, the growth rate of the money supply has been rapid which may foreshadow future inflation. Malaysia also shows some reluctance to give up its regulatory ways as evidenced by the relatively low ratings in Government Enterprises (IIb), Price Controls (IIc) and Equality before the Law (IIe).

All in all, Malaysia's impressive move toward economic liberalization is being rewarded by a vibrant and growing economy. With per capita GDP growth rates averaging over 3% per year in the 1980's and increasing to nearly 5% in the 1990's, Malaysia is earning the dividends of economic freedom.

171

# MAURITIUS

**Part 1: The Economic Freedom Ratings for the Components and Various Area and Summary Indexes: 1975, 1980, 1985, 1990 and 1993-95.**

(The numbers in parentheses indicate the actual values for the components.)

|  | **Summary Ratings** | | |
|---|---|---|---|
|  | **Ie** | **Is1** | **Is2** |
| 1975 | 3.7 | 3.9 | 3.1 |
| 1980 | 3.8 | 3.8 | 3.6 |
| 1985 | 6.0 | 6.0 | 5.5 |
| 1990 | 5.4 | 5.6 | 4.8 |
| 1993-1995 | 6.2 | 6.3 | 5.8 |

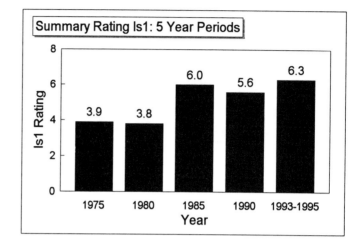

| Components of Economic Freedom | 1975 | | 1980 | | 1985 | | 1990 | | 1993-95 | |
|---|---|---|---|---|---|---|---|---|---|---|
| **I. Money and Inflation** | **0.6** | | **3.1** | | **6.0** | | **4.0** | | **4.8** | |
| (a) Annual Money Growth (last 5 yrs.) | 1 | (31.0) | 7 | (6.3) | 10 | (-0.8) | 2 | (16.2) | 6 | (7.9) |
| (b) Inflation Variablity (last 5 yrs.) | 1 | (20.1) | 3 | (8.0) | 9 | (1.4) | 10 | (1.3) | 9 | (1.7) |
| (c) Ownership of Foreign Currency | 0 | | 0 | | 0 | | 0 | | 0 | |
| (d) Maint. of Bank Account Abroad | 0 | | 0 | | 0 | | 0 | | 0 | |
| | | | | | | | | | | |
| **II. Government Operation** | **6.5** | | **6.0** | | **7.6** | | **4.7** | | **8.0** | |
| (a) Govern. Consumption (% of GDP) | 7 | (11.1) | 6 | (14.1) | 8 | (10.2) | 7 | (11.1) | 7 | (12.9) |
| (b) Government Enterprises | 6 | | 6 | | 6 | | 6 | | 6 | |
| (c) Price Controls | - | | - | | - | | - | | - | |
| (d) Entry Into Business | - | | - | | - | | - | | 10 | |
| (e) Legal System | - | | - | | - | | - | | 7.5 | |
| (f) Avoidance of Neg. Interest Rates | - | | - | | 10 | | 8 | | 10 | |
| | | | | | | | | | | |
| **III. Takings** | **6.2** | | **4.7** | | **7.0** | | **7.4** | | **7.5** | |
| (a) Transfers and Subsidies (% of GDP) | 5 | (6.6) | 5 | (6.5) | 6 | (5.2) | 7 | (4.2) | 6 | (4.9) |
| (b) Marginal Tax Rates (Top Rate) | - | | 3 | (50) | 7 | (35) | 7 | (35) | 8 | (30) |
| (c) Conscription | 10 | | 10 | | 10 | | 10 | | 10 | |
| | | | | | | | | | | |
| **IV. International Sector** | **3.1** | | **2.0** | | **3.7** | | **3.8** | | **3.9** | |
| (a) Taxes on International Trade (Avg.) | 4 | (7.1) | 1 | (9.6) | 1 | (9.6) | 3 | (7.6) | 3 | (7.5) |
| (b) Black Market Exchange Rates (Prem.) | 2 | (47) | 2 | (40) | 8 | (1) | 5 | (8) | 6 | (5) |
| (c) Size of Trade Sector (% of GDP) | 5 | (112.3) | 4 | (112.6) | 4 | (109.0) | 6 | (142.1) | 5 | (128.3) |
| (d) Capital Transactions with Foreigners | 2 | | 2 | | 2 | | 2 | | 2 | |

## Part 2: Recent Economic Indicators:

| | | | | |
|---|---|---|---|---|
| **Population 1994:** | 1.1 | **Real Per Capita GDP :** | 1994 = | $6,650 |
| (in millions) | | (in 1985 U.S. dollars) | | |
| Annual Rate of Change (1980-94): | 1.1% | Avg. Growth Rate: | 1980-90 = | 5.0% |
| | | | 1985-93 = | 5.4% |

| Economic Indicators: | 1987 | 1988 | 1989 | 1990 | 1991 | 1992 | 1993 | 1994 |
|---|---|---|---|---|---|---|---|---|
| Change in Real GDP:Aggregate | 10.2 | 6.8 | 4.6 | 7.2 | 4.1 | 6.3 | 5.4 | 4.6 |
| : Per Capita | 9.1 | 5.7 | 4.5 | 6.1 | 3.0 | 5.2 | 4.3 | 3.5 |
| Inflation Rate (CPI) | 0.5 | 9.2 | 12.7 | 13.5 | 7.0 | 4.6 | 10.5 | 7.3 |
| Change in Money Supply: (M1) | 29.3 | 22.1 | 20.4 | 19.6 | 24.1 | 11.5 | 6.2 | 7.4 |
| : (M2) | 32.2 | 29.4 | 19.1 | 19.9 | 21.3 | 19.7 | 14.5 | 16.4 |
| Investment/GDP Ratio | 25.3 | 30.6 | 30.7 | 30.4 | 27.7 | 28.5 | 29.4 | 31.7 |
| Central Government Budget Deficit (-) or Surplus (+) As a Percent of GDP | +0.3 | +0.3 | -1.6 | -0.5 | - | -0.8 | 0.0 | - |
| Unemployment Rate | 18.5 | 10.4 | 6.7 | 4.6 | 3.8 | | | |

This small island nation off the southeastern coast of Africa took substantial steps toward economic freedom between 1975 and 1985 and it has maintained its higher ratings into the 1990s. Based on the average of our three summary ratings, Mauritius ranked 31st (tied with several other countries) in 1993-1995. Its Is1 rating placed it even higher (tied for 21st).

What accounts for this relatively high ranking? While there is still room for improvement, the growth rate of the money supply has been moderate and the inflation rate relatively stable. The government consumption and transfer sectors are both relatively small and the legal structure provides for protection of property rights and freedom of entry into business. Taxes are relatively low; the top marginal tax rate is currently 30%, down from 50% in 1980. The record is not all positive. Tariff rates are high and there are restrictions on both the convertibility of the domestic currency and the movement of capital into and out of the country. All considered, however, it is not a bad record, probably the best among the African group of nations.

Like its economic freedom rating, Mauritius's growth rate has been impressive. Its per capita GDP grew at an annual rate of 5.0% during the 1980s and 5.4% during the last decade. With additional moves toward freedom, the economic future of this country would indeed be bright.

# MEXICO

**Part 1: The Economic Freedom Ratings for the Components and Various Area and Summary Indexes: 1975, 1980, 1985, 1990 and 1993-95.**

(The numbers in parentheses indicate the actual values for the components.)

### Summary Ratings

| | Ie | Is1 | Is2 |
|------|-----|-----|-----|
| 1975 | 4.8 | 5.0 | 4.5 |
| 1980 | 3.7 | 3.8 | 3.4 |
| 1985 | 4.0 | 4.1 | 3.7 |
| 1990 | 5.1 | 5.3 | 4.8 |
| 1993-95 | 5.7 | 5.8 | 5.7 |

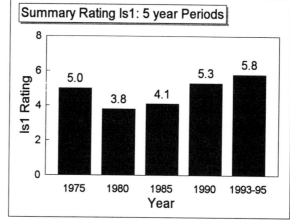

| Components of Economic Freedom | 1975 | | 1980 | | 1985 | | 1990 | | 1993-95 | |
|---|---|---|---|---|---|---|---|---|---|---|
| **I. Money and Inflation** | **5.8** | | **5.6** | | **4.0** | | **3.6** | | **4.6** | |
| (a) Annual Money Growth (last 5 yrs.) | 4 | (11.2) | 1 | (24.7) | 0 | (44.4) | 0 | (67.1) | 1 | (36.0) |
| (b) Inflation Variablity (last 5 yrs.) | 3 | (6.0) | 5 | (4.9) | 1 | (20.4) | 0 | (42.8) | 2 | (9.3) |
| (c) Ownership of Foreign Currency | 10 | | 10 | | 10 | | 10 | | 10 | |
| (d) Maint. of Bank Account Abroad | 10 | | 10 | | 10 | | 10 | | 10 | |
| | | | | | | | | | | |
| **II. Government Operation** | **5.4** | | **4.7** | | **5.1** | | **4.7** | | **6.4** | |
| (a) Govern. Consumption (% of GDP) | 9 | (9.3) | 8 | (10.0) | 9 | (9.2) | 9 | (8.4) | 9 | (9.3) |
| (b) Government Enterprises | 2 | | 2 | | 2 | | 4 | | 6 | |
| (c) Price Controls | - | | - | | - | | 0 | | 7 | |
| (d) Entry Into Business | - | | - | | - | | - | | 7.5 | |
| (e) Legal System | - | | - | | - | | - | | 0 | |
| (f) Avoidance of Neg. Interest Rates | - | | 4 | | 4 | | 8 | | 8 | |
| | | | | | | | | | | |
| **III. Takings** | **5.1** | | **4.7** | | **3.9** | | **5.3** | | **5.3** | |
| (a) Transfers and Subsidies (% of GDP) | 7 | (4.1) | 7 | (4.4) | 5 | (5.4) | 5 | (6.4) | 5 | (7.1) |
| (b) Marginal Tax Rates (Top Rate) | 5 | (47) | 4 | (55) | 4 | (55) | 7 | (40) | 7 | (35) |
| (c) Conscription | 0 | | 0 | | 0 | | 0 | | 0 | |
| | | | | | | | | | | |
| **IV. International Sector** | **4.2** | | **1.0** | | **3.8** | | **7.1** | | **6.5** | |
| (a) Taxes on International Trade (Avg.) | 3 | (7.9) | 0 | (17.6) | 7 | (2.6) | 8 | (2.0) | - | |
| (b) Black Market Exchange Rates (Prem.) | 10 | (0) | 1 | (92) | 3 | (25) | 10 | (0) | 10 | (0) |
| (c) Size of Trade Sector (% of GDP) | 0 | (14.7) | 1 | (23.7) | 2 | (25.7) | 4 | (32.7) | 3 | (30.7) |
| (d) Capital Transactions with Foreigners | 2 | | 2 | | 2 | | 5 | | 5 | |

## Part 2:  Recent Economic Indicators:

| | | | | | | | | |
|---|---|---|---|---|---|---|---|---|
| **Population 1994:** | 88.4 | | | **Real Per Capita GDP** : | | 1994= | $6,260 | |
| (in millions) | | | | (in 1985 U.S. dollars) | | | | |
| Annual Rate of Change (1980-94): | 2.0% | | | Avg. Growth Rate: | | 1980-90= | -0.3% | |
| | | | | | | 1985-94= | 1.2% | |

| Economic Indicators: | 1987 | 1988 | 1989 | 1990 | 1991 | 1992 | 1993 | 1994 |
|---|---|---|---|---|---|---|---|---|
| Change in Real GDP: Aggregate | 1.9 | 1.2 | 3.3 | 4.4 | 3.6 | 2.8 | 0.6 | 3.5 |
| : Per Capita | -0.2 | -0.8 | 1.3 | 2.4 | 1.6 | 0.9 | -1.2 | 1.5 |
| Inflation Rate (CPI) | 131.8 | 114.2 | 20.0 | 26.7 | 22.7 | 15.5 | 9.8 | 7.0 |
| Change in Money Supply (M1) | 106.5 | 110.1 | 30.6 | 47.9 | 91.6 | 70.3 | 17.3 | 10.9 |
| : (M2) | 126.5 | 77.8 | -10.2 | 104.1 | 72.4 | 34.7 | 21.5 | 21.7 |
| Investment/GDP Ratio | 19.3 | 20.4 | 21.4 | 21.9 | 22.4 | 23.3 | 20.4 | 21.5 |
| Central Government Budget Deficit (-) or Surplus (+) As a Percent of GDP | -13.6 | -10.3 | -5.2 | +0.7 | - | +4.5 | +0.7 | - |
| Unemployment Rate [a] | 3.9 | 3.6 | 3.0 | 2.8 | 2.6 | 2.8 | 3.6 | 3.8 |

a  If the Mexican unemployment rate was adjusted to the concepts of unemployment used in the United States, these rates would be between 1.5% and 2% higher.  For example, the U.S. Labor Department estimated that the Mexican unemployment rate during 1993 (second quarter) was 5.0% rather than the official Mexican figure of 3.1% during the period.  See Susan Fleck and Constance Sorrentino, "Employment and Unemployment in Mexico's Labor Force," Monthly Labor Review, Nov., 1994.

Based on its average for our three summary indexes, in 1993-95 Mexico ranked 45th among the 103 countries in our study.  Between 1975 and 1985, its rating declined, primarily because of an unstable monetary policy, higher taxes, and imposition of exchange rate controls. Beginning in the late 1980s, Mexico undertook a number of constructive moves toward a freer economy.  Exchange rate controls were eliminated.  Price controls were relaxed.  A number of government enterprises were privatized.  The top marginal tax rate was reduced from 55% in 1985 to 40% in 1990 and 35% in 1994.

However, a monetary system capable of providing confidence to domestics and foreigners alike was still absent.  During 1990-1994, the growth rate of the money supply was reduced and the inflation rate declined.  But monetary policy lacked credibility and it was severely tested when civil unrest and the assassination of several key political figures led to an outflow of capital.  If the monetary authorities had responded forcefully and shifted to a more restrictive monetary policy to protect the purchasing power of the peso, they could have offset these factors.  But they did not and a crisis ensued, eroding the confidence that was beginning to develop.  Mexican monetary policy desperately needs an anchor that will provide confidence and lead to a prolonged period of relative price stability.  At this point,  institutional change might well be helpful. Mexico would do well to follow the path of Argentina and tie its currency (and monetary policy) to the dollar or a basket of stable currencies.  Without stable money, Mexico will fail to achieve its full potential.

# NETHERLANDS

## Part 1: The Economic Freedom Ratings for the Components and Various Area and Summary Indexes: 1975, 1980, 1985, 1990 and 1993-95.

(The numbers in parentheses indicate the actual values for the components.)

### Summary Ratings

|  | Ie | Is1 | Is2 |
|------|------|------|------|
| 1975 | 6.3 | 5.7 | 7.1 |
| 1980 | 6.4 | 5.4 | 7.5 |
| 1985 | 6.6 | 5.6 | 7.6 |
| 1990 | 6.7 | 5.8 | 7.6 |
| 1993-95 | 7.2 | 6.4 | 7.9 |

**Summary Rating Is1: 5 Year Periods**

| Year | Is1 Rating |
|------|------|
| 1975 | 5.7 |
| 1980 | 5.4 |
| 1985 | 5.6 |
| 1990 | 5.8 |
| 1993-95 | 6.4 |

| Components of Economic Freedom | 1975 | | 1980 | | 1985 | | 1990 | | 1993-95 | |
|---|---|---|---|---|---|---|---|---|---|---|
| **I. Money and Inflation** | **8.8** | | **9.1** | | **9.1** | | **9.4** | | **9.4** | |
| (a) Annual Money Growth (last 5 yrs.) | 6 | (7.9) | 8 | (3.9) | 8 | (4.9) | 8 | (4.4) | 9 | (2.6) |
| (b) Inflation Variablity (last 5 yrs.) | 10 | (0.7) | 9 | (1.7) | 9 | (1.9) | 10 | (1.0) | 9 | (1.7) |
| (c) Ownership of Foreign Currency | 10 | | 10 | | 10 | | 10 | | 10 | |
| (d) Maint. of Bank Account Abroad | 10 | | 10 | | 10 | | 10 | | 10 | |
| | | | | | | | | | | |
| **II. Government Operation** | **4.8** | | **5.7** | | **6.1** | | **6.6** | | **7.3** | |
| (a) Govern. Consumption (% of GDP) | 3 | (16.9) | 3 | (17.4) | 4 | (15.7) | 5 | (14.5) | 5 | (14.9) |
| (b) Government Enterprises | 6 | | 6 | | 6 | | 6 | | 6 | |
| (c) Price Controls | - | | - | | - | | 7 | | 7 | |
| (d) Entry Into Business | - | | - | | - | | - | | 7.5 | |
| (e) Legal System | - | | - | | - | | - | | 10 | |
| (f) Avoidance of Neg. Interest Rates | 6 | | 10 | | 10 | | 10 | | 10 | |
| | | | | | | | | | | |
| **III. Takings** | **2.3** | | **0.0** | | **0.0** | | **0.0** | | **0.9** | |
| (a) Transfers and Subsidies (% of GDP) | 0 | (25.6) | 0 | (29.4) | 0 | (31.6) | 0 | (28.7) | 0 | (30.7) |
| (b) Marginal Tax Rates (Top Rate) | 5 | (46) | 0 | (72) | 0 | (72) | 0 | (72) | 2 | (60) |
| (c) Conscription | 0 | | 0 | | 0 | | 0 | | 0 | |
| | | | | | | | | | | |
| **IV. International Sector** | **8.2** | | **9.1** | | **9.5** | | **9.3** | | **9.7** | |
| (a) Taxes on International Trade (Avg.) | 9 | (1.3) | 10 | (0.0) | 10 | (0.0) | 10 | (0.0) | 10 | (0.0) |
| (b) Black Market Exchange Rates (Prem.) | 10 | (0) | 10 | (0) | 10 | (0) | 10 | (0) | 10 | (0) |
| (c) Size of Trade Sector (% of GDP) | 9 | (92.2) | 8 | (100.9) | 10 | (116.8) | 9 | (103.7) | 8 | (100.0) |
| (d) Capital Transactions with Foreigners | 5 | | 8 | | 8 | | 8 | | 10 | |

## Part 2: Recent Economic Indicators:

| | | | | |
|---|---|---|---|---|
| **Population 1994:** | 15.4 | **Real Per Capita GDP :** | 1994= | $13,505 |
| (in millions) | | (in 1985 U.S. dollars) | | |
| Annual Rate of Change (1980-94): | 0.6% | Avg. Growth Rate: | 1980-90= | 1.5% |
| | | | 1985-94= | 1.7% |

| Economic Indicators: | 1987 | 1988 | 1989 | 1990 | 1991 | 1992 | 1993 | 1994 |
|---|---|---|---|---|---|---|---|---|
| Change in Real GDP: Aggregate | 3.3 | 2.6 | 4.7 | 3.9 | 2.3 | 1.8 | 0.4 | 2.5 |
| : Per Capita | 2.7 | 2.0 | 4.1 | 3.4 | 1.5 | 1.2 | -0.2 | 1.9 |
| Inflation Rate (CPI) | -0.7 | 0.7 | 1.1 | 2.5 | 3.9 | 3.7 | 2.1 | 2.6 |
| Change in Money Supply: (M1) | 6.9 | 7.5 | 5.5 | 5.5 | 3.6 | 5.5 | 7.8 | 0.9 |
| : (M2) | 3.8 | 3.2 | 8.8 | 9.0 | 5.4 | 5.2 | 5.1 | 0.2 |
| Investment/GDP Ratio | 20.7 | 21.4 | 22.6 | 22.2 | 21.1 | 20.8 | 19.7 | 19.7 |
| Central Government Budget Deficit or Surplus (% of GDP) | -3.1 | -4.2 | -4.3 | -4.8 | -2.8 | -3.4 | -1.0 | 0.0 |
| Unemployment Rate | 9.6 | 9.1 | 8.3 | 7.5 | 7.0 | 6.7 | 8.3 | 7.8 |

During 1975-1990, the Is1 economic freedom summary rating of the Netherlands fluctuated within a narrow range between 5.5 and 5.8. During the 1990s, there has been some upward movement. Based on the average of our three economic freedom indexes, the Netherlands ranked 11th (between Japan and Germany) in 1993-1995. The Is1 summary index ranks it a little lower—in a tie with Bolivia and Germany for 18th place.

Netherlands gets exceedingly high marks in both the money and international areas. The justification for these high ratings is clear. The growth rate of the money supply has been low and relatively stable. Not surprisingly, the inflation rate has followed suit. Citizens are allowed to maintain foreign currency bank accounts both domestically and abroad. Tariffs are negligible; the currency is fully convertible; the trade sector is large; and there are virtually no restrictions on the mobility of capital.

Even in the government operations area, the rating of the Netherlands is not bad. While government consumption is large, this is offset by a strong legal system, competitive business practices, and a credit market that is well integrated with the global economy. In contrast with the other areas, the rating of the Netherlands in the takings area is one of the lowest in the world. Netherlands combines a huge transfer sector (only Sweden transfers a larger share of its GDP away from those who generate it), with high taxes (the top marginal tax rate is currently 60%, down from the 72% figure of 1990), and conscription. Typically, a large transfer sector leads to two unpleasant side effects—large budget deficits and high unemployment rates. To date, these effects have been moderate. However, if the current transfer policies remain in place, these negative side effects will almost certainly become more severe in the future.

# NEW ZEALAND

**Part 1: The Economic Freedom Ratings for the Components and Various Area and Summary Indexes: 1975, 1980, 1985, 1990 and 1993-95.**

(The numbers in parentheses indicate actual values for the components).

| | **Summary Ratings** | | |
|---|---|---|---|
| | **Ie** | **Is1** | **Is2** |
| 1975 | 4.5 | 4.3 | 4.6 |
| 1980 | 5.1 | 4.8 | 5.6 |
| 1985 | 4.6 | 4.1 | 4.9 |
| 1990 | 6.4 | 6.0 | 7.2 |
| 1993-95 | 8.4 | 8.0 | 9.1 |

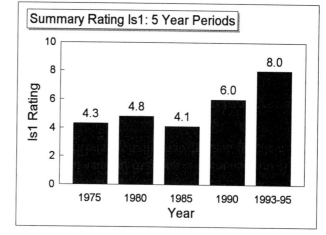

| Components of Economic Freedom | 1975 | | 1980 | | 1985 | | 1990 | | 1993-95 | |
|---|---|---|---|---|---|---|---|---|---|---|
| **I. Money and Inflation** | **2.9** | | **5.1** | | **3.5** | | **5.3** | | **9.4** | |
| (a) Annual Money Growth (last 5 yrs.) | 3 | (11.8) | 7 | (5.5) | 5 | (8.6) | 1 | (40.2) | 8 | (3.4) |
| (b) Inflation Variablity (last 5 yrs.) | 6 | (3.7) | 9 | (2.1) | 6 | (3.1) | 4 | (5.0) | 10 | (0.8) |
| (c) Ownership of Foreign Currency | 0 | | 0 | | 0 | | 10 | | 10 | |
| (d) Maint. of Bank Account Abroad | 0 | | 0 | | 0 | | 10 | | 10 | |
| | | | | | | | | | | |
| **II. Government Operation** | **5.0** | | **4.5** | | **5.7** | | **6.7** | | **8.7** | |
| (a) Govern. Consumption (% of GDP) | 4 | (15.6) | 2 | (17.9) | 4 | (16.2) | 3 | (17.0) | 5 | (15.2) |
| (b) Government Enterprises | 6 | | 6 | | 6 | | 6 | | 8 | |
| (c) Price Controls | - | | - | | - | | 9 | | 10 | |
| (d) Entry Into Business | - | | - | | - | | - | | 10 | |
| (e) Legal System | - | | - | | - | | - | | 10 | |
| (f) Avoidance of Neg. Interest Rates | - | | 6 | | 8 | | 10 | | 10 | |
| | | | | | | | | | | |
| **III. Takings** | **3.1** | | **2.7** | | **1.7** | | **4.6** | | **5.4** | |
| (a) Transfers and Subsidies (% of GDP) | 1 | (20.2) | 1 | (21.9) | 1 | (20.6) | 0 | (27.5) | 2 | (15.7) |
| (b) Marginal Tax Rates (Top Rate) | 3 | (60) | 2 | (60) | 0 | (66) | 7 | (33) | 7 | (33) |
| (c) Conscription | 10 | | 10 | | 10 | | 10 | | 10 | |
| | | | | | | | | | | |
| **IV. International Sector** | **6.2** | | **7.3** | | **6.3** | | **7.3** | | **8.9** | |
| (a) Taxes on International Trade (Avg.) | 8 | (2.4) | 8 | (2.5) | 8 | (2.0) | 8 | (1.7) | 9 | (1.2) |
| (b) Black Market Exchange Rates (Prem.) | 6 | (5) | 10 | (0) | 6 | (4) | 6 | (5) | 10 | (0) |
| (c) Size of Trade Sector (% of GDP) | 5 | (55.9) | 5 | (61.8) | 6 | (64.4) | 4 | (54.0) | 5 | (59.4) |
| (d) Capital Transactions with Foreigners | 5 | | 5 | | 5 | | 10 | | 10 | |

178

## Part 2:  Recent Economic Indicators:

| | | | | |
|---|---|---|---|---|
| **Population 1994:** | 3.5 | **Real Per Capita GDP :** | 1994= | $12,240 |
| (in millions): | | (in 1985 U.S. dollars) | | |
| Annual Rate of Change (1980-94): | 0.8% | Avg. Growth Rate: | 1980-90= | 1.0% |
| | | | 1985-94= | 0.8% |

| Economic Indicators: | 1987 | 1988 | 1989 | 1990 | 1991 | 1992 | 1993 | 1994 |
|---|---|---|---|---|---|---|---|---|
| Change in Real GDP: Aggregate | -0.8 | 1.2 | -1.0 | 0.2 | -2.0 | 1.6 | 5.2 | 6.0 |
| : Per Capita | -1.6 | 0.4 | -1.8 | -0.6 | -2.8 | 0.8 | 4.4 | 4.2 |
| Inflation Rate (CPI) | 15.7 | 6.4 | 5.7 | 6.1 | 2.6 | 1.0 | 1.3 | 1.7 |
| Change in Money Supply: (M1) | 30.6 | 44.8 | 39.7 | 27.7 | 1.3 | 2.7 | 3.7 | 10.3 |
| : (M2) | 31.5 | -8.6 | 8.9 | 62.2 | 30.4 | 11.7 | 3.8 | |
| Investment/GDP Ratio | 21.9 | 20.0 | 23.4 | 21.2 | 17.4 | 19.5 | 18.4 | |
| Central Government Budget Deficit (-) or Surplus (+) As a Percent of GDP | +1.0 | +2.0 | - | +4.0 | +1.9 | -2.3 | 0.0 | |
| Unemployment Rate | 4.1 | 5.6 | 7.1 | 7.7 | 10.2 | 10.3 | 9.5 | 7.7 [a] |

a  First 9 months of the year.

In 1985, New Zealand was plagued by an expansionary and unstable monetary policy, restrictions on foreign currency holdings, high marginal tax rates, a large transfer sector, exchange rate controls, and capital market restrictions.  Much has changed in the last decade.  Monetary reform—the central bank has a legislative mandate to keep the inflation rate low—has led to a dramatic improvement in price stability.  Foreign currency bank accounts are now legal. (Note: New Zealand's rating in the monetary area rose from 2.5 in 1985 to 9.4 in 1995.)  The top marginal tax rate has been sliced from 66% to 33%.  Exchange rate controls have been removed and the New Zealand dollar is now fully convertible.

Propelled by these changes, the Is1 summary index of New Zealand rose from 4.1 in 1975 to 8.0 in 1995, the largest increase in the world during this time period. New Zealand now ranks as the third most free economy, behind only Hong Kong and Singapore.   Government consumption expenditures and the transfer sector are still quite large, but even here some progress has been made.  These policies are now beginning to pay off.  After years of sluggish growth, real GDP increased at an annual rate of 5.2% in 1993 and 6% in 1994 (see Part 2, above).  Inflation has fallen to an annual rate of near 1% and the unemployment rate is falling.  If New Zealand stays on its current path, our analysis suggests its economic future will be bright.

# NICARAGUA

**Part 1: The Economic Freedom Ratings for the Components and Various Area and Summary Indexes:  1975, 1980, 1985, 1990 and 1993-95.**

(The numbers in parentheses indicate the actual values for the components.)

| | **Summary Ratings** | | |
| | **Ie** | **Is1** | **Is2** |
| 1975 | 6.0 | 6.4 | 5.5 |
| 1980 | 3.5 | 3.6 | 3.6 |
| 1985 | 1.2 | 1.8 | 0.6 |
| 1990 | 1.5 | 2.0 | 1.1 |
| 1993-95 | 2.7 | 3.3 | 2.2 |

**Summary Rating Is1: 5 Year Periods**

| Year | Is1 Rating |
| --- | --- |
| 1975 | 6.4 |
| 1980 | 3.6 |
| 1985 | 1.8 |
| 1990 | 2.0 |
| 1993-95 | 3.3 |

| Components of Economic Freedom | 1975 | | 1980 | | 1985 | | 1990 | | 1993-95 | |
| --- | --- | --- | --- | --- | --- | --- | --- | --- | --- | --- |
| **I.  Money and Inflation** | **5.2** | | **4.3** | | **0.0** | | **0.0** | | **0.0** | |
| (a) Annual Money Growth (last 5 yrs.) | 3 | (12.3) | 1 | (26.6) | 0 | (70.0) | 0 | (2073.5) | 0 | (322.9) |
| (b) Inflation Variablity (last 5 yrs.) | 2 | (8.8) | 1 | (15.9) | 0 | (60.3) | 0 | (4853.2) | 0 | (2875.9) |
| (c) Ownership of Foreign Currency | 10 | | 10 | | 0 | | 0 | | 0 | |
| (d) Maint. of Bank Account Abroad | 10 | | 10 | | 0 | | 0 | | 0 | |
| | | | | | | | | | | |
| **II.  Government Operation** | **7.5** | | **3.6** | | **0.0** | | **0.0** | | **2.1** | |
| (a) Govern. Consumption (% of GDP) | 9 | (9.1) | 1 | (19.7) | 0 | (35.7) | 0 | (32.6) | 4 | (15.9) |
| (b) Government Enterprises | 6 | | 6 | | 0 | | 0 | | 0 | |
| (c) Price Controls | - | | - | | - | | - | | 2 | |
| (d) Entry Into Business | - | | - | | - | | - | | 5.0 | |
| (e) Legal System | - | | - | | - | | - | | 0 | |
| (f) Avoidance of Neg. Interest Rates | - | | - | | - | | 0 | | 0 | |
| | | | | | | | | | | |
| **III.  Takings** | **7.9** | | **5.1** | | **4.3** | | **3.8** | | **7.1** | |
| (a) Transfers and Subsidies (% of GDP) | 8 | (2.4) | 7 | (4.1) | 5 | (6.2) | 5 | (6.8) | 5 | (6.2) |
| (b) Marginal Tax Rates (Top Rate) | 10 | (21) | 5 | (50) | 5 | (50) | - | | 8 | (30) |
| (c) Conscription | 0 | | 0 | | 0 | | 0 | | 10 | |
| | | | | | | | | | | |
| **IV.  International Sector** | **4.9** | | **1.4** | | **1.1** | | **3.5** | | **2.7** | |
| (a) Taxes on International Trade (Avg.) | 6 | (4.9) | 2 | (8.7) | 3 | (7.4) | 6 | (4.3) | 2 | (8.0) |
| (b) Black Market Exchange Rates (Prem.) | 4 | (21) | 1 | (91) | 0 | (382) | 4 | (10) | 6 | (4) |
| (c) Size of Trade Sector (% of GDP) | 4 | (65.7) | 3 | (67.5) | 1 | (36.5) | 4 | (68.5) | 3 | (65.2) |
| (d) Capital Transactions with Foreigners | 5 | | 0 | | 0 | | 0 | | 0 | |

180

## Part 2:  Recent Economic Indicators:

| | | | | | |
|---|---|---|---|---|---|
| **Population 1994:** | 4.4 | **Real Per Capita GDP** : | | 1994= | $1,165 |
| (in millions) | | (in 1985 U.S. dollars) | | | |
| Annual Rate of Change (1980-94): | 3.4% | Avg. Growth Rate: | | 1980-90= | -3.8% |
| | | | | 1985-94= | -3.8% |

| Economic Indicators: | 1987 | 1988 | 1989 | 1990 | 1991 | 1992 | 1993 | 1994 |
|---|---|---|---|---|---|---|---|---|
| Change in Real GDP: Aggregate | -0.7 | -12.4 | -1.7 | -0.1 | -0.2 | 0.4 | -0.9 | 3.2 |
| : Per Capita | -4.1 | -15.8 | -4.1 | -3.5 | -3.6 | -3.0 | -4.3 | 0.0 |
| Inflation Rate (CPI) | 911.9 | 10205.0 | 4770.4 | 7485.2 | 2742.2 | 20.3 | - | - |
| Change in Money Supply: (M1) | 562.8 | - | 2403.0 | - | 1330.0 | 11.5 | -4.6 | 36.1 |
| : (M2) | 487.1 | - | - | - | 1510.0 | 20.0 | 25.2 | 61.3 |
| Investment/GDP Ratio | 15.8 | 26.8 | 27.2 | 19.3 | 19.7 | 17.4 | 21.7 | 22.2 |
| Central Government Budget Deficit (-) or Surplus (+) As a Percent of GDP | - | -23.7 | -1.9 | -11.6 | - | -2.1 | +0.3 | - |
| Unemployment Rate | | | | | | | | |

The Nicaraguan experiment of the last two years provides a vivid portrait of what happens when economic freedom is lost.  In almost every area, policies that conflicted with economic freedom were adopted.  The government financed more and more of its expenditures with money creation.  Soaring money growth (the *annual* growth rate of the money supply rose from 12% during 1970-1975, to 26% in 1975-1980, to 70% in 1980-1985, and to more than 2000% during 1985-1990) predictably led to hyperinflation.  The government responded with price controls, higher taxes, and more spending.  Government consumption expenditures increased from 9% of GDP in 1975 to 36% in 1985.  By the mid-1980s, government enterprises dominated the economy and  the top marginal tax rate had been pushed to 50%, up from 21% in 1975.  Higher tariffs, rigid exchange rate controls (the black market exchange rate premium rose from 21% in 1975 to 382% in 1985), and capital market controls were also a part of this political economy experiment.

The results were disastrous.  Measured in 1985 dollars, the per capita income of Nicaragua fell from $2,531 in 1975 to $1,165 in 1994.  In 1975, Nicaragua's per capita income was nearly as large as that of Chile; by 1994 it was only one-fifth as large.  In the early 1990s, a few modest steps toward economic freedom have been taken, but much more will be required to restore the confidence of citizens and foreigners alike.

# NIGERIA

**Part 1: The Economic Freedom Ratings for the Components and Various Area and Summary Indexes: 1975, 1980, 1985, 1990 and 1993-95.**

(The numbers in parentheses indicate the actual values for the components.)

### Summary Ratings

|      | Ie  | Is1 | Is2 |
|------|-----|-----|-----|
| 1975 | 3.2 | 3.3 | 2.5 |
| 1980 | 3.0 | 2.8 | 2.7 |
| 1985 | 3.8 | 4.3 | 2.9 |
| 1990 | 3.3 | 3.3 | 2.9 |
| 1993-95 | 3.5 | 3.7 | 2.7 |

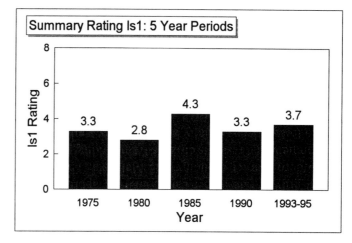

| Components of Economic Freedom | 1975 | | 1980 | | 1985 | | 1990 | | 1993-95 | |
|---|---|---|---|---|---|---|---|---|---|---|
| **I. Money and Inflation** | **0.6** | | **3.3** | | **3.1** | | **0.9** | | **0.6** | |
| (a) Annual Money Growth (last 5 yrs.) | 1 | (25.4) | 1 | (25.5) | 7 | (6.8) | 2 | (20.2) | 1 | (30.0) |
| (b) Inflation Variablity (last 5 yrs.) | 1 | (15.7) | 9 | (1.5) | 3 | (6.0) | 1 | (19.3) | 1 | (17.7) |
| (c) Ownership of Foreign Currency | 0 | | 0 | | 0 | | 0 | | 0 | |
| (d) Maint. of Bank Account Abroad | 0 | | 0 | | 0 | | 0 | | 0 | |
| | | | | | | | | | | |
| **II. Government Operation** | **4.7** | | **3.9** | | **4.0** | | **3.7** | | **4.0** | |
| (a) Govern. Consumption (% of GDP) | 7 | (12.6) | 7 | (11.9) | 6 | (13.5) | 7 | (11.4) | 10 | (5.3) |
| (b) Government Enterprises | 4 | | 2 | | 2 | | 2 | | 2 | |
| (c) Price Controls | - | | - | | - | | 4 | | 4 | |
| (d) Entry Into Business | - | | - | | - | | - | | 5.0 | |
| (e) Legal System | - | | - | | - | | - | | 0 | |
| (f) Avoidance of Neg. Interest Rates | 2 | | 2 | | 4 | | 0 | | 0 | |
| | | | | | | | | | | |
| **III. Takings** | **4.5** | | **2.2** | | **6.7** | | **3.8** | | **7.7** | |
| (a) Transfers and Subsidies (% of GDP) | 8 | (2.9) | - | | 10 | (1.4) | - | | - | |
| (b) Marginal Tax Rates (Top Rate) | 0 | (75) | 0 | (70) | 3 | (55) | 2 | (55) | 7 | (35) |
| (c) Conscription | 10 | | 10 | | 10 | | 10 | | 10 | |
| | | | | | | | | | | |
| **IV. International Sector** | **2.7** | | **2.0** | | **2.3** | | **4.3** | | **2.3** | |
| (a) Taxes on International Trade (Avg.) | 4 | (6.6) | 2 | (8.5) | 6 | (5.1) | 6 | (4.0) | - | |
| (b) Black Market Exchange Rates (Prem.) | 2 | (43) | 1 | (72) | 0 | (270) | 3 | (23) | 0 | (277) |
| (c) Size of Trade Sector (% of GDP) | 6 | (41.2) | 7 | (48.0) | 3 | (28.5) | 10 | (64.6) | 10 | (73.7) |
| (d) Capital Transactions with Foreigners | 0 | | 0 | | 0 | | 0 | | 0 | |

## Part 2: Recent Economic Indicators:

| Population 1994: | 107.9 | **Real Per Capita GDP** : | 1994= | $960 |
| (in millions) | | (in 1985 U.S. dollars) | | |
| Annual Rate of Change (1980-84): | 3.0% | Avg. Growth Rate: | 1980-90= | -2.0% |
| | | | 1985-94= | 1.1% |

| Economic Indicators: | 1987 | 1988 | 1989 | 1990 | 1991 | 1992 | 1993 | 1994 |
|---|---|---|---|---|---|---|---|---|
| Change in Real GDP: Aggregate | -0.5 | 9.9 | 7.4 | 8.2 | 4.7 | 3.6 | 2.6 | 1.3 |
| : Per Capita | -3.5 | 6.9 | 4.4 | 5.2 | 1.7 | 0.6 | -0.4 | -1.7 |
| Inflation Rate (CPI) | 11.3 | 54.5 | 50.5 | 7.4 | 13.0 | 44.6 | 57.2 | |
| Change in Money Supply: (M1) | 0.6 | 35.7 | 37.8 | 25.9 | 47.8 -- | | -- | |
| : (M2) | 7.7 | 32.9 | 22.5 | 21.8 | 42.8 -- | | -- | |
| Investment/GDP Ratio | 8.8 | 6.5 | 8.2 | 11.9 | 11.0 | 10.7 | 12.8 | 9.4 |
| Central Government Budget Deficit (-) or Surplus (+) As a Percent of GDP) | -8.9 | | | | | | | |
| Unemployment Rate | | | | | | | | |

The economic freedom of this resource rich country was low throughout the 1975-1995 period and there are few signs of improvement. Monetary instability, insecure property rights, rigid exchange rate controls, and capital market restrictions continue to undermine the Nigerian economy. Excessive monetary expansion (M1 grew by 30% annually during the most recent five-year period) has caused high and variable rates of inflation. In 1990, the inflation rate was 7%, but it rose to 45% in 1992 and 57% in 1993. It is difficult for either businesses or households to plan for the future in this environment. In addition the economy is characterized by inefficient state enterprises and legal restrictions (and subsidies) that retard competition from private firms. Nigeria's 1994 black market exchange rate premium (277%) was the second highest among the countries in our study. A highly politicized economy of this type almost inevitably leads to corruption that undermines the confidence of both domestics and foreigners. This is precisely what has happened to the Nigerian economy.

Measured in 1985 dollars, the per capita income of Nigeria has fallen from $1,438 in 1980 to $960 in 1994. Unless the current policies that are stifling both economic freedom and prosperity are reversed, the economic stagnation will almost surely continue.

# NORWAY

**Part 1: The Economic Freedom Ratings for the Components and Various Area and Summary Indexes: 1975, 1980, 1985, 1990 and 1993-95.**

(The numbers in parentheses indicate the actual values for the components.)

### Summary Ratings

|        | Ie  | Is1 | Is2 |
|--------|-----|-----|-----|
| 1975   | 3.8 | 3.6 | 3.8 |
| 1980   | 3.8 | 3.4 | 4.0 |
| 1985   | 4.3 | 3.9 | 4.4 |
| 1990   | 5.3 | 4.8 | 6.1 |
| 1993-95| 6.3 | 5.7 | 7.2 |

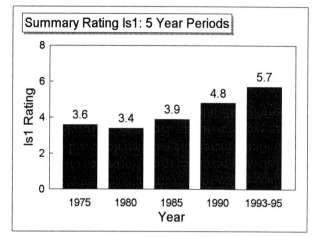

Summary Rating Is1: 5 Year Periods

| Components of Economic Freedom | 1975 | | 1980 | | 1985 | | 1990 | | 1993-95 | |
|---|---|---|---|---|---|---|---|---|---|---|
| **I. Money and Inflation** | **4.2** | | **5.4** | | **2.9** | | **6.3** | | **8.8** | |
| (a) Annual Money Growth (last 5 yrs.) | 4 | (10.2) | 10 | (1.6) | 3 | (12.7) | 2 | (17.1) | 7 | (5.7) |
| (b) Inflation Variablity (last 5 yrs.) | 9 | (2.1) | 7 | (3.0) | 6 | (3.3) | 6 | (3.5) | 9 | (1.9) |
| (c) Ownership of Foreign Currency | 0 | | 0 | | 0 | | 10 | | 10 | |
| (d) Maint. of Bank Account Abroad | 0 | | 0 | | 0 | | 10 | | 10 | |
| | | | | | | | | | | |
| **II. Government Operation** | **1.5** | | **2.8** | | **3.7** | | **3.8** | | **5.8** | |
| (a) Govern. Consumption (% of GDP) | 1 | (19.3) | 2 | (18.8) | 2 | (18.5) | 1 | (21.1) | 1 | (21.9) |
| (b) Government Enterprises | 2 | | 2 | | 2 | | 2 | | 2 | |
| (c) Price Controls | - | | - | | - | | 5 | | 7 | |
| (d) Entry Into Business | - | | - | | - | | - | | 7.5 | |
| (e) Legal System | - | | - | | - | | - | | 10 | |
| (f) Avoidance of Neg. Interest Rates | - | | 6 | | 10 | | 10 | | 10 | |
| | | | | | | | | | | |
| **III. Takings** | **0.0** | | **0.4** | | **0.9** | | **1.4** | | **1.9** | |
| (a) Transfers and Subsidies (% of GDP) | - | | 1 | (22.1) | 1 | (21.4) | 0 | (27.3) | 0 | (27.0) |
| (b) Marginal Tax Rates (Top Rate) | 0 | (74) | 0 | (75) | 1 | (64) | 3 | (54) | 4 | (42) |
| (c) Conscription | 0 | | 0 | | 0 | | 0 | | 0 | |
| | | | | | | | | | | |
| **IV. International Sector** | **6.9** | | **6.0** | | **8.4** | | **8.8** | | **9.1** | |
| (a) Taxes on International Trade (Avg.) | 9 | (0.5) | 9 | (0.3) | 10 | (0.3) | 10 | (0.3) | - | |
| (b) Black Market Exchange Rates (Prem.) | 8 | (1) | 6 | (3) | 10 | (0) | 10 | (0) | 10 | (0) |
| (c) Size of Trade Sector (% of GDP) | 9 | (90.3) | 7 | (88.5) | 8 | (86.0) | 6 | (81.1) | 6 | (79.0) |
| (d) Capital Transactions with Foreigners | 2 | | 2 | | 5 | | 8 | | 10 | |

## Part 2:  Recent Economic Indicators:

| | | | | |
|---|---|---|---|---|
| **Population 1994:** | 4.4 | **Real Per Capita GDP  :** | 1994= | $16,589 |
| (in millions) | | (in 1985 U.S. dollars) | | |
| Annual Rate of Change (1980-94): | 0.4% | Avg. Growth Rate: | 1980-90= | 1.8% |
| | | | 1985-94= | 1.3% |

| Economic Indicators: | 1987 | 1988 | 1989 | 1990 | 1991 | 1992 | 1993 | 1994 |
|---|---|---|---|---|---|---|---|---|
| Change in Real GDP: Aggregate | 2.0 | -0.5 | 0.6 | 1.7 | 1.6 | 3.3 | 2.5 | 5.1 |
| : Per Capita | 1.6 | -0.9 | 0.2 | 1.3 | 1.1 | 2.8 | 2.1 | 4.7 |
| Inflation Rate (CPI) | 8.7 | 6.7 | 4.6 | 4.1 | 3.4 | 2.3 | 2.3 | 1.5 |
| Change in Money Supply:  (M1) | 36.4 | 21.2 | 24.3 | 10.8 | 6.2 | 7.8 | 12.2 | 1.6 |
| : (M2) | 22.9 | 7.6 | 8.4 | 7.7 | 4.1 | 4.8 | 6.6 | 3.0 |
| Investment/GDP Ratio | 28.2 | 27.1 | 24.3 | 20.5 | 18.8 | 18.2 | 19.6 | 18.3 |
| Central Government Budget Deficit or Surplus (% of GDP) | +0.6 | -0.2 | -1.2 | +0.7 | -0.2 | -2.3 | -2.7 | -1.3 [a] |
| Unemployment Rate | 2.1 | 3.2 | 4.9 | 5.2 | 5.5 | 5.9 | 6.0 | 5.4 [a] |

a  First nine months of the year.

The average of our three summary indexes ranked Norway as the 22nd most free economy in 1993-1995.  The Is1 index placed it 41st.

Norway's rating has improved during the last decade, primarily as the result of a freer and more stable monetary regime.  During the last five years, monetary expansion has been low (5.7% after adjustment for the growth of real output, down from double-digit monetary growth throughout much of the 1975-1990 period.)  The recent inflation rate has been both low and relatively steady.  The restrictions on the maintenance of foreign currency bank accounts were abolished in the late 1980s.  As the result, Norway's rating in the money and inflation area rose from 2.9 in 1985 to 8.8 in 1995.

Norway's legal structure provides equal protection and restricts arbitrary authority.  Its credit market is integrated with the global market and its international sector is relatively free.  The major deficiencies of this economy are the huge government consumption and transfer sectors.  Government spending in these two areas now takes approximately 50% of the earnings of Norwegians—22% for government consumption and another 27% for transfers and subsidies.  To date, substantial revenues from North Sea oil have made it possible for Norway to avoid the large budget deficits, increasing national debt, and rising interest costs that have entrapped several other European welfare states.  However, if revenues from this source should decrease, Norway will almost surely fall into this same cycle.

# PAKISTAN

## Part 1: The Economic Freedom Ratings for the Components and Various Area and Summary Indexes: 1975, 1980, 1985, 1990 and 1993-95.
(The numbers in parentheses indicate the actual values for the components.)

### Summary Ratings

|       | Ie  | Is1 | Is2 |
|-------|-----|-----|-----|
| 1975  | 2.4 | 2.3 | 1.9 |
| 1980  | 3.6 | 3.5 | 3.2 |
| 1985  | 4.2 | 3.9 | 4.0 |
| 1990  | 4.5 | 4.2 | 4.3 |
| 1993-95 | 5.3 | 5.4 | 5.0 |

Summary Rating Is1: 5 Year Periods

| Components of Economic Freedom | 1975 | | 1980 | | 1985 | | 1990 | | 1993-95 | |
|---|---|---|---|---|---|---|---|---|---|---|
| **I.  Money and Inflation** | **1.9** | | **3.6** | | **4.8** | | **6.1** | | **5.8** | |
| (a) Annual Money Growth (last 5 yrs.) | 4 | (10.2) | 2 | (16.4) | 7 | (6.5) | 5 | (9.4) | 5 | (9.3) |
| (b) Inflation Variablity (last 5 yrs.) | 2 | (8.6) | 9 | (1.6) | 8 | (2.3) | 8 | (2.4) | 7 | (3.0) |
| (c) Ownership of Foreign Currency | 0 | | 0 | | 0 | | 10 | | 10 | |
| (d) Maint. of Bank Account Abroad | 0 | | 0 | | 0 | | 0 | | 0 | |
| | | | | | | | | | | |
| **II.  Government Operation** | **4.9** | | **5.2** | | **5.2** | | **4.8** | | **4.6** | |
| (a) Govern. Consumption (% of GDP) | 8 | (10.6) | 8 | (10.0) | 7 | (12.1) | 5 | (15.1) | 7 | (12.2) |
| (b) Government Enterprises | 2 | | 2 | | 2 | | 4 | | 4 | |
| (c) Price Controls | - | | - | | - | | - | | 4 | |
| (d) Entry Into Business | - | | - | | - | | - | | 5 | |
| (e) Legal System | - | | - | | - | | - | | 0 | |
| (f) Avoidance of Neg. Interest Rates | - | | 6 | | 8 | | 6 | | 8 | |
| | | | | | | | | | | |
| **III.  Takings** | **0.8** | | **3.8** | | **3.0** | | **4.5** | | **6.1** | |
| (a) Transfers and Subsidies (% of GDP) | - | | - | | - | | - | | - | |
| (b) Marginal Tax Rates (Top Rate) | 1 | (61) | 2 | (55) | 1 | (60) | 3 | (50) | 5 | (38) |
| (c) Conscription | 0 | | 10 | | 10 | | 10 | | 10 | |
| | | | | | | | | | | |
| **IV.  International Sector** | **2.3** | | **2.0** | | **3.0** | | **2.3** | | **6.1** | |
| (a) Taxes on International Trade (Avg.) | 0 | (15.3) | 0 | (15.3) | 0 | (14.7) | 0 | (16.5) | - | |
| (b) Black Market Exchange Rates (Prem.) | 4 | (17) | 3 | (27) | 6 | (4) | 4 | (14) | 10 | (0) |
| (c) Size of Trade Sector (% of GDP) | 4 | (33.1) | 4 | (36.6) | 5 | (34.0) | 4 | (35.0) | 6 | (41.6) |
| (d) Capital Transactions with Foreigners | 2 | | 2 | | 2 | | 2 | | 2 | |

## Part 2:  Recent Economic Indicators:

| | | | | |
|---|---|---|---|---|
| **Population 1994:** | 126.3 | **Real Per Capita GDP** : | 1994= | $1,435 |
| (in millions) | | (in 1985 U.S. dollars) | | |
| Annual Rate of Change (1980-84): | 3.1% | Avg. Growth Rate: | 1980-90= | 3.0% |
| | | | 1985-94= | 2.3% |

| Economic Indicators: | 1987 | 1988 | 1989 | 1990 | 1991 | 1992 | 1993 | 1994 |
|---|---|---|---|---|---|---|---|---|
| Change in Real GDP: Aggregate | 6.5 | 7.6 | 5.0 | 4.5 | 5.5 | 7.8 | 2.6 | 4.0 |
| : Per Capita | 3.4 | 4.5 | 1.9 | 1.4 | 2.4 | 4.7 | -0.5 | 0.9 |
| Inflation Rate (CPI) | 4.7 | 8.8 | 7.8 | 9.1 | 11.8 | 9.5 | 9.4 | 12.5 |
| Change in Money Supply: (M1) | 18.8 | 15.2 | 11.0 | 16.4 | 19.0 | 20.0 | 8.2 | 10.9 |
| : (M2) | 14.9 | 12.1 | 5.7 | 12.4 | 15.0 | 24.6 | 23.4 | 16.0 |
| Investment/GDP Ratio | 19.1 | 18.0 | 18.9 | 18.9 | 19.0 | 20.1 | 20.4 | 19.9 |
| Central Government Budget Deficit (-) or Surplus (+) As a Percent of GDP | -8.5 | -6.3 | -7.4 | -5.4 | -7.6 | -7.9 | -7.4 | -6.0 |
| Unemployment Rate* | 3.1 | 3.1 | 3.1 | 3.1 | 6.3 | 6.3 | - | - |

* From the United Nations, Statistical Yearbook.

Pakistan's summary economic freedom rating (Is1) improved from a very low 2.3 in 1975 to 5.4 in 1993-95.  Most of the improvement came in the 1990's.  In terms of the  rankings, Pakistan moved from 93rd in 1975 to 50th in the mid-1990s (or 51st based on the average of the three ratings).

The improvement in Pakistan's economic freedom rating can be attributed to a few components in the index.  First, top marginal tax rates have been reduced from 61% in 1975 (and 60% in 1985) to the current rate of 38%. A significant liberalization of the exchange rate system has reduced the black market exchange rate premium from a high of 27% in 1980 to zero (and a rating of 10) in 1993-94.  Some of the increase in the summary rating for 1993-95 may reflect the fact that the Taxes on International Trade (IVa) datum was not available for Pakistan in that year.  In all the previous periods, this component received a zero rating.  Its absence in the most recent period may have artificially inflated the summary rating slightly.

It is clear that there has been a slight move toward economic liberalization in Pakistan over the last two decades.  This improvement has allowed Pakistan to report modest, if unremarkable, annual growth rate of per capita GDP of approximately 2.5%.  For Pakistan to make the move into the modern market economy like Malaysia, Thailand, and Singapore, it must improve its regulatory environment that restricts citizens from holding bank accounts abroad, restricts prices and market entry, fails to treat citizens equally before the law, and interferes with the capital transactions with foreigners.

# PERU

**Part 1: The Economic Freedom Ratings for the Components and Various Area and Summary Indexes:    1975, 1980, 1985, 1990 and 1993-95.**

(The numbers in parentheses indicate the actual values for the components.)

|      | **Summary Ratings** | | |
|------|------|------|------|
|      | **Ie** | **Is1** | **Is2** |
| 1975 | 3.1 | 3.7 | 2.1 |
| 1980 | 3.0 | 3.4 | 2.0 |
| 1985 | 3.2 | 3.4 | 2.2 |
| 1990 | 3.4 | 4.0 | 2.4 |
| 1993-95 | 5.4 | 5.9 | 5.1 |

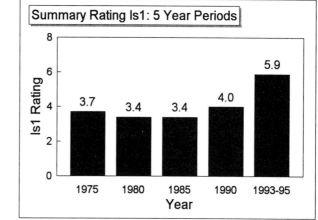

| **Components of Economic Freedom** | **1975** | | **1980** | | **1985** | | **1990** | | **1993-95** | |
|------|------|------|------|------|------|------|------|------|------|------|
| **I. Money and Inflation** | **1.9** | | **0.6** | | **1.9** | | **1.9** | | **3.6** | |
| (a) Annual Money Growth (last 5 yrs.) | 2 | (18.6) | 1 | (39.1) | 0 | (98.4) | 0 | (690.2) | 0 | (249.1) |
| (b) Inflation Variablity (last 5 yrs.) | 4 | (5.9) | 1 | (17.5) | 0 | (38.1) | 0 | (2302.8) | 0 | (2380.4) |
| (c) Ownership of Foreign Currency | 0 | | 0 | | 10 | | 10 | | 10 | |
| (d) Maint. of Bank Account Abroad | 0 | | 0 | | 0 | | 0 | | 10 | |
| | | | | | | | | | | |
| **II. Government Operation** | **5.5** | | **6.0** | | **6.4** | | **4.4** | | **5.8** | |
| (a) Govern. Consumption (% of GDP) | 7 | (12.4) | 8 | (10.5) | 9 | (9.5) | 10 | (6.4) | 10 | (5.7) |
| (b) Government Enterprises | 4 | | 4 | | 4 | | 4 | | 6 | |
| (c) Price Controls | - | | - | | - | | 2 | | 6 | |
| (d) Entry Into Business | - | | - | | - | | - | | 7.5 | |
| (e) Legal System | - | | - | | - | | - | | 0 | |
| (f) Avoidance of Neg. Interest Rates | - | | - | | - | | 0 | | 2 | |
| | | | | | | | | | | |
| **III. Takings** | **5.5** | | **4.5** | | **3.6** | | **5.1** | | **6.9** | |
| (a) Transfers and Subsidies (% of GDP) | 9 | (1.9) | 9 | (1.9) | 9 | (1.8) | 8 | (3.0) | 8 | (2.8) |
| (b) Marginal Tax Rates (Top Rate) | 4 | (51) | 2 | (65) | 0 | (65) | 4 | (45) | 8 | (30) |
| (c) Conscription | 0 | | 0 | | 0 | | 0 | | 0 | |
| | | | | | | | | | | |
| **IV. International Sector** | **1.7** | | **2.6** | | **2.3** | | **3.6** | | **6.3** | |
| (a) Taxes on International Trade (Avg.) | 1 | (9.5) | 1 | (10.6) | 2 | (8.3) | 6 | (3.9) | 6 | (4.4) |
| (b) Black Market Exchange Rates (Prem.) | 2 | (56) | 4 | (18) | 2 | (51) | 4 | (16) | 8 | (1) |
| (c) Size of Trade Sector (% of GDP) | 2 | (32.8) | 4 | (41.6) | 4 | (39.4) | 1 | (26.8) | 1 | (22.4) |
| (d) Capital Transactions with Foreigners | 2 | | 2 | | 2 | | 2 | | 8 | |

## Part 2: Recent Economic Indicators:

| Population 1994: | 23.3 | **Real Per Capita GDP** : | 1994= | $2,390 |
| (in millions) | | (in 1985 U.S. dollars) | | |
| Annual Rate of Change (1980-94): | 2.1% | Avg. Growth Rate: | 1980-90= | -2.8% |
| | | | 1985-94= | -0.7% |

| Economic Indicators: | 1987 | 1988 | 1989 | 1990 | 1991 | 1992 | 1993 | 1994 |
|---|---|---|---|---|---|---|---|---|
| Change in Real GDP: Aggregate | 8.3 | -8.2 | -11.0 | -4.3 | 2.8 | -2.3 | 6.4 | 13.0 |
| : Per Capita | 6.2 | -10.3 | -13.1 | -6.4 | 0.7 | -4.4 | 4.3 | 11.0 |
| Inflation Rate (CPI) | 85.8 | 667.0 | 3398.7 | 7481.7 | 409.5 | 73.5 | 48.6 | 23.7 |
| Change in Money Supply: (M1) | 96.2 | 261.2 | 1585.5 | 4930.1 | 476.4 | 78.2 | 76.5 | 30.7 |
| : (M2) | 79.1 | 271.0 | 2081.3 | 4825.2 | 628.3 | 107.2 | 98.5 | 46.0 |
| Investment/GDP Ratio | 22.0 | 24.2 | 17.9 | 15.5 | 16.6 | 16.6 | 18.5 | 20.4 |
| Central Government Budget Deficit (-) or Surplus (+) As a Percent of GDP | -6.2 | -3.6 | -5.6 | -3.7 | -1.4 | -1.8 | -0.8 | - |
| Unemployment Rate [a] | 4.8 | | 7.9 | | 5.8 | | | |

a From the United Nations, Statistical Yearbook.

Based on the average of our three indexes, Peru's 1993-95 economic freedom rating placed it 47th among the 103 countries in our study. This was a substantial improvement. During the last decade and particularly during the last five years, Peru has made dramatic moves toward a freer economy. As the accompanying data show, gains have been registered. Exchange rate controls have been relaxed (the black market premium fell from 51% in 1985 to 16% in 1990 and 1% in 1994). Tariffs have been reduced and capital market controls relaxed. The top marginal tax rate was cut from 65% in 1985 to 45% in 1990 and 30% in 1994.

While some progress has been made—monetary expansion was reduced from the colossal figures of 1988-91 (see above)—the growth rate of the money supply is still much too rapid. Like several other Latin American countries with a history of inflation, Peru's monetary policy needs a credible anchor. There are several ways this could be accomplished, including the establishment of a currency board (as in the case of Hong Kong) or the subjection of one's monetary policy to the maintenance of a pegged exchange rate (as Argentina has done). Unless institutional change of this type is taken, it will be difficult to convince decision-makers that monetary and price stability are important policy objectives. Without this credibility, the economy will fail to meet its full potential.

The changes to date are paying off. After years of decline (real per capita GDP fell from $3164 in 1975 to $2092 in 1992, *a reduction of 34%*), Peru achieved robust growth during 1993-1994. In fact, its 13% growth rate of real GDP in 1994 was probably the highest in the world. If additional steps are taken to achieve monetary stability and expand economic freedom, the long-term prospects for this economy are good.

# PHILIPPINES

## Part 1: The Economic Freedom Ratings for the Components and Various Area and Summary Indexes: 1975, 1980, 1985, 1990 and 1993-95.

(The numbers in parentheses indicate the actual values for the components.)

### Summary Ratings

|      | Ie  | Is1 | Is2 |
|------|-----|-----|-----|
| 1975 | 4.4 | 4.6 | 3.6 |
| 1980 | 4.7 | 4.8 | 3.8 |
| 1985 | 4.7 | 4.9 | 3.8 |
| 1990 | 5.2 | 5.6 | 4.3 |
| 1993-95 | 6.1 | 6.2 | 5.7 |

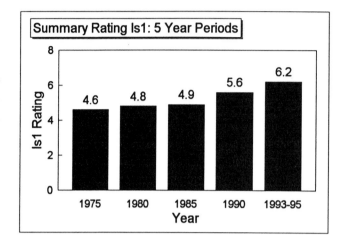

| Components of Economic Freedom | 1975 | | 1980 | | 1985 | | 1990 | | 1993-95 | |
|---|---|---|---|---|---|---|---|---|---|---|
| **I. Money and Inflation** | **1.6** | | **3.6** | | **2.1** | | **2.6** | | **6.6** | |
| (a) Annual Money Growth (last 5 yrs.) | 3 | (13.7) | 4 | (11.1) | 6 | (8.0) | 2 | (18.7) | 3 | (12.4) |
| (b) Inflation Variablity (last 5 yrs.) | 2 | (9.2) | 7 | (2.9) | 1 | (16.4) | 6 | (3.3) | 6 | (3.7) |
| (c) Ownership of Foreign Currency | 0 | | 0 | | 0 | | 0 | | 10 | |
| (d) Maint. of Bank Account Abroad | 0 | | 0 | | 0 | | 0 | | 10 | |
| | | | | | | | | | | |
| **II. Government Operation** | **8.1** | | **6.8** | | **6.3** | | **5.0** | | **4.9** | |
| (a) Govern. Consumption (% of GDP) | 8 | (10.7) | 9 | (9.1) | 10 | (7.6) | 8 | (10.1) | 9 | (8.6) |
| (b) Government Enterprises | 4 | | 4 | | 4 | | 4 | | 4 | |
| (c) Price Controls | - | | - | | - | | 2 | | 3 | |
| (d) Entry Into Business | - | | - | | - | | - | | 5 | |
| (e) Legal System | - | | - | | - | | - | | 0 | |
| (f) Avoidance of Neg. Interest Rates | 8 | | 8 | | 4 | | 8 | | 10 | |
| | | | | | | | | | | |
| **III. Takings** | **5.4** | | **4.5** | | **5.8** | | **8.6** | | **8.6** | |
| (a) Transfers and Subsidies (% of GDP) | 10 | (0.8) | 10 | (1.1) | 10 | (0.2) | 10 | (0.9) | 10 | (0.8) |
| (b) Marginal Tax Rates (Top Rate) | 3 | (56) | 1 | (70) | 1 | (60) | 7 | (35) | 7 | (35) |
| (c) Conscription | 0 | | 0 | | 10 | | 10 | | 10 | |
| | | | | | | | | | | |
| **IV. International Sector** | **2.9** | | **4.7** | | **4.7** | | **4.7** | | **5.0** | |
| (a) Taxes on International Trade (Avg.) | 0 | (13.4) | 4 | (6.8) | 5 | (6.2) | 4 | (6.6) | 2 | (8.2) |
| (b) Black Market Exchange Rates (Prem.) | 4 | (13) | 6 | (3) | 5 | (7) | 5 | (7) | 8 | (1) |
| (c) Size of Trade Sector (% of GDP) | 8 | (48.1) | 8 | (52.0) | 8 | (45.8) | 10 | (61.3) | 10 | (62.3) |
| (d) Capital Transactions with Foreigners | 2 | | 2 | | 2 | | 2 | | 2 | |

## Part 2:  Recent Economic Indicators:

| | | | |
|---|---|---|---|
| **Population 1994:** | 67.3 | **Real Per Capita GDP :** | 1994 = $1,720 |
| (in millions) | | (in 1985 U.S. dollars) | |
| Annual Rate of Change (1980-94): | 2.4% | Avg. Growth Rate: | 1980-90 = -0.7% |
| | | | 1985-94 = 0.8% |

| Economic Indicators: | 1987 | 1988 | 1989 | 1990 | 1991 | 1992 | 1993 | 1994 |
|---|---|---|---|---|---|---|---|---|
| Change in Real GDP:Aggregate | 4.3 | 6.8 | 6.2 | 2.7 | -0.5 | 0.6 | 2.0 | 4.3 |
| : Per Capita | 1.9 | 4.4 | 3.8 | -0.5 | -2.9 | -1.8 | -0.5 | 2.0 |
| Inflation Rate (CPI) | 3.8 | 8.8 | 12.2 | 14.1 | 18.0 | 8.9 | 7.6 | 9.1 |
| Change in Money Supply: (M1) | 24.6 | 19.2 | 18.9 | 21.4 | 18.2 | 15.4 | 15.5 | 13.9 |
| : (M2) | 13.0 | 21.3 | 27.8 | 25.7 | 20.9 | 12.8 | 18.7 | 23.8 |
| Investment/GDP Ratio | 18.0 | 18.8 | 18.8 | 24.8 | 20.4 | 21.3 | 24.1 | 25.2 |
| Central Government Budget Deficit (-) or Surplus (+) As a Percent of GDP | -2.5 | -2.9 | -2.1 | -3.5 | -2.1 | -1.2 | -1.5 | +1.1 |
| Unemployment Rate | - | 10.8 | 9.2 | 8.3 | 10.6 | 9.8 | 10.2 | 9.4 |

The average of our three indexes places the Philippines 36th among the countries in our study.  Like Indonesia, the Philippines ranks in the middle among the Asian economies, less free than Hong Kong, Singapore, Malaysia, Thailand, South Korea, and Taiwan, but more free than India, Bangladesh, and Nepal.

The economic freedom rating of the Philippines has shown modest but steady improvement during the last two decades.  The growth of per capita GDP, while still low, has changed from negative to positive.  The primary factors contributing to the rating improvement were legalization of foreign currency bank accounts, reduction in marginal tax rates (the top rate was reduced from 70% in 1980 and 60% in 1985 to the current rate of 35%), relaxation of exchange rate controls, and an increase in the size of the trade sector.  The major deficiencies are persistent monetary instability, excessive regulation (price controls, discriminatory tariffs, and restrictions on capital movements), and  particularly a legal system that is often arbitrary and discriminatory.  The problem of political favoritism is further complicated by the government enterprises that are spread throughout the economy.

If this economy is going to prosper in the future, it needs the security provided by rule of law, a strong dose of deregulation, and far greater reliance on markets.

191

# POLAND

## Part 1: The Economic Freedom Ratings for the Components and Various Area and Summary Indexes: 1975, 1980, 1985, 1990 and 1993-95.

(The numbers in parentheses indicate the actual values for the components.)

### Summary Ratings

|  | Ie | Is1 | Is2 |
|------|------|------|------|
| 1975 | N/R | N/R | N/R |
| 1980 | N/R | N/R | N/R |
| 1985 | 2.5 | 2.2 | 2.5 |
| 1990 | 3.1 | 3.3 | 2.7 |
| 1993-95 | 4.8 | 4.8 | 4.7 |

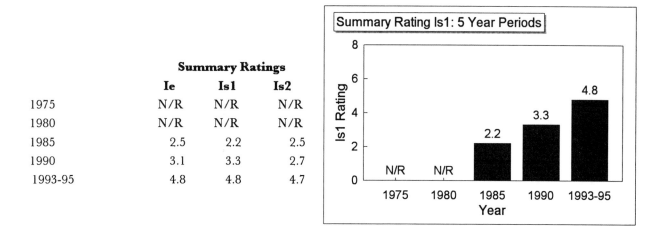

| Components of Economic Freedom | 1975 | 1980 | 1985 | | 1990 | | 1993-95 | |
|---|---|---|---|---|---|---|---|---|
| **I. Money and Inflation** | **10.0** | **10.0** | **3.9** | | **3.6** | | **3.6** | |
| (a) Annual Money Growth (last 5 yrs.) | - | - | 1 | (20.9) | 0 | (110.8) | 0 | (70.4) |
| (b) Inflation Variablity (last 5 yrs.) | - | - | 0 | (37.4) | 0 | (178.3) | 0 | (172.3) |
| (c) Ownership of Foreign Currency | 10 | 10 | 10 | | 10 | | 10 | |
| (d) Maint. of Bank Account Abroad | 10 | 10 | 10 | | 10 | | 10 | |
| | | | | | | | | |
| **II. Government Operation** | **0.0** | **4.4** | **4.4** | | **3.0** | | **5.7** | |
| (a) Govern. Consumption (% of GDP) | - | 9 (9.2) | 9 | (9.2) | 9 | (8.3) | 8 | (10.2) |
| (b) Government Enterprises | 0 | 0 | 0 | | 0 | | 2 | |
| (c) Price Controls | - | - | - | | 2 | | 5 | |
| (d) Entry Into Business | - | - | - | | - | | 7.5 | |
| (e) Legal System | - | - | - | | - | | 7.5 | |
| (f) Avoidance of Neg. Interest Rates | - | - | - | | 0 | | 4 | |
| | | | | | | | | |
| **III. Takings** | **0.0** | **0.0** | **0.0** | | **3.8** | | **3.1** | |
| (a) Transfers and Subsidies (% of GDP) | - | - | 0 | (27.4) | 5 | (7.2) | - | |
| (b) Marginal Tax Rates (Top Rate) | - | - | - | | - | | 4 | (45) |
| (c) Conscription | 0 | 0 | 0 | | 0 | | 0 | |
| | | | | | | | | |
| **IV. International Sector** | **0.0** | **1.6** | **1.1** | | **2.9** | | **5.6** | |
| (a) Taxes on International Trade (Avg.) | - | - | 2 | (8.6) | - | | - | |
| (b) Black Market Exchange Rates (Prem.) | 0 (3786) | 0 (298) | 0 | (301) | 5 | (9) | 10 | (0) |
| (c) Size of Trade Sector (% of GDP) | - | 7 (59.2) | 3 | (35.0) | 4 | (45.8) | 4 | (43.5) |
| (d) Capital Transactions with Foreigners | 0 | 0 | 0 | | 0 | | 2 | |

## Part 2: Recent Economic Indicators:

| | | | | |
|---|---|---|---|---|
| **Population 1994:** | 38.9 | **Real Per Capita GDP :** | 1994 = | $4,150 |
| (in millions) | | (in 1985 U.S. dollars) | | |
| Annual Rate of Change (1980-94): | 0.6% | Avg. Growth Rate: | 1980-90 = | -0.9% |
| | | | 1985-94 = | -0.4% |

| Economic Indicators: | 1987 | 1988 | 1989 | 1990 | 1991 | 1992 | 1993 | 1994 |
|---|---|---|---|---|---|---|---|---|
| Change in Real GDP:Aggregate | 2.1 | 4.0 | 0.2 | -11.5 | -7.0 | 1.5 | 4.5 | 5.0 |
| : Per Capita | 1.5 | 3.4 | -0.4 | -12.1 | -7.6 | 0.9 | 3.9 | 4.4 |
| Inflation Rate (CPI) | 26.4 | 58.7 | 244.6 | 555.4 | 76.7 | 45.3 | 36.9 | 32.2 |
| Change in Money Supply: (M1) | 26.8 | 40.5 | 137.0 | 556.1 | 65.7 | 31.4 | 31.8 | 35.6 |
| : (M2) | 34.6 | 50.1 | 238.8 | 384.3 | 67.5 | 49.7 | 42.6 | 35.3 |
| Investment/GDP Ratio | 28.8 | 32.6 | 38.5 | 27.5 | 21.5 | 15.0 | 15.4 | 15.6 |
| Central Government Budget Deficit (-) or Surplus (+) As a Percent of GDP | -1.5 | -2.4 | -7.4 | +3.5 | -6.2 | -7.0 | -4.8 | -1.8 |
| Unemployment Rate | - | - | - | 6.0 | 9.2 | 12.9 | 15.7 | 15.8 |

The average of our three indexes places Poland 57th among the countries in our study. Along with the Czech Republic, it is the freest of the former communist bloc economies.

The transition from a socialist to a market economy has not been easy. Large budget deficits financed with printing press money led to hyperinflation in 1989-1991. Fortunately, it is legal to maintain foreign currency bank accounts; dollars and other foreign currencies have been widely used both as a means of storing value and for transactions since the fall of communism. The inflation rate has now receded, but it is far too high (32% in 1994) for the smooth operation of a market economy. On the positive side, subsidies to enterprises have been sharply reduced, marginal tax rates are low for a European nation, and the Polish zloty is convertible. The private sector of the economy has been growing rapidly and now dominates the service and retail sectors. On the negative side, the privatization of middle and large scale state enterprises was handled poorly and this process has now slowed to a standstill. Employment taxes are high and compliance is low. This makes it difficult for an honest person to survive in business. Under central planning, a large segment of the economy was producing things that had little value relative to their cost. As the extremely high rate of unemployment (15.8% in 1994) illustrates, movement of resources out of these activities and into productive employment is a painful process.

The Polish economy, particularly the private sector, is now growing at a healthy rate-- approximately 5% during 1993-1994. If Poland does not revert to its prior restrictive practices, growth of the market sector will soon begin to upgrade living standards in this country that has suffered so much during the last 50 years.

# PORTUGAL

## Part 1: The Economic Freedom Ratings for the Components and Various Area and Summary Indexes: 1975, 1980, 1985, 1990 and 1993-95.

(The numbers in parentheses indicate the actual values for the components.)

### Summary Ratings

| | Ie | Is1 | Is2 |
|------|-----|-----|-----|
| 1975 | 2.4 | 2.4 | 2.0 |
| 1980 | 3.3 | 3.1 | 3.0 |
| 1985 | 3.9 | 3.5 | 3.7 |
| 1990 | 4.1 | 4.1 | 3.9 |
| 1993-95 | 5.7 | 5.5 | 6.1 |

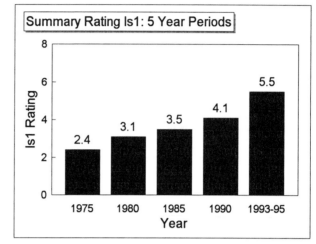

| Components of Economic Freedom | 1975 | | 1980 | | 1985 | | 1990 | | 1993-95 | |
|---|---|---|---|---|---|---|---|---|---|---|
| **I.  Money and Inflation** | **2.2** | | **2.9** | | **3.3** | | **2.6** | | **6.2** | |
| (a) Annual Money Growth (last 5 yrs.) | 3 | (12.8) | 3 | (12.2) | 3 | (12.0) | 2 | (17.0) | 3 | (12.8) |
| (b) Inflation Variablity (last 5 yrs.) | 4 | (5.2) | 6 | (3.4) | 7 | (2.5) | 6 | (3.4) | 5 | (4.1) |
| (c) Ownership of Foreign Currency | 0 | | 0 | | 0 | | 0 | | 10 | |
| (d) Maint. of Bank Account Abroad | 0 | | 0 | | 0 | | 0 | | 10 | |
| | | | | | | | | | | |
| **II.  Government Operation** | **3.5** | | **3.6** | | **4.8** | | **3.8** | | **5.4** | |
| (a) Govern. Consumption (% of GDP) | 5 | (15.0) | 5 | (14.5) | 5 | (15.5) | 3 | (16.7) | 2 | (18.3) |
| (b) Government Enterprises | 2 | | 2 | | 2 | | 2 | | 2 | |
| (c) Price Controls | - | | - | | - | | 4 | | 6 | |
| (d) Entry Into Business | - | | - | | - | | - | | 7.5 | |
| (e) Legal System | - | | - | | - | | - | | 7.5 | |
| (f) Avoidance of Neg. Interest Rates | - | | 4 | | 10 | | 8 | | 10 | |
| | | | | | | | | | | |
| **III.  Takings** | **1.2** | | **0.8** | | **0.4** | | **3.1** | | **3.5** | |
| (a) Transfers and Subsidies (% of GDP) | 3 | (14.6) | 2 | (16.3) | 1 | (19.5) | 2 | (15.5) | 3 | (14.5) |
| (b) Marginal Tax Rates (Top Rate) | 0 | (82) | 0 | (84) | 0 | (69) | 5 | (40) | 5 | (40) |
| (c) Conscription | 0 | | 0 | | 0 | | 0 | | 0 | |
| | | | | | | | | | | |
| **IV.  International Sector** | **3.4** | | **5.7** | | **6.3** | | **6.6** | | **7.4** | |
| (a) Taxes on International Trade (Avg.) | 6 | (4.6) | 8 | (2.1) | 9 | (1.2) | 9 | (1.0) | 9 | (0.5) |
| (b) Black Market Exchange Rates (Prem.) | 2 | (42) | 7 | (2) | 7 | (2) | 6 | (3) | 10 | (0) |
| (c) Size of Trade Sector (% of GDP) | 3 | (53.2) | 5 | (69.4) | 7 | (78.7) | 6 | (81.8) | 4 | (67.5) |
| (d) Capital Transactions with Foreigners | 2 | | 2 | | 2 | | 5 | | 5 | |

## Part 2: Recent Economic Indicators:

| | | | | |
|---|---|---|---|---|
| Population 1994:<br>(in millions) | 9.8 | Real Per Capita GDP :<br>(in 1985 U.S. dollars) | 1994 = | $7,685 |
| Annual Rate of Change (1980-94): | 0.1% | Avg. Growth Rate: | 1980-90 = | 2.6% |
| | | | 1985-94 = | 3.3% |

| Economic Indicators: | 1987 | 1988 | 1989 | 1990 | 1991 | 1992 | 1993 | 1994 |
|---|---|---|---|---|---|---|---|---|
| Change in Real GDP:Aggregate | 5.1 | 4.0 | 4.9 | 4.1 | 2.1 | 1.1 | -1.0 | 1.0 |
| : Per Capita | 5.0 | 3.9 | 4.8 | 4.0 | 2.0 | 1.0 | -1.1 | 0.9 |
| Inflation Rate (CPI) | 9.4 | 9.6 | 12.6 | 13.4 | 11.4 | 8.9 | 6.5 | 4.9 |
| Change in Money Supply: (M1) | 27.8 | 12.9 | 8.9 | 12.9 | 21.3 | 16.3 | 14.2 | 4.6 |
| : (M2) | 18.1 | 14.3 | 12.5 | 13.1 | 20.8 | 24.9 | 16.8 | 8.6 |
| Investment/GDP Ratio | 27.4 | 29.8 | 29.1 | 29.1 | 28.3 | 28.3 | 27.5 | 28.5 |
| Central Government Budget<br>Deficit (-) or Surplus (+)<br>As a Percent of GDP | -10.4 | -8.7 | -4.0 | -5.3 | -6.1 | -3.8 | -8.0 | -7.1 |
| Unemployment Rate | 7.0 | 5.7 | 5.0 | 4.6 | 4.1 | 4.1 | 5.5 | 6.8 [a] |

a First 9 months of the year.

In 1975, only three countries (Uganda, Israel, and Pakistan) had a lower economic freedom rating (Is1) than Portugal. Since that time this country has moved steadily toward a freer economy. In 1993-1995, the average of our three indexes placed it 41st (the Is1 rankings placed it 47th) among the 103 countries in our study. In terms of economic freedom, Portugal is one of the most improved countries in the world.

The highlights of Portugal's advancement include:
- legalization of foreign currency accounts in the early 1990s;
- reduction of the top marginal tax rate from 82% in 1975 to 69% in 1985 and to the current 40% in the late 1980s;
- substantial reductions in tariffs;
- movement to a convertible currency and therefore the elimination of the black market in foreign exchange; and
- a sizeable increase in the size of the trade sector.

More needs to be done. Monetary policy is still far to expansionary—note the continued double digit growth rates of the money supply and inflationary side effects. Both the government consumption and transfer sectors are large and this spending is fueling the large and unsustainable budget deficits.

The movement to a freer economy has paid off. The country is on a strong growth path. Among the European countries, Portugal's 3.3% growth of per capita income during the last decade is one of the highest in Europe.

# SINGAPORE

## Part 1: The Economic Freedom Ratings for the Components and Various Area and Summary Indexes: 1975, 1980, 1985, 1990 and 1993-95.

(The numbers in parentheses indicate the actual values for the components.)

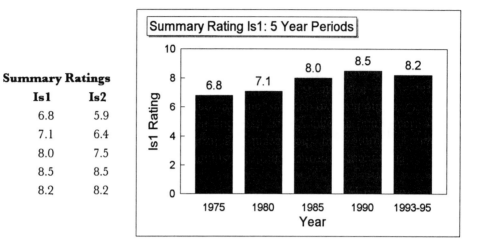

| | **Summary Ratings** | | |
|---|---|---|---|
| | **Ie** | **Is1** | **Is2** |
| 1975 | 6.5 | 6.8 | 5.9 |
| 1980 | 7.0 | 7.1 | 6.4 |
| 1985 | 7.9 | 8.0 | 7.5 |
| 1990 | 8.5 | 8.5 | 8.5 |
| 1993-95 | 8.2 | 8.2 | 8.2 |

| Components of Economic Freedom | 1975 | | 1980 | | 1985 | | 1990 | | 1993-95 | |
|---|---|---|---|---|---|---|---|---|---|---|
| **I. Money and Inflation** | **3.8** | | **4.7** | | **7.3** | | **8.4** | | **9.4** | |
| (a) Annual Money Growth (last 5 yrs.) | 7 | (5.2) | 9 | (3.1) | 10 | (0.1) | 8 | (4.6) | 8 | (4.5) |
| (b) Inflation Variablity (last 5 yrs.) | 5 | (4.7) | 6 | (3.7) | 7 | (2.7) | 7 | (2.8) | 10 | (0.4) |
| (c) Ownership of Foreign Currency | 0 | | 0 | | 10 | | 10 | | 10 | |
| (d) Maint. of Bank Account Abroad | 0 | | 0 | | 0 | | 10 | | 10 | |
| | | | | | | | | | | |
| **II. Government Operation** | **8.0** | | **8.4** | | **7.3** | | **8.3** | | **7.2** | |
| (a) Govern. Consumption (% of GDP) | 8 | (10.6) | 8 | (9.8) | 5 | (14.3) | 8 | (10.5) | 9 | (9.4) |
| (b) Government Enterprises | 8 | | 8 | | 8 | | 8 | | 8 | |
| (c) Price Controls | - | | - | | - | | 8 | | 8 | |
| (d) Entry Into Business | - | | - | | - | | - | | 7.5 | |
| (e) Legal System | - | | - | | - | | - | | 0 | |
| (f) Avoidance of Neg. Interest Rates | - | | 10 | | 10 | | 10 | | 10 | |
| | | | | | | | | | | |
| **III. Takings** | **5.9** | | **5.9** | | **7.3** | | **7.4** | | **7.4** | |
| (a) Transfers and Subsidies (% of GDP) | 10 | (1.4) | 10 | (1.1) | 9 | (1.8) | 8 | (2.6) | 8 | (2.9) |
| (b) Marginal Tax Rates (Top Rate) | 4 | (55) | 4 | (55) | 8 | (40) | 9 | (33) | 9 | (30) |
| (c) Conscription | 0 | | 0 | | 0 | | 0 | | 0 | |
| | | | | | | | | | | |
| **IV. International Sector** | **9.2** | | **9.2** | | **9.7** | | **10.0** | | **10.0** | |
| (a) Taxes on International Trade (Avg.) | 9 | (0.7) | 9 | (0.5) | 9 | (0.3) | 10 | (0.2) | 10 | (0.2) |
| (b) Black Market Exchange Rates (Prem.) | 10 | (0) | 10 | (0) | 10 | (0) | 10 | (0) | 10 | (0) |
| (c) Size of Trade Sector (% of GDP) | 10 | (289.1) | 10 | (423.3) | 10 | (318.0) | 10 | (372.7) | 10 | (340.8) |
| (d) Capital Transactions with Foreigners | 8 | | 8 | | 10 | | 10 | | 10 | |

## Part 2:  Recent Economic Indicators:

| | | | | |
|---|---|---|---|---|
| **Population 1994:** | 2.9 | **Real Per Capita GDP** : | 1994 = | $14,415 |
| (in millions) | | (in 1985 U.S. dollars) | | |
| Annual Rate of Change (1980-94): | 1.8% | Avg. Growth Rate: | 1980-90 = | 5.2% |
| | | | 1985-94 = | 5.9% |

| Economic Indicators: | 1987 | 1988 | 1989 | 1990 | 1991 | 1992 | 1993 | 1994 |
|---|---|---|---|---|---|---|---|---|
| Change in Real GDP:Aggregate | 9.4 | 11.1 | 9.2 | 8.3 | 7.0 | 6.1 | 9.9 | 7.2 |
| : Per Capita | 7.6 | 9.3 | 7.4 | 6.5 | 5.2 | 4.3 | 8.1 | 5.4 |
| Inflation Rate (CPI) | 0.5 | 1.5 | 2.4 | 3.4 | 3.4 | 2.3 | 2.4 | 3.6 |
| Change in Money Supply: (M1) | 18.3 | 6.1 | 14.3 | 11.8 | 4.4 | 14.0 | 17.8 | 11.5 |
| : (M2) | 17.4 | 12.8 | 22.8 | 21.9 | 14.3 | 11.7 | 6.2 | 11.6 |
| Investment/GDP Ratio | 39.0 | 36.9 | 35.5 | 39.5 | 38.0 | 40.4 | 43.8 | - |
| Central Government Budget Deficit (-) or Surplus (+) As a Percent of GDP | -2.6 | +6.7 | +9.9 | +10.6 | +8.7 | +12.5 | - | - |
| Unemployment Rate | 4.7 | 3.3 | 2.2 | 1.7 | 1.9 | 2.7 | - | - |

The average of our three indexes ranks Singapore's economy as the third most free in the world, behind only Hong Kong and New Zealand.  The Is1 index places it second.  Its ranking was persistently high throughout the last two decades.

Some may be troubled by Singapore's high rating.  After all, Freedom House has given it a relatively low rating with regard to both political and civil liberties in recent years.  In addition, there have been well publicized restrictive practices, such as the government imposed limitations on the domestic circulation of the *Wall Street Journal*.  The case of Singapore highlights the difference between economic liberty and political and civil liberty.  Consider the data underlying the rating of Singapore.  Monetary expansion has been modest (after adjustment for the growth of real GDP) and, as a result, the inflation is both low and stable. Citizens are free to maintain foreign currency bank accounts.  As a share of GDP, both government consumption expenditures and transfers and subsidies are low, particularly for a high-income nation.  Government-operated enterprises are few and they produce only a small portion of the total output. The top marginal tax rate of Singapore is 30%.  The Singapore dollar is freely convertible to other currencies.  There are virtually no tariffs; the size of the trade sector as a share of the economy is the largest in the world; and the restrictions on the movement of capital into and out of the country are minimal.  Singapore is not perfect.  It uses conscription, often fails to provide citizens with equal protection under the law, and its forced saving plan (which our index does not register) is also a violation of economic freedom.  All things considered, however, it is still one of the world's freest economies.

197

# SOUTH AFRICA

## Part 1: The Economic Freedom Ratings for the Components and Various Area and Summary Indexes: 1975, 1980, 1985, 1990 and 1993-95.

(The numbers in parentheses indicate the actual values for the components.)

### Summary Ratings

|        | Ie  | Is1 | Is2 |
|--------|-----|-----|-----|
| 1975   | 4.1 | 3.9 | 3.7 |
| 1980   | 4.4 | 4.6 | 3.7 |
| 1985   | 4.5 | 4.5 | 4.0 |
| 1990   | 4.4 | 4.6 | 4.1 |
| 1993-95| 4.9 | 4.9 | 4.8 |

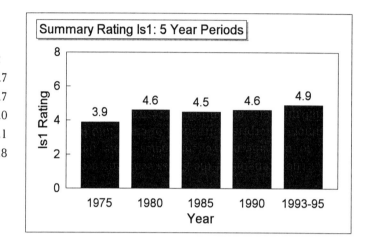

| Components of Economic Freedom | 1975 | | 1980 | | 1985 | | 1990 | | 1993-95 | |
|---|---|---|---|---|---|---|---|---|---|---|
| **I. Money and Inflation** | **3.2** | | **2.5** | | **3.6** | | **4.0** | | **3.9** | |
| (a) Annual Money Growth (last 5 yrs.) | 5 | (9.3) | 4 | (11.0) | 2 | (18.3) | 2 | (17.0) | 3 | (12.5) |
| (b) Inflation Variablity (last 5 yrs.) | 5 | (4.8) | 4 | (5.1) | 9 | (1.9) | 10 | (0.9) | 9 | (1.8) |
| (c) Ownership of Foreign Currency | 0 | | 0 | | 0 | | 0 | | 0 | |
| (d) Maint. of Bank Account Abroad | 0 | | 0 | | 0 | | 0 | | 0 | |
| | | | | | | | | | | |
| **II. Government Operation** | **5.0** | | **4.8** | | **4.5** | | **3.8** | | **4.4** | |
| (a) Govern. Consumption (% of GDP) | 6 | (13.8) | 6 | (13.5) | 3 | (17.3) | 1 | (19.5) | 1 | (21.1) |
| (b) Government Enterprises | 4 | | 4 | | 4 | | 4 | | 4 | |
| (c) Price Controls | - | | - | | - | | 4 | | 4 | |
| (d) Entry Into Business | - | | - | | - | | - | | 5 | |
| (e) Legal System | - | | - | | - | | - | | 5 | |
| (f) Avoidance of Neg. Interest Rates | - | | 4 | | 8 | | 8 | | 10 | |
| | | | | | | | | | | |
| **III. Takings** | **0.8** | | **4.1** | | **4.3** | | **4.7** | | **5.6** | |
| (a) Transfers and Subsidies (% of GDP) | - | | 8 | (3.2) | 6 | (4.8) | 6 | (4.8) | 6 | (5.0) |
| (b) Marginal Tax Rates (Top Rate) | 1 | (66) | 2 | (60) | 4 | (50) | 5 | (45) | 4 | (43) |
| (c) Conscription | 0 | | 0 | | 0 | | 0 | | 10 | |
| | | | | | | | | | | |
| **IV. International Sector** | **6.0** | | **6.3** | | **5.5** | | **5.5** | | **5.8** | |
| (a) Taxes on International Trade (Avg.) | 8 | (2.0) | 9 | (1.2) | 9 | (1.4) | 8 | (2.2) | - | |
| (b) Black Market Exchange Rates (Prem.) | 6 | (6) | 6 | (6) | 3 | (25) | 6 | (3) | 10 | (0) |
| (c) Size of Trade Sector (% of GDP) | 9 | (58.6) | 9 | (64.7) | 9 | (55.4) | 6 | (47.2) | 5 | (43.8) |
| (d) Capital Transactions with Foreigners | 2 | | 2 | | 2 | | 2 | | 2 | |

## Part 2: Recent Economic Indicators:

| | | | |
|---|---|---|---|
| **Population 1994:** | 41.5 | **Real Per Capita GDP :** | 1994 = $3,025 |
| (in millions) | | (in 1985 U.S. dollars) | |
| Annual Rate of Change (1980-94): | 2.4% | Avg. Growth Rate: 1980-90 = | -1.0% |
| | | 1985-94 = | -1.4% |

| Economic Indicators: | 1987 | 1988 | 1989 | 1990 | 1991 | 1992 | 1993 | 1994 |
|---|---|---|---|---|---|---|---|---|
| Change in Real GDP:Aggregate | 2.1 | 4.2 | 2.4 | -0.3 | -1.0 | -2.2 | 1.1 | 2.3 |
| : Per Capita | -0.3 | 1.8 | 0.0 | -2.7 | -3.4 | -4.6 | -1.3 | -0.1 |
| Inflation Rate (CPI) | 16.1 | 12.8 | 14.7 | 14.4 | 15.3 | 13.9 | 9.7 | 9.0 |
| Change in Money Supply: (M1) | 20.9 | 31.8 | 14.2 | 12.4 | | | | |
| : (M2) | 10.2 | 33.3 | 38.5 | 18.5 | | | | |
| Investment/GDP Ratio | 19.4 | 21.5 | 21.2 | 19.1 | 16.1 | 15.1 | 15.9 | 18.0 |
| Central Government Budget Deficit (-) or Surplus (+) As a Percent of GDP | -7.0 | -5.3 | -0.2 | -4.3 | -6.1 | -6.2 | -7.7 | -5.8 |
| Unemployment Rate | | | | | | | | |

The average of our three indexes places South Africa in a tie (with Greece and Cyprus) for 54th place. Its Is1 summary rating places it 56th. Thus South Africa ranks in the middle range among the 103 countries in our study. This rating has been relatively steady—there is no evidence of a consistent commitment to or movement toward economic freedom.

Of course, uncertainty about the future political stability of this racially divided country reduces the security of property rights and the incentive of both foreigners and domestics to invest. So, too, do policies that restrict economic freedom and undermine the workings of a market economy. Such policies abound in South Africa. During the last two decades, the monetary authorities have typically increased the money supply at annual rates between 10% and 20%. As the result of this excessive monetary growth, double-digit inflation rates have been common. Government consumption expenditures account for more than 30% of GDP and public enterprises operate in several sectors of the economy. These factors, along with the high taxes for their support, distort and weaken the operation of markets. In recent years, budget deficits have averaged around 6% of GDP. Deficits in this range are unsustainable. If they are not brought under control, they will eventually lead to printing-press finance of government and hyper-inflation.

The political future of this country is both uncertain and complex. From an economic viewpoint, the best thing South Africa could do would be to move swiftly and consistently toward a freer economy. Voluntary exchange tends to bring people together, while the political process pulls them apart. South Africa need more of the former and less of the latter.

# SOUTH KOREA

## Part 1: The Economic Freedom Ratings for the Components and Various Area and Summary Indexes: 1975, 1980, 1985, 1990 and 1993-95.

(The numbers in parentheses indicate the actual values for the components.)

### Summary Ratings

|       | Ie  | Is1 | Is2 |
|-------|-----|-----|-----|
| 1975  | 4.0 | 4.3 | 3.2 |
| 1980  | 4.0 | 4.0 | 3.2 |
| 1985  | 5.2 | 5.1 | 4.3 |
| 1990  | 5.1 | 5.2 | 4.5 |
| 1993-95 | 6.7 | 6.7 | 6.6 |

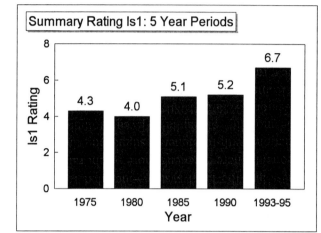

Summary Rating Is1: 5 Year Periods

| Components of Economic Freedom | 1975 | | 1980 | | 1985 | | 1990 | | 1993-95 | |
|---|---|---|---|---|---|---|---|---|---|---|
| **I. Money and Inflation** | **1.3** | | **2.6** | | **3.8** | | **2.8** | | **7.8** | |
| (a) Annual Money Growth (last 5 yrs.) | 1 | (21.3) | 2 | (18.2) | 7 | (6.8) | 7 | (6.8) | 5 | (9.3) |
| (b) Inflation Variablity (last 5 yrs.) | 3 | (7.1) | 6 | (3.3) | 5 | (4.9) | 2 | (10.2) | 8 | (2.2) |
| (c) Ownership of Foreign Currency | 0 | | 0 | | 0 | | 0 | | 10 | |
| (d) Maint. of Bank Account Abroad | 0 | | 0 | | 0 | | 0 | | 10 | |
| | | | | | | | | | | |
| **II. Government Operation** | **5.5** | | **6.0** | | **7.6** | | **6.2** | | **6.6** | |
| (a) Govern. Consumption (% of GDP) | 7 | (11.0) | 7 | (11.5) | 8 | (10.1) | 8 | (10.1) | 8 | (10.7) |
| (b) Government Enterprises | 6 | | 6 | | 6 | | 6 | | 6 | |
| (c) Price Controls | - | | - | | - | | 3 | | 4 | |
| (d) Entry Into Business | - | | - | | - | | - | | 7.5 | |
| (e) Legal System | - | | - | | - | | - | | 7.5 | |
| (f) Avoidance of Neg. Interest Rates | 2 | | 4 | | 10 | | 10 | | 8 | |
| | | | | | | | | | | |
| **III. Takings** | **4.5** | | **3.6** | | **4.5** | | **4.6** | | **5.5** | |
| (a) Transfers and Subsidies (% of GDP) | 9 | (2.0) | 9 | (2.0) | 9 | (2.2) | 8 | (2.9) | 8 | (2.6) |
| (b) Marginal Tax Rates (Top Rate) | 2 | (63) | 0 | (89) | 2 | (65) | 3 | (60) | 5 | (48) |
| (c) Conscription | 0 | | 0 | | 0 | | 0 | | 0 | |
| | | | | | | | | | | |
| **IV. International Sector** | **5.3** | | **4.2** | | **5.0** | | **6.6** | | **7.3** | |
| (a) Taxes on International Trade (Avg.) | 7 | (3.1) | 6 | (4.1) | 7 | (3.6) | 7 | (3.4) | 8 | (2.2) |
| (b) Black Market Exchange Rates (Prem.) | 7 | (2) | 4 | (11) | 4 | (11) | 8 | (1) | 10 | (0) |
| (c) Size of Trade Sector (% of GDP) | 8 | (64.4) | 8 | (75.5) | 8 | (67.8) | 6 | (60.0) | 5 | (58.7) |
| (d) Capital Transactions with Foreigners | 0 | | 0 | | 2 | | 5 | | 5 | |

## Part 2: Recent Economic Indicators:

| | | | | | | |
|---|---|---|---|---|---|---|
| **Population 1994:** | 44.7 | | **Real Per Capita GDP :** | 1994 = | $8,565 |
| (in millions) | | | (in 1985 U.S. dollars) | | |
| Annual Rate of Change (1980-94): | 1.1% | | Avg. Growth Rate: | 1980-90 = | 7.9% |
| | | | | 1985-94 = | 7.7 |

| Economic Indicators: | 1987 | 1988 | 1989 | 1990 | 1991 | 1992 | 1993 | 1994 |
|---|---|---|---|---|---|---|---|---|
| Change in Real GDP:Aggregate | 11.5 | 11.3 | 6.4 | 9.5 | 9.1 | 5.1 | 5.7 | 8.4 |
| : Per Capita | 10.4 | 10.2 | 5.3 | 8.4 | 8.0 | 4.0 | 4.6 | 7.3 |
| Inflation Rate (CPI) | 3.0 | 7.1 | 5.7 | 8.6 | 9.3 | 6.2 | 4.8 | 6.3 |
| Change in Money Supply: (M1) | 18.0 | 11.5 | 14.2 | 22.0 | 19.7 | 35.6 | 18.4 | 9.8 |
| : (M2) | 18.2 | 18.1 | 18.3 | 21.7 | 19.6 | 19.2 | 17.7 | 15.2 |
| Investment/GDP Ratio | 29.8 | 31.1 | 33.6 | 36.9 | 38.9 | 36.6 | 34.3 | 35.7 |
| Central Government Budget Deficit (-) or Surplus (+) As a Percent of GDP | +0.4 | +1.5 | +0.2 | -0.7 | -1.7 | -0.5 | +0.6 | - |
| Unemployment Rate | 3.1 | 2.5 | 2.6 | 2.4 | 2.3 | 2.4 | 2.8 | 2.5 |

Throughout the late 1970s and 1980s, South Korea ranked in the middle of the world in terms of economic freedom. Its Is1 summary economic freedom rating increased from 4.3 in 1975 to 5.2 in 1990—a modest but unremarkable increase. Its Is1 rating in 1993-95, however, increased to 6.7, placing South Korea in a tie for 12th place among the 102 countries rated that year. Based of the average of the three indexes, it ranks a little lower, in a tie with France for 20th place.

The recent improvement in the summary rating is primarily the result of a more stable monetary regime and the recent legalization of foreign currency bank accounts both domestically and abroad. Thus, its rating in the monetary area has jumped by 5 points since 1990. Over the last two decades, a more competitive and stable credit market, lower marginal tax rates (the top rate is now 48%, down from 89% in 1980), and some relaxation of restrictions of capital transactions with foreigners have also contributed to Korea's improved rating.

Like many other emerging economic powers in Asia, South Korea is not known for its political and civil freedoms. However, its recent move toward economic liberalization has increased per capita GDP to $8,565 and has resulted in extraordinary growth rates in per capita GDP of over 7% per year for well over a decade.

201

# SPAIN

**Part 1: The Economic Freedom Ratings for the Components and Various Area and Summary Indexes: 1975, 1980, 1985, 1990 and 1993-95.**

(The numbers in parentheses indicate the actual values for the components.)

| | **Summary Ratings** | | |
|---|---|---|---|
| | **Ie** | **Is1** | **Is2** |
| 1975 | 3.6 | 3.9 | 3.0 |
| 1980 | 4.0 | 3.9 | 3.8 |
| 1985 | 4.5 | 4.1 | 4.4 |
| 1990 | 4.8 | 4.7 | 4.7 |
| 1993-95 | 6.3 | 5.8 | 6.9 |

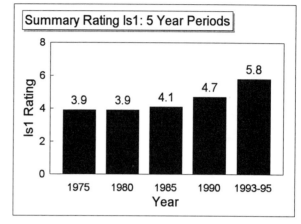

Summary Rating Is1: 5 Year Periods

| Components of Economic Freedom | 1975 | | 1980 | | 1985 | | 1990 | | 1993-95 | |
|---|---|---|---|---|---|---|---|---|---|---|
| **I. Money and Inflation** | **2.6** | | **2.9** | | **4.5** | | **3.6** | | **9.4** | |
| (a) Annual Money Growth (last 5 yrs.) | 2 | (15.7) | 3 | (12.3) | 5 | (8.3) | 2 | (15.9) | 8 | (3.7) |
| (b) Inflation Variablity (last 5 yrs.) | 6 | (3.7) | 6 | (3.5) | 9 | (2.1) | 9 | (2.0) | 10 | (1.2) |
| (c) Ownership of Foreign Currency | 0 | | 0 | | 0 | | 0 | | 10 | |
| (d) Maint. of Bank Account Abroad | 0 | | 0 | | 0 | | 0 | | 10 | |
| | | | | | | | | | | |
| **II. Government Operation** | **6.0** | | **5.2** | | **5.7** | | **5.8** | | **5.6** | |
| (a) Government Consumption (% of GDP) | 8 | (10.5) | 6 | (13.2) | 5 | (14.7) | 5 | (15.5) | 3 | (17.0) |
| (b) Government Enterprises | 4 | | 4 | | 4 | | 4 | | 4 | |
| (c) Price Controls | - | | - | | - | | 6 | | 6 | |
| (d) Entry Into Business | - | | - | | - | | - | | 7.5 | |
| (e) Legal System | - | | - | | - | | - | | 5 | |
| (f) Avoidance of Neg. Interest Rates | - | | 6 | | 10 | | 10 | | 10 | |
| | | | | | | | | | | |
| **III. Takings** | **3.1** | | **1.7** | | **1.3** | | **2.2** | | **2.2** | |
| (a) Transfers and Subsidies (% of GDP) | - | | 3 | (12.3) | 2 | (16.9) | 2 | (16.0) | 2 | (16.3) |
| (b) Marginal Tax Rates (Top Rate) | 4 | (55) | 1 | (66) | 1 | (66) | 3 | (56) | 3 | (56) |
| (c) Conscription | 0 | | 0 | | 0 | | 0 | | 0 | |
| | | | | | | | | | | |
| **IV. International Sector** | **4.3** | | **6.5** | | **6.1** | | **7.2** | | **8.0** | |
| (a) Taxes on International Trade (Avg.) | 5 | (6.1) | 7 | (2.7) | 7 | (3.0) | 9 | (1.3) | 9 | (0.9) |
| (b) Black Market Exchange Rates (Prem.) | 7 | (2) | 10 | (0) | 7 | (2) | 7 | (2) | 10 | (0) |
| (c) Size of Trade Sector (% of GDP) | 2 | (30.9) | 2 | (33.8) | 5 | (43.5) | 3 | (37.5) | 3 | (38.0) |
| (d) Capital Transactions with Foreigners | 2 | | 5 | | 5 | | 8 | | 8 | |

## Part 2: Recent Economic Indicators:

| | | | | |
|---|---|---|---|---|
| **Population 1994:** | 39.4 | **Real Per Capita GDP** : | 1994- | $9,990 |
| (in millions) | | (in 1985 U.S. dollars) | | |
| Annual Rate of Change (1980-94): | 0.4% | Avg. Growth Rate: | 1980-90= | 2.6% |
| | | | 1985-94= | 2.7% |

| Economic Indicators: | 1987 | 1988 | 1989 | 1990 | 1991 | 1992 | 1993 | 1994 |
|---|---|---|---|---|---|---|---|---|
| Change in Real GDP: Aggregate | 5.6 | 5.2 | 4.7 | 3.6 | 2.2 | 0.8 | -1.0 | 2.8 |
| : Per Capita | 5.2 | 4.8 | 4.5 | 3.6 | 2.1 | 0.5 | -1.2 | 2.4 |
| Inflation Rate (CPI) | 5.2 | 4.8 | 6.8 | 6.7 | 5.9 | 5.9 | 4.6 | 4.6 |
| Change in Money Supply: (M1) | 13.7 | 21.1 | 21.7 | 17.9 | 13.0 | 5.7 | -2.2 | 7.1 |
| : (M2) | 7.6 | 10.4 | 13.2 | 13.2 | 13.9 | 10.0 | 7.4 | 10.0 |
| Investment/GDP Ratio | 21.5 | 23.7 | 25.1 | 25.5 | 24.7 | 22.9 | 20.8 | 19.6 |
| Central Government Budget Deficit (-) or Surplus (+) As a Percent of GDP | -3.9 | -3.6 | -2.3 | -3.2 | -3.7 | -4.2 | -7.5 | -6.8 |
| Unemployment Rate | 20.5 | 19.5 | 17.3 | 16.3 | 16.4 | 18.4 | 22.7 | 24.1 |

After struggling with an economic freedom rating among the bottom one-third of countries during 1975-1985, Spain's summary rating has improved in recent years. In 1993-1995, the average of our three ratings ranked Spain's economy as the 23rd most free in the world. Our Is1 summary index placed it 36th.

Spain's improvement is almost exclusively the result of steps taken in the monetary and financial areas. In the 1990s, the monetary authorities reduced the rate of money growth and the inflation rate has declined accordingly. In addition, it is now legal for the Spanish to maintain foreign currency bank accounts both domestically and abroad. As the result of the increased monetary stability and the legalization of these foreign currency accounts, Spain's rating in the monetary area jumped from 3.6 in 1990 to 9.4 in 1995. In addition, exchange controls have been abolished, which eliminated the black market in this area.

More needs to be done. The government consumption and transfer sectors are quite large and the top marginal tax rate, though down a little from the mid-1980s, is still one of the highest in the world. Recent budget deficits have averaged around 6% of GDP, a level that is unsustainable. While the growth of per capita GDP has been strong (2.7% during the last decade), the unemployment rate has been near or above 20% since the mid-1980s. Interestingly, the unemployment rate of Portugal, Spain's next door neighbor, has been running around 6%—less than a third the Spanish rate—during this same period. When a growing economy has prolonged double-digit unemployment, it reflects transfer payments that reduce the cost of job search and/or regulations that make it expensive to hire and terminate employees. Spain desperately needs to revise its transfer system and deregulate the labor market. It will fail to reach its full potential until these steps are taken.

# SWEDEN

**Part 1: The Economic Freedom Ratings for the Components and Various Area and Summary Indexes: 1975, 1980, 1985, 1990 and 1993-95.**

(The numbers in parentheses indicate the actual values for the components.)

### Summary Ratings

|  | Ie | Is1 | Is2 |
|---|---|---|---|
| 1975 | 3.9 | 3.5 | 4.3 |
| 1980 | 4.0 | 3.4 | 4.4 |
| 1985 | 5.0 | 4.2 | 5.5 |
| 1990 | 5.2 | 4.5 | 5.8 |
| 1993-95 | 6.1 | 5.5 | 6.7 |

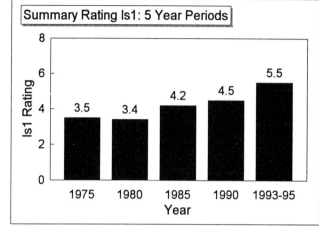

| Components of Economic Freedom | 1975 | | 1980 | | 1985 | | 1990 | | 1993-95 | |
|---|---|---|---|---|---|---|---|---|---|---|
| **I. Money and Inflation** | **5.8** | | **6.1** | | **7.4** | | **7.0** | | **6.9** | |
| (a) Annual Money Growth (last 5 yrs.) | 5 | (8.3) | 4 | (10.1) | 7 | (5.9) | 7 | (6.1) | 10 | (1.9) |
| (b) Inflation Variablity (last 5 yrs.) | 7 | (2.9) | 9 | (1.5) | 10 | (1.2) | 9 | (1.4) | 6 | (3.1) |
| (c) Ownership of Foreign Currency | 10 | | 10 | | 10 | | 10 | | 10 | |
| (d) Maint. of Bank Account Abroad | 0 | | 0 | | 0 | | 0 | | 0 | |
| | | | | | | | | | | |
| **II. Government Operation** | **2.5** | | **3.3** | | **3.7** | | **4.4** | | **6.7** | |
| (a) Govern. Consumption (% of GDP) | 0 | (24.2) | 0 | (29.3) | 0 | (27.9) | 0 | (27.4) | 0 | (27.3) |
| (b) Government Enterprises | 4 | | 4 | | 4 | | 4 | | 4 | |
| (c) Price Controls | - | | - | | - | | 6 | | 8 | |
| (d) Entry Into Business | - | | - | | - | | - | | 10 | |
| (e) Legal System | - | | - | | - | | - | | 10 | |
| (f) Avoidance of Neg. Interest Rates | 4 | | 8 | | 10 | | 10 | | 10 | |
| | | | | | | | | | | |
| **III. Takings** | **0.8** | | **0.0** | | **0.0** | | **0.0** | | **0.5** | |
| (a) Transfers and Subsidies (% of GDP) | 0 | (25.0) | 0 | (24.7) | 0 | (26.0) | 0 | (29.9) | 0 | (31.7) |
| (b) Marginal Tax Rates (Top Rate) | 1 | (70) | 0 | (87) | 0 | (80) | 0 | (72) | 1 | (56-63) |
| (c) Conscription | 0 | | 0 | | 0 | | 0 | | 0 | |
| | | | | | | | | | | |
| **IV. International Sector** | **6.2** | | **5.7** | | **7.3** | | **8.3** | | **8.7** | |
| (a) Taxes on International Trade (Avg.) | 9 | (1.0) | 9 | (0.7) | 9 | (0.3) | 9 | (0.4) | 9 | (0.6) |
| (b) Black Market Exchange Rates (Prem.) | 8 | (1) | 6 | (5) | 8 | (1) | 8 | (1) | 10 | (0) |
| (c) Size of Trade Sector (% of GDP) | 5 | (55.9) | 5 | (60.8) | 7 | (69.0) | 5 | (59.4) | 4 | (54.0) |
| (d) Capital Transactions with Foreigners | 2 | | 2 | | 5 | | 10 | | 10 | |

## Part 2:  Recent Economic Indicators:

| | | | | | | | |
|---|---|---|---|---|---|---|---|
| **Population 1994:** | 8.8 | | **Real Per Capita GDP** : | | 1994= | $13,930 | |
| (in millions) | | | (in 1985 U.S. dollars) | | | | |
| Annual Rate of Change (1980-94): | 0.4% | | Avg. Growth Rate: | | 1980-90= | 1.7% | |
| | | | | | 1985-94= | 0.4% | |

| Economic Indicators: | 1987 | 1988 | 1989 | 1990 | 1991 | 1992 | 1993 | 1994 |
|---|---|---|---|---|---|---|---|---|
| Change in Real GDP: Aggregate | 2.8 | 2.7 | 2.4 | 1.4 | -1.1 | -1.4 | -2.6 | 2.2 |
| : Per Capita | 2.4 | 2.3 | 1.7 | 0.5 | -1.7 | -2.0 | -3.0 | 1.8 |
| Inflation Rate (CPI) | 4.2 | 5.8 | 6.4 | 10.5 | 9.3 | 2.3 | 4.6 | 2.5 |
| Change in Money Supply: (M1) | 7.4 | 3.4 | 6.2 | - | - | - | - | - |
| : (M2) | 10.2 | 7.8 | 9.3 | 11.3 | 4.0 | 3.2 | 4.0 | 0.2 |
| Investment/GDP Ratio | 18.4 | 19.3 | 21.3 | 20.5 | 17.2 | 16.5 | 14.2 | 13.7 |
| Central Government Budget Deficit (-) or Surplus (+) As a Percent of GDP | +0.4 | +0.8 | +0.6 | +0.6 | -1.1 | -2.3 | -11.9 | - |
| Unemployment Rate | 1.9 | 1.6 | 1.4 | 1.5 | 2.7 | 4.8 | 8.2 | 8.0 |

Based on the average of our three economic freedom indexes, in 1993-1995 Sweden placed 31st among the countries in our study.  The Is1 summary rating ranked it 47th.  Sweden's economic freedom rating is the lowest of the 20 high-income industrial nations.  Its most recent rating is higher than prior figures.  However, this change is more apparent than real.  The higher 1993-1995 rating is primarily the result of its high ratings for the two new components—entry into business and the legal system—included for the first time in the most recent index.  The only component where Sweden's more recent rating was substantially higher than in 1980 was "capital transactions with foreigners", suggesting that there has been some relaxation of prior restrictions on the mobility of capital.  Even though its top marginal tax rate has been reduced from a confiscatory 87% in 1980 to the 60% range in 1994, it is still one of the highest in the world.  Only Romania, Cameroon, Gabon, and Zaire had lower or comparable 1994 ratings in this area.  Political rather than market choices allocate 27% of GDP.  Another 32% is taxed from the earner and transferred to someone else.  Thus, approximately 60% of the Swedish output is channelled through the government.  Again, this figure is one of the highest is the world.  Conscription and restrictions limiting the maintenance of bank accounts abroad further limit the economic freedom of Swedes.

These policies are taking a toll on economic growth, Sweden's 0.4% growth of per capita GDP during the last decade is the lowest among the high-income industrial nations.  In 1975, Sweden's per capita GDP was the fourth highest in the world, behind only United States, Switzerland, and Canada.  In 1994 it was 11th and it will almost certainly drop several more notches in the near future unless it begins to reverse its course and move toward a freer economy.

# SWITZERLAND

**Part 1: The Economic Freedom Ratings for the Components and Various Area and Summary Indexes: 1975, 1980, 1985, 1990 and 1993-95.**

(The numbers in parentheses indicate the actual values for the components.)

### Summary Ratings

| | Ie | Is1 | Is2 |
|------|-----|-----|-----|
| 1975 | 7.1 | 7.1 | 7.2 |
| 1980 | 7.3 | 7.1 | 7.9 |
| 1985 | 7.8 | 7.3 | 8.4 |
| 1990 | 7.7 | 7.3 | 8.2 |
| 1993-95 | 7.9 | 7.5 | 8.3 |

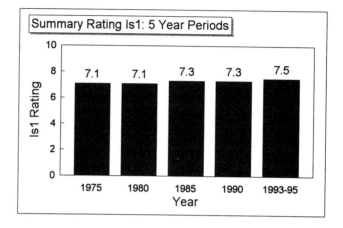

Summary Rating Is1: 5 Year Periods

| Components of Economic Freedom | 1975 | | 1980 | | 1985 | | 1990 | | 1993-95 | |
|---|---|---|---|---|---|---|---|---|---|---|
| **I. Money and Inflation** | **10.0** | | **9.1** | | **9.7** | | **10.0** | | **9.7** | |
| (a) Annual Money Growth (last 5 yrs.) | 10 | (1.9) | 7 | (5.2) | 10 | (0.1) | 10 | (0.6) | 10 | (0.2) |
| (b) Inflation Variablity (last 5 yrs.) | 10 | (1.1) | 10 | (1.1) | 9 | (2.0) | 10 | (1.2) | 9 | (1.9) |
| (c) Ownership of Foreign Currency | 10 | | 10 | | 10 | | 10 | | 10 | |
| (d) Maint. of Bank Account Abroad | 10 | | 10 | | 10 | | 10 | | 10 | |
| | | | | | | | | | | |
| **II. Government Operation** | **7.2** | | **7.2** | | **7.7** | | **7.5** | | **7.9** | |
| (a) Govern. Consumption (% of GDP) | 7 | (12.6) | 7 | (12.7) | 6 | (13.3) | 6 | (13.4) | 5 | (14.3) |
| (b) Government Enterprises | 8 | | 8 | | 8 | | 8 | | 8 | |
| (c) Price Controls | - | | - | | - | | 7 | | 6 | |
| (d) Entry Into Business | - | | - | | - | | - | | 10 | |
| (e) Legal System | - | | - | | - | | - | | 10 | |
| (f) Avoidance of Neg. Interest Rates | 6 | | 6 | | 10 | | 10 | | 10 | |
| | | | | | | | | | | |
| **III. Takings** | **5.5** | | **4.5** | | **4.5** | | **4.5** | | **5.0** | |
| (a) Transfers and Subsidies (% of GDP) | - | | 3 | (13.4) | 3 | (13.2) | 2 | (16.0) | 2 | (16.0) |
| (b) Marginal Tax Rates (Top Rate) | 7 | (38-42) | 7 | (31-44) | 7 | (33-46) | 8 | (33-43) | 9 | (26-32) |
| (c) Conscription | 0 | | 0 | | 0 | | 0 | | 0 | |
| | | | | | | | | | | |
| **IV. International Sector** | **6.2** | | **8.7** | | **8.9** | | **8.6** | | **8.6** | |
| (a) Taxes on International Trade (Avg.) | 7 | (3.5) | 8 | (2.4) | 8 | (2.0) | 8 | (1.9) | 8 | (1.9) |
| (b) Black Market Exchange Rates (Prem.) | 10 | (0) | 10 | (0) | 10 | (0) | 10 | (0) | 10 | (0) |
| (c) Size of Trade Sector (% of GDP) | 5 | (60.0) | 6 | (77.0) | 7 | (77.6) | 5 | (72.7) | 5 | (68.4) |
| (d) Capital Transactions with Foreigners | 2 | | 10 | | 10 | | 10 | | 10 | |

206

## Part 2:  Recent Economic Indicators:

| | | | | |
|---|---|---|---|---|
| **Population 1994:** | 7.0 | **Real Per Capita GDP** : | 1994= | $15,980 |
| (in millions) | | (in 1985 U.S. dollars) | | |
| Annual Rate of Change (1980-94): | 0.7% | Avg. Growth Rate: | 1980-90= | 1.5% |
| | | | 1985-94= | 0.7% |

| Economic Indicators: | 1987 | 1988 | 1989 | 1990 | 1991 | 1992 | 1993 | 1994 |
|---|---|---|---|---|---|---|---|---|
| Change in Real GDP: Aggregate | 2.0 | 2.9 | 3.9 | 2.3 | 0.0 | -0.3 | -0.6 | 2.6 |
| : Per Capita | 1.3 | 2.1 | 4.3 | 1.3 | -1.3 | -1.4 | -1.3 | 1.9 |
| Inflation Rate (CPI) | 1.4 | 1.9 | 3.2 | 5.4 | 5.8 | 4.1 | 3.3 | 1.4 |
| Change in Money Supply: (M1) | 8.0 | 12.4 | -5.5 | -4.4 | 1.1 | -0.2 | 10.9 | 5.0 |
| : (M2) | 9.2 | 8.5 | 5.8 | 1.7 | 2.6 | 2.1 | 5.5 | 3.4 |
| Investment/GDP Ratio | 27.2 | 27.9 | 29.7 | 29.3 | 27.0 | 23.5 | 21.9 | 22.9 |
| Central Government Budget Deficit (-) or Surplus (+) As a Percent of GDP | | | | | | | | |
| Unemployment Rate | 0.8 | 0.7 | 0.6 | 0.6 | 1.3 | 3.0 | 4.5 | 4.7 |

Our analysis indicates that Switzerland is economically the freest county in Europe and the fifth most free in the world (trailing only Hong Kong, Singapore, New Zealand and the United States). Moreover, its rating has been remarkably steady over a lengthy period of time. No doubt, the presence of a high level of economic freedom for many years provides the explanation for its high income per capita ($15,980 in 1994), which is also one of the highest in the world.

The strengths of the Swiss economy are a very stable monetary regime buttressed with the liberty to use alternative currencies (note the near perfect rating in the monetary area), few government enterprises, freedom of entry into business, equal treatment under the law, competitive financial markets, and minimal restraints on trade and capital mobility. Like most other high income countries, both government consumption expenditures and transfers are large relative to GDP. Conscription is used to obtain military personnel. Thus, the Swiss rating is low for these components.

The Swiss growth rate has been relatively low—approximately 1% throughout the period. To a degree, however, this may reflect the tendency of high-income economies to converge toward a relatively low long-run equilibrium rate of growth.

# SYRIA

## Part 1: The Economic Freedom Ratings for the Components and Various Area and Summary Indexes: 1975, 1980, 1985, 1990 and 1993-95.

(The numbers in parentheses indicate the actual values for the components.)

### Summary Ratings

| | Ie | Is1 | Is2 |
|------|-----|-----|-----|
| 1975 | 3.9 | 3.7 | 4.5 |
| 1980 | 3.4 | 3.1 | 3.9 |
| 1985 | 2.8 | 2.7 | 3.3 |
| 1990 | 3.2 | 3.2 | 2.6 |
| 1993-95 | 2.6 | 2.6 | 2.1 |

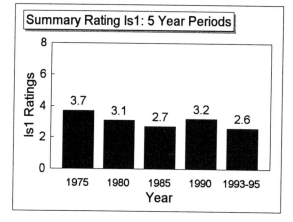

| Components of Economic Freedom | 1975 | | 1980 | | 1985 | | 1990 | | 1993-95 | |
|---|---|---|---|---|---|---|---|---|---|---|
| **I. Money and Inflation** | **4.9** | | **6.3** | | **5.6** | | **4.5** | | **3.9** | |
| (a) Annual Money Growth (last 5 yrs.) | 2 | (15.9) | 2 | (15.9) | 2 | (15.5) | 2 | (14.5) | 2 | (15.5) |
| (b) Inflation Variablity (last 5 yrs.) | 2 | (12.2) | 6 | (3.8) | 4 | (5.3) | 6 | (3.2) | 4 | (15.1) |
| (c) Ownership of Foreign Currency | 10 | | 10 | | 10 | | 10 | | 10 | |
| (d) Maint. of Bank Account Abroad | 10 | | 10 | | 10 | | 0 | | 0 | |
| | | | | | | | | | | |
| **II. Government Operation** | **3.6** | | **2.0** | | **1.0** | | **3.5** | | **1.9** | |
| (a) Govern. Consumption (% of GDP) | 1 | (21.1) | 0 | (23.2) | 0 | (23.8) | 5 | (14.4) | 5 | (14.4) |
| (b) Government Enterprises | 6 | | 4 | | 2 | | 2 | | 2 | |
| (c) Price Controls | - | | - | | - | | - | | 0 | |
| (d) Entry Into Business | - | | - | | - | | - | | 2.5 | |
| (e) Legal System | - | | - | | - | | - | | 0 | |
| (f) Avoidance of Neg. Interest Rates | - | | - | | - | | - | | - | |
| | | | | | | | | | | |
| **III. Takings** | **0.0** | | **0.0** | | **0.0** | | **0.0** | | **0.0** | |
| (a) Transfers and Subsidies (% of GDP) | - | | - | | - | | - | | - | |
| (b) Marginal Tax Rates (Top Rate) | - | | - | | - | | - | | - | |
| (c) Conscription | 0 | | 0 | | 0 | | 0 | | 0 | |
| | | | | | | | | | | |
| **IV. International Sector** | **3.5** | | **1.9** | | **2.0** | | **2.7** | | **2.9** | |
| (a) Taxes on International Trade (Avg.) | 2 | (8.5) | 3 | (7.1) | 6 | (5.6) | 7 | (2.9) | 7 | (3.6) |
| (b) Black Market Exchange Rates (Prem.) | 8 | (1) | 2 | (35) | 0 | (251) | 0 | (301) | 0 | (283) |
| (c) Size of Trade Sector (% of GDP) | 4 | (55.4) | 3 | (53.7) | 1 | (37.2) | 4 | (55.1) | 5 | (64.0) |
| (d) Capital Transactions with Foreigners | 0 | | 0 | | 0 | | 0 | | 0 | |

## Part 2: Recent Economic Indicators:

| Population 1994: | 13.7 | **Real Per Capita GDP** : | | 1993= | $4,270 |
|---|---|---|---|---|---|

(in millions)  (in 1985 U.S. dollars)

Annual Rate of Change (1980-94):  3.3%  Avg. Growth Rate:  1980-90= -1.2%

1985-93= 0.6%

| Economic Indicators: | 1987 | 1988 | 1989 | 1990 | 1991 | 1992 | 1993 | 1994 |
|---|---|---|---|---|---|---|---|---|
| Change in Real GDP: Aggregate | 1.9 | 13.3 | -9.0 | 7.6 | 11.6 | 9.6 | 3.9 | - |
| : Per Capita | -1.4 | -10.0 | -12.3 | 4.3 | 8.3 | 6.3 | 0.6 | - |
| Inflation Rate (CPI) | 59.5 | 34.6 | 11.4 | 19.4 | 7.7 | 9.5 | 11.8 | 8.7 |
| Change in Money Supply: (M1) | 13.3 | 14.0 | 17.5 | 21.6 | 27.6 | 27.6 | 23.9 | |
| : (M2) | 14.0 | 16.9 | 20.1 | 22.7 | 33.4 | 25.8 | 21.0 | - |
| Investment/GDP Ratio | 18.2 | 14.0 | 16.2 | 16.5 | 17.7 | 23.6 | 25.7 | |
| Central Government Budget Deficit (-) or Surplus (+) As a Percent of GDP | -2.6 | +1.3 | -0.6 | +0.3 | +1.4 | +1.9 | | |
| Unemployment Rate | | | | | | | | |

Syria's 2.6 freedom rating (Is1 index) in 1993-1995 placed it 99th among the 103 countries in our study. It was one of only nine countries that never managed to achieve a rating as high as 4.0 during the period of our study.

Several factors underlie Syria's persistently low ratings. Monetary policy has generally been both erratic and highly expansionary, although there is some evidence of improvement during the last few years. Government enterprises are widespread and legal restraints limit the freedom of private firms to compete in several areas. Government consumption expenditures are large, particularly for a low-income country. Conscription, exchange rate controls (note that the black market premium has persistently exceeded 250% during the last decade), and restrictions on trade and capital mobility also contributed to Syria's low rating.

Predictably, the economy is stagnating. Syria's 1993 per capita income was actually slightly lower than its 1980 figure. Like several other countries in this region, Syria is paying a price for ignoring the laws of economics and the path to prosperity.

# TAIWAN

## Part 1: The Economic Freedom Ratings for the Components and Various Area and Summary Indexes: 1975, 1980, 1985, 1990 and 1993-95.

(The numbers in parentheses indicate the actual values for the components.)

### Summary Ratings

|  | Ie | Is1 | Is2 |
|------|------|------|------|
| 1975 | 4.9 | 4.9 | 4.8 |
| 1980 | 5.4 | 5.3 | 5.4 |
| 1985 | 5.8 | 5.5 | 5.8 |
| 1990 | 6.1 | 5.9 | 6.4 |
| 1993-95 | 6.8 | 6.6 | 7.0 |

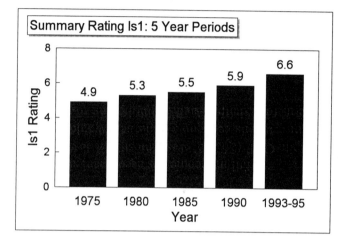

Summary Rating Is1: 5 Year Periods

| Components of Economic Freedom | 1975 | | 1980 | | 1985 | | 1990 | | 1993-95 | |
|---|---|---|---|---|---|---|---|---|---|---|
| **I. Money and Inflation** | **4.9** | | **5.9** | | **7.4** | | **7.6** | | **10.0** | |
| (a) Annual Money Growth (last 5 yrs.) | 2 | (19.1) | 2 | (15.1) | 7 | (5.0) | 3 | (13.1) | 10 | (0.1) |
| (b) Inflation Variablity (last 5 yrs.) | 2 | (12.6) | 5 | (4.3) | 5 | (4.8) | 9 | (1.3) | 10 | (0.4) |
| (c) Ownership of Foreign Currency | 10 | | 10 | | 10 | | 10 | | 10 | |
| (d) Maint. of Bank Account Abroad | 10 | | 10 | | 10 | | 10 | | 10 | |
| | | | | | | | | | | |
| **II. Government Operation** | **4.8** | | **4.8** | | **5.3** | | **5.0** | | **5.7** | |
| (a) Govern. Consumption (% of GDP) | 4 | (15.8) | 4 | (15.9) | 4 | (16.2) | 2 | (17.6) | 4 | (16.0) |
| (b) Government Enterprises | 4 | | 4 | | 4 | | 4 | | 4 | |
| (c) Price Controls | - | | - | | - | | 6 | | 7 | |
| (d) Entry Into Business | - | | - | | - | | - | | 7.5 | |
| (e) Legal System | - | | - | | - | | - | | 2.5 | |
| (f) Avoidance of Neg. Interest Rates | 8 | | 8 | | 10 | | 10 | | 10 | |
| | | | | | | | | | | |
| **III. Takings** | **5.0** | | **4.6** | | **4.6** | | **4.7** | | **5.3** | |
| (a) Transfers and Subsidies (% of GDP) | 9 | (2.2) | 8 | (2.6) | 8 | (3.6) | 6 | (4.7) | 5 | (5.9) |
| (b) Marginal Tax Rates (Top Rate) | 3 | (60) | 3 | (60) | 3 | (60) | 5 | (50) | 7 | (40) |
| (c) Conscription | 0 | | 0 | | 0 | | 0 | | 0 | |
| | | | | | | | | | | |
| **IV. International Sector** | **4.8** | | **6.0** | | **5.4** | | **7.3** | | **7.3** | |
| (a) Taxes on International Trade (Avg.) | 6 | (4.8) | 7 | (3.6) | 7 | (2.8) | 8 | (2.1) | 8 | (2.0) |
| (b) Black Market Exchange Rates (Prem.) | 6 | (5) | 8 | (1) | 6 | (3) | 10 | (0) | 10 | (0) |
| (c) Size of Trade Sector (% of GDP) | 5 | (82.5) | 7 | (106.3) | 7 | (96.6) | 5 | (90.5) | 5 | (86.5) |
| (d) Capital Transactions with Foreigners | 2 | | 2 | | 2 | | 5 | | 5 | |

## Part 2: Recent Economic Indicators:

| | | | | |
|---|---|---|---|---|
| **Population 1994:** | 21.3 | **Real Per Capita GDP :** | 1994 = | $10,152 |
| (in millions) | | (in 1985 U.S. dollars) | | |
| Annual Rate of Change (1980-94): | 1.0% | Avg. Growth Rate: | 1980-90 = | 6.5% |
| | | | 1985-94 = | 6.7% |

| Economic Indicators: | 1987 | 1988 | 1989 | 1990 | 1991 | 1992 | 1993 | 1994 |
|---|---|---|---|---|---|---|---|---|
| Change in Real GDP:Aggregate | 12.7 | 7.8 | 8.2 | 5.4 | 7.6 | 6.8 | 6.3 | 7.0 |
| : Per Capita | 11.7 | 6.8 | 7.2 | 4.4 | 6.6 | 5.8 | 5.3 | 6.0 |
| Inflation Rate (CPI) | 0.5 | 1.3 | 4.4 | 4.1 | 3.6 | 4.5 | 2.9 | 3.4 |
| Change in Money Supply: (M1) | 37.8 | 24.4 | 6.1 | -6.7 | 12.1 | 12.4 | 15.3 | |
| : (M2) | | | | | | | | |
| Investment/GDP Ratio | 20.6 | 23.7 | 23.4 | 23.1 | 23.3 | 24.9 | 25.2 | |
| Central Government Budget | | | | | | | | |
| Deficit (-) or Surplus (+) | | | | | | | | |
| As a Percent of GDP | +1.4 | +2.9 | +3.6 | +0.8 | +0.5 | +0.2 | +0.6 | |
| Unemployment Rate | 2.0 | 1.7 | 1.6 | 1.7 | 1.5 | 1.5 | 1.5 | |

The Taiwanese economic freedom rating has continuously improved during the last two decades. The Is1 index rose from 4.8 1975 to 5.5 in 1985 and 6.6 in 1993-95. This improvement propelled Taiwan into a tie (with Panama) for 15th place among the 103 countries of our study.

Improvements in the monetary and international areas account for most of the gains. In the 1970s, money growth was rapid (15% or more even after adjustment for the long-term growth of real GDP) and inflation was a persistent problem. This is no longer the case. During the last five years, the inflation rate has remained within a narrow band between 2.9% and 4.5%. (Note the perfect 10 rating in the money and inflation area in 1993-1995.) In the international area, lower tariffs, elimination of exchange rate controls, and a relaxation of various restrictions on capital movements have led to a higher rating. Large government expenditures, state-operated enterprises, and conscription are the major factors pulling down the overall Taiwanese rating.

Rapid economic growth has accompanied the steady expansion in economic freedom. Since 1980, the per capita GDP of Taiwan has increased at an annual rate of 6.5%. The Taiwanese economy is now one of the fastest growing in the world.

# TANZANIA

## Part 1: The Economic Freedom Ratings for the Components and Various Area and Summary Indexes: 1975, 1980, 1985, 1990 and 1993-95.

(The numbers in parentheses indicate the actual values for the components.)

### Summary Ratings

|       | Ie  | Is1 | Is2 |
|-------|-----|-----|-----|
| 1975  | 3.0 | 3.3 | 2.4 |
| 1980  | 3.4 | 4.0 | 2.3 |
| 1985  | 1.6 | 1.9 | 0.9 |
| 1990  | 2.3 | 2.3 | 1.5 |
| 1993-95 | 3.3 | 3.7 | 2.6 |

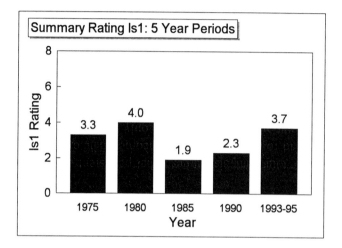

| Components of Economic Freedom | 1975 | | 1980 | | 1985 | | 1990 | | 1993-95 | |
|---|---|---|---|---|---|---|---|---|---|---|
| **I.  Money and Inflation** | **1.9** | | **1.6** | | **2.3** | | **1.0** | | **1.0** | |
| (a) Annual Money Growth (last 5 yrs.) | 2 | (15.3) | 1 | (22.1) | 3 | 12.3) | 1 | (30.0) | 1 | (26.6) |
| (b) Inflation Variablity (last 5 yrs.) | 4 | (5.8) | 4 | (5.7) | 4 | (5.9) | 2 | (9.5) | 2 | (8.9) |
| (c) Ownership of Foreign Currency | 0 | | 0 | | 0 | | 0 | | 0 | |
| (d) Maint. of Bank Account Abroad | 0 | | 0 | | 0 | | 0 | | 0 | |
| | | | | | | | | | | |
| **II. Government Operation** | **2.5** | | **4.3** | | **1.9** | | **2.7** | | **3.2** | |
| (a) Govern. Consumption (% of GDP) | 3 | (17.2) | 7 | (13.0) | 5 | (15.4) | 8 | (10.4) | 7 | (11.3) |
| (b) Government Enterprises | 2 | | 2 | | 0 | | 0 | | 0 | |
| (c) Price Controls | - | | - | | - | | 0 | | 4 | |
| (d) Entry Into Business | - | | - | | - | | - | | 2.5 | |
| (e) Legal System | - | | - | | - | | - | | 2.5 | |
| (f) Avoidance of Neg. Interest Rates | - | | 4 | | 0 | | 4 | | - | |
| | | | | | | | | | | |
| **III. Takings** | **5.3** | | **10.0** | | **2.4** | | **2.3** | | **6.2** | |
| (a) Transfers and Subsidies (% of GDP) | 10 | (0.1) | 10 | (0.1) | 6 | (5.2) | - | | - | |
| (b) Marginal Tax Rates (Top Rate) | 0 | (80) | - | | 0 | (95) | 3 | (50) | 8 | (30) |
| (c) Conscription | 10 | | 10 | | 0 | | 0 | | 0 | |
| | | | | | | | | | | |
| **IV. International Sector** | **2.2** | | **1.4** | | **1.2** | | **2.7** | | **4.7** | |
| (a) Taxes on International Trade (Avg.) | 3 | (7.3) | 3 | (7.7) | 4 | (6.3) | - | | - | |
| (b) Black Market Exchange Rates (Prem.) | 1 | (203) | 0 | (224) | 0 | (259) | 1 | (78) | 6 | (6) |
| (c) Size of Trade Sector (% of GDP) | 6 | (52.1) | 3 | (39.5) | 0 | (21.0) | 10 | (76.0) | 10 | (85.8) |
| (d) Capital Transactions with Foreigners | 0 | | 0 | | 0 | | 0 | | 0 | |

## Part 2:  Recent Economic Indicators:

| | | | | | |
|---|---|---|---|---|---|
| **Population 1994:** | 27.5 | **Real Per Capita GDP** : | 1993 = | $470 |
| (in millions) | | (in 1985 U.S. dollars) | | |
| Annual Rate of Change (1980-94): | 3.0% | Avg. Growth Rate: | 1980-90 = | 0.6% |
| | | | 1985-93 = | 0.5% |

| Economic Indicators: | 1987 | 1988 | 1989 | 1990 | 1991 | 1992 | 1993 | 1994 |
|---|---|---|---|---|---|---|---|---|
| Change in Real GDP:Aggregate | 5.1 | 4.2 | 4.0 | 4.8 | 3.9 | 3.6 | -9.0 | |
| : Per Capita | 2.1 | 1.2 | 1.0 | 1.8 | 0.9 | 0.6 | -12.0 | |
| Inflation Rate (CPI) | 30.0 | 31.2 | 25.8 | 19.7 | 22.3 | 22.1 | 23.5 | |
| Change in Money Supply: (M1) | 33.5 | 34.3 | 35.7 | 32.9 | 32.9 | 26.2 | 30.7 | |
| : (M2) | 29.2 | 30.4 | 40.2 | 39.8 | 40.6 | 23.9 | 27.5 | |
| Investment/GDP Ratio | 30.4 | 30.6 | 34.4 | 46.6 | 38.5 | 42.4 | 57.0 | |
| Central Government Budget Deficit (-) or Surplus (+) As a Percent of GDP | | | | | | | | |
| Unemployment Rate | | | | | | | | |

Despite the recent improvement, the economic freedom rating of Tanzania is still one of the lowest in the world.  In 1985, Tanzania's Is1 rating fell to 1.9, fourth lowest  (only Nicaragua, Somalia, and Uganda had lower ratings) among the countries in our study.  Its 1990 rating was only slightly higher.  Since 1990, Tanzania's rating has risen from 2.3 to 3.7.

The major factors contributing to the recent improvement were lower marginal tax rates, relaxation of exchange rate controls, and a substantial increase in the size of the trade sector. Tanzania's astronomical 95% top marginal tax rate of 1985 was cut to 50% in 1990 and 30% in 1994.  Its black market exchange rate premium is now  at single digit levels, down from 259% in 1985 and 78% in 1990.  The exchange rate controls of the mid-1980s virtually stifled the ability of Tanzanians to engage in international trade.  Thus, the growth of the trade sector as the controls were relaxed is not surprising.

A highly unstable monetary policy (in recent years money growth has generally exceeded 30% and the inflation rate 20%), legal restraints imposed on private sector business, insecure property rights, inefficient state-operated enterprises, price controls, conscription, and  restrictions on capital mobility continue to plague this extremely poor country.  Major changes are needed if this nation is going to throw off the curse of both state oppression and poverty.

# THAILAND

**Part 1: The Economic Freedom Ratings for the Components and Various Area and Summary Indexes: 1975, 1980, 1985, 1990 and 1993-95.**

(The numbers in parentheses indicate the actual values for the components.)

### Summary Ratings

|  | Ie | Is1 | Is2 |
|------|------|------|------|
| 1975 | 4.6 | 4.9 | 3.7 |
| 1980 | 4.7 | 5.0 | 3.9 |
| 1985 | 5.3 | 5.3 | 4.6 |
| 1990 | 6.2 | 6.3 | 5.5 |
| 1993-95 | 6.9 | 7.0 | 6.7 |

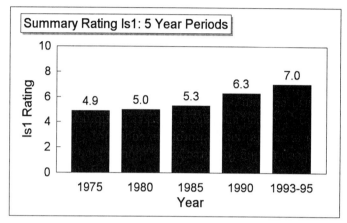

| Components of Economic Freedom | 1975 | | 1980 | | 1985 | | 1990 | | 1993-95 | |
|---|---|---|---|---|---|---|---|---|---|---|
| **I. Money and Inflation** | **3.1** | | **3.9** | | **5.4** | | **6.4** | | **8.8** | |
| (a) Annual Money Growth (last 5 yrs.) | 8 | (4.9) | 5 | (8.8) | 9 | (-2.9) | 5 | (10.0) | 7 | (5.8) |
| (b) Inflation Variablity (last 5 yrs.) | 2 | (8.4) | 7 | (2.8) | 8 | (2.5) | 9 | (1.7) | 9 | (1.8) |
| (c) Ownership of Foreign Currency | 0 | | 0 | | 0 | | 10 | | 10 | |
| (d) Maint. of Bank Account Abroad | 0 | | 0 | | 0 | | 0 | | 10 | |
| | | | | | | | | | | |
| **II. Government Operation** | **7.0** | | **6.0** | | **6.8** | | **6.5** | | **5.5** | |
| (a) Govern. Consumption (% of GDP) | 8 | (10.3) | 7 | (12.3) | 6 | (13.5) | 9 | (9.4) | 8 | (10.3) |
| (b) Government Enterprises | 6 | | 6 | | 6 | | 6 | | 6 | |
| (c) Price Controls | - | | - | | - | | 4 | | 5 | |
| (d) Entry Into Business | - | | - | | - | | - | | 5 | |
| (e) Legal System | - | | - | | - | | - | | 0 | |
| (f) Avoidance of Neg. Interest Rates | - | | 4 | | 10 | | 8 | | 10 | |
| | | | | | | | | | | |
| **III. Takings** | **5.4** | | **5.4** | | **4.9** | | **5.9** | | **7.3** | |
| (a) Transfers and Subsidies (% of GDP) | 10 | (0.6) | 10 | (0.7) | 10 | (1.2) | 10 | (1.0) | 10 | (0.9) |
| (b) Marginal Tax Rates (Top Rate) | 3 | (60) | 3 | (60) | 2 | (65) | 4 | (55) | 7 | (37) |
| (c) Conscription | 0 | | 0 | | 0 | | 0 | | 0 | |
| | | | | | | | | | | |
| **IV. International Sector** | **4.5** | | **4.5** | | **4.5** | | **6.7** | | **7.5** | |
| (a) Taxes on International Trade (Avg.) | 4 | (7.0) | 4 | (6.9) | 4 | (6.5) | 6 | (5.4) | 6 | (3.9) |
| (b) Black Market Exchange Rates (Prem.) | 7 | (2) | 6 | (5) | 6 | (3) | 10 | (0) | 10 | (0) |
| (c) Size of Trade Sector (% of GDP) | 5 | (41.4) | 7 | (54.5) | 7 | (49.1) | 10 | (75.5) | 10 | (77.1) |
| (d) Capital Transactions with Foreigners | 2 | | 2 | | 2 | | 2 | | 5 | |

214

## Part 2:  Recent Economic Indicators:

| Population 1994: | 60.0 | **Real Per Capita GDP** : | 1994 = | $4,450 |
| (in millions) | | (in 1985 U.S. dollars) | | |
| Annual Rate of Change (1980-94): | 1.8% | Avg. Growth Rate: | 1980-90 = | 5.9% |
| | | | 1985-94 = | 7.6% |

| Economic Indicators: | 1987 | 1988 | 1989 | 1990 | 1991 | 1992 | 1993 | 1994 |
|---|---|---|---|---|---|---|---|---|
| Change in Real GDP:Aggregate | 9.5 | 13.2 | 12.0 | 10.0 | 6.7 | 6.8 | 8.0 | 8.4 |
| : Per Capita | 7.7 | 11.4 | 10.2 | 8.2 | 4.9 | 5.0 | 6.2 | 6.6 |
| Inflation Rate (CPI) | 2.5 | 3.9 | 5.4 | 5.9 | 5.7 | 4.1 | 3.6 | 5.3 |
| Change in Money Supply: (M1) | 22.9 | 18.5 | 19.7 | 16.8 | 2.4 | 19.7 | 10.1 | 20.1 |
| : (M2) | 16.1 | 18.5 | 23.3 | 29.2 | 20.2 | 18.2 | 16.1 | 13.0 |
| Investment/GDP Ratio | 23.9 | 28.8 | 31.5 | 36.8 | - | - | - | - |
| Central Government Budget Deficit (-) or Surplus (+) As a Percent of GDP | -2.3 | 0.7 | 3.1 | 4.7 | 4.9 | 2.9 | - | - |
| Unemployment Rate [a] | 6.3 | 4.6 | 3.6 | 2.2 | 3.5 | 3.6 | | |

a Data for 1987-90 are based on an average of a few months during each year.

As the result of substantial improvement during the last two decades, the Thai economy is now one of the world's most free. In 1995 its Is1 economic freedom rating was 7.0, up from 4.5 in 1975.  This places Thailand in a tie for sixth (with United Kingdom and Malaysia) among the countries in our study.

Thailand has improved in almost every area.  Its price level is now more stable—the inflation rate has fluctuated between 4% and 6% during the last five years.  Beginning in the late 1980s, Thais were permitted to own foreign currency bank accounts domestically and the maintenance of bank accounts abroad was authorized in the early 1990s.  These moves contributed to a jump in the money and inflation area rating. Deregulation of the credit market has integrated the domestic financial markets with the global economy.  The negative interest rates of the late 70s are now a thing of the past.  The top marginal tax rate was reduced from 65% in 1985 to 55% in 1990 and 37% in 1994.  Tariff rates have been reduced; the Thai baht is now fully convertible; the size of the trade sector *as a share of GDP* has nearly doubled since the mid-70s; and restrictions on the flow of capital were relaxed in the early 1990s. All of these factors  contributed to the growth of economic freedom.

The economy has responded.  The annual growth rate of per capita GDP was 7.6% during 1985-1994, up from 3.7% during 1970-1985.  The central government has generally run a budget surplus in recent years and the  unemployment rate is relatively low.

215

# TURKEY

## Part 1: The Economic Freedom Ratings for the Components and Various Area and Summary Indexes: 1975, 1980, 1985, 1990 and 1993-95.

(The numbers in parentheses indicate the actual values for the components.)

### Summary Ratings

| | Ie | Is1 | Is2 |
|---|---|---|---|
| 1975 | 2.5 | 2.8 | 1.9 |
| 1980 | 2.0 | 2.3 | 1.4 |
| 1985 | 3.8 | 3.8 | 3.0 |
| 1990 | 4.5 | 4.6 | 4.4 |
| 1993-95 | 4.2 | 4.2 | 4.3 |

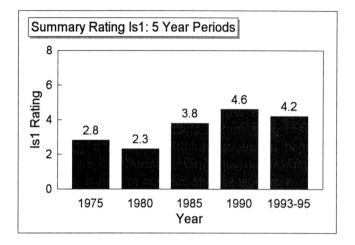

Summary Rating Is1: 5 Year Periods

| Components of Economic Freedom | 1975 | | 1980 | | 1985 | | 1990 | | 1993-95 | |
|---|---|---|---|---|---|---|---|---|---|---|
| **I. Money and Inflation** | **2.3** | | **0.6** | | **1.0** | | **4.0** | | **4.0** | |
| (a) Annual Money Growth (last 5 yrs.) | 2 | (20.2) | 1 | (39.7) | 1 | (31.7) | 0 | (48.9) | 0 | (59.0) |
| (b) Inflation Variablity (last 5 yrs.) | 5 | (4.4) | 1 | (31.4) | 2 | (8.4) | 1 | (13.9) | 1 | (18.8) |
| (c) Ownership of Foreign Currency | 0 | | 0 | | 0 | | 10 | | 10 | |
| (d) Maint. of Bank Account Abroad | 0 | | 0 | | 0 | | 10 | | 10 | |
| | | | | | | | | | | |
| **II. Government Operation** | **4.7** | | **4.3** | | **6.8** | | **4.9** | | **3.8** | |
| (a) Govern. Consumption (% of GDP) | 7 | (12.3) | 7 | (12.6) | 9 | (8.6) | 6 | (14.1) | 2 | (18.6) |
| (b) Government Enterprises | 4 | | 4 | | 4 | | 4 | | 4 | |
| (c) Price Controls | - | | - | | - | | 6 | | 3 | |
| (d) Entry Into Business | - | | - | | - | | - | | 7.5 | |
| (e) Legal System | - | | - | | - | | - | | 0 | |
| (f) Avoidance of Neg. Interest Rate | 2 | | 0 | | 8 | | 2 | | 6 | |
| | | | | | | | | | | |
| **III. Takings** | **3.8** | | **2.0** | | **3.0** | | **4.7** | | **3.9** | |
| (a) Transfers and Subsidies (% of GDP) | 5 | (6.0) | 5 | (6.0) | 4 | (10.3) | 7 | (3.9) | 5 | (5.8) |
| (b) Marginal Tax Rates (Top Rate) | - | | 0 | (75) | 3 | (60) | 4 | (50) | 4 | (55) |
| (c) Conscription | 0 | | 0 | | 0 | | 0 | | 0 | |
| | | | | | | | | | | |
| **IV. International Sector** | **1.3** | | **2.3** | | **4.7** | | **4.8** | | **5.4** | |
| (a) Taxes on International Trade (Avg.) | 0 | (14.4) | 4 | (6.3) | 7 | (3.0) | 7 | (2.8) | 8 | (2.3) |
| (b) Black Market Exch. Rates (Prem.) | 4 | (11) | 4 | (16) | 6 | (3) | 7 | (2) | 8 | (1) |
| (c) Size of Trade Sector (% of GDP) | 1 | (19.3) | 0 | (20.6) | 6 | (44.4) | 5 | (42.0) | 5 | (44.4) |
| (d) Capital Transactions with Foreigners | 0 | | 0 | | 0 | | 0 | | 0 | |

216

## Part 2: Recent Economic Indicators:

| | | | |
|---|---|---|---|
| **Population 1994:** (in millions) | 60.9 | **Real Per Capita GDP** : (in 1985 U.S. dollars) | 1994= $3,665 |
| Annual Rate of Change (1980-94): | 2.3% | Avg. Growth Rate: 1980-90= | 3.2% |
| | | 1985-94= | 2.9% |

| Economic Indicators: | 1987 | 1988 | 1989 | 1990 | 1991 | 1992 | 1993 | 1994 |
|---|---|---|---|---|---|---|---|---|
| Change in Real GDP: Aggregate | 7.4 | 3.8 | 1.3 | 9.2 | 0.3 | 5.1 | 6.0 | -5.4 |
| : Per Capita | 5.1 | 1.5 | -1.0 | 6.9 | -2.0 | 3.8 | 3.7 | -7.7 |
| Inflation Rate (CPI) | 38.8 | 73.7 | 63.3 | 60.3 | 66.0 | 70.1 | 66.1 | 106.3 |
| Change in Money Supply: (M1) | 62.6 | 44.4 | 63.7 | 71.4 | 45.9 | 59.2 | 78.4 | 84.4 |
| : (M2) | 49.4 | 57.1 | 74.8 | 61.3 | 66.5 | 88.3 | 66.7 | 128.4 |
| Investment/GDP Ratio | 25.2 | 24.0 | 22.7 | 23.9 | 22.4 | 23.2 | 26.2 | 27.5 |
| Central Government Budget Deficit (-) or Surplus (+) As a Percent of GDP | -4.0 | -3.8 | -4.5 | -4.2 | -5.2 | -4.3 | - | - |
| Unemployment Rate | - | 8.3 | 8.5 | 7.4 | 8.3 | 7.8 | | |

The average of our three indexes places Turkey in a tie (with Bangladesh and Israel) for 66th place in our 1993-1995 rankings. Its Is1 summary rating places it 70th. Thus, Turkey ranks in the lower-middle range among the 103 countries in our study. Its 1975 and 1980 rankings were even lower. During the 1980s, Turkey took some significant steps toward a freer economy (note the increase in its summary ratings). The key elements of Turkey's improvement during this period were:

- legalization of foreign currency bank accounts;
- reductions in tax rates—the top marginal rate was cut from 75% in 1980 to 50% in 1990 (recently it has been increased to 55%);
- lower tariffs—the average tax on international trade fell from 14.4% in 1975 to 2.3% during the most recent period;
- relaxation of exchange rate controls—the black market in this area has virtually disappeared; and
- a substantial increase in the size of the trade sector.

The most serious obstacle to further advancement is the current mismanagement of both monetary and fiscal policy. During the last five years, the Turkish monetary authorities have expanded the money supply at almost a 70% annual rate. Predictably, the price level has increased by a similar magnitude. The 1994 Turkish inflation rate of 106% was one of the highest in the world. After making significant progress toward economic freedom and experiencing a healthy growth rate (per capita GDP increased 3.2% annually during the 1980s), it would be tragic if these policy failures once again sent the economy into stagnation and regression.

# UNITED KINGDOM

**Part 1: The Economic Freedom Ratings for the Components and Various Area and Summary Indexes: 1975, 1980, 1985, 1990 and 1993-95.**

(The numbers in parentheses indicate the actual values for the components.)

### Summary Ratings

|        | Ie  | Is1 | Is2 |
|--------|-----|-----|-----|
| 1975   | 4.7 | 5.0 | 4.7 |
| 1980   | 4.7 | 4.5 | 5.3 |
| 1985   | 6.8 | 6.0 | 7.9 |
| 1990   | 7.0 | 6.6 | 7.8 |
| 1993-95| 7.5 | 7.0 | 8.3 |

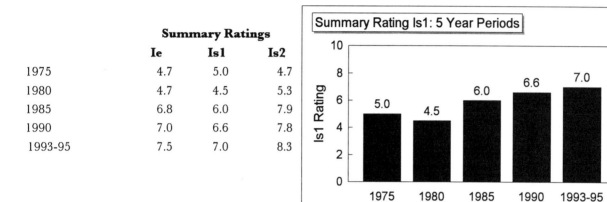

Summary Rating Is1: 5 Year Periods

| Components of Economic Freedom | 1975 | | 1980 | | 1985 | | 1990 | | 1993-95 | |
|---|---|---|---|---|---|---|---|---|---|---|
| **I. Money and Inflation** | **2.2** | | **3.6** | | **7.2** | | **7.0** | | **8.8** | |
| (a) Annual Money Growth (last 5 yrs.) | 4 | (10.4) | 4 | (10.3) | 4 | (10.9) | 1 | (28.0) | 7 | (5.3) |
| (b) Inflation Variablity (last 5 yrs.) | 3 | (7.4) | 7 | (2.6) | 7 | (2.5) | 9 | (1.4) | 9 | (1.6) |
| (c) Ownership of Foreign Currency | 0 | | 0 | | 10 | | 10 | | 10 | |
| (d) Maint. of Bank Account Abroad | 0 | | 0 | | 10 | | 10 | | 10 | |
| | | | | | | | | | | |
| **II. Government Operation** | **2.8** | | **2.8** | | **4.9** | | **5.9** | | **6.8** | |
| (a) Govern. Consumption (% of GDP) | 1 | (22.4) | 1 | (21.6) | 1 | (21.1) | 1 | (20.6) | 1 | (21.5) |
| (b) Government Enterprises | 4 | | 4 | | 6 | | 6 | | 6 | |
| (c) Price Controls | - | | - | | - | | 8 | | 9 | |
| (d) Entry Into Business | - | | - | | - | | - | | 10 | |
| (e) Legal System | - | | - | | - | | - | | 5 | |
| (f) Avoidance of Neg. Interest Rates | 4 | | 4 | | 10 | | 10 | | 10 | |
| | | | | | | | | | | |
| **III. Takings** | **5.8** | | **2.1** | | **3.1** | | **4.9** | | **4.5** | |
| (a) Transfers and Subsidies (% of GDP) | 3 | (15.0) | 2 | (15.8) | 2 | (17.9) | 3 | (14.9) | 2 | (17.3) |
| (b) Marginal Tax Rates (Top Rate) | 7 | (41) | 0 | (83) | 2 | (60) | 5 | (40) | 5 | (40) |
| (c) Conscription | 10 | | 10 | | 10 | | 10 | | 10 | |
| | | | | | | | | | | |
| **IV. International Sector** | **7.4** | | **9.2** | | **9.7** | | **9.2** | | **9.2** | |
| (a) Taxes on International Trade (Avg.) | 10 | (0.0) | 10 | (0.0) | 10 | (0.0) | 10 | (0.0) | 10 | (0.1) |
| (b) Black Market Exchange Rates (Prem.) | 10 | (0) | 10 | (0) | 10 | (0) | 10 | (0) | 10 | (0) |
| (c) Size of Trade Sector (% of GDP) | 7 | (53.6) | 5 | (52.3) | 8 | (56.6) | 5 | (51.4) | 5 | (49.0) |
| (d) Capital Transactions with Foreigners | 2 | | 10 | | 10 | | 10 | | 10 | |

## Part 2: Recent Economic Indicators:

| | | | | |
|---|---|---|---|---|
| **Population 1994:** | 58.0 | **Real Per Capita GDP :** | 1994= | $13,430 |
| (in millions) | | (in 1985 U.S. dollars) | | |
| Annual Rate of Change (1980-94): | 0.2% | Avg. Growth Rate: | 1980-90= | 2.5% |
| | | | 1985-94= | 1.8% |

| Economic Indicators: | 1987 | 1988 | 1989 | 1990 | 1991 | 1992 | 1993 | 1994 |
|---|---|---|---|---|---|---|---|---|
| Change in Real GDP: Aggregate | 4.8 | 5.0 | 2.2 | 0.4 | -2.2 | -0.6 | 2.0 | 3.9 |
| : Per Capita | 4.5 | 4.7 | 1.9 | 0.1 | -2.6 | -0.8 | 1.8 | 3.7 |
| Inflation Rate (CPI) | 4.1 | 4.9 | 7.8 | 7.5 | 5.9 | 3.7 | 1.6 | 3.3 |
| Change in Money Supply: (M1) | 26.5 | 13.7 | 10.8 | 11.5 | 9.2 | 5.7 | 3.8 | 6.5 |
| : (M2) | 23.6 | 15.9 | 18.7 | 15.6 | 8.1 | 1.6 | 5.4 | 4.3 |
| Investment/GDP Ratio | 18.0 | 20.3 | 21.0 | 19.2 | 15.9 | 15.2 | 14.9 | 14.9 |
| Central Government Budget Deficit (-) or Surplus (+) As a Percent of GDP | -0.7 | +1.6 | +1.5 | +0.7 | -1.0 | -5.0 | -6.9 | -5.6 |
| Unemployment Rate | 10.3 | 8.6 | 7.3 | 6.9 | 8.8 | 10.0 | 10.4 | 9.4 |

Our analysis indicates that in the mid-1990s the economy of the United Kingdom is one of the most free in the world. Among the countries in our study, each of our three indexes ranked it sixth. Since 1980, the UK economic freedom rating has improved steadily. The Is1 rating jumped from 4.5 in 1980 to 6.6 in 1990 and 7.0 in 1993-1995. The major factors underlying this improvement were greater monetary and price stability, removal of restrictions limiting the use of foreign currencies, privatization, and the sharp reduction in marginal tax rates (the top rate was sliced from 83% in 1980 to 60% in 1985 and 40% later in the decade).

Growth since 1980 has been impressive even though the British economy was hard hit by the 1990-92 recession. Between 1980 and 1994, the annual growth of *per capita* GDP averaged 1.9%, compared to, for example, 1.8% for Germany and 1.4% for France. Both these economies had grown more rapidly than the UK between 1960 and 1980.

The UK economy still confronts serious problems. Its government consumption and transfer sectors are among the largest in the world. Employment regulations and a complex web of social benefits reduce worker mobility and labour market flexibility. Unemployment, which has been falling for three years, though high by U.S. and Japanese standards, is nevertheless lower than in several major European countries. The extent to which the size of the government sector can be reduced and labour market flexibility increased will determine the future direction of the British economy.

# UNITED STATES

**Part 1: The Economic Freedom Ratings for the Components and Various Area and Summary Indexes: 1975, 1980, 1985, 1990 and 1993-95.**

(The numbers in parentheses indicate the actual values for the components).

### Summary Ratings

| | Ie | Is1 | Is2 |
|------|-----|-----|-----|
| 1975 | 6.6 | 6.0 | 7.9 |
| 1980 | 6.9 | 6.2 | 8.2 |
| 1985 | 7.0 | 6.5 | 8.1 |
| 1990 | 7.8 | 7.4 | 8.7 |
| 1993-95 | 8.0 | 7.7 | 8.6 |

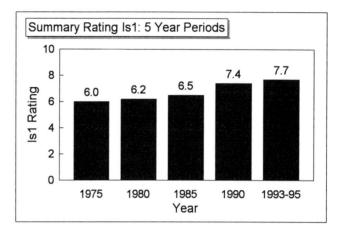

Summary Rating Is1: 5 Year Periods

| Components of Economic Freedom | 1975 | | 1980 | | 1985 | | 1990 | | 1993-95 | |
|---|---|---|---|---|---|---|---|---|---|---|
| **I. Money and Inflation** | **8.7** | | **9.1** | | **8.4** | | **9.7** | | **9.1** | |
| (a) Annual Money Growth (last 5 yrs.) | 8 | (3.5) | 8 | (4.8) | 7 | (5.8) | 9 | (3.2) | 7 | (5.6) |
| (b) Inflation Variablity (last 5 yrs.) | 8 | (2.1) | 9 | (1.3) | 8 | (2.4) | 10 | (0.7) | 10 | (0.7) |
| (c) Ownership of Foreign Currency | 10 | | 10 | | 10 | | 10 | | 10 | |
| (d) Maint. of Bank Account Abroad | 10 | | 10 | | 10 | | 10 | | 10 | |
| | | | | | | | | | | |
| **II. Government Operation** | **5.7** | | **6.1** | | **6.1** | | **6.7** | | **7.6** | |
| (a) Govern. Consumption (% of GDP) | 2 | (18.6) | 2 | (17.6) | 2 | (18.1) | 2 | (17.8) | 3 | (17.4) |
| (b) Government Enterprises | 8 | | 8 | | 8 | | 8 | | 8 | |
| (c) Price Controls | - | | - | | - | | 8 | | 8 | |
| (d) Entry Into Business | - | | - | | - | | - | | 10 | |
| (e) Legal System | - | | - | | - | | - | | 7.5 | |
| (f) Avoidance of Neg. Interest Rates | 8 | | 10 | | 10 | | 10 | | 10 | |
| | | | | | | | | | | |
| **III. Takings** | **2.5** | | **2.5** | | **4.4** | | **5.8** | | **5.8** | |
| (a) Transfers and Subsidies (% of GDP) | 3 | (11.1) | 3 | (10.0) | 3 | (12.5) | 3 | (12.7) | 3 | (14.3) |
| (b) Marginal Tax Rates (Top Rate) | 0 | (70-75) | 0 | (70-75) | 4 | (50-59) | 7 | (33-42) | 7 | (40-47) |
| (c) Conscription | 10 | | 10 | | 10 | | 10 | | 10 | |
| | | | | | | | | | | |
| **IV. International Sector** | **8.4** | | **8.6** | | **8.1** | | **8.6** | | **8.6** | |
| (a) Taxes on International Trade (Avg.) | 9 | (1.5) | 9 | (1.1) | 8 | (1.7) | 9 | (1.5) | 9 | (1.4) |
| (b) Black Market Exchange Rates (Prem.) | 10 | (0) | 10 | (0) | 10 | (0) | 10 | (0) | 10 | (0) |
| (c) Size of Trade Sector (% of GDP) | 2 | (16.4) | 3 | (21.1) | 2 | (17.7) | 3 | (21.4) | 3 | (21.8) |
| (d) Capital Transactions with Foreigners | 10 | | 10 | | 10 | | 10 | | 10 | |

## Part 2: Recent Economic Indicators:

| | | | | |
|---|---|---|---|---|
| **Population 1994:** | 260.7 | **Real Per Capita GDP :** | 1994= | $18,850 |
| (in millions) | | (in 1985 U.S. dollars) | | |
| Annual Rate of Change (1980-94): | 1.0% | Avg. Growth Rate: | 1980-90= | 1.7% |
| | | | 1985-94= | 1.6% |

| Economic Indicators: | 1987 | 1988 | 1989 | 1990 | 1991 | 1992 | 1993 | 1994 |
|---|---|---|---|---|---|---|---|---|
| Change in Real GDP: Aggregate | 3.1 | 3.9 | 2.7 | 1.2 | -1.2 | 3.4 | 3.0 | 4.0 |
| : Per Capita | 2.1 | 2.9 | 1.7 | 0.8 | -1.7 | 2.4 | 2.0 | 3.0 |
| Inflation Rate (CPI) | 3.7 | 4.0 | 4.8 | 5.4 | 4.2 | 3.0 | 3.0 | 2.6 |
| Change in Money Supply: (M1) | 9.4 | 4.7 | 0.7 | 3.9 | 6.1 | 11.7 | 12.6 | 1.7 |
| : (M2) | 6.2 | 6.5 | 4.6 | 5.9 | 4.5 | 2.3 | 1.1 | 0.9 |
| Investment/GDP Ratio | 18.9 | 18.4 | 18.2 | 16.9 | 15.3 | 15.7 | 16.5 | 15.3 |
| Central Government Budget Deficit (-) or Surplus (+) As a Percent of GDP | -3.3 | -3.2 | -2.8 | -4.0 | -4.8 | -4.9 | -4.1 | -3.3 |
| Unemployment Rate | 6.2 | 5.5 | 5.3 | 5.5 | 6.7 | 7.4 | 6.8 | 6.1 |

Other than Hong Kong and Switzerland, no economy has achieved more persistently high ratings throughout the last two decades than the United States. The U.S. ranked in the Top Ten during each of our rating years and its ranking has improved. It moved from 10th in 1975 to 6th in 1985 to 4th in the mid-1990s. Only Hong Kong, Singapore, and New Zealand were rated higher in our most recent rating year.

The U. S. received below average ratings for only two components: size of the transfer sector and international trade as a share of GDP. Increased price stability (the inflation rate has generally been between 2% and 4% for more than a decade) and a reduction in the top marginal tax rate (the combined federal and state top rate was reduced from over 70% in 1980 to the 40% range) were the primary factors contributing to the increase in the U.S. rating. Compared to the high-income industrial nations of Europe, the size of the government consumption and transfer sectors are slightly smaller in the United States. In addition, the labor market is more flexible and therefore the unemployment rate of the United States has persistently been lower than the rates of most industrial nations.

Our analysis suggests that persistent economic freedom *over a prolonged time period* will lead to a high per capita income. The experience of the United States is consistent with this viewpoint. The U.S. is not only one of the two or three persistently most free economies, the per capita income of Americans ($18,850 in 1994) is still the highest in the world. Economic freedom leads to progress.

# VENEZUELA

## Part 1: The Economic Freedom Ratings for the Components and Various Area and Summary Indexes: 1975, 1980, 1985, 1990 and 1993-95.

(The numbers in parentheses indicate the actual values for the components.)

### Summary Ratings

| | Ie | Is1 | Is2 |
|------|-----|-----|-----|
| 1975 | 6.4 | 6.9 | 6.3 |
| 1980 | 6.3 | 6.6 | 6.1 |
| 1985 | 5.0 | 5.2 | 4.7 |
| 1990 | 5.2 | 5.5 | 5.0 |
| 1993-95 | 4.0 | 4.5 | 3.2 |

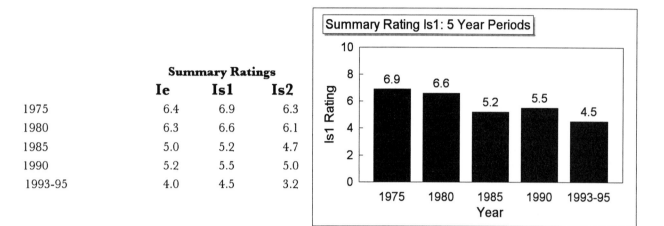

Summary Rating Is1: 5 Year Periods

| Components of Economic Freedom | 1975 | | 1980 | | 1985 | | 1990 | | 1993-95 | |
|---|---|---|---|---|---|---|---|---|---|---|
| **I. Money and Inflation** | **4.3** | | **5.5** | | **5.9** | | **4.6** | | **0.6** | |
| (a) Annual Money Growth (last 5 yrs.) | 1 | (25.5) | 3 | (13.6) | 3 | (13.3) | 2 | (19.9) | 1 | (39.8) |
| (b) Inflation Variablity (last 5 yrs.) | 1 | (15.0) | 3 | (7.4) | 4 | (5.2) | 1 | (30.4) | 1 | (13.9) |
| (c) Ownership of Foreign Currency | 10 | | 10 | | 10 | | 10 | | 0 | |
| (d) Maint. of Bank Account Abroad | 10 | | 10 | | 10 | | 10 | | 0 | |
| | | | | | | | | | | |
| **II. Government Operation** | **6.5** | | **5.5** | | **6.0** | | **4.2** | | **3.9** | |
| (a) Govern. Consumption (% of GDP) | 7 | (11.5) | 7 | (11.8) | 8 | (10.5) | 9 | (8.4) | 10 | (7.3) |
| (b) Government Enterprises | 6 | | 4 | | 4 | | 2 | | 2 | |
| (c) Price Controls | - | | - | | - | | 4 | | 2 | |
| (d) Entry Into Business | - | | - | | - | | - | | 5 | |
| (e) Legal System | - | | - | | - | | - | | 0 | |
| (f) Avoidance of Neg. Interest Rates | - | | - | | - | | 0 | | 4 | |
| | | | | | | | | | | |
| **III. Takings** | **7.8** | | **6.8** | | **6.0** | | **5.2** | | **6.1** | |
| (a) Transfers and Subsidies (% of GDP) | 8 | (2.3) | 9 | (2.0) | 7 | (4.5) | 5 | (5.8) | 6 | (5.3) |
| (b) Marginal Tax Rates (Top Rate) | 10 | (20) | 7 | (45) | 7 | (45) | 7 | (45) | 8 | (30) |
| (c) Conscription | 0 | | 0 | | 0 | | 0 | | 0 | |
| | | | | | | | | | | |
| **IV. International Sector** | **7.6** | | **7.8** | | **3.1** | | **7.6** | | **6.3** | |
| (a) Taxes on International Trade (Avg.) | 6 | (3.7) | 7 | (3.0) | 1 | (9.1) | 8 | (2.2) | 6 | (3.8) |
| (b) Black Market Exchange Rates (Prem.) | 10 | (0) | 10 | (0) | 3 | (25) | 10 | (0) | 8 | (1) |
| (c) Size of Trade Sector (% of GDP) | 6 | (50.7) | 5 | (50.7) | 4 | (40.7) | 7 | (59.6) | 6 | (54.3) |
| (d) Capital Transactions with Foreigners | 8 | | 8 | | 5 | | 5 | | 5 | |

222

## Part 2: Recent Economic Indicators:

| | | | | | |
|---|---|---|---|---|---|
| **Population 1994:** | 21.2 | **Real Per Capita GDP** : | | 1994= | $6,395 |
| (in millions) | | (in 1985 U.S. dollars) | | | |
| Annual Rate of Change (1980-94): | 2.6% | Avg. Growth Rate: | 1980-90= | -1.7% | |
| | | | 1985-94= | 0.2% | |

| Economic Indicators: | 1987 | 1988 | 1989 | 1990 | 1991 | 1992 | 1993 | 1994 |
|---|---|---|---|---|---|---|---|---|
| Change in Real GDP: Aggregate | 4.5 | 6.2 | -7.8 | 6.9 | 9.7 | 6.8 | -1.0 | -3.3 |
| : Per Capita | 1.9 | 3.6 | -10.4 | 4.3 | 7.1 | 4.2 | -3.6 | -6.9 |
| Inflation Rate (CPI) | 28.1 | 29.5 | 84.2 | 40.8 | 34.2 | 31.4 | 38.1 | 60.8 |
| Change in Money Supply: (M1) | 21.9 | 18.4 | 20.7 | 25.0 | 52.6 | 26.5 | -2.5 | 101.4 |
| : (M2) | 20.6 | 16.6 | 35.2 | 49.7 | 56.9 | 25.1 | 21.8 | 56.0 |
| Investment/GDP Ratio | 25.2 | 27.9 | 12.9 | 10.2 | 18.7 | 23.2 | 18.0 | 15.8 |
| Central Government Budget Deficit (-) or Surplus (+) As a Percent of GDP | -5.9 | -7.7 | -1.6 | +1.1 | +4.4 | -3.2 | -3.0 | - |
| Unemployment Rate | 9.1 | 7.3 | 9.2 | 10.4 | 9.5 | 7.8 | - | - |

While most South American countries have been moving toward greater economic freedom, Venezuela is a clear exception to the trend. In 1975, Venezuela's 6.9 Is1 summary rating placed it as the 5th freest economy in the world. Since that time, the freedom rating of this economy has gone steadily down. In 1993-1995, Venezuela's 4.5 Is1 summary rating placed it in a tie with India and Kenya for 63rd place. Based on the average of our three indexes, Venezuela's ranking is even lower, 75th. Except for Brazil, Venezuela now has the least free economy in South America.

Why did Venezuela's rating decline? The major contributing factors were: monetary and price instability, removal in the early 1990s of the freedom to maintain foreign currency bank accounts, and increased use of price controls. Low ratings for the widespread use of public sector enterprises, a weak and often arbitrary legal system, interest rate controls, and conscription also pull down the summary rating. There are a few bright spots. The size of government consumption as a share of GDP is relatively small and the top marginal tax rate is only 30%, down from 45% in 1990.

A fall in income has accompanied Venezuela's decline in economic freedom. Its 1994 per capita GDP ($6,395) was almost 15% less than the 1980 figure ($7,401). If prosperity is going to return to this economy, Venezuela would do well to emulate several of its neighbors—Chile and Peru, for example—and begin moving toward a freer economy.

# ZAIRE

## Part 1: The Economic Freedom Ratings for the Components and Various Area and Summary Indexes: 1975, 1980, 1985, 1990 and 1993-95.

(The numbers in parentheses indicate the actual values for the components.)

### Summary Ratings

|         | Ie  | Is1 | Is2 |
|---------|-----|-----|-----|
| 1975    | 3.2 | 3.6 | 2.3 |
| 1980    | 3.1 | 3.5 | 2.0 |
| 1985    | 3.5 | 3.3 | 2.9 |
| 1990    | 2.8 | 3.4 | 1.9 |
| 1993-95 | 1.8 | 1.9 | 2.0 |

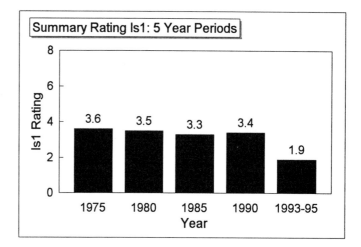

Summary Rating Is1: 5 Year Periods

| Components of Economic Freedom | 1975 | | 1980 | | 1985 | | 1990 | | 1993-95 | |
|---|---|---|---|---|---|---|---|---|---|---|
| **I. Money and Inflation** | **2.3** | | **0.6** | | **0.3** | | **0.3** | | **0.0** | |
| (a) Annual Money Growth (last 5 yrs.) | 2 | (17.1) | 1 | (22.3) | 0 | (52.7) | 0 | (99.1) | 0 | (550.0) |
| (b) Inflation Variablity (last 5 yrs.) | 5 | (4.0) | 1 | (25.8) | 1 | (25.1) | 1 | (28.0) | 0 | (8765.4) |
| (c) Ownership of Foreign Currency | 0 | | 0 | | 0 | | 0 | | 0 | |
| (d) Maint. of Bank Account Abroad | 0 | | 0 | | 0 | | 0 | | 0 | |
| | | | | | | | | | | |
| **II. Government Operation** | **4.4** | | **5.4** | | **4.7** | | **3.5** | | **1.5** | |
| (a) Govern. Consumption (% of GDP) | 7 | (11.6) | 9 | (8.4) | 10 | (7.7) | 7 | (11.5) | 1 | (21.7) |
| (b) Government Enterprises | 2 | | 2 | | 2 | | 2 | | 2 | |
| (c) Price Controls | - | | - | | - | | - | | - | |
| (d) Entry Into Business | - | | - | | - | | - | | 2.5 | |
| (e) Legal System | - | | - | | - | | - | | 0 | |
| (f) Avoidance of Neg. Interest Rates | - | | - | | - | | - | | - | |
| | | | | | | | | | | |
| **III. Takings** | **6.3** | | **5.8** | | **3.0** | | **5.8** | | **3.0** | |
| (a) Transfers and Subsidies (% of GDP) | 10 | (1.0) | 10 | (0.6) | - | | 10 | (1.0) | - | |
| (b) Marginal Tax Rates (Top Rate) | 2 | (60) | 1 | (60) | 1 | (60) | 1 | (60) | 1 | (60) |
| (c) Conscription | 10 | | 10 | | 10 | | 10 | | 10 | |
| | | | | | | | | | | |
| **IV. International Sector** | **1.0** | | **1.6** | | **4.3** | | **1.9** | | **3.5** | |
| (a) Taxes on International Trade (Avg.) | 0 | (19.0) | 1 | (10.3) | 2 | (8.4) | 1 | (9.1) | - | |
| (b) Black Market Exchange Rates (Prem.) | 1 | (120) | 1 | (131) | 6 | (6) | 4 | (20) | 5 | (9) |
| (c) Size of Trade Sector (% of GDP) | 1 | (25.1) | 3 | (32.0) | 9 | (53.1) | 0 | (18.6) | - | |
| (d) Capital Transactions with Foreigners | 2 | | 2 | | 2 | | 2 | | 2 | |

224

## Part 2:  Recent Economic Indicators:

| | | | | | | | | |
|---|---|---|---|---|---|---|---|---|
| **Population 1994:** | 42.0 | | **Real Per Capita GDP** [a] **:** | | | 1992 = | $300 (est.) | |
| (in millions) | | | (in 1985 U.S. dollars) | | | | | |
| Annual Rate of Change (1980-94): | 3.0% | | Avg. Growth Rate: | | | 1980-90 = | -2.0% | |
| | | | | | | 1985-92 = | -5.3% | |

| Economic Indicators: | 1987 | 1988 | 1989 | 1990 | 1991 | 1992 | 1993 | 1994 |
|---|---|---|---|---|---|---|---|---|
| Change in Real GDP:Aggregate | 2.6 | 0.6 | -1.4 | -2.5 | -12.3 | -10.4 | - | |
| : Per Capita | -0.4 | -2.4 | -4.4 | -5.5 | -15.3 | -13.4 | | |
| Inflation Rate (CPI) | 90.4 | 82.7 | 104.1 | 81.3 | 2154.4 | 4129.2 | 1986.9 | 23773.0 |
| Change in Money Supply: (M1) | 79.7 | 97.7 | 105.3 | 86.7 | 1083.4 | 5497.6 | 1658.0 | 8377.0 |
| : (M2) | 82.6 | 99.0 | 105.9 | 94.1 | 1171.1 | 4987.5 | 1716.5 | |
| Investment/GDP Ratio | 14.2 | 14.4 | 14.3 | 9.1 | 5.6 | 6.9 | - | |
| Central Government Budget Deficit (-) or Surplus (+) As a Percent of GDP | - | - | -8.0 | - | -6.5 | -14.4 | -12.1 | - |
| Unemployment Rate* | | | | | | | | |

a  Derived by purchasing power parity method.

In 1993-1995, this country ranked last among the 102 nations that we were able to rate.  It is easy to see why.  Economic freedom is restricted in almost every area.  Monetary expansion of more than 1,000% per year has led to hyperinflation.  Citizens are prohibited from using other currencies.  Government expenditures consume more than one-fifth of GDP.  The legal structure is arbitrary (it is under the control of an authoritarian political regime) and corrupt.  Restrictions abound.  Interest and exchange rate controls, restrictions on entry into business, political control of capital movements, and  high marginal tax rates (the top rate is currently 60%) are all part of this economic tragedy.  This is a politically controlled economy run by an authoritarian leader.

The results have been tragic.  Already one of the world's poorest nations,  income  has persistently declined during the last two decades. Per capita GDP is now approximately one-half the figure of the mid-1970s.  Until there is a dramatic change in political and economic structure, the suffering will continue.

# ZIMBABWE

## Part 1: The Economic Freedom Ratings for the Components and Various Area and Summary Indexes: 1975, 1980, 1985, 1990 and 1993-95.

(The numbers in parentheses indicate the actual values for the components.)

### Summary Ratings

| | Ie | Is1 | Is2 |
|---|---|---|---|
| 1975 | N/R | N/R | N/R |
| 1980 | 3.7 | 3.7 | 3.4 |
| 1985 | 3.0 | 2.6 | 2.9 |
| 1990 | 2.6 | 2.3 | 2.6 |
| 1993-95 | 3.5 | 3.4 | 3.3 |

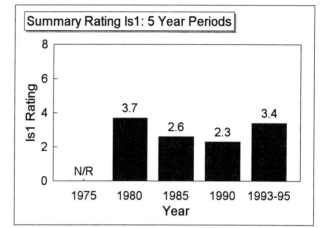

Summary Rating Is1: 5 Year Periods

| Components of Economic Freedom | 1975 | | 1980 | | 1985 | | 1990 | | 1993-95 | |
|---|---|---|---|---|---|---|---|---|---|---|
| **I. Money and Inflation** | **3.4** | | **3.3** | | **3.1** | | **1.9** | | **1.3** | |
| (a) Annual Money Growth (last 5 yrs.) | - | | 3 | (11.5) | 6 | (7.4) | 2 | (15.8) | 1 | (29.4) |
| (b) Inflation Variablity (last 5 yrs.) | 7 | (2.7) | 7 | (2.7) | 4 | (5.5) | 4 | (5.7) | 3 | (7.0) |
| (c) Ownership of Foreign Currency | 0 | | 0 | | 0 | | 0 | | 0 | |
| (d) Maint. of Bank Account Abroad | 0 | | 0 | | 0 | | 0 | | 0 | |
| | | | | | | | | | | |
| **II. Government Operation** | **5.5** | | **3.3** | | **3.7** | | **3.2** | | **3.6** | |
| (a) Govern. Consumption (% of GDP) | 7 | (12.8) | 1 | (19.7) | 1 | (21.5) | 1 | (22.5) | 2 | (18.8) |
| (b) Government Enterprises | 4 | | 4 | | 4 | | 4 | | 4 | |
| (c) Price Controls | - | | - | | - | | 2 | | 2 | |
| (d) Entry Into Business | - | | - | | - | | - | | 5.0 | |
| (e) Legal System | - | | - | | - | | - | | 2.5 | |
| (f) Avoidance of Negative Interest Rates | - | | 6 | | 8 | | 8 | | 8 | |
| | | | | | | | | | | |
| **III. Takings** | | | **3.5** | | **1.6** | | **0.8** | | **2.3** | |
| (a) Transfers and Subsidies (% of GDP) | - | | 3 | (11.4) | 4 | (10.0) | - | | - | |
| (b) Marginal Tax Rates (Top Rate) | - | | 5 | (45) | 0 | (63) | 1 | (60) | 3 | (50) |
| (c) Conscription | - | | 0 | | 0 | | 0 | | 0 | |
| | | | | | | | | | | |
| **IV. International Sector** | **5.5** | | **4.3** | | **2.7** | | **2.9** | | **6.0** | |
| (a) Taxes on International Trade (Avg.) | 8 | (2.1) | 8 | (1.7) | 2 | (8.0) | 1 | (9.2) | - | |
| (b) Black Market Exchange Rates (Prem) | 2 | (54) | 1 | (84) | 2 | (42) | 4 | (15) | 8 | (1) |
| (c) Size of Trade Sector (% of GDP) | 7 | (60.2) | 7 | (63.6) | 6 | (56.4) | 6 | (59.0) | 9 | (74.8) |
| (d) Capital Transactions with Foreigners | - | | 2 | | 2 | | 2 | | 2 | |

## Part 2: Recent Economic Indicators:

| Population 1994: | 11.0 | **Real Per Capita GDP :** | 1992 = | $1,162 |
| (in millions) | | (in 1985 U.S. dollars) | | |
| Annual Rate of Change (1980-94): | 3.3% | Avg. Growth Rate: | 1980-90 = | |
| | | | 1985-92 = | -0.8% |

| Economic Indicators: | 1987 | 1988 | 1989 | 1990 | 1991 | 1992 | 1993 | 1994 |
|---|---|---|---|---|---|---|---|---|
| Change in Real GDP:Aggregate | -1.0 | 9.2 | 5.0 | 3.4 | 8.8 | -3.6 | - | |
| : Per Capita | -4.3 | 5.9 | 1.7 | 0.1 | 5.5 | -6.9 | | |
| Inflation Rate (CPI) | 12.5 | 7.4 | 12.9 | 17.4 | 23.3 | 42.1 | 27.6 | 22.3 |
| Change in Money Supply: (M1) | 8.5 | 25.3 | 20.0 | 26.6 | 34.2 | 11.6 | 39.0 | 58.0 |
| : (M2) | 8.7 | 24.2 | 23.2 | 18.4 | 18.9 | 1.3 | 37.9 | 54.7 |
| Investment/GDP Ratio | 18.5 | 17.0 | 19.8 | - | - | - | - | - |
| Central Government Budget | | | | | | | | |
| Deficit (-) or Surplus (+) | | | | | | | | |
| As a Percent of GDP | -8.1 | -11.1 | -10.0 | -9.2 | -8.0 | - | - | - |
| Unemployment Rate | - | - | - | - | - | - | - | - |

This country has consistently followed policies that conflict with economic freedom. Even through its 1993-1995 summary ratings increased by approximately a point, Zimbabwe still ranked 85th among the 102 nations we were able to rate. Excessive monetary expansion (the M1 money supply has increased at an annual rate of approximately 30% in recent years) has fueled inflation. Use of foreign currencies is restricted. Government consumption takes approximately 20% of GDP, an exceedingly high figure for a poor less developed nation. Government enterprises operate in many sectors of the economy. The legal system is authoritarian and provides little protection for the property rights of either blacks or the few whites who remain. Price controls, foreign exchange controls, and restrictions on capital movements are also part of this economic tragedy.

Per capita GDP has declined during the last decade and there is no hope for improvement until there is a dramatic shift in policies and institutional arrangements.

# Appendix I:

# The Ratings for Each of the Components

# and the Summary Ratings for 1990,

# 1985, 1980 and 1975

*List of Tables—Appendix I*

## Table A1-1: Component and Summary Index Ratings: 1990

| INDUSTRIAL COUNTRIES | I A | I B | I C | I D | II A | II B | II C | II F | III A | III B | III C | IV A | IV B | IV C | IV D | Summary Ratings (Ie) | (Is1) | (Is2) |
|---|---|---|---|---|---|---|---|---|---|---|---|---|---|---|---|---|---|---|
| United States | 9 | 10 | 10 | 10 | 2 | 8 | 8 | 10 | 3 | 7 | 10 | 9 | 10 | 3 | 10 | 7.8 | 7.4 | 8.7 |
| Canada | 8 | 10 | 10 | 10 | 1 | 6 | 8 | 10 | 2 | 5 | 10 | 9 | 10 | 9 | 8 | 7.5 | 6.9 | 8.5 |
| Australia | 3 | 9 | 10 | 10 | 2 | 6 | 6 | 10 | 3 | 3 | 10 | 7 | 10 | 5 | 8 | 6.5 | 6.0 | 7.3 |
| Japan | 9 | 10 | 10 | 10 | 9 | 8 | 6 | 10 | 4 | 2 | 10 | 9 | 10 | 1 | 8 | 7.4 | 6.9 | 7.9 |
| New Zealand | 1 | 4 | 10 | 10 | 3 | 6 | 9 | 10 | 0 | 7 | 10 | 8 | 6 | 4 | 10 | 6.4 | 6.0 | 7.2 |
| Austria | 8 | 10 | 10 | 10 | 2 | 2 | 5 | 10 | 0 | 4 | 0 | 9 | 10 | 8 | 5 | 6.0 | 5.4 | 6.7 |
| Belgium | 9 | 10 | 10 | 10 | 5 | 6 | 2 | 10 | 0 | 2 | 0 | 10 | 10 | 10 | 10 | 6.7 | 5.9 | 7.5 |
| Denmark | 6 | 10 | 10 | 10 | 0 | 4 | 6 | 10 | 0 | 0 | 0 | 10 | 10 | 3 | 5 | 5.4 | 4.6 | 6.4 |
| Finland | 7 | 10 | 10 | 10 | 1 | 6 | 6 | 10 | 2 | 0 | 0 | 9 | 10 | 2 | 2 | 5.5 | 4.8 | 6.3 |
| France | 9 | 10 | 10 | 10 | 2 | 6 | 6 | 8 | 0 | 3 | 0 | 10 | 10 | 5 | 5 | 6.2 | 5.5 | 7.0 |
| Germany | 5 | 10 | 10 | 10 | 2 | 6 | 9 | 10 | 2 | 3 | 0 | 10 | 10 | 8 | 10 | 7.0 | 6.3 | 7.8 |
| Iceland | 1 | 6 | 10 | 10 | 1 | 4 | - | 6 | 4 | - | 10 | 6 | 6 | 2 | 2 | 4.8 | 4.7 | 5.4 |
| Ireland | 8 | 7 | 0 | 0 | 5 | 4 | 7 | 10 | 2 | 1 | 10 | 7 | 8 | 8 | 5 | 5.5 | 5.0 | 5.7 |
| Italy | 7 | 10 | 10 | 10 | 3 | 2 | 5 | 10 | 0 | 5 | 0 | 10 | 10 | 4 | 5 | 5.9 | 5.4 | 6.4 |
| Netherlands | 8 | 10 | 10 | 10 | 5 | 6 | 7 | 10 | 0 | 0 | 0 | 10 | 10 | 9 | 8 | 6.7 | 5.8 | 7.6 |
| Norway | 2 | 6 | 10 | 10 | 1 | 2 | 5 | 10 | 0 | 3 | 0 | 10 | 10 | 6 | 8 | 5.3 | 4.8 | 6.1 |
| Spain | 2 | 9 | 0 | 0 | 5 | 4 | 6 | 10 | 2 | 3 | 0 | 9 | 7 | 3 | 8 | 4.8 | 4.7 | 4.7 |
| Sweden | 7 | 9 | 10 | 0 | 0 | 4 | 6 | 10 | 0 | 0 | 0 | 9 | 8 | 5 | 10 | 5.2 | 4.5 | 5.8 |
| Switzerland | 10 | 10 | 10 | 10 | 6 | 8 | 7 | 10 | 2 | 8 | 0 | 8 | 10 | 5 | 10 | 7.7 | 7.3 | 8.2 |
| United Kingdom | 1 | 9 | 10 | 10 | 1 | 6 | 8 | 10 | 3 | 5 | 10 | 10 | 10 | 5 | 10 | 7.0 | 6.6 | 7.8 |

### CENTRAL/SOUTH AMERICA

| | I A | I B | I C | I D | II A | II B | II C | II F | III A | III B | III C | IV A | IV B | IV C | IV D | (Ie) | (Is1) | (Is2) |
|---|---|---|---|---|---|---|---|---|---|---|---|---|---|---|---|---|---|---|
| Argentina | 0 | 0 | 10 | 10 | 10 | 4 | 0 | 0 | 4 | 7 | 0 | 0 | 10 | 0 | 0 | 3.4 | 3.8 | 3.2 |
| Belize | 6 | 7 | 0 | 0 | 1 | 8 | - | 10 | 10 | 4 | 10 | 1 | 3 | 3 | 8 | 5.2 | 5.4 | 5.1 |
| Bolivia | 1 | 0 | 10 | 10 | 6 | 4 | 6 | 8 | 8 | 10 | 0 | 8 | 10 | 5 | 2 | 5.8 | 6.3 | 5.5 |
| Brazil | 0 | 0 | 0 | 0 | 5 | 2 | 0 | 0 | 3 | 9 | 0 | 6 | 4 | 0 | 0 | 2.1 | 2.9 | 1.4 |
| Chile | 1 | 6 | 10 | 10 | 9 | 8 | 8 | 8 | 4 | 3 | 0 | 6 | 10 | 7 | 2 | 6.1 | 5.7 | 6.3 |
| Colombia | 1 | 8 | 0 | 0 | 8 | 4 | 6 | 8 | 7 | 8 | 0 | 3 | 4 | 3 | 0 | 4.4 | 4.8 | 3.5 |
| Costa Rica | 3 | 6 | 10 | 10 | 2 | 8 | - | 8 | 6 | 9 | 10 | 4 | 10 | 3 | 5 | 6.5 | 6.6 | 7.1 |
| Dominican Rep | 1 | 1 | 0 | 0 | 9 | 6 | 4 | - | 9 | 0 | 10 | 2 | 1 | 2 | 2 | 3.4 | 3.6 | 2.7 |
| Ecuador | 1 | 1 | 10 | 10 | 9 | 6 | 0 | 0 | 7 | 5 | 0 | 6 | 10 | 5 | 2 | 4.6 | 4.9 | 4.3 |
| El Salvador | 3 | 2 | 0 | 0 | 7 | 8 | - | 8 | 10 | 2 | 0 | 6 | 3 | 0 | 2 | 4.0 | 4.3 | 3.1 |
| Guatemala | 2 | 1 | 10 | 10 | 10 | 8 | 6 | 8 | 9 | 7 | 0 | 7 | 10 | 1 | 5 | 6.3 | 6.6 | 6.0 |
| Haiti | 5 | 3 | 10 | 10 | - | 6 | 2 | - | - | 9 | 10 | 4 | 7 | 0 | 0 | 5.1 | 5.4 | 5.2 |
| Honduras | 2 | 3 | 10 | 10 | 7 | 8 | - | 8 | 9 | 5 | 0 | - | 10 | 5 | 0 | 5.9 | 6.0 | 5.7 |
| Jamaica | 2 | 4 | 0 | 0 | 6 | 4 | 4 | 8 | 9 | 7 | 10 | - | 3 | 5 | 2 | 4.7 | 5.2 | 3.8 |
| Mexico | 0 | 0 | 10 | 10 | 9 | 4 | 0 | 8 | 5 | 7 | 0 | 8 | 10 | 4 | 5 | 5.1 | 5.3 | 4.8 |
| Nicaragua | 0 | 0 | 0 | 0 | 0 | 0 | - | 0 | 5 | - | 0 | 6 | 4 | 4 | 0 | 1.5 | 2.0 | 1.1 |
| Panama | 10 | 10 | 10 | 10 | 2 | 6 | 2 | 10 | 5 | 3 | 10 | 6 | 10 | 3 | 10 | 6.7 | 6.3 | 7.5 |

230

| CENTRAL/- SOUTH AMERICA (con't) | I A | B | C | D | II A | B | C | F | III A | B | C | IV A | B | C | D | Summary Ratings (Ie) | (Is1) | (Is2) |
|---|---|---|---|---|---|---|---|---|---|---|---|---|---|---|---|---|---|---|
| Paraguay | 1 | 6 | 10 | 10 | 10 | 8 | 4 | 2 | 9 | 8 | 0 | 7 | 3 | 8 | 5 | 6.1 | 6.4 | 5.6 |
| Peru | 0 | 0 | 10 | 0 | 10 | 4 | 2 | 0 | 8 | 4 | 0 | 6 | 4 | 1 | 2 | 3.4 | 4.0 | 2.4 |
| Trinidad/Tobago | 8 | 4 | 0 | 0 | 4 | 2 | 4 | 6 | 4 | 7 | 10 | 7 | 2 | 1 | 0 | 4.0 | 4.3 | 3.5 |
| Uruguay | 0 | 2 | 10 | 10 | 6 | 6 | 4 | 8 | 3 | 10 | 10 | 6 | 10 | 1 | 10 | 6.1 | 6.3 | 6.5 |
| Venezuela | 2 | 1 | 10 | 10 | 9 | 2 | 4 | 0 | 5 | 7 | 0 | 8 | 10 | 7 | 5 | 5.2 | 5.5 | 5.0 |
| **EUROPE/MIDDLE EAST** | | | | | | | | | | | | | | | | | | |
| Bulgaria | 3 | 2 | 0 | 0 | 2 | 0 | 0 | - | 0 | - | 0 | 9 | 1 | 4 | 0 | 1.7 | 1.6 | 1.4 |
| Cyprus | 9 | 10 | 0 | 0 | 6 | 6 | 0 | 10 | 4 | 0 | 0 | 6 | 6 | 2 | 0 | 4.0 | 3.8 | 3.7 |
| Czechoslovakia | 10 | 5 | 0 | 0 | 1 | 0 | 0 | - | 0 | 4 | 0 | 6 | 2 | 6 | 0 | 2.5 | 2.4 | 2.4 |
| Czech Rep | - | - | - | - | - | - | - | - | - | - | - | - | - | - | - | N/R | N/R | N/R |
| Slovakia | - | - | - | - | - | - | - | - | - | - | - | - | - | - | - | N/R | N/R | N/R |
| Egypt | 6 | 9 | 10 | 10 | 7 | 2 | 2 | 6 | 4 | 2 | 0 | 5 | 2 | 10 | 0 | 4.7 | 4.2 | 4.7 |
| Greece | 2 | 7 | 10 | 0 | 1 | 2 | 0 | 8 | 0 | 4 | 0 | 10 | 6 | 3 | 2 | 3.5 | 3.4 | 3.5 |
| Hungary | 3 | 3 | 0 | 0 | 8 | 0 | 6 | 6 | 0 | 3 | 0 | 6 | 4 | 5 | 0 | 3.1 | 3.0 | 2.7 |
| Iran | 2 | 6 | 10 | 10 | 7 | 2 | 2 | - | 7 | 0 | 0 | 3 | 0 | 4 | 0 | 3.2 | 3.2 | 3.0 |
| Israel | 1 | 2 | 10 | 0 | 0 | 2 | 0 | 6 | 2 | 4 | 0 | 9 | 6 | 2 | 2 | 2.9 | 3.0 | 2.8 |
| Jordan | 5 | 2 | 0 | 0 | 0 | 6 | 2 | 4 | 7 | 5 | 10 | 6 | 4 | 10 | 2 | 4.2 | 4.4 | 4.1 |
| Malta | 10 | 10 | 0 | 0 | 2 | 4 | 0 | 10 | 2 | 0 | 10 | 6 | 7 | 4 | 2 | 4.3 | 3.8 | 4.5 |
| Poland | 0 | 0 | 10 | 10 | 9 | 0 | 2 | 0 | 5 | - | 0 | - | 5 | 4 | 0 | 3.1 | 3.3 | 2.7 |
| Portugal | 2 | 6 | 0 | 0 | 3 | 2 | 4 | 8 | 2 | 5 | 0 | 9 | 6 | 6 | 5 | 4.1 | 4.1 | 3.9 |
| Romania | 6 | 3 | 0 | 0 | 6 | 0 | 0 | - | 1 | - | 0 | 9 | 0 | 1 | 0 | 2.1 | 2.2 | 1.5 |
| Syria | 2 | 6 | 10 | 0 | 5 | 2 | - | - | - | - | 0 | 7 | 0 | 4 | 0 | 3.2 | 3.2 | 2.6 |
| Turkey | 0 | 1 | 10 | 10 | 6 | 4 | 6 | 2 | 7 | 4 | 0 | 7 | 7 | 5 | 0 | 4.5 | 4.6 | 4.4 |
| **ASIA** | | | | | | | | | | | | | | | | | | |
| Bangladesh | 9 | 8 | 0 | 0 | 6 | 6 | 0 | 10 | - | - | 10 | 1 | 1 | 1 | 0 | 4.0 | 3.8 | 3.6 |
| Fiji | 3 | 9 | 0 | 0 | 3 | 6 | 6 | 6 | 10 | 3 | 10 | 4 | 6 | 8 | 2 | 5.2 | 5.3 | 4.8 |
| Hong Kong | 4 | 7 | 10 | 10 | 10 | 10 | 10 | - | 10 | 9 | 10 | 9 | 10 | 10 | 10 | 9.2 | 9.3 | 9.2 |
| India | 5 | 9 | 0 | 0 | 7 | 0 | 3 | 8 | 5 | 2 | 10 | 0 | 4 | 3 | 2 | 3.7 | 3.7 | 3.3 |
| Indonesia | 3 | 4 | 10 | 10 | 9 | 2 | 6 | 10 | 9 | 7 | 0 | 8 | 10 | 10 | 2 | 6.5 | 6.6 | 6.0 |
| Malaysia | 7 | 4 | 10 | 10 | 6 | 6 | 5 | 10 | 8 | 6 | 10 | 7 | 10 | 10 | 5 | 7.3 | 7.1 | 7.4 |
| Nepal | 2 | 9 | 0 | 0 | 7 | 4 | - | 10 | - | - | 10 | 2 | 4 | 1 | 0 | 4.1 | 4.1 | 3.6 |
| Pakistan | 5 | 8 | 10 | 0 | 5 | 4 | - | 6 | - | 3 | 10 | 0 | 4 | 4 | 2 | 4.5 | 4.2 | 4.3 |
| Philippines | 2 | 6 | 0 | 0 | 8 | 4 | 2 | 10 | 10 | 7 | 10 | 4 | 5 | 10 | 2 | 5.4 | 5.7 | 4.4 |
| Singapore | 8 | 7 | 10 | 10 | 8 | 8 | 8 | 10 | 8 | 9 | 0 | 10 | 10 | 10 | 10 | 8.5 | 8.5 | 8.5 |
| South Korea | 7 | 2 | 0 | 0 | 8 | 6 | 3 | 10 | 8 | 3 | 0 | 7 | 8 | 6 | 5 | 5.1 | 5.2 | 4.5 |
| Sri Lanka | 3 | 5 | 0 | 0 | 9 | 4 | - | 8 | 5 | - | 10 | 2 | 3 | 5 | 0 | 4.2 | 4.2 | 3.4 |
| Taiwan | 3 | 9 | 10 | 10 | 2 | 4 | 6 | 10 | 6 | 5 | 0 | 8 | 10 | 5 | 5 | 6.1 | 5.9 | 6.4 |
| Thailand | 5 | 9 | 10 | 0 | 9 | 6 | 4 | 8 | 10 | 4 | 0 | 6 | 10 | 10 | 2 | 6.2 | 6.3 | 5.5 |

231

| | I | | | | II | | | | III | | | IV | | | | Summary Ratings | | |
|---|---|---|---|---|---|---|---|---|---|---|---|---|---|---|---|---|---|---|
| | A | B | C | D | A | B | C | F | A | B | C | A | B | C | D | (Ie) | (Is1) | (Is2) |
| **AFRICA** | | | | | | | | | | | | | | | | | | |
| Algeria | 9 | 2 | 0 | 0 | 3 | 4 | - | - | - | - | 0 | - | 1 | 7 | 0 | 2.9 * | 2.7 * | 2.6 * |
| Benin | 10 | 8 | 0 | 0 | 6 | 4 | - | 8 | - | - | 0 | - | 6 | 2 | 0 | 4.3 | 4.4 | 3.8 |
| Botswana | 2 | 2 | 0 | 0 | 2 | 6 | 6 | 4 | 5 | 3 | 10 | 4 | 5 | 10 | 5 | 4.4 | 4.3 | 4.4 |
| Burundi | 10 | 3 | 0 | 0 | 8 | 4 | - | - | - | - | 10 | 0 | 6 | 0 | 0 | 3.7 | 3.9 | 3.4 |
| Cameroon | 9 | 5 | 0 | 0 | 7 | 4 | 2 | 8 | 8 | 1 | 10 | 6 | 6 | 2 | 0 | 4.4 | 4.5 | 3.9 |
| C African Rep | 10 | 3 | 0 | 0 | 8 | 6 | - | 10 | - | - | 0 | 1 | 6 | 3 | 0 | 4.3 | .4.2 | 3.7 |
| Chad | 7 | 3 | 0 | 0 | 1 | 4 | - | 8 | 10 | - | 0 | 6 | 6 | 8 | 0 | 4.4 | 4.7 | 3.7 |
| Congo Peoples | 8 | 1 | 0 | 0 | 2 | 0 | 0 | 10 | - | 4 | 10 | - | 6 | 6 | 0 | 3.4 | 3.3 | 3.1 |
| Cote d' Ivoire | 9 | 7 | 0 | 0 | 2 | 4 | - | 8 | - | 4 | 0 | 1 | 6 | 5 | 0 | 3.8 | 3.7 | 3.7 |
| Gabon | 10 | 2 | 0 | 0 | 3 | 6 | - | 8 | 10 | 1 | 10 | 6 | 6 | 5 | 0 | 4.8 | 4.9 | 4.4 |
| Ghana | 1 | 5 | 10 | 0 | 8 | 2 | 0 | 2 | 8 | 2 | 10 | 1 | 5 | 1 | 0 | 3.3 | 3.6 | 2.6 |
| Kenya | 3 | 9 | 0 | 0 | 2 | 4 | 2 | 10 | 8 | 3 | 10 | 4 | 6 | 6 | 0 | 4.4 | 4.5 | 4.0 |
| Madagascar | 2 | 5 | 0 | 0 | 10 | 6 | - | - | 9 | - | 0 | 0 | 5 | 5 | 0 | 3.9 | 4.4 | 2.7 |
| Malawi | 1 | 4 | 0 | 0 | 5 | 4 | 2 | 6 | 8 | 3 | 10 | 5 | 4 | 3 | 2 | 3.8 | 4.1 | 3.2 |
| Mali | 7 | 5 | 0 | 0 | 6 | 4 | - | 8 | 10 | - | 0 | 6 | 6 | 6 | 2 | 4.9 | 5.4 | 4.0 |
| Mauritius | 2 | 10 | 0 | 0 | 7 | 6 | - | 8 | 7 | 7 | 10 | 3 | 5 | 6 | 2 | 5.4 | 5.6 | 4.8 |
| Morocco | 5 | 7 | 0 | 0 | 5 | 2 | 0 | 0 | 8 | 0 | 0 | 2 | 4 | 6 | 5 | 3.0 | 3.2 | 2.5 |
| Niger | 10 | 4 | 0 | 0 | 5 | 6 | - | - | - | - | 0 | - | 6 | 3 | 0 | 3.8 | 3.9 | 3.5 |
| Nigeria | 2 | 1 | 0 | 0 | 7 | 2 | 4 | 0 | - | 2 | 10 | 6 | 3 | 10 | 0 | 3.3 * | 3.3 * | 2.9 * |
| Rwanda | 10 | 6 | 0 | 0 | 5 | 6 | - | 10 | 8 | - | 10 | 0 | 3 | 0 | 0 | 4.6 | 4.7 | 4.1 |
| Senegal | 9 | 7 | 0 | 0 | 5 | 6 | 4 | 8 | - | 4 | 0 | - | 6 | 3 | 0 | 4.3 | 4.3 | 4.0 |
| Sierra Leone | 0 | 0 | 0 | 0 | 10 | 6 | 2 | 0 | 9 | - | 10 | 5 | 1 | 1 | 0 | 3.2 | 3.9 | 2.2 |
| Somalia | 0 | 0 | 0 | 0 | - | 4 | 0 | 0 | - | - | 0 | - | 1 | 3 | 0 | 0.9 | 0.8 | 0.9 |
| South Africa | 2 | 10 | 0 | 0 | 1 | 4 | 4 | 8 | 6 | 5 | 0 | 8 | 6 | 6 | 2 | 4.4 | 4.6 | 4.1 |
| Tanzania | 1 | 2 | 0 | 0 | 8 | 0 | 0 | 4 | - | 3 | 0 | - | 1 | 10 | 0 | 2.3 | 2.3 | 1.5 |
| Togo | 9 | 9 | 0 | 0 | 5 | 4 | 2 | 8 | - | - | 0 | 1 | 6 | 4 | 0 | 3.9 | 3.8 | 3.6 |
| Tunisia | 10 | 9 | 0 | 0 | 4 | 4 | 4 | - | 4 | - | 0 | 1 | 5 | 8 | 5 | 4.5 | 4.3 | 4.3 |
| Uganda | 0 | 0 | 0 | 0 | 9 | 2 | - | 0 | - | 3 | 10 | - | 2 | 1 | 0 | 2.2 | 2.5 | 1.5 |
| Zaire | 0 | 1 | 0 | 0 | 7 | 2 | - | - | 10 | 1 | 10 | 1 | 4 | 0 | 2 | 2.8 | 3.4 | 1.9 |
| Zambia | 0 | 1 | 0 | 0 | 2 | 0 | 0 | 0 | - | 0 | 10 | 6 | 0 | 9 | 2 | 1.9 | 1.8 | 1.8 |
| Zimbabwe | 2 | 4 | 0 | 0 | 1 | 4 | 2 | 8 | - | 1 | 0 | 1 | 4 | 6 | 2 | 2.6 | 2.3 | 2.6 |

* These summary ratings should be interpreted with caution because they are based on data for only ten of the potential fifteen components in the index for this year.

## Table A1-2: Component and Summary Index Ratings: 1985

| INDUSTRIAL COUNTRIES | I A | B | C | D | II A | B | F | III A | B | C | IV A | B | C | D | Summary Ratings (Ie) | (Is1) | (Is2) |
|---|---|---|---|---|---|---|---|---|---|---|---|---|---|---|---|---|---|
| United States | 7 | 8 | 10 | 10 | 2 | 8 | 10 | 3 | 4 | 10 | 8 | 10 | 2 | 10 | 7.0 | 6.5 | 8.1 |
| Canada | 4 | 6 | 10 | 10 | 1 | 6 | 10 | 2 | 3 | 10 | 8 | 10 | 10 | 8 | 6.7 | 5.9 | 7.7 |
| Australia | 8 | 8 | 10 | 10 | 2 | 6 | 10 | 3 | 2 | 10 | 7 | 10 | 6 | 5 | 6.6 | 5.9 | 7.5 |
| Japan | 10 | 10 | 10 | 0 | 9 | 8 | 10 | 4 | 1 | 10 | 9 | 10 | 3 | 5 | 6.9 | 6.5 | 7.0 |
| New Zealand | 5 | 6 | 0 | 0 | 4 | 6 | 8 | 1 | 0 | 10 | 8 | 6 | 6 | 5 | 4.6 | 4.1 | 4.9 |
| Austria | 9 | 10 | 10 | 0 | 2 | 2 | 10 | 0 | 2 | 0 | 9 | 10 | 9 | 2 | 5.3 | 4.6 | 5.5 |
| Belgium | 10 | 10 | 10 | 10 | 3 | 6 | 10 | 0 | 0 | 0 | 10 | 10 | 10 | 10 | 6.9 | 5.8 | 8.1 |
| Denmark | 3 | 8 | 0 | 0 | 0 | 4 | 10 | 1 | 0 | 0 | 10 | 10 | 4 | 5 | 4.1 | 3.7 | 4.4 |
| Finland | 4 | 9 | 10 | 0 | 1 | 6 | 10 | 2 | 1 | 0 | 9 | 10 | 4 | 2 | 4.9 | 4.4 | 5.1 |
| France | 6 | 8 | 0 | 0 | 1 | 4 | 8 | 0 | 1 | 0 | 10 | 6 | 6 | 2 | 3.9 | 3.4 | 4.1 |
| Germany | 9 | 10 | 10 | 10 | 1 | 6 | 10 | 1 | 2 | 0 | 10 | 10 | 9 | 10 | 6.9 | 6.0 | 8.0 |
| Iceland | 1 | 1 | 0 | 0 | 3 | 4 | 4 | 3 | - | 10 | 6 | 4 | 4 | 2 | 3.2 | 3.3 | 3.1 |
| Ireland | 9 | 5 | 0 | 0 | 2 | 4 | 10 | 1 | 0 | 10 | 8 | 6 | 9 | 5 | 4.9 | 4.2 | 5.3 |
| Italy | 5 | 6 | 0 | 0 | 4 | 2 | 6 | 0 | 0 | 0 | 10 | 10 | 6 | 5 | 4.0 | 3.6 | 4.1 |
| Netherlands | 8 | 9 | 10 | 10 | 4 | 6 | 10 | 0 | 0 | 0 | 10 | 10 | 10 | 8 | 6.6 | 5.6 | 7.6 |
| Norway | 3 | 6 | 0 | 0 | 2 | 2 | 10 | 1 | 1 | 0 | 10 | 10 | 8 | 5 | 4.3 | 3.9 | 4.4 |
| Spain | 5 | 9 | 0 | 0 | 5 | 4 | 10 | 2 | 1 | 0 | 7 | 7 | 5 | 5 | 4.5 | 4.1 | 4.4 |
| Sweden | 7 | 10 | 10 | 0 | 0 | 4 | 10 | 0 | 0 | 0 | 9 | 8 | 7 | 5 | 5.0 | 4.2 | 5.5 |
| Switzerland | 10 | 9 | 10 | 10 | 6 | 8 | 10 | 3 | 7 | 0 | 8 | 10 | 7 | 10 | 7.8 | 7.3 | 8.4 |
| United Kingdom | 4 | 7 | 10 | 10 | 1 | 6 | 10 | 2 | 2 | 10 | 10 | 10 | 8 | 10 | 6.8 | 6.0 | 7.9 |

### CENTRAL/SOUTH AMERICA

| | I A | B | C | D | II A | B | F | III A | B | C | IV A | B | C | D | (Ie) | (Is1) | (Is2) |
|---|---|---|---|---|---|---|---|---|---|---|---|---|---|---|---|---|---|
| Argentina | 0 | 0 | 10 | 10 | 7 | 4 | 0 | 3 | 2 | 0 | 0 | 2 | 1 | 0 | 2.5 | 2.5 | 2.6 |
| Belize | 8 | 3 | - | - | 0 | 8 | 8 | 8 | 4 | 10 | 1 | 1 | 2 | 8 | 5.0 | 4.9 | 5.5 |
| Bolivia | 0 | 0 | 0 | 0 | 6 | 4 | 0 | 9 | 8 | 0 | 4 | 5 | 2 | 2 | 3.2 | 4.2 | 2.2 |
| Brazil | 0 | 0 | 0 | 0 | 8 | 2 | 0 | 4 | 1 | 0 | 7 | 2 | 2 | 0 | 2.0 | 2.3 | 1.2 |
| Chile | 6 | 2 | 10 | 10 | 6 | 8 | 8 | 2 | 1 | 0 | 5 | 4 | 5 | 2 | 4.8 | 4.1 | 5.3 |
| Colombia | 2 | 9 | 10 | 0 | 8 | 4 | - | 7 | 5 | 0 | 3 | 5 | 1 | 0 | 4.2 | 4.6 | 3.3 |
| Costa Rica | 1 | 1 | 10 | 10 | 4 | 8 | 6 | 5 | 3 | 10 | 4 | 3 | 2 | 5 | 4.8 | 4.6 | 5.3 |
| Dominican Rep | 2 | 2 | 0 | 10 | 9 | 6 | - | 8 | 0 | 10 | 4 | 4 | 3 | 2 | 4.4 | 4.3 | 4.3 |
| Ecuador | 2 | 2 | 10 | 10 | 7 | 6 | 0 | 7 | 2 | 0 | 5 | 2 | 3 | 2 | 4.0 | 4.0 | 3.9 |
| El Salvador | 4 | 5 | 0 | 0 | 5 | 8 | 8 | 9 | 3 | 0 | 3 | 1 | 1 | 2 | 3.9 | 4.1 | 3.2 |
| Guatemala | 4 | 4 | 10 | 10 | 10 | 8 | 8 | 10 | 5 | 0 | 3 | 1 | 0 | 5 | 5.6 | 5.7 | 5.1 |
| Haiti | 5 | 6 | 10 | 10 | 7 | 6 | - | 5 | - | 10 | 2 | 2 | 0 | 0 | 4.9 | 4.8 | 5.0 |
| Honduras | 9 | 10 | 10 | 10 | 6 | 8 | 10 | 9 | 5 | 0 | - | 1 | 2 | 0 | 6.2 | 6.0 | 6.0 |
| Jamaica | 2 | 2 | 0 | 0 | 5 | 2 | 4 | 10 | 1 | 10 | 8 | 4 | 8 | 2 | 4.1 | 4.4 | 3.3 |
| Mexico | 0 | 1 | 10 | 10 | 9 | 2 | 4 | 5 | 4 | 0 | 7 | 3 | 2 | 2 | 4.0 | 4.1 | 3.7 |
| Nicaragua | 0 | 0 | 0 | 0 | 0 | 0 | - | 5 | 5 | 0 | 3 | 0 | 1 | 0 | 1.2 | 1.8 | 0.6 |
| Panama | 10 | 10 | 10 | 10 | 1 | 6 | - | 6 | 3 | 10 | 6 | 10 | 3 | 10 | 7.0 | 6.6 | 8.0 |

233

| CENTRAL/-SOUTH AMERICA (con't) | I A | B | C | D | II A | B | F | III A | B | C | IV A | B | C | D | Summary Ratings (Ie) | (Is1) | (Is2) |
|---|---|---|---|---|---|---|---|---|---|---|---|---|---|---|---|---|---|
| Paraquay | 5 | 3 | 10 | 10 | 10 | 8 | - | 9 | 8 | 0 | 8 | 0 | 4 | 5 | 6.2 | 6.5 | 5.7 |
| Peru | 0 | 0 | 10 | 0 | 9 | 4 | - | 9 | 0 | 0 | 2 | 2 | 4 | 2 | 3.2 | 3.4 | 2.2 |
| Trinidad/Tobago | 6 | 1 | 0 | 0 | 1 | 2 | 8 | 3 | 4 | 10 | 5 | 2 | 1 | 0 | 3.0 | 3.1 | 2.9 |
| Uruguay | 1 | 1 | 10 | 10 | 5 | 6 | 8 | 4 | 10 | 10 | 5 | 10 | 1 | 10 | 6.3 | 6.5 | 6.7 |
| Venezuela | 3 | 4 | 10 | 10 | 8 | 4 | - | 7 | 7 | 0 | 1 | 3 | 4 | 5 | 5.0 | 5.2 | 4.7 |
| **EUROPE/MIDDLE EAST** | | | | | | | | | | | | | | | | | |
| Bulgaria | - | 7 | 0 | 0 | 9 | 0 | - | 2 | - | 0 | 6 | 0 | 5 | 0 | 2.8 | 2.9 | 1.8 |
| Cyprus | 8 | 7 | 0 | 0 | 6 | 6 | 8 | 4 | 1 | 0 | 6 | 8 | 3 | 0 | 4.3 | 4.1 | 4.0 |
| Czechoslovakia | 9 | 8 | 0 | 0 | 1 | 0 | - | - | - | 0 | - | 0 | 7 | 0 | 2.7 * | 2.4 * | 2.4 * |
| Czech Rep | - | - | - | - | - | - | - | - | - | - | - | - | - | - | N/R | N/R | N/R |
| Slovakia | - | - | - | - | - | - | - | - | - | - | - | - | - | - | N/R | N/R | N/R |
| Egypt | 6 | 6 | 10 | 10 | 3 | 2 | 6 | 3 | 2 | 0 | 1 | 1 | 8 | 0 | 3.9 | 3.3 | 4.2 |
| Greece | 2 | 8 | 10 | 0 | 1 | 2 | 6 | 2 | 1 | 0 | 9 | 3 | 4 | 2 | 3.5 | 3.2 | 3.4 |
| Hungary | 8 | 10 | 0 | 0 | 8 | 0 | - | 0 | - | 0 | 6 | 0 | 9 | 0 | 3.6 | 3.3 | 3.0 |
| Iran | 1 | 3 | 10 | 10 | 5 | 2 | - | 8 | 0 | 0 | 0 | 0 | 0 | 0 | 2.6 | 2.7 | 2.5 |
| Israel | 0 | 0 | 10 | 0 | 0 | 2 | 0 | 1 | 3 | 0 | 7 | 5 | 5 | 2 | 2.4 | 2.5 | 2.5 |
| Jordan | 10 | 4 | 10 | 0 | 0 | 6 | - | 6 | - | 10 | 5 | 6 | 9 | 2 | 5.6 | 5.4 | 5.7 |
| Malta | 9 | 6 | 0 | 0 | 2 | 4 | 10 | 2 | 0 | 10 | 6 | 5 | 3 | 2 | 4.2 | 3.7 | 4.4 |
| Poland | 1 | 0 | 10 | 10 | 9 | 0 | - | 0 | - | 0 | 2 | 0 | 3 | 0 | 2.5 | 2.2 | 2.5 |
| Portugal | 3 | 7 | 0 | 0 | 5 | 2 | 10 | 1 | 0 | 0 | 9 | 7 | 7 | 2 | 3.9 | 3.5 | 3.7 |
| Romania | 9 | 5 | 0 | 0 | 10 | 0 | - | 4 | - | 0 | - | 0 | 1 | 0 | 3.1 | 3.2 | 1.9 |
| Syria | 2 | 4 | 10 | 10 | 0 | 2 | - | - | - | 0 | 6 | 0 | 1 | 0 | 2.8 | 2.7 | 3.3 |
| Turkey | 1 | 2 | 0 | 0 | 9 | 4 | 8 | 4 | 3 | 0 | 7 | 6 | 6 | 0 | 3.8 | 3.8 | 3.0 |
| **ASIA** | | | | | | | | | | | | | | | | | |
| Bangladesh | 3 | 7 | 0 | 0 | 10 | 6 | 6 | - | 1 | 10 | 0 | 1 | 1 | 0 | 3.5 | 3.3 | 3.0 |
| Fiji | 8 | 5 | 0 | 0 | 2 | 6 | 8 | 7 | 3 | 10 | 3 | 5 | 4 | 5 | 4.8 | 4.8 | 4.8 |
| Hong Kong | 9 | 7 | 10 | 10 | 10 | 10 | - | 10 | 9 | 10 | 9 | 10 | 10 | 10 | 9.5 | 9.5 | 9.5 |
| India | 4 | 10 | 0 | 0 | 7 | 0 | 8 | 5 | 0 | 10 | 0 | 4 | 2 | 2 | 3.5 | 3.4 | 3.1 |
| Indonesia | 5 | 7 | 10 | 10 | 7 | 2 | - | 8 | 7 | 0 | 8 | 5 | 9 | 2 | 6.0 | 6.1 | 5.6 |
| Malaysia | 10 | 7 | 10 | 0 | 5 | 6 | 10 | 8 | 6 | 10 | 5 | 10 | 10 | 5 | 7.2 | 7.1 | 7.0 |
| Nepal | 4 | 8 | 0 | 0 | 8 | 6 | 6 | - | - | 10 | 3 | 4 | 1 | 0 | 4.3 | 4.4 | 3.8 |
| Pakistan | 7 | 8 | 0 | 0 | 7 | 2 | 8 | - | 1 | 10 | 0 | 6 | 5 | 2 | 4.2 | 3.9 | 4.0 |
| Philippines | 6 | 1 | 0 | 0 | 10 | 4 | 4 | 10 | 1 | 10 | 5 | 5 | 8 | 2 | 4.7 | 4.9 | 3.8 |
| Singapore | 10 | 7 | 10 | 0 | 5 | 8 | 10 | 9 | 8 | 0 | 9 | 10 | 10 | 10 | 7.9 | 8.0 | 7.5 |
| South Korea | 7 | 5 | 0 | 0 | 8 | 6 | 10 | 9 | 2 | 0 | 7 | 4 | 8 | 2 | 5.2 | 5.1 | 4.3 |
| Sri Lanka | 5 | 3 | 0 | 0 | 8 | 4 | 8 | 6 | 0 | 10 | 1 | 4 | 5 | 0 | 3.8 | 3.6 | 3.3 |
| Taiwan | 7 | 5 | 10 | 10 | 4 | 4 | 10 | 8 | 3 | 0 | 7 | 6 | 7 | 2 | 5.8 | 5.5 | 5.8 |
| Thailand | 9 | 8 | 0 | 0 | 6 | 6 | 10 | 10 | 2 | 0 | 4 | 6 | 7 | 2 | 5.3 | 5.3 | 4.6 |

234

| | I | | | | II | | | III | | | IV | | | | Summary Ratings | | |
|---|---|---|---|---|---|---|---|---|---|---|---|---|---|---|---|---|---|
| | A | B | C | D | A | B | F | A | B | C | A | B | C | D | (Ie) | (Is1) | (Is2) |
| **AFRICA** | | | | | | | | | | | | | | | | | |
| Algeria | 3 | 5 | 0 | 0 | 4 | 4 | - | - | - | 0 | - | 0 | 6 | 0 | 2.5 * | 2.4 * | 2.1 * |
| Benin | 5 | 3 | 0 | 0 | 5 | 4 | 8 | - | - | 0 | - | 8 | 5 | 0 | 3.8 | 3.7 | 3.3 |
| Botswana | 8 | 2 | 0 | 0 | 0 | 8 | 8 | 5 | 2 | 10 | 3 | 4 | 10 | 5 | 4.7 | 4.4 | 5.1 |
| Burundi | 5 | 3 | 0 | 0 | 10 | 4 | 6 | - | - | 10 | 0 | 3 | 0 | 0 | 3.4 | 3.5 | 2.8 |
| Cameroon | 7 | 9 | 0 | 0 | 9 | 4 | 6 | 10 | 2 | 10 | 5 | 8 | 5 | 0 | 5.4 | 5.6 | 4.6 |
| C African Rep | 6 | 3 | 0 | 0 | 6 | 6 | 8 | - | - | 0 | - | 8 | 7 | 0 | 4.4 | 4.4 | 3.9 |
| Chad | 2 | 2 | 0 | 0 | 3 | 4 | 8 | - | - | 0 | - | 8 | 8 | 0 | 3.5 | 3.3 | 3.1 |
| Congo Peoples R | 6 | 2 | 0 | 0 | 3 | 0 | 8 | - | - | 10 | - | 8 | 10 | 0 | 4.2 | 4.0 | 3.8 |
| Cote d' Ivoire | 8 | 5 | 0 | 0 | 6 | 4 | 10 | - | 5 | 0 | 1 | 8 | 8 | 0 | 4.5 | 4.4 | 4.0 |
| Gabon | 3 | 6 | 0 | 0 | 2 | 6 | 8 | - | - | 10 | 4 | 8 | 7 | 0 | 4.6 | 4.5 | 4.5 |
| Ghana | 1 | 0 | 0 | 0 | 9 | 0 | 0 | 10 | 1 | 10 | 0 | 1 | 0 | 0 | 2.1 | 2.8 | 1.0 |
| Kenya | 8 | 10 | 0 | 0 | 3 | 4 | 10 | 6 | 0 | 10 | 3 | 7 | 5 | 0 | 4.7 | 4.3 | 4.6 |
| Madagascar | 5 | 3 | 0 | 0 | 8 | 6 | - | - | - | 0 | - | 5 | 2 | 0 | 3.3 * | 3.5 * | 2.7 * |
| Malawi | 6 | 7 | 0 | 0 | 2 | 4 | 8 | 8 | 3 | 10 | 2 | 3 | 3 | 2 | 4.2 | 4.3 | 3.9 |
| Mali | 4 | 5 | 0 | 0 | 7 | 4 | 6 | 8 | - | 0 | 6 | 8 | 9 | 2 | 4.9 | 5.2 | 4.0 |
| Mauritius | 10 | 9 | 0 | 0 | 8 | 6 | 10 | 6 | 7 | 10 | 1 | 8 | 4 | 2 | 6.0 | 6.0 | 5.5 |
| Morocco | 7 | 10 | 0 | 0 | 4 | 2 | 6 | 7 | 0 | 0 | 4 | 5 | 7 | 5 | 4.2 | 4.1 | 3.9 |
| Niger | 9 | 4 | 0 | 0 | 5 | 4 | - | - | - | 0 | - | 8 | 7 | 0 | 4.1 * | 4.1 * | 3.6 * |
| Nigeria | 7 | 3 | 0 | 0 | 6 | 2 | 4 | 10 | 3 | 10 | 6 | 0 | 3 | 0 | 3.8 | 4.3 | 2.9 |
| Rwanda | 10 | 4 | 0 | 0 | 7 | 6 | 8 | - | - | 10 | - | 2 | 0 | 0 | 4.4 | 4.4 | 3.9 |
| Senegal | 8 | 9 | 0 | 0 | 3 | 4 | 6 | - | 1 | 0 | 2 | 8 | 6 | 0 | 3.8 | 3.5 | 3.8 |
| Sierra Leone | 1 | 1 | 0 | 0 | 10 | 6 | 0 | 10 | - | 10 | 1 | 1 | 0 | 0 | 3.1 | 3.9 | 2.1 |
| Somalia | 1 | 1 | 0 | 0 | 2 | 4 | 0 | - | - | 0 | - | 1 | 0 | 0 | 1.0 | 1.1 | 0.9 |
| South Africa | 2 | 9 | 0 | 0 | 3 | 4 | 8 | 6 | 4 | 0 | 9 | 3 | 9 | 2 | 4.5 | 4.5 | 4.0 |
| Tanzania | 3 | 4 | 0 | 0 | 5 | 0 | 0 | 6 | 0 | 0 | 4 | 0 | 0 | 0 | 1.6 | 1.9 | 0.9 |
| Togo | 7 | 4 | 0 | 0 | 6 | 4 | 8 | - | - | 0 | 2 | 8 | 8 | 0 | 4.2 | 4.1 | 3.7 |
| Tunisia | 3 | 6 | 0 | 0 | 3 | 2 | 6 | 5 | 2 | 0 | 0 | 4 | 6 | 0 | 2.8 | 2.8 | 2.4 |
| Uganda | 0 | 0 | 0 | 0 | 7 | 2 | 0 | - | 0 | 10 | 1 | 3 | 0 | 0 | 1.6 | 1.7 | 1.3 |
| Zaire | 0 | 1 | 0 | 0 | 10 | 2 | - | - | 1 | 10 | 2 | 6 | 9 | 2 | 3.5 | 3.3 | 2.9 |
| Zambia | 2 | 2 | 0 | 0 | 0 | 0 | 0 | 7 | 0 | 10 | 4 | 2 | 10 | 2 | 2.6 | 2.7 | 2.4 |
| Zimbabwe | 6 | 4 | 0 | 0 | 1 | 4 | 8 | 4 | 0 | 0 | 2 | 2 | 6 | 2 | 3.0 | 2.6 | 2.9 |

N/R = No rating given because data were available for less than ten of the components of the index.

* These summary ratings should be interpreted with caution because they are based on ratings for only ten of the fourteen components in the index for this year.

235

# Table A1-3: Component and Summary Index Ratings: 1980

| | I | | | | II | | | III | | | IV | | | | Summary Ratings | | |
|---|---|---|---|---|---|---|---|---|---|---|---|---|---|---|---|---|---|
| **INDUSTRIAL COUNTRIES** | A | B | C | D | A | B | F | A | B | C | A | B | C | D | (Ie) | (Is1) | (Is2) |
| United States | 8 | 9 | 10 | 10 | 2 | 8 | 10 | 3 | 0 | 10 | 9 | 10 | 3 | 10 | 6.9 | 6.2 | 8.2 |
| Canada | 10 | 9 | 10 | 10 | 2 | 6 | 10 | 3 | 4 | 10 | 8 | 10 | 9 | 8 | 7.5 | 6.8 | 8.5 |
| Australia | 5 | 9 | 10 | 10 | 2 | 6 | 10 | 4 | 2 | 10 | 7 | 8 | 5 | 2 | 6.0 | 5.5 | 6.8 |
| Japan | 9 | 9 | 10 | 0 | 8 | 8 | 10 | 4 | 0 | 10 | 9 | 10 | 3 | 2 | 6.4 | 5.9 | 6.4 |
| New Zealand | 7 | 9 | 0 | 0 | 2 | 6 | 6 | 1 | 2 | 10 | 8 | 10 | 5 | 5 | 5.1 | 4.8 | 5.6 |
| Austria | 10 | 10 | 10 | 0 | 2 | 2 | 8 | 1 | 2 | 0 | 9 | 10 | 7 | 2 | 5.2 | 4.6 | 5.4 |
| Belgium | 10 | 9 | 10 | 10 | 2 | 6 | 10 | 0 | 0 | 0 | 10 | 10 | 10 | 10 | 6.8 | 5.7 | 8.0 |
| Denmark | 7 | 10 | 0 | 0 | 0 | 4 | 10 | 1 | 0 | 0 | 10 | 7 | 3 | 5 | 4.3 | 3.8 | 4.6 |
| Finland | 7 | 9 | 10 | 0 | 2 | 6 | 8 | 3 | 1 | 0 | 9 | 8 | 5 | 2 | 5.0 | 4.6 | 5.2 |
| France | 4 | 10 | 10 | 0 | 2 | 4 | 8 | 0 | 3 | 0 | 10 | 6 | 5 | 2 | 4.6 | 4.2 | 4.7 |
| Germany | 8 | 10 | 10 | 10 | 1 | 6 | 10 | 2 | 3 | 0 | 10 | 10 | 6 | 8 | 6.6 | 6.0 | 7.6 |
| Iceland | 1 | 3 | 0 | 0 | 3 | 4 | 4 | 4 | - | 10 | 4 | 5 | 2 | 2 | 3.2 | 3.4 | 3.1 |
| Ireland | 3 | 6 | 0 | 0 | 2 | 4 | 6 | 2 | 1 | 10 | 7 | 10 | 7 | 5 | 4.5 | 4.2 | 4.8 |
| Italy | 2 | 8 | 0 | 0 | 5 | 2 | 4 | 1 | 0 | 0 | 10 | 10 | 5 | 5 | 3.8 | 3.6 | 3.8 |
| Netherlands | 8 | 9 | 10 | 10 | 3 | 6 | 10 | 0 | 0 | 0 | 10 | 10 | 8 | 8 | 6.4 | 5.4 | 7.5 |
| Norway | 10 | 7 | 0 | 0 | 2 | 2 | 6 | 1 | 0 | 0 | 9 | 6 | 7 | 2 | 3.8 | 3.4 | 4.0 |
| Spain | 3 | 6 | 0 | 0 | 6 | 4 | 6 | 3 | 1 | 0 | 7 | 10 | 2 | 5 | 4.0 | 3.9 | 3.8 |
| Sweden | 4 | 9 | 10 | 0 | 0 | 4 | 8 | 0 | 0 | 0 | 9 | 6 | 5 | 2 | 4.0 | 3.4 | 4.4 |
| Switzerland | 7 | 10 | 10 | 10 | 7 | 8 | 6 | 3 | 7 | 0 | 8 | 10 | 6 | 10 | 7.3 | 7.1 | 7.9 |
| United Kingdom | 4 | 7 | 0 | 0 | 1 | 4 | 4 | 2 | 0 | 10 | 10 | 10 | 5 | 10 | 4.7 | 4.5 | 5.3 |
| **CENTRAL/- SOUTH AMERICA** | | | | | | | | | | | | | | | | | |
| Argentina | 0 | 0 | 10 | 10 | 6 | 4 | 0 | 4 | 6 | 0 | 1 | 8 | 0 | 0 | 3.3 | 3.6 | 3.4 |
| Belize | - | 6 | - | - | 3 | 8 | 8 | 8 | - | 10 | 2 | 3 | 3 | 8 | 5.8 | 5.9 | 6.1 |
| Bolivia | 1 | 2 | 10 | 10 | 6 | 6 | 6 | 9 | 3 | 0 | 3 | 4 | 2 | 2 | 4.4 | 4.5 | 4.3 |
| Brazil | 1 | 1 | 0 | 0 | 9 | 4 | - | 3 | 4 | 0 | 1 | 4 | 2 | 0 | 2.5 | 2.7 | 1.7 |
| Chile | 0 | 0 | 10 | 0 | 7 | 8 | 8 | 3 | 2 | 0 | 7 | 6 | 4 | 2 | 4.1 | 3.9 | 3.8 |
| Colombia | 1 | 5 | 0 | 0 | 8 | 4 | - | 8 | 2 | 0 | 3 | 4 | 2 | 0 | 3.1 | 3.5 | 2.1 |
| Costa Rica | 2 | 5 | 10 | 10 | 2 | 8 | - | 5 | 5 | 10 | 6 | 1 | 2 | 2 | 4.9 | 4.8 | 5.4 |
| Dominican Rep | 8 | 5 | 0 | 10 | 10 | 6 | - | 9 | - | 10 | 1 | 2 | 1 | 2 | 5.3 | 5.5 | 4.9 |
| Ecuador | 2 | 5 | 10 | 10 | 5 | 6 | - | 6 | 5 | 0 | 3 | 4 | 3 | 2 | 4.6 | 4.6 | 4.7 |
| El Salvador | 2 | 3 | 0 | 0 | 6 | 8 | - | 8 | 3 | 0 | 4 | 1 | 2 | 2 | 3.4 | 3.7 | 2.6 |
| Guatemala | 4 | 6 | 10 | 10 | 9 | 8 | 8 | 10 | 8 | 0 | 6 | 4 | 1 | 5 | 6.4 | 6.8 | 6.0 |
| Haiti | 2 | 2 | 10 | 10 | 8 | 6 | - | - | - | 10 | 1 | 4 | 1 | 0 | 4.5 | 4.3 | 4.6 |
| Honduras | 3 | 7 | 10 | 10 | 7 | 8 | - | - | 8 | 10 | 4 | 4 | 5 | 0 | 6.1 | 6.1 | 6.1 |
| Jamaica | 2 | 4 | 0 | 0 | 1 | 2 | 4 | - | 0 | 10 | 9 | 2 | 4 | 2 | 2.9 | 2.8 | 2.9 |
| Mexico | 1 | 5 | 10 | 10 | 8 | 2 | 4 | 7 | 4 | 0 | 0 | 1 | 1 | 2 | 3.7 | 3.8 | 3.4 |
| Nicaragua | 1 | 1 | 10 | 10 | 1 | 6 | - | 7 | 5 | 0 | 2 | 1 | 3 | 0 | 3.5 | 3.6 | 3.6 |
| Panama | 5 | 7 | 10 | 10 | 2 | 6 | - | 6 | 3 | 10 | 7 | 10 | 5 | 10 | 6.6 | 6.3 | 7.5 |
| Paraguay | 2 | 4 | 10 | 10 | 10 | 8 | - | 9 | - | 0 | 5 | 5 | 2 | 5 | 5.8 | 6.1 | 5.5 |

236

| CENTRAL/- S. AMERICA (con't) | I A | I B | I C | I D | II A | II B | II F | III A | III B | III C | IV A | IV B | IV C | IV D | Summary Ratings (Ie) | (Is1) | (Is2) |
|---|---|---|---|---|---|---|---|---|---|---|---|---|---|---|---|---|---|
| Peru | 1 | 1 | 0 | 0 | 8 | 4 | - | 9 | 2 | 0 | 1 | 4 | 4 | 2 | 3.0 | 3.4 | 2.0 |
| Trinidad/Tobago | 1 | 2 | 0 | 0 | 7 | 2 | - | 5 | - | 10 | 7 | 2 | 1 | 0 | 3.0 | 3.4 | 2.2 |
| Uruguay | 0 | 2 | 10 | 10 | 7 | 6 | 6 | 4 | 10 | 10 | 2 | 10 | 0 | 10 | 6.0 | 6.3 | 6.4 |
| Venezuela | 3 | 3 | 10 | 10 | 7 | 4 | - | 9 | 7 | 0 | 7 | 10 | 5 | 8 | 6.3 | 6.6 | 6.1 |
| **EUROPE/- MIDDLE EAST** | | | | | | | | | | | | | | | | | |
| Bulgaria | - | - | 0 | 0 | 10 | 0 | - | - | 0 | 0 | - | 1 | 2 | 0 | N/R | N/R | N/R |
| Cyprus | 2 | 8 | 0 | 0 | 6 | 6 | 4 | 5 | 1 | 0 | 6 | 6 | 3 | 0 | 3.6 | 3.6 | 3.2 |
| Czechoslovakia | - | - | 0 | 0 | 2 | 0 | - | - | - | 0 | - | 0 | - | 0 | N/R | N/R | N/R |
| Czech Rep | - | - | - | - | - | - | - | - | - | - | - | - | - | - | N/R | N/R | N/R |
| Slovakia | - | - | - | - | - | - | - | - | - | - | - | - | - | - | N/R | N/R | N/R |
| Egypt | 1 | 5 | 10 | 10 | 4 | 2 | 4 | 2 | 0 | 0 | 0 | 5 | 10 | 0 | 3.5 | 2.8 | 3.9 |
| Greece | 2 | 8 | 10 | 0 | 4 | 2 | 6 | 3 | 3 | 0 | 7 | 5 | 2 | 2 | 3.8 | 3.8 | 3.5 |
| Hungary | - | 6 | 0 | 0 | 8 | 0 | 6 | - | - | 0 | 6 | 0 | 8 | 0 | 3.3 | 3.2 | 2.3 |
| Iran | 1 | 3 | 10 | 10 | 1 | 2 | - | 5 | - | 0 | 0 | 1 | 2 | 0 | 2.6 | 2.5 | 2.9 |
| Israel | 1 | 0 | 10 | 0 | 0 | 2 | 0 | 1 | 1 | 0 | 6 | 8 | 4 | 2 | 2.4 | 2.3 | 2.6 |
| Jordan | 2 | 7 | 10 | 0 | 0 | 6 | - | 5 | - | 10 | 4 | 10 | 10 | 2 | 5.3 | 5.3 | 5.6 |
| Malta | 7 | 7 | - | - | 4 | 4 | 6 | 3 | 0 | 10 | 6 | 4 | 4 | 2 | 4.5 | 4.0 | 4.8 |
| Poland | - | - | 10 | 10 | 9 | 0 | - | - | - | 0 | - | 0 | 7 | 0 | N/R | N/R | N/R |
| Portugal | 3 | 6 | 0 | 0 | 5 | 2 | 4 | 2 | 0 | 0 | 8 | 7 | 5 | 2 | 3.3 | 3.1 | 3.0 |
| Romania | 8 | 7 | 0 | 0 | 10 | 0 | - | 3 | - | 0 | - | 0 | 5 | 0 | 3.2 * | 3.2 * | 2.2 * |
| Syria | 2 | 6 | 10 | 10 | 0 | 4 | - | - | - | 0 | 3 | 2 | 3 | 0 | 3.4 | 3.1 | 3.9 |
| Turkey | 1 | 1 | 0 | 0 | 7 | 4 | 0 | 5 | 0 | 0 | 4 | 4 | 0 | 0 | 2.0 | 2.3 | 1.4 |
| **ASIA** | | | | | | | | | | | | | | | | | |
| Bangladesh | 2 | 1 | 0 | 0 | 10 | 6 | 6 | - | 1 | 10 | 0 | 1 | 1 | 0 | 2.9 | 2.8 | 2.4 |
| Fiji | 10 | 4 | 0 | 0 | 4 | 6 | 6 | 8 | 2 | 10 | 5 | 4 | 4 | 5 | 4.9 | 5.0 | 4.7 |
| Hong Kong | 9 | 4 | 10 | 10 | 10 | 10 | - | 10 | 10 | 10 | 9 | 10 | 9 | 10 | 9.3 | 9.4 | 9.2 |
| India | 6 | 5 | 0 | 0 | 9 | 0 | 8 | 6 | 1 | 10 | 0 | 6 | 2 | 2 | 3.8 | 3.8 | 3.2 |
| Indonesia | 1 | 2 | 10 | 10 | 8 | 2 | 2 | 8 | 3 | 0 | 7 | 7 | 10 | 2 | 4.9 | 5.0 | 4.6 |
| Malaysia | 5 | 6 | 10 | 10 | 3 | 4 | 6 | 6 | 2 | 10 | 3 | 10 | 10 | 5 | 6.0 | 5.6 | 6.7 |
| Nepal | 2 | 4 | 0 | 0 | 10 | 6 | 6 | - | - | 10 | 2 | 10 | 1 | 0 | 4.3 | 4.6 | 3.8 |
| Pakistan | 2 | 9 | 0 | 0 | 8 | 2 | 6 | - | 2 | 10 | 0 | 3 | 4 | 2 | 3.6 | 3.5 | 3.2 |
| Philippines | 4 | 7 | 0 | 0 | 9 | 4 | 8 | 10 | 1 | 0 | 4 | 6 | 8 | 2 | 4.7 | 4.8 | 3.8 |
| Singapore | 9 | 6 | 0 | 0 | 8 | 8 | 10 | 10 | 4 | 0 | 9 | 10 | 10 | 8 | 7.0 | 7.1 | 6.4 |
| South Korea | 2 | 6 | 0 | 0 | 7 | 6 | 4 | 9 | 0 | 0 | 6 | 4 | 8 | 0 | 4.0 | 4.0 | 3.2 |
| Sri Lanka | 2 | 6 | 0 | 0 | 9 | 4 | 4 | 4 | 0 | 10 | 1 | 5 | 8 | 0 | 3.7 | 3.5 | 3.3 |
| Taiwan | 2 | 5 | 10 | 10 | 4 | 4 | 8 | 8 | 3 | 0 | 7 | 8 | 7 | 2 | 5.4 | 5.3 | 5.4 |
| Thailand | 5 | 7 | 0 | 0 | 7 | 6 | 4 | 10 | 3 | 0 | 4 | 6 | 7 | 2 | 4.7 | 5.0 | 3.9 |

| | I | | | | II | | | III | | | IV | | | | Summary Ratings | | |
|---|---|---|---|---|---|---|---|---|---|---|---|---|---|---|---|---|---|
| | A | B | C | D | A | B | F | A | B | C | A | B | C | D | (Ie) | (Is1) | (Is2) |
| **AFRICA** | | | | | | | | | | | | | | | | | |
| Algeria | 2 | 4 | 0 | 0 | 6 | 4 | - | - | - | 0 | - | 0 | 9 | 0 | 2.8 * | 2.7 * | 2.2 * |
| Benin | 6 | 7 | 0 | 0 | 9 | 4 | 6 | - | - | - | 1 | 7 | 3 | 0 | 4.1 | 4.2 | 3.5 |
| Botswana | 3 | 2 | 0 | 0 | 1 | 8 | 4 | 6 | 0 | 10 | 0 | 4 | 10 | 5 | 3.8 | 3.5 | 4.1 |
| Burundi | 2 | 3 | 0 | - | 9 | 4 | 2 | - | - | 10 | 0 | 2 | 0 | 0 | 2.8 | 2.9 | 2.4 |
| Cameroon | 2 | 9 | 0 | 0 | 9 | 4 | 6 | 10 | - | 10 | 1 | 7 | 3 | 0 | 4.7 | 5.3 | 3.7 |
| C African Rep | 1 | 3 | 0 | 0 | 5 | 6 | - | - | - | 0 | 1 | 7 | 6 | 0 | 3.0 | 3.0 | 2.7 |
| Chad | 3 | 10 | 0 | 0 | 0 | 4 | - | - | - | 10 | - | 7 | 8 | 0 | 4.2 * | 4.2 * | 4.3 * |
| Congo Peoples Rep | 6 | 3 | 0 | 0 | 2 | 0 | 6 | - | - | 10 | 6 | 7 | 9 | 0 | 4.0 | 4.0 | 3.7 |
| Cote d' Ivoire | 2 | 2 | 0 | 0 | 3 | 4 | 8 | 7 | 5 | 10 | 0 | 7 | 7 | 0 | 4.0 | 4.1 | 3.5 |
| Gabon | 9 | 2 | 0 | 0 | 6 | 6 | 6 | - | - | 10 | 3 | 7 | 5 | 0 | 4.6 | 4.6 | 4.3 |
| Ghana | 1 | 1 | 0 | 0 | 7 | 0 | 0 | 8 | 1 | 10 | 0 | 0 | 0 | 0 | 1.8 | 2.3 | 1.0 |
| Kenya | 6 | 3 | 0 | 0 | 1 | 4 | 8 | 8 | 1 | 10 | 5 | 4 | 7 | 0 | 4.0 | 4.0 | 3.8 |
| Madagascar | 2 | 7 | 0 | 0 | 7 | 6 | - | - | - | 0 | 2 | 2 | 4 | 0 | 3.1 | 3.1 | 2.5 |
| Malawi | 10 | 4 | 0 | 0 | 1 | 4 | 4 | 9 | - | 10 | 4 | 2 | 3 | 2 | 4.1 | 4.5 | 3.8 |
| Mali | 6 | 10 | 0 | 0 | 8 | 4 | 4 | 8 | 4 | 10 | 6 | 6 | 5 | 2 | 5.3 | 5.5 | 4.6 |
| Mauritius | 7 | 3 | 0 | 0 | 6 | 6 | - | 5 | 3 | 10 | 1 | 2 | 4 | 2 | 3.8 | 3.8 | 3.6 |
| Morocco | 5 | 5 | 0 | 0 | 2 | 4 | - | 7 | 3 | 0 | 1 | 8 | 4 | 2 | 3.4 | 3.7 | 3.1 |
| Niger | 1 | 6 | 0 | 0 | 8 | 4 | 2 | 8 | 2 | 0 | 2 | 7 | 8 | 0 | 3.6 | 3.9 | 2.8 |
| Nigeria | 1 | 9 | 0 | 0 | 7 | 2 | 2 | - | 0 | 10 | 2 | 1 | 7 | 0 | 3.0 | 2.8 | 2.7 |
| Rwanda | 2 | 6 | 0 | 0 | 7 | 6 | 6 | 10 | 0 | 10 | 0 | 1 | 1 | 0 | 3.5 | 3.7 | 2.8 |
| Senegal | 4 | 7 | 0 | 0 | 1 | 4 | 8 | - | - | 0 | 1 | 7 | 5 | 0 | 3.3 | 3.2 | 3.3 |
| Sierra Leone | 2 | 5 | 0 | 0 | 9 | 6 | 6 | - | - | 10 | 0 | 1 | 2 | 0 | 3.5 | 3.5 | 2.9 |
| Somalia | 1 | 0 | 0 | 0 | 4 | 4 | 0 | - | - | 10 | 1 | 2 | 10 | 0 | 2.6 | 2.5 | 2.5 |
| South Africa | 4 | 4 | 0 | 0 | 6 | 4 | 4 | 8 | 2 | 0 | 9 | 6 | 9 | 2 | 4.4 | 4.6 | 3.7 |
| Tanzania | 1 | 4 | 0 | 0 | 7 | 2 | 4 | 10 | - | 10 | 3 | 0 | 3 | 0 | 3.4 | 4.0 | 2.3 |
| Togo | 2 | 2 | 0 | 0 | 5 | 4 | 8 | - | - | 0 | 0 | 7 | 6 | 0 | 3.1 | 2.9 | 2.7 |
| Tunisia | 6 | 6 | 0 | 0 | 5 | 2 | 4 | 5 | 2 | 0 | 1 | 4 | 7 | 0 | 3.2 | 3.1 | 2.7 |
| Uganda | 1 | 0 | 0 | 0 | - | 2 | 0 | - | - | 10 | 7 | 0 | 4 | 0 | 2.1 | 2.2 | 1.9 |
| Zaire | 1 | 1 | 0 | 0 | 9 | 2 | - | 10 | 1 | 10 | 1 | 1 | 3 | 2 | 3.1 | 3.5 | 2.0 |
| Zambia | 6 | 5 | 0 | 0 | 0 | 0 | 4 | 4 | 0 | 10 | 8 | 1 | 10 | 2 | 3.4 | 3.1 | 3.4 |
| Zimbabwe | 3 | 7 | 0 | 0 | 1 | 4 | 6 | 3 | 5 | 0 | 8 | 1 | 7 | 2 | 3.7 | 3.7 | 3.4 |

N/R = No rating given because data were available for less than ten of the components of the index.

* These summary ratings should be interpreted with caution because they are based on ratings for only ten of the fourteen components in the index for this year.

# Table A1-4:  Component and Summary Index Ratings:  1975

| INDUSTRIAL COUNTRIES | I A | I B | I C | I D | II A | II B | II F | III A | III B | III C | IV A | IV B | IV C | IV D | Summary Ratings (Ie) | (Is1) | (Is2) |
|---|---|---|---|---|---|---|---|---|---|---|---|---|---|---|---|---|---|
| United States | 8 | 8 | 10 | 10 | 2 | 8 | 8 | 3 | 0 | 10 | 9 | 10 | 2 | 10 | 6.6 | 6.0 | 7.9 |
| Canada | 7 | 5 | 10 | 10 | 1 | 6 | 6 | 4 | 4 | 10 | 6 | 10 | 9 | 8 | 6.5 | 6.1 | 7.5 |
| Australia | 7 | 5 | 10 | 10 | 3 | 6 | 4 | 4 | 2 | 10 | 6 | 8 | 4 | 2 | 5.4 | 5.0 | 6.1 |
| Japan | 4 | 4 | 10 | 0 | 8 | 8 | 4 | 4 | 1 | 10 | 9 | 10 | 3 | 2 | 5.3 | 5.2 | 5.3 |
| New Zealand | 3 | 6 | 0 | 0 | 4 | 6 | - | 1 | 3 | 10 | 8 | 6 | 5 | 5 | 4.5 | 4.3 | 4.6 |
| Austria | 6 | 10 | 10 | 0 | 3 | 2 | 6 | 1 | 4 | 0 | 8 | 10 | 6 | 2 | 4.8 | 4.6 | 4.9 |
| Belgium | 6 | 7 | 10 | 10 | 3 | 6 | 6 | 0 | 2 | 0 | 10 | 10 | 9 | 10 | 6.2 | 5.5 | 7.3 |
| Denmark | 5 | 9 | 0 | 0 | 0 | 4 | 8 | 2 | 1 | 0 | 9 | 8 | 3 | 5 | 4.1 | 3.8 | 4.3 |
| Finland | 2 | 4 | 10 | 0 | 3 | 6 | - | 3 | 2 | 0 | 8 | 8 | 4 | 2 | 4.0 | 3.9 | 4.0 |
| France | 5 | 7 | 0 | 0 | 3 | 4 | 8 | 0 | 5 | 0 | 10 | 10 | 4 | 2 | 4.4 | 4.3 | 4.4 |
| Germany | 6 | 10 | 10 | 10 | 1 | 6 | 8 | 2 | 4 | 0 | 10 | 10 | 6 | 8 | 6.4 | 5.9 | 7.3 |
| Iceland | 1 | 2 | 0 | 0 | 3 | 4 | 2 | 4 | - | 10 | 2 | 1 | 3 | 2 | 2.6 | 2.7 | 2.4 |
| Ireland | 6 | 5 | 0 | 0 | 2 | 4 | 4 | 2 | 0 | 10 | 6 | 10 | 6 | 5 | 4.2 | 3.9 | 4.6 |
| Italy | 3 | 4 | 0 | 0 | 6 | 2 | 6 | 2 | 5 | 0 | 10 | 5 | 5 | 5 | 4.0 | 4.1 | 3.6 |
| Netherlands | 6 | 10 | 10 | 10 | 3 | 6 | 6 | 0 | 5 | 0 | 9 | 10 | 9 | 5 | 6.3 | 5.7 | 7.1 |
| Norway | 4 | 9 | 0 | 0 | 1 | 2 | - | - | 0 | 0 | 9 | 8 | 9 | 2 | 3.8 | 3.6 | 3.8 |
| Spain | 2 | 6 | 0 | 0 | 8 | 4 | - | - | 4 | 0 | 5 | 7 | 2 | 2 | 3.6 | 3.9 | 3.0 |
| Sweden | 5 | 7 | 10 | 0 | 0 | 4 | 4 | 0 | 1 | 0 | 9 | 8 | 5 | 2 | 3.9 | 3.5 | 4.3 |
| Switzerland | 10 | 10 | 10 | 10 | 7 | 8 | 6 | - | 7 | 0 | 7 | 10 | 5 | 2 | 7.1 | 7.1 | 7.2 |
| United Kingdom | 4 | 3 | 0 | 0 | 1 | 4 | 4 | 3 | 7 | 10 | 10 | 10 | 7 | 2 | 4.7 | 5.0 | 4.7 |
| **CENTRAL/- S.AMERICA** | | | | | | | | | | | | | | | | | |
| Argentina | 0 | 0 | 10 | 10 | 7 | 6 | - | 4 | 4 | 0 | 0 | 1 | 0 | 0 | 3.1 | 3.1 | 3.1 |
| Belize | - | 2 | - | - | - | 8 | - | - | - | - | - | 3 | - | - | N/R | N/R | N/R |
| Bolivia | 2 | 1 | 10 | 10 | 8 | 6 | - | 10 | - | 0 | 2 | 6 | 8 | 2 | 5.3 | 5.5 | 4.9 |
| Brazil | 1 | 3 | 0 | 0 | 8 | 4 | - | - | 5 | 0 | 5 | 2 | 2 | 0 | 2.8 | 3.2 | 2.0 |
| Chile | 0 | 0 | 0 | 0 | 4 | 6 | - | 4 | 0 | 0 | 6 | 6 | 5 | 2 | 2.8 | 2.8 | 2.5 |
| Colombia | 2 | 4 | 0 | 0 | 9 | 6 | - | 8 | 6 | 0 | 3 | 3 | 2 | 0 | 3.7 | 4.3 | 2.6 |
| Costa Rica | 2 | 2 | 10 | 10 | 5 | 8 | - | - | 5 | 10 | 5 | 5 | 3 | 2 | 5.3 | 5.2 | 5.6 |
| Dominican Rep | 5 | 3 | 0 | 0 | 10 | 6 | - | - | 5 | 0 | 0 | 3 | 2 | 2 | 3.4 | 3.6 | 2.7 |
| Ecuador | 2 | 1 | 10 | 10 | 5 | 6 | - | - | 5 | 0 | 2 | 6 | 5 | 2 | 4.4 | 4.3 | 4.6 |
| El Salvador | 3 | 5 | 0 | 0 | 7 | 8 | - | 8 | 4 | - | 4 | 4 | 3 | 2 | 4.3 | 4.7 | 3.6 |
| Guatemala | 5 | 3 | 0 | 10 | 10 | 8 | - | 10 | 9 | 0 | 6 | 4 | 2 | 5 | 5.9 | 6.5 | 5.3 |
| Haiti | 2 | 4 | 10 | 0 | 9 | 6 | - | - | - | 10 | 1 | 10 | 0 | 0 | 4.5 | 4.8 | 4.1 |
| Honduras | 7 | 4 | 10 | 10 | 7 | 8 | - | 10 | 9 | - | 6 | 10 | 5 | 0 | 7.1 | 7.4 | 6.8 |
| Jamaica | 2 | 2 | 0 | 0 | 2 | 2 | - | 5 | 2 | 10 | 6 | 4 | 3 | 2 | 3.0 | 3.2 | 2.8 |
| Mexico | 4 | 3 | 10 | 10 | 9 | 2 | - | 7 | 5 | 0 | 3 | 10 | 0 | 2 | 4.8 | 5.0 | 4.5 |
| Nicaragua | 3 | 2 | 10 | 10 | 9 | 6 | - | 8 | 10 | 0 | 6 | 4 | 4 | 5 | 6.0 | 6.4 | 5.5 |
| Panama | 7 | 6 | 10 | 10 | 2 | 8 | - | 7 | 4 | 10 | 7 | 10 | 7 | 10 | 7.3 | 7.0 | 8.2 |
| Paraguay | 2 | 3 | 10 | 10 | 10 | 8 | - | 9 | - | 0 | 2 | 4 | 1 | 5 | 5.3 | 5.6 | 5.0 |

239

Table 1-4: 1975 (Continued)

| CENTRAL/- S. AMERICA (con't) | I | | | | II | | | III | | | IV | | | | Summer Ratings | | |
|---|---|---|---|---|---|---|---|---|---|---|---|---|---|---|---|---|---|
| | A | B | C | D | A | B | F | A | B | C | A | B | C | D | (Ie) | (Is1) | (Is2) |
| Peru | 2 | 4 | 0 | 0 | 7 | 4 | - | 9 | 4 | 0 | 1 | 2 | 2 | 2 | 3.1 | 3.7 | 2.1 |
| Trinidad/Tobago | 2 | 1 | 0 | 0 | 7 | 2 | - | - | - | 10 | 7 | 2 | 2 | 0 | 2.9 | 3.2 | 2.3 |
| Uruguay | 0 | 0 | 10 | 10 | 6 | 6 | - | 3 | 7 | 10 | 7 | 10 | 1 | 8 | 5.7 | 5.8 | 6.2 |
| Venezuela | 1 | 1 | 10 | 10 | 7 | 6 | - | 8 | 10 | 0 | 6 | 10 | 6 | 8 | 6.4 | 6.9 | 6.3 |
| **EUROPE/- MIDDLE EAST** | | | | | | | | | | | | | | | | | |
| Bulgaria | - | - | 0 | 0 | - | 0 | - | - | - | 0 | - | 1 | - | 0 | N/R | N/R | N/R |
| Cyprus | 7 | 7 | 0 | 0 | 3 | 6 | - | 4 | 3 | 0 | 7 | 6 | 2 | 0 | 3.8 | 3.9 | 3.6 |
| Czechoslavakia | - | - | 0 | 0 | - | 0 | 8 | - | - | - | - | 0 | - | 0 | N/R | N/R | N/R |
| Czech Rep | - | - | - | - | - | - | - | - | - | - | - | - | - | - | N/R | N/R | N/R |
| Slovakia | - | - | - | - | - | - | - | - | - | - | - | - | - | - | N/R | N/R | N/R |
| Egypt | 2 | 6 | 0 | 0 | 0 | 4 | - | 0 | - | 0 | 0 | 8 | 10 | 0 | 2.7 | 2.4 | 3.0 |
| Greece | 3 | 3 | 10 | 0 | 5 | 2 | - | 4 | 4 | 0 | 7 | 6 | 2 | 2 | 3.7 | 3.9 | 3.2 |
| Hungary | - | 7 | 0 | 0 | 8 | 0 | 4 | - | - | 0 | - | 0 | 10 | 0 | 3.1 * | 3.0 * | 2.1 * |
| Iran | 2 | - | 10 | 0 | 0 | 4 | - | 4 | 8 | 0 | 7 | 7 | 10 | 5 | 4.9 | 5.0 | 4.8 |
| Israel | 2 | 2 | 10 | 0 | 0 | 2 | - | - | - | 0 | 2 | 2 | 4 | 2 | 2.2 | 2.1 | 2.3 |
| Jordan | 2 | 4 | 0 | 0 | 0 | 6 | - | - | - | 10 | 4 | 8 | 10 | 2 | 4.3 | 4.2 | 4.4 |
| Malta | 6 | 8 | - | - | 2 | 4 | - | 3 | - | - | 6 | 6 | 5 | 0 | N/R | N/R | N/R |
| Poland | - | - | 10 | 10 | - | 0 | - | - | - | 0 | - | 0 | - | 2 | N/R | N/R | N/R |
| Portugal | 3 | 4 | 0 | 0 | 5 | 2 | - | 3 | 0 | 0 | 6 | 2 | 3 | 0 | 2.3 | 2.2 | 1.8 |
| Romania | - | - | 0 | 0 | - | 0 | - | - | - | 0 | - | 0 | - | 0 | N/R | N/R | N/R |
| Syria | 2 | 2 | 10 | 10 | 1 | 6 | - | - | - | 0 | 2 | 8 | 4 | 0 | 3.9 | 3.7 | 4.5 |
| Turkey | 2 | 5 | 0 | 0 | 7 | 4 | 2 | 5 | - | 0 | 0 | 4 | 1 | 0 | 2.5 | 2.8 | 1.9 |
| **ASIA** | | | | | | | | | | | | | | | | | |
| Bangladesh | - | 1 | 0 | 0 | 10 | 6 | - | - | - | 10 | 3 | 2 | 0 | 0 | 3.3 * | 3.5 * | 2.5 * |
| Fiji | 3 | 2 | 0 | 0 | 7 | 6 | 0 | 9 | 3 | 10 | 4 | 4 | 4 | 5 | 4.1 | 4.6 | 3.6 |
| Hong Kong | 5 | 5 | 10 | 10 | 10 | 10 | - | 10 | 10 | 10 | 9 | 10 | 9 | 10 | 9.0 | 9.2 | 9.0 |
| India | 5 | 3 | 0 | 0 | 9 | 0 | - | 7 | 0 | 10 | 0 | 5 | 1 | 2 | 3.0 | 3.3 | 2.3 |
| Indonesia | 1 | 1 | 10 | 10 | 9 | 4 | 2 | 9 | 4 | 0 | 6 | 5 | 9 | 2 | 5.0 | 5.2 | 4.6 |
| Malaysia | 5 | 2 | 0 | 10 | 3 | 4 | - | 5 | 4 | 10 | 4 | 10 | 10 | 5 | 5.4 | 5.2 | 5.9 |
| Nepal | 3 | 2 | 0 | 0 | 10 | 6 | - | - | - | 10 | 2 | 2 | 0 | 0 | 3.2 | 3.4 | 2.6 |
| Pakistan | 4 | 2 | 0 | 0 | 8 | 2 | - | - | 1 | 10 | 0 | 4 | 4 | 2 | 3.0 | 2.9 | 2.6 |
| Philippines | 3 | 2 | 0 | 0 | 8 | 4 | 8 | 10 | 3 | 10 | 0 | 4 | 8 | 2 | 4.4 | 4.6 | 3.6 |
| Singapore | 7 | 5 | 0 | 0 | 8 | 8 | - | 10 | 4 | 0 | 9 | 10 | 10 | 8 | 6.5 | 6.8 | 5.9 |
| South Korea | 1 | 3 | 0 | 0 | 7 | 6 | 2 | 9 | 2 | 0 | 7 | 7 | 8 | 0 | 4.0 | 4.3 | 3.2 |
| Sri Lanka | 8 | 3 | 0 | 0 | 9 | 2 | - | 4 | - | 10 | 1 | 1 | 5 | 0 | 3.6 | 3.6 | 2.8 |
| Taiwan | 2 | 2 | 10 | 10 | 4 | 4 | 8 | 9 | 3 | 0 | 6 | 6 | 5 | 2 | 4.9 | 4.9 | 4.8 |
| Thailand | 8 | 2 | 0 | 0 | 8 | 6 | - | 10 | 3 | 0 | 4 | 7 | 5 | 2 | 4.6 | 4.9 | 3.7 |

Table 1-4: 1975 (con't)

| | I | | | | II | | | III | | | IV | | | | Summary Ratings | | |
|---|---|---|---|---|---|---|---|---|---|---|---|---|---|---|---|---|---|
| | A | B | C | D | A | B | F | A | B | C | A | B | C | D | (Ie) | (Is1) | (Is2) |
| **AFRICA** | | | | | | | | | | | | | | | | | |
| Algeria | 2 | 1 | 0 | 0 | 7 | 4 | - | - | - | 10 | - | 2 | 10 | 0 | 3.6 * | 3.5 * | 3.0 * |
| Benin | 1 | 4 | 0 | 0 | 9 | 4 | - | - | - | 10 | 1 | 7 | 3 | 0 | 3.5 | 3.8 | 3.0 |
| Botswana | - | 3 | 0 | 0 | 2 | 8 | - | 6 | 0 | 10 | 1 | 2 | 10 | - | 3.9 | 3.5 | 4.0 |
| Burundi | 9 | 1 | - | - | 7 | 4 | - | - | - | - | 1 | 2 | 0 | 0 | N/R | N/R | N/R |
| Cameroon | 4 | 4 | 0 | 0 | 8 | 4 | - | 9 | - | 10 | 0 | 7 | 4 | 0 | 4.2 | 4.7 | 3.3 |
| C African Rep | 6 | 3 | 0 | 0 | 3 | 6 | - | - | - | - | - | 7 | 7 | 0 | N/R | N/R | N/R |
| Chad | 3 | 9 | 0 | 0 | 0 | 4 | - | - | - | 10 | 1 | 7 | 8 | 0 | 3.8 | 3.7 | 4.0 |
| Congo Peoples Rep | 7 | 10 | 0 | 0 | 2 | 0 | - | - | - | 10 | 6 | 7 | 8 | 0 | 4.5 | 4.5 | 4.2 |
| Cote d' Ivoire | 5 | 2 | 0 | 0 | 3 | 4 | - | - | - | 10 | - | 7 | 8 | 0 | 3.9 * | 3.9 * | 3.8 * |
| Gabon | 2 | 1 | 0 | 0 | 7 | 6 | - | - | - | 10 | 2 | 7 | 6 | 0 | 3.8 | 3.9 | 3.4 |
| Ghana | 1 | 2 | 0 | 0 | 7 | 0 | - | 8 | 0 | 10 | 0 | 1 | 1 | 0 | 2.1 | 2.5 | 1.3 |
| Kenya | 9 | 2 | 0 | 0 | 2 | 4 | 4 | - | 0 | 10 | 6 | 5 | 8 | 0 | 3.8 | 3.4 | 3.9 |
| Madagascar | 7 | 3 | - | 0 | 8 | 6 | 4 | - | - | - | 0 | 3 | 4 | 0 | 3.7 | 3.6 | 3.2 |
| Malawi | 3 | 4 | 0 | 0 | 6 | 4 | - | 10 | 0 | 10 | 6 | 3 | 6 | 2 | 4.1 | 4.3 | 3.4 |
| Mali | 2 | 4 | 0 | 0 | 8 | 4 | - | 8 | - | 10 | 0 | 5 | 5 | 2 | 4.0 | 4.4 | 3.2 |
| Mauritius | 1 | 1 | 0 | 0 | 7 | 6 | - | 5 | - | 10 | 4 | 2 | 5 | 2 | 3.7 | 3.9 | 3.1 |
| Morocco | 2 | 2 | 0 | 0 | 4 | 4 | - | 5 | 8 | 0 | 3 | 6 | 6 | 0 | 3.4 | 3.9 | 2.8 |
| Niger | 2 | 1 | 0 | 0 | 8 | 4 | - | - | - | 10 | 4 | 7 | 6 | 0 | 3.8 | 4.0 | 3.3 |
| Nigeria | 1 | 1 | 0 | 0 | 7 | 4 | 2 | 8 | 0 | 10 | 4 | 2 | 6 | 0 | 3.2 | 3.3 | 2.5 |
| Rwanda | 3 | 1 | - | 0 | 3 | 6 | - | 10 | - | 10 | 0 | 2 | 0 | 0 | 3.1 | 3.8 | 2.5 |
| Senegal | 2 | 4 | 0 | 0 | 5 | 4 | - | 9 | - | - | 2 | 7 | 7 | 0 | 3.8 | 4.3 | 3.0 |
| Sierra Leone | 3 | 3 | 0 | 0 | 7 | 6 | - | 9 | - | 10 | 1 | 2 | 3 | 0 | 3.8 | 4.2 | 2.9 |
| Somalia | 3 | 5 | 0 | 0 | 1 | 4 | 4 | - | - | 10 | 0 | 3 | 2 | 0 | 2.6 | 2.6 | 2.7 |
| South Africa | 5 | 5 | 0 | 0 | 6 | 4 | - | - | 1 | 0 | 8 | 6 | 9 | 2 | 4.1 | 3.9 | 3.7 |
| Tanzania | 2 | 4 | 0 | 0 | 3 | 2 | - | 10 | 0 | 10 | 3 | 1 | 6 | 0 | 3.0 | 3.3 | 2.4 |
| Togo | 3 | 1 | 0 | 0 | 5 | 4 | - | - | - | - | 3 | 7 | 6 | 0 | 3.1 * | 3.2 * | 2.7 * |
| Tunisia | 3 | 3 | 0 | 0 | 5 | 2 | - | 9 | - | 0 | 1 | 4 | 5 | 0 | 2.9 | 3.4 | 1.9 |
| Uganda | 1 | 1 | 0 | 0 | - | 2 | - | - | - | 10 | 0 | 0 | 0 | 0 | 1.2 * | 1.2 * | 1.3 * |
| Zaire | 2 | 5 | 0 | 0 | 7 | 2 | - | 10 | 2 | 10 | 0 | 1 | 1 | 2 | 3.2 | 3.6 | 2.3 |
| Zambia | 5 | 2 | 0 | 0 | 0 | 0 | 4 | 5 | 0 | 10 | 7 | 1 | 10 | 2 | 3.1 | 2.9 | 3.0 |
| Zimbabwe | - | 7 | 0 | 0 | 7 | 4 | - | - | - | - | 8 | 2 | 7 | - | N/R | N/R | N/R |

N/R= No rating given because data were available for less than ten of the components of the index.

* These summary ratings should be interpreted with caution because they are based on ratings for only ten of the fourteen components in the index for this year.

241

# Appendix II:

# The Underlying Data and Country

# Ratings for Each of the

# 17 Components in

# the Index

## List of Tables

## Table I-A: The Expansion in the Money Supply (M1) Minus the Annual Growth Rate of Potential Real GDP: 1971-75, 1976-80, 1981-85, 1986-90, and 1990-94

| INDUSTRIAL COUNTRIES | Annual Growth Rate of the Money Supply (M1) Minus Annual Growth Rate of Potential Real GDP (The rating of each country is in parenthesis) | | | | | | | | | |
|---|---|---|---|---|---|---|---|---|---|---|
| | 1971-75 | | 1976-80 | | 1981-85 | | 1986-90 | | 1990-94 | |
| United States | 3.5 | (8) | 4.8 | (8) | 5.8 | (7) | 3.2 | (9) | 5.6 | (7) |
| Canada | 6.0 | (7) | 1.6 | (10) | 11.3 | (4) | 4.0 | (8) | 2.5 | (9) |
| Australia | 7.0 | (7) | 8.7 | (5) | 3.3 | (8) | 11.9 | (3) | 9.6 | (5) |
| Japan | 10.8 | (4) | 2.4 | (9) | 0.9 | (10) | 2.0 | (9) | 2.4 | (9) |
| New Zealand | 11.8 | (3) | 5.5 | (7) | 8.6 | (5) | 40.2 | (1) | 3.4 | (8) |
| Austria | 8.0 | (6) | 1.0 | (10) | 2.3 | (9) | 4.2 | (8) | 4.9 | (8) |
| Belgium | 7.9 | (6) | 1.5 | (10) | 1.7 | (10) | 2.9 | (9) | 3.3 | (8) |
| Denmark | 9.6 | (5) | 7.0 | (7) | 12.5 | (3) | 7.3 | (6) | 2.4 | (9) |
| Finland | 18.9 | (2) | 5.5 | (7) | 10.3 | (4) | 6.8 | (7) | 29.1 | (1) |
| France | 8.4 | (5) | 10.2 | (4) | 8.1 | (6) | 3.0 | (9) | -1.2 | (10) |
| Germany | 7.5 | (6) | 4.5 | (8) | 3.1 | (9) | 9.6 | (5) | 8.7 | (5) |
| Iceland | 24.8 | (1) | 36.7 | (1) | 41.4 | (1) | 26.9 | (1) | 10.2 | (4) |
| Ireland | 7.7 | (6) | 12.9 | (3) | 2.8 | (9) | 4.3 | (8) | 2.1 | (9) |
| Italy | 12.6 | (3) | 17.2 | (2) | 9.8 | (5) | 7.0 | (7) | 3.7 | (8) |
| Netherlands | 7.9 | (6) | 3.9 | (8) | 4.9 | (8) | 4.4 | (8) | 2.6 | (9) |
| Norway | 10.2 | (4) | 1.6 | (10) | 12.7 | (3) | 17.1 | (2) | 5.7 | (7) |
| Spain | 15.7 | (2) | 12.3 | (3) | 8.3 | (5) | 15.9 | (2) | 3.7 | (8) |
| Sweden | 8.3 | (5) | 10.1 | (4) | 5.9 | (7) | 6.1 | (7) | 1.9 | (10) |
| Switzerland | 1.9 | (10) | 5.2 | (7) | 0.1 | (10) | 0.6 | (10) | 0.2 | (10) |
| United Kingdom | 10.4 | (4) | 10.3 | (4) | 10.9 | (4) | 28.0 | (1) | 5.3 | (7) |

### CENTRAL/SOUTH AMERICA

| | 1971-75 | | 1976-80 | | 1981-85 | | 1986-90 | | 1990-94 | |
|---|---|---|---|---|---|---|---|---|---|---|
| Argentina | 78.2 | (0) | 150.0 | (0) | 295.3 | (0) | 515.4 | (0) | 371.6 | (0) [a] |
| Belize | - | | - | | 3.3 | (8) | 7.9 | (6) | 1.0 | (10) |
| Bolivia | 19.3 | (2) | 21.3 | (1) | 569.5 | (0) | 38.1 | (1) | 33.0 | (1) |
| Brazil | 28.9 | (1) | 41.6 | (1) | 137.8 | (0) | 648.6 | (0) | 1232.5 | (0) [a] |
| Chile | 210.7 | (0) | 93.5 | (0) | 7.3 | (6) | 24.7 | (1) | 18.3 | (2) [a] |
| Colombia | 15.7 | (2) | 23.8 | (1) | 16.9 | (2) | 27.7 | (1) | 27.9 | (1) [a] |
| Costa Rica | 16.0 | (2) | 15.7 | (2) | 32.1 | (1) | 13.0 | (3) | 15.9 | (2) |
| Dominican Republic | 9.4 | (5) | 3.7 | (8) | 13.9 | (2) | 37.4 | (1) | 18.6 | (2) |
| Ecuador | 16.9 | (2) | 14.6 | (2) | 19.0 | (2) | 38.9 | (1) | 46.3 | (0) [a] |
| El Salvador | 12.1 | (3) | 13.9 | (2) | 10.4 | (4) | 12.4 | (3) | 15.1 | (2) |
| Guatemala | 9.7 | (5) | 10.7 | (4) | 10.1 | (4) | 18.3 | (2) | 21.1 | (1) |
| Haiti | 14.1 | (2) | 14.3 | (2) | 8.6 | (5) | 8.7 | (5) | 20.6 | (2) [a] |
| Honduras | 6.4 | (7) | 12.9 | (3) | 2.6 | (9) | 15.7 | (2) | 17.8 | (2) |
| Jamaica | 17.1 | (2) | 18.3 | (2) | 18.1 | (2) | 19.5 | (2) | 44.7 | (0) |
| Mexico | 11.2 | (4) | 24.7 | (1) | 44.4 | (0) | 67.1 | (0) | 36.0 | (1) |

Table I-A: Money Supply (continued)

### Annual Growth Rate of the Money Supply (M1) Minus Annual Growth Rate of Potential Real GDP

(The rating of each country is in parenthesis)

| CENTRAL/-S. AMERICA | 1971-75 | | 1976-80 | | 1981-85 | | 1986-90 | | 1990-94 | |
|---|---|---|---|---|---|---|---|---|---|---|
| Nicaragua | 12.3 | (3) | 26.6 | (1) | 70.0 | (0) | 2073.5 | (0) | 322.9 | (0) |
| Panama | 6.0 | (7) | 8.6 | (5) | -0.5 | (10) | 0.4 | (10) | 18.7 | (2) |
| Paraguay | 14.1 | (2) | 19.7 | (2) | 8.8 | (5) | 32.0 | (1) | 22.4 | (1) |
| Peru | 18.6 | (2) | 39.1 | (1) | 98.4 | (0) | 690.2 | (0) | 249.1 | (0) |
| Trinidad & Tobago | 17.3 | (2) | 21.6 | (1) | 8.0 | (6) | 4.6 | (8) | 13.0 | (3) |
| Uruguay | 60.3 | (0) | 58.3 | (0) | 38.0 | (1) | 75.8 | (0) | 67.8 | (0) |
| Venezuela | 25.5 | (1) | 13.6 | (3) | 13.3 | (3) | 19.9 | (2) | 39.8 | (1) |
| **EUROPE/MIDDLE EAST** | | | | | | | | | | |
| Bulgaria | - | | - | | - | | 13.1 | (3) | 67.0 | (0) |
| Cyprus | 6.0 | (7) | 16.0 | (2) | 4.6 | (8) | 2.3 | (9) | 3.2 | (9) a |
| Czechoslovakia | - | | - | | 3.0 | (9) | 0.4 | (10) | - | |
| Czech Republic | - | | - | | - | | - | | 13.9 | (2) |
| Slovakia | - | | - | | - | | - | | 13.5 | (3) |
| Egypt | 13.8 | (2) | 21.5 | (1) | 7.8 | (6) | 7.3 | (6) | 8.4 | (5) |
| Greece | 12.9 | (3) | 14.1 | (2) | 16.5 | (2) | 18.6 | (2) | 16.5 | (2) |
| Hungary | - | | - | | 4.4 | (8) | 11.9 | (3) | 23.5 | (1) |
| Iran | 18.1 | (2) | 35.1 | (1) | 23.4 | (1) | 14.8 | (2) | 18.9 | (2) a |
| Israel | 18.2 | (2) | 40.0 | (1) | 169.3 | (0) | 42.6 | (1) | 17.0 | (2) |
| Jordan | 15.1 | (2) | 14.1 | (2) | -0.7 | (10) | 9.0 | (5) | 3.3 | (8) |
| Malta | 7.1 | (6) | 5.5 | (7) | -2.1 | (9) | -0.2 | (10) | 0.6 | (10) |
| Poland | - | | - | | 20.9 | (1) | 110.5 | (0) | 70.4 | (0) |
| Portugal | 12.8 | (3) | 12.2 | (3) | 12.0 | (3) | 17.0 | (2) | 12.8 | (3) |
| Romania | - | | 4.0 | (8) | 2.3 | (9) | 7.4 | (6) | 93.2 | (0) |
| Syria | 15.9 | (2) | 15.9 | (2) | 15.5 | (2) | 14.5 | (2) | 15.5 | (2) a |
| Turkey | 20.2 | (2) | 39.7 | (1) | 31.7 | (1) | 48.9 | (0) | 59.0 | (0) |
| **ASIA** | | | | | | | | | | |
| Bangladesh | - | | 18.0 | (2) | 13.3 | (3) | 2.7 | (9) | 10.8 | (4) |
| Fiji | 11.9 | (3) | -1.3 | (10) | 4.5 | (8) | 12.1 | (3) | 2.6 | (9) |
| Hong Kong | 9.3 | (5) | 2.9 | (9) | 2.9 | (9) | 10.3 | (4) | 9.9 | (5) |
| India | 8.7 | (5) | 7.8 | (6) | 10.8 | (4) | 9.4 | (5) | 12.7 | (3) |
| Indonesia | 32.6 | (1) | 24.8 | (1) | 8.8 | (5) | 13.1 | (3) | 13.2 | (3) a |
| Malaysia | 8.9 | (5) | 9.7 | (5) | 0.9 | (10) | 6.5 | (7) | 14.0 | (2) |
| Nepal | 11.6 | (3) | 14.4 | (2) | 10.8 | (4) | 15.2 | (2) | 15.5 | (2) a |
| Pakistan | 10.2 | (4) | 16.4 | (2) | 6.5 | (7) | 9.4 | (5) | 9.3 | (5) |
| Philippines | 13.7 | (3) | 11.1 | (4) | 8.0 | (6) | 18.7 | (2) | 12.4 | (3) |
| Singapore | 5.2 | (7) | 3.1 | (9) | 0.1 | (10) | 4.6 | (8) | 4.5 | (8) |
| South Korea | 21.3 | (1) | 18.2 | (2) | 6.8 | (7) | 6.8 | (7) | 9.3 | (5) |
| Sri Lanka | 3.6 | (8) | 20.4 | (2) | 9.5 | (5) | 11.8 | (3) | 10.8 | (4) |
| Taiwan | 19.1 | (2) | 15.1 | (2) | 5.0 | (7) | 13.1 | (3) | 0.1 | (10) |
| Thailand | 4.9 | (8) | 8.8 | (5) | -2.9 | (9) | 10.0 | (5) | 5.8 | (7) |

Table I-A: Money Supply (continued)

## Annual Growth Rate of the Money Supply (M1) Minus Annual
## Growth Rate of Potential Real GDP

(The rating of each country is in parenthesis)

| AFRICA | 1971-75 | | 1976-80 | | 1981-85 | | 1986-90 | | 1990-94 | |
|---|---|---|---|---|---|---|---|---|---|---|
| Algeria | 18.2 | (2) | 15.8 | (2) | 13.3 | (3) | 3.2 | (9) | 13.8 | (2) |
| Benin | 21.6 | (1) | 8.1 | (6) | 9.9 | (5) | 0.9 | (10) | 13.1 | (3) |
| Botswana | - | | 11.9 | (3) | 4.2 | (8) | 15.4 | (2) | 0.5 | (10) |
| Burundi | 2.2 | (9) | 19.7 | (2) | 8.3 | (5) | 0.2 | (10) | 11.1 | (4) a |
| Cameroon | 10.3 | (4) | 15.1 | (2) | 6.3 | (7) | -3.2 | (9) | -2.9 | (9) |
| Cent Afriican Rep | 7.3 | (6) | 21.9 | (1) | 7.2 | (6) | -0.7 | (10) | 11.7 | (3) |
| Chad | 11.8 | (3) | 13.6 | (3) | 19.3 | (2) | -6.4 | (7) | -6.0 | (7) |
| Congo | 6.7 | (7) | 7.9 | (6) | 8.1 | (6) | -3.7 | (8) | 6.2 | (7) |
| Cote d'Ivoire | 9.6 | (5) | 13.9 | (2) | 4.9 | (8) | -3.1 | (9) | 9.7 | (5) |
| Gabon | 18.4 | (2) | 2.2 | (9) | 13.3 | (3) | -0.9 | (10) | 1.3 | (10) |
| Ghana | 25.6 | (1) | 42.8 | (1) | 43.9 | (1) | 37.9 | (1) | 25.0 | (1) |
| Kenya | 3.2 | (9) | 7.2 | (6) | 4.5 | (8) | 12.2 | (3) | 23.1 | (1) |
| Madagascar | 6.0 | (7) | 15.9 | (2) | 9.7 | (5) | 18.7 | (2) | 20.7 | (1) |
| Malawi | 11.6 | (3) | -0.5 | (10) | 7.9 | (6) | 21.2 | (1) | 24.6 | (1) |
| Mali | 15.6 | (2) | 8.9 | (5) | 11.0 | (4) | -5.6 | (7) | 6.1 | (7) |
| Mauritius | 31.0 | (1) | 6.3 | (7) | -0.8 | (10) | 16.2 | (2) | 7.9 | (6) |
| Morocco | 13.8 | (2) | 9.0 | (5) | 6.3 | (7) | 9.8 | (5) | 10.0 | (5) |
| Niger | 18.5 | (2) | 25.2 | (1) | 3.0 | (9) | 0.0 | (10) | 1.8 | (10) |
| Nigeria | 25.4 | (1) | 25.5 | (1) | 6.8 | (7) | 20.2 | (2) | 30.0 | (1) b |
| Rwanda | 12.6 | (3) | 15.0 | (2) | -1.5 | (10) | 0.7 | (10) | 5.7 | (7) a |
| Senegal | 14.2 | (2) | 10.9 | (4) | 4.9 | (8) | -2.1 | (9) | 3.8 | (8) |
| Sierra Leone | 13.3 | (3) | 18.8 | (2) | 41.8 | (1) | 72.0 | (0) | 33.7 | (1) |
| Somalia | 13.5 | (3) | 23.8 | (1) | 25.3 | (1) | 92.0 | (0) | - | |
| South Africa | 9.3 | (5) | 11.0 | (4) | 18.3 | (2) | 17.0 | (2) | 12.5 | (3) |
| Tanzania | 15.3 | (2) | 22.1 | (1) | 12.3 | (3) | 30.0 | (1) | 26.6 | (1) a |
| Togo | 12.4 | (3) | 16.4 | (2) | 6.1 | (7) | -3.0 | (9) | 8.5 | (5) |
| Tunisia | 11.5 | (3) | 7.5 | (6) | 11.4 | (3) | 1.7 | (10) | 0.6 | (10) |
| Uganda | 23.9 | (1) | 35.7 | (1) | 75.1 | (0) | 410.0 | (0) | 61.0 | (0) b |
| Zaire | 17.1 | (2) | 22.3 | (1) | 52.7 | (0) | 99.1 | (0) | 550.0 | (0) |
| Zambia | 9.8 | (5) | 7.9 | (6) | 18.5 | (2) | 58.1 | (0) | 60.0 | (0) b |
| Zimbabwe | - | | 11.5 | (3) | 7.4 | (6) | 15.8 | (2) | 29.4 | (1) |

a Indicates data are for 1989-1993 data.
b Indicates data are for 1988-1992 data.

Source: The actual growth rate of real GDP during the last 10 years was used as the estimate for the growth rate of "potential real GDP". Thus, this variable is the annual rate of growth in the M1 money supply during the last 5 years minus the annual growth rate of real GDP during the last 10 years.

When they were available, the money supply (narrow definition) and real GDP data from the World Bank, *World Tables, 1994* were utilized. If the money supply data were unavailable from the World Bank, the money supply figures from the International Monetary Fund, *International Financial Statistics Yearbook, 1994* (or the monthly version) were used. The base year for the rating of each country was 1985. The following conversion table divided the 1985 data into eleven intervals of equal size:

Table I-A: (Con't)

| Percent Growth Rate of the Money Supply minus Percent Change in Real GDP | Rating |
|---|---|
| -7.01 - -8.20 | 6 |
| -4.91 - -7.00 | 7 |
| -3.21 - -4.90 | 8 |
| -1.91 - -3.20 | 9 |
| -1.90 - 1.90 | 10 |
| 1.91 - 3.20 | 9 |
| 3.21 - 4.90 | 8 |
| 4.91 - 7.00 | 7 |
| 7.01 - 8.20 | 6 |
| 8.21 - 10.00 | 5 |
| 10.01 - 11.30 | 4 |
| 11.31 - 13.75 | 3 |
| 13.76 - 20.60 | 2 |
| 20.61 - 44.25 | 1 |
| > 44.25 | 0 |

## Table I-B: The Standard Deviation of the Annual Rate of Inflation As Measured by the GDP Deflator (1971-75, 1976-80, 1981-85, 1986-90 and 1990-94)

| | Standard Deviation of the Inflation Rate (percent) | | | | | | | | |
|---|---|---|---|---|---|---|---|---|---|
| INDUSTRIAL | (The rating of each country is in parenthesis) | | | | | | | | |
| COUNTRIES | 1971-75 | | 1976-80 | | 1981-85 | | 1986-90 | | 1990-94 |
| United States | 2.1 | (8) | 1.3 | (9) | 2.4 | (8) | 0.7 | (10) | 0.7 | (10) |
| Canada | 4.0 | (5) | 1.9 | (9) | 3.2 | (6) | 1.1 | (10) | 1.1 | (10) |
| Australia | 4.2 | (5) | 1.6 | (9) | 2.2 | (8) | 1.9 | (9) | 0.8 | (10) |
| Japan | 5.6 | (4) | 1.7 | (9) | 0.8 | (10) | 0.9 | (10) | 0.6 | (10) |
| New Zealand | 3.7 | (6) | 2.1 | (9) | 3.1 | (6) | 5.0 | (4) | 0.8 | (10) |
| Austria | 1.1 | (10) | 0.6 | (10) | 1.3 | (10) | 0.9 | (10) | 0.4 | (10) |
| Belgium | 3.0 | (7) | 1.6 | (9) | 0.8 | (10) | 1.0 | (10) | 0.4 | (10) |
| Denmark | 2.1 | (9) | 0.8 | (10) | 2.4 | (8) | 0.8 | (10) | 0.4 | (10) |
| Finland | 5.5 | (4) | 1.9 | (9) | 1.9 | (9) | 0.9 | (10) | 1.9 | (9) |
| France | 2.6 | (7) | 0.8 | (10) | 2.3 | (8) | 0.9 | (10) | 0.5 | (10) |
| Germany | 0.9 | (10) | 0.5 | (10) | 1.0 | (10) | 0.7 | (10) | 0.6 | (10) |
| Iceland | 11.1 | (2) | 7.7 | (3) | 17.2 | (1) | 3.6 | (6) | 4.6 | (5) |
| Ireland | 4.7 | (5) | 3.5 | (6) | 4.8 | (5) | 2.5 | (7) | 1.5 | (9) |
| Italy | 5.2 | (4) | 2.2 | (8) | 3.8 | (6) | 0.8 | (10) | 1.7 | (9) |
| Netherlands | 0.7 | (10) | 1.7 | (9) | 1.9 | (9) | 1.0 | (10) | 1.7 | (9) |
| Norway | 2.1 | (9) | 3.0 | (7) | 3.3 | (6) | 3.5 | (6) | 1.9 | (9) |
| Spain | 3.7 | (6) | 3.5 | (6) | 2.1 | (9) | 2.0 | (9) | 1.2 | (10) |
| Sweden | 2.9 | (7) | 1.5 | (9) | 1.2 | (10) | 1.4 | (9) | 3.1 | (6) |
| Switzerland | 1.1 | (10) | 1.1 | (10) | 2.0 | (9) | 1.2 | (10) | 1.9 | (9) |
| United Kingdom | 7.4 | (3) | 2.6 | (7) | 2.5 | (7) | 1.4 | (9) | 1.6 | (9) |
| **CENTRAL/S. AMERICA** | | | | | | | | | |
| Argentina | 61.8 | (0) | 119.8 | (0) | 207.6 | (0) | 1185.0 | (0) | 793.4 | (0) |
| Belize | 8.3 | (2) | 3.6 | (6) | 6.5 | (3) | 2.8 | (7) | 1.8 | (9) |
| Bolivia | 21.0 | (1) | 11.0 | (2) | 4349.2 | (0) | 91.2 | (0) | 4.3 | (5) |
| Brazil | 6.9 | (3) | 16.6 | (1) | 53.1 | (0) | 909.8 | (0) | 956.5 | (0) |
| Chile | 234.0 | (0) | 80.6 | (0) | 9.6 | (2) | 3.2 | (6) | 4.1 | (5) |
| Colombia | 5.7 | (4) | 4.2 | (5) | 1.7 | (9) | 2.2 | (8) | 3.2 | (6) |
| Costa Rica | 8.9 | (2) | 4.5 | (5) | 24.2 | (1) | 3.3 | (6) | 6.1 | (3) |
| Dominican Rep | 6.8 | (3) | 4.7 | (5) | 13.1 | (2) | 16.7 | (1) | 22.7 | (1) |
| Ecuador | 14.6 | (1) | 4.3 | (5) | 10.2 | (2) | 16.7 | (1) | 9.8 | (2) |
| El Salvador | 4.5 | (5) | 7.5 | (3) | 4.7 | (5) | 8.2 | (2) | 5.0 | (4) |
| Guatemala | 7.8 | (3) | 3.6 | (6) | 5.3 | (4) | 15.2 | (1) | 13.2 | (2) |
| Haiti | 5.9 | (4) | 8.3 | (2) | 3.1 | (6) | 8.1 | (3) | 14.0 | (1) |
| Honduras | 5.4 | (4) | 3.0 | (7) | 1.3 | (10) | 6.7 | (3) | 6.7 | (3) |
| Jamaica | 9.9 | (2) | 5.1 | (4) | 10.2 | (2) | 5.0 | (4) | 12.9 | (2) |
| Mexico | 6.0 | (3) | 4.9 | (5) | 20.4 | (1) | 42.8 | (0) | 9.3 | (2) |
| Nicaragua | 8.8 | (2) | 15.9 | (1) | 60.3 | (0) | 4853.2 | (0) | 2875.9 | (0) |
| Panama | 3.2 | (6) | 2.5 | (7) | 1.3 | (10) | 0.8 | (10) | 1.0 | (10) |

248

Table I-B: Annual Rate of Inflation (continued)

**Standard Deviation of the Inflation Rate (percent)**

(The rating of each country is in parenthesis)

| CENTRAL- S. AMERICA (con't) | 1971-75 | | 1976-80 | | 1981-85 | | 1986-90 | | 1990-94 | |
|---|---|---|---|---|---|---|---|---|---|---|
| Paraguay | 7.5 | (3) | 5.3 | (4) | 8.0 | (3) | 3.6 | (6) | 8.2 | (3) |
| Peru | 5.9 | (4) | 17.5 | (1) | 38.1 | (0) | 2302.8 | (0) | 2380.4 | (0) |
| Trinidad/Tobago | 18.5 | (1) | 9.6 | (2) | 13.9 | (1) | 5.6 | (4) | 5.9 | (4) |
| Uruguay | 36.6 | (0) | 11.9 | (2) | 20.4 | (1) | 12.6 | (2) | 23.7 | (1) |
| Venezuela | 15.0 | (1) | 7.4 | (3) | 5.2 | (4) | 30.4 | (1) | 13.9 | (1) |
| **EUROPE/MIDDLE EAST** | | | | | | | | | | |
| Bulgaria | - | | - | | 2.5 | (7) | 11.3 | (2) | 82.1 | (0) |
| Cyprus | 3.0 | (7) | 2.3 | (8) | 2.8 | (7) | 0.7 | (10) | 0.6 | (10) |
| Czechoslovakia | - | | - | | 2.2 | (8) | 4.0 | (5) | - | |
| Czech Republic | - | | - | | - | | - | | 17.4 | (1) |
| Slovakia | - | | - | | - | | - | | 18.5 | (1) |
| Egypt | 3.5 | (6) | 4.4 | (5) | 3.4 | (6) | 1.6 | (9) | 5.4 | (4) |
| Greece | 7.3 | (3) | 2.4 | (8) | 2.3 | (8) | 2.9 | (7) | 3.4 | (6) |
| Hungary | 2.9 | (7) | 3.8 | (6) | 1.0 | (10) | 7.8 | (3) | 8.7 | (2) |
| Iran | - | | 6.1 | (3) | 6.8 | (3) | 3.6 | (6) | 4.3 | (5) |
| Israel | 9.4 | (2) | 33.2 | (0) | 101.7 | (0) | 13.0 | (2) | 3.6 | (6) |
| Jordan | 5.8 | (4) | 2.6 | (7) | 5.1 | (4) | 8.3 | (2) | 2.4 | (8) |
| Malta | 2.3 | (8) | 3.0 | (7) | 3.1 | (6) | 0.7 | (10) | 1.1 | (10) |
| Poland | - | | - | | 37.4 | (0) | 178.3 | (0) | 172.3 | (0) |
| Portugal | 5.2 | (4) | 3.4 | (6) | 2.5 | (7) | 3.4 | (6) | 4.1 | (5) |
| Romania | - | | 2.8 | (7) | 4.8 | (5) | 6.0 | (3) | 75.5 | (0) |
| Syria | 12.2 | (2) | 3.8 | (6) | 5.3 | (4) | 3.2 | (6) | 5.1 | (4) |
| Turkey | 4.4 | (5) | 31.4 | (1) | 8.4 | (2) | 13.9 | (1) | 18.8 | (1) |
| **ASIA** | | | | | | | | | | |
| Bangladesh | 31.5 | (1) | 14.4 | (1) | 3.0 | (7) | 2.1 | (8) | 2.4 | (8) |
| Fiji | 9.0 | (2) | 5.7 | (4) | 3.9 | (5) | 2.0 | (9) | 2.7 | (7) |
| Hong Kong | 3.9 | (5) | 5.2 | (4) | 2.5 | (7) | 2.9 | (7) | 4.5 | (5) |
| India | 7.2 | (3) | 4.8 | (5) | 1.1 | (10) | 1.4 | (9) | 2.1 | (9) |
| Indonesia | 16.3 | (1) | 10.2 | (2) | 3.0 | (7) | 5.1 | (4) | 0.9 | (10) |
| Malaysia | 8.3 | (2) | 3.1 | (6) | 2.6 | (7) | 5.2 | (4) | 1.1 | (10) |
| Nepal | 11.3 | (2) | 5.4 | (4) | 2.2 | (8) | 1.9 | (9) | 3.9 | (5) |
| Pakistan | 8.6 | (2) | 1.6 | (9) | 2.3 | (8) | 2.4 | (8) | 3.0 | (7) |
| Philippines | 9.2 | (2) | 2.9 | (7) | 16.4 | (1) | 3.3 | (6) | 3.7 | (6) |
| Singapore | 4.7 | (5) | 3.7 | (6) | 2.7 | (7) | 2.8 | (7) | 0.4 | (10) |
| South Korea | 7.1 | (3) | 3.3 | (6) | 4.9 | (5) | 10.2 | (2) | 2.2 | (8) |
| Sri Lanka | 8.1 | (3) | 3.6 | (6) | 6.2 | (3) | 4.7 | (5) | 4.2 | (5) |
| Taiwan | 12.6 | (2) | 4.3 | (5) | 4.8 | (5) | 1.3 | (9) | 0.4 | (10) |
| Thailand | 8.4 | (2) | 2.8 | (7) | 2.5 | (8) | 1.7 | (9) | 1.8 | (9) |

Table I-B: Annual Rate of Inflation (continued)

## Standard Deviation of the Inflation Rate (percent)

(The rating of each country is in parenthesis)

| AFRICA | 1971-75 | | 1976-80 | | 1981-85 | | 1986-90 | | 1990-94 | |
|---|---|---|---|---|---|---|---|---|---|---|
| Algeria | 17.3 | (1) | 5.7 | (4) | 4.2 | (5) | 9.5 | (2) | 12.3 | (2) |
| Benin | 5.7 | (4) | 3.0 | (7) | 6.8 | (3) | 2.4 | (8) | 0.8 | (10) |
| Botswana | 7.7 | (3) | 8.8 | (2) | 8.8 | (2) | 8.7 | (2) | 2.5 | (7) |
| Burundi | 16.6 | (1) | 6.0 | (3) | 7.3 | (3) | 6.9 | (3) | 4.1 | (5) |
| Cameroon | 5.3 | (4) | 1.9 | (9) | 1.5 | (9) | 4.2 | (5) | 4.1 | (5) |
| C African Rep | 6.7 | (3) | 6.4 | (3) | 6.5 | (3) | 6.0 | (3) | 2.8 | (7) |
| Chad | 2.0 | (9) | 0.8 | (10) | 9.4 | (2) | 8.2 | (3) | 3.5 | (6) |
| Congo Peoples Rep | 0.9 | (10) | 7.2 | (3) | 11.0 | (2) | 14.5 | (1) | 3.0 | (7) |
| Cote d' Ivoire | 9.6 | (2) | 10.1 | (2) | 3.9 | (5) | 3.0 | (7) | 11.6 | (2) |
| Gabon | 26.3 | (1) | 11.4 | (2) | 3.6 | (6) | 13.0 | (2) | 3.5 | (6) |
| Ghana | 8.7 | (2) | 16.9 | (1) | 38.2 | (0) | 4.8 | (5) | 8.6 | (2) |
| Kenya | 9.3 | (2) | 6.1 | (3) | 1.2 | (10) | 1.4 | (9) | 7.5 | (3) |
| Madagascar | 7.6 | (3) | 2.8 | (7) | 7.9 | (3) | 4.8 | (5) | 10.5 | (2) |
| Malawi | 5.5 | (4) | 5.9 | (4) | 2.6 | (7) | 5.9 | (4) | 4.6 | (5) |
| Mali | 5.9 | (4) | 1.3 | (10) | 4.5 | (5) | 3.8 | (5) | 4.1 | (5) |
| Mauritius | 20.1 | (1) | 8.0 | (3) | 1.4 | (9) | 1.3 | (10) | 1.7 | (9) |
| Morocco | 8.4 | (2) | 4.5 | (5) | 0.9 | (10) | 2.6 | (7) | 1.0 | (10) |
| Niger | 16.6 | (1) | 3.3 | (6) | 5.7 | (4) | 5.3 | (4) | 15.9 | (1) |
| Nigeria | 15.7 | (1) | 1.5 | (9) | 6.0 | (3) | 19.3 | (1) | 17.7 | (1) |
| Rwanda | 30.0 | (1) | 3.3 | (6) | 5.3 | (4) | 3.8 | (6) | 5.7 | (4) |
| Senegal | 5.4 | (4) | 2.5 | (7) | 1.7 | (9) | 2.7 | (7) | 12.4 | (2) |
| Sierra Leone | 7.9 | (3) | 4.4 | (5) | 28.0 | (1) | 38.9 | (0) | 30.7 | (1) |
| Somalia | 4.8 | (5) | 35.8 | (0) | 18.7 | (1) | 67.5 | (0) | 63.2 | (0) a |
| South Africa | 4.8 | (5) | 5.1 | (4) | 1.9 | (9) | 0.9 | (10) | 1.8 | (9) |
| Tanzania | 5.8 | (4) | 5.7 | (4) | 5.9 | (4) | 9.5 | (2) | 8.9 | (2) |
| Togo | 16.8 | (1) | 11.2 | (2) | 5.0 | (4) | 1.6 | (9) | 1.8 | (9) |
| Tunisia | 7.8 | (3) | 3.5 | (6) | 3.8 | (6) | 1.8 | (9) | 0.9 | (10) |
| Uganda | 15.5 | (1) | 33.8 | (0) | 45.7 | (0) | 67.7 | (0) | 17.8 | (1) |
| Zaire | 4.0 | (5) | 25.8 | (1) | 25.1 | (1) | 28.0 | (1) | 8765.4 | (0) |
| Zambia | 12.1 | (2) | 4.6 | (5) | 12.6 | (2) | 23.3 | (1) | 38.3 | (0) |
| Zimbabwe | 2.7 | (7) | 2.7 | (7) | 5.5 | (4) | 5.7 | (4) | 7.0 | (3) |

a Indicates data are for 1988-1992.

Source:  Prior to 1994 the inflation rate was derived from the data on the GDP Deflator of the World Bank, *World Tables, 1994*. The base year for the rating of each country was 1985. Since they were available for most all countries, the CPI data from the IMF, *Monthly International Financial Statistics*, were used to derive the inflation rates for 1994. The following conversion table divided the 1985 data into eleven intervals of equal size:

Table I-B: (Con't):

| Standard Deviation of the Inflation Rate | Rating |
|---|---|
| 0.000% - 1.30% | 10 |
| 1.31 - 2.12 | 9 |
| 2.13 - 2.49 | 8 |
| 2.50 - 3.05 | 7 |
| 3.06 - 3.81 | 6 |
| 3.82 - 4.95 | 5 |
| 4.96 - 5.95 | 4 |
| 5.96 - 8.20 | 3 |
| 8.21 - 13.53 | 2 |
| 13.54 - 32.70 | 1 |
| > 32.70 | 0 |

## Table I-C: Freedom of Residents to Own Foreign Currencies Domestically
(Countries Where Citizens are Free to Own Foreign Currencies are Given a Rating of 10; Countries that Restrict This Freedom are Given a Rating of Zero.)

**Is It Legal (without restrictions) for Citizens to Own Foreign Money Domestically?**

| INDUSTRIAL COUNTRIES | 1975 | | 1980 | | 1985 | | 1990 | | 1993-94 | |
|---|---|---|---|---|---|---|---|---|---|---|
| United States | Yes | 10 | Yes | 10 | Yes | 10 | Yes | 10 | Yes | 10 |
| Canada | Yes | 10 | Yes | 10 | Yes | 10 | Yes | 10 | Yes | 10 |
| Australia | Yes | 10 | Yes | 10 | Yes | 10 | Yes | 10 | Yes | 10 |
| Japan | Yes | 10 | Yes | 10 | Yes | 10 | Yes | 10 | Yes | 10 |
| New Zealand | No | 0 | No | 0 | No | 0 | Yes | 10 | Yes | 10 |
| Austria | Yes | 10 | Yes | 10 | Yes | 10 | Yes | 10 | Yes | 10 |
| Belgium | Yes | 10 | Yes | 10 | Yes | 10 | Yes | 10 | Yes | 10 |
| Denmark | No | 0 | No | 0 | No | 0 | Yes | 10 | Yes | 10 |
| Finland | Yes | 10 | Yes | 10 | Yes | 10 | Yes | 10 | Yes | 10 |
| France | No | 0 | No | 0 | No | 0 | Yes | 10 | Yes | 10 |
| Germany | Yes | 10 | Yes | 10 | Yes | 10 | Yes | 10 | Yes | 10 |
| Iceland | No | 0 | No | 0 | No | 0 | Yes | 10 | Yes | 10 |
| Ireland | No | 0 | No | 0 | No | 0 | No | 0 | Yes | 10 |
| Italy | No | 0 | No | 0 | No | 0 | Yes | 10 | Yes | 10 |
| Netherlands | Yes | 10 | Yes | 10 | Yes | 10 | Yes | 10 | Yes | 10 |
| Norway | No | 0 | No | 0 | No | 0 | Yes | 10 | Yes | 10 |
| Spain | No | 0 | No | 0 | No | 0 | No | 0 | Yes | 10 |
| Sweden | Yes | 10 | Yes | 10 | Yes | 10 | Yes | 10 | Yes | 10 |
| Switzerland | Yes | 10 | Yes | 10 | Yes | 10 | Yes | 10 | Yes | 10 |
| United Kingdom | No | 0 | No | 0 | Yes | 10 | Yes | 10 | Yes | 10 |
| **CENTRAL/SOUTH AMERICA** | | | | | | | | | | |
| Argentina | Yes | 10 | Yes | 10 | Yes | 10 | Yes | 10 | Yes | 10 |
| Belize | - | | - | | - | | No | 0 | No | 0 |
| Bolivia | Yes | 10 | Yes | 10 | No | 0 | Yes | 10 | Yes | 10 |
| Brazil | No | 0 | No | 0 | No | 0 | No | 0 | No | 0 |
| Chile | No | 0 | Yes | 10 | Yes | 10 | Yes | 10 | Yes | 10 |
| Colombia | No | 0 | No | 0 | Yes | 10 | No | 0 | Yes | 10 |
| Costa Rica | Yes | 10 | Yes | 10 | Yes | 10 | Yes | 10 | Yes | 10 |
| Dominican Rep | No | 0 | No | 0 | No | 0 | No | 0 | No | 0 |
| Ecuador | Yes | 10 | Yes | 10 | Yes | 10 | Yes | 10 | Yes | 10 |
| El Salvador | No | 0 | No | 0 | No | 0 | No | 0 | Yes | 10 |
| Guatemala | No | 0 | Yes | 10 | Yes | 10 | Yes | 10 | Yes | 10 |
| Haiti | Yes | 10 | Yes | 10 | Yes | 10 | Yes | 10 | Yes | 10 |
| Honduras | Yes | 10 | Yes | 10 | Yes | 10 | Yes | 10 | Yes | 10 |
| Jamaica | No | 0 | No | 0 | No | 0 | No | 0 | Yes | 10 |
| Mexico | Yes | 10 | Yes | 10 | Yes | 10 | Yes | 10 | Yes | 10 |
| Nicaragua | Yes | 10 | Yes | 10 | No | 0 | No | 0 | No | 0 |
| Panama | Yes | 10 | Yes | 10 | Yes | 10 | Yes | 10 | Yes | 10 |

Table I-C: Freedom to Own Foreign Money (continued)

## Is It Legal (without restrictions) for Citizens to
## Own Foreign Money Domestically?

| CENTRAL/- | 1975 | | 1980 | | 1985 | | 1990 | | 1993-94 | |
|---|---|---|---|---|---|---|---|---|---|---|
| **S. AMERICA (con't)** | | | | | | | | | | |
| Paraguay | Yes | 10 | Yes | 10 | Yes | 10 | Yes | 10 | Yes | 10 |
| Peru | No | 0 | No | 0 | No | 10 | Yes | 10 | Yes | 10 |
| Trinidad/Tobago | No | 0 | No | 0 | No | 0 | No | 0 | Yes | 10 |
| Uraguay | Yes | 10 | Yes | 10 | Yes | 10 | Yes | 10 | Yes | 10 |
| Venezuela | Yes | 10 | Yes | 10 | Yes | 10 | Yes | 10 | No | 0 |
| | | | | | | | | | | |
| **EUROPE/MIDDLE EAST** | | | | | | | | | | |
| Bulgaria | No | 0 | No | 0 | No | 0 | No | 0 | Yes | 10 |
| Cyprus | No | 0 | No | 0 | No | 0 | No | 0 | No | 0 |
| Czechoslovakia | No | 0 | No | 0 | No | 0 | No | 0 | - | |
| Czech Rep | - | | - | | - | | - | | Yes | 10 |
| Slovakia | - | | - | | - | | - | | Yes | 10 |
| Egypt | No | 0 | Yes | 10 | Yes | 10 | Yes | 10 | Yes | 10 |
| Greece | Yes | 10 | Yes | 10 | Yes | 10 | Yes | 10 | Yes | 10 |
| Hungary | No | 0 | No | 0 | No | 0 | No | 0 | No | 0 |
| Iran | Yes | 10 | Yes | 10 | Yes | 10 | Yes | 10 | No | 0 |
| Israel | Yes | 10 | Yes | 10 | Yes | 10 | Yes | 10 | Yes | 10 |
| Jordan | No | 0 | Yes | 10 | Yes | 10 | No | 0 | No | 0 |
| Malta | - | | - | | No | 0 | No | 0 | Yes | 10 |
| Poland | Yes | 10 | Yes | 10 | Yes | 10 | Yes | 10 | Yes | 10 |
| Portugal | No | 0 | No | 0 | No | 0 | No | 0 | Yes | 10 |
| Romania | No | 0 | No | 0 | No | 0 | No | 0 | Yes | 10 |
| Syria | Yes | 10 | Yes | 10 | Yes | 10 | Yes | 10 | Yes | 10 |
| Turkey | No | 0 | No | 0 | No | 0 | Yes | 10 | Yes | 10 |
| | | | | | | | | | | |
| **ASIA** | | | | | | | | | | |
| Bangladesh | No | 0 | No | 0 | No | 0 | No | 0 | No | 0 |
| Fiji | No | 0 | No | 0 | No | 0 | No | 0 | No | 0 |
| Hong Kong | Yes | 10 | Yes | 10 | Yes | 10 | Yes | 10 | Yes | 10 |
| India | No | 0 | No | 0 | No | 0 | No | 0 | No | 0 |
| Indonesia | Yes | 10 | Yes | 10 | Yes | 10 | Yes | 10 | Yes | 10 |
| Malaysia | No | 0 | Yes | 10 | Yes | 10 | Yes | 10 | Yes | 10 |
| Nepal | No | 0 | No | 0 | No | 0 | No | 0 | No | 0 |
| Pakistan | No | 0 | No | 0 | No | 0 | Yes | 10 | Yes | 10 |
| Philippines | No | 0 | No | 0 | No | 0 | No | 0 | Yes | 10 |
| Singapore | No | 0 | No | 0 | Yes | 10 | Yes | 10 | Yes | 10 |
| South Korea | No | 0 | No | 0 | No | 0 | No | 0 | Yes | 10 |
| Sri Lanka | No | 0 | No | 0 | No | 0 | No | 0 | No | 0 |
| Taiwan | Yes | 10 | Yes | 10 | Yes | 10 | Yes | 10 | Yes | 10 |
| Thailand | No | 0 | No | 0 | No | 0 | Yes | 10 | Yes | 10 |

Table I-C: Freedom to Own Foreign Money (continued)

## Is It Legal (without restrictions) for Citizens to Own Foreign Money Domestically?

| COUNTRY | 1975 | | 1980 | | 1985 | | 1990 | | 1993-94 | |
|---|---|---|---|---|---|---|---|---|---|---|
| **AFRICA (cont)** | | | | | | | | | | |
| Algeria | No | 0 | No | 0 | No | 0 | No | 0 | No | 0 |
| Benin | No | 0 | No | 0 | No | 0 | No | 0 | No | 0 |
| Botswana | No | 0 | No | 0 | No | 0 | No | 0 | No | 0 |
| Burundi | - | | No | 0 | No | 0 | No | 0 | No | 0 |
| Cameroon | No | 0 | No | 0 | No | 0 | No | 0 | No | 0 |
| C African Rep | No | 0 | No | 0 | No | 0 | No | 0 | No | 0 |
| Chad | No | 0 | No | 0 | No | 0 | No | 0 | No | 0 |
| Congo Peoples Rep | No | 0 | No | 0 | No | 0 | No | 0 | No | 0 |
| Cote d' Ivoire | No | 0 | No | 0 | No | 0 | No | 0 | No | 0 |
| Gabon | No | 0 | No | 0 | No | 0 | No | 0 | No | 0 |
| Ghana | No | 0 | No | 0 | No | 0 | Yes | 10 | Yes | 10 |
| Kenya | No | 0 | No | 0 | No | 0 | No | 0 | No | 0 |
| Madagascar | - | | No | 0 | No | 0 | No | 0 | No | 0 |
| Malawi | No | 0 | No | 0 | No | 0 | No | 0 | No | 0 |
| Mali | No | 0 | No | 0 | No | 0 | No | 0 | No | 0 |
| Mauritius | No | 0 | No | 0 | No | 0 | No | 0 | No | 0 |
| Morocco | No | 0 | No | 0 | No | 0 | No | 0 | No | 0 |
| Niger | No | 0 | No | 0 | No | 0 | No | 0 | No | 0 |
| Nigeria | No | 0 | No | 0 | No | 0 | No | 0 | No | 0 |
| Rwanda | - | | No | 0 | No | 0 | No | 0 | Yes | 10 |
| Senegal | No | 0 | No | 0 | No | 0 | No | 0 | No | 0 |
| Sierra Leone | No | 0 | No | 0 | No | 0 | No | 0 | Yes | 10 |
| Somalia | No | 0 | No | 0 | No | 0 | No | 0 | No | 0 |
| South Africa | No | 0 | No | 0 | No | 0 | No | 0 | No | 0 |
| Tanzania | No | 0 | No | 0 | No | 0 | No | 0 | No | 0 |
| Togo | No | 0 | No | 0 | No | 0 | No | 0 | No | 0 |
| Tunisia | No | 0 | No | 0 | No | 0 | No | 0 | No | 0 |
| Uganda | No | 0 | No | 0 | No | 0 | No | 0 | No | 0 |
| Zaire | No | 0 | No | 0 | No | 0 | No | 0 | No | 0 |
| Zambia | No | 0 | No | 0 | No | 0 | No | 0 | No | 0 |
| Zimbabwe | No | 0 | No | 0 | No | 0 | No | 0 | No | 0 |

Source: International Currency Analysis, *World Currency Yearbook*, (various issues) and International Monetary Fund, *Exchange Arrangements and Exchange Restrictions: Annual Report 1994.*

## Table I-D: Freedom of Citizens to Maintain Bank Balances Abroad
(Countries That Permit Their Citizens to Maintain Bank Balances Abroad Are Given a Rating of 10; Those That Restrict This Freedom are Given a Rating of Zero.)

**Is It Legal (without restrictions) for Citizens to Maintain Bank Balances Abroad?**

| INDUSTRIAL COUNTRIES | 1975 | | 1980 | | 1985 | | 1990 | | 1993-94 | |
|---|---|---|---|---|---|---|---|---|---|---|
| United States | Yes | 10 | Yes | 10 | Yes | 10 | Yes | 10 | Yes | 10 |
| Canada | Yes | 10 | Yes | 10 | Yes | 10 | Yes | 10 | Yes | 10 |
| Australia | Yes | 10 | Yes | 10 | Yes | 10 | Yes | 10 | Yes | 10 |
| Japan | No | 0 | No | 0 | No | 0 | Yes | 10 | Yes | 10 |
| New Zealand | No | 0 | No | 0 | No | 0 | Yes | 10 | Yes | 10 |
| Austria | No | 0 | No | 0 | No | 0 | Yes | 10 | Yes | 10 |
| Belgium | Yes | 10 | Yes | 10 | Yes | 10 | Yes | 10 | Yes | 10 |
| Denmark | No | 0 | No | 0 | No | 0 | Yes | 10 | Yes | 10 |
| Finland | No | 0 | No | 0 | No | 0 | Yes | 10 | Yes | 10 |
| France | No | 0 | No | 0 | No | 0 | Yes | 10 | Yes | 10 |
| Germany | Yes | 10 | Yes | 10 | Yes | 10 | Yes | 10 | Yes | 10 |
| Iceland | No | 0 | No | 0 | No | 0 | Yes | 10 | Yes | 10 |
| Ireland | No | 0 | No | 0 | No | 0 | No | 0 | Yes | 10 |
| Italy | No | 0 | No | 0 | No | 0 | Yes | 10 | Yes | 10 |
| Netherlands | Yes | 10 | Yes | 10 | Yes | 10 | Yes | 10 | Yes | 10 |
| Norway | No | 0 | No | 0 | No | 0 | Yes | 10 | Yes | 10 |
| Spain | No | 0 | No | 0 | No | 0 | No | 0 | Yes | 10 |
| Sweden | No | 0 | No | 0 | No | 0 | No | 0 | No | 0 |
| Switzerland | Yes | 10 | Yes | 10 | Yes | 10 | Yes | 10 | Yes | 10 |
| United Kingdom | No | 0 | No | 0 | Yes | 10 | Yes | 10 | Yes | 10 |

**CENTRAL/SOUTH AMERICA**

| | 1975 | | 1980 | | 1985 | | 1990 | | 1993-94 | |
|---|---|---|---|---|---|---|---|---|---|---|
| Argentina | Yes | 10 | Yes | 10 | Yes | 10 | Yes | 10 | Yes | 10 |
| Belize | - | | - | | - | | No | 0 | No | 0 |
| Bolivia | Yes | 10 | Yes | 10 | No | 0 | Yes | 10 | Yes | 10 |
| Brazil | No | 0 | No | 0 | No | 0 | No | 0 | No | 0 |
| Chile | No | 0 | No | 0 | Yes | 10 | Yes | 10 | Yes | 10 |
| Colombia | No | 0 | No | 0 | No | 0 | No | 0 | Yes | 10 |
| Costa Rica | Yes | 10 | Yes | 10 | Yes | 10 | Yes | 10 | Yes | 10 |
| Dominican Rep | No | 0 | Yes | 10 | Yes | 10 | No | 0 | No | 0 |
| Ecuador | Yes | 10 | Yes | 10 | Yes | 10 | Yes | 10 | Yes | 10 |
| El Salvador | No | 0 | No | 0 | No | 0 | No | 0 | Yes | 10 |
| Guatemala | Yes | 10 | Yes | 10 | Yes | 10 | Yes | 10 | Yes | 10 |
| Haiti | No | 0 | Yes | 10 | Yes | 10 | Yes | 10 | Yes | 10 |
| Honduras | Yes | 10 | Yes | 10 | Yes | 10 | Yes | 10 | Yes | 10 |
| Jamaica | No | 0 | No | 0 | No | 0 | No | 0 | Yes | 10 |
| Mexico | Yes | 10 | Yes | 10 | Yes | 10 | Yes | 10 | Yes | 10 |
| Nicaragua | Yes | 10 | Yes | 10 | No | 0 | No | 0 | No | 0 |
| Panama | Yes | 10 | Yes | 10 | Yes | 10 | Yes | 10 | Yes | 10 |

Table I-D:   Freedom to Maintain Bank Balances (continued)

**Is It Legal (without restrictions) for Citizens to Maintain Bank Balances Abroad?**

| CENTRAL/-<br>S. AMERICA (con't) | 1975 | | 1980 | | 1985 | | 1990 | | 1993-94 | |
|---|---|---|---|---|---|---|---|---|---|---|
| Paraguay | Yes | 10 | Yes | 10 | Yes | 10 | Yes | 10 | Yes | 10 |
| Peru | No | 0 | No | 0 | No | 0 | No | 0 | Yes | 10 |
| Trinidad/Tobago | No | 0 | No | 0 | No | 0 | No | 0 | Yes | 10 |
| Uraguay | Yes | 10 | Yes | 10 | Yes | 10 | Yes | 10 | Yes | 10 |
| Venezuela | Yes | 10 | Yes | 10 | Yes | 10 | Yes | 10 | No | 0 |
| **EUROPE/MIDDLE EAST** | | | | | | | | | | |
| Bulgaria | No | 0 | No | 0 | No | 0 | No | 0 | Yes | 10 |
| Cyprus | No | 0 | No | 0 | No | 0 | No | 0 | No | 0 |
| Czechoslovakia | No | 0 | No | 0 | No | 0 | No | 0 | - | |
|   Czech Rep | - | | - | | - | | - | | Yes | 10 |
|   Slovakia | - | | - | | - | | - | | Yes | 10 |
| Egypt | No | 0 | Yes | 10 | Yes | 10 | Yes | 10 | Yes | 10 |
| Greece | No | 0 | No | 0 | No | 0 | No | 0 | No | 0 |
| Hungary | No | 0 | No | 0 | No | 0 | No | 0 | No | 0 |
| Iran | No | 0 | Yes | 10 | Yes | 10 | Yes | 10 | No | 0 |
| Israel | No | 0 | No | 0 | No | 0 | No | 0 | No | 0 |
| Jordan | No | 0 | No | 0 | No | 0 | No | 0 | No | 0 |
| Malta | - | | - | | No | 0 | No | 0 | No | 0 |
| Poland | Yes | 10 | Yes | 10 | Yes | 10 | Yes | 10 | Yes | 10 |
| Portugal | No | 0 | No | 0 | No | 0 | No | 0 | Yes | 10 |
| Romania | No | 0 | No | 0 | No | 0 | No | 0 | No | 0 |
| Syria | Yes | 10 | Yes | 10 | Yes | 10 | No | 0 | No | 0 |
| Turkey | No | 0 | No | 0 | No | 0 | Yes | 10 | Yes | 10 |
| **ASIA** | | | | | | | | | | |
| Bangladesh | No | 0 | No | 0 | No | 0 | No | 0 | No | 0 |
| Fiji | No | 0 | No | 0 | No | 0 | No | 0 | No | 0 |
| Hong Kong | Yes | 10 | Yes | 10 | Yes | 10 | Yes | 10 | Yes | 10 |
| India | No | 0 | No | 0 | No | 0 | No | 0 | No | 0 |
| Indonesia | Yes | 10 | Yes | 10 | Yes | 10 | Yes | 10 | Yes | 10 |
| Malaysia | Yes | 10 | Yes | 10 | No | 0 | Yes | 10 | Yes | 10 |
| Nepal | No | 0 | No | 0 | No | 0 | No | 0 | No | 0 |
| Pakistan | No | 0 | No | 0 | No | 0 | No | 0 | No | 0 |
| Philippines | No | 0 | No | 0 | No | 0 | No | 0 | Yes | 10 |
| Singapore | No | 0 | No | 0 | No | 0 | Yes | 10 | Yes | 10 |
| South Korea | No | 0 | No | 0 | No | 0 | No | 0 | Yes | 10 |
| Sri Lanka | No | 0 | No | 0 | No | 0 | No | 0 | No | 0 |
| Taiwan | Yes | 10 | Yes | 10 | Yes | 10 | Yes | 10 | Yes | 10 |
| Thailand | No | 0 | No | 0 | No | 0 | No | 0 | Yes | 10 |

Table I-D: Freedom to Maintain Bank Balances (continued)

**Is It Legal (without restrictions) for Citizens to**
**Maintain Bank Balances Abroad?**

| COUNTRY | 1975 | | 1980 | | 1985 | | 1990 | | 1993-94 | |
|---|---|---|---|---|---|---|---|---|---|---|
| **AFRICA (cont)** | | | | | | | | | | |
| Algeria | No | 0 | No | 0 | No | 0 | No | 0 | No | 0 |
| Benin | No | 0 | No | 0 | No | 0 | No | 0 | No | 0 |
| Botswana | No | 0 | No | 0 | No | 0 | No | 0 | No | 0 |
| Burundi | - | | - | | No | 0 | No | 0 | No | 0 |
| Cameroon | No | 0 | No | 0 | No | 0 | No | 0 | No | 0 |
| C African Rep | No | 0 | No | 0 | No | 0 | No | 0 | No | 0 |
| Chad | No | 0 | No | 0 | No | 0 | No | 0 | No | 0 |
| Congo Peoples Rep | No | 0 | No | 0 | No | 0 | No | 0 | No | 0 |
| Cote d' Ivoire | No | 0 | No | 0 | No | 0 | No | 0 | No | 0 |
| Gabon | No | 0 | No | 0 | No | 0 | No | 0 | No | 0 |
| Ghana | No | 0 | No | 0 | No | 0 | No | 0 | No | 0 |
| Kenya | No | 0 | No | 0 | No | 0 | No | 0 | No | 0 |
| Madagascar | No | 0 | No | 0 | No | 0 | No | 0 | No | 0 |
| Malawi | No | 0 | No | 0 | No | 0 | No | 0 | No | 0 |
| Mali | No | 0 | No | 0 | No | 0 | No | 0 | No | 0 |
| Mauritius | No | 0 | No | 0 | No | 0 | No | 0 | No | 0 |
| Morocco | No | 0 | No | 0 | No | 0 | No | 0 | No | 0 |
| Niger | No | 0 | No | 0 | No | 0 | No | 0 | No | 0 |
| Nigeria | No | 0 | No | 0 | No | 0 | No | 0 | No | 0 |
| Rwanda | No | 0 | No | 0 | No | 0 | No | 0 | No | 0 |
| Senegal | No | 0 | No | 0 | No | 0 | No | 0 | No | 0 |
| Sierra Leone | No | 0 | No | 0 | No | 0 | No | 0 | No | 0 |
| Somalia | No | 0 | No | 0 | No | 0 | No | 0 | No | 0 |
| South Africa | No | 0 | No | 0 | No | 0 | No | 0 | No | 0 |
| Tanzania | No | 0 | No | 0 | No | 0 | No | 0 | No | 0 |
| Togo | No | 0 | No | 0 | No | 0 | No | 0 | No | 0 |
| Tunisia | No | 0 | No | 0 | No | 0 | No | 0 | No | 0 |
| Uganda | No | 0 | No | 0 | No | 0 | No | 0 | No | 0 |
| Zaire | No | 0 | No | 0 | No | 0 | No | 0 | No | 0 |
| Zambia | No | 0 | No | 0 | No | 0 | No | 0 | No | 0 |
| Zimbabwe | No | 0 | No | 0 | No | 0 | No | 0 | No | 0 |

Source:  International Currency Analysis, *World Currency Yearbook*, (various issues) and International Monetary Fund, *Exchange Arrangements and Exchange Restrictions:  Annual Report 1994.*

## Table II-A:  General Government Consumption Expenditures As A Percent of GDP

| | Government Consumption As A Percent of GDP | | | | | | | | | |
|---|---|---|---|---|---|---|---|---|---|---|
| | (The rating of each country is in parenthesis) | | | | | | | | | |
| **INDUSTRIAL COUNTRIES** | 1975 | | 1980 | | 1985 | | 1990 | | 1994 | |
| United States | 18.6 | (2) | 17.6 | (2) | 18.1 | (2) | 17.8 | (2) | 17.4 | (3) |
| Canada | 19.5 | (1) | 19.2 | (2) | 20.1 | (1) | 20.3 | (1) | 20.1 | (1) |
| Australia | 17.2 | (3) | 18.0 | (2) | 18.9 | (2) | 17.8 | (2) | 19.0 | (2) |
| Japan | 10.0 | (8) | 9.8 | (8) | 9.6 | (9) | 9.1 | (9) | 9.8 | (8) |
| New Zealand | 15.6 | (4) | 17.9 | (2) | 16.2 | (4) | 17.0 | (3) | 15.2 | (5) [a] |
| Austria | 17.2 | (3) | 18.0 | (2) | 18.9 | (2) | 17.8 | (2) | 19.0 | (2) |
| Belgium | 16.5 | (3) | 17.8 | (2) | 17.1 | (3) | 14.5 | (5) | 15.0 | (5) |
| Denmark | 24.6 | (0) | 26.7 | (0) | 25.3 | (0) | 25.3 | (0) | 25.3 | (0) |
| Finland | 17.0 | (3) | 18.0 | (2) | 20.2 | (1) | 21.1 | (1) | 22.4 | (1) |
| France | 16.6 | (3) | 18.1 | (2) | 19.4 | (1) | 17.9 | (2) | 19.8 | (1) |
| Germany | 20.5 | (1) | 20.3 | (1) | 20.1 | (1) | 18.3 | (2) | 17.5 | (3) |
| Iceland | 16.5 | (3) | 16.9 | (3) | 17.5 | (3) | 19.4 | (1) | 20.8 | (1) |
| Ireland | 17.7 | (2) | 18.9 | (2) | 17.6 | (2) | 15.1 | (5) | 16.4 | (4) [a] |
| Italy | 14.1 | (6) | 14.7 | (5) | 16.4 | (4) | 17.4 | (3) | 17.6 | (2) [b] |
| Netherlands | 16.9 | (3) | 17.4 | (3) | 15.7 | (4) | 14.5 | (5) | 14.9 | (5) |
| Norway | 19.3 | (1) | 18.8 | (2) | 18.5 | (2) | 21.1 | (1) | 21.9 | (1) |
| Spain | 10.5 | (8) | 13.2 | (6) | 14.7 | (5) | 15.5 | (5) | 17.0 | (3) |
| Sweden | 24.2 | (0) | 29.3 | (0) | 27.9 | (0) | 27.4 | (0) | 27.3 | (0) |
| Switzerland | 12.6 | (7) | 12.7 | (7) | 13.3 | (6) | 13.4 | (6) | 14.3 | (5) |
| United Kingdom | 22.4 | (1) | 21.6 | (1) | 21.1 | (1) | 20.6 | (1) | 21.5 | (1) |
| **CENTRAL/SOUTH AMERICA** | | | | | | | | | | |
| Argentina | 12.6 | (7) | 13.4 | (6) | 12.0 | (7) | 5.6 | (10) | 5.1 | (10) |
| Belize | - | | 17.2 | (3) | 22.8 | (0) | 19.6 | (1) | 19.6 | (1) [a] |
| Bolivia | 10.5 | (8) | 14.1 | (6) | 13.3 | (6) | 14.0 | (6) | 15.2 | (5) [a] |
| Brazil | 10.6 | (8) | 9.2 | (9) | 9.9 | (8) | 15.5 | (5) | 16.5 | (3) [a] |
| Chile | 15.7 | (4) | 12.5 | (7) | 13.4 | (6) | 9.6 | (9) | 9.3 | (9) |
| Colombia | 8.9 | (9) | 10.1 | (8) | 10.7 | (8) | 10.3 | (8) | 12.8 | (7) [a] |
| Costa Rica | 15.2 | (5) | 18.2 | (2) | 15.8 | (4) | 18.2 | (2) | 17.3 | (3) |
| Dominican Republic | 6.2 | (10) | 7.6 | (10) | 8.0 | (9) | 9.3 | (9) | 10.9 | (8) [a] |
| Ecuador | 14.5 | (5) | 14.5 | (5) | 11.5 | (7) | 8.6 | (9) | 7.3 | (10) |
| El Salvador | 11.2 | (7) | 14.0 | (6) | 15.5 | (5) | 11.3 | (7) | 9.3 | (9) |
| Guatemala | 6.9 | (10) | 8.0 | (9) | 7.1 | (10) | 6.8 | (10) | 6.4 | (10) [a] |
| Haiti | 9.0 | (9) | 10.1 | (8) | 11.9 | (7) | - | | - | |
| Honduras | 12.4 | (7) | 12.7 | (7) | 13.1 | (6) | 12.9 | (7) | 10.6 | (8) |
| Jamaica | 18.6 | (2) | 20.2 | (1) | 15.5 | (5) | 14.1 | (6) | 13.1 | (6) [a] |
| Mexico | 9.3 | (9) | 10.0 | (8) | 9.2 | (9) | 8.4 | (9) | 9.3 | (9) [a] |
| Nicaragua | 9.1 | (9) | 19.7 | (1) | 35.7 | (0) | 32.6 | (0) | 15.9 | (4) |

Table II-A: (continued)

## Government Consumption As A Percent of GDP

(The rating of each country is in parenthesis)

| CENTRAL/-SOUTH AMERICA (con't) | 1975 | | 1980 | | 1985 | | 1990 | | 1994 | |
|---|---|---|---|---|---|---|---|---|---|---|
| Panama | 19.2 | (2) | 18.9 | (2) | 21.1 | (1) | 18.8 | (2) | 19.8 | (1) [a] |
| Paraguay | 6.3 | (10) | 6.0 | (10) | 5.6 | (10) | 6.2 | (10) | 9.3 | (9) [a] |
| Peru | 12.4 | (7) | 10.5 | (8) | 9.5 | (9) | 6.4 | (10) | 5.7 | (10) |
| Trinidad & Tobago | 12.3 | (7) | 12.1 | (7) | 22.7 | (1) | 16.2 | (4) | 16.5 | (3) [a] |
| Uruguay | 14.0 | (6) | 12.5 | (7) | 14.5 | (5) | 13.9 | (6) | 13.4 | (6) |
| Venezuela | 11.5 | (7) | 11.8 | (7) | 10.5 | (8) | 8.4 | (9) | 7.3 | (10) |

| EUROPE/MIDDLE EAST | | | | | | | | | | |
|---|---|---|---|---|---|---|---|---|---|---|
| Bulgaria | - | | 5.6 | (10) | 8.5 | (9) | 18.2 | (2) | 17.3 | (3) [a] |
| Cyprus | 17.5 | (3) | 13.7 | (6) | 14.1 | (6) | 13.3 | (6) | 14.3 | (5) [b] |
| Czechoslovakia | - | | 19.5 | (2) | 20.9 | (1) | 22.5 | (1) | - | |
| Czech Republic | - | | - | | - | | - | | 22.3 | (1) |
| Slovakia | - | | - | | - | | - | | 25.8 | (0) |
| Egypt | 24.9 | (0) | 15.7 | (4) | 17.2 | (3) | 11.7 | (7) | 15.0 | (5) |
| Greece | 15.2 | (5) | 16.4 | (4) | 20.4 | (1) | 21.1 | (1) | 19.7 | (1) [b] |
| Hungary | 10.4 | (8) | 10.3 | (8) | 10.1 | (8) | 10.6 | (8) | 13.1 | (6) [a] |
| Iran | 24.2 | (0) | 20.8 | (1) | 15.5 | (5) | 11.1 | (7) | 17.3 | (3) [a] |
| Israel | 40.2 | (0) | 38.5 | (0) | 34.4 | (0) | 28.8 | (0) | 27.1 | (0) [a] |
| Jordan | 29.2 | (0) | 29.0 | (0) | 26.8 | (0) | 25.2 | (0) | 22.9 | (0) |
| Malta | 18.4 | (2) | 16.2 | (4) | 17.7 | (2) | 17.6 | (2) | 20.1 | (1) [a] |
| Poland | - | | 9.2 | (9) | 9.2 | (9) | 8.3 | (9) | 10.2 | (8) [a] |
| Portugal | 15.0 | (5) | 14.5 | (5) | 15.5 | (5) | 16.7 | (3) | 18.3 | (2) [b] |
| Romania | - | | 5.0 | (10) | 3.9 | (10) | 13.3 | (6) | 14.6 | (5) [a] |
| Syria | 21.1 | (1) | 23.2 | (0) | 23.8 | (0) | 14.4 | (5) | 14.4 | (5) [a] |
| Turkey | 12.3 | (7) | 12.6 | (7) | 8.6 | (9) | 14.1 | (6) | 18.6 | (2) [a] |

| ASIA | | | | | | | | | | |
|---|---|---|---|---|---|---|---|---|---|---|
| Bangladesh | 3.2 | (10) | 6.3 | (10) | 7.3 | (10) | 14.0 | (6) | 13.9 | (6) [a] |
| Fiji | 12.0 | (7) | 15.9 | (4) | 19.2 | (2) | 16.6 | (3) | 18.9 | (2) [a] |
| Hong Kong | 7.5 | (10) | 6.5 | (10) | 7.6 | (10) | 6.2 | (10) | 6.9 | (10) [b] |
| India | 9.4 | (9) | 9.6 | (9) | 11.1 | (7) | 11.6 | (7) | 11.8 | (7) [a] |
| Indonesia | 9.0 | (9) | 10.5 | (8) | 11.2 | (7) | 9.0 | (9) | 8.2 | (9) |
| Malaysia | 17.7 | (2) | 16.5 | (3) | 15.3 | (5) | 14.0 | (6) | 13.0 | (7) |
| Nepal | 7.6 | (10) | 6.7 | (10) | 9.8 | (8) | 11.4 | (7) | 10.6 | (8) [a] |
| Pakistan | 10.6 | (8) | 10.0 | (8) | 12.1 | (7) | 15.1 | (5) | 12.2 | (7) |
| Philippines | 10.7 | (8) | 9.1 | (9) | 7.6 | (10) | 10.1 | (8) | 8.6 | (9) |
| Singapore | 10.6 | (8) | 9.8 | (8) | 14.3 | (5) | 10.5 | (8) | 9.4 | (9) [a] |
| South Korea | 11.0 | (7) | 11.5 | (7) | 10.1 | (8) | 10.1 | (8) | 10.7 | (8) |
| Sri Lanka | 9.3 | (9) | 8.6 | (9) | 10.0 | (8) | 9.6 | (9) | 9.7 | (8) |
| Taiwan | 15.8 | (4) | 15.9 | (4) | 16.2 | (4) | 17.6 | (2) | 16.0 | (4) [a] |
| Thailand | 10.3 | (8) | 12.3 | (7) | 13.5 | (6) | 9.4 | (9) | 10.3 | (8) |

Table II-A: (continued)

## Government Consumption As A Percent of GDP

(The rating of each country is in parenthesis)

| AFRICA | 1975 | | 1980 | | 1985 | | 1990 | | 1994 | |
|---|---|---|---|---|---|---|---|---|---|---|
| Algeria | 12.9 | (7) | 13.8 | (6) | 15.7 | (4) | 16.6 | (3) | 18.5 | (2) a |
| Benin | 9.3 | (9) | 8.6 | (9) | 15.4 | (5) | 13.2 | (6) | 11.5 | (7) a |
| Botswana | 18.8 | (2) | 19.3 | (1) | 24.2 | (0) | 19.1 | (2) | 24.6 | (0) a |
| Burundi | 11.6 | (7) | 9.2 | (9) | 7.8 | (10) | 10.4 | (8) | 10.4 | (8) a |
| Cameroon | 10.9 | (8) | 8.7 | (9) | 9.0 | (9) | 12.9 | (7) | 13.6 | (6) a |
| Central African Rep | 17.3 | (3) | 15.1 | (5) | 13.8 | (6) | 9.9 | (8) | 9.8 | (8) a |
| Chad | 25.3 | (0) | 25.4 | (0) c | 16.7 | (3) | 20.9 | (1) | 16.6 | (3) a |
| Congo Peoples Rep | 18.0 | (2) | 17.6 | (2) | 16.5 | (3) | 19.2 | (2) | 22.3 | (1) a |
| Cote d'Ivoire | 17.0 | (3) | 16.9 | (3) | 13.9 | (6) | 18.1 | (2) | 20.4 | (1) a |
| Gabon | 12.2 | (7) | 13.2 | (6) | 18.6 | (2) | 16.9 | (3) | 19.3 | (1) a |
| Ghana | 13.0 | (7) | 11.2 | (7) | 9.4 | (9) | 10.9 | (8) | 11.7 | (7) a |
| Kenya | 18.3 | (2) | 19.8 | (1) | 17.5 | (3) | 18.7 | (2) | 13.1 | (6) a |
| Madagascar | 10.8 | (8) | 12.1 | (7) | 9.8 | (8) | 6.2 | (10) | 5.6 | (10) |
| Malawi | 14.1 | (6) | 19.3 | (1) | 17.7 | (2) | 15.2 | (5) | 16.9 | (3) a |
| Mali | 10.3 | (8) | 10.4 | (8) | 12.4 | (7) | 13.5 | (6) | 12.8 | (7) a |
| Mauritius | 11.1 | (7) | 14.1 | (6) | 10.2 | (8) | 11.1 | (7) | 12.9 | (7) a |
| Morocco | 16.3 | (4) | 18.3 | (2) | 15.8 | (4) | 15.4 | (5) | 16.5 | (3) a |
| Niger | 10.8 | (8) | 10.3 | (8) | 15.0 | (5) | 15.0 | (5) | 16.6 | (3) a |
| Nigeria | 12.6 | (7) | 11.9 | (7) | 13.5 | (6) | 11.4 | (7) | 5.3 | (10) |
| Rwanda | 16.6 | (3) | 12.5 | (7) | 11.3 | (7) | 15.4 | (5) | 26.4 | (0) b |
| Senegal | 15.2 | (5) | 22.0 | (1) | 16.8 | (3) | 14.6 | (5) | 12.5 | (7) a |
| Sierra Leone | 11.1 | (7) | 8.4 | (9) | 7.2 | (10) | 6.6 | (10) | 11.2 | (7) a |
| Somalia | 20.3 | (1) | 15.6 | (4) | 18.0 | (2) | - | | - | |
| South Africa | 13.8 | (6) | 13.5 | (6) | 17.3 | (3) | 19.5 | (1) | 21.1 | (1) |
| Tanzania | 17.2 | (3) | 13.0 | (7) | 15.4 | (5) | 10.4 | (8) | 11.3 | (7) a |
| Togo | 15.0 | (5) | 14.8 | (5) | 13.1 | (6) | 15.2 | (5) | 16.5 | (3) a |
| Tunisia | 14.6 | (5) | 14.5 | (5) | 16.5 | (3) | 16.4 | (4) | 16.6 | (3) |
| Uganda | - | | - | | 11.9 | (7) | 8.8 | (9) | 10.0 | (8) a |
| Zaire | 11.6 | (7) | 8.4 | (9) | 7.7 | (10) | 11.5 | (7) | 21.7 | (1) b |
| Zambia | 26.8 | (0) | 25.5 | (0) | 23.9 | (0) | 19.0 | (2) | 14.7 | (5) b |
| Zimbabwe | 12.8 | (7) | 19.7 | (1) | 21.5 | (1) | 22.5 | (1) | 18.8 | (2) a |

a Indicates data are for 1993.
b Indicates data are for 1992.
c The 1980 data were unavailable. These data are for 1978, the closest year for which data were available.

Source: Both the general government consumption expenditures and the GDP data used to derived the ratio are from the World Bank, *World Tables, 1994*. In cases where the 1994 data were not yet available from the World Bank, data from the International Monetary Fund, *Monthly International Financial Statistics*, were used. The base year for the rating of each country was 1985. The following conversion table divided the 1985 data into eleven intervals of equal size.

Table II-A (con't)

| General Government Consumption Expenditures As A Percent of GDP | Rating |
|---|---|
| 0.000% - 7.90% | 10 |
| 7.91 - 9.67 | 9 |
| 9.68 - 10.91 | 8 |
| 10.92 - 13.07 | 7 |
| 13.08 - 14.16 | 6 |
| 14.17 - 15.50 | 5 |
| 15.51 - 16.45 | 4 |
| 16.46 - 17.56 | 3 |
| 17.57 - 19.26 | 2 |
| 19.27 - 22.78 | 1 |
| > 22.78 | 0 |

**Table II-B: The Role of Government Enterprises in the Economy**

### Size of Government Enterprises As A Share of Economy

(A higher rating indicates that government enterprises play a less significant role.)

| INDUSTRIAL COUNTRIES | 1975 | 1980 | 1985 | 1990 | 1995 |
|---|---|---|---|---|---|
| United States | (8) | (8) | (8) | (8) | (8) |
| Canada | (6) | (6) | (6) | (6) | (6) |
| Australia | (6) | (6) | (6) | (6) | (6) |
| Japan | (8) | (8) | (8) | (8) | (8) |
| New Zealand | (6) | (6) | (6) | (6) | (8) |
| Austria | (2) | (2) | (2) | (2) | (2) |
| Belgium | (6) | (6) | (6) | (6) | (6) |
| Denmark | (4) | (4) | (4) | (4) | (4) |
| Finland | (6) | (6) | (6) | (6) | (6) |
| France | (4) | (4) | (4) | (6) | (6) |
| Germany | (6) | (6) | (6) | (6) | (6) |
| Iceland | (4) | (4) | (4) | (4) | (4) |
| Ireland | (4) | (4) | (4) | (4) | (4) |
| Italy | (2) | (2) | (2) | (2) | (2) |
| Netherlands | (6) | (6) | (6) | (6) | (6) |
| Norway | (2) | (2) | (2) | (2) | (2) |
| Spain | (4) | (4) | (4) | (4) | (4) |
| Sweden | (4) | (4) | (4) | (4) | (4) |
| Switzerland | (8) | (8) | (8) | (8) | (8) |
| United Kingdom | (4) | (4) | (6) | (6) | (6) |

| CENTRAL/SOUTH AMERICA | | | | | |
|---|---|---|---|---|---|
| Argentina | (6) | (4) | (4) | (4) | (6) |
| Belize | (8) | (8) | (8) | (8) | (8) |
| Bolivia | (6) | (6) | (4) | (4) | (4) |
| Brazil | (4) | (4) | (2) | (2) | (2) |
| Chile | (6) | (8) | (8) | (8) | (8) |
| Colombia | (6) | (4) | (4) | (4) | (4) |
| Costa Rica | (8) | (8) | (8) | (8) | (8) |
| Dominican Rep | (6) | (6) | (6) | (6) | (6) |
| Ecuador | (6) | (6) | (6) | (6) | (6) |
| El Salvador | (8) | (8) | (8) | (8) | (8) |
| Guatemala | (8) | (8) | (8) | (8) | (8) |
| Haiti | (6) | (6) | (6) | (6) | (4) |
| Honduras | (8) | (8) | (8) | (8) | (8) |
| Jamaica | (2) | (2) | (2) | (4) | (4) |
| Mexico | (2) | (2) | (2) | (4) | (6) |
| Nicaragua | (6) | (6) | (0) | (0) | (0) |

Table II-B: (continued)

**Size of Government Enterprises As A Share of Economy**

(A higher rating indicates that government enterprises play a less significant role.)

| CENTRAL/-<br>S. AMERICA (cont) | 1975 | 1980 | 1985 | 1990 | 1995 |
|---|---|---|---|---|---|
| Panama | (8) | (6) | (6) | (6) | (6) |
| Paraguay | (8) | (8) | (8) | (8) | (8) |
| Peru | (4) | (4) | (4) | (4) | (6) |
| Trinidad/Tobago | (2) | (2) | (2) | (2) | (2) |
| Uraguay | (6) | (6) | (6) | (6) | (6) |
| Venezuela | (6) | (4) | (4) | (2) | (2) |
| **EUROPE/MIDDLE EAST** | | | | | |
| Bulgaria | (0) | (0) | (0) | (0) | (0) |
| Cyprus | (6) | (6) | (6) | (6) | (6) |
| Czechoslovakia | (0) | (0) | (0) | (0) | - |
|    Czech Republic | - | - | - | - | (4) |
|    Slovakia | - | - | - | - | (4) |
| Egypt | (4) | (2) | (2) | (2) | (2) |
| Greece | (2) | (2) | (2) | (2) | (2) |
| Hungary | (0) | (0) | (0) | (0) | (2) |
| Iran | (4) | (2) | (2) | (2) | (2) |
| Israel | (2) | (2) | (2) | (2) | (2) |
| Jordan | (6) | (6) | (6) | (6) | (6) |
| Malta | (4) | (4) | (4) | (4) | (4) |
| Poland | (0) | (0) | (0) | (0) | (2) |
| Portugal | (2) | (2) | (2) | (2) | (2) |
| Romania | (0) | (0) | (0) | (0) | (0) |
| Syria | (6) | (4) | (2) | (2) | (2) |
| Turkey | (4) | (4) | (4) | (4) | (4) |
| **ASIA** | | | | | |
| Bangladesh | (6) | (6) | (6) | (6) | (6) |
| Fiji | (6) | (6) | (6) | (6) | (6) |
| Hong Kong | (10) | (10) | (10) | (10) | (10) |
| India | (0) | (0) | (0) | (0) | (2) |
| Indonesia | (4) | (2) | (2) | (2) | (2) |
| Malaysia | (4) | (4) | (6) | (6) | (6) |
| Nepal | (6) | (6) | (6) | (4) | (4) |
| Pakistan | (2) | (2) | (2) | (4) | (4) |
| Philippines | (4) | (4) | (4) | (4) | (4) |
| Singapore | (8) | (8) | (8) | (8) | (8) |
| South Korea | (6) | (6) | (6) | (6) | (6) |
| Sri Lanka | (2) | (4) | (4) | (4) | (4) |
| Taiwan | (4) | (4) | (4) | (4) | (4) |
| Thailand | (6) | (6) | (6) | (6) | (6) |

Table II-B: (continued)

**Size of Government Enterprises As A Share of Economy**

(A higher rating indicates that government enterprises play a less significant role.)

| | 1975 | 1980 | 1985 | 1990 | 1995 |
|---|---|---|---|---|---|
| **AFRICA** | | | | | |
| Algeria | (4) | (4) | (4) | (4) | (4) |
| Benin | (4) | (4) | (4) | (4) | (4) |
| Botswana | (8) | (8) | (8) | (6) | (6) |
| Burundi | (4) | (4) | (4) | (4) | (4) |
| Cameroon | (4) | (4) | (4) | (4) | (4) |
| C African Rep | (6) | (6) | (6) | (6) | (6) |
| Chad | (4) | (4) | (4) | (4) | (4) |
| Congo Rep | (0) | (0) | (0) | (0) | (0) |
| Cote d' Ivoire | (4) | (4) | (4) | (4) | (4) |
| Gabon | (6) | (6) | (6) | (6) | (6) |
| Ghana | (0) | (0) | (0) | (2) | (2) |
| Kenya | (4) | (4) | (4) | (4) | (4) |
| Madagascar | (6) | (6) | (6) | (6) | (6) |
| Malawi | (4) | (4) | (4) | (4) | (4) |
| Mali | (4) | (4) | (4) | (4) | (4) |
| Mauritius | (6) | (6) | (6) | (6) | (6) |
| Morocco | (4) | (4) | (2) | (2) | (2) |
| Niger | (4) | (4) | (4) | (6) | (6) |
| Nigeria | (4) | (2) | (2) | (2) | (2) |
| Rwanda | (6) | (6) | (6) | (6) | (6) |
| Senegal | (4) | (4) | (4) | (6) | (6) |
| Sierra Leone | (6) | (6) | (6) | (6) | (6) |
| Somalia | (4) | (4) | (4) | (4) | (4) |
| South Africa | (4) | (4) | (4) | (4) | (4) |
| Tanzania | (2) | (2) | (0) | (0) | (0) |
| Togo | (4) | (4) | (4) | (4) | (4) |
| Tunisia | (2) | (2) | (2) | (4) | (4) |
| Uganda | (2) | (2) | (2) | (2) | (2) |
| Zaire | (2) | (2) | (2) | (2) | (2) |
| Zambia | (0) | (0) | (0) | (0) | (0) |
| Zimbabwe | (4) | (4) | (4) | (4) | (4) |

Source and Explanation of Ratings:

The rating for each country was designed to reflect the following:

| Rating | Role of Government Enterprises in Country |
|---|---|
| 10 | There are very few government-operated enterprises and they produce less then 1 percent of the country's total output. |
| 8 | There are very few government-operated enterprises other than power-generating plants and those operating in industries where economies of scale generally reduce the effectiveness of competition. |
| 6 | Government enterprises are generally present in power generating, transportation (airlines, railroads, and bus lines), communications (television and radio stations, telephone companies, and post offices) and the development of energy sources, but private enterprises dominates other sectors of the economy. |
| 4 | There are a substantial number of government-operated enterprises in many sectors of the economy, including the manufacturing sector. Most of the large enterprises of the economy are operated by the government; private enterprises are generally small. Employment and output in the government-operated enterprises generally comprises between 10 and 20 percent of the total non-agricultural employment and output. |
| 2 | Numerous government enterprises of all sizes are present and they operate in many sectors of the economy, including manufacturing and retail sales. Employment and output in the government-operated enterprises generally comprises between 20 and 30 percent of the total non-agricultural employment and output. |
| 0 | The economy is dominated by government-operated enterprises. Employment and output in the government-operated enterprises generally exceeds 30 percent of the total non-agricultural employment and output. |

Data on the number of government enterprises and the activities of these enterprises from the International Monetary Fund, *Government Finance Statistics Yearbook*, (various issues) were used to assist with the determination of the rating for each country. In addition, the following publications were helpful in determining the proper classification for various countries: V.V. Ramanadham, ed., *Privatization in Developing Countries*, London: Routledge, 1989; Rexford A. Ahene and Bernard S. Katz, eds., *Privatization and Investment in Sub-Saharan Africa*, New York: Praeger, 1992; Manuel Sanchez and Rossana Corona, eds., *Privatization in Latin America*, Washington, D.C.: Inter-American Development Bank, 1993; Iliya Harik and Denis J. Sullivan, eds., *Privatization and Liberalization in the Middle East*, Bloomington, IN: Indiana University Press, 1992; *OECD Economic Surveys*, Italy; Organization for Economic Co-Operation and Development, January 1994; John R. Nellis, "Public Enterprises in Sub-Saharan Africa," *World Bank Discussion Paper*, no. 1 (Washington, DC: November, 1986); Bos Dieter, *Public Enterprise Economics*, New York: North Holland, 1989; and Raymond Vernon, editor, *The Promise of Privatization: A Challenge for American Foreign Policy*, New York: Council on Foreign Relations, 1988.

## Table II-C: The Extent Countries Imposed Price Controls on Various Goods and Services, (1989 and 1994)

| INDUSTRIAL COUNTRIES | Rating (Ten indicates little or no use of price controls) | | CENTRAL/- S. AMERICA (con't) | Rating (Ten indicates little or no use of price controls) | |
|---|---|---|---|---|---|
| | 1989 | 1994 | | 1989 | 1994 |
| United States | 8 | 8 | Peru | 2 | 6 |
| Canada | 8 | 8 | Trinidad/Tobago | 4 | 4 |
| Australia | 6 | 7 | Uruguay | 4 | 6 |
| Japan | 6 | 5 | Venezuela | 4 | 2 |
| New Zealand | 9 | 10 | | | |
| Austria | 5 | 6 | **EUROPE/MIDDLE EAST** | | |
| Belgium | 2 | 5 | Bulgaria | 0 | 4 |
| Denmark | 6 | 8 | Cyprus | 0 | 2 |
| Finland | 6 | 8 | Czechoslovakia | 0 | - |
| France | 6 | 7 | Czech Rep | - | 5 |
| Germany | 9 | 9 | Slovakia | - | 4 |
| Iceland | - | - | Egypt | 2 | 2 |
| Ireland | 7 | 8 | Greece | 0 | 6 |
| Italy | 5 | 5 | Hungary | 6 | 7 |
| Netherlands | 7 | 7 | Iran | 2 | - |
| Norway | 5 | 7 | Israel | 0 | 4 |
| Spain | 6 | 6 | Jordan | 2 | 2 |
| Sweden | 6 | 8 | Malta | 0 | 2 |
| Switzerland | 7 | 6 | Poland | 2 | 5 |
| United Kingdom | 8 | 9 | Portugal | 4 | 6 |
| | | | Romania | 0 | 4 |
| **CENTRAL/S. AMERICA** | | | Syria | - | 0 |
| Argentina | 0 | 8 | Turkey | 6 | 3 |
| Belize | - | 6 | | | |
| Bolivia | 6 | 8 | **ASIA** | | |
| Brazil | 0 | 4 | Bangladesh | 0 | 0 |
| Chile | 8 | 8 | Fiji | 6 | 6 |
| Colombia | 6 | 6 | Hong Kong | 10 | 9 |
| Costa Rica | - | 6 | India | 3 | 3 |
| Dominican Republic | 4 | 6 | Indonesia | 6 | 3 |
| Ecuador | 0 | 0 | Malaysia | 5 | 4 |
| El Salvador | - | 6 | Nepal | - | - |
| Guatemala | 6 | 6 | Pakistan | - | 4 |
| Haiti | 2 | 0 | Philippines | 2 | 3 |
| Honduras | - | 4 | Singapore | 8 | 8 |
| Jamaica | 4 | 4 | South Korea | 3 | 4 |
| Mexico | 0 | 7 | Sri Lanka | - | 6 |
| Nicaragua | - | 2 | Taiwan | 6 | 7 |
| Panama | 2 | 4 | Thailand | 4 | 5 |
| Paraguay | 4 | 4 | | | |

266

Table II-C: (continued)

| AFRICA | Rating (Ten indicates little or no use of price controls) | | AFRICA (cont) | Rating (Ten indicates little or no use of price controls) | |
|---|---|---|---|---|---|
| | 1989 | 1994 | | 1989 | 1994 |
| Algeria | - | - | Morocco | 0 | 4 |
| Benin | - | 2 | Niger | - | - |
| Botswana | 6 | 6 | Nigeria | 4 | 4 |
| Burundi | - | - | Rwanda | - | - |
| Cameroon | 2 | 2 | Senegal | 4 | 4 |
| C African Rep | - | - | Sierra Leone | 2 | 2 |
| Chad | - | - | Somalia | 0 | - |
| Congo Peoples Rep | 0 | 0 | South Africa | 4 | 4 |
| Cote d' Ivoire | - | 4 | Tanzania | 0 | 4 |
| Gabon | - | 4 | Togo | 2 | 2 |
| Ghana | 0 | 6 | Tunisia | 4 | 6 |
| Kenya | 2 | 4 | Uganda | - | - |
| Madagascar | - | - | Zaire | - | - |
| Malawi | 2 | 2 | Zambia | 0 | 2 |
| Mali | - | - | Zimbabwe | 2 | 2 |
| Mauritius | - | - | | | |

Source: The foundation for these ratings was provided by the data of the World Economic Forum, *The World Competitiveness Report*, (1989 and 1994) and Price Waterhouse, *Doing Business Series*. *The World Competitiveness Report* contains survey data indicating the "extent to which companies can set their prices freely: 0 = not at all, to 100 = very much so". Thirty-two countries were rated in the 1989 survey and 41 countries in the 1994 survey. Since these data were the most comprehensive quantifiable indicators of the presence or absence of price controls which we could find, we used them to rate the following countries: Austria, Australia, Belgium, Brazil, Canada, Denmark, Finland, France, Germany, Greece, Hong Kong, India, Indonesia, Ireland, Italy, Japan, Malaysia, Mexico, Netherlands, New Zealand, Norway, Portugal, Singapore, Spain, Sweden, Switzerland, Taiwan, Thailand, Turkey, United Kingdom, and United States for both 1989 and 1994. These data were also used to rate Argentina, Columbia, Chile, Czech Republic, Hungary, Denmark, Poland, Philippines, South Africa, and Venezuela in 1994. The following table indicates the relationship between the World Economic Forum survey data and our 0 to 10 rating system.

| Percent Indicating Companies Can Set Prices Freely | Rating |
|---|---|
| more than 90% | 10 |
| 85 - 90 | 9 |
| 80 - 85 | 8 |
| 75 - 80 | 7. |
| 70 - 75 | 6 |
| 65 - 70 | 5 |
| 60 - 65 | 4 |
| 55 - 60 | 3 |
| 50 - 55 | 2 |
| 45 - 50 | 1 |
| less than 40% | 0 |

The Price Waterhouse booklet provided a verbal description on the general presence or absence of price controls which helped us classify other countries. In some instances, this information was supplemented with similar information which was available from country sources. These descriptive data were used to classify countries and place them into the following categories:

| General Characteristics of Country | Rating |
|---|---|
| No Price controls or marketing boards are present. | 10 |
| Except in industries (e.g., electric power generation) where economics of scale may reduce the effectiveness of competition, prices are generally determined by market forces. | 8 |
| Price controls are often applied in energy markets; marketing boards often influence prices of agricultural products; controls are also present in a few other areas, but most prices are determined by market forces. | 6 |
| Price controls are levied on energy, agricultural, and many stable products (e. g. food products, clothing and housing) that are widely purchased by households; but most other prices are set by market forces. | 4 |
| Price controls apply to a significant number of products in both agricultural and manufacturing industries. | 2 |
| There is widespread use of price controls throughout the economy. | 0 |

## Table II-D: Freedom of Businesses and Cooperatives to Compete in the Marketplace

**Are Businesses and Cooperatives Free to Compete?**

(1994-95 Rating--the Higher the Rating the Greater the Freedom to Compete)

| INDUSTRIAL COUNTRIES | | CENTRAL/- S. AMERICA (con't) | |
|---|---|---|---|
| United States | 10.0 | Paraguay | 7.5 |
| Canada | 7.5 | Peru | 7.5 |
| Australia | 10.0 | Trinidad/Tobago | 10.0 |
| Japan | 7.5 | Uruguay | 7.5 |
| New Zealand | 10.0 | Venezuela | 5.0 |
| Austria | 7.5 | | |
| Belgium | 7.5 | **EUROPE/MIDDLE EAST** | |
| Denmark | 10.0 | Bulgaria | 7.5 |
| Finland | 7.5 | Cyprus | 10.0 |
| France | 7.5 | Czech Republic | 5.0 |
| Germany | 7.5 | Egypt | 2.5 |
| Iceland | 10.0 | Greece | 7.5 |
| Ireland | 7.5 | Hungary | 5.0 |
| Italy | 7.5 | Iran | 2.5 |
| Netherlands | 7.5 | Israel | 7.5 |
| Norway | 7.5 | Jordan | 5.0 |
| Spain | 7.5 | Malta | 7.5 |
| Sweden | 10.0 | Poland | 7.5 |
| Switzerland | 10.0 | Portugal | 7.5 |
| United Kingdom | 10.0 | Romania | 5.0 |
| | | Slovakia | 5.0 |
| | | Syria | 2.5 |
| **CENTRAL/SOUTH AMERICA** | | Turkey | 7.5 |
| Argentina | 10.0 | | |
| Belize | 10.0 | **ASIA** | |
| Bolivia | 7.5 | Bangladesh | 7.5 |
| Brazil | 7.5 | Fiji | 7.5 |
| Chile | 10.0 | Hong Kong | 10.0 |
| Colombia | 7.5 | India | 5.0 |
| Costa Rica | 10.0 | Indonesia | 2.5 |
| Dominican Rep | 7.5 | Malaysia | 7.5 |
| Ecuador | 7.5 | Nepal | 5.0 |
| El Salvador | 5.0 | Pakistan | 5.0 |
| Guatemala | 7.5 | Philippines | 5.0 |
| Haiti | 2.5 | Singapore | 7.5 |
| Honduras | 7.5 | South Korea | 7.5 |
| Jamaica | 7.5 | Sri Lanka | 5.0 |
| Mexico | 7.5 | Taiwan | 7.5 |
| Nicaragua | 5.0 | Thailand | 5.0 |
| Panama | 7.5 | | |

Table II-D: (Con't)

**Are Businesses and Cooperatives Free to Compete?**

(1994-95 Rating--the Higher the Rating the Greater the Freedom to Compete)

COUNTRY

**AFRICA (cont)**

| Country | Rating | Country | Rating |
|---|---|---|---|
| Algeria | 2.5 | Morocco | 5.0 |
| Benin | 5.0 | Niger | 5.0 |
| Botswana | 7.5 | Nigeria | 5.0 |
| Burundi | 2.5 | Rwanda | 2.5 |
| Cameroon | 5.0 | Senegal | 5.0 |
| C African Rep | 5.0 | Sierra Leone | 5.0 |
| Chad | 5.0 | Somalia | 2.5 |
| Congo Rep | 5.0 | South Africa | 5.0 |
| Cote d' Ivoire | 5.0 | Tanzania | 2.5 |
| Gabon | 7.5 | Togo | 5.0 |
| Ghana | 5.0 | Tunisia | 5.0 |
| Kenya | 5.0 | Uganda | 5.0 |
| Madagascar | 5.0 | Zaire | 2.5 |
| Malawi | 7.5 | Zambia | 5.0 |
| Mali | 5.0 | Zimbabwe | 5.0 |
| Mauritius | 10.0 | | |

Source: See Freedom House, *Freedom in the World: The Annual Survey of Political Rights and Civil Liberties, 1994-95*. The survey team of Freedom House ranked countries with regard to the economic freedom of businesses and cooperatives to compete in the marketplace (Item 9 on their checklist of 13 civil liberty categories). Each country was given a rating of 0 to 4 with a rating of 4 indicating the countries for which businesses and cooperatives were most free to compete. We transformed the 0 to 4 rating of Freedom House to our 0 to 10 scale (0 = 0, 1 = 2.5, 2 = 5, 3 = 7.5 and 4 = 10). The actual ratings for the specific checklist items were unavailable in the Annual Survey publication. However, Joseph Ryan, a senior scholar at the Freedom House, graciously supplied them to us.

## Table II-E: Equality of Citizens Under the Law and Access to a Nondiscriminatory Judiciary

**Equality of Citizens Under the Law**

(1994-1995: the higher rating indicates greater equality under the law)

| INDUSTRIAL COUNTRIES | | CENTRAL/- S. AMERICA (con't) | |
|---|---|---|---|
| United States | 7.5 | Paraguay | 2.5 |
| Canada | 7.5 | Peru | 0.0 |
| Australia | 7.5 | Trinidad/Tobago | 7.5 |
| Japan | 7.5 | Uruguay | 5.0 |
| New Zealand | 10.0 | Venezuela | 0.0 |
| Austria | 7.5 | | |
| Belgium | 10.0 | **EUROPE/MIDDLE EAST** | |
| Denmark | 10.0 | Bulgaria | 7.5 |
| Finland | 10.0 | Cyprus | 7.5 |
| France | 7.5 | Czech Republic | 7.5 |
| Germany | 7.5 | Egypt | 0.0 |
| Iceland | 10.0 | Greece | 5.0 |
| Ireland | 7.5 | Hungary | 7.5 |
| Italy | 7.5 | Iran | 0.0 |
| Netherlands | 10.0 | Israel | 5.0 |
| Norway | 10.0 | Jordan | 2.5 |
| Spain | 5.0 | Malta | 10.0 |
| Sweden | 10.0 | Poland | 7.5 |
| Switzerland | 10.0 | Portugal | 7.5 |
| United Kingdom | 5.0 | Romania | 5.0 |
| | | Slovakia | 5.0 |
| **CENTRAL/SOUTH AMERICA** | | Syria | 0.0 |
| Argentina | 2.5 | Turkey | 0.0 |
| Belize | 7.5 | | |
| Bolivia | 2.5 | **ASIA** | |
| Brazil | 0.0 | Bangladesh | 5.0 |
| Chile | 5.0 | Fiji | 5.0 |
| Colombia | 0.0 | Hong Kong | 7.5 |
| Costa Rica | 7.5 | India | 2.5 |
| Dominican Rep | 2.5 | Indonesia | 0.0 |
| Ecuador | 2.5 | Malaysia | 2.5 |
| El Salvador | 2.5 | Nepal | 0.0 |
| Guatemala | 0.0 | Pakistan | 0.0 |
| Haiti | 0.0 | Philippines | 0.0 |
| Honduras | 2.5 | Singapore | 0.0 |
| Jamaica | 2.5 | South Korea | 7.5 |
| Mexico | 0.0 | Sri Lanka | 0.0 |
| Nicaragua | 0.0 | Taiwan | 2.5 |
| Panama | 2.5 | Thailand | 0.0 |

Table II-E: (continued)

## Equality of Citizens Under the Law

(1994-1995:  the higher rating indicates greater equality under the law)

### AFRICA

| | | | | |
|---|---|---|---|---|
| Algeria | 0.0 | | Morocco | 0.0 |
| Benin | 5.0 | | Niger | 0.0 |
| Botswana | 5.0 | | Nigeria | 0.0 |
| Burundi | 0.0 | | Rwanda | 0.0 |
| Cameroon | 0.0 | | Senegal | 2.5 |
| C African Rep | 2.5 | | Sierra Leone | 0.0 |
| Chad | 0.0 | | Somalia | 0.0 |
| Congo Rep | 2.5 | | South Africa | 5.0 |
| Cote d' Ivoire | 0.0 | | Tanzania | 2.5 |
| Gabon | 0.0 | | Togo | 0.0 |
| Ghana | 2.5 | | Tunisia | 0.0 |
| Kenya | 0.0 | | Uganda | 0.0 |
| Madagascar | 2.5 | | Zaire | 0.0 |
| Malawi | 5.0 | | Zambia | 0.0 |
| Mali | 0.0 | | Zimbabwe | 2.5 |
| Mauritius | 7.5 | | | |

Source:  These data are from the annual survey of political and civil liberties conducted by the Freedom House.  Item 5 of the 13 item civil liberties checklist is:  "Are citizens equal under the law, do they have access to an independent, non-discriminatory judiciary, and are they respected by the security forces?"  Countries were given ratings ranging from 0 to 4.  The higher the rating, the greater the degree of equality under the law.  We transformed the 0 to 4 ratings of the Freedom House to our 0 to 10 scale (0 = 0, 1 = 2.5, 2 = 5, 3 = 7.5, and 4 = 10).  We are indebted to Joseph Ryan of the Freedom House for supplying the rating for each country to us.  See Freedom House, *Survey of Political Rights and Civil Liberties, 1994-95.*  This variable was not available for the early periods of our study.

## Table II-F: Freedom from Government Regulations and Policies
## That Cause Negative Interest Rates

| | Have Government Regulations, Interest Rate Controls, and Inflationary Monetary Policy Caused Negative Interest Rates and Credit Market Disruptions? ( When this is the case, a country is given a low rating.) | | | | |
|---|---|---|---|---|---|
| | 1973-75 | 1978-80 | 1983-85 | 1988-90 | 1991-93 |
| **INDUSTRIAL COUNTRIES** | | | | | |
| United States | 8 | 10 | 10 | 10 | 10 |
| Canada | 6 | 10 | 10 | 10 | 10 |
| Australia | 4 | 10 | 10 | 10 | 10 |
| Japan | 4 | 10 | 10 | 10 | 10 |
| New Zealand | - | 6 | 8 | 10 | 10 |
| Austria | 6 | 8 | 10 | 10 | 6 |
| Belgium | 6 | 10 | 10 | 10 | 10 |
| Denmark | 8 | 10 | 10 | 10 | 10 |
| Finland | - | 8 | 10 | 10 | 10 |
| France | 8 | 8 | 8 | 8 | 8 |
| Germany | 8 | 10 | 10 | 10 | 10 |
| Iceland | 2 | 4 | 4 | 6 | 6 |
| Ireland | 4 | 6 | 10 | 10 | 10 |
| Italy | 6 | 4 | 6 | 10 | 10 |
| Netherlands | 6 | 10 | 10 | 10 | 10 |
| Norway | - | 6 | 10 | 10 | 10 |
| Spain | - | 6 | 10 | 10 | 10 |
| Sweden | 4 | 8 | 10 | 10 | 10 |
| Switzerland | 6 | 6 | 10 | 10 | 10 |
| United Kingdom | 4 | 4 | 10 | 10 | 10 |
| | | | | | |
| **CENTRAL/SOUTH AMERICA** | | | | | |
| Argentina | - | 0 | 0 | 0 | 8 |
| Belize | - | 8 | 8 | 10 | 10 |
| Bolivia | - | 6 | 0 | 8 | 8 |
| Brazil | - | - | 0 | 0 | 0 |
| Chile | - | 8 | 8 | 8 | 10 |
| Colombia | - | - | - | 8 | 8 |
| Costa Rica | - | - | 6 | 8 | 8 |
| Dominican Rep | - | - | - | - | - |
| Ecuador | - | - | 0 | 0 | 6 |
| El Salvador | - | - | 8 | 8 | 10 |
| Guatemala | - | 8 | 8 | 8 | 8 |
| Haiti | - | - | - | - | - |
| Honduras | - | - | 10 | 8 | 6 |
| Jamaica | - | 4 | 4 | 8 | 4 |
| Mexico | - | 4 | 4 | 8 | 8 |
| Nicaragua | - | - | - | 0 | 0 |
| Panama | - | - | - | 10 | 10 |

Table II-F: (continued)

## Have Government Regulations, Interest Rate Controls, and Inflationary Monetary Policy Caused Negative Interest Rates and Credit Market Disruptions?

( When this is the case, a country is given a low rating.)

| | 1973-75 | 1978-80 | 1983-85 | 1988-90 | 1991-93 |
|---|---|---|---|---|---|
| **CTRL/S. AMERICA** | | | | | |
| Paraguay | - | - | - | 2 | 8 |
| Peru | - | - | - | 0 | 2 |
| Trinidad/Tobago | - | - | 8 | 6 | 8 |
| Uraguay | - | 6 | 8 | 8 | 6 |
| Venezuela | - | - | - | 0 | 4 |
| | | | | | |
| **EUROPE/MIDDLE EAST** | | | | | |
| Bulgaria | - | - | - | - | - |
| Cyprus | 8 | 4 | 8 | 10 | 8 |
| Czechoslovakia | - | - | - | - | - |
|   Czech Rep | - | - | - | - | 6 |
|   Slovakia | - | - | - | - | 4 |
| Egypt | - | 4 | 6 | 6 | 8 |
| Greece | 4 | 6 | 6 | 8 | 8 |
| Hungary | - | 6 | - | 6 | 6 |
| Iran | - | - | - | - | - |
| Israel | - | 0 | 0 | 6 | 8 |
| Jordan | - | - | - | 4 | 6 |
| Malta | - | 6 | 10 | 10 | 10 |
| Poland | - | - | - | 0 | 4 |
| Portugal | - | 4 | 10 | 8 | 10 |
| Romania | - | - | - | - | - |
| Syria | - | - | - | - | - |
| Turkey | 2 | 0 | 8 | 2 | 6 |
| | | | | | |
| **ASIA** | | | | | |
| Bangladesh | - | 6 | 6 | 10 | 10 |
| Fiji | 0 | 6 | 8 | 6 | 6 |
| Hong Kong | - | - | - | - | - |
| India | - | 8 | 8 | 8 | 10 |
| Indonesia | 2 | 2 | - | 10 | 10 |
| Malaysia | - | 6 | 10 | 10 | 10 |
| Nepal | - | 6 | 6 | 10 | - |
| Pakistan | - | 6 | 8 | 6 | 8 |
| Philippines | 8 | 8 | 4 | 8 | 10 |
| Singapore | - | 10 | 10 | 10 | 10 |
| South Korea | 2 | 4 | 10 | 10 | 8 |
| Sri Lanka | - | 4 | 8 | 8 | 10 |
| Taiwan | 8 | 8 | 10 | 10 | 10 |
| Thailand | - | 4 | 10 | 8 | 10 |

Table II-F: (continued)

## Have Government Regulations, Interest Rate
## Controls, and Inflationary Monetary Policy Caused
## Negative Interest Rates and Credit Market Disruptions?

( When this is the case, a country is given a low rating.)

| | 1973-75 | 1978-80 | 1983-85 | 1988-90 | 1992-94 |
|---|---|---|---|---|---|
| **AFRICA (cont)** | | | | | |
| Algeria | - | - | - | - | - |
| Benin | - | 6 | 8 | 8 | - |
| Botswana | - | 4 | 8 | 4 | 6 |
| Burundi | - | 2 | 6 | - | - |
| Cameroon | - | 6 | 6 | 8 | 8 |
| C African Rep | - | - | 8 | 10 | 8 |
| Chad | - | - | 8 | 8 | 8 |
| Congo Peoples Rep | - | 6 | 8 | 10 | 6 |
| Cote d' Ivoire | - | 8 | 10 | 8 | 8 |
| Gabon | - | 6 | 8 | 8 | 8 |
| Ghana | - | 0 | 0 | 2 | 8 |
| Kenya | 4 | 8 | 10 | 10 | - |
| Madagascar | - | - | - | - | - |
| Malawi | - | 4 | 8 | 6 | 4 |
| Mali | - | 4 | 6 | 8 | 8 |
| Mauritius | - | - | 10 | 8 | 10 |
| Morocco | - | - | 6 | - | - |
| Niger | - | 2 | - | 8 | 8 |
| Nigeria | 2 | 2 | 4 | 0 | 0 |
| Rwanda | - | 6 | 8 | 10 | 6 |
| Senegal | - | 8 | 6 | 8 | 8 |
| Sierra Leone | - | 6 | 0 | 0 | 2 |
| Somalia | 4 | 0 | 0 | 0 | - |
| South Africa | - | 4 | 8 | 8 | 10 |
| Tanzania | - | 4 | 0 | 4 | - |
| Togo | - | 8 | 8 | 8 | 8 |
| Tunisia | - | 4 | 6 | - | - |
| Uganda | - | 0 | 0 | 0 | - |
| Zaire | - | - | - | - | - |
| Zambia | 4 | 4 | 0 | 0 | 0 |
| Zimbabwe | - | 6 | 8 | 8 | 8 |

Source and
Explanation
of Ratings: This rating seeks to identify how credit market regulations, interest rate controls, and government operation of the banking system stifle and distort exchange in the credit market. When interest rates are determined by market forces and monetary policy is relatively stable, positive *real* borrowing and lending rates will emerge consistently in credit markets. When this is the case, the country is given a high rating. There are several ways that regulations and controls can restrict exchanges between potential borrowers and lenders. The most damaging is the combination of an inflationary monetary policy coupled with interest rate controls that lead to substantial, persistently *negative real* deposit and lending interest rates. Thus, countries with persistently large *negative real* deposit and lending interest rates are rated low. In addition, regulations and controls that drive a wedge between the deposit rate and the lending rate will stifle exchange. Thus, a country is given a lower rating if the differential between the deposit and the lending rate is abnormally large. The inflation rate, deposit rate, and lending rate data of the International Monetary Fund, *International Financial Statistics Yearbook* (or the monthly version of this publication) were used to estimate the real interest rates. The real interest rate is simply the nominal rate (either the deposit rate or the lending rate) minus the rate of inflation during the year. The following table indicates the relationship between the rating and the characteristics in the credit market.

| Rating | Characteristics in Credit Market |
|---|---|
| 10 | Interest rates are determined primarily by market forces and real interest rates are consistently positive. |
| 8 | Interest rates are determined primarily by market forces, but real interest rates are sometimes slightly (less than 5%) negative and/or regulatory policies result in a persistent abnormally large differential (8% or more) between the deposit and the lending interest rate. |
| 6 | Either the deposit or lending real interest rate is persistently negative by a single-digit amount. |
| 4 | Both the deposit and lending real interest rates are persistently negative by single-digit amounts. |
| 2 | Either the deposit or lending real interest rate is persistently negative by a double-digit amount. |
| 0 | Both the deposit and lending real interest rates are persistently negative by double-digit amounts or hyperinflation has virtually eliminated the operation of the credit market. |

## Table III-A: Transfers and Subsides As A Percent of GDP
### (1975, 1980, 1985, 1990, and 1992)

| | Transfers and Subsidies As A Percent of GDP | | | | | | | | | |
| | (Rating in parenthesis) | | | | | | | | | |
| INDUSTRIAL COUNTRIES | 1975 | | 1980 | | 1985 | | 1990 | | 1992 | |
|---|---|---|---|---|---|---|---|---|---|---|
| United States | 11.1 | (3) | 10.9 | (3) | 12.5 | (3) | 12.7 | (3) | 14.3 | (3) |
| Canada | 9.1 | (4) | 14.5 | (3) | 16.3 | (2) | 15.6 | (2) | 17.7 | (2) b |
| Australia | 8.5 | (4) | 10.1 | (4) | 10.9 | (3) | 10.7 | (3) | 13.4 | (3) |
| Japan | 9.6 | (4) | 10.0 | (4) | 10.4 | (4) | 9.9 | (4) | 10.0 | (4) |
| New Zealand | 20.2 | (1) | 21.9 | (1) | 20.6 | (1) | 27.5 | (0) | 15.7 | (2) |
| Austria | 19.4 | (1) | 22.1 | (1) | 23.1 | (0) | 22.4 | (0) | 23.4 | (0) |
| Belgium | 28.5 | (0) | 26.0 | (0) | 27.6 | (0) | 25.0 | (0) | 26.6 | (0) |
| Denmark | 17.8 | (2) | 20.8 | (1) | 20.4 | (1) | 22.6 | (0) | 24.6 | (0) |
| Finland | 14.1 | (3) | 14.3 | (3) | 15.8 | (2) | 16.0 | (2) | 21.1 | (1) |
| France | 24.0 | (0) | 26.1 | (0) | 26.8 | (0) | 25.2 | (0) | 26.9 | (0) |
| Germany | 17.4 | (2) | 17.6 | (2) | 19.0 | (1) | 17.9 | (2) | 22.4 | (0) |
| Iceland | 9.9 | (4) | 10.6 | (4) | 11.7 | (3) | 10.1 | (4) | 11.0 | (3) |
| Ireland | 18.3 | (2) | 17.7 | (2) | 20.5 | (1) | 17.1 | (2) | 18.1 | (2) b |
| Italy | 17.5 | (2) | 20.9 | (1) | 28.5 | (0) | 27.1 | (0) | 28.6 | (0) |
| Netherlands | 25.6 | (0) | 29.4 | (0) | 31.6 | (0) | 28.7 | (0) | 30.7 | (0) |
| Norway | - | | 22.1 | (1) | 21.4 | (1) | 27.3 | (0) | 27.0 | (0) |
| Spain | - | | 12.3 | (3) | 16.9 | (2) | 16.0 | (2) | 16.3 | (2) b |
| Sweden | 25.0 | (0) | 24.7 | (0) | 26.0 | (0) | 29.9 | (0) | 31.7 | (0) |
| Switzerland | - | | 13.4 | (3) | 13.2 | (3) | 16.0 | (2) | 16.0 | (2) |
| United Kingdom | 15.0 | (3) | 15.8 | (2) | 17.9 | (2) | 14.9 | (3) | 17.3 | (2) |

### CENTRAL/SOUTH AMERICA

| | 1975 | | 1980 | | 1985 | | 1990 | | 1992 | |
|---|---|---|---|---|---|---|---|---|---|---|
| Argentina | 7.9 | (4) | 9.7 | (4) | 11.7 | (3) | 8.5 | (4) a | 12.8 | (3) |
| Belize | - | | 2.6 | (8) | 3.6 | (8) | 1.2 | (10) | 1.2 | (10) |
| Bolivia | 1.3 | (10) | 1.6 | (9) | 1.8 | (9) | 2.8 | (8) | 2.6 | (8) |
| Brazil | - | | 12.4 | (3) | 10.0 | (4) | 10.7 | (3) | 11.8 | (3) b |
| Chile | 10.5 | (4) | 12.9 | (3) | 15.3 | (2) | 10.5 | (4) | 10.8 | (3) |
| Colombia | 3.0 | (8) | 2.9 | (8) | 4.4 | (7) | 4.6 | (7) | 5.7 | (5) |
| Costa Rica | - | | 6.0 | (5) | 7.2 | (5) | 5.0 | (6) | 4.7 | (6) |
| Dominican Republic | - | | 1.6 | (9) | 2.5 | (8) | 1.5 | (9) | 1.4 | (9) |
| Ecuador | - | | 5.2 | (6) | 4.0 | (7) | 4.3 | (7) | 3.0 | (8) |
| El Salvador | 2.5 | (8) | 2.7 | (8) | 2.0 | (9) | 1.4 | (10) | 1.5 | (9) |
| Guatemala | 0.8 | (10) | 1.2 | (10) | 1.3 | (10) | 1.8 | (9) a | 1.9 | (9) |
| Haiti | - | | - | | 7.4 | (5) | - | | - | |
| Honduras | 0.5 | (10) | - | | 2.3 | (9) | 2.2 | (9) | 4.0 | (7) |
| Jamaica | 7.0 | (5) | - | | 0.6 | (10) | 2.0 | (9) | 3.9 | (7) |
| Mexico | 4.1 | (7) | 4.4 | (7) | 5.4 | (5) | 6.4 | (5) | 7.1 | (5) |
| Nicaragua | 2.4 | (8) | 4.1 | (7) | 6.2 | (5) | 6.8 | (5) | 6.2 | (5) |
| Panama | 3.8 | (7) | 4.9 | (6) | 4.8 | (6) | 7.4 | (5) | 9.8 | (4) |

Table III-A: (con't)

## Transfers and Subsidies As A Percent of GDP
### (Rating in parenthesis)

| CENTRAL/-<br>SOUTH AMERICA | 1975 | | 1980 | | 1985 | | 1990 | | 1992 | |
|---|---|---|---|---|---|---|---|---|---|---|
| Paraguay | 2.0 | (9) | 2.0 | (9) | 2.1 | (9) | 1.8 | (9) | 3.3 | (8) |
| Peru | 1.9 | (9) | 1.9 | (9) | 1.8 | (9) | 3.0 | (8) | 2.8 | (8) |
| Trinidad & Tobago | - | | 6.0 | (5) | 14.9 | (3) | 10.0 | (4) | 8.3 | (4) |
| Uruguay | 11.8 | (3) | 9.1 | (4) | 10.0 | (4) | 12.0 | (3) | 15.9 | (2) |
| Venezuela | 2.3 | (8) | 2.0 | (9) | 4.5 | (7) | 5.8 | (5) | 5.3 | (6) |
| | | | | | | | | | | |
| **EUROPE/MIDDLE EAST** | | | | | | | | | | |
| Bulgaria | - | | - | | 17.5 | (2) | 27.2 | (0) | 15.6 | (2) |
| Cyprus | 10.3 | (4) | 6.6 | (5) | 8.1 | (4) | 8.3 | (4) | 9.9 | (4) b |
| Czechoslovakia | - | | - | | - | | 37.2 | (0) | - | |
| Czech Republic | - | | - | | - | | - | | - | |
| Slovakia | - | | - | | - | | - | | - | |
| Egypt | 25.0 | (0) | 17.2 | (2) | 13.9 | (3) | 8.9 | (4) | 10.6 | (4) |
| Greece | 8.5 | (4) | 12.5 | (3) | 18.0 | (2) | 27.1 | (0) | 15.6 | (2) |
| Hungary | - | | - | | 33.3 | (0) | 28.7 | (0) | 25.0 | (0) |
| Iran | 8.9 | (4) | 7.0 | (5) | 3.0 | (8) | 4.4 | (7) | - | |
| Israel | - | | 20.8 | (1) | 19.7 | (1) | 16.7 | (2) | 15.2 | (2) |
| Jordan | - | | 6.3 | (5) | 5.1 | (6) | 3.7 | (7) | 3.1 | (8) |
| Malta | 14.7 | (3) | 12.2 | (3) | 15.6 | (2) | 15.6 | (2) | 15.2 | (2) b |
| Poland | - | | - | | 27.4 | (0) | 7.2 | (5) | - | |
| Portugal | 14.6 | (3) | 16.3 | (2) | 19.5 | (1) | 15.5 | (2) | 14.5 | (3) |
| Romania | - | | 14.1 | (3) | 8.0 | (4) | 18.6 | (1) | 20.9 | (1) |
| Syria | - | | - | | - | | - | | - | |
| Turkey | 6.0 | (5) | 6.0 | (5) | 10.3 | (4) | 3.9 | (7) | 5.8 | (5) |
| | | | | | | | | | | |
| **ASIA** | | | | | | | | | | |
| Bangladesh | - | | - | | - | | - | | - | |
| Fiji | 1.9 | (9) | 2.5 | (8) | 4.5 | (7) | 1.0 | (10) | 1.0 | (10) |
| Hong Kong | 1.1 | (10) | 0.6 | (10) | 0.9 | (10) | 0.9 | (10) | 1.2 | (10) |
| India | 3.8 | (7) | 5.4 | (6) | 6.5 | (5) | 6.5 | (5) | 6.7 | (5) b |
| Indonesia | 1.5 | (9) | 3.3 | (8) | 2.5 | (8) | 2.0 | (9) | 0.7 | (10) |
| Malaysia | 6.4 | (5) | 4.8 | (6) | 3.6 | (8) | 2.4 | (8) | 4.2 | (7) |
| Nepal | - | | - | | - | | - | | - | |
| Pakistan | - | | - | | - | | - | | - | |
| Philippines | 0.8 | (10) | 1.1 | (10) | 0.2 | (10) | 0.9 | (10) | 0.8 | (10) |
| Singapore | 1.4 | (10) | 1.1 | (10) | 1.8 | (9) | 2.6 | (8) | 2.9 | (8) |
| South Korea | 2.0 | (9) | 2.0 | (9) | 2.2 | (9) | 2.9 | (8) | 2.6 | (8) |
| Sri Lanka | 8.1 | (4) | 8.4 | (4) | 5.1 | (6) | 6.0 | (5) | 6.0 | (5) |
| Taiwan | 2.2 | (9) | 2.6 | (8) | 3.6 | (8) | 4.7 | (6) | 5.9 | (5) |
| Thailand | 0.6 | (10) | 0.7 | (10) | 1.2 | (10) | 1.0 | (10) | 0.9 | (10) |

Table III-A: (con't)

## Transfers and Subsidies As A Percent of GDP

(Rating in parenthesis)

| | 1975 | 1980 | 1985 | 1990 | 1992 |
|---|---|---|---|---|---|
| **AFRICA** | | | | | |
| Algeria | - | - | - | - | - |
| Benin | - | - | - | - | - |
| Botswana | 5.5 (6) | 4.9 (6) | 7.3 (5) | 6.6 (5) | 6.9 (5) |
| Burundi | - | - | - | - | - |
| Cameroon | 1.4 (9) | 0.8 (10) | 0.6 (10) | 2.7 (8) | 2.7 (8) |
| Central African Rep | - | - | - | - | - |
| Chad | - | - | - | 0.9 (10) | 0.9 (10) b |
| Congo | - | - | - | - | - |
| Cote d'Ivoire | - | 4.2 (7) | - | - | - |
| Gabon | - | - | - | 1.2 (10) | 1.2 (10) b |
| Ghana | 3.1 (8) | 2.4 (8) | 1.3 (10) | 2.6 (8) | 3.3 (7) |
| Kenya | - | 2.3 (8) | 4.7 (6) | 2.8 (8) | 1.7 (9) |
| Madagascar | - | - | - | 1.4 (9) | 1.4 (9) b |
| Malawi | 1.0 (10) | 2.1 (9) | 2.3 (8) | 2.4 (8) a | - |
| Mali | 2.3 (8) | 2.3 (8) | 2.3 (8) | 0.6 (10) | - |
| Mauritius | 6.6 (5) | 6.5 (5) | 5.2 (6) | 4.2 (7) | 4.9 (6) |
| Morocco | 6.0 (5) | 4.1 (7) | 4.6 (7) | 2.3 (8) | - |
| Niger | | 2.5 (8) | - | - | - |
| Nigeria | 2.9 (8) | - | 1.4 (10) | - | - |
| Rwanda | 0.4 (10) | 0.4 (10) | - | 3.5 (8) | 2.2 (9) |
| Senegal | 1.9 (9) | - | - | - | - |
| Sierra Leone | 1.6 (9) | - | 0.6 (10) | 1.6 (9) | 3.3 (8) |
| Somalia | - | - | - | - | - |
| South Africa | - | 3.2 (8) | 4.8 (6) | 4.8 (6) | 5.0 (6) b |
| Tanzania | 0.1 (10) | 0.1 (10) | 5.2 (6) | - | - |
| Togo | - | - | - | - | - |
| Tunisia | 1.9 (9) | 5.6 (5) | 6.8 (5) | 9.3 (4) | 8.3 (4) b |
| Uganda | - | - | - | - | - |
| Zaire | 1.0 (10) | 0.6 (10) | - | 1.0 (10) | - |
| Zambia | 7.0 (5) | 8.7 (4) | 4.2 (7) | - | - |
| Zimbabwe | - | 11.4 (3) | 10.0 (4) | - | - |

a  Indicates data are for 1989.
b  Indicates data are for 1991.

Source: The GDP data are from the World Bank, *World Tables, 1994*. The data on transfers and subsidies are from International Monetary Fund, *Government Finance Statistics Yearbook*, (various years). In addition, supplementary data on transfers and subsides from Inter-American Development Bank, *Economic and Social Progress in Latin America*, 1994, were also utilized. The 1992 data were the most recent available at the time this study was completed. The base year for the rating of each country was 1985. The following conversion table divided the 1985 data into eleven intervals of equal size:

Table III-A: (con't)

| Transfers and Subsidies As a Percent of GDP | Rating |
|---|---|
| 0.0% - 1.3% | 10 |
| 1.4 - 2.2 | 9 |
| 2.3 - 3.6 | 8 |
| 3.7 - 4.6 | 7 |
| 4.7 - 5.3 | 6 |
| 5.4 - 7.7 | 5 |
| 7.8 - 10.6 | 4 |
| 10.7 - 15.1 | 3 |
| 15.2 - 18.5 | 2 |
| 18.6 - 22.3 | 1 |
| > 22.3 | 0 |

## Table III-B: Top Marginal Tax Rate and Income Threshold  (Measured in 1982-84 dollars) at which Top Rate Takes Affect

| | 1974 | | | | 1979 | | |
| | Top Marginal Tax Rate | Threshold Income Level | Rating | | Top Marginal Tax Rate | Threshold Income Level | Rating |
|---|---|---|---|---|---|---|---|
| **INDUSTRIAL COUNTRIES** | | | | | | | |
| United States | 70-75 | 185,000 | 0 | | 70-75 | 82,645 | 0 |
| Canada | 43-61 | 130,109 | 4 | | 47-62 | 115,840 | 4 |
| Australia | 64 | 74,348 | 2 | | 62 | 51,928 | 2 |
| Japan | 68 | 185,000 | 1 | | 75 | 546,694 | 0 |
| New Zealand | 60 | 83,642 | 3 | | 60 | 31,818 | 2 |
| Austria | 54 | 185,000 | 4 | | 62 | 153,581 | 2 |
| Belgium | 64 | 185,000 | 2 | | 76 | 187,879 | 0 |
| Denmark | 63 | 37,174 | 1 | | 66 | 37,052 | 0 |
| Finland | 61-68 | 111,522 | 2 | | 65-71 | 88,843 | 1 |
| France | 48 | 130,109 | 5 | | 60 | 126,722 | 3 |
| Germany | 56 | 167,283 | 4 | | 56 | 193,939 | 3 |
| Iceland | | | | | | | |
| Ireland | 80 | 46,468 | 0 | | 60 | 19,559 | 1 |
| Italy | 48 | 185,000 | 5 | | 72 | 819,559 | 0 |
| Netherlands | 46 | 185,000 | 5 | | 72 | 127,548 | 0 |
| Norway | 74 | 111,522 | 0 | | 75 | 82,645 | 0 |
| Spain | 55 | 185,000 | 4 | | 66 | 195,592 | 1 |
| Sweden | 70 | 74,348 | 1 | | 87 | 53,306 | 0 |
| Switzerland | 38-42 | 111,522 | 7 | | 31-44 | 76,171 | 7 |
| United Kingdom | 41 | 185,000 | 7 | | 83 | 66,942 | 0 |
| | | | | | | | |
| **CENTRAL/SOUTH AMERICA** | | | | | | | |
| Argentina | 51 | 65,055 | 4 | | 45 | 101,515 | 6 |
| Belize | | | | | | | |
| Bolivia | | | | | 48 | 15,152 | 3 |
| Brazil | 50 | 65,055 | 5 | | 55 | 105,234 | 4 |
| Chile | 80 | 185,000 | 0 | | 60 | 42,424 | 2 |
| Colombia | 41 | 111,522 | 6 | | 56 | 36,501 | 2 |
| Costa Rica | 50 | 83,642 | 5 | | 50 | 56,061 | 5 |
| Dominican Rep | 49 | 185,000 | 5 | | | | |
| Ecuador | 50 | 148,696 | 5 | | 50 | 150,000 | 5 |
| El Salvador | 55 | 185,000 | 4 | | 60 | 137,741 | 3 |
| Guatemala | 34 | 185,000 | 9 | | 40 | 688,700 | 8 |
| Haiti | | | | | | | |
| Honduras | 27 | 185,000 | 9 | | 40 | 688,700 | 8 |
| Jamaica | 60 | 27,881 | 2 | | 80 | 23,967 | 0 |

281

Table III-B: (continued)

| | 1974 | | | 1979 | | |
|---|---|---|---|---|---|---|
| CENTRAL/-S. AMERICA (con't) | Top Marginal Tax Rate | Threshold Income Level | Rating | Top Marginal Tax Rate | Threshold Income Level | Rating |
| Mexico | 47 | 83,642 | 5 | 55 | 90,634 | 4 |
| Nicaragua | 21 | 185,000 | 10 | 50 | 275,482 | 5 |
| Panama | 52 | 185,000 | 4 | 56 | 275,482 | 3 |
| Paraguay | | | | | | |
| Peru | 51 | 55,761 | 4 | 65 | 53,719 | 2 |
| Trinidad/Tobago | | | | | | |
| Uruguay | 41 | 185,000 | 7 | 0 | | 10 |
| Venezuela | 20 | 185,000 | 10 | 45 | 1,350,000 | 7 |
| | | | | | | |
| **EUROPE/MIDDLE EAST** | | | | | | |
| Bulgaria | | | | | | |
| Cyprus | 54 | 37,174 | 3 | 60 | 19,146 | 1 |
| Czechoslovakia | | | | | | |
|    Czech Republic | | | | | | |
|    Slovakia | | | | | | |
| Egypt | | | | 80 | 196,832 | 0 |
| Greece | 52 | 130,109 | 4 | 60 | 113,223 | 3 |
| Hungary | | | | | | |
| Iran | 40 | 150,900 | 8 | | | |
| Israel | | | | 66 | 70,000 | 1 |
| Jordan | | | | | | |
| Malta | | | | 65 | 18,000 | 0 |
| Poland | | | | | | |
| Portugal | 82 | 167,283 | 0 | 84 | 28,788 | 0 |
| Romania | | | | | | |
| Syria | | | | | | |
| Turkey | | | | 75 | 60,000 | 0 |
| | | | | | | |
| **ASIA** | | | | | | |
| Bangladesh | | | | 60 | 10,000 | 1 |
| Fiji | 53 | 27,000 | 3 | 53 | 13,774 | 2 |
| Hong Kong | 15 | 27,881 | 10 | 15 | 28,512 | 10 |
| India | 77 | 13,940 | 0 | 60 | 16,529 | 1 |
| Indonesia | 48 | 37,174 | 4 | 50 | 21,212 | 3 |
| Malaysia | 50 | 46,468 | 4 | 60 | 47,383 | 2 |
| Nepal | | | | | | |
| Pakistan | 61 | 27,881 | 1 | 55 | 6,887 | 2 |
| Philippines | 56 | 167,000 | 3 | 70 | 94,353 | 1 |
| Singapore | 55 | 83,642 | 4 | 55 | 255,096 | 4 |
| South Korea | 63 | 110,000 | 2 | 89 | 238,567 | 0 |
| Sri Lanka | | | | 60.5 | 3,500 | 0 |
| Taiwan | 60 | 111,500 | 3 | 60 | 110,000 | 3 |
| Thailand | 60 | 100,000 | 3 | 60 | 68,871 | 3 |

Table III-B: (continued)

| | 1974 | | | | 1979 | | |
|---|---|---|---|---|---|---|---|
| | Top Marginal Tax Rate | Threshold Income Level | Rating | | Top Marginal Tax Rate | Threshold Income Level | Rating |
| **AFRICA** | | | | | | | |
| Algeria | | | | | | | |
| Benin | | | | | | | |
| Botswana | 75 | 83,642 | 0 | | 75 | 66,116 | 0 |
| Burundi | | | | | | | |
| Cameroon | | | | | | | |
| C African Rep | | | | | | | |
| Chad | | | | | | | |
| Congo Peoples Rep | | | | | | | |
| Cote d' Ivoire | | | | | 45 | 38,500 | 5 |
| Gabon | | | | | | | |
| Ghana | 70 | 22,000 | 0 | | 60 | 700 | 1 |
| Kenya | 70 | 46,468 | 0 | | 65 | 27,500 | 1 |
| Madagascar | | | | | | | |
| Malawi | 69 | 27,881 | 0 | | 45 | 20,937 | 4 |
| Mali | | | | | | | |
| Mauritius | | | | | 50 | 20,000 | 3 |
| Morocco | 39 | 185,000 | 8 | | 64 | 261,570 | 2 |
| Niger | | | | | | | |
| Nigeria | 75 | 74,348 | 0 | | 70 | 62,000 | 0 |
| Rwanda | | | | | | | |
| Senegal | | | | | | | |
| Sierra Leone | | | | | | | |
| Somalia | | | | | | | |
| South Africa | 66 | 83,642 | 1 | | 60 | 45,868 | 2 |
| Tanzania | 80 | 74,000 | 0 | | | | |
| Togo | | | | | | | |
| Tunisia | | | | | 62.3 | 300,000 | 2 |
| Uganda | | | | | | | |
| Zaire | 60 | 37,200 | 2 | | 60 | 8,540 | 1 |
| Zambia | 70 | 37,175 | 0 | | 70 | 22,452 | 0 |
| Zimbabwe | | | | | 45 | 34,435 | 5 |

Table III-B: (continued)

| INDUSTRIAL COUNTRIES | 1984 | | | 1989 | | | 1994 | | |
|---|---|---|---|---|---|---|---|---|---|
| | Top Marginal Tax Rate | Threshold Income Level | Rating | Top Marginal Tax Rate | Threshold Income Level | Rating | Top Marginal Tax Rate | Threshold Income Level | Rating |
| United States | 50-59 | 156,300 | 4 | 33-42 | 58,937 | 7 | 40-47 | 168,900 | 7 |
| Canada | 49-60 | 43,100 | 3 | 42-47 | 35,888 | 5 | 44-54 | 30,250 | 4 |
| Australia | 60 | 28,400 | 2 | 49 | 23,555 | 3 | 47 | 33,675 | 4 |
| Japan | 70 | 305,500 | 1 | 65 | 178,000 | 2 | 65 | 178,571 | 2 |
| New Zealand | 66 | 17,200 | 0 | 33 | 15,194 | 7 | 33 | 16,981 | 7 |
| Austria | 62 | 65,350 | 2 | 50 | 42,728 | 4 | 50 | 57,660 | 5 |
| Belgium | 76 | 60,600 | 0 | 55-65 | 46,379 | 2 | 55-65 | 67,017 | 2 |
| Denmark | 73 | 21,400 | 0 | 68 | 24,802 | 0 | 65 | 51,118 | 2 |
| Finland | 64-70 | 59,300 | 1 | 63-69 | 47,128 | 0 | 55-61 | 48,405 | 2 |
| France | 65 | 30,700 | 1 | 53 | 29,929 | 3 | 57 | 103,060 | 3 |
| Germany | 56 | 39,650 | 2 | 56 | 114,764 | 3 | 53 | 139,073 | 4 |
| Iceland | | | | | | | | | |
| Ireland | 65 | 19,000 | 0 | 58 | 20,214 | 1 | 48 | 14,570 | 3 |
| Italy | 81 | 248,200 | 0 | 50 | 180,906 | 5 | 51 | 118,798 | 4 |
| Netherlands | 72 | 59,100 | 0 | 72 | 90,675 | 0 | 60 | 30,113 | 2 |
| Norway | 64 | 32,600 | 1 | 54 | 28,117 | 3 | 42 | 23,602 | 4 |
| Spain | 66 | 67,700 | 1 | 56 | 57,114 | 3 | 56 | 52,244 | 3 |
| Sweden | 80 | 38,100 | 0 | 72 | 24,346 | 0 | 56-63 | 16,072 | 1 |
| Switzerland | 33-46 | 145,300 | 7 | 33-43 | 176,000 | 8 | 26-32 | 522,687 | 9 |
| United Kingdom | 60 | 40,100 | 2 | 40 | 24,700 | 5 | 40 | 23,621 | 5 |
| **CENTRAL/SOUTH AMERICA** | | | | | | | | | |
| Argentina | 62 | 65,400 | 2 | 35 | 40,465 | 7 | 30 | 80,972 | 9 |
| Belize | 50 | 30,000 | 4 | 45 | 23,980 | 4 | 45 | 20,243 | 4 |
| Bolivia | 30 | 45 | 8 | 10 | 1 a | 10 | 13 | 1 a | 10 |
| Brazil | 60 | 10,400 | 1 | 25 | 1,434 | 9 | 35 | 83,936 | 8 |
| Chile | 57 | 3,600 | 1 | 50 | 3,709 | 3 | 48 | 3,522 | 3 |
| Colombia | 49 | 55,400 | 5 | 30 | 32,822 | 8 | 37 | 22,707 | 5 |
| Costa Rica | 50 | 2,200 | 3 | 25 | 9,843 | 9 | 25 | 9,407 | 9 |
| Dominican Rep | 73.1 | 497,238 | 0 | 73 | 183,000 | 0 | 27 | 8,097 | 8 |
| Ecuador | 58 | 27,800 | 2 | 40 | 21,787 | 5 | 25 | 38,121 | 9 |
| El Salvador | 48 | 11,700 | 3 | 60 | 39,370 | 2 | 30 | 15,406 | 8 |
| Guatemala | 48 | 324,350 | 5 | 34 | 3,791 | 7 | 25 | 7,522 | 9 |
| Haiti | | | | 30 | 193,000 | 9 | | | |
| Honduras | 46 | 476,400 | 5 | 46 | 393,701 | 5 | 46 | 91,804 | 5 |
| Jamaica | 58 | 2,400 | 1 | 33 | 1,489 | 7 | 25 | 382 | 9 |
| Mexico | 55 | 59,300 | 4 | 40 | 89,000 | 7 | 35 | 18,572 | 7 |
| Nicaragua | 50 | 67,600 | 5 | | | | 30 | 19,128 | 8 |
| Panama | 56 | 192,500 | 3 | 56 | 157,480 | 3 | 30 | 134,953 | 9 |
| Paraguay | 30 | 8,200 | 8 | 30 | 3,822 | 8 | 30 | 10,182 a | 8 |
| Peru | 65 | 40 | 0 | 45 | 12,558 | 4 | 30 | 28,545 | 8 |
| Trinidad/Tobago | 50 | 34,600 | 4 | 35 | 9,330 | 7 | 40 | 4,590 | 5 |
| Uruguay | 0 | | 10 | 0 | | 10 | 0 | | 10 |
| Venezuela | 45 | 1,110,000 | 7 | 45 | 234,000 | 7 | 30 | 27,054 | 8 |

284

Table III-B: (continued)

| EUROPE/-MIDDLE EAST | 1984 Top Marginal Tax Rate | 1984 Threshold Income Level | 1984 Rating | 1989 Top Marginal Tax Rate | 1989 Threshold Income Level | 1989 Rating | 1994 Top Marginal Tax Rate | 1994 Threshold Income Level | 1994 Rating |
|---|---|---|---|---|---|---|---|---|---|
| Bulgaria | | | | | | | | | |
| Cyprus | 60 | 20,900 | 1 | 62 | 18,547 | 0 | 40 | 10,391 | 5 |
| Czechoslovakia | | | | 55 | 52,500 | 4 | | | |
|    Czech Republic | | | | | | | 44 | 24,324 | 4 |
|    Slovakia | | | | | | | 47 | 22,000 | 3 |
| Egypt | 65 | 148,000 | 2 | 65 | 61,750 | 2 | 50 | 13,575 | 3 |
| Greece | 63 | 36,500 | 1 | 50 | 28,594 | 4 | 40 | 18,997 | 5 |
| Hungary | | | | 50 | 9,900 | 3 | 44 | 3,694 | 4 |
| Iran | 90 | 59,700 | 0 | 75 | 140,827 | 0 | 54 | 116,434 | 4 |
| Israel | 60 | 55,000 | 3 | 51 | 82,000 | 4 | 50 | 34,575 | 4 |
| Jordan | | | | 45 | 49,000 | 5 | | | |
| Malta | 65 | 10,000 | 0 | 65 | 3,030 | 0 | 35 | 1,333 | 7 |
| Poland | | | | | | | 45 | 5,741 | 4 |
| Portugal | 69 | 39,900 | 0 | 40 | 16,171 | 5 | 40 | 21,216 | 5 |
| Romania | | | | | | | 60 | 4,400 | 1 |
| Syria | | | | | | | | | |
| Turkey | 60 | 53,800 | 3 | 50 | 32,800 | 4 | 55 | 112,009 | 4 |
| **ASIA** | | | | | | | | | |
| Bangladesh | 60 | 8,200 | 1 | | | | | | |
| Fiji | 50 | 16,650 | 3 | 50 | 21,872 | 3 | 35 | 6,482 | 7 |
| Hong Kong | 25 | 4,900 | 9 | 25 | 7,066 | 9 | 25 | 6,996 | 9 |
| India | 62 | 7,700 | 0 | 53 | 5,194 | 2 | 45 | 2,158 | 4 |
| Indonesia | 35 | 44,750 | 7 | 35 | 22,731 | 7 | 35 | 15,990 | 7 |
| Malaysia | 45 | 117,300 | 6 | 45 | 90,161 | 6 | 34 | 24,872 | 7 |
| Nepal | | | | | | | | | |
| Pakistan | 60 | 6,500 | 1 | 50 | 8,394 | 3 | 38 | 6,680 | 5 |
| Philippines | 60 | 24,350 | 1 | 35 | 18,031 | 7 | 35 | 12,180 | 7 |
| Singapore | 40 | 325,000 | 8 | 33 | 161,850 | 9 | 30 | 168,061 | 9 |
| South Korea | 65 | 69,600 | 2 | 60 | 110,000 | 3 | 48 | 53,473 | 5 |
| Sri Lanka | 60.5 | 2,220 | 0 | | | | | | |
| Taiwan | 60 | 100,000 | 3 | 50 | 97,658 | 5 | 40 | 75,901 | 7 |
| Thailand | 65 | 70,700 | 2 | 55 | 62,270 | 4 | 37 | 105,473 | 7 |
| **AFRICA** | | | | | | | | | |
| Algeria | | | | | | | | | |
| Benin | | | | | | | | | |
| Botswana | 60 | 34,300 | 2 | 50 | 16,472 | 3 | 40 | 13,126 | 5 |
| Burundi | | | | | | | | | |
| Cameroon | 60 | 30,000 | 2 | 60 | 20,600 | 1 | 60 | 17,155 | 1 |

285

Table III-B: (continued)

| | 1984 | | | 1989 | | | 1994 | | |
|---|---|---|---|---|---|---|---|---|---|
| | Top Marginal Tax Rate | Threshold Income Level | Rating | Top Marginal Tax Rate | Threshold Income Level | Rating | Top Marginal Tax Rate | Threshold Income Level | Rating |
| **AFRICA (cont)** | | | | | | | | | |
| C African Rep | | | | | | | | | |
| Chad | | | | | | | | | |
| Congo Peoples Rep | | | | 50 | 34,250 | 4 | 50 | 18,299 | 3 |
| Cote d' Ivoire | 45 | 25,050 | 5 | 45 | 14,500 | 4 | 50 | 5,500 | 3 |
| Gabon | | | | 60 | 15,000 | 1 | 66 | 2,745 | 0 |
| Ghana | 60 | 400 | 1 | 55 | 3,700 | 2 | 35 | 11,588 | 7 |
| Kenya | 65 | 9,900 | 0 | 50 | 400 | 3 | 40 | 2,970 | 5 |
| Madagascar | | | | | | | | | |
| Malawi | 50 | 13,500 | 3 | 50 | 7,194 | 3 | 35 | 5,337 | 7 |
| Mali | | | | | | | | | |
| Mauritius | 35 | 10,000 | 7 | 35 | 2,750 | 7 | 30 | 2,006 | 8 |
| Morocco | 87 | 75,500 | 0 | 87 | 28,699 | 0 | 47 | 8,537 | 3 |
| Niger | | | | | | | | | |
| Nigeria | 55 | 40,000 | 3 | 55 | 4,200 | 2 | 35 | 3,067 | 7 |
| Rwanda | | | | | | | | | |
| Senegal | 65 | 39,000 | 1 | 48 | 31,000 | 4 | 50 b | 31,700 b | 4 |
| Sierra Leone | | | | | | | | | |
| Somalia | | | | | | | | | |
| South Africa | 50 | 32,250 | 4 | 45 | 26,456 | 5 | 43 | 16,006 | 4 |
| Tanzania | 95 | 19,293 | 0 | 50 | 1,200 | 3 | 30 | 422 | 8 |
| Togo | | | | | | | | | |
| Tunisia | 62.3 | 351,300 | 2 | | | | | | |
| Uganda | 70 | 4,440 | 0 | 50 | 2,020 | 3 | 30 | 2,464 | 8 |
| Zaire | 60 | 1,350 | 1 | 60 | 854 | 1 | 60 b | 100 b | 1 |
| Zambia | 80 | 10,700 | 0 | 75 | 2,375 | 0 | 35 | 867 | 7 |
| Zimbabwe | 63 | 22,200 | 0 | 60 | 13,287 | 1 | 50 | 3,744 | 3 |

a    Flat tax rate on all taxable income.
b    Based on the 1993 data.

Source: The data are from Price Waterhouse, *Individual Taxes: A Worldwide Summary,* (various issues). The exchange rate at beginning of the year was used to convert the income threshold data to U.S. dollars, and the U.S. Consumer Price Index was used to convert the threshold to real 1982-84 dollars. The following conversion table/matrix was devised to transform the marginal tax rate/income threshold data for each country into the zero to ten rating system:

Table III-B (con't)

| Top Marginal Tax Rate | Income Threshold Level (1982-84 U.S. Dollars) | | | |
|---|---|---|---|---|
| | Less than 25,000 | 25,000 to 50,000 | 50,000 to 150,000 | more than 150,000 |
| 20% or less | 10 | 10 | 10 | 10 |
| 21 to 25 | 9 | 9 | 10 | 10 |
| 26 to 30 | 8 | 8 | 9 | 9 |
| 31 to 35 | 7 | 7 | 8 | 9 |
| 36 to 40 | 5 | 6 | 7 | 8 |
| 41 to 45 | 4 | 5 | 6 | 7 |
| 46 to 50 | 3 | 4 | 5 | 5 |
| 51 to 55 | 2 | 3 | 4 | 4 |
| 56 to 60 | 1 | 2 | 3 | 3 |
| 61 to 65 | 0 | 1 | 2 | 2 |
| 66 to 70 | 0 | 0 | 1 | 1 |
| more than 70% | 0 | 0 | 0 | 0 |

## Table III-C: The Use of Conscription to Obtain Military Personnel
(Countries with Voluntary Military Service are given a Rating of
10; Countries that Use Conscription to Obtain Military Personnel
are Given a Rating of Zero.)

| | Are Individuals Conscripted into the Military? | | | | | | | | | |
|---|---|---|---|---|---|---|---|---|---|---|
| **INDUSTRIAL COUNTRIES** | 1974-75 | | 1979-80 | | 1984-85 | | 1989-90 | | 1993-94 | |
| United States | No | 10 | No | 10 | No | 10 | No | 10 | No | 10 |
| Canada | No | 10 | No | 10 | No | 10 | No | 10 | No | 10 |
| Australia | No | 10 | No | 10 | No | 10 | No | 10 | No | 10 |
| Japan | No | 10 | No | 10 | No | 10 | No | 10 | No | 10 |
| New Zealand | No | 10 | No | 10 | No | 10 | No | 10 | No | 10 |
| Austria | Yes | 0 | Yes | 0 | Yes | 0 | Yes | 0 | Yes | 0 |
| Belgium | Yes | 0 | Yes | 0 | Yes | 0 | Yes | 0 | Yes | 0 |
| Denmark | Yes | 0 | Yes | 0 | Yes | 0 | Yes | 0 | Yes | 0 |
| Finland | Yes | 0 | Yes | 0 | Yes | 0 | Yes | 0 | Yes | 0 |
| France | Yes | 0 | Yes | 0 | Yes | 0 | Yes | 0 | Yes | 0 |
| Germany | Yes | 0 | Yes | 0 | Yes | 0 | Yes | 0 | Yes | 0 |
| Iceland | No | 10 | No | 10 | No | 10 | No | 10 | No | 10 |
| Ireland | No | 10 | No | 10 | No | 10 | No | 10 | No | 10 |
| Italy | Yes | 0 | Yes | 0 | Yes | 0 | Yes | 0 | Yes | 0 |
| Netherlands | Yes | 0 | Yes | 0 | Yes | 0 | Yes | 0 | Yes | 0 |
| Norway | Yes | 0 | Yes | 0 | Yes | 0 | Yes | 0 | Yes | 0 |
| Spain | Yes | 0 | Yes | 0 | Yes | 0 | Yes | 0 | Yes | 0 |
| Sweden | Yes | 0 | Yes | 0 | Yes | 0 | Yes | 0 | Yes | 0 |
| Switzerland | Yes | 0 | Yes | 0 | Yes | 0 | Yes | 0 | Yes | 0 |
| United Kingdom | No | 10 | No | 10 | No | 10 | No | 10 | No | 10 |
| **CENTRAL/S. AMERICA** | | | | | | | | | | |
| Argentina | Yes | 0 | Yes | 0 | Yes | 0 | Yes | 0 | Yes | 0 |
| Belize | - | | No | 10 | No | 10 | No | 10 | No | 10 |
| Bolivia | Yes | 0 | Yes | 0 | Yes | 0 | Yes | 0 | Yes | 0 |
| Brazil | Yes | 0 | Yes | 0 | Yes | 0 | Yes | 0 | Yes | 0 |
| Chile | Yes | 0 | Yes | 0 | Yes | 0 | Yes | 0 | Yes | 0 |
| Colombia | Yes | 0 | Yes | 0 | Yes | 0 | Yes | 0 | Yes | 0 |
| Costa Rica | No | 10 | No | 10 | No | 10 | No | 10 | No | 10 |
| Dominican Rep | Yes | 0 | No | 10 | No | 10 | No | 10 | No | 10 |
| Ecuador | Yes | 0 | Yes | 0 | Yes | 0 | Yes | 0 | Yes | 0 |
| El Salvador | - | | Yes | 0 | Yes | 0 | Yes | 0 | Yes | 0 |
| Guatemala | Yes | 0 | Yes | 0 | Yes | 0 | Yes | 0 | Yes | 0 |
| Haiti | No | 10 | No | 10 | No | 10 | No | 10 | No | 10 |
| Honduras | - | | No | 10 | Yes | 0 | Yes | 0 | Yes | 0 |
| Jamaica | No | 10 | No | 10 | No | 10 | No | 10 | No | 10 |
| Mexico | Yes | 0 | Yes | 0 | Yes | 0 | Yes | 0 | Yes | 0 |

Table III-C: (continued)

| | **Are Individuals Conscripted into the Military?** | | | | | | | | | |
|---|---|---|---|---|---|---|---|---|---|---|
| **CENTRAL/-** | 1974-75 | | 1979-80 | | 1984-85 | | 1989-90 | | 1993-94 | |
| **S. AMERICA (con't)** | | | | | | | | | | |
| Nicaraqua | Yes | 0 | Yes | 0 | Yes | 0 | Yes | 0 | No | 10 |
| Panama | No | 10 | No | 10 | No | 10 | No | 10 | No | 10 |
| Paraguay | Yes | 0 | Yes | 0 | Yes | 0 | Yes | 0 | Yes | 0 |
| Peru | Yes | 0 | Yes | 0 | Yes | 0 | Yes | 0 | Yes | 0 |
| Trinidad/Tobago | No | 10 | No | 10 | No | 10 | No | 10 | No | 10 |
| Uruguay | No | 10 | No | 10 | No | 10 | No | 10 | No | 10 |
| Venezuela | Yes | 0 | Yes | 0 | Yes | 0 | Yes | 0 | Yes | 0 |
| | | | | | | | | | | |
| **EUROPE/MIDDLE EAST** | | | | | | | | | | |
| Bulgaria | Yes | 0 | Yes | 0 | Yes | 0 | Yes | 0 | Yes | 0 |
| Cyprus | - | | Yes | 0 | Yes | 0 | Yes | 0 | Yes | 0 |
| Czechoslovakia | Yes | 0 | Yes | 0 | Yes | 0 | Yes | 0 | - | |
| Czech Republic | - | | - | | - | | - | | Yes | 0 |
| Slovakia | - | | - | | - | | - | | Yes | 0 |
| Egypt | Yes | 0 | Yes | 0 | Yes | 0 | Yes | 0 | Yes | 0 |
| Greece | Yes | 0 | Yes | 0 | Yes | 0 | Yes | 0 | Yes | 0 |
| Hungary | Yes | 0 | Yes | 0 | Yes | 0 | Yes | 0 | Yes | 0 |
| Iran | Yes | 0 | Yes | 0 | Yes | 0 | Yes | 0 | Yes | 0 |
| Israel | Yes | 0 | Yes | 0 | Yes | 0 | Yes | 0 | Yes | 0 |
| Jordan | No | 10 | No | 10 | No | 10 | No | 10 | No | 10 |
| Malta | - | | No | 10 | No | 10 | No | 10 | No | 10 |
| Poland | Yes | 0 | Yes | 0 | Yes | 0 | Yes | 0 | Yes | 0 |
| Portugal | Yes | 0 | Yes | 0 | Yes | 0 | Yes | 0 | Yes | 0 |
| Romania | Yes | 0 | Yes | 0 | Yes | 0 | Yes | 0 | Yes | 0 |
| Syria | Yes | 0 | Yes | 0 | Yes | 0 | Yes | 0 | Yes | 0 |
| Turkey | Yes | 0 | Yes | 0 | Yes | 0 | Yes | 0 | Yes | 0 |
| | | | | | | | | | | |
| **ASIA** | | | | | | | | | | |
| Bangladesh | No | 10 | No | 10 | No | 10 | No | 10 | No | 10 |
| Fiji | - | | No | 10 | No | 10 | No | 10 | No | 10 |
| Hong Kong | No | 10 | No | 10 | No | 10 | No | 10 | No | 10 |
| India | No | 10 | No | 10 | No | 10 | No | 10 | No | 10 |
| Indonesia | Yes | 0 | Yes | 0 | Yes | 0 | Yes | 0 | Yes | 0 |
| Malaysia | No | 10 | No | 10 | No | 10 | No | 10 | No | 10 |
| Nepal | No | 10 | No | 10 | No | 10 | No | 10 | No | 10 |
| Pakistan | Yes | 0 | No | 10 | No | 10 | No | 10 | No | 10 |
| Philippines | Yes | 0 | Yes | 0 | No | 10 | No | 10 | No | 10 |
| Singapore | Yes | 0 | Yes | 0 | Yes | 0 | Yes | 0 | Yes | 0 |
| South Korea | Yes | 0 | Yes | 0 | Yes | 0 | Yes | 0 | Yes | 0 |
| Sri Lanka | No | 10 | No | 10 | No | 10 | No | 10 | No | 10 |
| Taiwan | Yes | 0 | Yes | 0 | Yes | 0 | Yes | 0 | Yes | 0 |
| Thailand | Yes | 0 | Yes | 0 | Yes | 0 | Yes | 0 | Yes | 0 |

Table III-C: (continued)

| AFRICA | Are Individuals Conscripted into the Military? | | | | | | | | | |
|---|---|---|---|---|---|---|---|---|---|---|
| | 1974-75 | | 1979-80 | | 1984-85 | | 1989-90 | | 1993-94 | |
| Algeria | No | 10 | Yes | 0 | Yes | 0 | Yes | 0 | Yes | 0 |
| Benin | - | | - | | Yes | 0 | Yes | 0 | Yes | 0 |
| Botswana | No | 10 | No | 10 | No | 10 | No | 10 | No | 10 |
| Burundi | No | 10 | No | 10 | No | 10 | No | 10 | No | 10 |
| Cameroon | No | 10 | No | 10 | No | 10 | No | 10 | No | 10 |
| C African Rep | - | | Yes | 0 | Yes | 0 | Yes | 0 | Yes | 0 |
| Chad | No | 10 | No | 10 | Yes | 0 | Yes | 0 | Yes | 0 |
| Congo Peoples Rep | No | 10 | No | 10 | No | 10 | No | 10 | No | 10 |
| Cote d' Ivoire | No | 10 | No | 10 | Yes | 0 | Yes | 0 | Yes | 0 |
| Gabon | No | 10 | No | 10 | No | 10 | No | 10 | No | 10 |
| Ghana | No | 10 | No | 10 | No | 10 | No | 10 | No | 10 |
| Kenya | No | 10 | No | 10 | No | 10 | No | 10 | No | 10 |
| Madagascar | - | | Yes | 0 | Yes | 0 | Yes | 0 | Yes | 0 |
| Malawi | No | 10 | No | 10 | No | 10 | No | 10 | No | 10 |
| Mali | No | 10 | No | 10 | Yes | 0 | Yes | 0 | Yes | 0 |
| Mauritius | No | 10 | No | 10 | No | 10 | No | 10 | No | 10 |
| Morocco | Yes | 0 | Yes | 0 | Yes | 0 | Yes | 0 | Yes | 0 |
| Niger | No | 10 | Yes | 0 | Yes | 0 | Yes | 0 | Yes | 0 |
| Nigeria | No | 10 | No | 10 | No | 10 | No | 10 | No | 10 |
| Rwanda | No | 10 | No | 10 | No | 10 | No | 10 | No | 10 |
| Senegal | - | | Yes | 0 | Yes | 0 | Yes | 0 | Yes | 0 |
| Sierra Leone | No | 10 | No | 10 | No | 10 | No | 10 | No | 10 |
| Somalia | No | 10 | No | 10 | Yes | 0 | Yes | 0 | Yes | 0 |
| South Africa | Yes | 0 | Yes | 0 | Yes | 0 | Yes | 0 | No | 10 |
| Tanzania | No | 10 | No | 10 | Yes | 0 | Yes | 0 | Yes | 0 |
| Togo | - | | Yes | 0 | Yes | 0 | Yes | 0 | Yes | 0 |
| Tunisia | Yes | 0 | Yes | 0 | Yes | 0 | Yes | 0 | Yes | 0 |
| Uganda | No | 10 | No | 10 | No | 10 | No | 10 | No | 10 |
| Zaire | No | 10 | No | 10 | No | 10 | No | 10 | No | 10 |
| Zambia | No | 10 | No | 10 | No | 10 | No | 10 | No | 10 |
| Zimbabwe | - | | Yes | 0 | Yes | 0 | Yes | 0 | Yes | 0 |

Source: International Institute for Strategic Studies, *The Military Balance*, (various issues).

## Table IV-A: The Average Tax Rate on International Trade

**Taxes on Trade As A Percent of Exports Plus Imports**

(The rating of each country is in parenthesis)

| INDUSTRIAL COUNTRIES | 1975 | | 1980 | | 1985 | | 1990 | | 1992 | |
|---|---|---|---|---|---|---|---|---|---|---|
| United States | 1.50 | (9) | 1.13 | (9) | 1.73 | (8) | 1.45 | (9) | 1.37 | (9) |
| Canada | 3.67 | (6) | 2.38 | (8) | 1.67 | (8) | 1.18 | (9) | 1.20 | (9) b |
| Australia | 4.36 | (6) | 3.60 | (7) | 3.22 | (7) | 3.07 | (7) | 2.26 | (8) |
| Japan | 1.25 | (9) | 0.89 | (9) | 0.82 | (9) | 0.93 | (9) | 0.90 | (9) |
| New Zealand | 2.42 | (8) | 2.51 | (8) | 2.01 | (8) | 1.65 | (8) | 1.19 | (9) |
| Austria | 1.65 | (8) | 0.71 | (9) | 0.60 | (9) | 0.65 | (9) | 0.67 | (9) |
| Belgium | 0.01 | (10) | 0.00 | (10) | 0.00 | (10) | 0.01 | (10) | 0.00 | (10) |
| Denmark | 0.92 | (9) | 0.05 | (10) | 0.04 | (10) | 0.04 | (10) | 0.04 | (10) |
| Finland | 1.61 | (8) | 0.81 | (9) | 0.42 | (9) | 0.59 | (9) | 0.57 | (9) |
| France | 0.05 | (10) | 0.05 | (10) | 0.03 | (10) | 0.01 | (10) | 0.00 | (10) |
| Germany | 0.02 | (10) | 0.01 | (10) | 0.00 | (10) | 0.00 | (10) | 0.00 | (10) |
| Iceland | 8.06 | (2) | 6.54 | (4) | 4.57 | (6) | 3.96 | (6) | 4.16 | (6) |
| Ireland | 4.82 | (6) | 2.98 | (7) | 2.53 | (8) | 2.61 | (7) | 2.38 | (8) b |
| Italy | 0.26 | (10) | 0.04 | (10) | 0.02 | (10) | 0.01 | (10) | 0.02 | (10) |
| Netherlands | 1.33 | (9) | 0.00 | (10) | 0.00 | (10) | 0.00 | (10) | 0.00 | (10) |
| Norway | 0.51 | (9) | 0.30 | (9) | 0.25 | (10) | 0.27 | (10) | - | |
| Spain | 6.11 | (5) | 2.69 | (7) | 2.97 | (7) | 1.33 | (9) | 0.90 | (9) b |
| Sweden | 0.95 | (9) | 0.66 | (9) | 0.32 | (9) | 0.39 | (9) | 0.62 | (9) |
| Switzerland | 3.50 | (7) | 2.42 | (8) | 1.95 | (8) | 1.87 | (8) | 1.93 | (8) b |
| United Kingdom | 0.00 | (10) | 0.04 | (10) | 0.00 | (10) | 0.04 | (10) | 0.06 | (10) |

| CENTRAL/SOUTH AMERICA | | | | | | | | | | |
|---|---|---|---|---|---|---|---|---|---|---|
| Argentina | 12.90 | (0) | 9.50 | (1) | 12.72 | (0) | 12.76 | (0) a | - | |
| Belize | - | | 8.70 | (2) | 10.86 | (1) | 10.76 | (1) | 9.56 | (1) |
| Bolivia | 8.90 | (2) | 7.80 | (3) | 7.01 | (4) | 2.31 | (8) | 2.82 | (7) |
| Brazil | 5.65 | (5) | 10.00 | (1) | 3.22 | (7) | 3.66 | (6) | 3.24 | (7) b |
| Chile | 5.56 | (6) | 2.79 | (7) | 5.69 | (5) | 3.69 | (6) | 3.73 | (6) |
| Colombia | 7.39 | (3) | 7.77 | (3) | 7.46 | (3) | 7.09 | (3) a | - | |
| Costa Rica | 5.91 | (5) | 5.30 | (6) | 6.92 | (4) | 7.03 | (4) | 5.03 | (6) |
| Dominican Rep | 16.12 | (0) | 9.76 | (1) | 6.45 | (4) | 8.20 | (2) | - | |
| Ecuador | 8.88 | (2) | 7.20 | (3) | 6.21 | (5) | 3.95 | (6) | - | |
| El Salvador | 6.40 | (4) | 6.24 | (4) | 7.13 | (3) | 4.13 | (6) | 3.79 | (6) |
| Guatemala | 5.62 | (6) | 4.81 | (6) | 7.47 | (3) | 3.55 | (7) | 3.58 | (7) b |
| Haiti | 9.30 | (1) | 9.86 | (1) | 8.03 | (2) | 6.70 | (4) a | - | |
| Honduras | 5.32 | (6) | 6.70 | (4) | - | | - | | - | |
| Jamaica | 3.99 | (6) | 0.87 | (9) | 1.71 | (8) | - | | - | |
| Mexico | 7.87 | (3) | 17.56 | (0) | 2.57 | (7) | 1.95 | (8) | - | |
| Nicaragua | 4.88 | (6) | 8.70 | (2) | 7.38 | (3) | 4.30 | (6) | 7.97 | (2) |

Table IV-A: (contined)

## Taxes on Trade As A Percent of Exports Plus Imports

(The rating of each country is in parenthesis)

| CENTRAL/-S. AMERICA (cont) | 1975 | | 1980 | | 1985 | | 1990 | | 1992 | |
|---|---|---|---|---|---|---|---|---|---|---|
| Panama | 3.20 | (7) | 3.07 | (7) | 4.14 | (6) | 4.45 | (6) | 4.14 | (6) |
| Paraguay | 8.81 | (2) | 6.04 | (5) | 2.22 | (8) | 3.26 | (7) | 3.52 | (7) |
| Peru | 9.52 | (1) | 10.62 | (1) | 8.30 | (2) | 3.86 | (6) | 4.35 | (6) |
| Trinidad/Tobago | 2.60 | (7) | 3.17 | (7) | 5.71 | (5) | 2.68 | (7) a | - | |
| Uruguay | 3.41 | (7) | 8.87 | (2) | 5.82 | (5) | 5.61 | (6) | 5.03 | (6) |
| Venezuela | 3.74 | (6) | 2.98 | (7) | 9.14 | (1) | 2.21 | (8) | 3.76 | (6) |
| **EUROPE/MIDDLE EAST** | | | | | | | | | | |
| Bulgaria | - | | - | | 5.40 | (6) | 1.30 | (9) | 2.22 | (8) |
| Cyprus | 3.45 | (7) | 4.00 | (6) | 4.42 | (6) | 4.15 | (6) | 4.20 | (6) b |
| Czechoslovakia | - | | - | | - | | 3.99 | (6) | - | |
| Czech Republic | - | | - | | - | | - | | - | |
| Slovakia | - | | - | | - | | - | | - | |
| Egypt | 16.73 | (0) | 13.08 | (0) | 12.06 | (1) | 5.92 | (5) | 6.42 | (4) |
| Greece | 3.46 | (7) | 3.23 | (7) | 0.33 | (9) | 0.05 | (10) | 0.07 | (10) |
| Hungary | - | | 4.97 | (6) | 3.74 | (6) | 4.97 | (6) | | |
| Iran | 3.59 | (7) | 16.95 | (0) | 14.18 | (0) | 7.32 | (3) | 8.67 | (2) |
| Israel | 7.96 | (2) | 5.05 | (6) | 2.85 | (7) | 0.92 | (9) | 1.05 | (9) |
| Jordan | 6.75 | (4) | 7.06 | (4) | 6.09 | (5) | 4.96 | (6) | 9.23 | (1) |
| Malta | 4.59 | (6) | 4.87 | (6) | 4.46 | (6) | 4.85 | (6) | 4.76 | (6) |
| Poland | - | | - | | 8.59 | (2) | - | | - | |
| Portugal | 4.61 | (6) | 2.11 | (8) | 1.24 | (9) | 1.02 | (9) | 0.47 | (9) b |
| Romania | - | | - | | - | | 0.44 | (9) | 2.27 | (8) |
| Syria | 8.48 | (2) | 7.12 | (3) | 5.63 | (6) | 2.93 | (7) | 3.63 | (7) |
| Turkey | 14.43 | (0) | 6.33 | (4) | 2.96 | (7) | 2.81 | (7) | 2.26 | (8) |
| **ASIA** | | | | | | | | | | |
| Bangladesh | 7.90 | (3) | 13.41 | (0) | 17.88 | (0) | 12.11 | (1) a | - | |
| Fiji | 6.58 | (4) | 5.78 | (5) | 7.87 | (3) | 6.43 | (4) | 5.91 | (5) |
| Hong Kong | 0.70 | (9) | 0.50 | (9) | 0.60 | (9) | 0.40 | (9) | 0.30 | (9) |
| India | 14.77 | (0) | 15.52 | (0) | 24.19 | (0) | 20.73 | (0) | 16.98 | (0) |
| Indonesia | 4.00 | (6) | 2.89 | (7) | 1.59 | (8) | 2.46 | (8) | 1.86 | (8) |
| Malaysia | 7.04 | (4) | 7.71 | (3) | 5.65 | (5) | 3.20 | (7) | 2.81 | (7) |
| Nepal | 8.90 | (2) | 8.60 | (2) | 7.71 | (3) | 8.80 | (2) | - | |
| Pakistan | 15.32 | (0) | 15.29 | (0) | 14.74 | (0) | 16.45 | (0) | - | |
| Philippines | 13.38 | (0) | 6.75 | (4) | 6.20 | (5) | 6.64 | (4) | 8.16 | (2) |
| Singapore | 0.74 | (9) | 0.47 | (9) | 0.32 | (9) | 0.15 | (10) | 0.17 | (10) |
| South Korea | 3.07 | (7) | 4.14 | (6) | 3.55 | (7) | 3.42 | (7) | 2.21 | (8) |
| Sri Lanka | 11.13 | (1) | 11.72 | (1) | 10.59 | (1) | 8.81 | (2) | 6.99 | (4) |
| Taiwan | 4.83 | (6) | 3.60 | (7) | 2.80 | (7) | 2.14 | (8) | 1.97 | (8) |
| Thailand | 7.00 | (4) | 6.88 | (4) | 6.48 | (4) | 5.40 | (6) | 3.86 | (6) |

Table IV-A: (continued)

## Taxes on Trade As A Percent of Exports Plus Imports

(The rating of each country is in parenthesis)

| | 1975 | | 1980 | | 1985 | | 1990 | | 1992 | |
|---|---|---|---|---|---|---|---|---|---|---|
| **AFRICA** | | | | | | | | | | |
| Algeria | - | | - | | - | | - | | - | |
| Benin | 9.17 | (1) | 10.60 | (1) | - | | - | | - | |
| Botswana | 10.39 | (1) | 12.80 | (0) | 7.12 | (3) | 6.61 | (4) | 9.59 | (1) b |
| Burundi | 12.18 | (1) | 18.08 | (0) | 17.01 | (0) | 22.90 | (0) a | - | |
| Cameroon | 13.44 | (0) | 11.00 | (1) | 6.07 | (5) | 5.39 | (6) | 7.71 | (3) |
| C African Rep | - | | 10.60 | (1) | - | | 11.50 | (1) a | - | |
| Chad | 9.16 | (1) | - | | - | | 3.87 | (6) | 2.17 | (8) b |
| Congo Peoples Re | 5.43 | (6) | 3.80 | (6) | - | | - | | - | |
| Cote d' Ivoire | - | | 12.78 | (0) | 11.79 | (1) | 10.92 | (1) | - | |
| Gabon | 8.20 | (2) | 7.25 | (3) | 6.43 | (4) | 4.78 | (6) | 6.32 | (4) b |
| Ghana | 20.58 | (0) | 17.27 | (0) | 21.67 | (0) | 11.59 | (1) | 8.60 | (2) |
| Kenya | 5.47 | (6) | 6.06 | (5) | 7.38 | (3) | 6.26 | (4) | 3.70 | (6) |
| Madagascar | 13.80 | (0) | 8.50 | (2) | - | | 14.00 | (0) | 8.69 | (2) b |
| Malawi | 3.75 | (6) | 6.58 | (4) | 8.80 | (2) | 5.65 | (5) | - | |
| Mali | 14.09 | (0) | 3.81 | (6) | 4.97 | (6) | 4.60 | (6) a | - | |
| Mauritius | 7.06 | (4) | 9.55 | (1) | 9.64 | (1) | 7.61 | (3) | 7.50 | (3) |
| Morocco | 7.51 | (3) | 10.68 | (1) | 6.39 | (4) | 8.59 | (2) | - | |
| Niger | 6.70 | (4) | 8.40 | (2) | - | | - | | - | |
| Nigeria | 6.64 | (4) | 8.50 | (2) | 5.09 | (6) | 4.00 | (6) a | - | |
| Rwanda | 16.49 | (0) | 13.30 | (0) | - | | 14.15 | (0) | 14.63 | (0) |
| Senegal | 8.66 | (2) | 11.40 | (1) | 8.30 | (2) | - | | - | |
| Sierra Leone | 10.44 | (1) | 13.33 | (0) | 11.90 | (1) | 5.97 | (5) | 8.27 | (2) |
| Somalia | 14.01 | (0) | 10.50 | (1) | - | | - | | - | |
| South Africa | 2.02 | (8) | 1.21 | (9) | 1.41 | (9) | 2.22 | (8) | - | |
| Tanzania | 7.33 | (3) | 7.72 | (3) | 6.25 | (4) | - | | - | |
| Togo | 7.20 | (3) | 12.43 | (0) | 8.63 | (2) | 9.20 | (1) a | - | |
| Tunisia | 10.70 | (1) | 8.99 | (1) | 13.30 | (0) | 9.49 | (1) | 9.91 | (1) b |
| Uganda | 20.40 | (0) | 3.07 | (7) | 11.60 | (1) | - | | - | |
| Zaire | 19.02 | (0) | 10.28 | (1) | 8.39 | (2) | 9.10 | (1) | - | |
| Zambia | 2.61 | (7) | 2.39 | (8) | 6.40 | (4) | 4.20 | (6) a | - | |
| Zimbabwe | 2.10 | (8) | 1.67 | (8) | 8.03 | (2) | 9.19 | (1) | - | |

a Data are for 1989.
b Data are for 1991.

Source: The data on tax revenue are from the International Monetary Fund, *Government Finance Statistics Yearbook*, (various issues), Table A, line 6 entitled, "Taxes on International Trade Transactions." The data on the volume of exports and imports are from the World Bank, *World Tables, 1994*. The following conversion table divided the 1985 base year data into eleven intervals of equal size:

Table IV-A: (con't)

| Average Tax Rate | Rating |
|---|---|
| 0.000% - 0.285% | 10 |
| 0.285 - 1.500 | 9 |
| 1.500 - 2.550 | 8 |
| 2.550 - 3.645 | 7 |
| 3.645 - 5.640 | 6 |
| 5.640 - 6.230 | 5 |
| 6.230 - 7.065 | 4 |
| 7.065 - 7.950 | 3 |
| 7.950 - 8.970 | 2 |
| 8.970 - 12.390 | 1 |
| > 12.390 | 0 |

## Table IV-B: The Black Market Exchange Rate Premium

(The premium one must pay to exchange the domestic currency for dollars in the black market relative to the official exchange rate. The data are year-end except for the 1995 figures.)

| | | | | | | |
|---|---|---|---|---|---|---|
| **Black Market Exchange Rate Premium** | | | | | | |
| *(The rating of each country is in parenthesis)* | | | | | | |
| **INDUSTRIAL COUNTRIES** | 1975 | 1980 | 1985 | 1988 | 1990 | 1992 | 1995 (March) |

| INDUSTRIAL COUNTRIES | 1975 | 1980 | 1985 | 1988 | 1990 | 1992 | 1995 (March) |
|---|---|---|---|---|---|---|---|
| United States | 0 (10) | 0 (10) | 0 (10) | 0 (10) | 0 (10) | 0 (10) | 0 (10) |
| Canada | 0 (10) | 0 (10) | 0 (10) | 0 (10) | 0 (10) | 0 (10) | 0 (10) |
| Australia | 1 (8) | 1 (8) | 0 (10) | 0 (10) | 0 (10) | 0 (10) | 0 (10) |
| Japan | 0 (10) | 0 (10) | 0 (10) | 0 (10) | 0 (10) | 0 (10) | 0 (10) |
| New Zealand | 5 (6) | 0 (10) | 4 (6) | 0 (10) | 5 (6) | 0 (10) | 0 (10) |
| Austria | 0 (10) | 0 (10) | 0 (10) | 0 (10) | 0 (10) | 0 (10) | 0 (10) |
| Belgium | 0 (10) | 0 (10) | 0 (10) | 0 (10) | 0 (10) | 0 (10) | 0 (10) |
| Denmark | 1 (8) | 2 (7) | 0 (10) | 0 (10) | 0 (10) | 0 (10) | 0 (10) |
| Finland | 1 (8) | 1 (8) | 0 (10) | 0 (10) | 0 (10) | 0 (10) | 0 (10) |
| France | 0 (10) | 3 (6) | 4 (6) | 2 (7) | 0 (10) | 0 (10) | 0 (10) |
| Germany | 0 (10) | 0 (10) | 0 (10) | 0 (10) | 0 (10) | 0 (10) | 0 (10) |
| Iceland | 106 (1) | 9 (5) | 16 (4) | 5 (6) | 3 (6) | 3 (6) | 1 (8) |
| Ireland | 0 (10) | 0 (10) | 3 (6) | 2 (7) | 1 (8) | 0 (10) | 0 (10) |
| Italy | 9 (5) | 0 (10) | 0 (10) | 1 (8) | 0 (10) | 0 (10) | 0 (10) |
| Netherlands | 0 (10) | 0 (10) | 0 (10) | 0 (10) | 0 (10) | 0 (10) | 0 (10) |
| Norway | 1 (8) | 3 (6) | 0 (10) | 1 (8) | 0 (10) | 1 (8) | 0 (10) |
| Spain | 2 (7) | 0 (10) | 2 (7) | 2 (7) | 2 (7) | 0 (10) | 0 (10) |
| Sweden | 1 (8) | 5 (6) | 1 (8) | 0 (10) | 1 (8) | 0 (10) | 0 (10) |
| Switzerland | 0 (10) | 0 (10) | 0 (10) | 0 (10) | 0 (10) | 0 (10) | 0 (10) |
| United Kingdom | 0 (10) | 0 (10) | 0 (10) | 0 (10) | 0 (10) | 0 (10) | 0 (10) |
| **CENTRAL/SOUTH AMERICA** | | | | | | | |
| Argentina | 124 (1) | 1 (8) | 40 (2) | 50 (2) | 0 (10) | 0 (10) | 0 (10) |
| Belize | 32 (3) | 34 (3) | 63 (1) | 25 (3) | 25 (3) | 14 (4) | 6 (6) |
| Bolivia | 5 (6) | 22 (4) | 9 (5) | 6 (6) | 0 (10) | 0 (10) | 1 (8) |
| Brazil | 49 (2) | 18 (4) | 49 (2) | 57 (2) | 10 (4) | 9 (5) | 5 (6) |
| Chile | 5 (6) | 6 (6) | 22 (4) | 29 (3) | 0 (10) | 5 (6) | 4 (6) |
| Colombia | 29 (3) | 16 (4) | 9 (5) | 15 (4) | 17 (4) | 9 (5) | 1 (8) |
| Costa Rica | 8 (5) | 69 (1) | 24 (3) | 23 (3) | 0 (10) | 4 (6) | 1 (8) |
| Dominican Rep | 28 (3) | 37 (2) | 14 (4) | 12 (4) | 66 (1) | 3 (6) | 2 (7) |
| Ecuador | 5 (6) | 13 (4) | 48 (2) | 25 (3) | 0 (10) | 5 (6) | 1 (8) |
| El Salvador | 20 (4) | 100 (1) | 195 (1) | 195 (1) | 24 (3) | 13 (4) | 18 (4) |
| Guatemala | 10 (4) | 10 (4) | 89 (1) | 28 (3) | 0 (10) | 4 (6) | 4 (6) |
| Haiti | 0 (10) | 20 (4) | 60 (2) | 151 (1) | 2 (7) | 78 (1) | 224 (0) |
| Honduras | 0 (10) | 20 (4) | 65 (1) | 85 (1) | 0 (10) | 5 (6) | 3 (6) |
| Jamaica | 22 (4) | 61 (2) | 19 (4) | 22 (4) | 27 (3) | 12 (4) | 1 (8) |
| Mexico | 0 (10) | 92 (1) | 25 (3) | 15 (4) | 0 (10) | 2 (7) | 0 (10) |
| Nicaragua | 21 (4) | 91 (1) | 382 (0) | 416 (0) | 10 (4) | 27 (3) | 4 (6) |

295

Table IV-B: (Continued)

## Black Market Exchange Rate Premium

(The rating of each country is in parenthesis)

| CENTRAL/- S. AMERICA (con't) | 1975 | | 1980 | | 1985 | | 1988 | | 1990 | | 1992 | | 1995 (March) | |
|---|---|---|---|---|---|---|---|---|---|---|---|---|---|---|
| Panama | 0 | (10) | 0 | (10) | 0 | (10) | 0 | (10) | 0 | (10) | 0 | (10) | 0 | (10) |
| Paraguay | 13 | (4) | 7 | (5) | 213 | (0) | 127 | (1) | 26 | (3) | 14 | (4) | 12 | (4) |
| Peru | 56 | (2) | 18 | (4) | 51 | (2) | 240 | (0) | 16 | (4) | 12 | (4) | 1 | (8) |
| Trinidad/Tobago | 43 | (2) | 49 | (2) | 39 | (2) | 57 | (2) | 40 | (2) | 15 | (4) | 0 | (10) |
| Uraguay | 0 | (10) | 0 | (10) | 0 | (10) | 0 | (10) | 0 | (10) | --- | | 1 | (8) |
| Venezuela | 0 | (10) | 0 | (10) | 25 | (3) | 0 | (10) | 0 | (10) | 5 | (6) | 1 | (8) |

### EUROPE/MIDDLE EAST

| | 1975 | | 1980 | | 1985 | | 1988 | | 1990 | | 1992 | | 1995 | |
|---|---|---|---|---|---|---|---|---|---|---|---|---|---|---|
| Bulgaria | 175 | (1) | 175 | (1) | 435 | (0) | 691 | (0) | 100 | (1) | -- | | 5 | (6) |
| Cyprus | 6 | (6) | 4 | (6) | 1 | (8) | 3 | (6) | 5 | (6) | 8 | (5) | -- | |
| Czechoslovkia | 359 | (0) | 387 | (0) | 423 | (0) | 763 | (0) | 61 | (2) | 31 | (3) | -- | |
| Czech Republic | -- | | -- | | -- | | -- | | -- | | -- | | 0 | (10) |
| Slovakia | -- | | -- | | -- | | -- | | -- | | -- | | 9 | (5) |
| Egypt | 1 | (8) | 9 | (5) | 146 | (1) | 248 | (0) | 56 | (2) | 1 | (8) | 1 | (8) |
| Greece | 3 | (6) | 7 | (5) | 25 | (3) | 8 | (5) | 3 | (6) | 1 | (8) | 0 | (10) |
| Hungary | 317 | (0) | 244 | (0) | 210 | (0) | 56 | (2) | 22 | (4) | 7 | (5) | 9 | (5) |
| Iran | 2 | (7) | 164 | (1) | 533 | (0) | 1030 | (0) | 2197 | (0) | 3034 | (0) | 156 | (1) |
| Israel | 60 | (2) | 1 | (8) | 7 | (5) | 18 | (4) | 4 | (6) | 0 | (10) | 1 | (8) |
| Jordan | 1 | (8) | 0 | (10) | 3 | (6) | 10 | (4) | 11 | (4) | 7 | (5) | 1 | (8) |
| Malta | 5 | (6) | 12 | (4) | 7 | (5) | 3 | (6) | 2 | (7) | 1 | (8) | 4 | (6) |
| Poland | 3786 | (0) | 298 | (0) | 301 | (0) | 537 | (0) | 9 | (5) | 47 | (2) | 0 | (10) |
| Portugal | 42 | (2) | 2 | (7) | 2 | (7) | 13 | (4) | 3 | (6) | 0 | (10) | 0 | (10) |
| Romania | 596 | (0) | 628 | (0) | 1246 | (0) | 561 | (0) | 416 | (0) | 41 | (2) | 25 | (3) |
| Syria | 1 | (8) | 35 | (2) | 251 | (0) | 354 | (0) | 301 | (0) | 273 | (0) | 283 | (0) |
| Turkey | 11 | (4) | 16 | (4) | 3 | (6) | 8 | (5) | 2 | (7) | 3 | (6) | 1 | (8) |

### ASIA

| | 1975 | | 1980 | | 1985 | | 1988 | | 1990 | | 1992 | | 1995 | |
|---|---|---|---|---|---|---|---|---|---|---|---|---|---|---|
| Bangladesh | 51 | (2) | 111 | (1) | 168 | (1) | 318 | (0) | 165 | (1) | 113 | (1) | 30 | (3) |
| Fiji | 17 | (4) | 18 | (4) | 8 | (5) | 13 | (4) | 4 | (6) | 1 | (8) | 1 | (8) |
| Hong Kong | 0 | (10) | 0 | (10) | 0 | (10) | 0 | (10) | 0 | (10) | 0 | (10) | 0 | (10) |
| India | 9 | (5) | 5 | (6) | 14 | (4) | 14 | (4) | 10 | (4) | 23 | (3) | 0 | (10) |
| Indonesia | 7 | (5) | 2 | (7) | 7 | (5) | 16 | (4) | 0 | (10) | 16 | (4) | 2 | (7) |
| Malaysia | 0 | (10) | 0 | (10) | 0 | (10) | 0 | (10) | 0 | (10) | 0 | (10) | 0 | (10) |
| Nepal | 40 | (2) | 0 | (10) | 11 | (4) | 61 | (2) | 16 | (4) | 50 | (2) | 25 | (3) |
| Pakistan | 17 | (4) | 27 | (3) | 4 | (6) | 10 | (4) | 14 | (4) | 13 | (4) | 0 | (10) |
| Philippines | 13 | (4) | 3 | (6) | 7 | (5) | 3 | (6) | 7 | (5) | 2 | (7) | 1 | (8) |
| Singapore | 0 | (10) | 0 | (10) | 0 | (10) | 0 | (10) | 0 | (10) | 0 | (10) | 0 | (10) |
| South Korea | 2 | (7) | 11 | (4) | 11 | (4) | 10 | (4) | 1 | (8) | 4 | (6) | 0 | (10) |
| Sri Lanka | 92 | (1) | 9 | (5) | 20 | (4) | 36 | (2) | 24 | (3) | 13 | (4) | 0 | (10) |
| Taiwan | 5 | (6) | 1 | (8) | 3 | (6) | 1 | (8) | 0 | (10) | 0 | (10) | 0 | (10) |
| Thailand | 2 | (7) | 5 | (6) | 3 | (6) | 1 | (8) | 0 | (10) | 0 | (10) | 0 | (10) |

Table IV-B: (Continued)

## Black Market Exchange Rate Premium

(The rating of each country is in parenthesis)

| AFRICA | 1975 | | 1980 | | 1985 | | 1988 | | 1990 | | 1992 | | 1995 (March) | |
|---|---|---|---|---|---|---|---|---|---|---|---|---|---|---|
| Algeria | 56 | (2) | 263 | (0) | 335 | (0) | 416 | (0) | 140 | (1) | 339 | (0) | 205 | (1) |
| Benin | 2 | (7) | 2 | (7) | 1 | (8) | 2 | (7) | 4 | (6) | 1 | (8) | 1 | (8) |
| Botswana | 44 | (2) | 10 | (4) | 22 | (4) | 53 | (2) | 7 | (5) | 16 | (4) | 1 | (8) |
| Burundi | 46 | (2) | 45 | (2) | 25 | (3) | 25 | (3) | 6 | (6) | 54 | (2) | 42 | (2) |
| Cameroon | 2 | (7) | 2 | (7) | 1 | (8) | 2 | (7) | 4 | (6) | 1 | (8) | 1 | (8) |
| C African Rep | 2 | (7) | 2 | (7) | 1 | (8) | 2 | (7) | 4 | (6) | 1 | (8) | 1 | (8) |
| Chad | 2 | (7) | 2 | (7) | 1 | (8) | 2 | (7) | 4 | (6) | 1 | (8) | 1 | (8) |
| Congo Peoples Rep | 2 | (7) | 2 | (7) | 1 | (8) | 2 | (7) | 4 | (6) | 1 | (8) | 1 | (8) |
| Cote d' Ivoire | 2 | (7) | 2 | (7) | 1 | (8) | 2 | (7) | 4 | (6) | 1 | (8) | 1 | (8) |
| Gabon | 2 | (7) | 2 | (7) | 1 | (8) | 2 | (7) | 4 | (6) | 1 | (8) | 1 | (8) |
| Ghana | 67 | (1) | 304 | (0) | 142 | (1) | 36 | (2) | 7 | (5) | 11 | (4) | 2 | (7) |
| Kenya | 8 | (5) | 10 | (4) | 2 | (7) | 13 | (4) | 6 | (6) | 107 | (1) | 6 | (6) |
| Madagascar | 23 | (3) | 51 | (2) | 9 | (5) | 16 | (4) | 7 | (5) | 7 | (5) | 30 | (3) |
| Malawi | 28 | (3) | 48 | (2) | 30 | (3) | 27 | (3) | 14 | (4) | 34 | (3) | 21 | (4) |
| Mali | 7 | (5) | 5 | (6) | 1 | (8) | 2 | (7) | 4 | (6) | 1 | (8) | 1 | (8) |
| Mauritius | 47 | (2) | 40 | (2) | 1 | (8) | 3 | (6) | 8 | (5) | 5 | (6) | 5 | (6) |
| Morocco | 3 | (6) | 1 | (8) | 7 | (5) | 4 | (6) | 13 | (4) | 1 | (8) | 4 | (6) |
| Niger | 2 | (7) | 2 | (7) | 1 | (8) | 2 | (7) | 4 | (6) | 1 | (8) | 1 | (8) |
| Nigeria | 43 | (2) | 72 | (1) | 270 | (0) | 87 | (1) | 23 | (3) | 43 | (2) | 277 | (0) |
| Rwanda | 45 | (2) | 67 | (1) | 49 | (2) | 30 | (3) | 28 | (3) | 99 | (1) | 105 | (1) |
| Senegal | 2 | (7) | 2 | (7) | 1 | (8) | 2 | (7) | 4 | (6) | 1 | (8) | 1 | (8) |
| Sierra Leone | 53 | (2) | 62 | (1) | 206 | (1) | 1406 | (0) | 165 | (1) | 1 | (8) | 1 | (8) |
| Somalia | 28 | (3) | 41 | (2) | 147 | (1) | 48 | (2) | 200 | (1) | -- | | -- | |
| South Africa | 6 | (6) | 6 | (6) | 25 | (3) | 5 | (6) | 3 | (6) | 1 | (8) | 0 | (10) |
| Tanzania | 203 | (1) | 224 | (0) | 259 | (0) | 100 | (1) | 78 | (1) | 19 | (4) | 6 | (6) |
| Togo | 2 | (7) | 2 | (7) | 1 | (8) | 2 | (7) | 4 | (6) | 1 | (8) | 1 | (8) |
| Tunisia | 11 | (4) | 18 | (4) | 12 | (4) | 12 | (4) | 8 | (5) | 4 | (6) | 5 | (6) |
| Uganda | 390 | (0) | 360 | (0) | 25 | (3) | 261 | (0) | 40 | (2) | 17 | (4) | 12 | (4) |
| Zaire | 120 | (1) | 131 | (1) | 6 | (6) | 15 | (4) | 20 | (4) | 202 | (1) | 9 | (5) |
| Zambia | 140 | (1) | 70 | (1) | 38 | (2) | 900 | (0) | 212 | (0) | 1 | (8) | 1 | (8) |
| Zimbabwe | 54 | (2) | 84 | (1) | 42 | (2) | 47 | (2) | 15 | (4) | 30 | (3) | 1 | (8) |

Source: International Currency Analysis, Inc., *World Currency Yearbook* (various issues of the yearbook and the monthly report supplement) and Inter-national Monetary Fund, *International Financial Statistics* (various monthly issues). The 1985 base year data were used to derive the rating intervals. The following conversion table divided the 1985 data into eleven intervals of equal size:

Table IV-B: (con't)

| Black Market Exchange Rate Premium (percent) | Rating |
|:---:|:---:|
| 0 | 10 |
| 1 | 8 |
| 2 | 7 |
| 3 - 6 | 6 |
| 7 - 9 | 5 |
| 10 - 22 | 4 |
| 23 - 34 | 3 |
| 35 - 61 | 2 |
| 62 - 208 | 1 |
| 210 or more | 0 |

## Table IV-C: The Actual Size of the Trade Sector (Exports plus Imports divided by GDP) Compared to the Expected Size: 1975, 1980, 1990, and 1993

| | 1975 | | | | 1980 | | | |
|---|---|---|---|---|---|---|---|---|
| | Actual Trade | Expected Trade | Actual-Expected Expected | | Actual Trade | Expected Trade | Actual-Expected Expected | |
| **INDUSTRIAL COUNTRIES** | | | | | | | | |
| United States | 16.4 | 21.8 | -24.8% | (2) | 21.1 | 24.4 | -13.5% | (3) |
| Canada | 47.2 | 31.5 | 49.8% | (9) | 55.1 | 35.2 | 56.5% | (9) |
| Australia | 28.8 | 28.8 | 0.0% | (4) | 33.9 | 32.2 | 5.3% | (5) |
| Japan | 25.6 | 29.0 | -11.8% | (3) | 28.3 | 32.5 | -13.0% | (3) |
| New Zealand | 55.9 | 52.4 | 6.7% | (5) | 61.8 | 58.9 | 4.9% | (5) |
| Austria | 63.1 | 52.7 | 19.7% | (6) | 75.6 | 59.4 | 27.3% | (7) |
| Belgium | 107.0 | 67.4 | 58.8% | (9) | 128.3 | 75.9 | 69.0% | (10) |
| Denmark | 61.1 | 72.0 | -15.1% | (3) | 66.5 | 81.0 | -17.9% | (3) |
| Finland | 54.0 | 58.1 | -7.1% | (4) | 67.2 | 65.3 | 2.9% | (5) |
| France | 36.9 | 36.9 | 0.0% | (4) | 44.3 | 41.4 | 7.0% | (5) |
| Germany | 46.5 | 37.9 | 22.7% | (6) | 53.3 | 42.7 | 24.8% | (6) |
| Iceland | 78.9 | 87.5 | -9.8% | (3) | 72.6 | 97.9 | -25.8% | (2) |
| Ireland | 87.3 | 73.3 | 19.1% | (6) | 107.5 | 81.8 | 31.4% | (7) |
| Italy | 41.1 | 39.1 | 5.1% | (5) | 46.5 | 44.0 | 5.7% | (5) |
| Netherlands | 92.2 | 62.8 | 46.8% | (9) | 100.9 | 70.4 | 43.3% | (8) |
| Norway | 90.3 | 59.9 | 50.8% | (9) | 88.5 | 67.2 | 31.7% | (7) |
| Spain | 30.9 | 39.6 | -21.9% | (2) | 33.8 | 44.3 | -23.7% | (2) |
| Sweden | 55.9 | 51.7 | 2.6% | (5) | 60.8 | 58.2 | 4.5% | (5) |
| Switzerland | 60.0 | 58.5 | 2.6% | (5) | 77.0 | 66.0 | 16.7% | (6) |
| United Kingdom | 53.6 | 41.1 | 30.4% | (7) | 52.3 | 46.3 | 13.0% | (5) |
| **CENTRAL/SOUTH AMERICA** | | | | | | | | |
| Argentina | 11.8 | 34.5 | -65.8% | (0) | 11.6 | 38.4 | -69.7% | (0) |
| Belize | - | - | | | 124.0 | 149.9 | -17.3% | (3) |
| Bolivia | 58.2 | 42.5 | 36.9% | (8) | 37.7 | 47.0 | -19.8% | (2) |
| Brazil | 19.0 | 24.5 | -22.4% | (2) | 20.4 | 27.1 | -24.7% | (2) |
| Chile | 52.9 | 47.2 | 12.1% | (5) | 49.8 | 52.5 | -5.1% | (4) |
| Colombia | 29.8 | 38.5 | -22.6% | (2) | 31.8 | 42.7 | -25.5% | (2) |
| Costa Rica | 68.6 | 81.7 | -16.0% | (3) | 63.3 | 90.0 | -29.7% | (2) |
| Dominican Republic | 57.7 | 71.0 | -18.7% | (2) | 48.1 | 78.5 | -38.7% | (1) |
| Ecuador | 58.9 | 55.7 | 5.7% | (5) | 50.6 | 61.4 | -17.6% | (3) |
| El Salvador | 71.5 | 80.5 | -11.2% | (3) | 67.4 | 89.3 | -24.5% | (2) |
| Guatemala | 45.3 | 63.3 | -28.4% | (2) | 47.1 | 69.9 | -32.6% | (1) |
| Haiti | 37.5 | 75.8 | -50.5% | (0) | 52.1 | 84.3 | -38.2% | (1) |
| Honduras | 70.4 | 70.1 | 0.4% | (5) | 80.3 | 76.8 | 4.6% | (5) |
| Jamaica | 80.9 | 96.3 | -16.0% | (3) | 105.3 | 107.7 | -2.2% | (4) |
| Mexico | 14.7 | 31.6 | -53.5% | (0) | 23.7 | 34.9 | -32.1% | (1) |
| Nicaragua | 65.7 | 71.5 | -8.1% | (4) | 67.5 | 78.7 | -14.2% | (3) |

299

Table IV-C: (Continued)

| | 1975 | | | | 1980 | | | |
|---|---|---|---|---|---|---|---|---|
| CENTRAL/- S. AMERICA (cont) | Actual Trade | Expected Trade | Actual-Expected Expected | | Actual Trade | Expected Trade | Actual-Expected Expected | |
| Panama | 102.0 | 79.6 | 28.1% | (7) | 91.6 | 881.0 | -89.6% | (5) |
| Paraguay | 31.9 | 52.0 | -38.7% | (1) | 44.0 | 57.2 | -23.1% | (2) |
| Peru | 32.8 | 40.8 | -19.6% | (2) | 41.6 | 46.0 | -9.6% | (4) |
| Trinidad & Tobago | 88.2 | 116.7 | -24.4% | (2) | 89.4 | 130.1 | -31.3% | (1) |
| Uruguay | 37.1 | 67.5 | -45.0% | (1) | 35.7 | 75.7 | -52.8% | (0) |
| Venezuela | 50.7 | 43.5 | 16.6% | (6) | 50.7 | 47.8 | 6.1% | (5) |
| **EUROPE/MIDDLE EAST** | | | | | | | | |
| Bulgaria | - | - | - | | 66.4 | 82.9 | -19.9% | (2) |
| Cyprus | 92.2 | 118.3 | -22.1% | (2) | 108.3 | 132.7 | -18.4% | (3) |
| Czechoslovakia | - | - | - | | - | - | - | |
| Czech Republic | - | - | - | | - | - | - | |
| Slovakia | - | - | - | | - | - | - | |
| Egypt | 61.5 | 36.6 | 68.0% | (10) | 73.4 | 40.5 | 81.2% | (10) |
| Greece | 43.7 | 58.3 | -25.0% | (2) | 47.1 | 65.0 | -27.5% | (2) |
| Hungary | 90.4 | 49.5 | 82.6% | (10) | 80.3 | 55.6 | 44.4% | (8) |
| Iran | 75.0 | 35.2 | 113.1% | (10) | 29.7 | 38.6 | -23.1% | (2) |
| Israel | 77.4 | 82.6 | -6.3% | (4) | 90.4 | 91.4 | -1.1% | (4) |
| Jordan | 128.8 | 77.9 | 65.3% | (10) | 146.6 | 85.3 | 71.9% | (10) |
| Malta | 179.1 | 178.5 | 0.3% | (5) | 187.4 | 197.9 | -5.3% | (4) |
| Poland | - | - | - | | 59.2 | 47.0 | 26.0% | (7) |
| Portugal | 53.2 | 60.0 | -11.3% | (3) | 69.4 | 67.5 | 2.8% | (5) |
| Romania | - | - | | | 75.3 | 66.3 | 13.6% | (5) |
| Syria | 55.4 | 57.9 | -4.3% | (4) | 53.7 | 63.6 | -15.6% | (3) |
| Turkey | 19.3 | 37.1 | -48.0% | (1) | 20.6 | 41.1 | -49.9% | (0) |
| **ASIA** | | | | | | | | |
| Bangladesh | 11.0 | 41.5 | -73.5% | (0) | 24.1 | 45.9 | -47.5% | (1) |
| Fiji | 86.6 | 91.1 | -4.9% | (4) | 100.0 | 101.2 | -1.2% | (4) |
| Hong Kong | 162.5 | 111.1 | 46.3% | (9) | 180.7 | 122.5 | 47.5% | (9) |
| India | 12.8 | 20.8 | -38.3% | (1) | 16.6 | 23.6 | -29.7% | (2) |
| Indonesia | 44.2 | 28.0 | 57.9% | (9) | 53.3 | 31.0 | 71.9% | (10) |
| Malaysia | 86.8 | 50.3 | 72.6% | (10) | 112.6 | 55.7 | 102.2% | (10) |
| Nepal | 22.3 | 45.9 | -51.4% | (0) | 30.3 | 50.7 | -40.2% | (1) |
| Pakistan | 33.1 | 33.9 | -2.4% | (4) | 36.6 | 37.3 | -1.9% | (4) |
| Philippines | 48.1 | 34.5 | 39.4% | (8) | 52.0 | 38.2 | 36.1% | (8) |
| Singapore | 289.1 | 124.9 | 131.5% | (10) | 423.3 | 138.3 | 206.1% | (10) |
| South Korea | 64.4 | 48.8 | 32.0% | (8) | 75.5 | 54.3 | 39.0% | (8) |
| Sri Lanka | 62.5 | 57.4 | 8.9% | (5) | 87.0 | 63.8 | 36.4% | (8) |
| Taiwan | 82.5 | 76.2 | 8.3% | (5) | 106.3 | 84.6 | 25.6% | (7) |
| Thailand | 41.4 | 38.6 | 7.3% | (5) | 54.5 | 42.7 | 27.6% | (7) |

Table IV-C: (Continued)

| | 1975 | | | | 1980 | | | |
|---|---|---|---|---|---|---|---|---|
| | **Actual Trade** | **Expected Trade** | **Actual-Expected Expected** | | **Actual Trade** | **Expected Trade** | **Actual-Expected Expected** | |
| **AFRICA** | | | | | | | | |
| Algeria | 76.5 | 37.8 | 102.4% | (10) | 64.7 | 41.6 | 55.5% | (9) |
| Benin | 59.9 | 70.1 | -14.6% | (3) | 66.3 | 77.4 | -14.3% | (3) |
| Botswana | 109.1 | 60.8 | 79.4% | (10) | 116.4 | 66.7 | 74.5% | (10) |
| Burundi | 27.3 | 66.4 | -58.9% | (0) | 32.1 | 73.5 | -56.3% | (0) |
| Cameroon | 48.2 | 52.0 | -7.3% | (4) | 51.3 | 57.4 | -10.6% | (3) |
| Central African Rep | 65.3 | 51.8 | 26.1% | (7) | 68.9 | 52.2 | 32.0% | (6) |
| Chad | 57.2 | 43.1 | 32.7% | (8) | 65.1 | 47.8 | 36.2% | (8) |
| Congo Peoples Rep | 99.6 | 69.6 | 43.1% | (8) | 120.1 | 76.6 | 56.8% | (9) |
| Cote d'Ivoire | 73.3 | 55.3 | 32.5% | (8) | 76.2 | 60.5 | 26.0% | (7) |
| Gabon | 97.4 | 81.1 | 20.1% | (6) | 96.4 | 88.3 | 9.2% | (5) |
| Ghana | 37.8 | 53.9 | -29.9% | (1) | 17.6 | 59.9 | -70.6% | (0) |
| Kenya | 64.3 | 46.5 | 38.3% | (8) | 67.0 | 50.9 | 31.6% | (7) |
| Madagascar | 36.8 | 41.9 | -12.2% | (3) | 43.1 | 46.2 | -6.7% | (4) |
| Malawi | 75.0 | 64.1 | 17.0% | (6) | 63.7 | 70.5 | -9.6% | (3) |
| Mali | 41.3 | 40.8 | 1.2% | (5) | 51.1 | 45.2 | 13.1% | (5) |
| Mauritius | 112.3 | 108.5 | 3.5% | (5) | 112.6 | 120.6 | -6.6% | (4) |
| Morocco | 55.9 | 44.8 | 24.8% | (6) | 45.3 | 49.6 | -8.7% | (4) |
| Niger | 50.3 | 40.9 | 23.0% | (6) | 65.9 | 45.0 | 46.4% | (8) |
| Nigeria | 41.2 | 34.1 | 20.8% | (6) | 48.0 | 37.5 | 28.0% | (7) |
| Rwanda | 26.9 | 65.1 | -58.7% | (0) | 40.8 | 71.6 | -43.1% | (1) |
| Senegal | 78.4 | 61.5 | 27.5% | (7) | 72.3 | 67.8 | 6.6% | (5) |
| Sierra Leone | 61.1 | 74.0 | -17.4% | (3) | 65.7 | 82.1 | -20.0% | (2) |
| Somalia | 39.3 | 53.8 | -27.0% | (2) | 121.7 | 59.3 | 105.2% | (10) |
| South Africa | 58.6 | 37.8 | 55.0% | (9) | 64.7 | 41.7 | 55.2% | (9) |
| Tanzania | 52.1 | 42.1 | 23.8% | (6) | 39.5 | 46.2 | -14.5% | (3) |
| Togo | 97.1 | 78.9 | 23.1% | (6) | 107.4 | 87.1 | 23.3% | (6) |
| Tunisia | 66.7 | 61.2 | 9.0% | (5) | 85.8 | 67.6 | 26.9% | (7) |
| Uganda | 18.5 | 44.3 | -58.2% | (0) | 44.7 | 48.9 | -8.6% | (4) |
| Zaire | 25.1 | 35.7 | -29.7% | (1) | 32.0 | 39.4 | -18.8% | (3) |
| Zambia | 92.9 | 44.4 | 109.2% | (10) | 86.8 | 48.9 | 77.5% | (10) |
| Zimbabwe | 60.2 | 46.1 | 30.6% | (7) | 63.6 | 50.8 | 25.2% | (7) |

Table IV-C: (Continued)

| INDUSTRIAL COUNTRIES | 1985 Actual Trade | 1985 Expected Trade | 1985 Actual-Expected Expected | | 1990 Actual Trade | 1990 Expected Trade | 1990 Actual-Expected Expected | | 1993 Actual Trade | 1993 Expected Trade | 1993 Actual-Expected Expected | |
|---|---|---|---|---|---|---|---|---|---|---|---|---|
| United States | 17.7 | 22.2 | -20.3% | (2) | 21.4 | 23.7 | -9.7% | (3) | 21.8 | 24.1 | -9.5% | (3) |
| Canada | 54.4 | 32.1 | 69.5% | (10) | 51.2 | 34.3 | 49.3% | (9) | 54.0 | 34.8 | 55.2% | (9) |
| Australia | 35.2 | 29.2 | 20.5% | (6) | 34.3 | 31.1 | 10.3% | (5) | 37.4 | 31.6 | 18.4% | (6) |
| Japan | 25.5 | 29.7 | -14.3% | (3) | 21.0 | 31.8 | -34.0% | (1) | 18.0 | 32.5 | -44.6% | (1) |
| New Zealand | 64.4 | 53.7 | 19.9% | (6) | 54.0 | 57.6 | -6.2% | (4) | 59.4 | 58.6 | 1.4% | (5) |
| Austria | 81.2 | 54.5 | 49.0% | (9) | 79.1 | 58.5 | 35.2% | (8) | 77.8 | 59.6 | 30.5% | (7) |
| Belgium | 151.2 | 69.7 | 116.9% | (10) | 145.0 | 75.0 | 93.3% | (10) | 135.6 | 76.4 | 77.5% | (10) |
| Denmark | 73.0 | 74.4 | -1.9% | (4) | 65.5 | 80.0 | -18.1% | (3) | 66.4 | 81.7 | -18.7% | (2) |
| Finland | 58.1 | 59.8 | -2.8% | (4) | 47.6 | 64.2 | -25.9% | (2) | 52.5 | 65.4 | -19.7% | (2) |
| France | 47.1 | 38.0 | 23.9% | (6) | 46.1 | 40.6 | 13.5% | (5) | 45.0 | 41.4 | 8.7% | (5) |
| Germany | 61.5 | 39.3 | 56.5% | (9) | 58.0 | 42.1 | 37.8% | (8) | 59.9 | 43.0 | 39.3% | (8) |
| Iceland | 81.8 | 89.2 | -8.3% | (4) | 69.4 | 95.1 | -27.0% | (2) | 64.3 | 96.8 | -33.6% | (1) |
| Ireland | 113.4 | 74.7 | 51.8% | (9) | 113.5 | 80.5 | 41.0% | (8) | 116.1 | 82.1 | 41.4% | (8) |
| Italy | 46.0 | 40.3 | 14.1% | (6) | 41.4 | 43.4 | -4.6% | (4) | 39.8 | 44.2 | -10.0% | (3) |
| Netherlands | 116.8 | 64.5 | 81.1% | (10) | 103.7 | 69.0 | 50.3% | (9) | 100.0 | 70.3 | 42.2% | (8) |
| Norway | 86.0 | 61.6 | 39.6% | (8) | 81.1 | 66.1 | 22.7% | (6) | 79.0 | 67.4 | 17.2% | (6) |
| Spain | 43.5 | 40.5 | 7.4% | (5) | 37.5 | 43.5 | -13.8% | (3) | 38.0 | 44.4 | -14.4% | (3) |
| Sweden | 69.0 | 53.4 | 28.5% | (7) | 59.4 | 57.2 | 3.8% | (5) | 54.0 | 58.3 | -7.4% | (4) |
| Switzerland | 77.6 | 60.4 | 28.5% | (7) | 72.7 | 64.6 | 12.5% | (5) | 68.4 | 65.7 | 4.1% | (5) |
| United Kingdom | 56.6 | 42.5 | 33.2% | (8) | 51.4 | 45.6 | 12.7% | (5) | 49.0 | 46.6 | 5.2% | (5) |
| **CENTRAL/SOUTH AMERICA** | | | | | | | | | | | | |
| Argentina | 18.0 | 35.0 | -48.6% | (1) | 15.3 | 37.1 | -58.8% | (0) | 14.8 | 37.8 | -60.8% | (0) |
| Belize | 109.7 | 135.1 | -18.8% | (2) | 127.3 | 142.5 | -10.7% | (3) | 128.1 | 144.4 | -11.3% | (3) |
| Bolivia | 30.2 | 42.3 | -28.6% | (2) | 46.8 | 44.7 | 4.7% | (5) | 40.4 | 45.3 | -10.8% | (3) |
| Brazil | 19.3 | 24.5 | -21.2% | (2) | 12.6 | 26.0 | -51.5% | (0) | 16.5 | 26.4 | -37.5% | (1) |
| Chile | 53.8 | 47.6 | 13.0% | (5) | 65.4 | 50.6 | 29.2% | (7) | 60.0 | 51.4 | 16.7% | (6) |
| Colombia | 26.3 | 38.6 | -31.9% | (1) | 35.3 | 41.0 | -13.9% | (3) | 35.3 | 41.6 | -15.1% | (3) |
| Costa Rica | 63.2 | 80.9 | -21.9% | (2) | 75.4 | 85.2 | -11.5% | (3) | 82.0 | 86.3 | -5.0% | (4) |
| Dominican Republic | 64.2 | 71.0 | -9.6% | (3) | 59.2 | 75.1 | -21.2% | (2) | 64.5 | 76.3 | -15.5% | (3) |
| Ecuador | 47.6 | 55.2 | -13.8% | (3) | 60.1 | 58.3 | 3.1% | (5) | 59.2 | 59.1 | 0.2% | (4) |
| El Salvador | 52.2 | 81.5 | -36.0% | (1) | 43.0 | 86.5 | -50.3% | (0) | 42.8 | 87.8 | -51.3% | (0) |
| Guatemala | 25.0 | 62.8 | -60.2% | (0) | 43.4 | 66.1 | -34.3% | (1) | 45.0 | 67.0 | -32.8% | (1) |
| Haiti | 38.4 | 76.4 | -49.7% | (0) | 34.4 | 81.0 | -57.5% | (0) | - | - | | |
| Honduras | 54.1 | 68.7 | -21.3% | (2) | 75.2 | 72.1 | 4.3% | (5) | 65.3 | 73.0 | -10.5% | (3) |
| Jamaica | 132.5 | 98.0 | 35.2% | (8) | 111.0 | 104.7 | 6.0% | (5) | 153.0 | 106.7 | 43.4% | (8) |
| Mexico | 25.7 | 31.5 | -18.4% | (2) | 32.7 | 33.4 | -2.1% | (4) | 30.7 | 34.0 | -9.7% | (3) |
| Nicaragua | 36.5 | 70.8 | -48.4% | (1) | 68.5 | 74.7 | -8.3% | (4) | 65.2 | 75.7 | -13.9% | (3) |
| Panama | 71.0 | 79.6 | -10.8% | (3) | 73.1 | 84.3 | -13.3% | (3) | 75.6 | 85.6 | -11.7% | (3) |
| Paraguay | 49.5 | 51.2 | -3.3% | (4) | 75.5 | 6.0 | 1158.3% | (8) | 61.7 | 54.6 | 13.0% | (5) |
| Peru | 39.4 | 40.6 | -3.0% | (4) | 26.8 | 43.0 | -37.7% | (1) | 22.4 | 43.7 | -48.7% | (1) |
| Trinidad & Tobago | 61.0 | 118.4 | -48.5% | (1) | 73.8 | 126.1 | -41.5% | (1) | 69.8 | 128.3 | -45.6% | (1) |
| Uruguay | 86.0 | 69.2 | 24.3% | (1) | 46.2 | 74.1 | -37.7% | (1) | 42.7 | 75.6 | -43.5% | (1) |
| Venezuela | 40.7 | 43.0 | -5.3% | (4) | 59.6 | 45.4 | 31.3% | (7) | 54.3 | 46.0 | 18.0% | (6) |

Table IV-C: (con't)

| | 1985 | | | | 1990 | | | | 1993 | | | |
|---|---|---|---|---|---|---|---|---|---|---|---|---|
| EUROPE/- MIDDLE EAST | Actual Trade | Expected Trade | Actual-Expected Expected | | Actual Trade | Expected Trade | Actual-Expected Expected | | Actual Trade | Expected Trade | Actual-Expected Expected | |
| Bulgaria | 86.0 | 76.1 | 13.0% | (5) | 69.8 | 82.3 | -15.2% | (4) | 97.1 | 84.3 | 15.2% | (6) |
| Cyprus | 107.5 | 121.0 | -11.2% | (3) | 101.7 | 129.0 | -21.2% | (2) | 108.2 | 131.3 | -17.6% | (3) |
| Czechoslovakia | 69.7 | 57.3 | 21.6% | (7) | 68.8 | 61.5 | 11.9% | (6) | - | - | - | |
| Czech Republic | - | - | - | | - | - | - | | 110.5 | 62.5 | 76.8% | (10) |
| Slovakia | - | - | - | | - | - | - | | 139.7 | 80.0 | 74.6% | (10) |
| Egypt | 52.0 | 36.5 | 42.5% | (8) | 65.0 | 38.5 | 68.8% | (10) | 65.1 | 39.1 | 66.5% | (10) |
| Greece | 53.9 | 59.5 | -9.4% | (4) | 54.2 | 63.8 | -15.0% | (3) | 56.1 | 65.0 | -13.7% | (3) |
| Hungary | 82.3 | 51.2 | 60.7% | (9) | 59.6 | 55.1 | 8.2% | (5) | 74.2 | 56.5 | 31.3% | (7) |
| Iran | 16.0 | 34.6 | -53.8% | (0) | 35.2 | 36.1 | -2.5% | (4) | 31.1 | 36.5 | -14.9% | (3) |
| Israel | 85.8 | 83.0 | 3.4% | (5) | 69.0 | 78.9 | -12.5% | (2) | 64.4 | 88.5 | -27.2% | (2) |
| Jordan | 113.5 | 76.1 | 49.1% | (9) | 144.4 | 79.2 | 82.3% | (10) | 135.2 | 78.6 | 72.0% | (10) |
| Malta | 160.8 | 183.5 | -12.4% | (3) | 184.1 | 196.0 | -6.1% | (4) | 191.5 | 199.0 | -3.8% | (4) |
| Poland | 35.0 | 42.9 | -18.4% | (3) | 45.8 | 46.0 | -0.4% | (4) | 43.5 | 47.0 | -7.4% | (4) |
| Portugal | 78.7 | 61.6 | 27.8% | (7) | 81.8 | 66.6 | 22.8% | (6) | 67.5 | 68.1 | -0.9% | (4) |
| Romania | 41.6 | 60.7 | -31.5% | (1) | 42.8 | 65.1 | -34.3% | (1) | 58.0 | 66.7 | -13.0% | (3) |
| Syria | 37.2 | 57.0 | -34.7% | (1) | 55.1 | 59.8 | -7.9% | (4) | 64.0 | 60.5 | 5.8% | (5) |
| Turkey | 44.4 | 37.0 | 20.0% | (6) | 42.0 | 39.2 | 7.1% | (5) | 44.4 | 39.8 | 11.6% | (5) |
| **ASIA** | | | | | | | | | | | | |
| Bangladesh | 25.7 | 41.4 | -37.9% | (1) | 26.9 | 43.8 | -38.6% | (1) | 26.6 | 44.4 | -40.1% | (1) |
| Fiji | 89.1 | 91.6 | -2.7% | (4) | 129.6 | 97.6 | 32.8% | (8) | 109.8 | 99.6 | 10.2% | (5) |
| Hong Kong | 209.5 | 111.2 | 88.4% | (10) | 262.9 | 118.8 | 121.3% | (10) | 285.8 | 121.0 | 136.2% | (10) |
| India | 15.0 | 20.8 | -27.9% | (2) | 18.7 | 22.0 | -15.0% | (3) | 21.2 | 22.4 | -5.4% | (4) |
| Indonesia | 42.6 | 28.0 | 52.1% | (9) | 52.6 | 29.7 | 77.1% | (10) | 55.8 | 30.2 | 84.8% | (10) |
| Malaysia | 104.6 | 50.1 | 108.8% | (10) | 151.2 | 53.5 | 182.6% | (10) | 154.2 | 53.7 | 187.2% | (10) |
| Nepal | 31.0 | 45.6 | -32.0% | (1) | 33.7 | 48.1 | -29.9% | (1) | 48.7 | 48.8 | -0.2% | (4) |
| Pakistan | 34.0 | 33.4 | 1.8% | (5) | 35.0 | 35.1 | -0.3% | (4) | 41.6 | 35.6 | 16.9% | (6) |
| Philippines | 45.8 | 34.4 | 33.1% | (8) | 61.3 | 36.4 | 68.4% | (10) | 62.3 | 37.0 | 68.4% | (10) |
| Singapore | 318.0 | 125.5 | 153.4% | (10) | 372.7 | 133.3 | 179.6% | (10) | 340.8 | 135.3 | 151.9% | (10) |
| South Korea | 67.8 | 49.4 | 37.2% | (8) | 60.0 | 52.7 | 13.9% | (6) | 58.7 | 53.7 | 9.3% | (5) |
| Sri Lanka | 63.0 | 58.0 | 8.6% | (5) | 67.3 | 61.7 | 9.1% | (5) | 71.6 | 62.8 | 14.0% | (6) |
| Taiwan | 96.6 | 76.8 | 25.8% | (7) | 90.5 | 81.9 | 10.5% | (5) | 86.5 | 83.4 | 3.7% | (5) |
| Thailand | 49.1 | 38.6 | 27.2% | (7) | 75.5 | 41.0 | 84.1% | (10) | 77.1 | 41.7 | 84.9% | (10) |
| **AFRICA** | | | | | | | | | | | | |
| Algeria | 43.8 | 37.3 | 17.4% | (6) | 50.1 | 39.3 | 27.5% | (7) | 52.8 | 39.8 | 32.7% | (8) |
| Benin | 76.8 | 69.4 | 10.7% | (5) | 52.3 | 73.0 | -28.4% | (2) | 56.4 | 73.8 | -23.6% | (2) |
| Botswana | 115.0 | 59.6 | 93.0% | (10) | 118.1 | 62.4 | 89.3% | (10) | 106.0 | 63.2 | 67.7% | (10) |
| Burundi | 30.8 | 66.1 | -53.4% | (0) | 35.3 | 69.5 | -49.2% | (0) | 39.2 | 70.4 | -44.3% | (1) |
| Cameroon | 57.6 | 51.7 | 11.4% | (5) | 41.5 | 54.3 | -23.6% | (2) | 40.6 | 55.0 | -26.2% | (2) |
| Central African Rep | 65.1 | 51.5 | 26.4% | (7) | 49.0 | 54.3 | -9.8% | (3) | 33.6 | 55.0 | -38.9% | (1) |
| Chad | 61.4 | 43.1 | 42.5% | (8) | 60.0 | 45.5 | 31.9% | (8) | 56.4 | 46.1 | 22.3% | (6) |
| Congo | 112.7 | 68.9 | 63.6% | (10) | 86.5 | 72.3 | 19.6% | (6) | 87.4 | 73.1 | 19.6% | (6) |
| Cote d'Ivoire | 78.1 | 53.9 | 44.9% | (8) | 64.0 | 56.4 | 13.5% | (5) | 61.5 | 56.9 | 8.1% | (5) |
| Gabon | 100.0 | 78.4 | 27.6% | (7) | 83.5 | 82.7 | 1.0% | (5) | 77.8 | 83.7 | -7.0% | (4) |

Table IV-C: (Continued)

| | 1985 | | | | 1990 | | | | 1993 | | | |
|---|---|---|---|---|---|---|---|---|---|---|---|---|
| | Actual Trade | Expected Trade | Actual-Expected / Expected | | Actual Trade | Expected Trade | Actual-Expected / Expected | | Actual Trade | Expected Trade | Actual-Expected / Expected | |
| **AFRICA (con't)** | | | | | | | | | | | | |
| Ghana | 21.2 | 53.7 | -60.5% | (0) | 39.4 | 56.3 | -30.0% | (1) | 42.8 | 57.0 | -24.9% | (2) |
| Kenya | 51.6 | 45.4 | 13.7% | (5) | 57.5 | 47.1 | 22.1% | (6) | 54.0 | 48.3 | 11.8% | (5) |
| Madagascar | 30.5 | 41.6 | -26.7% | (2) | 44.0 | 43.6 | 0.9% | (5) | 41.1 | 44.2 | -7.0% | (4) |
| Malawi | 54.0 | 63.3 | -14.7% | (3) | 57.8 | 66.3 | -12.8% | (3) | 63.0 | 67.1 | -6.1% | (4) |
| Mali | 62.2 | 40.8 | 52.5% | (9) | 50.6 | 43.0 | 17.7% | (6) | 46.8 | 43.5 | 7.6% | (5) |
| Mauritius | 109.0 | 110.0 | -0.9% | (4) | 142.1 | 117.3 | 21.1% | (6) | 128.3 | 119.4 | 7.5% | (5) |
| Morocco | 58.4 | 44.7 | 30.6% | (7) | 54.5 | 47.1 | 15.7% | (6) | 52.0 | 47.8 | 8.8% | (5) |
| Niger | 51.1 | 40.2 | 27.1% | (7) | 38.0 | 42.3 | -10.2% | (3) | 32.0 | 42.8 | -25.2% | (2) |
| Nigeria | 28.5 | 33.7 | -15.4% | (3) | 64.6 | 35.4 | 82.5% | (10) | 73.7 | 36.0 | 104.7% | (10) |
| Rwanda | 30.6 | 64.3 | -52.4% | (0) | 22.2 | 67.6 | -67.2% | (0) | 29.4 | 68.5 | -57.1% | (0) |
| Senegal | 70.6 | 61.0 | 15.7% | (6) | 55.6 | 64.1 | -13.3% | (3) | 50.7 | 65.0 | -22.0% | (2) |
| Sierra Leone | 19.5 | 74.1 | -73.7% | (0) | 44.8 | 78.2 | -42.7% | (1) | 50.4 | 79.3 | -36.4% | (1) |
| Somalia | 25.6 | 53.2 | -51.9% | (0) | 47.5 | 56.0 | -15.2% | (3) | - | - | | |
| South Africa | 55.4 | 37.5 | 47.7% | (9) | 47.2 | 39.6 | 19.2% | (6) | 43.8 | 40.2 | 9.0% | (5) |
| Tanzania | 21.0 | 41.4 | -49.3% | (0) | 76.0 | 43.6 | 74.3% | (10) | 85.8 | 47.0 | 82.6% | (10) |
| Togo | 105.5 | 78.2 | 34.9% | (8) | 78.4 | 81.8 | -4.2% | (4) | 67.7 | 82.7 | -18.1% | (3) |
| Tunisia | 71.3 | 61.0 | 16.9% | (6) | 89.3 | 64.5 | 38.4% | (8) | 81.1 | 65.5 | 23.8% | (6) |
| Uganda | 21.6 | 44.7 | -51.7% | (0) | 24.5 | 46.5 | -47.3% | (1) | 25.2 | 47.1 | -46.5% | (1) |
| Zaire | 53.1 | 35.3 | 50.4% | (9) | 18.6 | 36.6 | -49.2% | (0) | - | - | | |
| Zambia | 76.9 | 43.7 | 76.0% | (10) | 74.1 | 46.0 | 61.1% | (9) | 66.7 | 46.5 | 43.4% | (8) |
| Zimbabwe | 56.4 | 45.4 | 24.2% | (6) | 59.0 | 47.7 | 23.7% | (6) | 74.8 | 48.3 | 54.9% | (9) |

Source: The data for exports, imports, and GDP used to derive the actual size of the international trade sector are from the World Bank, *World Tables, 1994* (or International Monetary Fund, *Monetary International Financial Statistics*. The expected size of the trade sector was derived by methods explained in the text. The rating of each country is indicated in parenthesis. The 1985 base year data were used to derive the rating intervals. The following conversion table divided the 1985 data into eleven intervals of equal size.

| Actual Relative to Expected (Percent Difference) | Rating |
|---|---|
| > 61.2% | 10 |
| 46.1 to 61.2 | 9 |
| 31.9 to 46.0 | 8 |
| 25.0 to 31.8 | 7 |
| 13.9 to 24.9 | 6 |
| -0.3 to 13.8 | 5 |
| -0.4 to -9.4 | 4 |
| -9.5 to -18.4 | 3 |
| -18.5 to -29.7 | 2 |
| -29.8 to -49.0 | 1 |
| < -49.0 | 0 |

## Table IV-D: Freedom to Engage in Capital (Investment) Transactions with Foreigners

| | Freedom to Engage in Capital Transactions with Foreigners (Countries with Fewer Restrictions on this Freedom are Rated Higher). | | | | |
|---|---|---|---|---|---|
| **INDUSTRIAL COUNTRIES** | 1975 | 1980 | 1985 | 1990 | 1993-94 |
| United States | 10 | 10 | 10 | 10 | 10 |
| Canada | 8 | 8 | 8 | 8 | 8 |
| Australia | 2 | 2 | 5 | 8 | 8 |
| Japan | 2 | 2 | 5 | 8 | 8 |
| New Zealand | 5 | 5 | 5 | 10 | 10 |
| Austria | 2 | 2 | 2 | 5 | 8 |
| Belgium | 10 | 10 | 10 | 10 | 10 |
| Denmark | 5 | 5 | 5 | 5 | 10 |
| Finland | 2 | 2 | 2 | 2 | 8 |
| France | 2 | 2 | 2 | 5 | 8 |
| Germany | 8 | 8 | 10 | 10 | 10 |
| Iceland | 2 | 2 | 2 | 2 | 5 |
| Ireland | 5 | 5 | 5 | 5 | 10 |
| Italy | 5 | 5 | 5 | 5 | 8 |
| Netherlands | 5 | 8 | 8 | 8 | 10 |
| Norway | 2 | 2 | 5 | 8 | 10 |
| Spain | 2 | 5 | 5 | 8 | 8 |
| Sweden | 2 | 2 | 5 | 10 | 10 |
| Switzerland | 2 | 10 | 10 | 10 | 10 |
| United Kingdom | 2 | 10 | 10 | 10 | 10 |
| **CENTRAL/SOUTH AMERICA** | | | | | |
| Argentina | 0 | 0 | 0 | 0 | 10 |
| Belize | -- | 8 | 8 | 8 | 8 |
| Bolivia | 2 | 2 | 2 | 2 | 5 |
| Brazil | 0 | 0 | 0 | 0 | 0 |
| Chile | 2 | 2 | 2 | 2 | 5 |
| Colombia | 0 | 0 | 0 | 0 | 5 |
| Costa Rica | 2 | 2 | 5 | 5 | 5 |
| Dominican Rep | 2 | 2 | 2 | 2 | 2 |
| Ecuador | 2 | 2 | 2 | 2 | 5 |
| El Salvador | 2 | 2 | 2 | 2 | 8 |
| Guatemala | 5 | 5 | 5 | 5 | 8 |
| Haiti | 0 | 0 | 0 | 0 | 2 |
| Honduras | 0 | 0 | 0 | 0 | 5 |
| Jamaica | 2 | 2 | 2 | 2 | 8 |
| Mexico | 2 | 2 | 2 | 5 | 5 |

Table IV-D: (Contined)

**Freedom to Engage in Capital Transactions with Foreigners**
(Countries with Fewer Restrictions on this Freedom are Rated Higher).

| CENTRAL/-<br>S. AMERICA (con't) | 1975 | 1980 | 1985 | 1990 | 1993-94 |
|---|---|---|---|---|---|
| Nicaragua | 5 | 0 | 0 | 0 | 0 |
| Panama | 10 | 10 | 10 | 10 | 10 |
| Paraguay | 5 | 5 | 5 | 5 | 5 |
| Peru | 2 | 2 | 2 | 2 | 8 |
| Trinidad/Tobago | 0 | 0 | 0 | 0 | 8 |
| Uraguay | 8 | 10 | 10 | 10 | 10 |
| Venezuela | 8 | 8 | 5 | 5 | 5 |
| | | | | | |
| **EUROPE/MIDDLE EAST** | | | | | |
| Bulgaria | 0 | 0 | 0 | 0 | 5 |
| Cyprus | 0 | 0 | 0 | 0 | 0 |
| Czechoslovakia | 0 | 0 | 0 | 0 | -- |
| Czech Rep | -- | -- | -- | -- | 5 |
| Slovakia | -- | -- | -- | -- | 0 |
| Egypt | 0 | 0 | 0 | 0 | 0 |
| Greece | 2 | 2 | 2 | 2 | 5 |
| Hungary | 0 | 0 | 0 | 0 | 0 |
| Iran | 5 | 0 | 0 | 0 | 0 |
| Israel | 2 | 2 | 2 | 2 | 2 |
| Jordan | 2 | 2 | 2 | 2 | 2 |
| Malta | 2 | 2 | 2 | 2 | 2 |
| Poland | 0 | 0 | 0 | 0 | 2 |
| Portugal | 2 | 2 | 2 | 5 | 5 |
| Romania | 0 | 0 | 0 | 0 | 5 |
| Syria | 0 | 0 | 0 | 0 | 0 |
| Turkey | 0 | 0 | 0 | 0 | 0 |
| | | | | | |
| **ASIA** | | | | | |
| Bangladesh | 0 | 0 | 0 | 0 | 0 |
| Fiji | 5 | 5 | 5 | 2 | 2 |
| Hong Kong | 10 | 10 | 10 | 10 | 10 |
| India | 2 | 2 | 2 | 2 | 2 |
| Indonesia | 2 | 2 | 2 | 2 | 2 |
| Malaysia | 5 | 5 | 5 | 5 | 5 |
| Nepal | 0 | 0 | 0 | 0 | 0 |
| Pakistan | 2 | 2 | 2 | 2 | 2 |
| Philippines | 2 | 2 | 2 | 2 | 2 |
| Singapore | 8 | 8 | 10 | 10 | 10 |
| South Korea | 0 | 0 | 2 | 5 | 5 |
| Sri Lanka | 0 | 0 | 0 | 0 | 0 |
| Taiwan | 2 | 2 | 2 | 5 | 5 |
| Thailand | 2 | 2 | 2 | 2 | 5 |

Table IV-D: (Con't)

## Freedom to Engage in Capital Transactions with Foreigners

(Countries with Fewer Restrictions on this Freedom are Rated Higher).

| | 1975 | 1980 | 1985 | 1990 | 1993-94 |
|---|---|---|---|---|---|
| **AFRICA** | | | | | |
| Algeria | 0 | 0 | 0 | 0 | 2 |
| Benin | 0 | 0 | 0 | 0 | 0 |
| Botswana | -- | 5 | 5 | 5 | 5 |
| Burundi | 0 | 0 | 0 | 0 | 0 |
| Cameroon | 0 | 0 | 0 | 0 | 0 |
| C African Rep | 0 | 0 | 0 | 0 | 0 |
| Chad | 0 | 0 | 0 | 0 | 0 |
| Congo Peoples Rep | 0 | 0 | 0 | 0 | 0 |
| Cote d' Ivoire | 0 | 0 | 0 | 0 | 0 |
| Gabon | 0 | 0 | 0 | 0 | 0 |
| Ghana | 0 | 0 | 0 | 0 | 0 |
| Kenya | 0 | 0 | 0 | 0 | 0 |
| Madagascar | 0 | 0 | 0 | 0 | 0 |
| Malawi | 2 | 2 | 2 | 2 | 2 |
| Mali | 2 | 2 | 2 | 2 | 2 |
| Mauritius | 2 | 2 | 2 | 2 | 2 |
| Morocco | 2 | 2 | 5 | 5 | 5 |
| Niger | 0 | 0 | 0 | 0 | 0 |
| Nigeria | 0 | 0 | 0 | 0 | 0 |
| Rwanda | 0 | 0 | 0 | 0 | 0 |
| Senegal | 0 | 0 | 0 | 0 | 0 |
| Sierra Leone | 0 | 0 | 0 | 0 | 0 |
| Somalia | 0 | 0 | 0 | 0 | 0 |
| South Africa | 2 | 2 | 2 | 2 | 2 |
| Tanzania | 0 | 0 | 0 | 0 | 0 |
| Togo | 0 | 0 | 0 | 0 | 0 |
| Tunisia | 0 | 0 | 0 | 5 | 5 |
| Uganda | 0 | 0 | 0 | 0 | 0 |
| Zaire | 2 | 2 | 2 | 2 | 2 |
| Zambia | 2 | 2 | 2 | 2 | 2 |
| Zimbabwe | - | 2 | 2 | 2 | 2 |

Source: International Monetary Fund, *Exchange Arrangements and Exchange Restrictions* (various issues) and Price-Waterhouse, *Doing Business Series* (booklets for various countries), were used to rate each country. These publications provided the descriptive characteristics of the capital market arrangements for each country. These descriptions were used to classify and rate each country as follows:

Table IV-D: (con't)

| Rating | Characteristics of Capital Market |
|--------|-----------------------------------|
| 10 | Foreigners are free to undertake domestic investments and nationals are free to undertake investments abroad. |
| 8 | With the exception of a few industries (e.g., banking, defense-related, telecommunications) and/or minor administrative procedures, foreigners are free to undertake domestic investments and nationals are free to undertake investments abroad. |
| 5 | Both domestic investments by foreigners and investments by nationals abroad are authorized, but there are regulatory restrictions (e.g., divesture after a period of time, investment must be of a specific size, limitations on the percentage share of a firm that can be owned by foreigners, or registration is required for repatriation of profits or earnings from investments) that retard the mobility of capital. |
| 2 | Either (but not both) (a) foreigners are prohibited from undertaking domestic investments or (b) nationals are prohibited from undertaking investments abroad *without the approval of governmental authorities.* |
| 0 | Regulations (including restrictions on the remittance of earnings) substantially reduce the freedom of both foreigners to undertake domestic investments and of nationals to undertake investments aboard. Generally neither are allowed *without the approval of government officials.* |